FOCUS ON EARTH SCIENCE

SECOND EDITION

Margaret S. Bishop
University of Houston
Houston, Texas

Phyllis G. Lewis
Associated with Phoenix Union High School System
Phoenix, Arizona

Richmond L. Bronaugh, Consultant
Baylor University
Waco, Texas

CHARLES E. MERRILL PUBLISHING CO.
A Division of Bell & Howell Company
Columbus, Ohio

A Merrill Science Text

Focus on Earth Science
Focus on Earth Science, Teacher's Annotated
Edition and Solutions Manual
Focus on Earth Science, Spirit Duplicating Test Booklet
Earth Science, Activity - Centered Program, Teacher's Guide
Earth Science, A Learning Strategy
for the Laboratory
Behavioral Objectives Booklet
Earth and Space Science Skillcards

Focus on Life Science Program
Focus on Physical Science Program

ISBN O-675-07455-X

Copyright © 1972, 1969 by
CHARLES E. MERRILL PUBLISHING CO.
A Division of Bell & Howell Company
Columbus, Ohio 43216

Focus on Earth Science is a study of the planet earth—its features, its forces, its place in the solar system, and its place in the universe. The study proceeds from an overview of the characteristics of the earth, through an in-depth study of its matter and processes, to a survey of matter and processes in the universe. This presentation examines and explains concepts in a vocabulary suited to the language sophistication of the student.

This approach to earth science was developed to cultivate an observing eye and an inquiring mind through a carefully planned sequence of learning. Each of the twenty-four chapters demonstrates the importance of observation and experimentation in the development of scientific principles. Organization of the areas encourages the student to apply his newly acquired skill and insight to an interpretation of the never-ending changes of his environment.

The scope of the text leads from familiar experiences and observations to an understanding of abstract concepts such as geologic time, astronomical distances, and inferences about celestial bodies. Basic principles of chemistry and physics are introduced early to form the framework for understanding the changes that occur in minerals, rocks, and celestial bodies. Within the six units, the materials and processes of the earth and the universe are explained in terms of matter and energy.

Focus on Earth Science is a suitable introduction to interpretation of the matter and processes of the earth. Complex ideas are presented simply and then developed. Scientific principles are reinforced immediately by experiments and activities which are placed appropriately within the text. The student repeatedly uses his experiences in observation, data gathering, and cause and effect relationships to interpret his environment. Experiments and activities have been devised to use inexpensive materials that are readily available. Each laboratory segment is effective without being either overwhelming or time-consuming.

Throughout the text, memorization is minimized and problem-solving is emphasized. A clear distinction is made between scientific laws and theories. For example, the origin of the earth and evolution are treated as a series of theories rather than as scientific facts. Theories and hypotheses to explain natural phenomena are presented from the historical viewpoint. It is this aspect which acquaints the student with the scientific endeavors of past investigators and fosters his appreciation of scientific observation.

Self-study aids are incorporated in the text. Each chapter contains a summary of main ideas as well as a variety of questions and a bibliography. These aids are designed to help the student recall factual material and to encourage his independent thinking. Important concepts printed in the margins of each page are useful for reference and review. Photographs, tables, and drawings have been selected carefully to help the student visualize the ideas presented in the accompanying text and to assist him to read with understanding. New terms associated with the scientific presentation of earth study are defined and spelled phonetically in the text and in an accompanying glossary. Appendices and an extensive index are included.

During the writing of *Focus on Earth Science*, the authors have had many helpful suggestions from students, teachers, and colleagues. To them, as well as to the editors and reviewers who have contributed to the accuracy and usefulness of the text, the authors offer their thanks.

CONTENTS

Chapter 6   Sedimentary Rocks

Chapter 7   Metamorphic Rocks

Chapter 8   Products of the Lithosphere

UNIT Three   The Atmosphere and the Hydrosphere

Chapter 9   The Atmosphere

Chapter 15 Glaciers

Chapter 16 Wind

Chapter 17 Crustal Movements

Chapter 18 Earthquakes

Cover and Unit Opening Photo Credits and Descriptions

COVER   Sunset at a Swiss lake   *Fred Wirz*

UNIT 1   Earth's surface from 470 nautical miles   *NASA*

         Earth's curvature   *NASA*

         Earth over the moon's horizon   *NASA*

UNIT 2   Ocean shore, Monterey, California   *Caterpillar News*

         Bryce Canyon   *Union Pacific Railroad Photo*

         Rainforest   *Union Pacific Railroad Photo*

UNIT 3   Storm clouds over Kauai, Hawaii   *American Airlines*

         Nevada desert   *Nevada State Highway Department*

         Cloud formations over Santa Catalina Island, California   *Official U.S. Navy Photograph*

UNIT 4   Colorado River meander in Utah   *U.S. Department of the Interior Geological Survey*

         Glacier, Alberta, Canada   *William Huber*

         Saracens Tent, Luray Caverns, Virginia   *Luray Caverns Corp.*

UNIT 5   Cave painting   *Art Reference Bureau, Inc.*

         Ammonite fossil   *Ward's Natural Science Est.*

         Dinosaur tracks   *Ward's Natural Science Est.*

UNIT 6   Moon   *Lick Observatory*

         Galaxy   *Official U.S. Naval Observatory Photograph*

         Edwin Aldrin on the moon   *NASA*

The Planet Earth

Science represents the world as man gradually comes to discover it.

Joseph Wood Krutch (1893-1970)

Man has always wondered about his world. What is its shape? What is its size? Does it move or stand still? How was the earth made?

Primitive men developed myths to answer questions about the earth. Gradually, as methods of observation improved, myths gave way to more accurate answers to these age-old questions.

Every age has contributed to man's store of knowledge about the earth. Long before man-made satellites were used to photograph the earth from space, scholars had found ways to calculate the size and shape of this planet. But no era has contributed more to man's knowledge than the twentieth century. Planck and Einstein among others have revolutionized man's picture of the earth. Yet each new bit of information opens new avenues of scientific investigation.

UNIT One

Origin and Motions of the Earth

In 1571, a Danish scientist and teacher named Peter Severinus gave his students the following advice: "Go my sons, sell your lands, your houses, your garments, and your jewelry; burn your books. On the other hand buy yourselves stout shoes, get away to the mountains, search the valleys, the deserts, the shores of the seas, and the deepest recesses of the world; mark well the distinctions between animals, the differences among plants, the various kinds of minerals, the properties and modes of origin of everything that exists. Be not ashamed to learn by heart the astronomy and terrestrial philosophy of the peasantry. Lastly purchase coals, build furnaces, watch and experiment without wearying. In this way and no other will you arrive at a knowledge of things and their properties."

What did Severinus really expect of his students? Did he intend that they burn their books and abandon their homes? Probably not. Instead he was encouraging them to learn about their environment through *observation* and *experimentation*. He did not want his students to accept myths and superstitions as explanations of natural events.

1:1 *Earth Science*

Learning associated with the out-of-doors was a new idea. Before Severinus' time, education stressed reading, writing, and discussion, but included very little experimentation and observation of nature. Since the sixteenth century, however, investigations and measurements of the environment have become an important part of learning.

Recall that Severinus wanted his students to learn the terrestrial philosophy (te res′tree ul · fi lahs′a fee) * of the peasantry.

Terrestrial means of the earth.

Philosophy is the science which investigates facts and principles underlying all knowledge and being.

*See Pronunciation Key, p. 540.

4

His point was that peasants observed the forces of nature every day. They planted their crops and reaped their harvests according to nature's cycles. Their observations would be correct, even though their explanations might depend upon imagination. Severinus wanted his students to have firsthand knowledge of "things" and their properties. He wanted them to observe nature just as the peasants did.

Modern geologists and earth scientists benefit from the observations and experiments of earlier scientists. But they still search the mountains and the valleys, the deserts and the oceans to learn more about nature. They continue to discover new facts based upon actual observations and measurements.

Earth science is the study of the planet earth—its land masses, its seas, and its atmosphere. It is not a new science; men have always been curious about their surroundings. Ancient men tried to explain their environment by myths, legends, and tales. Modern men study their surroundings in an attempt to

Robert F. Moseley, Jr.

Figure 1-1. Man's curiosity about earth, sea, and air has led him to probe his environment and revise his old ideas in light of his new findings.

Knowledge of the earth comes through observation and experimentation.

understand the laws of nature that govern their environment. However, the environment is so complex that no one scientist can fully study all its parts. Many fields of investigation are related to the study of the earth. *Lithology* (lith ahl'a jee) is the study of rocks. *Structure* is the study of the position and distribution of rocks. *Historical geology* is the study of changes that have occurred on the planet earth since its beginning. *Meteorology* (meet ee a rahl'a jee) is the study of the atmosphere, and *oceanography* is the study of the earth's seas and their influence on the land masses.

Chemistry is the science concerned with the composition of matter. **Physics** is the science concerned with facts about matter and motion. **Biology** is the study of living matter in all its forms. **Astronomy** is the science of the celestial bodies, their motions, distances, positions, and magnitudes. **Geologic history** is the study of the development of earth.

Earth science deals with changes in the materials of the earth and the causes of such changes. It depends upon both chemistry and physics for an understanding of these materials. Earth science depends upon biology for an understanding of life processes. It looks to geologic history for the story of change in both plants and animals. Modern earth science also includes those areas of astronomy that concern the earth and its relationship to the universe.

Have you ever wondered why volcanoes erupt? Why do glaciers creep across the land? Why do oceans build some shores but wear down others? Why do rivers flood certain lands and cut canyons elsewhere? Earth science is a study of the causes and effects of such events.

1:2 *Origin of the Earth*

No one knows how the earth began. Although many facts about the origin of the earth have been learned, much remains unknown. A number of *hypotheses* (hie pahth'e seez') have been suggested to explain the known facts. A **hypothesis** (hie pahth'e sis) is an explanation for a problem based on a limited amount of information. A hypothesis is often called an *educated guess* because it has not been proved. Modern explanations of the origin of the earth are called *theories* (thee'a rees) instead of hypotheses. A **scientific theory** is an explanation which has stood the test of time. A theory is supported by more information than a hypothesis is.

Discovery of new facts often shows old hypotheses and theories to be wrong. For example, ancient men tried to explain the trembling of the earth. Some thought it was caused by movements of a great giant who supported the earth on his toe. Occasionally the giant tired of holding the earth in a rigid posi-

Figure 1-2. Hypotheses of solar system origin: (a.) near collision, (b.) nebular, (c.) dust cloud. All hypotheses of solar system origin must account for the observed distribution of angular momentum.

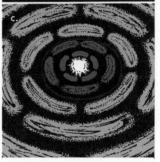

tion. When his muscles relaxed, the earth shook and trembled, causing an earthquake. No one questions that earthquakes occur. This is a fact. The cause of an earthquake, however, is no longer explained by the old "giant hypothesis." Scientists have proved that rocks crack and move upward, downward, or sideward. Movements of rocks within the earth cause earthquake tremors (trem'ers). The "giant hypothesis" is just one example of the way in which hypotheses change. Explanations of the origin of the earth also have undergone many changes as astronomers learned more and more about the universe.

One of the earliest of the modern hypotheses for the origin of the earth was proposed by George de Buffon in 1749. This French naturalist thought that a comet had come close to the sun and pulled away some of the sun's matter. Buffon supposed that the planets were formed from the sun's matter. Few scientists have taken Buffon's idea seriously. But his suggestion was the forerunner of the **near-collision hypothesis.** This hypothesis was proposed at the beginning of this century by two American scientists, T. C. Chamberlin and F. R. Moulton. Their hypothesis was accepted as sound until the early 1940's. Chamberlin and Moulton believed that a second star had nearly collided with the star called the sun. During the near-collision, particles of the sun's matter were pulled away. These particles, called **planetesimals** (plan e tes'i mals), then revolved around the sun. They were held in place by the sun's gravitational attraction for the planetesimals. Gradually, the planetesimals collected and formed larger and larger masses which became the planets.

The planetesimal hypothesis suggests that planets were formed from particles of matter from the sun.

An entirely different hypothesis for the origin of the solar system was suggested in 1755 by Immanuel Kant, a German philosopher. Kant's idea was expanded later by Pierre de Laplace, a French mathematician. The Kant-Laplace hypothesis is similar in many respects to today's most accepted idea of the origin of the solar system. Kant and Laplace pictured a large cloud of hot gas rotating in space. Gradually, the gas cooled and contracted. Some rings of gas were left behind as the main mass condensed and formed the sun. These gas rings were thrown outward by the centrifugal force of the whirling mass of gas

Centrifugal force causes an object to fly outward from the center of rotation.

as it contracted. Each separate gas ring supposedly condensed into a planet. But hot gases do not tend to condense. Instead, hot gases expand into space. In spite of its weaknesses, the Kant-Laplace hypothesis was an important step forward in the understanding of the universe. It was known as the **nebular** (neb'ye ler) **hypothesis.** It suggested that large clouds of gas called *nebulae* (neb'ye lee) existed in outer space.

In 1943, Carl von Weizsacker, a German physicist, suggested the basic ideas of the modern **dust cloud theory.** Astronomers have found that clouds of gas and dust do exist in outer space.

Planet means wanderer; all celestial bodies move, but stars are so far away that they appear static.

Mount Wilson and Palomar Observatories

Figure 1-3.   These four nebulae in the constellation Leo are about 20 million light-years away.

But the gaseous material is cold, not hot, as Kant thought it was. Weizsacker's theory answers some early questions. According to Weizsacker's theory, the planets in the solar system revolve in the same direction, they have nearly circular orbits, and all of them orbit in nearly the same plane.

Gerard Kuiper, an American astronomer, expanded Weizsacker's theory in 1951. Both Kuiper and Weizsacker deserve credit for the modern theories of the origin of the solar system. Today many scientists believe that the solar system developed from a large mass of rotating gas and dust. At first the rate of rotation was slow, but gradually the rate grew faster and faster. Particles within the dust cloud bumped into one another more and more often as the rate of rotation increased. Many of the particles clung together because of their gravitational attraction for each other. Small clumps or knots of matter developed in this way. These clumps gradually increased in size as they attracted more and more particles. Eventually, the solar system developed from these masses of matter.

Astronomers believe that, early in the history of the nebula, the cloud flattened into the shape of a disk. During this stage, matter in the nebula began to rotate in the same plane and in nearly the same direction. *Eddies* (ed'ees), or whirlpools, like the circular currents within a swiftly moving river, began to separate the nebula into parts. Each part became a clump of matter as the particles were swept closer and closer together. Eventually each major eddy became a planet, rotating around its own center and carrying itself forward around the center of the dust cloud.

Gas at the center of the nebula condensed into the largest mass of the solar system. In this mass, particles of matter came into contact so often that the temperature began to rise. As the temperature rose higher and higher, changes similar to those within a nuclear bomb occurred. The mass began to radiate energy in the form of heat and light. Thus, the star called the *sun* was born.

All these theories are based on the best information available today. Theories are subject to change in light of any new scientific information.

Modern theories, based on ideas of Weizsacker and Kuiper, suggest that: (1) a combination of cool gas and dust formed the planets, (2) planets formed from eddies in the nebula, (3) center of the nebula became the sun and, because of nuclear reactions, began to radiate energy.

Figure 1-4. Matter within large eddies is believed to have condensed to form the planets which are spaced within the solar system in a mathematical relationship known as Bode's law.

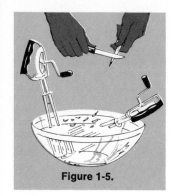

Figure 1-5.

ACTIVITY. Compare the movement of particles on water with the presumed movements in the solar system's nebula. Place two egg beaters in a shallow bowl. Add water to the bowl to cover the webs of the beaters. Gently and evenly, distribute some pencil shavings onto the water. Start one beater in the center of the bowl. Stir slowly and then gradually increase the speed. Notice which shavings move first. Where do they move? What force causes the movement? Do all the shavings move at the same rate? Does the size of a shaving have any effect on its movement? Stop the beater and observe which shavings stop moving first.

Resume the beating in the center of the bowl. Have a friend start the second egg beater rotating slowly near the outer edge of the bowl. How are the shavings affected by this second center of movement? Alternate the speeds of both beaters and record the results. How is the movement of the shavings affected?

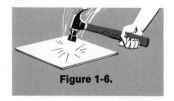

Figure 1-6.

ACTIVITY. Test the relationship between collision and temperature. Hammer on a piece of sheet metal for several minutes. Feel the sheet metal. What has happened to its temperature? Explain the change.

1:3 Gravity

Vacuum is an area in which there is little matter present.

Acceleration is the rate at which velocity increases in a unit of time. **Velocity** is the distance traveled in a unit of time. **Mass** is the quantity of matter present in a body.

Aristotle (384-322 B.C.), a Greek philosopher, suggested that a heavy body (large mass) falls faster than a lightweight body (small mass). Aristotle's theory was generally accepted until early in the seventeenth century. Then an Italian astronomer and physicist named Galileo demonstrated that the increasing speed, or **acceleration** (ik sel a rae'shun), of a falling object does *not* depend upon its mass. A falling body near the surface of the earth has an acceleration of 980 centimeters (32 feet*) per second per second in a vacuum. This means that the **velocity** (ve lahs'et ee) of the body increases 980 cm (32 ft) per second for every second that it falls. In other words, the farther an object falls, the faster it falls. Bodies that fall in air do not fall as fast as bodies in a vacuum. Friction between the body and air decreases its speed slightly. For most problems, an acceleration of 980 cm (32 ft)/sec/sec is exact enough. (Figure 1-7.)

* See Appendix A, p. 528.

Galileo's experiments did not explain why bodies fall or why their rate of fall is not related to their mass. But his efforts laid the groundwork for the explanation of gravity developed later by the English scientist Sir Isaac Newton.

In 1680, Newton explained the relationships that exist between all *observable* bodies. His explanations are called the *laws of motion*. They are the basic ideas of physics. Study of outer space has contributed some new ideas to physics. But Newton's ideas still explain the motions of observable bodies.

One of Newton's laws states that all bodies at rest resist motion. But if a body is set in motion by some outside force, it tends to continue to move in a straight line. This property of matter is called **inertia** (in er'shuh). Force must be applied to make a body move, change the direction of its motion, or to stop. The amount of force required depends upon the *mass* of the body. Mass is the property of a body that gives it its inertia. Mass also is a measure of the quantity of matter in a body.

All particles or objects attract all other particles or objects. This mutual attraction between all matter is known as **gravitation** (grav i tae'shun). The force of gravitation that pulls bodies toward one another corresponds to the product of the mass of the bodies divided by the square of the distance between them. This relationship is known as Newton's **law of gravitation.** It may be written mathematically as follows:

$$F \; :: \frac{M \times m}{d^2}.$$

In this equation, F represents the gravitational force or attraction, : : represents "is proportional to," M represents the mass of one body or object, m represents the mass of the second body or object, and d represents the distance between the centers of the two bodies or objects.

Gravitational attraction between small bodies, such as oranges, apples, and even automobiles, is not measurable by ordinary methods. However, objects of large mass have an extremely large gravitational attraction. For example, the gravitational attraction between earth and moon is several trillion tons. Gravitational attraction of the earth for objects near its surface is called *gravity*. A measure of this gravitational pull of the earth on bodies near its surface is called *weight*.

Bodies may be observed falling to earth. Planetary bodies may be observed moving through the sky. Newton's laws of motion explain both motions in terms of gravitational attraction.

Figure 1-7. In a vacuum, would a feather and a steel ball fall with the same acceleration?

PROBLEM

1. If you were standing on top of Mt. Everest (elevation about 29,000 ft above sea level), would the gravitational

attraction between you and the earth be greater or less than it would be at sea level? Why?

Newton's laws led to the discovery of unknown planets. The laws supplied an explanation of ocean tides. They predicted the true shape of the earth and gave a reason for the slow change in the direction of the axis on which the earth turns. Newton explained the *how* of movements of all observable bodies, including the bodies of the solar system.

1:4 *Motions of the Earth*

Movements of bodies in space are determined by the gravitational attraction of one body for another. Bodies of small mass tend to move toward bodies of greater mass. The sun has the greatest mass of all the bodies in the solar system. For example, the mass of the sun is 333,500 times the mass of the earth. Therefore, the earth tends to move toward the sun. In fact, each planet is pulled inward toward the sun which is at the center of the solar system. If there were no gravitational attraction of the sun, inertia of the planets would tend to keep them moving in a straight line. The gravitational attraction of the sun exerts a force on the planet. The difference between the planet's inertia and the gravitational force determines the direction of movement. As a result of these two forces, planets

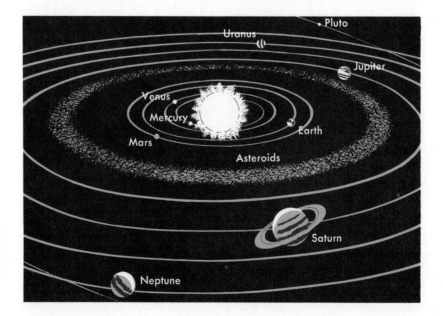

Figure 1-8. The gravitational attraction of the sun controls several thousand independent bodies. But the volume of space occupied by the solar system is so vast that it may be considered nearly empty.

follow a curved path. Because the planets do not move at uniform speeds, their paths are *elliptical* (e lip'ti kal). (Figure 1–8.) As viewed from the North Star, the motion of the planets is in a counterclockwise direction. Planets orbit the sun approximately in the plane of the sun's equator. This plane of orbit is called the *plane of the ecliptic* (i klip'tik).

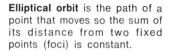

Elliptical orbit is the path of a point that moves so the sum of its distance from two fixed points (foci) is constant.

ACTIVITY.   Hold a ball in your hand. Then let the ball drop without giving it a push. What force causes the ball to fall? Throw the ball horizontally. What happens to the ball? What kind of path does the ball follow? What forces determine the path of the ball?

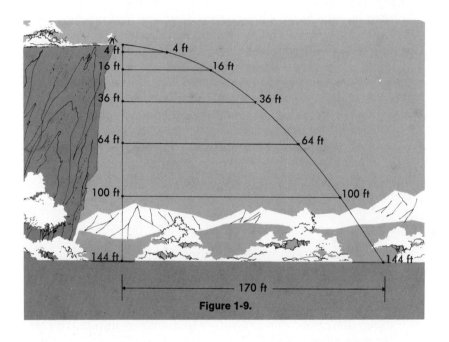

Figure 1-9.

Figure 1–9 illustrates the combined effect of gravity and horizontal movement. Two balls are released at the same time from an overhanging cliff 144 ft high. One ball is allowed to fall freely. The other ball is thrown horizontally from the cliff. As shown in the diagram, the positions of the two balls are photographed every one-half second. Compare the vertical fall of one ball with that of the other ball. (This rate of fall is indicated in feet per every one-half second.) How far does each ball fall in 3 sec? What force determines the vertical movement? What forces determine the horizontal movement of the second ball? Is the path followed by the second ball circular or is it elliptical?

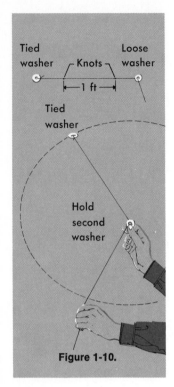

Tied washer — Knots — Loose washer

1 ft

Tied washer

Hold second washer

Figure 1-10.

The combination of forces illustrated is the same as the forces acting on the planets. What was the direction of forces that determined the planets' orbits? What were the forces?

ACTIVITY. Tie knots about 1 ft apart in a string at least 4 ft long. Tie a heavy iron washer at one end of the string and thread the loose end through another washer. Do not tie the second washer to the string. Hold the free end of the string in one hand and the loose washer in the other hand. (Figure 1–10.) Swing the tied washer in a circle over your head. Be sure you do not hit anyone. Increase the speed of the moving washer until the string is taut. Now gradually shorten the string, one section at a time, by pulling it down through the washer in your hand. Continue to rotate the tied washer. To keep the string taut, do you need to increase or decrease the speed of the swinging washer?

Replace the large washer at the end of the string with a small washer and repeat the first part of the activity. Does the size of the washer affect the speed necessary to keep the string taut? Compare the materials used in your activity to the parts of the solar system. What does the washer in your hand represent? What do the string and the tied washer represent? How is the size of a planet and its distance from the sun related to this activity? What effects do a planet's mass and its distance from the sun have on its velocity?

PROBLEMS

2. If all the planets were the same size, but were different distances from the sun, which ones would move fastest around the sun?
3. If all the planets were their actual sizes, but were the same distance from the sun, which ones would move fastest around the sun?
4. Why is the sun at the center of the solar system?

Figure 1-11. Solar system distances can be expressed in miles, kilometers, astronomical units, or light-years.

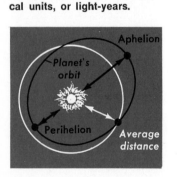

Aphelion

Planet's orbit

Perihelion

Average distance

Two familiar motions of the earth are *revolution* and *rotation*. **Revolution** (rev a loo'shun) is the movement of the earth around the sun. **Rotation** (roh tae'shun) is the spinning motion of the earth on its axis. The earth revolves around the sun in a path called an *orbit*. The shape of the orbit is elliptical. The distance between earth and sun depends upon the position of the earth in the ellipse. (Figure 1–11.) In January, the earth is nearest the sun. This point in the ellipse is called **perihelion** (per i heel'yan). At perihelion, the earth is 91.5 million mi away from the sun. In this position, the earth moves more rapidly than when it is farther from the sun. In July, the distance between the earth and the sun is 94.5 million mi. This point in the orbit is called **aphelion** (a feel′yan). At aphelion, the earth is farthest from the sun. The mean or average distance between the earth and the sun is 93 million mi. This mean distance is called one *astronomical unit*. It is often used to express distances within the solar system. For example, the mean distance between Mars and the sun is 1.524 astronomical units (142 million mi).

Mean or average distance between earth and sun is 93 million mi **(one astronomical unit).**

One *earth year* is the period of time required for the earth to make one revolution around the sun. If the starting point in the orbit is determined by sighting on a star, the orbital period is called the *sidereal* (sie dir′ee al) *year*, or the *star year*. If the starting point is measured in relation to the position of the sun, the orbital period is called the *solar year*, or the *tropical year*. The tropical year is the basis for our calendars. One complete tropical year requires approximately 365¼ days.

Time periods measured by sighting on a star **(sidereal time)** are shorter than those measured by sighting on the sun or moon.

Once every 24 hours, the earth rotates or turns on its axis, if the starting point is measured in relation to the sun. The day is slightly shorter if the period of rotation is measured in relation to a star. This is the *sidereal day*. The axis on which the earth rotates is tilted in relation to its plane of orbit. The angle of tilt, or *inclination*, is 23½° measured from a perpendicular to the plane of the earth's orbit. It is 66½° measured from the axis to the orbital plane. (Figure 1–12.)

The tilt of the axis is the cause of the difference in the length of daylight in winter and summer. In the northern hemisphere, there are more than 12 hours of daylight from about March 21 to September 23 (spring and summer). There are fewer than 12 hours of daylight from about September 22 to March 21 (fall

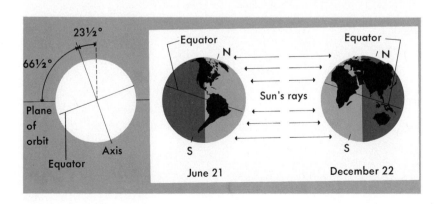

Figure 1-12. Earth's axis maintains its 23½° inclination from the vertical to its plane of orbit and points at all times to the north celestial pole.

and winter). The southern hemisphere has more than 12 hours of daylight from about September 23 through March 21 (spring and summer). It has fewer than 12 hours of daylight from about March 21 to September 23 (fall and winter). The seasons are opposite in the two hemispheres because the position of the sun changes in relation to the axis of the earth.

Earth has a natural *satellite* (sat'el iet), or moon, which makes one revolution around the earth in 29½ days measured from new moon to new moon. This orbital period takes slightly over 2 days longer than the *sideral orbit* which is measured in relation to a star. The *month* is a unit of time corresponding nearly to the orbit of the moon around the earth.

The orbital plane of the moon is inclined, or tipped, approximately 5° from the ecliptic plane of the earth. Therefore, the moon and the earth seldom lie between one another and the sun. When the two bodies are in a direct line with the sun, an *eclipse* (i klips') occurs. A *lunar eclipse* occurs when the earth is directly between the moon and the sun. Then the shadow of the earth falls across the moon and darkens it. A *solar eclipse* occurs when the moon is directly between the earth and the sun. Then the shadow of the moon falls on the surface of the earth. Areas of the earth are darkened. It is called a solar eclipse because, in the darkened areas, part or all of the sun is hidden by the moon's disk.

Earth and its moon are so close together that they form an earth-moon system. The earth and its moon are 232,271 mi apart as measured by one Apollo laser experiment. The mean distance is 238,857 mi which is very small compared to the 93 million mi between the earth and the sun. The earth-moon system revolves around the sun. But the center of gravity for the

Eclipse or darkening of either earth or moon may occur if one or the other body lies in direct line with the sun and cuts off the sun's light.

Figure 1-13. A multiple exposure showing the 1970 solar eclipse from beginning to end. This was the first total eclipse seen on the eastern seaboard of the United States in 92 years.

NASA

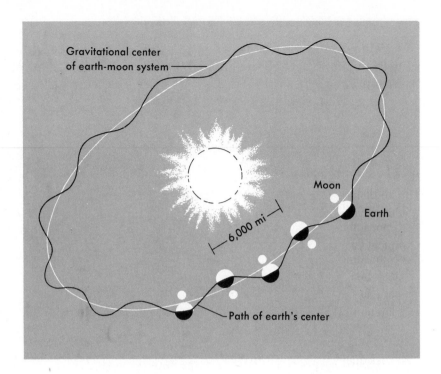

Figure 1-14. Center of gravity for the earth-moon system traces a smooth ellipse during its yearly orbit around the sun, but the center of the moon and center of the earth have an intertwined path as the moon orbits the earth.

system does not lie at the true center of the earth. Instead, the gravitational center of the earth-moon system is approximately 1,000 mi below the earth's surface or 3,000 mi from the true center of the earth. Thus, the center of gravity for the earth-moon system is 3,000 mi closer to the moon than the true center of the earth is.

Several motions result from the earth-moon relationship. The gravitational center of the earth-moon system traces a smooth ellipse around the sun. The center of the earth traces an S-shaped curve along the ellipse. The range of this S-curve movement is approximately 6,000 mi. (Figure 1–14.) It takes 18.6 years for the moon to alternately pass from south to north and then south of the earth. This movement is known as **nutation** (neu tae'shun).

Precession (pree sesh'un) refers to the motion of the earth's axis as it traces a cone-shaped pattern during a 25,800-year cycle. (Table 1–1.) The north pole of the earth now points to the star Polaris. Thus, *Polaris* is called the North Star. In approximately 13,000 years, the north pole of the earth will have changed its position and will point toward the star *Vega* (vee'ga). Then Vega will be called the North Star. In still about another 13,000 years, the north pole again will be pointing to the star Polaris.

Figure 1-15. At present, the earth's north pole points toward Polaris. However, the pole traces a cone-shaped pattern in the sky. In about 13,000 years, the north pole will point toward Vega.

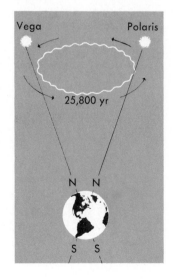

Nutation and precession are irregularities in the path traced by the earth's axis.

In another movement through space, the earth and the sun move in an orbit through the Milky Way Galaxy. This journey requires 200 million years. During this cycle, the solar system rushes onward in space at a rate of 150 mi/sec!

Table 1–1. *Motions of the Earth*

Mean distance from sun	93,000,000 mi (1 astronomical unit)
Mean distance from moon	238,857 mi
Sidereal year (measured from star position)	365d 6h 9m 9s*
Tropical year (measured from equinox**)	365d 5h 48m
Sidereal day	23h 56m 4s
Solar day	24h
Inclination of axis from perpendicular to plane of orbit	23½°
Orbital velocity	18.5 mi/sec
Precessional cycle***	25,800y

* y=year, d=day, h=hour, m=minute, s=second

** Equinox—the two points at which the plane of the ecliptic cuts the *celestial equator.* (Section 22:3.) Spring begins when the sun passes the vernal equinox (about March 21). Fall begins when the sun passes the autumnal equinox (about September 22). During the equinoxes, day and night are equal.

*** Precession—often referred to as "precession of the equinoxes." Because the earth's axis is moving in space, the intersection of the ecliptic and the celestial equator is gradually moving westward.

MAIN IDEAS

1. A study of earth science requires observation and investigation of earth processes and earth materials. Earth science depends upon many other fields of science.

2. Hypotheses change with the discovery of new facts that add to the understanding of natural processes.

3. Scientific theories explain many related facts and are based on more evidence than hypotheses are.

4. Early hypotheses about the earth's origin suggested that the planets were formed from the sun's matter. The matter was either pulled off by a passing star or left behind during the condensation of hot gases.

5. According to Weizsacker and Kuiper, all members of the solar system came from the same original nebula which consisted of cool gas and dust.

6. An experiment by Galileo led to an understanding of acceleration of bodies during free fall. All bodies near the earth's surface fall at an increasing rate of speed which is 980 cm/sec/sec.

7. Sir Isaac Newton proposed the first explanation that reasonably accounts for the motions of the solar system. Newton's law of gravitation led to an explanation for the movements of all observable bodies. Newton's mathematical expression of his law is $F : : \dfrac{M \times m}{d^2}$.

8. The planets are held in the solar system and their movements are governed by the gravitational attraction of the massive sun. Inertia carries a planet forward; gravitation pulls the planet inward. The effect of these two forces and variation in speed causes elliptical orbits.

9. Time is measured by motions of the earth. The earth revolves around the sun in $365\frac{1}{4}$ days, a period of one year. The moon revolves around the earth in a period known as one lunar month. The earth rotates on its axis in a unit of time known as one day.

10. The center of gravity for the earth-moon system is 3,000 miles closer to the moon than the true center of the earth is. The earth-moon relationship causes an imbalance in the rotation of the earth.

VOCABULARY

Write a sentence in which you use correctly each of the following words or terms.

acceleration	inertia	physics
aphelion	lithology	planetesimals
center of gravity	mass	precession
condense	meteorology	satellite
eclipse	nebulae	scientific theory
gravity	nutation	terrestrial
hypothesis	perihelion	velocity

STUDY QUESTIONS

A. True or False

Determine whether each of the following sentences is true or false. (Do not write in this book.)

1. Myths and legends are scientific explanations.
2. The nebulae in space contain mostly gases, but they also contain particles similar to the earth's matter.
3. The body in space known as the earth is a planet.
4. Cold gases tend to condense.
5. A hypothesis is based on more reliable information than a scientific theory.
6. As a result of his experiments, Galileo was able to explain why bodies fall toward the earth.
7. Newton discovered that all objects are attracted to all other objects.
8. The calendar month is not the same length as the moon's orbit around the earth.
9. The earth's greatest distance from the sun is 93 million miles.
10. All planets move counterclockwise around the sun.

B. Multiple Choice

Choose the word or phrase which completes correctly each of the following sentences. (Do not write in this book.)

1. An idea which is thought to be true, but which cannot be demonstrated, is called a (*fact, hypothesis, philosophy*).
2. Clouds of gas and dust that exist in outer space are called (*planets, astronomical units, nebulae*).
3. The force which keeps the planets revolving around the sun is the result of the sun's gravitational attraction and the planet's (*atmosphere, inertia, rotation*).
4. The most accepted theory for the origin of the earth is the work of (*Newton and Galileo, Chamberlin and Moulton, Kuiper and Weizsacker*).
5. The center of gravity for the earth-moon system is (*3,000 miles below the surface of the earth, 1,000 miles below the surface of the moon, 3,000 miles nearer the moon than the true center of the earth is*).

6. The point in the earth's orbit where the earth is farthest from the sun is the (*perihelion, equinox, aphelion, plane of the ecliptic*).

7. Acceleration of any falling body near the earth's surface is (*860 cm/sec/sec, 980 cm/sec/sec, 480 cm/sec/sec*).

8. A lunar month is (*27⅓, 28⅖, 29½*) days.

9. The motion of the earth which in time will change the north star from Polaris to Vega is called (*precession, nutation, acceleration, revolution*).

10. The attraction between the sun and the earth is known as the force of (*acceleration, inertia, gravitation, velocity*).

C. Completion

Complete each of the following sentences with a word or phrase which will make the sentence correct. (Do not write in this book.)

1. Time measured by sighting on stars is called ___?___.

2. The scientist who was responsible for formulating the Law of Gravitation was ___?___.

3. The force which acts along with the sun's gravitational attraction and keeps the planets revolving around the sun in elliptical orbits is ___?___.

4. The formula for the gravitational attraction between observable bodies is ___?___.

5. Because of ___?___, all bodies resist movement.

6. The plane of the earth's orbit around the sun is the ___?___.

7. The nodding of the axis of the earth because of the moon's influence is called ___?___.

8. Scientific methods of study require both ___?___ and ___?___.

9. The 16th century scientist who advised students to follow scientific methods of study was ___?___.

10. ___?___ is the quantity of matter present in a body.

D. How and Why

1. If the sun were to lose mass but the earth stayed the same, what would happen? Why? If the earth were to lose mass but the sun stayed the same, what would happen? Why? Do the other bodies in the solar system have an attraction for one another?

2. Why did Severinus advise his students to go to the mountains, the valleys, the deserts, and the seashores for their information?

3. What was the most important contribution of Newtonian physics?

4. Why is the greatest concentration of gas in the center of the nebula?

5. Why do artificial satellites eventually fall toward the earth?

6. Why does the United States have more hours of daylight in June than in January?

7. Why are the orbits of the planets elliptical rather than circular?

8. Account for the fact that the sidereal year, month, and day is shorter than similar time units measured by sighting on the sun or moon.

9. Discuss the difference between a hypothesis, a scientific theory, and a scientific law.

10. How does modern scientific study differ from the study that preceded the sixteenth century?

11. Name some fields of study that are related to the study of the earth. What is each field concerned with? Why is the study of the earth broken down into many fields of study?

INVESTIGATIONS

1. Obtain information in a library about a myth which illustrates the ideas ancient men had about such things as earthquakes, volcanic eruptions, floods, seasonal changes, day and night, or the shape of the earth.

2. Discuss the difference between chemistry and physics. Is either science more closely related to earth science than the other is? Explain your answer.

3. Look up the word *philosophy* in a complete dictionary and discuss the meanings you find there. Is earth science a philosophy? Explain your answer.

INTERESTING READING

Asimov, Isaac, *Great Ideas of Science*. Boston, Houghton Mifflin Company, 1969.

*Barnett, Lincoln, *The World We Live In*. New York, Golden Press, 1956.

*Bergamini, David, *The Universe*. Life Nature Library. New York, Time Inc., 1969.

Fenton, Carroll Lane, *Our Amazing Earth*. Garden City, N.Y., Doubleday & Company, Inc., 1945.

Gamow, George, *A Planet Called Earth*. New York, The Viking Press, Inc., 1963.

Gamow, George, *Gravity: Classic and Modern Views*. Garden City, N.Y., Doubleday & Company, Inc., 1962.

*Huxley, Julian, ed., *Motion, Matter & Energy—Man and Science*. The Illustrated Libraries of Human Knowledge. Columbus, Ohio, Charles E. Merrill Publishing Co., 1968.

*Sagan, Carl and Leonard, and Norton, Jonathan, *Planets*. Life Science Library. New York, Time Inc., 1966.

Sutton, Felix, *The How and Why Wonder Book of Our Earth*. Columbus, Ohio, Charles E. Merrill Publishing Co., 1960.

Zim, Herbert S., and Baker, Robert H., *Stars*. A Golden Nature Guide. New York, Golden Press, 1951.

---

* Well-illustrated material.

Form and Layers of the Earth

Discovering the dimensions and the shape of the earth has been a difficult problem for students and for earth scientists. Measuring an object as large as the earth requires instruments that are not common. You would need a tape measure almost 25,000 mi long to circle the earth at the equator. To measure the diameter, you would need more than 13 million yardsticks. Devices such as yardsticks or tape measures are neither accurate nor convenient for measuring objects as large as the earth. But the need for accuracy is increasingly important in an age of rapid transportation and space exploration. Without accurate instruments and earth measurements, planes would miss their landings, ships at sea could not be located, and spacecraft landing sites could not be determined exactly.

2:1 *Shape*

Earth's great size makes calculation of its dimensions difficult. Geodetic surveys supply accurate measurements made by modern methods.

Scientists constantly are trying to improve the accuracy of their measurements of the earth. The great dimensions involved in a survey of the earth are measured by a variety of instruments. The scientists making these measurements are *geodesists* (jee ahd'e sists). The measurements are called a *geodetic* (jee a det'ik) *survey*.

Today, few people have difficulty picturing the planet earth as a ball, or *sphere* (sfir). Data relayed from artificial satellites and pictures taken by astronauts have confirmed the teaching of geography about the size and shape of the earth.

Even without modern instruments, satellites, and photographs, some ancient philosophers reasoned that the earth is curved. About 500 B.C., Pythagoras, a Greek philosopher, concluded that the earth is a sphere. He compared the earth with the spherical shape of the moon. Aristotle, another Greek teacher who lived about 300 B.C., also taught his students that the earth is a sphere. He based his conclusions on his observation of the moon during an eclipse. (Section 1:4.) Aristotle saw that the earth cast a curved shadow on the moon as the earth passed between the moon and the sun. About 200 B.C., Eratosthenes, an astronomer of Alexandria, Egypt, not only demonstrated the earth's curvature, but also computed its size.

Scientists were not alone in recognizing that the earth is curved. A few observant sailors knew that the earth is not flat. If you have watched a ship sail away from shore toward the horizon, you may have seen the effect of the curvature of the

By studying the shape of the moon and watching eclipses, some ancient philosophers concluded that the earth is a sphere.

NASA

Figure 2-1. View of the earth from 22,300 miles above its surface. Portions of North America, South America, Europe, and Africa are visible through the cloud cover.

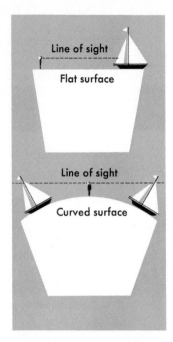

Figure 2-2. Around 500 B.C., Philolaus correctly guessed the earth to have the shape of a ball. Others thought the earth was a flat circular plate or short cylinder, floating in and surrounded by water.

Jean Richer, using a pendulum clock, proved that gravitational attraction of the earth is less at the equator than at points distant from the equator.

earth. As the ship sails away, first the lower part disappears from view. Then the upper part disappears below the horizon. As the ship approaches the shore, the upper part comes into view first. Then more and more of the lower part appears, until finally the entire ship becomes visible. (Figure 2–2.)

Unfortunately, much of the early knowledge of the earth was lost in the six centuries after the fall of the Roman Empire (A.D. 476). This period is called the Dark Ages. Many records of Greek and Roman culture were burned. Others were hidden away in monasteries. Few people could read the language in which the available records were written, even after they were found. Mere existence was a problem during this difficult period in the earth's history. The skills of the past were forgotten. People were confined to their immediate area of land. They did not realize that the earth is curved since they did not travel on the oceans.

When Columbus sailed westward from Spain in search of India in 1492, he began a great period of exploration and investigation. Many discoveries about the earth followed. In 1522, Magellan, a Portuguese navigator, proved the earth to be spherical by sailing completely around it. Magellan had no measurements to determine the exact shape of the earth, but his successful voyage around the globe supported the idea that the earth was a sphere. Eventually, enough evidence was obtained to show that the earth is an *oblate spheroid* and not a true sphere. An **oblate spheroid** (ahb'laet · sfir'awid) is a sphere that bulges at the equator and is flattened at the poles.

Proof of the bulge at the equator was the result of a scientific expedition sponsored by the French Academy of Science in 1672. Jean Richer, a French astronomer, went to French Guiana to observe the planet Mars. During his astronomical studies of the stars, Richer noticed that his pendulum clock lost about $2\frac{1}{2}$ minutes per day. Pendulum clocks depend on gravity. They are accurate unless the force of gravity varies. A *pendulum* (pen'je lum) is a mass suspended on a long wire. The wire hangs from a point so that the mass can swing freely in a circular arc. Gravity pulls the pendulum toward its rest position. Inertia carries the pendulum beyond its rest position until gravity pulls it back toward its rest position again. Thus, the pendulum swings back and forth in an arc. The time required for the complete swing of the pendulum is called its *period*. The period of a pendulum depends upon the length of the pendulum wire and the gravitational attraction of the earth.

Richer knew that the length of the pendulum had not changed. The clock had not been damaged in shipment. Therefore, the difference in period must have been related to a change in the gravitational attraction of the earth. Richer concluded that the force of gravity was weaker in French Guiana, near the equator, than in Paris, nearly 3,700 mi north of the equator.

Sir Isaac Newton suggested a reason for the weaker gravitational attraction at the equator. He suggested that the earth bulges at the equator. Newton reasoned that near the equator the rotational speed of 1,000 mi/hr partially overcomes the pull of gravity toward the center of the earth. This force pulling matter away from the center of the earth is called **centrifugal** (sen trif′ye gal) **force.** Consequently, matter tends to bulge outward around the equator. Particles of matter at the poles are pulled toward the center of the earth more than matter at the equator. This is because gravity is the only acting force at the poles. There is no rotational speed at the poles and, therefore, no centrifugal force. Therefore, the poles should be flatter than the equator. According to Newton's reasoning, the diameter of the earth should be greater at the equator than at the poles because of the equatorial bulge. In Newton's law of gravitation (Section 1:3), the gravitational attraction between two objects becomes less as the distance between the two objects becomes greater. This is another reason that the gravitational

Rotational speed of the earth at points between the equator and the poles is less than 1,000 mi/hr and greater than zero. Exact rotational speed depends on latitude.

Centrifugal means to flee from the center.

The diameter of a sphere is a straight line from one surface to another through the center of the sphere.

$$F :: \frac{M \times m}{d^2}$$

United Nations

Figure 2-3. The Foucault pendulum appears to shift its plane gradually clockwise, but the plane in which the pendulum swings does not change. Instead the earth beneath is rotating and causing the apparent shift.

The equator divides the globe into north and south latitudes. Imaginary lines (latitude and longitude) divide the earth into units for convenience in locating places on the globe and for measuring time.

Latitude lines would always intercept the same distances on the earth's surface if the earth were a perfect sphere. An arc of 1° intercepts distances that increase in length toward the poles.

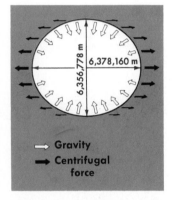

Figure 2-4. From the equator to the pole, the decrease in radius of the earth causes a change in weight of 0.5 percent.

attraction for bodies on the earth's surface is least at the equator and greatest at the poles. (Figure 2–4.)

Not all scientists accepted Newton's idea about the shape of the earth. To settle the question, expeditions were sent out to make actual measurements. These expeditions were sponsored by the French Royal Academy of Sciences. In 1735, one group went to Peru (now Ecuador), near the equator. The other group went to Lapland, above the Arctic Circle, near the Gulf of Bothnia. The purpose of the expeditions was to measure the width of one degree (1°) of latitude. If the earth were a perfect sphere, the widths would not vary. If the earth were an oblate spheroid, the widths would increase toward the poles.

Both the expedition in the Arctic and the one near the equator measured 1° latitude along a line of longitude. These are the results of their measurements:

Near the equator, 1° latitude = 68.704 mi
Near the north pole, 1° latitude = 69.407 mi

These measurements were additional proof that the earth is an oblate spheroid and not a perfect sphere.

Recent data from satellites indicate that the southern hemisphere is slightly larger than the northern hemisphere. From these data, the planet earth has been described as pear-shaped. However, the difference between the hemispheres is so slight that oblate spheroid is still the most exact description of the shape of the earth.

Locations on the earth's surface are indicated by the use of imaginary lines. These imaginary lines are called **latitude** lines and **longitude** lines. Latitude is measured in degrees north and south of the equator. The equator is zero latitude. The north pole lies at 90° north latitude. The south pole is at 90° south latitude. All latitude lines are parallel to the equator.

Lines of longitude, called meridians, refer to locations east or west in degrees. The longitude line which passes through Greenwich (Grin'ij), England, is called the *prime meridian*, 0° longitude. Opposite the prime meridian, at 180°, is another important line. This is the *international date line*. It varies slightly through populated areas. Lines of longitude divide the earth into 24 units. Each unit is 15° wide (15° × 24 = 360°). For each 15° of longitude, there is 1 hr of difference in time from the previous meridian. At the international date line, one day is lost or gained, depending upon the direction of travel.

PROBLEMS

1. When it is 12 noon on Sunday at 90° west longitude, what time is it at 90° east longitude? Is it the same day at Greenwich, England?
2. On a map of the world, draw 24 longitude lines equally far apart. How many degrees apart are they?
3. Assume that you leave the prime meridian at midnight and fly west at a rate of 1,000 mi/hr along a latitude line where the circumference of the earth measures exactly 24,000 mi. Give the hour at which you arrive at each of the longitude lines on the map. How many hours will it take you to return to your starting point? On which day and hour would you arrive at the prime meridian if you left there at 6 A.M. on Monday, June 1?

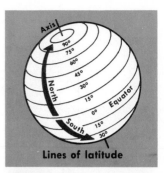

Figure 2-5. Lines of latitude are parallel to the equator. Longitude positions lie on great circles that pass through both poles.

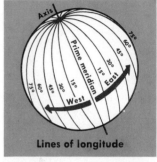

Figure 2-6. Time zones do not exactly follow longitude lines. They are modified to lessen confusion within states, counties, and towns.

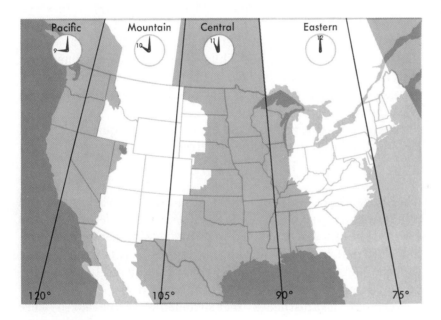

2:2 *Size*

Study of the shape of the earth led to questions about the size of the earth. From repeated scientific measurements, man's knowledge of the size of the earth increased. Ancient maps show far different outlines for the continents and the oceans than do modern maps. Values, or numerical measurements, for the size of the earth also have undergone change.

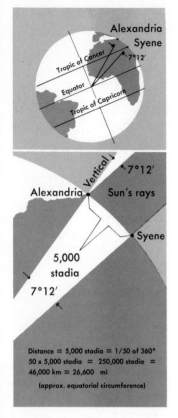

Distance = 5,000 stadia = 1/50 of 360°
50 x 5,000 stadia = 250,000 stadia =
46,000 km = 26,600 mi

(approx. equatorial circumference)

Figure 2-7.   Medieval figures for the earth's circumference were much smaller than Eratosthenes' nearly accurate calculations.

The circumference of the earth at the equator is approximately 24,902 mi.

About 200 B.C., the Greek astronomer Eratosthenes made the first measurements of the earth's circumference. His results were amazingly close to the presently accepted figures. The slight difference may be because the *stadium* (staed'ee um), an ancient unit of distance equal to about 185 meters, cannot be related directly to our modern units of distance.* Also, Eratosthenes may not have measured accurately the distance between Alexandria and Syene (now Aswân), Egypt. Another possibility is that the well walls may not have been perfectly perpendicular.

Eratosthenes knew that Syene (Sie ee'nee) was about 5,000 stadia south of Alexandria. He also knew that at noon on the vernal equinox the sun shone directly into a deep well in Syene and cast no shadow. At noon on the same day in Alexandria, the sun did cast a shadow. Eratosthenes determined that the angle between the sun's rays and a vertical post was seven degrees, twelve minutes (7° 12'). He assumed correctly that because of the sun's great distance from earth, all rays from the sun are nearly parallel. Thus, Eratosthenes reasoned that the earth must be curved because the sun's rays were perpendicular to earth at Syene and they made an angle with earth at Alexandria. (Figure 2–7.)

He calculated that an angle of 7° 12' was equal to 1/50 of the 360° in the circumference of a circle:

$$\frac{7° \ 12'}{360°} = \frac{7.2°}{360°} = 1/50$$

Therefore, the distance of 5,000 stadia between Alexandria and Syene was an arc equal to 1/50 of the circumference of the earth. If stadia are converted to miles, Eratosthenes' measurement is equal to 26,660 mi (approximately). This value is close to the 24,902 mi (approximately) now considered to be the correct circumference of the earth at the equator.

Although Eratosthenes' measurements of the earth were nearly exact, the data were not well known. Eratosthenes' measurements were not used in making early maps, and ancient maps were extremely inaccurate. Furthermore, the data were lost during the Dark Ages. No new measurements of the earth were made until the nineteenth century.

Eratosthenes' method of computing the size of the earth is still used. For greater accuracy, however, sightings today are made with a star as a reference point rather than the sun.

---

* See Appendix A, p. 528.

In 1830, Sir George Everest, the British surveyor after whom Mt. Everest was named, calculated values for the size of the earth that are still used. In 1909, the United States Geological Survey computed another series of values. These were adopted in 1924 as the International Standard. These figures are still in use, although they were revised in 1960 by the United States Army Map Service. Data from earth satellites were used for the latest revision. (Table 2–1 and 2–2.) Differences in the values represent variations in methods and instruments rather than actual changes in earth's size.

Earth measurements are always subject to revision in light of new data.

Table 2–1. *Values for Earth's Axes*

	North-South Axis	Equatorial Axis
Everest (1830)	6,356,075 m	6,377,276 m
International Standard (1909)	6,356,912 m	6,378,388 m
U.S. Army Map Service (1960)	6,356,778 m	6,378,160 m

Table 2–2. *Values for Earth's Radii**

Polar radius	6,357 km	3,951 mi
Equatorial radius	6,378 km	3,964 mi
Mean radius	6,367 km	3,960 mi

* As adopted by the International Union of Geodesy and Geophysics.

The values in Table 2–2 are used to determine values approximately equal to ($\cong$) earth measurements as follows:

Equatorial circumference $= 2 \pi r \cong 2 \times 3.14 \times 3,964 \text{ mi} \cong 24,902 \text{ mi}$
Polar circumference $= 2 \pi r \cong 2 \times 3.14 \times 3,951 \text{ mi} \cong 24,860 \text{ mi}$
Area $= 4 \pi r^2 \cong 4 \times 3.14 \times (3,960 \text{ mi})^2 \cong 197,000,000 \text{ mi}^2$
Volume $= \dfrac{4 \pi r^3}{3} \cong \dfrac{4 \times 3.14 \times (3,960)^3}{3} \cong 260 \text{ billion mi}^3$

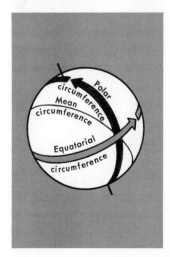

Figure 2-8.   Differences between the polar circumference and the equatorial circumference are so slight that the earth viewed from space appears nearly spherical.

PROBLEM

4. If the angle measured by Eratosthenes had been 10° instead of 7° 12′ and the distance had been 5,000 stadia, what would the value of the circumference of the earth have been? Give the answer in kilometers.

2:3 Mass

Mass and weight are not the same.

Knowledge of the size and shape of the earth made it possible to measure its mass. **Mass** is the amount of matter present in a body. It is a physical property that depends on the number, kind, and arrangement of particles within the body. Mass is also described as *inertia*, the resistance a body offers to movement. (Section 1:3.) Greater force is required to move a heavy or dense body than is required to move a lightweight or less dense body. The mass of a body may be measured on a balance by comparing it with the mass of an international standard.

Mass and weight are two terms which often are used interchangeably. But mass and weight are not the same. **Weight** on the earth is a measure of the gravitational attraction of the earth for an object on or near its surface. Mass is a constant property, but weight is a changing property. The weight of a body changes with its distance from the center of the earth. (Figure 2–9.) A body weighs more at sea level than on a mountain top; it weighs more at the poles than at the equator.

Weightlessness simply means that some force has overcome gravity. An astronaut in orbit experiences weightlessness. The pull on his body toward the earth is balanced by the outward force which sends him into orbit. When the centrifugal force and the attraction of gravity are in balance, the satellite orbits the earth. Then the net force acting on an astronaut is zero gravity.

Weight may be measured with a spring scale. The greater the gravitational attraction of the earth for the body, the more the spring is pulled downward. A balance that measures mass will register the same measurement for a body at any latitude or elevation.

Measurement of the mass of the earth is made by indirect methods. If man had an extremely sensitive instrument, he could compute earth's mass from the length of a pendulum and the amount of its *deflection* (di flek′shun) toward another body. However, the amount of deflection is too small to be measured accurately. Although the calculations are simple, the actual measurements are complex.

Accurate measurements of earth's mass have been made in a more practical way on a beam balance. This method of measurement was devised in 1914 by John Henry Poynting, a British physicist. (Figure 2–10.) With the Poynting balance, the difference between the gravitational pull of the earth and the

Figure 2-9. As the distance from the center of the earth increases, the weight of a body decreases.

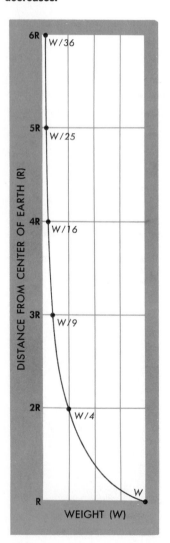

gravitational pull of a second large mass was determined. A large mass was placed on one pan of the balance. Then masses were placed on the other pan until both pans were balanced. A second larger mass was placed beneath one pan. The distance between the first mass and the second mass was measured. Then masses were added to the other pan to balance the beam which had been disturbed by the presence of the second mass. The additional masses represented the gravitational attraction between the mass on the pan and the mass below it. All measurements, except the mass of the earth, had been determined. The mass of the earth was found by using the following formula:

$$\frac{M_1 \times M_2}{d^2} = \frac{M \times m}{r^2}$$

In this equation, M_1 represents the first mass, M_2 represents the second mass, M represents the mass of the earth, m represents the masses added to achieve balance after placing the second mass below the pan, d represents the distance between the centers of M_1 and M_2, and r represents the radius of the earth. Solving the equation for M, the mass of the planet earth is found to be approximately 5.96×10^{24} kilograms (5,960,000,000,000,000,000,000,000 kilograms).

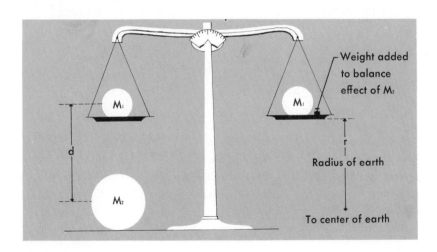

Figure 2-10. Poynting experimented for 12 years before he was able to demonstrate the method by which the mass of the earth has been determined.

2:4 Density

After the mass of the earth was determined, its density could be calculated. **Density** is the mass of a body divided by its volume, or mass per unit volume. Density is expressed in grams

Mass of a body divided by its
volume gives a ratio which represents the density of the body.

Mass of a body divided by its
volume gives a ratio which represents the density of the body.

$$D = \frac{M}{V}$$

Density of water is 1.0 g/cm³.

Average density of the earth is
5.52 g/cm³.

Specific gravity is a comparison
between the mass of a body and
the mass of an equal volume of
water.

per cubic centimeter (g/cm^3), slugs per cubic foot $(slugs/ft^3)$, or any other similar ratio of units in the same system. For example, the density of water may be expressed as $1.0\,g/cm^3$ or $1.9\,slugs/ft^3$.

To find the density of the earth, its mass of 5.96×10^{24} kg is divided by its volume of 1.08×10^{12} km³. If kilograms are converted to grams, and cubic kilograms are converted to cubic centimeters, the density of the earth is found to equal 5.52 g/cm³.

Specific gravity is the ratio, or relationship, between the mass of a given substance and the mass of an equal volume of water. Specific gravity is not expressed in units. It is simply a ratio that indicates whether a given substance is heavier or lighter than water. Because the density of water at 4°C (39°F) is 1 g/cm³, it is a convenient unit for comparison. The density of the earth is 5.52 times the density of water. Therefore, the specific gravity of the earth is 5.52. That is, the matter of the earth is 5.52 times as heavy or dense as water. (Table 2–3.)

PROBLEM

5. Find the density of a 108-kg rock that has the dimensions 3 m by 4 m by 2 m. What is the density in grams per cubic centimeter? What is the specific gravity of the rock?

Table 2–3. The Earth

Mean diameter	12,734 km	7,920 mi
Circumference (polar)	40,009 km	24,860 mi
Circumference (equatorial)	40,076 km	24,902 mi
Density	5.52 g/cm³	10.7 slugs/ft³
Area of surface	510,000,000 km²	197,000,000 mi²
Volume	11×10^{11} km³	26×10^{10} mi³
Mass	6×10^{24} kg	4.1×10^{23} slugs
Atmospheric pressure at sea level (decreases approximately 0.5 lb/in.² for every 3.5 mi above sea level)	1,033.4 g/cm²	14.7 lb/in.²

Mean temperature (increases approximately 0.56° C, or 1° F, for every 60 ft below the surface)

EXPERIMENT. *Cut a block of wood and a block of foam rubber to the same size (volume). Cover each of the pans of a laboratory balance with a piece of paper. Put the block of wood on one pan and the block of rubber on the other pan. Which has the greater mass? Which weighs more? Remove the rubber block and add enough iron filings to the paper on the pan to balance the wood block. Compare the volume of the wood block with the volume of the iron filings. Which has the greater volume? Compare the density of the rubber, the wood, and the iron. What effect does size have on density?*

Figure 2-11.

2:5 *Layers*

Information about the interior of the earth has been obtained by indirect methods. By means of an instrument called a seismograph (seiz'ma graf), geophysicists have studied vibrations coming from within the earth during earthquakes. A seismograph produces a recording called a *seismogram*. Seismograms indicate that the interior of the earth has layers of different densities. Rocks at the surface are the least dense (approximately 2.7 g/cm³). Densities increase downward until, at the center of the earth, the density is approximately 11.5 g/cm³.

Figure 2–12 shows the different densities within the earth as suggested by seismographic studies. The **crust** is the outer layer of the earth. It is the only layer about which scientists have direct knowledge. Materials of the crust remain in a solid state because both temperature and pressure are relatively low. The **mantle** is the layer directly beneath the crust. It has some

Geophysicists are scientists who study the physics of the earth, particularly the matter and motions of the earth.

Information about the layers of the earth is obtained from data recorded by a seismograph.

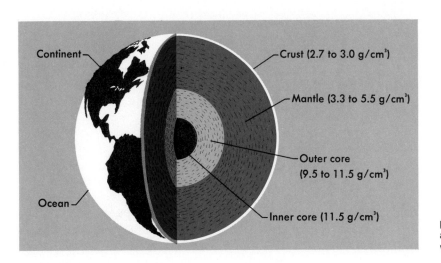

Figure 2-12. **Densities computed for the earth's interior are believed to be accurate to within about 10 percent.**

properties of a solid and some properties of a plastic or pliable material. Density of the mantle increases with depth. At the base of the crust, the density of the mantle is 3.5 g/cm³. At the contact between the **outer core** and the mantle, the density of the mantle is 5.5 g/cm³. The outer core is believed to be in the liquid state. Its density increases with depth from 9.5 g/cm³ at its contact with the base of the mantle to 11.5 g/cm³ at its contact with the **inner core.** Density of the inner core is approximately 11.5 g/cm³. Data from seismograms suggest that the inner core is in the solid state.

Density is the only clue to the composition, or makeup, of the inner layers of the earth. Geologists have suggested that the mantle has a composition similar to the rock known as *peridotite* (pa rid'a tiet) (Section 5:5) because the densities are the same. On the basis of recorded densities, geologists also suggest that the core may be mostly iron and nickel.

Iron has a density of about 7.8 g/cm³. The inner core density of about 11.5 g/cm³ is possible if pressure is considered.

Mantle of the earth appears to be composed of peridotite.

EXPERIMENT. Put ¼ cup of water, ¼ cup of cooking oil, and ¼ cup of syrup in a glass jar. Shake the jar and let it stand for 15 or 20 minutes. How are the substances arranged in the jar? Do you need to weigh the substances to determine their relative densities? Put the block of wood, the block of foam rubber, and the iron filings used in the experiment in Section 2:4 in a dry glass jar. Shake the jar and observe the arrangement of the materials. Are these substances arranged according to density? Why do liquids rearrange themselves in order of density?

Figure 2-13.

PROBLEM

 6. Examine the diagram of the layers of the earth in Figure 2–12. Offer an explanation for the arrangement of the layers with the iron-nickel core at the center.

MAIN IDEAS

1. As early as 500 B.C., philosophers and scholars were convinced that the earth is a sphere.

2. Columbus' voyages indicated that the earth is not flat, and Magellan supported the idea that the earth is a sphere by sailing around it.

3. The force of gravity is less at the equator than at other latitudes because the earth is an oblate spheroid which bulges in the region of the equator.

4. The imaginary surface line called the equator divides the earth into north latitude and south latitude.

5. Imaginary surface lines running from pole to pole divide the earth into east longitude and west longitude. The plane of the prime meridian, the longitude line at Greenwich, England, extended to the opposite side of the globe forms the international date line.

6. The circumference of the earth as calculated by modern methods is approximately 24,902 mi.

7. The mass or amount of matter in the earth is approximately 5.96×10^{24} kilograms.

8. Weight changes with distance from the center of the earth because of the changing of the force of gravity. However, mass does not change.

9. The average density of the earth (mass divided by volume) is 5.52 g/cm³.

10. Specific gravity is a comparison between the mass of a body and the mass of an equal volume of water. The specific gravity of the earth is 5.52; that is, 5.52 times the mass of an equal volume of water.

11. According to seismographic studies, the density of the matter of the earth increases from 2.7 g/cm³ at the surface to 11.5 g/cm³ at the center.

12. Information about the interior of the earth is obtained by seismographs. The core of the earth is probably a combination of iron and nickel.

13. Earth is sometimes described as pear-shaped because the southern hemisphere of the earth is larger than the northern hemisphere. However, oblate spheroid is a more accurate term to use.

VOCABULARY

Write a sentence in which you use correctly each of the following words or terms.

crust	mass
deflection	oblate spheroid
density	pendulum
geodesists	period
international date line	prime meridian
latitude	seismograph
longitude	specific gravity
mantle	weight

STUDY QUESTIONS

A. True or False

Determine whether each of the following sentences is true or false. (Do not write in this book.)

1. The period called the Dark Ages preceded the age of the Greek scholars.
2. A pendulum swings back and forth because of the forces of gravity and inertia.
3. At the equator, the same pendulum swings more slowly than it does at the poles.
4. Measurements of mass and weight are identical at all points on the surface of the earth.
5. Density of a substance depends upon its mass and its volume.
6. The specific gravity of a substance is expressed in units, such as pounds or grams.
7. The interior of the earth is divided into exact layers of equal depths.
8. The most recent data indicate that the earth is slightly pear-shaped.

9. The interior of the earth is much denser than 2.7 g/cm³, the density of the crust.

10. Rocks in the outer layer of earth appear to have hardened or crystallized because of low temperature and little pressure.

B. Multiple Choice

Choose the word or phrase which completes correctly each of the following sentences. (Do not write in this book.)

1. The average density of the earth is about *(3.4 g/cm³, 5.5 g/cm³, 7.5 g/cm³)*.

2. The layer of the earth about 1,800 miles below the surface is the *(mantle, outer core, inner core)*.

3. The density of the mantle is believed to be *(less than, more than, the same as)* the density of the core.

4. The true shape of the earth is a(n) *(sphere, oval, oblate spheroid, plane)*.

5. If you are traveling from east to west and you cross the international date line, you *(lose one, gain one, lose two, gain two)* day(s).

6. Distances north or south of the equator are measured on *(latitude lines, longitude lines, seismograms, meridians)*.

7. The amount of matter in a given body is its *(weight, mass, volume)*.

8. The measurement which changes with distance from the center of the earth is *(weight, mass, volume)*.

9. The property of matter which resists movement is *(acceleration, inertia, density)*.

10. The force of gravity *(increases, decreases, remains the same)* with an increase in mass.

C. Completion

Complete each of the following sentences with a word or phrase which will make the sentence correct. (Do not write in this book.)

1. The circumference of the earth is about ___?___ miles.

2. Density of a body is its ___?___ divided by its ___?___.

3. Specific gravity is the mass of a substance compared to the mass of an equal volume of ___?___.

4. Magellan's voyage around the earth suggested that the earth is __?__.

5. The period of a pendulum depends upon the __?__ of the pendulum and the __?__ of the earth.

6. The forces which cause the earth to bulge at the equator are __?__ and __?__.

7. Information about the interior of the earth is obtained from earthquake tremors that are recorded by a __?__.

8. The layers of the earth are called the __?__, __?__, __?__, and __?__.

9. The density of the earth __?__ with depth.

10. __?__ as well as __?__ of an object may be determined with a balance; __?__ of an object may be measured with a spring scale.

D. How and Why

1. What evidence have you observed to indicate that the earth is a sphere?

2. What causes a pendulum to swing back and forth in a regular period?

3. Why does time change when you cross the international date line?

4. On a world globe, find the latitude and longitude of your own locality.

5. Why is it important that the earth's size and shape be measured accurately?

6. Would you weigh less or more on the top of Mt. Everest than in your own home? Why do astronauts experience weightlessness?

7. What measurements must you know to calculate the density of a body? What measurements do you need to know to compute the specific gravity of a body?

8. How has information about the density of materials inside the earth been obtained?

9. Why are scientists convinced that the crust, the mantle, and the inner core show increasing densities with depth?

10. Do scientists actually know what kinds of materials are present in the interior of the earth?

11. Explain the difference between mass and weight. How have measurements of the earth's mass been obtained?

12. Why did Newton first propose that earth bulges at the equator? How was it proved that the planet earth has an equatorial bulge?

INVESTIGATIONS

1. Discuss several types of maps of the earth: a globe, a relief map, a homolographic projection, and a Mercator projection. Which map would be best for a sailor? Which for a flier? Which would be most useful for short distances? Which would be best for a person walking? Which flat map gives the truest idea of what the land areas of the earth are like?

2. Plan a jet plane flight from New York to Paris and one from New York to San Francisco. Find out the usual time the flight takes and, using the same departure time for each trip, figure out what time you would arrive at each destination in their local time. If you were flying to Japan, what time and day would you arrive?

INTERESTING READING

Adler, Irving, *Seeing the Earth from Space*. New York, The John Day Company, Inc., 1962.

*Beiser, Arthur, *The Earth*. Life Nature Library. New York, Time Inc., 1962.

*Huxley, Julian, ed., *Earth-Man and Science*. The Illustrated Libraries of Human Knowledge. Columbus, Ohio, Charles E. Merrill Publishing Co., 1968.

Liberty, Gene, *The How and Why Wonder Book of Time*. Columbus, Ohio, Charles E. Merrill Publishing Co., 1963.

*Wyckoff, Jerome, *Rock, Time, and Landforms*. New York, Harper & Row, Publishers, 1966.

---

* Well-illustrated material.

The Lithosphere

Give me matter and I will construct a world out of it.

Immanuel Kant (1724-1804)

What is matter? Are there many kinds of matter? Or is all matter made of the same substance? Look at all the variety in the world. Could this diverse earth be made entirely of one or even a few basic materials?

Man has long sought to separate everything in his environment into simple basic components. At one time, water was believed basic; at another time, air was favored. Aristotle believed four basic components—air, fire, water, and earth—combined to form all the materials of the world.

Today, scientists have developed methods for classifying matter on the basis of chemical and physical qualities. These qualities or properties help scientists study the differences and similarities among various substances. In place of Aristotle's four basics, scientists now separate matter into over one hundred basic elements. Man's knowledge of these tiny units of matter helps him to understand the wide variety of shapes and combinations in his environment.

UNIT
Two

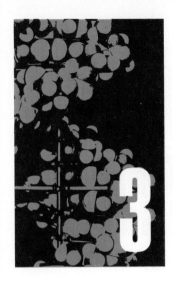

3 Matter

Look about you. How many different kinds of things can you see? In ancient times fire, water, air, and earth were considered the basic materials from which all things were made. Fire, water, air, and earth are completely different in their appearance and in the way they behave. The relationships among the varied things of the earth have challenged scientists from the time of the early Greek philosophers to the present. Like Severinus, scientists have gone to the mountains, the seashores, the deserts, and the laboratories to study the nature of earth's materials. Many questions are still unanswered, but scientists are learning gradually to understand matter.

When Severinus advised his students to gain a knowledge of "things" and their properties, he was telling them to study matter. Everything that Severinus mentioned—the mountains, valleys, deserts, shores, plants, animals, and minerals—is composed of matter. Each kind of matter is recognized by its physical characteristics and its behavior.

3:1 *Forms of Matter*

Matter exists in several forms including mixtures, chemical compounds, and elements.

Matter is anything that has mass and occupies space. **Matter** is also defined as anything that has inertia, or that resists movement or a change in the direction of movement. Matter is the term used by scientists to include all known materials of whatever origin. Matter exists in an almost limitless variety of patterns. Much of the matter of the earth consists of rocks and minerals. Matter also includes air, water, and all living things. The forms of matter include mixtures, chemical compounds, and elements.

Figure 3-1. Matter includes all known materials of the earth. What kinds of matter are present in this coastal seascape?

Mixtures consist of a variety of particles combined in any proportions. Each particle in a mixture has recognizable boundaries or edges. Particles in a mixture can be separated by a mechanical or manual process. One familiar mixture is soil. Soil is a combination of decayed plant and animal matter and weathered rock. Another common mixture is rock, which is a combination of minerals. Rocks can be broken apart into individual mineral grains. Soil and water can be separated by allowing the soil to settle and pouring off the water.

Mixtures are combinations of different kinds of particles that may be separated into their component parts by a manual process.

Compounds are composed of two or more kinds of particles combined in a definite ratio by mass. Compounds cannot be changed into simpler components (kam poh'nents) by a mechanical process. Instead, chemical changes, or reactions, are necessary. Components separated from a compound through a chemical process are completely different from the original compound. For example, common table salt is a compound and so is water. Salt can be separated into its components, sodium and chlorine. Sodium is a white metal; chlorine is a dark gas with a stinging, or pungent (pun'jent), odor. Water also can be separated into its components, hydrogen and oxygen. Both hydrogen and oxygen are gases which are completely different from water. The tiny particles which combine into compounds are called **atoms.** A substance which contains more than one kind of atom is called a compound. A substance which contains only one kind of atom is called an **element.**

Compounds are combinations of elements in which definite ratios of elements are present.

There are about 88 different kinds of atoms in the earth's crust.

45

Elements are unique substances that cannot be separated into simpler components by either chemical or mechanical means.

Atoms combine to form chemical compounds which are completely different from the combining elements, or atoms.

Subatomic particles are known through their electrical properties but are too small to be observed.

Figure 3-2. Each molecule of hydrogen gas (H₂) or oxygen gas (O₂) contains two atoms of the element.

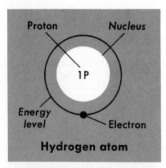

Hydrogen atom

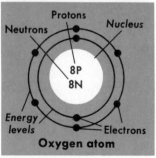

Oxygen atom

Elements are the basic materials of the earth. Each element differs from all others. Sodium, chlorine, hydrogen, and oxygen are four of the more than one hundred known elements. The smallest unit in which an element can exist is an atom. Atoms may be compared to building blocks or bricks. A building made of one kind of brick is similar to an element. A building made of several kinds of brick is similar to a chemical compound. Atoms are like building blocks which can be combined into more complex forms of matter.

Atoms are the smallest units of an element that enter into chemical reactions. Compounds always consist of two or more kinds of atoms. **Molecules** (mahl'i keuls) are the smallest units of a compound. Molecules of most compounds can be separated into atoms of different elements through chemical reactions. Atoms of the same element also can combine to form molecules, but the molecules of an element separate into atoms of the same kind. Both elements and compounds are called *substances*.

Elements cannot be reduced to simpler substances by either chemical or mechanical processes. However, atoms of elements are composed of many small particles called *subatomic particles*. All subatomic particles are too small to be seen with any known instrument. Only their behavior can be observed. Even atoms are too small to be observed by ordinary microscopes. Billions of atoms would be needed to cover the head of a pin. But in spite of the small sizes of atoms, scientists have obtained some idea of their size and shape through the use of X rays.

Experiments indicate that atoms of elements consist of particles with different electrical properties. Three of the particles are the *protons* (proh'tahns), *neutrons* (neu'trahns), and *electrons* (i lek'trahns). **Protons** are positively charged particles; **electrons** are negatively charged particles; **neutrons** are particles with no electrical charge. Protons, electrons, and neutrons are the smallest particles of matter of interest in the study of rocks and minerals. Still smaller particles have been discovered, but they are not important now to your understanding of the earth's matter.

3:2 *Structure of Matter*

In 1913, Niels Bohr, a Danish physicist, described the hydrogen atom. His model of hydrogen led to our present ideas of atomic structure. In the Bohr model, the center of the atom is pictured as a small, dense nucleus, or central part. The nucleus consists of protons and neutrons. It contains 99.9 percent of the mass of the atom. The nucleus of the atom usually has a number of positive charges equal to the number of protons it contains. Opposite electrical charges attract each other. The nucleus of an atom, therefore, attracts a number of negatively charged electrons. The electrons are outside the nucleus. The number of electrons is equal to the number of protons.

Electrons vibrate around the nucleus at approximately the speed of light. Not all of the electrons move about the nucleus at the same distance from its center. Instead, electrons may vibrate in a series of shells called *energy levels*. The number of shells used by the electrons depends upon the number of electrons in the atom. An atom of hydrogen, which has only one electron, has just one shell. Other kinds of atoms may have as many as seven shells. Some electrons are close to the nucleus; other electrons are farther away. The average distance between the nucleus and the outermost electrons determines the size of the atom. Most of an atom is empty space between the electrons and the nucleus and between the electrons themselves. Nevertheless, an atom behaves as a unit.

Bohr's model of the atom does not explain that electrons behave, in some ways, more like light waves than particles. Particles have true orbits, and it is possible to predict the position of the particle within the orbit at any moment. However, electrons move through space as waves, and the location of an electron cannot be determined exactly. Instead, its most probable location, or where the electron will be most often, determines the position of an energy level. The term *electron cloud* describes the movement of electrons better than the term electron orbit. Many physicists believe that electrons are vibrating particles that change position as energy levels change.

Speed of light is about 186,000 mi/sec.

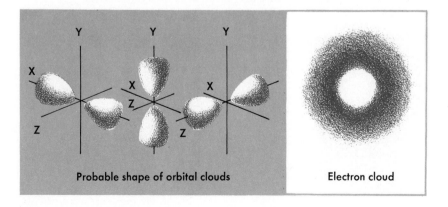

Probable shape of orbital clouds

Electron cloud

Figure 3-3.   Bohr's early concept showed electrons orbiting the nucleus in various subshells. The electron cloud model is the modern idea of the way electrons appear.

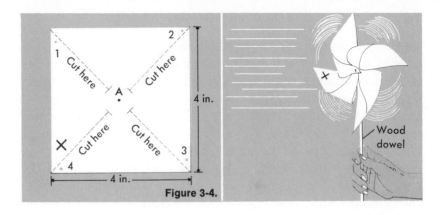

Figure 3-4.

ACTIVITY. Purchase or construct a pinwheel. Place an X on one of its tips. (Figure 3–4.) Blow on the pinwheel or hold it in front of an electric fan until it is revolving as rapidly as possible. Have another student use a stopwatch or the second hand on a clock. Without stopping the pinwheel, plot the position of the X during a period of 60 sec. Describe the plot. Can you determine the exact position of the X while the pinwheel is in motion? Compare your results with the movement of an electron. What is similar to the electron movement? What is different from the electron movement?

Any given atom has a different mass from isotopes of the same element.

The number of protons is always the same for each atom of a given element. The number of electrons is always equal to the number of protons. However, the number of neutrons may vary for atoms of the same element. **Isotopes** (ie'so tohps) are atoms of the same element that have different mass. The mass varies because each isotope has a different number of neutrons in its nucleus. Every element has at least two isotopes. For example, hydrogen has three isotopes. Most hydrogen atoms contain one proton, one electron, and no neutron. Some hydrogen atoms have one proton, one electron, and one neutron. A few hydrogen atoms have one proton, one electron, and two neutrons.

Figure 3-5. The hydrogen isotopes—protium, deuterium, and tritium—are alike in their chemical properties. How do they differ?

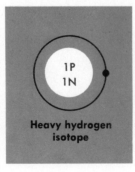

Ordinary hydrogen isotope

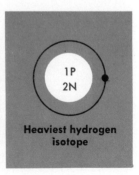

Heavy hydrogen isotope

Heaviest hydrogen isotope

Neutrons and protons determine the mass of an atom. The mass of a proton is 1.672×10^{-24} g. A neutron has approximately the same mass as a proton. Both a proton and a neutron have a very small mass, but that small mass is 1837 times the mass of an electron. Thus, electrons are not counted in determining the mass of an atom because their mass is too small.

3:3   *Chemical Properties*

Although electron mass is very small, electrons in the outer shell of an atom control its chemical properties. *Chemical properties* determine the way an atom behaves in contact with other atoms. Because of electron behavior, atoms can join together and form compounds, dissolve between molecules of a liquid, or substitute for other atoms. The process of filling the outer shell with electrons is known as a **chemical reaction.**

Each atom tends to have an equal number of protons and electrons. If positively charged protons are balanced by negatively charged electrons, the atom is said to be electrically neutral. But some atoms lose electrons and become positively charged particles. Other atoms gain electrons and become negatively charged particles. Both positively and negatively charged particles are called **ions** (ie′ans). Positively charged ions combine with negatively charged ions to form compounds. The number of positive charges is always balanced by an equal number of negative charges in a compound. Chemical properties can be determined only during chemical reactions.

Behavior of an atom depends upon the number of electrons in its outer shell.

Figure 3-6.   A positively charged sodium ion combines with a negatively charged chloride ion to form the compound sodium chloride, the mineral halite.

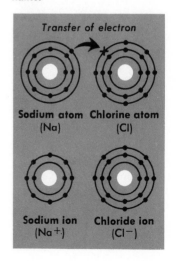

PROBLEMS

1. An atom of oxygen gains two electrons. What kind of charges does the oxide ion have? How many charges?
2. A silicon atom loses four of its electrons. How many electrical charges does the silicon ion have? What kind of charges does it have?
3. How many oxide ions are required to balance one silicon ion?
4. A sodium atom loses one electron when it becomes an ion. How many electrical charges does the sodium ion have? Is the sodium ion positive or negative?
5. A chlorine atom adds one electron when it becomes a chloride ion. How many electrical charges does a chloride ion have? Is the chloride ion positive or negative?

3:4   *Physical Properties*

Physical properties of a substance depend upon the kind and arrangement of its atoms. Chemical properties depend upon the number and arrangement of electrons in the outer shell of an atom. Physical properties can be seen and measured. Physical properties may be recognized by one or more of the senses of sight, smell, touch, taste, or hearing. Some physical properties are mass, density, taste, and reflection of light.

Hydrogen is the smallest and simplest kind of atom. Its common isotope consists of one proton and one electron. (Figure 3–5.) All other elements may be constructed by adding protons and neutrons to the nucleus, and electrons to the energy shells. Elements increase in mass as protons and neutrons are added. The *atomic number* of an element is the total number of protons in the nucleus of each atom of the element. The *atomic mass number* is the total number of protons and neutrons in the nucleus of each atom of the element. (Table 3–1.) As protons, neutrons, and electrons are added, atoms increase in mass as well as in size. Thus, atoms of great mass are larger than atoms of small mass.

Table 3–1.   *Atomic Table of Selected Elements*

Element	Symbol	Atomic Number (protons)	Atomic Mass Number (protons + neutrons)
Aluminum	Al	13	27
Calcium	Ca	20	40
Carbon	C	6	12
Chlorine	Cl	17	35
Helium	He	2	4
Hydrogen	H	1	1
Iron	Fe	26	56
Lead	Pb	82	206
Magnesium	Mg	12	24
Nitrogen	N	7	14
Oxygen	O	8	16
Potassium	K	19	39
Silicon	Si	14	28
Sodium	Na	11	23
Uranium	U	92	238

PROBLEMS

6. Refer to Table 3–1. How many electrons does aluminum have? How many neutrons?

7. Silicon has a mass number of 28. How many neutrons does it have? How many electrons? How many neutrons does oxygen have? How many electrons? How many protons does a molecule of silicon dioxide (SiO_2) have?

8. How many protons must be added to hydrogen to produce helium? How many neutrons must be added?

Physical changes alter only the physical appearance of a substance. Large masses may be divided into smaller pieces. But each small piece has the same physical properties as the large mass. But on the other hand, chemical changes produce new substances which have different properties. Physical changes depend primarily on the substance itself. Chemical changes depend primarily on the presence of a second substance.

3:5 *States of Matter*

Each kind of matter occurs in one of three physical states: solid, liquid, or gas. In a *solid*, the atoms or molecules have a rigid, fixed geometric pattern in relation to each other. Each atom or molecule vibrates around a fixed point. But the atom or molecule is held in place by the attraction between its negatively charged electrons and the positively charged nuclei of nearby atoms or molecules. A solid resists both change in shape and change in volume because its atoms are not free to move. Ice is one example of a solid. Other examples are wood, rocks, and minerals.

In a *liquid*, atoms or molecules are free to move about, but they remain in contact with each other. Liquids resist changes in volume, but they adopt the shape of their containers. Some familiar liquids are water, gasoline, and oil. In a *gas*, atoms cling together in molecules, but the molecules move about independently. Gases expand to fill all available space in a container of any shape or size. Gas molecules move so rapidly that they cannot be held in any fixed position. Gases offer no resistance to change in shape and less resistance than a liquid to change in volume. Differences between solids, liquids, and gases are: (1) distance between the atoms or molecules, and (2)

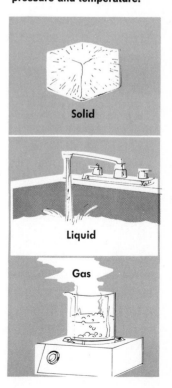

Figure 3-7. The physical state of a substance depends on both pressure and temperature.

Solid

Liquid

Gas

Figure 3-8.   Earth's temperature range allows water to exist in a gaseous, liquid, and solid state. In which states does water appear in this scene?

movement of the atoms or molecules. Both distance and movement change with changes in temperature and pressure.

Increases in temperature increase molecular movement, and as molecules become more mobile, a solid becomes a liquid, then a gas.

Physical states for each form of matter depend upon both the temperature of the matter and the pressure used on the matter. Molecules move faster and faster as temperature rises. Falling temperatures slow down the movement of molecules. With rising temperatures, solids become liquids. As molecular velocity increases, the molecules slide past each other and the attraction of nearby molecules becomes ineffective. Liquids boil and become gases as molecules separate and move about independently. With falling temperatures, molecules slow down. As the molecules come into contact with each other, the gas becomes a liquid. Liquids become solids as molecules travel too slowly to overcome the attraction of nearby nuclei. The relationship between temperature and molecular movement still receives a great amount of study.

As pressure on matter increases, the molecules are forced into closer and closer contact until, eventually, molecules can vibrate only around a fixed point. Gases become liquids, and liquids become solids under applications of pressure. Release of pressure produces the opposite effect. Depending upon the temperature, molecules may be free to move as pressure lessens. Solids become liquids, and liquids become gases.

EXPERIMENT.　*Place two large ice cubes in a shallow pan. Place a key or heavy nail on one ice cube and put the pan in the freezing compartment of a refrigerator. Leave the pan in the refrigerator for several hours or overnight. Examine the ice cubes. Where is the key or nail? Explain what has happened.*

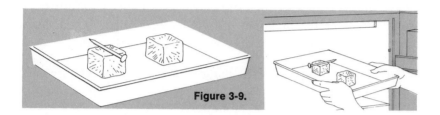

Figure 3-9.

The temperature at which a solid changes to a liquid is called its *melting point*. The temperature at which a liquid becomes a solid is its *freezing point*. Liquids change to gas at the *boiling point*. Both temperature and pressure may bring about changes in physical states. Thus, the melting point, freezing point, and boiling point for each substance vary with pressure. Water freezes at 0°C (32°F) at sea level. A slight increase in pressure raises the freezing point, and melting may occur. Water boils at 100°C (212°F) at sea level. On the top of Pikes Peak (14,000 ft above sea level), air pressure is reduced. There, water boils at 85°C (185°F).

Water exists as a solid, a liquid, and a gas at the surface of the earth. Its freezing, melting, and boiling points are reached between the maximum and minimum pressures and temperatures possible in nature. Many substances exist only as solids, liquids, or gases within the range of high and low temperatures that are possible in nature. Some substances can be changed to a different physical state only under laboratory conditions. In the laboratory, it is possible to raise the temperature and pressure to produce conditions that do not exist at the surface of the earth. These conditions might resemble or simulate many conditions within the interior. Even in the laboratory, temperatures and pressures that are similar to those of the earth's core

Temperatures at which changes in state occur are called the melting, boiling, and freezing points. These points vary with pressure.

Present ideas of the physical state of the earth's interior are derived from calculations and laboratory experiments.

cannot be reached. However, conditions of the mantle may be attained. Scientists depend on laboratory experiments to learn how changes in physical state occur in rock materials.

Scientists also study matter by making models to help them picture, or visualize, objects they cannot see. Models may be objects, like model cars and airplanes, or drawings and diagrams such as Figure 3–6. Models actually cannot represent particles of matter because the particles are so tiny and always in motion. However, you can learn the number, relative size, and arrangement of particles in different kinds of matter by studying atomic models. Particles in real atoms cling together because of their electrical charges and other factors that are not completely understood. Parts of an atomic model must be supported by wire or some other means, or the model falls apart. Thus, models are never exactly like real atoms.

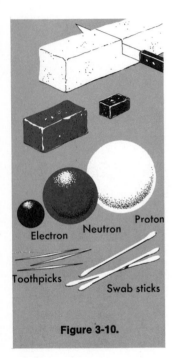

Figure 3-10.

ACTIVITY. To construct models of atoms, you will need one package of round toothpicks or one package of pipe cleaners, one package of swab sticks, and blue, green, and white plasticine modeling clay. Cut the white clay into pieces 1½ in. × 1½ in. × 3 in., the blue clay into pieces 1 in. × 1 in. × 2 in., and the green clay into pieces ½ in. × ½ in. × 1 in. Mold the clay into spheres. The white spheres represent protons, the blue spheres represent neutrons, and the green spheres represent electrons.

You can substitute small styrofoam spheres for the clay spheres. The styrofoam spheres should have diameters of approximately 3 in., 2 in., and 1 in. With felt-tipped pens, color the 2 in. spheres blue and the 1 in. spheres green. You will need 31 white spheres, 31 green spheres, and 23 blue spheres to construct all of the following models.

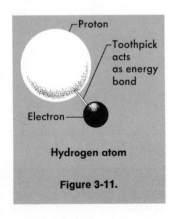

Hydrogen atom

Figure 3-11.

The Hydrogen Atom—*Push one end of a toothpick into a white sphere. Attach a green sphere to the other end of the toothpick. Look at Table 3–1. The atomic number of hydrogen is 1 and the atomic mass number of hydrogen is 1. From these values, you can determine that the normal hydrogen atom has one proton, one normal electron, and no neutrons.*

Protons and electrons are not actually held together by a physical bond, such as a toothpick. They are held together by an energy bond. But this model is one way to visualize how hydrogen compares in size and complexity with the atoms of other elements. Even the various spheres do not represent the true size relationships.

The Helium Atom—*Table 3–1 lists the atomic number and the atomic mass number for helium. From these you can calculate that there are two protons, two neutrons, and two electrons in every atom of helium. To form the nucleus of a helium atom, press two white spheres and two blue spheres together until they stick. Attach a toothpick to each white sphere and put a green sphere on the other end of each toothpick.*

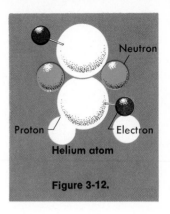

Figure 3-12.

Protons and electrons are believed to be held together by opposite electrical charges. The neutrons have no charge, so the electrons do not attract or repel them. Opposite charges attract, and like charges repel. Do you think the protons would cling to one another if there were no neutrons present? If neutrons are neutral, how do they hold the protons?

The Carbon Atom—*Use six white spheres and six blue spheres. Arrange them in a compact mass so that the colors alternate. Attach two green spheres to two of the white ones by using toothpicks. Attach four green spheres to the remaining four white spheres by using the longer swab sticks.*

Compare the diameter of the carbon atom with that of the helium and the hydrogen atoms. Note that the carbon atom has a greater mass than either the hydrogen or the helium atom because it has more protons, electrons, and neutrons. Also notice that the electrons vibrate around the nucleus on two different levels. A maximum of two electrons travel in the first level. A maximum of eight electrons travel in the second level.

Construct two more models. Use seven blue spheres for one carbon atom model and eight blue spheres for another. Do not change the number of protons or electrons.

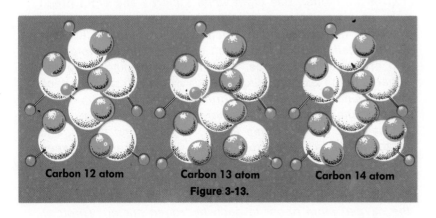

Carbon 12 atom   Carbon 13 atom   Carbon 14 atom

Figure 3-13.

You now have constructed three *isotopes* of the carbon atom. Each atom has similar electrical and chemical properties, but each differs in mass. The different isotopes are recognized by their different *atomic mass numbers;* that is, the sum of particles in the nucleus. If you assume each neutron weighs one gram, you can see that some isotopes weigh more than others.

The first model of carbon you constructed was *carbon 12*, the most abundant stable isotope of carbon. The second model was *carbon 13*, also a stable isotope. The third model was *carbon 14*, the most useful radioactive isotope of carbon. A **radioactive isotope** is unstable and emits, or gives off, particles from the nucleus. Eventually, a radioactive isotope of an element will change to another element. Carbon 14 eventually changes to nitrogen.

Eighty-eight elements have been found in the earth's crust. These elements have joined to form thousands of combinations. The combinations of different elements form new substances called *compounds*. A molecule is the smallest combination of atoms which can exist separately and still keep its distinct composition. A molecule also may be thought of as the smallest combination of atoms that will form a given compound.

Water is made up of two atoms of hydrogen and one atom of oxygen in each of its molecules. Both hydrogen and oxygen are gases found in the air. When they unite in the proper ratio, water is formed. Water is entirely different from either of the gases. Name a few of the differences between water and the elements which compose it.

The Water Molecule—Construct the oxygen atom first. Omit the eight neutrons in the nucleus in order to simplify construction of the model. Use eight white spheres and eight green spheres. Form the nucleus with the eight white spheres. The electrons vibrate around the nucleus on two different levels or energy shells. Attach two green spheres with toothpicks to two of the white spheres. Attach the remaining six green spheres to the six remaining spheres with swab sticks. Attach the remaining six electrons, three on each side, with space between them for the electrons of the hydrogen atoms.

Construct two hydrogen atoms like your first model, one proton joined to one electron. Place the oxygen atom between two hydrogen atoms so that electrons from the hydrogen atoms occupy the spaces between the electrons in the oxygen atom. Rotate the three atoms, keeping an electron from the oxygen atom opposite each hydrogen nucleus (proton).

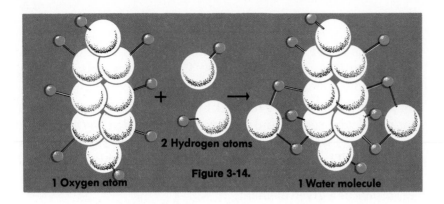

1 Oxygen atom   +   2 Hydrogen atoms   →   1 Water molecule

Figure 3-14.

Scientists picture the combining of oxygen and hydrogen to form water in this manner. Oxygen and hydrogen atoms are held together, or *bonded*, because their electrons belong to both nuclei. Demonstrate the bonding between the hydrogen and oxygen until you are sure you understand it. Then fasten toothpicks from the hydrogen electrons to the oxygen nucleus and from the hydrogen nucleus to two of the oxygen electrons. This will give you a more stable model to keep.

Few elements exist in nature in an uncombined form. Future models should be constructed with one sphere representing the entire atom. The models would become too cluttered and complex if some detail were not left out.

MAIN IDEAS

1. Matter is anything that has mass and occupies space.

2. Matter exists as mixtures, compounds, or elements. Mixtures may be separated into individual particles by mechanical processes. Compounds may be separated into their component elements by chemical processes. Elements cannot be separated into simpler components by either chemical or mechanical processes.

3. Atoms are the smallest units in which an element can exist. Atoms are composed of many subatomic particles. Three of the subatomic particles are protons, electrons, and neutrons. Protons have positive electrical charges; electrons have negative electrical charges; neutrons have no electrical charge.

4. It is believed that negatively charged electrons are attracted to the nucleus of an atom by the positive charges of the protons in the nucleus.

5. Atoms of one element may combine with atoms of different elements to form compounds. The smallest unit of a compound is a molecule.

6. Each atom (except normal hydrogen) has a nucleus composed of protons and neutrons surrounded by a cloud of electrons which vibrate around the nucleus at varying distances. The number of electrons equals the number of protons in an atom. These numbers are always the same for atoms of a given element.

7. The number of neutrons in the nucleus of an atom of a given element may vary. Therefore, atoms of the same element may differ from each other in their mass. Isotopes are atoms of the same element that have different masses. They have different numbers of neutrons in their nuclei.

8. Atoms are ordinarily electrically neutral because numbers of protons and electrons are equal. Ions are particles formed when atoms lose or gain electrons. Ions that lose electrons have positive charges equal to the number of electrons that have been lost. Ions that gain electrons have negative charges equal to the number of electrons that have been gained. Ions with opposite charges join to form compounds in which numbers of protons are balanced by numbers of electrons present.

9. Chemical properties determine the behavior of an atom in the presence of different kinds of atoms. All atoms of a given element have the same chemical properties and exhibit the same kind of behavior.

10. Elements differ from each other in mass as the number of protons and neutrons in the nucleus increases. The atomic mass number of an element indicates the total number of neutrons and protons present in each of its atoms. The atomic number indicates the number of protons present in the nucleus of each atom of a given element.

11. Matter occurs in one of three physical states: solid, liquid, or gas. In the solid state, atoms vibrate about a point but have fixed positions. Solids resist changes in volume and changes in shape. In the liquid state, atoms move about more freely but remain in contact. Liquids resist changes in volume but have no resistance to changes in shape. In a gas, molecules move rapidly and independently and have no resistance to change in shape and little resistance to change in volume.

12. Substances may change from one physical state to another if changes in temperature and/or pressure occur. If pressure remains constant, an increased temperature tends to allow molecules to move about more readily. Then the substance may go from the solid to the liquid to the gaseous state. If temperature remains at a certain point, increased pressure slows the movement of molecules. Then gases may become liquids, and liquids may become solids.

13. Models constructed to represent atoms cannot reproduce actual conditions or forms, but they assist in an understanding of atomic structure.

VOCABULARY

Write a sentence in which you use correctly each of the following words or terms.

atomic number	isotopes
boiling point	matter
electron cloud	mixtures
electrons	models
elements	molecules
energy levels	neutrons
helium	protons
hydrogen	stable
ions	subatomic particles

STUDY QUESTIONS

A. True or False

Determine whether each of the following sentences is true or false. (Do not write in this book.)

1. Matter has the property of inertia.
2. Matter of the earth consists of rocks, minerals, water, air, and living things.
3. Mixtures are the same as compounds.
4. Compounds may be separated into elements by crushing.
5. No two elements have the same number of protons.
6. Electrons contribute the greatest mass to the atom.
7. Protons have no electrical charge.

8. Electrons have a negative electrical charge.

9. Protons and electrons form the nucleus of an atom.

10. Ions have an electrical charge.

B. Multiple Choice

Choose the word or phrase which completes correctly each of the following sentences. (Do not write in this book.)

1. Unique combinations of the subatomic particles of matter are called (*elements, mixtures, neutrons*).

2. The smallest unit with the special characteristics of a compound is a(n) (*molecule, atom, electron*).

3. The smallest unit with the special characteristics of an element is a(n) (*molecule, atom, electron*).

4. When atoms lose or gain electrons, they become (*ions, neutrons, compounds*).

5. Physical properties include (*density, solubility, electrical charges*).

6. The physical state of matter depends on its (*temperature and pressure, solubility, chemical properties*).

7. Most substances in nature are (*elements, compounds, mixtures*).

8. Rearrangement of atoms occurs during (*filtering, chemical reactions, grinding*).

9. The mass of a proton is (*less than, greater than, the same as*) the mass of an electron.

10. Positive ions unite with negative ions to form (*mixtures, compounds, elements*).

C. Completion

Complete each of the following sentences with a word or phrase which will make the sentence correct. (Do not write in this book.)

1. Three subatomic particles of matter are the ___?___, ___?___, and ___?___.

2. An element is determined by the number of ___?___ in its atom.

3. Two or more elements combine to form a(n) ___?___.

4. Neutrons contribute ___?___ to the atom.

5. Atoms are balanced and have no ___?___.
6. Physical state of a substance depends on its ___?___ and ___?___.
7. Liquids may become ___?___ if the pressure is constant and the temperature increases.
8. Chemical reactions involve the rearrangement of ___?___.
9. A compound may be separated into elements by ___?___.
10. Mixtures may be separated into their individual components by ___?___.

D. How and Why

1. What is the main difference between a mixture and a compound?
2. What is the difference between an ion and an atom of a given element?
3. What do neutrons contribute to an atom?
4. Why is a compound called a balanced unit of matter?
5. What is the effect of temperature on the physical state?
6. Would hammering on a piece of metal change its chemical properties? Explain.
7. Do the chemical characteristics of a solid change when it becomes a liquid?
8. What kind of property is mass?
9. How does pressure affect a substance if the temperature remains constant?
10. Discuss what might happen to a substance if both temperature and pressure increase.

INVESTIGATIONS

1. Discuss the origin of the term "X ray." How was the X ray discovered?
2. Report on the work of Madam Marie Curie and her husband Pierre in their study of radioactive materials.
3. Discuss some milestones in the development of the use of atomic energy.

INTERESTING READING

Asimov, Isaac, *Inside the Atom*, rev. ed. New York, Abelard-Schuman Limited, 1961.

Bush, George L., and Silvidi, Anthony A., *The Atom: A Simplified Description*. New York, Barnes & Noble, Inc., 1961.

*Huxley, Julian, ed., *Chemical Universe-Man and Science*. The Illustrated Libraries of Human Knowledge. Columbus, Ohio, Charles E. Merrill Publishing Co., 1968.

Jaffe, Bernard, *Chemistry Creates a New World*. New York, Thomas Y. Crowell Company, 1957.

Keen, Martin L., *Let's Experiment*. New York, Grosset & Dunlap, Inc., 1968.

*Lapp, Ralph E., *Matter*. Life Science Library. New York, Time Inc., 1969.

Lessing, Lawrence, *Understanding Chemistry*. New York, John Wiley & Sons, Inc., 1959.

Romer, Alfred, *The Restless Atom*. Garden City, N. Y., Doubleday & Company, Inc., 1960.

---

* Well-illustrated material.

Matter of the Lithosphere

The crust of the earth consists of matter in the form of rocks and minerals. Recall that all matter consists of protons, neutrons, and electrons combined to form atoms. Matter made of only one kind of atom is an element. Elements may be combined to form chemical compounds. Chemical compounds or elements may be mingled in various proportions to form mixtures. In the earth's crust, single elements and chemical compounds occur as minerals. Minerals and mixtures of minerals occur as rocks. If you examine the ground that lies beneath you everywhere, you are likely to find boulders in some places. But more often you will find soil. Boulders and soil appear to be different from one another. Both of them, however, have come from the original rock materials of the crust.

4:1 *Minerals*

The **lithosphere** (lith'a sfir) is the outer crust of the earth. The Greek word *lithos* means rock or stone. Thus, the word lithosphere means that the earth's sphere is made of rock. Approximately 2,000 minerals have been recognized in the lithosphere, but only 88 elements* have been found. Eight of the 88 elements make up 98.58 percent of the matter of the crust. (Table 4–1.) The other 80 elements constitute only 1.42 percent of the lithosphere.

Of the 2,000 known minerals, only 12 are widespread or abundant enough to be essential to the earth's crust. These twelve minerals are called *rock-formers* because they make up the bulk of the lithosphere. If all of the other minerals were

Of the 2,000 known minerals, only 12 minerals are essential rock-formers. These are feldspars, quartz, amphiboles, pyroxenes, olivine, mica, clay (kaolinite), calcite, dolomite, gypsum, halite, and hematite.

---

* More than 100 elements have been recognized by chemists, but only 88 occur in the earth's crust.

absent from the crust, continents would look the same and have approximately the same characteristics. Many of the uncommon minerals are important to industry, to our way of life, and to our material welfare. But they are not abundant components of the lithosphere.

Table 4–1. Abundant Elements of the Lithosphere

Element	Symbol	Percentage by Weight
Oxygen	O	46.60
Silicon	Si	27.72
Aluminum	Al	8.13
Iron	Fe	5.00
Calcium	Ca	3.63
Sodium	Na	2.82
Potassium	K	2.59
Magnesium	Mg	2.09

Rocks are mixtures; minerals are compounds or elements.

Minerals are either elements or chemical compounds that are: (1) inorganic, (2) formed in nature, (3) solid, (4) of a definite internal atomic pattern, (5) of a definite constant chemical composition within certain well-defined limits.

1. *Minerals are inorganic.* This means that minerals consist of matter other than animal or vegetable material. Minerals are not alive and the processes by which they form are not life processes. Some marine animals, such as corals and mollusks (mahl'usks), use certain minerals taken from seawater to make their shells. Shells consist of the same chemical substances that are called minerals. However, because the shell was formed by a living animal, the shell material is not called a mineral.

2. *Minerals are formed in nature.* Man has learned to manufacture many artificial or imitation gems and other substances that have exactly the same characteristics as minerals formed by natural processes. These artificial substances are not properly classed as minerals. Gems found in nature have greater value than those made by man.

3. *Minerals are solids.* In Section 3:5, you read that a solid resists a change in shape or a change in volume because its atoms are arranged in fixed positions. The size and arrangement of its atoms determine the outward shape of a solid. Solids have geometric patterns, all of which belong to one of six crystal systems. (Figure 4–12.)

4. *Minerals have definite internal atomic patterns.* The atoms of each mineral are arranged in a characteristic pattern. Because a mineral is a solid, its atomic arrangement is always the same. If a mineral melts or dissolves in a liquid, its atoms lose their rigid pattern and no longer form a mineral. However, the same atoms are present in the liquid that were present in the mineral.

Figure 4-1. Tourmaline crystal.

The internal pattern of atoms in a mineral may be so small that it can be observed only by means of X-ray diffraction. Or the atomic pattern may be repeated over and over until it is large enough to be seen by the naked eye. The repetition of the same combination of atoms is similar to the repetition of a pattern in tile or linoleum. If the atomic pattern can be recognized, the resulting shape is called a **crystal.** A given mineral always occurs in the same general crystal shape. Museums frequently display large crystals that have formed in nature. Such crystals show the internal atomic pattern of the mineral.

Figure 4-2. Pyrite crystals.

Large crystals are uncommon because sometimes, when crystals start to form, they interfere with each other. Then, instead of growing into large, recognizable crystals, the minerals occur as masses of minute crystals. Such minerals are described as *massive.* Under a microscope, the crystal form often can be recognized. Occasionally, however, the crystals are so small they can be seen only by means of X-ray diffraction.

5. *Minerals have specific or exact chemical compositions.* A mineral always is composed of the same kind of atoms, in the same proportions, arranged in the same way. For example, every specimen of *quartz* (kwawrts), a very common mineral, has atoms in the ratio of two atoms of oxygen to one atom of silicon. Actually, a specimen of quartz contains billions of oxygen atoms and billions of silicon atoms. But the ratio of these two kinds of atoms is always two oxygen atoms to one silicon atom. Chemists use a kind of shorthand to indicate the composition of a chemical substance. Minerals are either elements or chemical compounds, so *symbols* or *formulas* are used to indicate the composition of a mineral. For quartz, the formula is SiO_2 (Si for silicon, O for oxygen). Tables 4–4 and 4–5 give the symbols or formulas for several minerals.

Minerals always have the same kind of atoms arranged in the same way.

Geologists define a mineral as having a specific chemical composition within certain, well-defined limits. You have seen what is meant by a specific chemical composition. But what is meant by well-defined limits? In nature, one kind of atom may

Substitution of one atom for another in an atomic pattern may occur only for ions of the same radius and with the same electrical charges.

Amount of substitution that may occur without having a mineral name change depends upon arbitrary decisions by mineralogists who study mineral characteristics.

Silicates are the most common minerals, carbonates are next, and oxides are least common. All of these minerals are combinations of one or more of the most abundant elements and some other elements which may or may not be among the eight most abundant elements.

Figure 4-3.   The tetrahedron (a figure with four triangular faces) is the basic unit of all silicate structures. (a.) Double tetrahedral structure (Si_2O_7). (b.) Single tetrahedral structure (SiO_4).

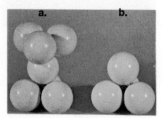

a.   b.

Ward's Natural Science Establishment, Inc.

Figure 4-4.   The SiO_4 tetrahedron has one oxygen ion situated on each of the four corners of a tetrahedron. The silicon ion is at the center.

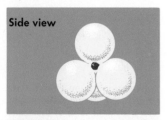

Side view

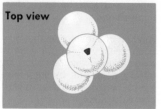

Top view

be so similar to another kind of atom that the two can substitute for one another. However, the ions must be of the same radius and have the same electrical charges to be exchangeable. Substitution may occur up to a certain point without changing the mineral characteristics. Picture atoms as building blocks and the atomic pattern as a building made of these blocks. As long as the blocks were the same shape and size, a blue block could take the place of a white block without disturbing the structure of the building. You would have the same pattern of blocks and a largely white building unless you kept substituting blue blocks for white ones. Eventually, the building would be blue if you exchanged all of the blocks.

Substitution of one element for another element takes place in some minerals. If substitution is carried to a point where the mineral color or another characteristic is changed, then the combination is given a new name. The point at which the name is changed is set by *mineralogists*, scientists who specialize in the study of minerals. For example, within the feldspar family, sodium substitutes for calcium. When the substitution of sodium for calcium reaches 10%, a new mineral name is assigned. For each additional 20% substitution, another name is used. Thus, the feldspar family includes anorthite, bytownite, labradorite, andesine, oligoclase, and albite.

Review the five points of the definition of a mineral. Note that all five conditions must be met if a substance is to be called a mineral.

Minerals that contain mainly the eight abundant elements listed in Table 4–1 are common. Minerals composed mainly of the other 80 elements found in the earth's crust are rare. The largest group of minerals are called *silicates* (sil'i kaets). **Silicates** are combinations of silicon (Si) and oxygen (O) and some other elements. For example, the feldspar which contains calcium, aluminum, silicon, and oxygen is a silicate. Because silicates are present in most rocks, they are called rockformers. In the earth's crust, 87 percent of the minerals are silicates.

Combinations of carbon and oxygen and some other elements such as calcium, magnesium, or iron are called *carbonates* (kahr'ba naets). **Carbonates,** such as calcite $CaCO_3$, are next in abundance after the silicates. *Oxides* (ahk'sieds) also are important minerals, but are much less common than either silicates or carbonates. **Oxides,** such as hematite Fe_2O_3, are combinations of oxygen and some other element.

ACTIVITY. To construct some mineral models, you will need four times as much white plasticine modeling clay as the other three colors. Cut the clay into pieces as follows: white—1½ in. × 1½ in. × 3 in.; blue—1 in. × 1 in. × 2 in.; green—½ in. × ½ in. × 1 in.; red—¼ in. × ¼ in. × ½ in. Roll the plasticine into spheres. White spheres represent negatively charged ions; the other spheres represent positively charged ions of different diameters. First use a red sphere as the center of an atomic unit. Arrange white spheres around the red one so that each white sphere is in contact with the red sphere and with two other white ones. Place this unit flat on the table. Using a ruler, place it tangent (tan'jent) to or touching two white spheres and draw a line. (Figure 4–5.) Continue drawing similar lines for each two white spheres. As you look down on the outline of the model, what is its shape?

Repeat the model construction, but this time use a blue sphere as the center ion. Make a third model using a green sphere as the center ion surrounded by white spheres. How does the diameter of the center ion affect the number of ions which surround it? What controls the arrangement and size of the crystals of a mineral?

In constructing the following model, let the white sphere represent the complete atom. Arrange four white spheres in a pyramid. This geometric form is called a tetrahedron (te tra hee'dron). It can be turned in any direction without changing the shape or size of the unit. Make four tetrahedra and arrange them in a chain. Remove one corner atom from one tetrahedron. Let the corner atom of another tetrahedron take its place. (Figure 4–6.) Continue this procedure until all four tetrahedra are joined in a chain. How many atoms did you remove to make a continuous chain? How many atoms are left?

Construct four more tetrahedra. Now make a double chain in which two tetrahedra are joined at two corners. (Figure 4–7b.) How many atoms did you remove in making the double chain? How many remain?

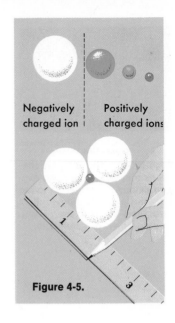

Negatively charged ion | Positively charged ions

Figure 4-5.

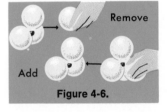

Remove

Add

Figure 4-6.

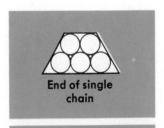

End of single chain

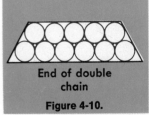

End of double chain

Figure 4-10.

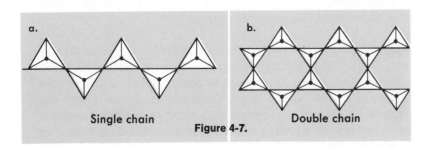

a.   Single chain   b.   Double chain

Figure 4-7.

Ward's Natural Science Establishment, Inc.

Figure 4-9. The SiO$_4$ tetrahedrons may join by sharing oxygen atoms with neighboring tetrahedra. Left: single chain structure of pyroxene. Right: double chain of amphibole.

The single and double chains are the basic units for two common mineral families, the *pyroxenes* (pie rahk'seens) and the *amphiboles* (am'fi bohls). Pyroxenes contain the single chains; amphiboles contain the double chains. Pyroxene minerals break along smooth plane surfaces. This type of break is called *cleavage*. Pyroxene cleavage surfaces are parallel to the single chain. Amphiboles cleave parallel to the double chain.

University of Houston

Figure 4-10. Cleavages occur along directions of weak bonding in the atomic structure of the minerals pyroxene (a.) and amphibole (b.).

With the help of another student, trace the outline of the base of each of your chains. Measure the angles. What measurement might be a clue to help you distinguish between amphibole and pyroxene minerals?

One of the earliest discoveries about minerals was that the angle between *crystal faces* (the flat surfaces which join at well defined angles) is always the same number of degrees regardless of the size of the mineral crystal.

ACTIVITY: Use two or three large crystals of quartz or calcite (kal'siet). Count the sides of the minerals. Trace the outline of a crystal on a sheet of paper. Measure the angles bounded by the crystal faces. Compare your results with the results of several other students. What is the measurement range? Find the average of the measurements determined by five students.

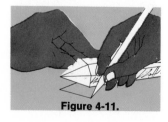

Figure 4-11.

ACTIVITY. Look at the diagrams showing the six crystal systems. (Figure 4–12.) Measure the length of each side of the cube. How do these lengths compare? Measure the length of each side of the tetragonal *(te trag'an l) system. How do these lengths compare? Make similar measurements for each system, and keep a record of them. Each crystal system has a variety of forms. Corners may be cut off, and ends may be pointed. But the relationship between axes remains the same within each system. (See Figure 4–19.)*

Using your largest plasticine spheres for corners, and toothpicks for edges, construct models of each of the first four crystal systems. Use a protractor to be sure that the angles are properly measured at the corners. The angles should be 90°, except for the hexagonal system, in which the angles are 60°.

On your model of the cubic *system, make two diagonals across the top of the cube, using thread. Then make diagonals across the bottom. Place a sphere on the top and bottom of the cube where the diagonals cross, or intersect. Connect these spheres with a toothpick. The central toothpick is the* axis *of the cube. It is parallel to the sides, and the same length as the sides. Continue this construction of axes for the other sides of the cube. When you have constructed the three axes, measure them, and determine the angles made by the intersecting axes. Write a definition for a cube, using the information you have determined about the axes and the sides.*

Figure 4-13. Models of copper (a.), halite (b.), and pyrite (c.) illustrate various arrangements of atoms, all of which are in the cubic system. Sketches of copper (d.), halite (e.), and pyrite (f.) illustrate the basic units of these minerals which are repeated numerous times to form visible crystals.

Ward's Natural Science Establishment, Inc.

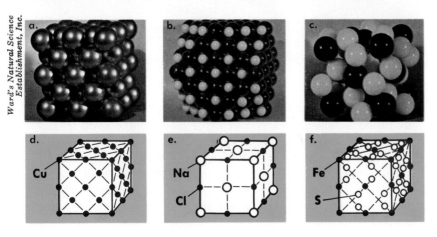

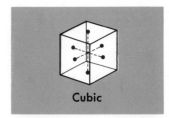

Cubic

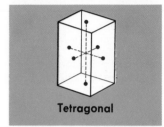

Tetragonal

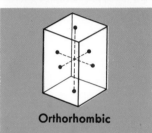

Orthorhombic

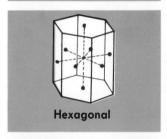

Hexagonal

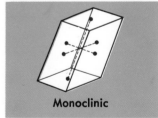

Monoclinic

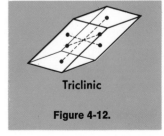

Triclinic

Figure 4-12.

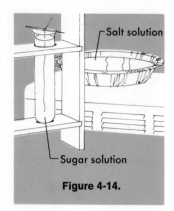

Salt solution

Sugar solution

Figure 4-14.

Construct the axes for the tetragonal, orthorhombic (awr tha rahm'bik), and hexagonal (hek sag'an l) systems. The longest axis is called the c axis; the one pointing toward you is the a axis, and the other axis is the b axis. Define each of the four crystal systems in terms of the a, b, and c axes, and indicate their relationship to the sides.

EXPERIMENT.   Dissolve 1 cup of sugar in ½ cup of boiling water. When all of the sugar has dissolved, fill a test tube with the solution. Set the solution in a test tube rack and place a toothpick across the top of the tube. Suspend a thread from the toothpick and carefully lower the thread into the sugar solution so it does not touch the sides or bottom of the test tube. (Figure 4–14.) Let the solution stand for 24 hours. Examine the thread. What has happened? Look at the material under a high-powered magnifying glass. Explain what has occurred.

Dissolve 1 cup of salt in ½ cup of warm water or until no more will go into solution. The solution is saturated, or loaded to capacity, when salt remains in the bottom of the cup even after vigorous stirring. Pour the saturated solution of salt water into a shallow dish and place it in the sun or near a warm radiator. Record what happens. Compare the results of this experiment with your experiment on sugar crystals. Is the process of crystallization exactly the same?

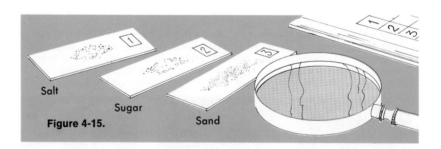

Salt

Sugar

Sand

Figure 4-15.

ACTIVITY.   Use salt crystals from the previous experiment or place a few grains of salt on a clean glass slide. Place crystals of sugar on another slide, and a few grains of sand on a third slide. Examine each slide under a microscope or strong magnifying glass. Note the differences and similarities among the crystals. Number the slides, and put the numbers in your notebook with the descriptions and the drawings of the observed grains.

4:2 *Identification of Minerals*

Minerals are identified or recognized by their physical properties. You can learn to recognize particular minerals through their appearance, smell, taste, feel, or sound when tapped. Appearance and feel are the most useful physical properties, but taste and smell are important clues to the identity of some minerals.

Minerals are recognized by physical properties which include those characteristics that can be seen and measured or recognized by one of the five senses.

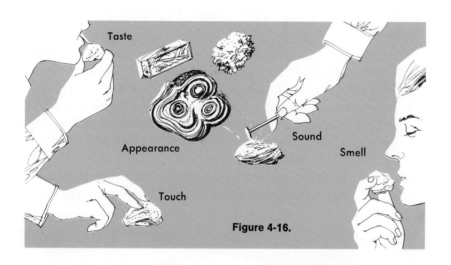

Figure 4-16.

ACTIVITY. You will be given mineral samples to examine with and without a microscope. List all of the characteristics that you think would be useful in recognizing the minerals. Base your answers on principles developed from model construction and crystal growing.

The appearance of a mineral is its most useful characteristic for identification. You can learn to recognize minerals just as you learn to recognize your friends, by the way they look. Physical properties by which you can recognize most minerals include crystal form, hardness, luster, cleavage and fracture, streak, and specific gravity or heft. The following discussion leads you through a series of tests which pinpoint the identifying characteristics of a number of common minerals.

Physical properties of minerals include crystal form, hardness, luster, cleavage or fracture, streak, and specific gravity.

Physical properties of thousands of minerals have been listed or cataloged by mineralogists and arranged in charts similar to Tables 4–4 and 4–5. To identify an unknown mineral specimen, ask yourself the following eight questions:

1. Is the mineral shiny? Luster refers to the way light is reflected from a mineral. If a mineral shines like a highly polished surface, it has **metallic luster.** If it is dull and does not reflect light, or if it allows light to pass through in the way window glass does, the mineral has **nonmetallic luster.** Nonmetallic luster may be described as dull, pearly, silky, glassy, or sparkling. Metallic luster is common among minerals that contain one of the metals, such as gold, silver, or lead. If the unknown mineral is shiny, turn to the first part of the chart where minerals with metallic luster are described. If the unknown mineral is not shiny, turn to the descriptions of minerals with nonmetallic luster.

Minerals that reflect light as though from a polished surface have metallic luster.

2. Can you streak the mineral? Rub the unknown mineral sample on a piece of unglazed porcelain, such as the back of a porcelain tile or a *streak plate*. Does the rubbing cause a streak? **Streak** is the color of the powdered mineral. Streak is a very important property in minerals that are softer than the porcelain streak plate. Streak is an especially useful aid for identifying metallic minerals. If no streak appears, the mineral is said to have a colorless or white streak. Locate the color of the streak of your unknown mineral in the mineral chart.

Streak, the color of the powdered mineral, is an important characteristic for minerals below 5 in hardness.

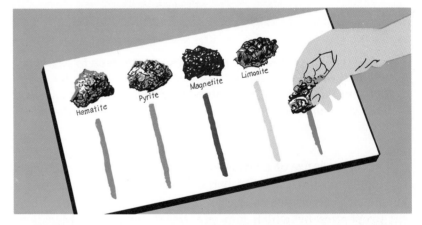

Figure 4-17. Color of the streak may be a very different color from the mineral. Only the mineral, not the matrix, should be rubbed on the streak plate.

Figure 4-18. Only fresh surfaces of a mineral should be used to test its hardness.

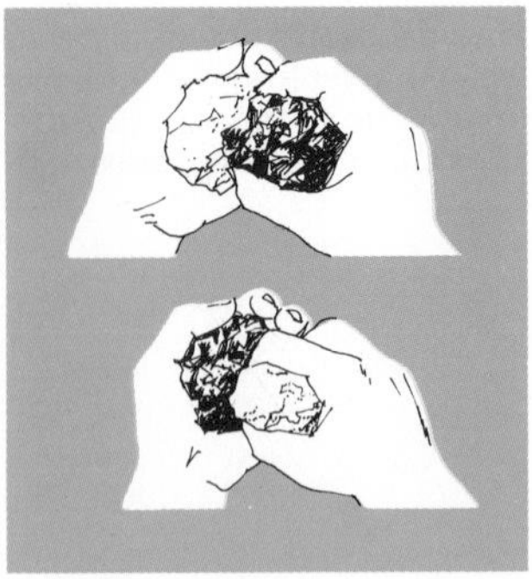

3. How hard is the mineral? Hardness is one of the most useful means for identifying minerals. **Hardness** is the resistance of a mineral to being scratched. A harder mineral always scratches a softer mineral. Fredrich Mohs, a German mineralogist, worked out a scale of hardness. The scale gives numbers to ten reference minerals in the order of increasing hardness. (Table 4–2.) Each mineral will scratch any mineral which has a lower number on the Mohs scale. You can determine the hardness of an unknown mineral sample by scratching its edge against the surface of each mineral in a set of hardness minerals. Minerals in a set of hardness minerals are assigned numbers corresponding to the Mohs scale. The unknown has the hardness of a mineral which it cannot scratch, and by which it cannot be scratched. The unknown mineral is softer than a mineral which scratches it. And it is harder than a mineral which it can scratch.

Table 4–2. *MOHS SCALE OF HARDNESS*

1—Talc	6—Orthoclase
2—Gypsum	7—Quartz
3—Calcite	8—Topaz
4—Fluorite	9—Corundum
5—Apatite	10—Diamond

If you are collecting rocks and minerals on a field trip, you may not have the Mohs set of minerals with you. Then the scale in Table 4–3, called the *field scale*, is convenient to use. However, the hardness determinations are not quite as exact as comparisons with a Mohs set of hardness minerals.

Table 4–3. *FIELD SCALE OF HARDNESS*

1—Soft, greasy, flakes on fingers
2—Scratched by fingernail
3—Cuts easily with knife or nail, or scratched by penny
4—Scratched easily by knife
5—Scratched by knife, but with difficulty
6—Scratched by steel file or piece of glass
7—Scratches steel file
8—Scratches quartz
No approximations above 8

4. What is the shape of the mineral? **Shape** refers to the geometric pattern or crystal habit characteristic of certain minerals. If your unknown mineral has a geometric shape that you can see, it means that the atomic pattern has been repeated over and over. Recall that solids exist in one of six crystal sys-

Minerals may occur as crystalline or massive solids.

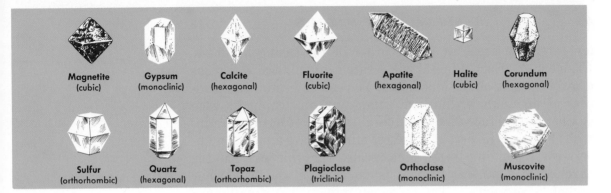

Magnetite
(cubic)

Gypsum
(monoclinic)

Calcite
(hexagonal)

Fluorite
(cubic)

Apatite
(hexagonal)

Halite
(cubic)

Corundum
(hexagonal)

Sulfur
(orthorhombic)

Quartz
(hexagonal)

Topaz
(orthorhombic)

Plagioclase
(triclinic)

Orthoclase
(monoclinic)

Muscovite
(monoclinic)

Figure 4-19. Crystal habits of several minerals.

Amorphous substances do not have a recognizable internal atomic structure and are properly called mineraloids.

Figure 4-20. Chalcopyrite.

University of Houston

Figure 4-21. Malachite.

University of Houston

tems. Compare your unknown mineral with the models of crystal systems and the drawings in Figure 4–19. If the unknown specimen has no recognizable crystal form, it may be *massive*. Massive minerals do not have visible crystalline forms. But with enough magnification, the crystals can be recognized. Examine the specimen with a magnifying glass to see whether you can recognize its form. Massive specimens may be described by terms that suggest their appearance, such as compact, fibrous, or granular. *Amorphous* (a mawr'fus) minerals properly should be called *mineraloids* (min'ra lawids). They have no recognizable crystal form, even when examined by X-ray diffraction. Mineraloids are often glassy and smooth. They cool so quickly that no regular pattern is formed.

5. *Does the mineral have any broken surfaces?* The way in which a mineral breaks is described by its *cleavage* and its *fracture* (frak'chur). Minerals that break along smooth flat planes are said to **cleave.** Cleavage planes may meet in angles that form a geometric pattern. Or cleavage may occur in only one or two directions. Basal cleavage is cleavage parallel to the base of a crystal. Cleavage may be cubic, octahedral (ok ta hee'dral), rhombohedral (rahm boh hee'dral), or any of the other forms in which solids occur. Recall that in an Activity in Section 4:1 you outlined the cleavage angles for pyroxenes and amphiboles. You also found these angles important means of distinguishing between the two mineral families. **Fracture** is breakage along an irregular surface which may be described as rough, conchoidal (kan kawid'l) (curved), or hackly (thin jagged points jutting upward).

6. *What is the color of the mineral?* Color is important for the identification of only a few minerals. Color of most minerals varies with the impurities included in the mineral when it crystallized or with the amount of surface tarnish. A few minerals have constant color and may be recognized by this property.

Pyrite, gold, and chalcopyrite (kal ka pier′iet) are always metallic yellow. The copper mineral azurite (azh′a riet) is a deep blue. For most minerals, streak is a more reliable clue than the color of the mineral in mass.

7. Is the mineral heavy? **Specific gravity** refers to the ratio of the mass of a mineral to the mass of an equal volume of water. (Section 2:4.) Specific gravity is useful in the recognition of very heavy minerals, such as galena. In general, minerals with specific gravities above 4 usually contain metals. The *heft* or relative weight can be judged by picking up the mineral. Specific gravity is not a useful characteristic for identification of nonmetallic minerals because their specific gravities are too similar. Specific gravity is useful, however, in some laboratory identifications where measurements are very precise.

8. Does the mineral have some unique characteristics? Be sure to check the column labeled Other Properties in Tables 4–4 and 4–5. Here you will find unusual features that may be helpful in recognizing certain minerals. Some minerals can be identified by special properties, such as *taste* for halite, *odor* for sulfur, and the bell-like *ringing* of jade when tapped. The properties in this column will help you to distinguish among several mineral descriptions that otherwise seem to fit your unknown mineral.

Octahedral means that the solid has eight plane faces with all angles less than right angles. **Rhombohedral** means that the solid is a six-sided figure with angles greater than or less than right angles.

Minerals which contain metals often have a high specific gravity. Lead and iron add mass to their minerals.

ACTIVITY. Identify some of the minerals you were given for inspection and the minerals you have acquired. First ask yourself the eight questions discussed in this section. Follow all of the suggestions given and find each unknown in Tables 4–4 or 4–5. Put a small square of white paint on your own specimen. The room specimen will have been labeled with a number. After you have used all of the tests, check with the teacher to be sure of your identification. Then number your minerals as the room minerals are numbered. In your notebook, write the numbers and the name of the mineral with the number. For your tests, you will need a powerful magnifying glass or microscope, unglazed porcelain (tile or streak plate), 15 percent hydrochloric acid, and a set of hardness minerals. Check for hardness with a nail, a penny, and a piece of glass and prove your conclusion on the hardness minerals listed in Table 4–3. In this way you will become familiar with the field scale which will be most useful to you in your own collecting. You may want to arrange the minerals in a display to exhibit some particular characteristic of mineral formation.

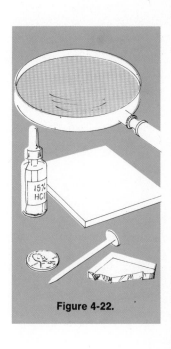

Figure 4-22.

Table 4-4. Minerals With Metallic Luster

Mineral	Color	Streak	Hardness	Specific Gravity	Shape	Breakage Pattern	Other Properties
Graphite C	Black to gray	Black	1-2	2.3	Hexagonal	Perfect basal cleavage	Greasy, soft, smudges fingers
Hematite (specular) Fe_2O_3	Silver gray	Reddish brown	6	5.3	Hexagonal massive	Uneven fracture, no cleavage	Earthy, brittle, source of iron
Pyrite FeS_2	Light brassy yellow	Greenish black	6.5	5.0	Cubic, massive	Conchoidal fracture	Alters to limonite, "fool's gold"
Magnetite Fe_3O_4	Black	Black	6	5.2	Cubic, granular	Conchoidal fracture	Naturally magnetic, source of iron
Galena PbS	Gray	Gray	2.5	7.5	Cubic, massive, granular, fibrous	Cubic cleavage, even fracture (rare)	Source of lead, often with sphalerite (zinc-containing mineral)
Bornite Cu_5FeS_4	Bronze, yellow, tarnishes to dark blue, purple	Grayish black	3	5.0	Cubic, massive, compact	Uneven fracture, poor octahedral cleavage	Purple-tarnished surface looks like hard coal and gives rise to name "peacock ore"
Copper Cu	Copper red, tarnishes to black	Copper red	3	8.1	Cubic, wire-like form	Hackly fracture	Malleable and ductile

Figure 4-23.   Graphite Schist.

University of Houston

Figure 4-24.   Pyrite (massive).

University of Houston

Figure 4-25.   Magnetite (massive).

University of Houston

Figure 4-26.   Galena.

University of Houston

Table 4-5. *Minerals With Nonmetallic Luster*

Mineral	Color	Streak	Hardness	Specific Gravity	Shape	Breakage Pattern	Other Properties
Talc $Mg_3(OH)_2Si_4O_{10}$	White, greenish	White	1	2.8	Monoclinic, massive, granular	Cleavage in one direction, thin sheets, uneven fracture	Pearly, soapy, easily cut
Gypsum $CaSO_4 \cdot 2H_2O$	White, gray, brown	White	2	2.3	Monoclinic, massive	Basal cleavage, fibrous fracture	Pearly, silky, dull, glassy
Calcite $CaCO_3$	White (pure), varied (impure)	White	3	2.7	Hexagonal, massive	Rhombohedral cleavage, conchoidal fracture	Dull or pearly, releases CO_2 when HCl is added
Fluorite CaF_2	White, green, yellow, purple, red, blue	Colorless	4	3-3.3	Cubic, octahedral	Octahedral cleavage, conchoidal fracture	Glassy to dull, brittle, fluorescent, phosphorescent, twin crystals common
Apatite $Ca_5(Cl,F)(PO_4)_3$	White, yellow, brown, blue, green	White	5	3.2	Hexagonal, massive	Conchoidal fracture	Glassy to dull, brittle, granular
Feldspar (orthoclase) $KAlSi_3O_8$	White to gray, red, green (rare)	Colorless	6	2.5	Monoclinic, massive	Two cleavage planes meet at 90° angles, conchoidal fracture	Common in igneous rock
Feldspar (plagioclase) $(Na,Ca)(Al,Si)AlSi_2O_8$	Gray, green, white	Colorless	6	2.5	Monoclinic, massive	Two cleavage planes meet at 90° angles, conchoidal fracture	Fine parallel lines on cleavage surface distinguish feldspar (plagioclase) from feldspar (orthoclase)
*Garnet (pyrope) $Mg_3Al_2Si_3O_{12}$	Deep yellow-red	Colorless	7.5	3.5	Cubic	Uneven to conchoidal fracture, no cleavage	Glassy, very common mineral, pyrope used in garnet sandpaper

*Valuable as gems or semi-precious stones.

Figure 4-27.   Talc.

University of Houston

Figure 4-28.   Gypsum.

University of Houston

Figure 4-29.   Fluorite.

University of Houston

Figure 4-30.   Apatite.

University of Houston

Figure 4-31.   Orthoclase Feldspar.

University of Houston

Table 4-5. Minerals With Nonmetallic Luster (Continued)

Mineral	Color	Streak	Hardness	Specific Gravity	Shape	Breakage Pattern	Other Properties
*Quartz SiO_2	Colorless through various colors	Colorless	7	2.65	Hexagonal, massive	Conchoidal fracture	Waxy or glassy, species includes chalcedony, agate, and onyx; rock crystal and amethyst are crystalline varieties.
*Topaz Al_2SiO_4 $(F,OH)_2$	White, yellow, pale blue, pink	Colorless	8	3.5-3.6	Orthorhombic, massive	Perfect basal cleavage, conchoidal fracture	Glassy
*Corundum Al_2O_3	Brown, green, pink, blue, red, black, violet	Colorless	9	3.9-4.1	Hexagonal, massive	Conchoidal or uneven fracture, no cleavage	Barrel-shaped, dull in some varieties, may sparkle in gem varieties (ruby, sapphire), brittle, often tough
*Tourmaline series (Na,Ca) $(Al,Fe,Li,Mg)_3$ B_3Al_3 $(Al_3Si_6O_{27})$ $(O,OH,F)_4$	Black, green, brown, white, red, blue	Colorless	7-7.5	3.0-3.3	Hexagonal, massive	Uneven to conchoidal fracture	Glassy, long direction often has fine parallel lines, brittle
Sulfur S	Yellow	Yellow to white	2.5	2.0	Orthorhombic, massive	Conchoidal fracture	Brittle, odor of sulfur, melts easily
Dolomite $CaMg(CO_3)_2$	White to pink to gray, green or black	White	3.5-4	2.8	Hexagonal	Rhombohedral cleavage, conchoidal fracture	Glassy to dull, will bubble with hot acid
Halite $NaCl$	Colorless, reddish, white, blue	Colorless	2.5	2.1	Cubic	Cubic cleavage, conchoidal fracture	Glassy to dull, salty taste, soluble in water
Hematite (red ocher) Fe_2O_3	Reddish brown to black	Reddish brown	6	5.3	Hexagonal massive	Uneven to conchoidal fracture, no cleavage	Dull to earthy, source of iron

*Valuable as gems or semi-precious stones.

Figure 4-32. Quartz.

University of Houston

Figure 4-33. Topaz.

University of Houston

Figure 4-34. Tourmaline.

University of Houston

Figure 4-35. Sulfur.

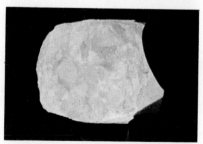

Texas Gulf Sulphur Company

Figure 4-36. Halite.

University of Houston

Table 4-5. *Minerals With Nonmetallic Luster (Continued)*

Mineral	Color	Streak	Hardness	Specific Gravity	Shape	Breakage Pattern	Other Properties
Limonite (yellow ocher) $2Fe_2O_3 \cdot H_2O$	Yellow, brown, or black	Yellow brown	5.5	4.0	Massive, often powdery	No cleavage, conchoidal to earthy fracture	Dull to glassy, iron-rust appearance, coloring matter of soils
Serpentine $Mg_3Si_2O_5(OH)_4$	White, red, green, black, brown, yellow	Colorless	2-5	2.2-2.6	Monoclinic	Conchoidal fracture, none to fibrous cleavage	Silky, greasy to waxy
Asbestos (serpentine, chrysotile) $Mg_3Si_2O_5(OH)_4$	Green to yellow green	Colorless	2	2.2	Monoclinic	Fibrous cleavage	Silky, separates into thread-like fibers
Bauxite $Al(OH)_3$	Gray, red, white, brown	Gray	1-3	2.0-2.5	Rounded masses	Earthy fracture	Dull, source of aluminum
Hornblende $CaNa(Mg,Fe)_4$ $(Al,Fe,Ti)_3Si_6$ $O_{22}(O,OH)_2$	Green to black	Gray to white	5-6	3.4	Monoclinic	Cleavage in two directions, uneven to subconchoidal fracture	Glassy to silky
Kaolinite $Al_2Si_2O_5(OH)_4$	Red or reddish-brown to white or black	White	2	2.6	Triclinic	Earthy fracture, perfect basal cleavage	Dull, earthy odor, often pliable, greasy, used in ceramics
Augite (Ca,Mg,Al,Fe) $(Al,Si)_2O_6$	Black to dark green	Colorless	6	3.5	Monoclinic	Cleavage in two directions	Dull, granular
*Olivine $(Mg,Fe)_2SiO_4$	Olive green	Colorless	6.5	3.5	Orthorhombic, granular	Imperfect cleavage, conchoidal fracture	Glassy, common in meteorites
Muscovite $KAl_3Si_3O_{10}(OH)_2$	White to light gray	Colorless	2.5	2.8	Monoclinic	Perfect basal cleavage	Plates flexible and elastic, large crystals in pegmatites, member of mica group
Biotite $K(Mg,Fe)_3$ $AlSi_3O_{10}(OH)_2$	Black to dark brown	Colorless	2.5	2.8-3.4	Monoclinic	Perfect basal cleavage	Plates flexible and elastic, common mineral of pegmatites, member of mica group

*Valuable as gems or semi-precious stones.

Figure 4-37.   Limonite.

University of Houston

Figure 4-38.   Kaolinite.

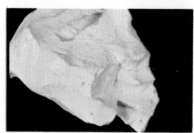

University of Houston

Figure 4-39.   Olivine.

University of Houston

Figure 4-40.   Muscovite.

University of Houston

Figure 4-41.   Biotite.

University of Houston

4:3 Rocks

Rocks are single minerals or mixtures of several minerals that make up an essential part of the earth's crust. You may not have seen rocks exposed at the surface of the earth, because rocks often are covered by soil or vegetation. Nevertheless, at some depth below the surface, rocks are present everywhere. In mountainous areas, exposed rocks extend skyward to great altitudes. In other regions, hundreds or even thousands of feet of sediment cover hard rocks below.

If you have seen rocks exposed at the surface, you may have observed that rocks are not all alike. Some look like hardened beach sand. Some look like chalkboard chalk. Some are hard, dense mixtures in which the minerals of which they are composed are easily recognizable. Other rocks look like cinders. Why are there differences among the rocks?

All rock materials originated beneath the present surface of the earth. All parent rock material, at one time in its history, was a liquid. The parent rock-forming liquid was carried to the surface and hardened there, or it hardened beneath the surface. When the liquid hardened, it formed *igneous* (ig'nee us) *rock*. Other kinds of rock have formed from the parent igneous rock.

The name igneous comes from the Latin word *igneus*, which means fire. Vulcan (Vul'kan), the Roman god of fire, was supposed to be responsible for sending liquid rock upward from his kingdom within the earth to form volcanoes. From the name Vulcan comes the term *volcanic* to describe the material which erupts or flows from a volcano. Not all liquid rock reaches the surface. Much of it hardens at great depths. But all igneous rocks have hardened from liquid material.

Chemical and mechanical changes called *weathering* occur when igneous rocks are exposed at the surface of the earth. Rock is broken into fragments by mechanical processes, or it undergoes chemical reactions. It may be formed into new and different chemical compounds. Soil is produced by such changes. Materials formed during weathering are carried away by winds, waves, and rivers. Later the materials are deposited as sediments. Sand deposited on a beach and mud deposited by a flooding river are two examples of sediments. Eventually, older sediments are buried under layers of younger sediments. The weight of overlying sediments hardens the buried materials into *sedimentary* (sed i ment'a ree) *rock*.

Marginal notes:

Rocks are single minerals or mixtures of minerals.

Rocks differ from one another according to their origin.

Igneous rocks have hardened from a liquid.

Sedimentary rocks consist of older rock materials changed mechanically or chemically at the surface of the earth.

Robert F. Moseley, Jr.

American Airlines

Figure 4-42. Igneous rock that hardened near the surface but within a volcano remains as a high hill after softer surrounding rocks are worn away.

Figure 4-43. Sedimentary rocks have been uplifted and exposed to weathering and erosion after they were buried and hardened into rock.

When sedimentary rocks are buried to depths of 8 mi to 10 mi below the surface of the earth, they are subjected to great heat and pressure. Heat and pressure may cause physical and chemical changes that form new kinds of rock. Rocks changed by great heat and pressure beneath the surface of the earth are called *metamorphic* (met e mawr'fik) *rocks. Metamorphism* (met e mawr'fiz um) is a process that transforms sedimentary rocks and igneous rocks into new forms. Most metamorphic changes occur 8 mi to 10 mi below the surface. However, metamorphism occasionally occurs adjacent, or next, to hot igneous masses that are moving upward through sedimentary rocks that are close to the surface.

Metamorphosis is a Greek word that means to transform.

During the rock cycle, rocks are changed from one kind to another as environmental conditions change. There is no beginning and no end; nothing is lost, but everything undergoes change.

Figure 4–44 illustrates the never-ending cycle of rock change and re-formation. Sedimentary rocks are placed at the top of the triangle because they form at or near the top of the earth's surface. Igneous rocks and metamorphic rocks occupy the lower points of the triangle because these rocks are formed far below the earth's surface. Other kinds of rock may be transformed into metamorphic rocks by heat and pressure. However, metamorphic changes occur while the rock remains solid and temperatures are below the melting point. If temperatures rise to the melting point and the rock becomes a liquid and then hardens, the new rock is called igneous. Upward-pointing arrows indicate that both igneous and metamorphic rocks may be changed to sedimentary rocks if they are exposed at the earth's surface. Downward-pointing arrows indicate that sedimentary rocks may be metamorphosed and form metamorphic rock far below the surface. Or rocks may be melted at great depths to form igneous rock.

No cycle diagram can show all of the complex history of rock change and re-formation. For example, this diagram does not show that volcanic rock which forms at the surface may be metamorphosed if it is buried. However, the diagram shows how the majority of rocks are formed. Notice that none of the

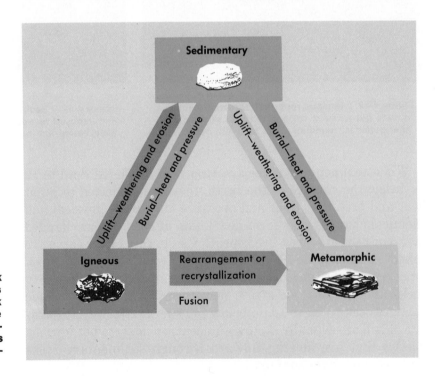

Figure 4-44. The cycle of rock change and re-formation is never-ending. Each kind of rock occupies a peak of the triangle for a short time before it is subjected to change and becomes a different kind of rock, occupying a new position.

matter of the crust is permanently lost and none remains permanently in one form. All matter is subject to chemical change or rearrangement of its particles, but the elements still remain the same.

Rock identification follows the same general principles as mineral identification. In the following activity, you will examine mixtures of several minerals in the rocks. The first step in rock identification is to classify, or group, similar materials. All members of one group must have a common characteristic. Different groups have different characteristics. The purpose of classification is to simplify the understanding of materials.

ACTIVITY. Examine from five to eight rock samples of different shapes and sizes. Group all rocks that have a common characteristic. Make at least three groupings of the rocks. Record the common characteristic on which you base each grouping. Compare your system of classification with the classification made by other students. Use a 10× magnifying glass to find characteristics not observable without the aid of magnification. Without a microscope, you cannot see all of the distinguishing features which geologists use for precise classification. However, you can see the same characteristics that early scientists used for rock classification.

Crush bits of the rocks. Examine the crushed rock with the magnifying glass. If you recognize any of the minerals, write their names in your notebook. Would you now change your classification or group your rocks any differently?

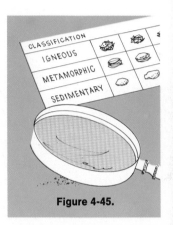

Figure 4-45.

MAIN IDEAS

1. The outer, solid crust of the earth, called the lithosphere, is composed of rocks and minerals. Rocks are made of single minerals or mixtures of minerals; minerals are elements or chemical compounds.

2. Only 12 of the 2,000 known minerals are common in the lithosphere.

3. Only 8 of the 88 crustal elements make up 98.58 percent of the lithosphere.

4. Minerals are naturally formed, inorganic solids that have a definite internal atomic pattern and a constant chemical composition.

5. Crystals of a given mineral always have the same kind of atoms arranged in the same pattern which is repeated over and over until the structure becomes visible.

6. One atom may substitute, up to a certain point, for another atom in a mineral if the ions involved have the same radius and the same electrical charges.

7. Given in order, the most common minerals of the lithosphere are silicates, carbonates, and oxides.

8. Minerals are recognized by the physical properties of form, hardness, luster, streak, fracture or cleavage, color, and specific gravity.

9. Mineraloids may occur as amorphous solids with no apparent internal atomic pattern. Mineraloids are not distinguished from minerals in most identification charts.

10. Cleavage is smooth, flat breakage in one or more directions. Fracture is uneven breakage with a curved (conchoidal), rough, or hackly surface.

11. Rocks are composed of single minerals or mixtures of minerals and are named igneous, sedimentary, or metamorphic according to their origin.

12. Igneous rocks, the source of all other rocks, are hardened from liquid rock material.

13. Sedimentary rock materials are formed by the mechanical breakdown and chemical changes which other kinds of rocks undergo when exposed at the surface. Sediments must be buried and hardened to form sedimentary rock.

14. Metamorphic rocks, which may have either igneous or sedimentary sources, result from deep burial and great heat and pressure.

15. The rock cycle is a never-ending process in which all rocks are changed, but matter is not lost.

VOCABULARY

Write a sentence in which you use correctly each of the following words or terms.

amorphous	igneous	sedimentary
cleavage	lithosphere	solid
crystal	luster	specific gravity
fracture	metamorphic	streak
hardness	mineraloid	weathering

STUDY QUESTIONS

A. True or False

Determine whether each of the following sentences is true or false. (Do not write in this book.)

1. Only 33 elements have been found in the earth's crust.
2. Oxygen is the most abundant element in the earth's crust.
3. Mohs scale of hardness is a convenient scale to use on a field trip.
4. Diamonds will scratch all other minerals.
5. Color is an excellent means of identifying most minerals.
6. The most common minerals on the surface of the earth are silicates.
7. Minerals do not change their internal atomic patterns.
8. Iron and oxygen combine to form silicates.
9. Quartz is a mineral.
10. Most minerals are chemical compounds.

B. Multiple Choice

Choose the word or phrase which completes correctly each of the following sentences. (Do not write in this book.)

1. The earth's crust contains (*77, 88, 99*) different elements.
2. Of the elements in the crust, only (*6, 8, 10*) are abundant.
3. Crystals of a given mineral (*always, occasionally, never*) appear in the same crystal system.
4. One mineral with a distinct taste is (*quartz, garnet, halite*).
5. (*Sedimentary, Igneous, Metamorphic*) rocks are the most abundant rocks.
6. In the rock cycle, none of the matter is (*permanently lost, changed, rearranged*).
7. (*Streak, Luster, Crystal habit*) is the color of the powdered mineral.
8. If a mineral breaks with a smooth plane surface, it is said to have (*luster, hardness, cleavage*).
9. An important means of distinguishing between the amphiboles and the pyroxenes is (*fracture, cleavage, streak*).
10. Odor is a unique characteristic of (*sulfur, halite, jade*).

C. Completion

Complete each of the following sentences with a word or phrase which will make the sentence correct. (Do not write in this book.)

1. A mineral must be: formed in nature, of a definite internal atomic pattern, of a constant composition, __?__, and __?__.

2. The two most abundant elements in the crust of the earth are __?__ and __?__.

3. Quartz is composed of __?__ and __?__.

4. Rocks may contain more than one __?__.

5. Hardness is a(n) __?__ property of a mineral.

6. The way in which a mineral breaks is called __?__ or __?__.

7. The way light is reflected from a mineral is termed __?__.

8. Minerals may occur as crystals or they may be __?__.

9. Minerals have geometric shapes which belong to one of the six __?__.

10. Gold has a(n) __?__ luster.

D. How and Why

1. How does a mineral differ from an element?

2. Is coral properly classified as a mineral?

3. How does a mineral differ from a rock?

4. Why are some minerals found as visible crystals and others in massive occurrences?

5. Why are silicate minerals the most common minerals?

6. What elements would you expect to combine most often with the silicates?

7. Why do igneous and metamorphic rocks change at the surface of the earth?

8. Explain the meaning of the rock cycle diagram in Figure 4–44.

9. Why do metamorphic rocks form at depths but not at the surface of the earth?

10. Discuss the physical characteristics that aid in identifying common minerals.

INVESTIGATIONS

1. Explain why rocks and minerals and many earth processes have Greek and Latin names.
2. Look up the myths of Pluto and Vulcan. Why are some rocks called plutonic?
3. List five minerals that are important in industry or as gems. Discuss why they are not among the rock-formers.
4. Discuss the difference between fracture and cleavage. Use a block of four soda crackers to demonstrate the difference in the appearance of the breaks.

INTERESTING READING

Clayton, Keith, *The Crust of the Earth: The Story of Geology.* Nature & Science Library. Garden City, N.Y., Natural History Press, 1967.

Gallant, R. A., and Schuberth, C. J., *Discovering Rock & Minerals.* Garden City, N.Y., Natural History Press, 1967.

*Hurlbut, C. S., Jr., *Mineralogy and Some of its Applications.* Cambridge, Mass., Mineralogical Society of America, Harvard University, n.d.

Keene, M., *The Beginner's Story of Minerals & Rocks.* New York, Harper & Row Publishers, Inc., 1966.

Matthews, William H., *The Story of the Earth.* Irvington-on-Hudson, N.Y., Harvey House, Inc., Publishers, 1968.

Pearl, Richard M., *One Thousand One Questions Answered About the Mineral Kingdom.* New York, Dodd, Mead & Co., 1959.

Pearl, Richard M., *Wonders of Rocks & Minerals.* New York, Dodd, Mead & Co., 1961.

Sanborn, W. B., *Handbook of Crystal & Mineral Collecting.* Mentone, Calif., Gembooks, 1966.

Sander, Lenore, *The Curious World of Crystals.* Englewood Cliffs, N.J., Prentice-Hall, Inc., 1964.

*Vanders, Iris, and Kerr, Paul, *Mineral Recognition.* New York, John Wiley & Sons, Inc., 1967.

Wohlrabe, R. A., *Crystals.* New York, J. B. Lippincott Co., 1962.

---

* Well-illustrated material.

Igneous Rocks

Igneous rocks have been forming since the earth was formed. They compose 95 percent by volume of the crust of the earth. They are the parent materials for all other kinds of rock. Most igneous rocks are hidden, but igneous rocks are still forming in regions of volcanic activity, such as Hawaii. Some scientists believe that all of the earth's crust is the result of volcanic activity. The rate at which volcanic material is accumulating in the Islands of Hawaii and around other volcanoes has been measured. The present volume of the crust of the earth could well have piled up during the approximately 4.5 billion years the earth has existed.

5:1 *Origin*

Igneous rock is formed by the solidification of liquid magma.

Rocks are called **igneous** (ig'nee us) if they have hardened or solidified from liquid rock. Liquid rock, called **magma** (mag'ma), forms within the upper mantle or near the bottom of the crust in certain regions. Magma then moves upward into the crust, or it flows out on the surface and solidifies as igneous rock. Melting of the mantle occurs where temperatures are raised to approximately 1400°C (2552°F), or where the pressure is lowered. If the pressure is lowered enough, the melting point of the mantle falls below 1400°C.

At depths of 35 mi below the surface, the temperature of the mantle is figured to be about 1400°C. This temperature is approximately equal to the melting point of rock being pressed down by a column of rock 35 mi thick. Where large amounts of radioactive elements are present, additional heat is produced. Then temperatures may be raised above 1400°C. Great thicknesses of sediment serve as a blanket to hold heat within

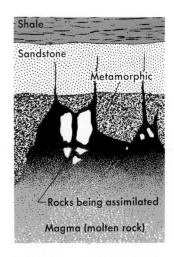

the earth. Thus, in areas of mountain building, temperatures also may rise above 1400°C. The melting point may fall below 1400°C where the earth's crust is broken by fractures that extend into the mantle. These fractures cause decreased pressure. Rocks melt at the lowered melting point. Magma moves upward along these fractures.

Magma moves upward from depths of 35 mi to 50 mi below the surface of the earth. Sometimes it moves upward because of the great pressures which accompany the uplift of mountains. More often, however, magma rises toward the surface because it is less dense than the solid material around it. Occasionally, magma moves along great fractures. If the fractures are open to the surface of the earth, the liquid rock flows out on the surface in a form called *lava* (lahv'a). Sometimes the magma seems to rise through the solid rock in a process called *stoping* (stohp'ing). During stoping, great blocks of overlying rock are surrounded by the hot liquid rock. The blocks break up, melt, and become part of the magma. Magma works upward through regions that formerly were occupied by solid rock.

Figure 5-1. Magma ascends along fractures which allow liquid rock to surround and melt great blocks of solid rock.

Fractures are breaks in rock caused by intense folding or cracking.

ACTIVITY.   Heat 2 cups of water until it boils. Then add ½ to ¾ cup of cream of wheat. The mixture should be very thick. As the cereal cooks, observe the surface. Why do craters form? How long do they remain? What gas escapes at the surface? Compare the processes that form the craters on the cream of wheat with processes that form volcanoes.

5:2   *Rock Bodies*

When magma cools, it solidifies and forms rock bodies of many different shapes and sizes. These rock bodies are named according to their dimensions and relationship to the surrounding rock. Some magma hardens and forms rock far below the surface of the earth. Some magma reaches the surface where it forms *volcanic mountains* and *volcanic plateaus* (pla tohs').

Batholiths (bath'a liths) are the largest rock bodies. They form several miles below the surface of the earth. They may be 50 mi across and extend hundreds of miles. Batholiths are exposed at the earth's surface only when miles of surface rock have been carried away from above them. **Stocks** have the same general characteristics as batholiths but are smaller.

Some liquids and gases are less dense than the main mass of the magma. These fluids rise to the top of the batholith. They

Figure 5-2.

Magma may be cooled and hardened below the surface, or it may pour out of volcanoes and harden on the surface.

Often, precious metals and other ores are found associated with the country rock surrounding the batholith.

often carry precious metals and valuable ores along with them. These liquids and gases move about more freely than the thicker rock magma. Thus they squeeze into the rock that surrounds the batholith. Metamorphic changes often result from *intrusion* (in troo'zhun), or forcing of liquids and gases into adjacent rock. This nearby rock is called **country rock** by miners and geologists. Some metamorphic changes in country rock may result from nearby intrusions.

Other rock bodies formed by igneous activity are *dikes, sills,* and *laccoliths.* When rock hardens in cracks that cut across the country rock, the body is called a **dike.** Sometimes magma squeezes between two rock layers. There it solidifies into a thin "sheet" known as a **sill.** A **laccolith** (lack'a lith) is formed in much the same way as a sill, but the magma develops a convex (kahn veks') upper surface before it hardens. Thus, the body becomes mushroom-shaped. These rock bodies are illustrated in Figure 5–3.

Volcanoes are rock bodies formed on the surface of the earth by magma that remains liquid until it reaches the surface. Some volcanoes are cone-shaped because the magma materials are blown out with explosive force from an opening in the earth. Fragments of rock settle back to earth around the opening. After many eruptions, mountains are formed from the cinders. Some volcanoes are shield-shaped. When the liquid rock reaches the surface, the lava flows out quietly around a

Rock bodies formed on the surface may be volcanoes (cone-shaped, shield-shaped, or a combination of these types) or volcanic plateaus.

Figure 5-3. Large igneous bodies tend to be coarse-grained because they cool slowly. Because dikes and sills cool more quickly than laccoliths and batholiths, they are finer grained. Heat and gases escaping from the batholith cause the enclosing rock to become metamorphosed.

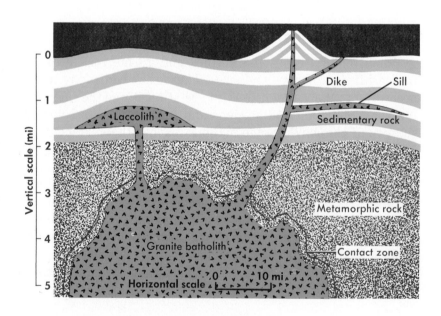

G. W. Stose, U.S. Geological Survey

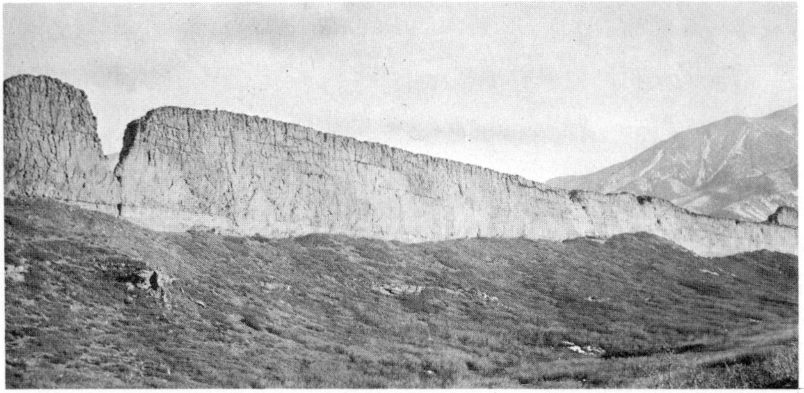

Figure 5-4. Dikes may form ridges at the surface that extend for miles after erosion has removed the less resistant surrounding rock.

central opening. Gradually, the hardened lava builds up a mound that resembles a warrior's shield. The Hawaiian Islands are typical shield volcanoes built up 30,000 ft above the ocean floor. Occasionally, lava flows out from long fractures extending for hundreds of miles. The hardened lava may be thousands of feet thick and hundreds of square miles in area. Such flows are called *volcanic plateaus*.

ACTIVITY. Set the large end of a funnel or the stem of a coffee percolator in a pan of water. Build a cone of modeling clay around the stem. Be sure not to cover the opening at the top. Set the pan over a Bunsen burner or an alcohol lamp and heat the water until it erupts from the opening at the top. What causes the eruption? Now cover the opening with a very thin piece of clay. (Squeeze the clay between your fingers until it is no thicker than a piece of paper.) The clay should just cover the opening. Repeat the activity. What happens to the clay covering the opening? Compare the processes you observe in this activity with those of a volcanic eruption.

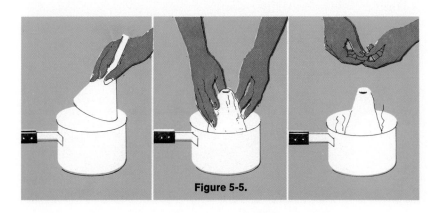

Figure 5-5.

5:3 *Texture*

The term **texture** (teks'cher) in igneous rock refers to the size of the mineral grains. Magma that solidifies at great depths cools slowly. Large masses of magma may require many millions of years to reach the temperature of the surrounding rock. During this slow cooling, minerals grow large and become recognizable. The rocks which contain large crystals are called **intrusives** (in troo'sivs) and are described as coarse-grained. Intrusive means forced in.

Magma that reaches the surface may solidify in a matter of days or even hours. Rocks formed during rapid cooling have small crystals or no crystals. These rocks are called **extrusives** (ik stroo'sivs) and are described as fine-grained or glass. Extrusive means forced out. Minerals in an extrusive rock can seldom be recognized without the aid of a microscope. Indeed, many extrusive rocks form so quickly that atoms have no opportunity to take on a geometric arrangement. Such rocks are called *glass*, and they have the same chemical and physical properties as man-made glass.

Occasionally, while the magma is still at great depth, some of the minerals crystallize. But before the entire magma solidifies, it rises to the surface. There the final cooling occurs rapidly. Rocks formed in this way are called *porphyries* (pawr'fa reez). They contain two or more different grain sizes.

Igneous rocks have many different mineral sizes because the size of the crystals depends upon the rate of cooling. The rate of cooling ranges from extremely slow at depths of several miles, to medium at depths of one mile or less, to very rapid at the surface. Batholiths cool very slowly and they have large crystals.

Intrusive igneous rocks harden slowly below the surface and have large mineral crystals.

Extrusive igneous rocks harden quickly at the surface and have small mineral crystals or no crystals.

Porphyries contain two or more noticeably different mineral grain sizes.

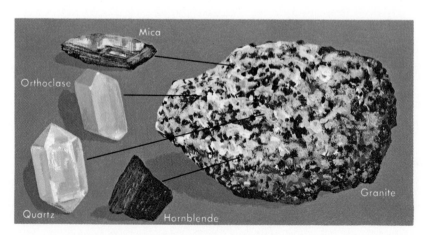

Figure 5-6. Granite forms from magma that cools slowly and each mineral component can be seen without magnification.

Laccoliths, sills, and dikes have recognizable crystals, but the grains are usually smaller than those of a batholith. Volcanic materials cool very rapidly. Their minerals can be recognized only with the aid of a microscope. If a glass forms, no crystals are visible.

Size of the mineral grains depends upon the rate of cooling of igneous rock.

Cook until it forms soft ball in water

Beat until thick and put in refrigerator

Figure 5-7.

ACTIVITY. Caution: This activity cannot be done successfully with packaged fudge. *Cook 2 cups of sugar, ¾ cup of milk, 2 squares of chocolate, and 2 tablespoons of light corn syrup slowly until the chocolate melts, stirring gently. Boil without stirring to 112°C (234°F) or until the mixture forms a soft ball when dropped into cold water. Remove the mixture from heat, add 2 tablespoons of butter, and let stand until cool. Pour half of the mixture into a pan and let stand. Pour the other half into a bowl and beat until thick. Place this half of the fudge in the refrigerator until hardened. Compare the textures of the two batches of fudge. Which one has the larger grains? Which batch is like an intrusive igneous rock? Which is similar to an extrusive igneous rock?*

EXPERIMENT. *Stir 2 yeast cakes in 2 cups of lukewarm water. Stir in enough flour to make a thick dough (6 to 7 cups of flour). Mix thoroughly and allow to rise in a warm place (near a radiator or on a sunny window sill) until double in size. The time required will be between 1 and 2 hours, depending on the temperature of the room. When the dough has risen, cut through the mass and observe what happens. What causes the holes? Where did the gas come from? Why did it tend to rise to the top of the dough? What rocks may be compared to the dough, so far as texture is concerned?*

Boil water

Stir yeast and then flour into lukewarm water

Cut through dough

Figure 5-8.

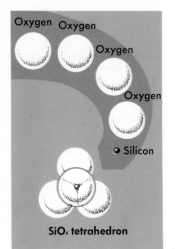

Figure 5-9. Oxygen and silicon atoms are the most abundant elements in a magma. They combine in a ratio of four oxygen atoms to one silicon atom to form the silicate tetrahedron. Atoms of other elements join the silicate tetrahedron to form a variety of rock-forming minerals.

5:4   *Composition*

Rock-forming minerals are combinations of the eight most abundant elements of the earth's crust: oxygen, silicon, aluminum, iron, calcium, sodium, potassium, and magnesium. (Table 4–1.) A mineral whose presence is necessary to classify and name a rock is called an *essential mineral*. A mineral whose presence is not necessary for classification and naming of a rock is called an *accessory mineral*. Accessory minerals may or may not be present. When they are present, their amount is small.

Oxygen and silicon, the most abundant elements in the earth's crust, join to form a unit called a *silicate tetrahedron* (sil'i kaet · te tra hee'dron). This silicate unit combines with one or more other elements to form the minerals found in igneous rocks. All igneous rocks contain one or more of the silicate minerals.

Members of the *feldspar family* are the most plentiful or abundant of the igneous rock minerals. The feldspar family includes several members. *Orthoclase* (awr'tha klaes) is the most common feldspar. *Plagioclase* (plae'ji klaes) feldspars include a number of different minerals. However, their characteristics

Figure 5-10. Granite rock exposed to erosion in the White Mountains of New Hampshire has formed a resistant profile known as "The Old Man of the Mountains."

American Airlines

are so similar it is not important to discuss them separately. Plagioclase feldspars have fine, closely spaced parallel lines across the mineral faces. These lines reflect light in a way that makes the mineral seem to change color. The parallel lines distinguish plagioclase feldspars from orthoclase.

Silicate minerals containing iron and magnesium ions in combination with the silicate tetrahedron include the *amphibole* and *pyroxene* families, as well as *biotite* (bie'a tiet) and *olivine* (ahl'i veen). Igneous rocks commonly contain one or more minerals that contain iron and magnesium.

Quartz is a mineral that forms only when excessive amounts of silicon and oxygen are present in a magma. Quartz is not present in all igneous rocks, but it is abundant in some of them.

Micas (mie'kas) are another mineral family. *Muscovite* (mus'ka viet) is the light-colored mica and *biotite* is the dark-colored mica. These two minerals look alike except for their color. Micas do not make up a large proportion of any igneous rock, but they usually are present.

Most igneous rock minerals contain silicates (silicon and oxygen) combined with some other elements.

Quartz is formed from any excess silicon and oxygen which remains after other rock-forming minerals have solidified.

Table 5–1. *Mineral Families in Igneous Rocks*

Name	Occurrence
Feldspar	Most rocks
Orthoclase	Light-colored rocks
Plagioclase	Dark-colored rocks
Olivine	Rare
Pyroxene	Many rocks
Amphibole	Many rocks
Mica	Small amounts in most rocks
Quartz	Common

The minerals listed in Table 5–1 occur in various combinations or mixtures in igneous rocks. Sometimes differences in igneous rocks occur because the magma cools slowly. Then the first minerals to crystallize sink to the bottom. The early-forming minerals occur together to form one kind of rock. The late-forming minerals solidify at the same time and form a different kind of rock. Differences in rock composition also result during the stoping process. Stoping occurs when country rock melts within a magma and the proportion of elements is changed. (Figure 5–1.) Rocks that solidify from such a magma have more silica than rocks that solidify from a magma that comes directly from the mantle.

Minerals may crystallize from a magma at different temperatures.

Composition of a magma may be altered by the melting of country rock.

Table 5–2 shows the order in which minerals of a magma tend to crystallize. Overlapping of minerals occurs, but, in general, rocks contain minerals which are grouped according to this simplified order of crystallization. Granites may overlie diorite, gabbro, and peridotite in this order. Peridotite and gabbro may be at depths too great to be seen. Sometimes materials are added to the magma during melting of rock as the magma moves upward. Then granite might occur without the other rocks being present, even at depth.

Olivine, or olivine and pyroxene, form *peridotite*. Pyroxene and anorthite form *gabbro* (gab'roh). Amphibole and either labradorite or albite, or a combination of these two feldspars, form *diorite* (die'a riet). Orthoclase and quartz form *granite*. Small amounts of amphibole or biotite may be present in granite. Small amounts of muscovite may be present in granite and diorite. Rock names are based on kind and amount of feldspar or, if feldspar is absent, on kind of iron-magnesian mineral.

Table 5–2. *Order of Crystallization from a Magma*

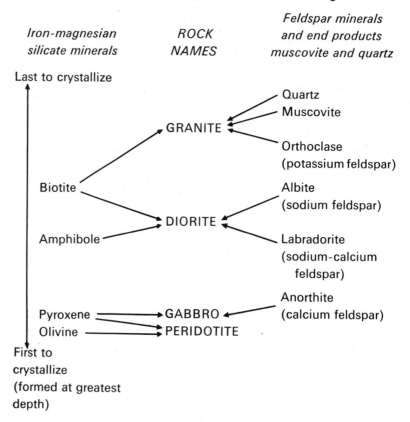

5:5 *Classification*

Classification means the grouping together of objects that are similar, and the separation of objects that are different. Igneous rocks are classified and named according to their texture and mineral content. The igneous rock chart (Table 5–3) lists the names of common mineral mixtures and textures.

Igneous rocks are classified by texture and mineral content.

Coarse-grained, or **intrusive,** rocks include peridotite, gabbro, diorite, and granite. Each of these rocks may be porphyritic; that is, they may contain large crystals in a fine-grained mass. *Peridotite* is a mixture of olivine and pyroxene. *Gabbro* contains pyroxene and small amounts of plagioclase feldspar. *Diorite* has equal amounts of amphibole and plagioclase feldspar. *Granite* is a mixture of orthoclase feldspar, quartz, and small amounts of either amphibole or biotite. Orthoclase is the most abundant mineral in granite.

Granite is the most abundant of the coarse-grained rocks. Diorite is the next most common rock among the intrusives. Batholiths, which are massive rock bodies, almost always are made up of granitic rocks.

Granite is the most abundant of the four common intrusive rocks which are granite, diorite, gabbro, and peridotite.

Fine-grained, or **extrusive,** rocks include basalt, andesite, and rhyolite. *Basalt* contains pyroxene, small amounts of plagioclase feldspar, and occasionally olivine. Basalt is similar to a gabbro in composition, but crystals cannot be seen in a basalt without magnification. *Andesite* (an'dee ziet) is fine-grained. Its composition, however, is like diorite. It contains amphibole and plagioclase feldspar in about equal amounts. *Rhyolite* (rie'a liet) is a mixture of orthoclase feldspar, quartz, and a small amount of either amphibole or biotite. Granite and rhyolite contain the same kind of minerals. But rhyolite is fine-grained and granite is coarse-grained.

Basalt is the most abundant of the extrusive rocks which are basalt, andesite, and rhyolite.

Paul W. Nesbit

Figure 5-11. A band of light igneous granitic rock intrudes into dark metamorphic rock.

Occasionally, fine-grained rocks such as basalt trap gases within the rock. When the gases escape, they leave behind a rock that is full of openings. *Scoria* (skohr'ee a) is the name given to basalts with this type of texture. The mineral composition characteristic of granite and rhyolite commonly forms glass when it is cooled rapidly on the surface. The glass is called *obsidian* (ab sid'ee an). If it contains many gas openings, it is known as *pumice* (pum'is). Pumice is so lightweight that it floats in water.

Intrusive rocks are more easily classified than extrusive rocks because the coarse grains can be identified. Minerals in many fine-grained rocks can be recognized with the aid of a microscope. But if the minerals cannot be identified, both rhyolite and andesite are called *felsites* (fel'siets). Felsites can be differentiated, or distinguished, from basalt by color and density. Felsites are lighter colored and less dense than basalts. Extrusive rocks are mostly basaltic rocks. The Hawaiian Islands and the Columbia Plateau lava flows of Oregon and Washington are examples of the immense volume of basalt that finds its way to the surface of the earth.

During cooling, fine-grained rocks may trap gas which leaves openings as it escapes. Scoria and pumice are examples of this.

Andesite and rhyolite are called felsite if their mineral grains are too small for identification. Felsites are lighter colored than basalts.

Figure 5-12.

ACTIVITY.   *Examine several specimens of igneous rock. Sort the rocks into groups labeled intrusive and extrusive. What is the basis for this grouping or classification? Examine each of the intrusive rocks and note the size of the crystals. Are all of the grains approximately the same size? If the sizes of the minerals vary noticeably, what type of rock is it?*

Indicate that the rocks are igneous by labeling them I with India ink in a small area of white paint. Write a number after the I and list the rocks in your notebook in the order in which they are numbered. Examine each rock and determine what minerals are present. Record the name, texture, and mineral content in your notebook.

Why do rocks of the same composition sometimes have different sizes of crystals? What is the difference between a basaltic rock and a gabbro? What is the difference between a gabbro and a granite? What is the difference between a granite and a pumice? What two characteristics determine the name of a rock? Color is the chief clue to differentiating between felsite and basalt. What minerals are present in the basalt that are absent in the felsite? Check Tables 4–4 and 4–5 for the composition of these minerals. What elements are responsible for the dark color of the basalt? What other rocks owe their dark color to the presence of these elements?

Table 5-3. *Igneous Rock*

Origin	Texture	Name	Dominant Minerals						
			Feldspars		Olivine	Pyroxine	Amphibole	Quartz	Mica
			Orthoclase	Plagioclase					
EXTRUSIVE	Glassy*	Obsidian	X				X	X	
		Pumice (with holes)	X				X	X	
		Scoria (with holes)		X	X	X			
	Fine-grained	Felsite Rhyolite (P)	X				X	X	X
		Andesite (P)		X			X		X
		Basalt (P)		X	X	X			X
INTRUSIVE	Coarse-grained	Granite (P)	X				X	X	X
		Diorite (P)		X		X	X		X
		Gabbro (P)		X		X			
		Peridotite			X	X			

(P) may also have a porphyritic form.

*Minerals do not form, but elements for these minerals are present.

Figure 5-13. Pumice.

University of Houston

Figure 5-14. Scoria.

University of Houston

Figure 5-15. Rhyolite.

University of Houston

Figure 5-16. Granite.

University of Houston

Figure 5-17. Diorite.

University of Houston

MAIN IDEAS

1. Igneous rock, which composes 95 percent by volume of the crust of the earth, is formed from liquid rock called magma.
2. Rock melts far below the surface when pressures are released by fracturing and the melting point is lowered or when the temperatures are raised above 1400°C.
3. Magma rises because it is under pressure or less dense than the surrounding rock. Magma may cool and solidify within the crust or on the surface.
4. Rock bodies formed beneath the surface include batholiths, laccoliths, sills, dikes, and stocks.
5. Lava is magma which reaches the surface of the earth. Lava may form volcanic peaks or volcanic plateaus.
6. Texture of igneous rocks is determined by the rate of cooling, which depends on depth and volume of the magma. Large rock bodies cooled below the surface (intrusives) tend to have large mineral crystals. Small rock bodies or rocks cooled on or near the surface (extrusives) tend to have small crystals or no crystals.
7. All igneous rock minerals contain silicon and oxygen. The silicate tetrahedron combines with other elements to form most igneous rock minerals. Quartz contains only silicon and oxygen.
8. The rock-forming minerals found in igneous rocks are: feldspars (orthoclase, plagioclase), micas (muscovite, biotite), olivine, pyroxine, amphibole, and quartz.
9. Igneous rocks are classified by texture (glassy, fine-grained, or coarse-grained) and the mineral content.
10. The most abundant intrusive igneous rock is granite. The most abundant extrusive igneous rock is basalt.

VOCABULARY

Write a sentence in which you use correctly each of the following words or terms.

accessory	intrusive	plateau
batholith	laccolith	porphyry
dike	lava	stoping
extrusive	magma	texture

STUDY QUESTIONS

A. True or False

Determine whether each of the following sentences is true or false. (Do not write in this book.)

1. Liquid rock is either lava or magma.
2. It is possible to see the crystals in pumice without aid of a microscope.
3. Pores in pumice are formed by escaping gases.
4. The crust of the earth has been built up by volcanic activity.
5. Stocks and batholiths differ only in size.
6. Rocks cooled on the surface have fine grains or none at all.
7. Porphyries are either intrusive or extrusive rocks.
8. All igneous rocks contain both silicon and oxygen.
9. Granite and basalt are both extrusive rocks.
10. Felsite is another name for basalt.

B. Multiple Choice

Choose the word or phrase which completes correctly each of the following sentences. (Do not write in this book.)

1. Igneous rocks which harden underground are called (*intrusive, extrusive, fine-grained*).
2. Pumice is a(n) (*intrusive, extrusive, coarse-grained*) igneous rock.
3. A slowly cooling magma produces a rock with (*large, small, no*) crystals.
4. Rock bodies which cut across country rock are called (*sills, dikes, laccoliths*).
5. Igneous rocks are named according to their mineral content and (*texture, color, hardness*).
6. All igneous rocks, except peridotite, contain some (*quartz, feldspar, pyroxene*).
7. All of the silicate minerals contain silicon and (*oxygen, iron, carbon*).
8. The most common of the intrusive igneous rocks is (*basalt, granite, felsite*).
9. The most common of the extrusive igneous rocks is (*basalt, granite, peridotite*).
10. Felsites include andesite and (*granite, rhyolite, obsidian*).

C. Completion

Complete each of the following sentences with a word or phrase which will make the sentence correct. (Do not write in this book.)

1. The composition of a magma may be changed during the process called ___?___.

2. Large crystals in igneous rock indicate that the rock is ___?___.

3. Molten rock which pours from a volcano is called ___?___.

4. ___?___ has many gas openings that give it a frothy appearance.

5. Magma forms during melting of the upper ___?___ or the base of the ___?___.

6. Magma may reach the surface of the earth by following great ___?___.

7. ___?___ refers to the size of the mineral grains in an igneous rock.

8. An intrusive rock body which has a convex surface is a(n) ___?___.

9. The most common mineral in igneous rocks is ___?___.

10. The rock-forming mineral which contains only silicon and oxygen is ___?___.

D. How and Why

1. Basalt, gabbro, and peridotite are among the darkest of the igneous rocks. What do these rocks have in common that might account for their color?

2. What changes in the country rock would you expect to find in the vicinity of a batholith?

3. Why are precious metals and other ores found near the top of a batholith rather than deep within it?

4. Why do the early-forming rock minerals sink to the bottom of the magma?

5. How could you distinguish between scoria and pumice without the aid of a microscope?

6. Why is it difficult to distinguish between andesite and rhyolite, even though diorite and granite may be rather easily identified?

7. Discuss reasons why rocks in a dike tend to be finer grained than rocks in a batholith.

8. Consult Table 5–2 before answering the following questions: Would olivine and quartz be present in the same rock? Would the calcium feldspar ever be present with quartz? Which iron-silicate mineral would form in association with the calcium-feldspar?

9. Man has reached depths of only 5 mi below the surface through drilling wells and mining operations. Discuss reasons why peridotite is the least common of all known rocks.

INVESTIGATIONS

1. Attach a thin slab of granite to a piece of cardboard with epoxy glue. Around the edge of the granite slab, draw and color an enlarged picture of any minerals you find in the granite. Attach a thread from the picture to the correct crystal in the slab. Make a diagram of basalt also if the basalt is porphyry or an amygdaloid (a mig'da lawid), a basalt in which the openings are filled with a different mineral. You will need a magnifying glass to see the basalt crystals. Display your investigation to the class.

2. Make a clay model of each of the various rock bodies described in this chapter. Explain the formation of each one for the class. Save the best models for a display.

3. If you have ever seen a volcano in action, describe what you saw to the class and explain the why and how of it.

INTERESTING READING

"Birth and Death of a Volcano: Myojin." *Life Magazine,* XXXIII (October 13, 1952), pp. 129–30.

Galt, T., *Volcano.* New York, Charles Scribner's Sons, 1946.

Hauser, E. O., "Will Vesuvius Blow Its Top Again?" *Saturday Evening Post*, CCXXVIII (February 11, 1956), pp. 36–37.

*Matthes, Francois E., *The Incomparable Valley: A Geologic Interpretation of the Yosemite.* Berkeley, Calif., University of California Press, 1950.

Thorarinsson, S., *Surtsey: The New Island in the North Atlantic.* New York, Viking Press, Inc., 1967.

Vaughan-Jackson, Genevieve, *Mountains of Fire.* New York, Hastings House Publishers, Inc., 1962.

---

* Well-illustrated material.

Sedimentary Rocks

Sedimentary rocks are exposed in many regions. In fact, they cover 75 percent of the surface of the earth. Although they are widespread, sedimentary rocks make up only 5 percent of the volume of the earth's crust. The sedimentary cover has an average thickness of about 2 mi. Igneous rocks have an average thickness of approximately 15 mi. You may have seen sedimentary rocks exposed along river banks or in excavations where highways are being cut through hills.

6:1 *Origin*

In the eighteenth century, James Hutton, a Scottish geologist, observed that the rocks of his native Highland area were changing constantly. He pointed out that the changes which rocks are undergoing now must be the same kind of changes that have occurred during all of geologic time. Hutton's observation led to the principle of **uniformitarianism** (eu ni fawr mi ter'ee a niz em). This principle says that *the present is the key to the past.* Geologists study the processes of the present for clues to the processes which were at work during past geologic time.

Have you ever seen a boulder with a crumbling surface, or the wind blowing dust and sand from place to place? Have you watched water flowing away after a rain and carrying mud and sand along with it? If so, you have observed some of the processes that change the surface of the earth.

Any rock that is exposed to sun, rain, air, plants, and animals undergoes change. Some changes are mechanical; some are chemical. The processes of change break down solid rock into small particles called **sediments.** Sediments then are buried and *consolidated* (kan sahl'i daet ed) or hardened into sedimentary rock.

All rocks exposed at the surface of the earth undergo either chemical or physical change.

Sedimentary rocks are formed from materials that are broken at the surface. The fragments then are carried away and deposited in a new environment. Sediments may consist of fragments of igneous, metamorphic, or older sedimentary rocks. Some sediments are sand grains or clay. Other sediments are the soluble products formed by chemical reactions at the earth's surface. Eventually, all of the products of change reach a new environment. There they may be buried under still younger sediments. During burial, the loose sediments are consolidated or hardened into solid rock.

6:2 *Weathering*

Weathering consists of two processes in which rock is broken up in place, at or near the surface of the earth. *Disintegration* (dis int e grae'shun) is a mechanical process. It breaks large masses of rock into small fragments. It does not change the mineral components of the rock. *Decomposition* (de kahm pa zish'un) is a chemical process. It changes the arrangement of atoms and forms new substances. Mechanical and chemical processes work together. In time, the two actions break down even the most resistant, or hardest, rocks.

Disintegration is weathering by mechanical means. Decomposition is weathering by chemical means.

Several factors determine the rate at which rocks weather. The *kind of rock* is an important factor. Igneous rocks that contain olivine, pyroxene, or amphibole decompose much more rapidly than others. Sedimentary rocks such as sandstones, shales, and limestones are subject to little chemical change. Metamorphic rocks, in general, decompose more rapidly than most igneous rocks.

Climate is also an important factor in the rate of weathering. Weathering is most rapid in tropical climates. There abundant moisture and high temperatures speed chemical reactions. Temperate climates also promote decomposition because water is present and temperatures are warm during the summer. Lack of moisture in deserts slows the weathering processes but does not stop it entirely. In frigid regions, however, low temperatures delay surface change even though abundant moisture is available.

Cracks in rocks hasten weathering. Such openings expose more surface area to chemical change. They also promote mechanical weathering. Water and plant roots enter the cracks and force the openings farther apart.

Figure 6-1. **What processes have caused weathering of these rocks?**

Edward J. Webster

Figure 6-2.   Water cascades over Bridal Veil Falls, cutting downward in the solid rock of Utah's fault block mountains.

Phyllis G. Lewis

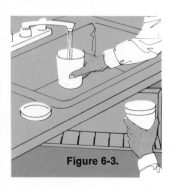

Figure 6-3.

A solution is a mixture formed by dissolving a substance (a mineral, in this case) in a solvent (water, in this case).

Soluble means that a substance can be dissolved by a solvent and carried in a solution.

6:3 Disintegration

Rocks are broken into fragments by plants, animals, water, and ice. Plants send their roots into any available opening. As the roots grow, they force the openings to widen. Burrowing animals make channels through rock, allowing water to reach greater depths. When water freezes, it expands. This ice wedging forces openings farther apart. In temperate climates, alternate freezing and thawing occur almost daily during the winter. The result is disintegration. The combination of forest fires followed by cooling rains may cause rocks to split into fragments. Disintegration changes the rocks from large solid masses into small pieces. But disintegration does not change the substances of which the rocks are made.

EXPERIMENT.   Fill a cardboard container completely with water. Cover it tightly and place it in the freezing compartment of a refrigerator. After one day, remove the container from the freezer. What is the shape of the container? What does this show about the volume of ice as compared with the volume of water? Which is more dense, ice or water? Why would a glass jar not be a suitable container in which to freeze water? Compare the results of your experiment with the effect of alternate freezing and thawing of water in the openings of a rock.

6:4 Decomposition

Rocks are subject to decomposition in the presence of water. Water is most plentiful in tropical regions. Even in arid regions, dew forms at night and chemical reactions between rocks and water are possible. Rainwater contains carbon dioxide in solution. This solution is a weak acid that reacts with rocks to form new chemical compounds. Decaying organic matter forms *humic* (heu'mik) *acid* in the soil. Humic acid also reacts with rock to form new substances. Some new compounds are carried away and only insoluble substances are left behind.

6:5 Products of Weathering

Both igneous and metamorphic rocks decompose to form clay and soluble forms of silica and carbonates. During the decomposition of rocks, iron is released from its combination with silicon and oxygen. Iron reacts with oxygen from the air to form a new mineral, limonite ($Fe_2O_3 \cdot H_2O$). Limonite is the brown substance commonly found in sediments. Clay is the most abundant substance formed during decomposition. It is formed from both the iron-magnesian minerals and the feldspars. Quartz is changed very little by weathering processes. When released from the solid rock in which it originally formed, it becomes one of the common sediments. Quartz grains in large amounts are known as sand.

Exfoliation domes are mountainous knobs of igneous rock. They can be seen in regions of little vegetation. Loose rock broken into thin plates covers the bare rock surface of the dome. (Figure 6–5.) Both mechanical and chemical processes produce exfoliation domes. Alternate wetting and drying loosen thin layers of surface material. After the overlying materials are removed and pressure lessens, similar layers are produced as the igneous rock expands.

Spheroidal boulders are formed by weathering along rock fractures. Water trickles into the cracks and hastens decomposition of the rock surface. Water also freezes in the openings and exerts pressure by expanding. Great rounded boulders are common in regions of exposed igneous rock that has been subjected to weathering. (Figure 6–4.)

Soil is the most familiar product of weathering. It covers most of the land surface. Soil forms on *mantle rock*, loose rock

Final products of decomposition are iron oxide, clay, and soluble forms of silica and carbonates.

W. T. Schaller, U.S. Geological Survey

Figure 6-4.　**Rapid weathering of exposed corners and edges of gabbro rock has formed this spheroidal boulder.**

F. C. Calkins, U.S. Geological Survey

Figure 6-5.　**Weathering of exposed mountain tops such as Half Dome in Yosemite National Park, California, causes layers of rock to split from the surface to form exfoliation domes.**

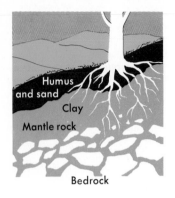

Figure 6-6. Soil, clay, and sand result from the weathering of hard rock. This type of soil profile forms in humid climates.

waste. Mantle rock which is formed by weathering is usually only a few feet thick.

Plants grow in the mantle rock as soon as it is weathered enough for roots to penetrate it. Decayed plant matter speeds the chemical change of feldspar and iron-magnesian minerals into clay and limonite. Soil is a mixture of *humus* (decayed organic matter), clay, limonite, and sand grains. Clay tends to move downward, carried by rainwater that enters the soil. The upper few inches of soil contain humus, sand grains, a little clay, and limonite. Soluble matter is carried away, except in arid regions.

Residual (ri zidj'wal) *soils* are soils that have formed in place. Such soils rest on mantle rock which grades downward into broken rock, and then into solid, unweathered rock called *bedrock*. Soil is called *transported soil* if it forms on loose rock that has been carried to the area by winds, rivers, or ice (glaciers). Transported soils and the mantle rock from which they form are not related to the solid rock beneath them. In humid regions where vegetation is abundant and slopes are gentle, the residual soils are thick. Soil is thin or absent on steep slopes because it is carried downward by rain or gravity as soon as it forms. Soil is also thin in arid regions and even in humid regions where the lands are plowed. Winds carry soil away if no vegetation is present to anchor it. During a period of drought in the early 1930's, great dust storms swept the Great Plains of the United States and carried away much of its fertile soil.

Sedimentary rocks are products of weathering that have been consolidated into hard layers. Like soils, sedimentary rocks consist of clay, sand grains, and limonite. Unlike soils, sedimentary rocks may consist of layers of substances which

Figure 6-7. Many farms have been abandoned when unprotected, dry topsoil is removed during widespread dust storms.

USDA Photo

were dissolved and have solidified due to chemical action. (Recall the experiment with salt and sugar crystals. (Section 4:1.)

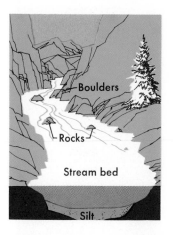

Figure 6-8. Boulders too heavy for the stream to carry are left in the stream bed. Finer materials are carried downstream.

6:6 *Clastics*

Clastics are sedimentary rocks made of pieces and grains of quartz, feldspar, shells, clay, and even pebbles and boulders. These materials are carried in suspension by rivers, winds, waves, or glaciers. With the exception of glaciers, the ability of these agents to carry materials depends on their speed or velocity. Materials are deposited as the speed of the carrying agent decreases. Usually the velocity decreases gradually and the clastics are sorted according to size and specific gravity. Large, heavy fragments are dropped first; medium sizes and weights are dropped next; and fine, lightweight sediments are deposited last. Materials transported by a glacier are not sorted because all sizes are dropped when the ice melts.

> *ACTIVITY. Stir sand, clay, and rock fragments in a glass jar of water. Allow the materials to settle. What is the appearance of the water after all of the materials have settled? What is the distribution of sediments? Compare this distribution with the layering of sediments in a quiet body of water.*

Figure 6-9.

Clastics include conglomerates, breccia, sandstone, siltstone, shale, and clay.

Clastic rocks are named according to the size and shape of the fragments they contain. They include conglomerate (kon glahm'e rit), breccia (brech'ee a), sandstone, siltstone, shale, and tillite (til'ite), a glacial deposit. (Table 6–1.) *Conglomerates* are mixtures of rounded pebbles and some clay or sand. The pebbles may be any kind of material. *Breccia* is similar to conglomerate in composition, but the shape of the fragments is angular instead of rounded. Conglomerates are more common than breccias because sharp edges tend to be worn during transportation. This results in rounded pebbles.

Sandstone consists of smaller grains than those of conglomerate. Beach sands and river sands are typical of the material in sandstone. Fragments of sand are easily seen and they feel gritty to the fingers. Sandstones usually are made of quartz, but they may contain feldspar, fragments of basalt, or even calcite. The composition depends upon the kind of rock from which they have been weathered.

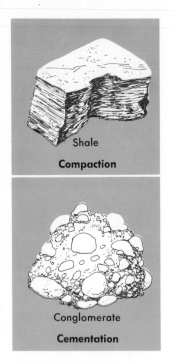

Figure 6-10. Compaction and cementation are effective lithifying processes.

Calcite and silica are the most common cementing agents. Clastics are often colored by iron stain, organic matter, or volcanic debris.

Siltstone is like sandstone except that the grains are much finer. It may be necessary to examine siltstone with a magnifying glass to see the texture. Usually the surface feels gritty. Some clay often is present.

Shale is made of thin layers consisting of clay fragments too small to be seen without magnification. Mica flakes also are common. Shale is distinguished from siltstone by its smooth, almost slippery feel.

Clastics are hardened or consolidated into rock by *compaction* (kom pak'shun) and *cementation*. Mud balls and mud pies demonstrate how easily clay is hardened simply by **compaction,** or squeezing, and drying. During burial of the original mud, water and air are squeezed out. Then tiny clay fragments become arranged in layers to form shale. Clay particles are pressed together so tightly that water does not move through shale. Siltstone, sandstone, and conglomerate undergo some compaction. But compaction alone does not produce hard rock from these materials.

Cementation, the deposition of cement between fragments, is necessary for the consolidation of siltstone, sandstone, and conglomerate. Waters that move through loose sediments carry cementing materials in solution. Chemical reactions cause these cementing substances to come out of solution. Cement is deposited around the various grains and pebbles and holds them together in a solid mass. Calcite is the most common cementing material; silica is the next most common. Clay or iron minerals hold some sediments together. Cement fills many former spaces between sediments, but sandstones and conglomerates tend to retain some openings through which water moves. Such rocks are both *porous* and *permeable* (pur'mee a bul). Porous rocks contain openings. Permeable rocks contain connected openings that allow liquids to flow or percolate through.

Figure 6-11. Oil and ground-water flow through permeable rocks such as sandstone but cannot flow through impermeable rocks such as shale.

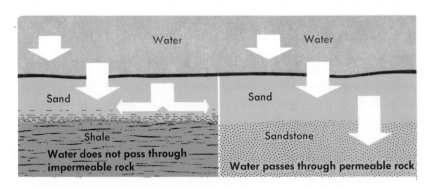

Clastics are colored red, yellow, or brown by iron stain or iron cement. They are colored black by organic matter, or green by decomposed volcanic fragments or debris. The most common colors are due to iron.

> *EXPERIMENT. Make six different mixtures of sand, gravel or pebbles, clay, patching plaster, and water. Be sure that you have one mixture of sand and water, one mixture of clay and water, one mixture of patching plaster and water. Other mixtures can be various combinations of gravel or pebbles with different amounts of clay and plaster or sand and plaster. Use just enough water to make a stiff mixture. Place each mixture in a paper cup or cut-off milk carton. Put all of the containers in an oven. If you use a gas oven, the pilot light will furnish sufficient heat. If you use an electric oven, set the temperature control at 200°F. When the oven has reached this temperature, turn off the heat. Let your mixtures stand until all of the water evaporates. Examine each mixture. Are any mixtures still loose? Are any of the mixtures cemented together? If so, what is the cementing agent? Label each of the synthetic rocks with the name of the sedimentary rock it resembles.*

Figure 6-12.

6:7   *Nonclastics*

Nonclastics are sedimentary rocks formed by chemical and organic processes. Chemical processes include both evaporation and precipitation (pri sip i tae'shun). Substances formerly carried in solution are deposited when the water in which they are dissolved evaporates. Products of evaporation are called *evaporites* (i vap'a riets). They are solid crystalline minerals of calcite, halite, and gypsum (jip'sum), or alabaster (al'a bas ter). *Precipitates* form when water moving through the ground comes in contact with certain substances that cause a chemical change in the solution. As a result of the change, solids are formed that precipitate, or separate from a solution. Much of the world's limestone is a precipitate consisting of the mineral calcite. Precipitates often include ores and minerals that are important in industry. (Section 8:2.)

Organic deposits may result from animal or plant processes. Animals form shells or bones from calcite or silica in seawater. They also build reef structures of calcite. Such materials may form hundreds or even thousands of feet of rock. Plant debris,

Nonclastics, formed by chemical or organic means, include precipitates, evaporites, and coal.

Precipitate means to separate a substance from a solution by a chemical reaction. **Precipitate** also means the substance which is separated by the chemical reaction.

Precipitates include limestones, some ore minerals, and chert.

Organic deposits include reefs, peat, lignite, and bituminous and anthracite coal.

Figure 6-13. Cochina lime-stone.

Figure 6-14. Fossiliferous limestone.

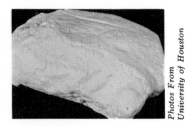

Figure 6-15. Chalk.

Photos From University of Houston

such as trees, twigs, and ferns, is buried in swamps. Vegetation partially decays beneath the swamp water, and eventually forms layers of peat, lignite, and coal.

Nonclastics are named according to their composition. They include *limestone*, composed of calcite; *flint* or *chert*, made of silica; *rock salt*, made of the mineral halite; and *alabaster*, made of either the mineral gypsum or anhydrite (an hie′driet). (Table 6–1.) Nonclastics are solid substances in which the crystals interlock during precipitation or evaporation. No open spaces are present in these nonclastics unless they form after the rock is deposited.

Coal, another nonclastic rock, is made of the remains of plants. The varieties of coal include *peat* and *lignite* (lig′niet), the lowest grades, and *bituminous* (bi too′me nes) and *anthracite* (an′thra siet), the preferred fuel types.

Nonclastic rocks may be crystalline, with the crystal form easily visible to the naked eye. Cave deposits commonly have beautiful crystals that are large and well developed. On the other hand, nonclastic rocks may be made of tiny or microscopic crystals or shells too fine to be seen without magnification. *Chalk* is a variety of limestone consisting of calcite and shells so small that they cannot be seen without the aid of a microscope. The rock has a white, powdery appearance.

ACTIVITY. Select sedimentary rocks from your own collection and unmarked rocks from the classroom collection. Group the rocks as clastic or nonclastic. Indicate that the rocks are sedimentary by labeling them S with India ink in a small area of white paint. Give each rock a number. List the rocks in your notebook (S-1, S-2, and so on). Name each rock. Check your samples for limestone and halite. Look for fossils, and note whether plants have been preserved in any of the specimens. Note any special features such as ripple marks, mud cracks, or concretions.

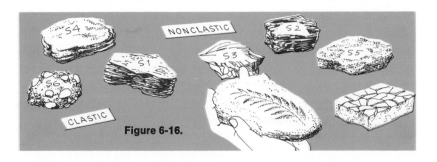

Figure 6-16.

6:8 *Features*

Sedimentary rocks are laid down in a series of distinct layers or beds similar to the layers in a cake. The individual layers, or **strata** (strae'ta), can be recognized because of differences in color, grain size, or composition. In a series of layered rock, the oldest bed lies at the bottom and the youngest bed lies at the top. Movement of the earth's crust can disturb the arrangement.

The top layer becomes covered by a new type of deposit— usually a finer-grained rock—as an area sinks beneath the sea. Some series consist of conglomerate covered by sandstone, and sandstone covered by shale. When shore zones are rising from the water instead of sinking, the series is often shale covered by sandstone, and sandstone covered by conglomerate. Conglomerates are less common than sandstone or shale, and they may be absent from the series. (Figure 6–17.)

Limestones may be present in a sedimentary sequence if the seas are warm and the water is clear with plenty of calcite in solution. If conditions are favorable for evaporation of seawater, limestone may form. Some limestone is formed from reworking a former limestone bed which has been eroded, or worn down, by waves and currents.

Fossils (fahs'ils) are important components of many sedimentary layers. A fossil is any record of past life such as a bone, shell, or some other hard part of an animal or plant. Fossils may also be prints of any of these hard parts, or of insects, leaves, or soft-bodied animals.

Fossils are most plentiful in limestone and somewhat less common in shales and sandstones. Marine shells or shell imprints are preserved more often than parts of land animals.

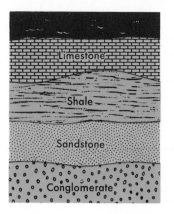

Figure 6-17. In cross section, sedimentary rocks show the layered effect resulting from changes in conditions of deposition.

Limestones are present only under certain conditions.

Figure 6-18. Fossils may be preserved in sedimentary rocks: a. fern, b. shells, predominantly *Exogyra*, c. bark of *Sigillaria*.

University of Houston

Fossils reveal many things about the past. From this information, a geologist can tell what kinds of plants and animals lived when a certain rock was being deposited. He also can learn something about the kind of environment in which deposition was made.

Other clues to the past are found in the sediments themselves. Conglomerates suggest disintegration of a rugged, mountainous land. Sandstones result from transportation by rivers, winds, or waves, and a gradual decrease in velocity along with good sorting. Shales suggest deposition in quiet bodies of water. Only the finest materials are carried into deep water. Sediments that form clays come from lands where decomposition has been almost completed.

Fossils record past life and supply clues to geologic history.

Ocean deposition is almost always covering dead sea animals with layers of sediment. Many sea animals have body parts that are readily preserved.

Figure 6-19.   The Turkey River in Iowa has deposited this 5 in. deep silt layer on its bottom lands.

USDA Photo

Figure 6-20.   Sand blown about by the wind forms asymmetrical ripple patterns.

Meston's Travels

Ripple marks and mud cracks form today as they have in the past. Ripple marks form in shallow water along shore zones and on the surface of sand dunes. Mud cracks form along shores where mud deposits are thoroughly dried out from time to time. Sand, blown or washed into the cracks, preserves them even when they are covered by water.

Concretions (kan kree′shuns) are sedimentary features found in the upper surface of a rock layer. They are formed from cementing materials precipitated layer upon layer around a central core. Concretions may be less than an inch or many feet in diameter. *Geodes* (jee′ohds) are hollow spherical bodies found commonly in limestone. The outer rim of the geode is hardened silica called *chalcedony* (kal sed′en ee). Clear quartz crystals grow inward from this outer rind. (Figure 6–21.)

Ward's Natural Science Establishment, Inc.

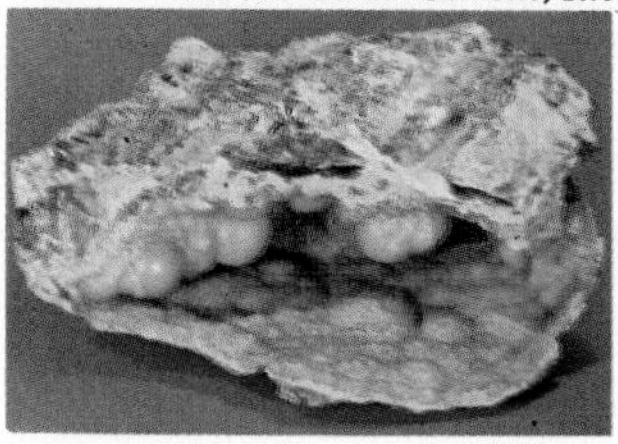

Figure 6-21. Quartz chalcedony mammillary geode.

EXPERIMENT. Put small fragments of limestone, granite, basalt, and quartz in a jar. Fill the jar with water and let it stand overnight. Next day, separate the various materials, putting the pieces of limestone in one jar, granite in a second jar, basalt in a third jar, and quartz in a fourth jar. Add enough 15 percent hydrochloric acid (HCl) to each jar to just cover the pieces, and let them stand overnight.

On the following day, examine the jars and record what has happened to the rocks in each jar. Compare your results with your experiment with clear water. From your experiment, describe the rocks that would be most likely to have caves formed by solution of the rock materials. Review the origin of acids in surface waters in Section 6:4. Would waters in the soil be most likely to be acid in tropical, in temperate, or in arid regions?

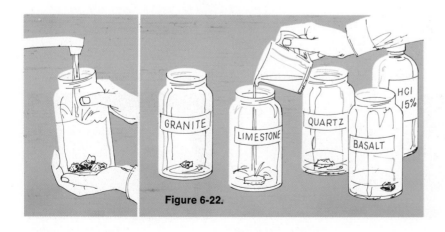

Figure 6-22.

Table 6-1. *Sedimentary Rock*

	Name	Texture	Composition	Comments
CLASTICS	Conglomerate	Round pebbles	Any kind of rock or minerals	Pebbles held together with sand, clay, and cement
	Breccia	Angular pebbles	Any kind of rock or minerals	
	Sandstone	Sand-size grains	Quartz (most common) or feldspar and quartz	Grains may be calcite
	Siltstone	Very fine grains	Mostly quartz, some clay	Gritty feel
	Shale	Microscopic grains and flakes	Mostly clay, some mica	Occurs in layers, no gritty feel
NONCLASTICS	Limestone	Coarse to microscopic crystals	Calcite or microscopic shells	Chalk—microscopic texture, a precipitate or evaporite
	Chert (flint)	Microscopic crystals	Chalcedony	Common as cement in rocks, or as masses, a precipitate
	Alabaster	Microscopic to coarse crystals	Gypsum or anhydrite	Evaporite
	Rock salt	Cubic crystals	Halite	Evaporite
	Peat, lignite, or coal	Coarse to microscopic plant fragments	Products of plant decay in absence of oxygen	Fragments of plants to fine-grained carbon compounds

Figure 6-23.　Conglomerate.

University of Houston

Figure 6-24.　Breccia.　　　**Figure 6-25.　Sandstone (red).**　　　**Figure 6-26.　Sandstone (banded).**

University of Houston　　　*University of Houston*　　　*University of Houston*

Figure 6-27. Sandstone (glau-conitic)

University of Houston

Figure 6-28. Limestone (massive).

University of Houston

Figure 6-29. Limestone (crystalline).

University of Houston

Figure 6-30. Chert.

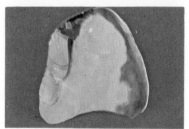

University of Houston

Figure 6-31. Coal.

National Coal Association

MAIN IDEAS

1. Rocks undergo constant change, as they have for billions of years since the earth began.

2. Breaking up of rock at or near the surface, called weathering, may be caused by mechanical or chemical means.

3. Weathering by mechanical means (disintegration) results from weather and climate conditions and the presence of plants, animals, and water.

4. Chemical weathering (decomposition) depends on the presence of water. Water aids the formation of carbonic acid and distributes humic acid from plants and animals. Both acids react with rock materials.

5. Decomposition produces insoluble iron oxide and clay, and silicas and carbonates in soluble form.

6. Weathering produces exfoliated rocks, spheroidal boulders, and both residual and transported soils.

7. Sedimentary rocks are formed when soil grains, fragments of rock, or soluble substances are hardened into solid rock.

8. A type of sedimentary rock, called clastic, is formed of fragments or grains that have been pressed together, or cemented, by silica or calcite.

9. Clastics are named according to the size and shape of the fragments of which they are composed. Clastics include conglomerate or breccia, sandstone, siltstone, shale, and tillite.

10. Nonclastics are formed by chemical and/or organic processes. They include evaporites, precipitates, and organic deposits.

11. Evaporites (calcite, halite, gypsum, and alabaster) are minerals left behind when the water which carried them evaporates. Precipitates (limestone, chert, and some ores) are formed by combinations of chemicals brought into contact by percolating water or in seawater. Organic deposits include limestone reefs and types of mineral fuels.

12. Unless crustal movements have taken place, sedimentary rocks are found in layers, progressing downward from the youngest deposit to the oldest deposit on the bottom.

13. Sedimentary rock records, such as fossils, ripple marks, mud cracks, geodes, and concretions, provide clues to the history of the earth.

VOCABULARY

Write a sentence in which you use correctly each of the following words or terms.

compaction	exfoliation	sediment
conglomerate	fossil	solution
decomposition	permeable	spheroidal
deposition	porous	strata
disintegration	precipitation	suspension
evaporation	residual	weathering

STUDY QUESTIONS

A. True or False

Determine whether each of the following statements is true or false. (Do not write in this book.)

1. Ice wedging is not an important weathering agent in Florida or Texas.

2. The effect of disintegration is more easily seen in arid climates than in humid climates.

3. Rainwater contains a weak acid.

4. Quartz does not break down into clay.

5. Chalk is a form of limestone.

6. The mantle rock and the inner mantle of the earth are about the same thickness.

7. Soil is a product of well developed weathering of the mantle rock.

8. Granite areas grade downward from residual soil, through mantle rock, to bedrock.

9. The formation of both evaporites and precipitates depends on the presence of water.

10. It is possible for the clastics breccia and conglomerate to have similar compositions.

B. Multiple Choice

Choose the word or phrase which completes correctly each of the following statements. (Do not write in this book.)

1. Spheroidal boulders are formed by (*precipitation of cementing material around a nucleus, weathering along joints, consolidation of conglomerates*).
2. Chemical weathering is most important in (*polar, desert, tropical*) areas.
3. Clay and mud are formed from decomposed (*igneous, limestone, sandstone*) rocks.
4. Decomposition is weathering by (*mechanical, chemical, physical*) means.
5. Rocks that contain (*pyroxene, quartz, feldspar*) decompose more slowly than other rocks.
6. The most common rock formed by precipitation is (*alabaster, rock salt, limestone*).
7. The sedimentary rock formed from decay of buried trees and plants is (*coal, chert, limestone*).
8. Hollow spherical bodies found in limestone are called (*exfoliation domes, geodes, spheroidal boulders*).
9. Deposits formed from plants are called (*precipitates, organic, evaporites*).
10. The composition of grains in sandstone is mainly (*quartz, mica, halite*).

C. Completion

Complete each of the following sentences with a word or phrase which will make the sentence correct. (Do not write in this book.)

1. ___?___ is the breaking up of rock in place, at or near the surface of the earth.
2. Disintegration means that rock is broken down by ___?___ means.
3. Plants and animals contribute ___?___ acid to the process of decomposition.
4. Thawing and freezing result in weathering called ___?___.
5. Sedimentary rocks formed by evaporation or precipitation are called ___?___.

6. Air and water are necessary for the weathering called ___?___.

7. Soil which is closely related to the bedrock below it is ___?___ soil.

8. Clastics are hardened into rock by ___?___ and ___?___.

9. Sedimentary layers may contain records of past life called ___?___.

10. Sandstones, shales, conglomerates, and limestones are ideally found in a sinking or subsiding basin in the following descending order: ___?___, ___?___, ___?___, and ___?___.

D. How and Why

1. What does James Hutton's term uniformitarianism mean? How does this term apply to sedimentary rocks and to extrusive igneous rocks? Does this term have any meaning in connection with intrusive igneous rocks or with metamorphic rocks?

2. Sedimentary rocks form a thin veneer or cover on the surface of the earth. How does their distribution compare with the distribution of igneous rocks? How does their volume compare with the volume of igneous rocks? Explain why sedimentary rocks are so widespread.

3. Why should ice wedging be more effective in Illinois than in Alaska?

4. How might forest fires contribute to weathering processes?

5. Why is the cover of sediments much thicker in the Mississippi Valley than on the Continental Divide?

6. If you wanted to drill a well to furnish water, would you try to drill to a sandstone or a shale layer? Why?

7. Under what conditions would breccia form rather than conglomerate?

8. Why do cave deposits often occur as large crystals?

9. In what kind of sedimentary rock would you be most likely to find well-preserved fossils? Why?

10. What conditions produce a series of sedimentary layers in which bottom layers are coarse conglomerates, the next layers are sandstones, and the top layer is shale?

INVESTIGATIONS

1. Collect pictures which illustrate types of weathering and prepare a bulletin board display. Include pictures of caves, trees growing out of rocks, cracks in pavement, and so on. Write a short explanation of each example and place it with the illustration. Indicate whether the weathering is disintegration or decomposition.

2. Draw a diagram of the ideal layering of sedimentary rock which has not been disturbed. Indicate in which layer you would expect to find the following: kaolinite, coal, coral, peat, gypsum, mica, breccia, and quartz.

INTERESTING READING

Evans, E. K., *Rock and Rock Collecting*. New York, Golden Press, 1970.

Fenton, Carroll L. and Mildred A., *The Rock Book*. New York, Doubleday & Company, Inc., 1940.

Herbert, D., and Bardossi, F., *Kilauea: Case History of a Volcano*. New York, Harper & Row Publishers, Inc., 1968.

Hood, Peter, *How the Earth Is Made*. Fair Lawn, N.J., Oxford University Press, Inc., 1954.

MacFall, R. P., *Gem Hunter's Guide*, 4th ed. New York, Thomas Y. Crowell Co., 1969.

Reed, William M., *The Earth for Sam*, rev. ed. New York, Harcourt Brace Jovanovich, Inc., 1960.

U. S. Department of Agriculture, *Soil (U.S.D.A. Yearbook, 1957)*. Washington, D. C., U. S. Government Printing Office, 1957.

White, A. T., *Rocks All Around Us*. New York, Random House, Inc., 1959.

Wyckoff, Jerome, *Geology: Our Changing Earth Through the Ages*. New York, Golden Press, 1967.

Metamorphic Rocks 7

Metamorphic rocks are the least abundant of the three rock classes. Like sedimentary rocks, the metamorphic rocks are formed by both chemical and mechanical processes. Unlike sedimentary rocks, metamorphic rocks form only at great depths or at high temperatures. Intrusive igneous rocks and metamorphic rocks form in similar environments. Both are unstable and are subject to weathering at the earth's surface.

7:1 *Origin*

Sedimentary rock and igneous rock may be changed or transformed into metamorphic rock. **Metamorphic rock** is rock that has been changed by great heat and pressure within the crust. Metamorphism occurs at temperatures ranging from 150°C (302°F) to approximately 800°C (1472°F) and at depths of from one mile to several miles. Occasionally, contact with an intruding magma may furnish enough heat for metamorphism within one mile of the surface. But, in general, metamorphism indicates deep burial.

Metamorphic rocks are derived from either sedimentary or igneous rocks.

During metamorphism, the parent rock undergoes a change in composition or in the size and arrangement of the mineral grains. Changes in both composition and texture occur while the rock remains in the solid state. If melting occurs, the rock that forms is called igneous rather than metamorphic. *Migmatites* are rocks that contain alternate layers of igneous and metamorphic rock.

Ward's Natural Science Establishment, Inc.

Figure 7-1. Migmatite.

7:2 *Metamorphic Processes*

High heat and great pressure cause metamorphism. Heat may come from the decay of radioactive elements in the mantle. Friction which occurs during mountain building may raise

Heat originates with radioactive decay of some elements in the mantle.

temperatures. Or heat may come from hot magma intruded into rock already in place. Of these three, decay of radioactive elements is believed to be the most important source of heat. During decay, radioactive elements spontaneously break down into other elements. An element changes to another element only when the nucleus of the atom changes. (Chapter 3.) Usually nuclear energy in the form of heat energy is released during the change.

Pressure results from the weight of overlying sediments or from forces associated with mountain building.

Pressure is associated with the uplift of mountains and the intrusion of large igneous masses. Pressure can crush, tear, and stretch. Such pressures may cause widespread metamorphic changes. Pressure also is exerted on deeply buried rocks by the weight of overlying material. The weight of overburden does not cause changes in composition. At depths of several miles, this overlying pressure may cause rearrangement of mineral grains.

Figure 7-2. Foliation is banding that results when unequal forces exert pressure on rocks after they have been buried and consolidated.

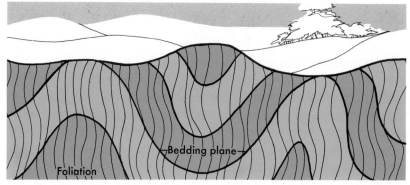

ACTIVITY. Arrange several dominoes or toy building bricks end to end. Place yardsticks or smooth flat boards on either side of the blocks to serve as guides. Hold a block of wood firmly at one end of the line of blocks. Push at the other end of the line with a second wooden block. One student should hold the yardsticks while another student pushes the line of blocks. What do the dominoes represent? Why are the yardsticks necessary? What is the source of energy in the experiment? Explain what happens to the dominoes.

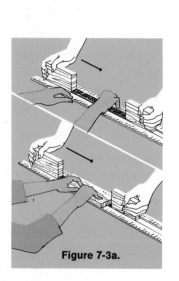

Figure 7-3a.

Realign the dominoes. Place a short flat board above the dominoes and have another student press downward on the flat board. Repeat the first part of the activity. Do the dominoes move into a vertical position? What does this indicate about the relative pressures to which rocks are subjected when they show evidence of flowage or rupture?

Try the activity again, using a slab of clay instead of the dominoes. Next, use a loaf of bread and try pushing against the bread with two wooden blocks. Two students should push against the bread, one from each end.

What observations can you make about the way similar pressures affect different materials? Which type of material would flow more readily under pressure, clay or granite? If you consider only the pressure, would you expect metamorphic changes in clay to occur at a lesser or greater depth than in granite?

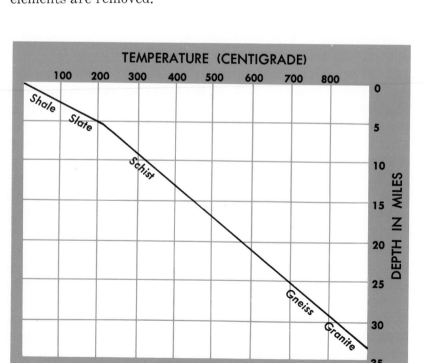

Figure 7-3b.

Thermal (thur'mal) *metamorphism* includes changes due to heat. In thermal metamorphism, heat rather than pressure determines the kind of metamorphic changes that occur. High temperatures cause a baking effect on the rock, creating a high gloss similar to the glaze on fine china. Enlargement of minerals, or *recrystallization*, is also typical of thermal metamorphism. Crystals of fine-grained rocks are enlarged by movements of certain ions from positions of greatest pressure to positions of least pressure. Original mineral crystals are made larger. No new elements, however, are added to the rock and no elements are removed.

Metamorphic processes include thermal, dynamic, and metasomatic changes.

Recrystallization is the enlargement of original mineral crystals and the formation of new mineral crystals during thermal metamorphism.

TEMPERATURE (CENTIGRADE)

100   200   300   400   500   600   700   800

Shale

Slate

Schist

Gneiss

Granite

DEPTH IN MILES

0

5

10

15

20

25

30

35

Figure 7-4.   As temperature rises with depth, rocks may change from sedimentary to metamorphic and eventually to igneous.

ACTIVITY. Caution: Perform this *activity* only under adult supervision. *Determine the effect of heat on minerals under pressure. Put 1 cup of water in a pressure cooker. Place the cooker over heat, and when some steam has escaped, put the pressure gauge on the cooker. Watch the pressure gauge pointer rise to the point marked HIGH. Turn off the heat. What happens to the gauge when the heat is turned off? Explain what occurs within the cooker to make the gauge rise and then fall.*

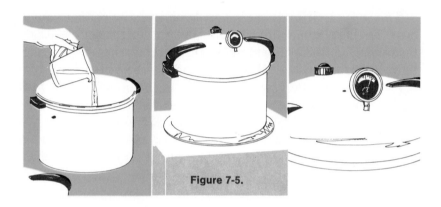

Figure 7-5.

Metasomatism is the growth of new minerals due to an exchange of ions between the original rock and high temperature fluids moving through the rock.

When fluids at high temperatures move through a rock, some ions may be removed from the parent rock. Other ions may be left behind. Many new minerals are formed in metamorphic rocks during this exchange, which is known as *metasomatism* (met e soh′ma tiz um). Some of the new minerals occur only in metamorphic rocks. Some of the new minerals are rare gems, such as rubies and sapphires. Garnets are among the rare minerals typical of metamorphic rocks.

Dynamic (die nam′ik) *metamorphism* includes changes caused primarily by pressure. Both temperature and pressure increase with depth. However, pressure is the main influence except near the core of mountain chains and next to igneous intrusions. Pressure may assist in recrystallization and influence the arrangement of mineral grains. Rocks appear to be hard and unyielding at the surface. But under high temperatures and great pressure they become pliable like modeling clay. Atoms slide into new positions, and minerals are redistributed to occupy the least possible space. All minerals having one axis longer than the other are realigned like toothpicks in a box. Such changes in mineral arrangement are called *foliation* (foh lee ae′shun).

7:3　Texture

Texture in metamorphic rock refers to the size, shape, and arrangement of grains. Rocks may be foliated, or recrystallized, or have a combination of the two textures. *Foliated textures* are bands or layers. The bands may be as close together as the pages of a book, or they may be several feet apart. Banding often results from the presence of dark-colored mica and light-colored mica. Micas occur in flakes that tend to line up in nearly parallel layers. Amphiboles also tend to be arranged in parallel bands. Rocks containing mica or amphibole often have dark layers alternating with lighter-colored minerals such as feldspar or quartz.

Recrystallized texture consists of large interlocking crystals. Recrystallization is most common for quartz, calcite, and feldspar. As these minerals increase in size, foliation bands appear farther apart.

Ward's Natural Science Establishment, Inc.

Figure 7-6.　Contorted gneiss.

Foliation may occur alone or it may occur in combination with recrystallization.

7:4　Composition

Minerals in metamorphic rocks include the same minerals that occur in igneous rocks. But metamorphic rocks also contain certain minerals not found in any other kind of rock.

Shale and sandstone layers contain the same elements as igneous rocks, but the elements are present in different combinations. Feldspars, amphiboles, quartz, and other minerals such as mica are formed from sedimentary rocks during metamorphism. Calcite and quartz recrystallize under pressure regardless of the temperature. Other minerals develop only during thermal metamorphism.

Metamorphic rocks contain many of the same minerals as igneous rocks.

7:5　Metamorphic Rank

Metamorphic intensity, or **rank,** differs from place to place. It is determined by the amount of pressure and the temperature. The higher the temperature and pressure, the greater the metamorphic change. Maximum metamorphism occurs close to the center of mountain building, where both temperature and pressure are greatest. The amount of metamorphism gradually decreases with distance from the center of uplift. *Regional metamorphism* is metamorphism that affects a large area. Mountain building usually is accompanied by regional metamorphism.

High rank metamorphism is associated with temperatures of 700°C to 800°C. Low rank metamorphism is associated with temperatures close to 150°C.

Regional metamorphism affects wide areas of mountain building and includes both high and low rank effects.

Figure 7-7. Abrupt contact between schist and granitic intrusion preserved in a weathered boulder.

Contact metamorphism occurs in narrow zones adjacent to igneous intrusions and includes only high rank effects.

Metasomatic changes and thermal metamorphism are at a maximum in the contact metamorphic zone.

Contact metamorphism occurs when intrusions of hot magma change the rock with which they come in contact. Metasomatic changes are characteristic. The hot magma contains liquids and gases that enter the adjacent rock and exchange ions with it. Contact metamorphism may be limited to a few inches, or it may include a zone about one mile wide. The width of the contact zone depends on the size of the igneous intrusion. The contact zone contains rocks of highest metamorphic rank; that is, rocks which represent the most extreme metamorphism. Temperatures are at a maximum (about 800°C or 1472°F) and rocks are changed both chemically and physically. Rare minerals are common in the contact zone. (Figure 7–7.)

7:6 *Classification*

Metamorphic rocks are grouped into foliated and nonfoliated rocks. **Foliated rocks** include rocks with banding. Examples of foliated rocks are slates, phyllites, schists, and gneisses.

Names are given to foliated rocks according to the width of the layers or bands. As the width between bands increases, recrystallization becomes more important.

Slates usually form from shale and have extremely fine foliation. Layering is difficult to recognize without the aid of a microscope. Occasionally, if a rock is broken across its foliation, layers can be recognized. Minerals, however, are usually too small to be seen. Slate represents the lowest rank of metamorphism, where temperatures are just high enough (150°C or 302°F) for metamorphism to occur. Slates are formed farthest from the mountain core during regional metamorphism. Or they may form from the weight and pressure of the overlying rock.

Phyllites are just one step above the slates in metamorphic rank. Layering is similar to that of slates. Mica flakes are present but are barely visible. Mica gives phyllite a shiny surface which contrasts with the dull surface of slate.

Schists are rocks in which recrystallization has occurred, but these changes were not great enough to erase foliation. Instead, layers of dark minerals, such as biotite or amphibole, are separated by lighter-colored minerals of feldspar or quartz. Layers are a fraction of an inch to as much as one inch apart. Recrystallized minerals are large enough to be identified. Schists are given a number of descriptive names, depending on the most abundant minerals. If quartz is present, the schist is a quartz schist; if one of the micas dominates, it is a mica schist. If garnets are present, the rock is a garnetiferous (gahr net if'e rus) schist.

Schists form closer to the mountain core than slates or phyllites do. They make up vast areas of regionally metamorphosed rocks. They represent intermediate temperatures of 200°C or 300°C (392°F or 572°F) up to relatively high temperatures of about 700°C (1292°F). Schists are the most common metamorphic rocks. They may come from a variety of parent materials such as shale, impure limestone, or even basalts.

Gneiss (nies) is a metamorphic rock that looks like granite. However, gneiss has rough layering of the dark constituents. Either biotite or amphibole may be present in widely separated layers which are inches or even feet apart. Gneiss represents the maximum rank of metamorphism, except for the contact zone. Gneiss occurs in association with the mountain core and may grade gradually into granite-type rocks. Gneisses commonly are confused with schists.

Nonfoliated rocks include rocks without banding. Two examples of nonfoliated rocks are marble and quartzite.

Marble is the recrystallized rock which comes from pure limestone. However, marble is harder than limestone and the crystals in marble are larger. Marble may be pure white or, when colored by impurities, it may be black, red, yellow, or green.

Quartzite is the recrystallized metamorphic rock which comes from quartz sandstone. It is a hard rock with a wide range of colors due to the various colors of iron stain or other impurities. Single-mineral rocks, such as sandstone and limestone, recrystallize without foliation because no contrasting minerals are present to form bands.

Paul W. Nesbit

Figure 7-8. Rocks from the mountain core often contain layers of schist intruded by granitic rock.

Nonfoliated rocks exhibit recrystallization without banding.

Serpentine, also called serpentine marble, is a green crystalline metamorphic rock. Serpentine forms during the alteration of a basalt. Serpentine may be associated with marble. If cut into slabs and polished, it is used as a decorative rock called green marble.

ACTIVITY. Examine several specimens of metamorphic rock. Use your collection of metamorphic rocks and some from the room collection. Classify the rocks into foliated and nonfoliated groups. Assign them names according to the metamorphic rock chart. (Table 7–1.)

Indicate that the rocks are metamorphic by labeling them M with India ink in a small area of white paint. Place a number after the M and write both the number and the name in your notebook. Indicate the possible source rock for each of the specimens. What are the characteristics by which you recognize each rock?

Put a drop of 15 percent hydrochloric acid (HCl) on each rock, wait for a reaction, and then quickly wipe it off. Record which of the rocks starts bubbling when HCl is dropped on it. Test each rock for hardness. (Table 4–3.) Which rocks cannot be scratched with a knife? Examine the fine-grained rocks with a magnifying glass to see whether you can identify the minerals. What mineral is present in the dark layer of the schist?

Write a paragraph in your notebook telling what similarities and differences you observe between metamorphic rock and igneous rock. Are any of the metamorphic rocks similar to sedimentary rocks?

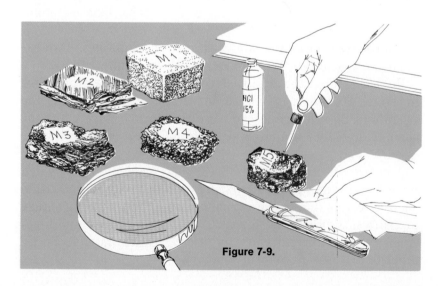

Figure 7-9.

Figure 7-10.

ACTIVITY. Use a set of identified and labeled rocks. The rocks should include chert, chalcedony, obsidian, granite, conglomerate, chalk, pumice, coal, basalt, slate, limestone, sandstone, gneiss, marble, and shale. Carefully break off a piece of each of the rocks to expose a fresh, unweathered surface. Test the surface with a steel knife for hardness. Put a drop of 15 percent hydrochloric acid on each sample. Examine the rock surface with a magnifying glass. Record your answers to the following questions about the rock samples:

1. Which rocks give off bubbles when tested with hydrochloric acid?
2. Which rocks have crystals?
3. Which rocks feel gritty to the fingers?
4. Which rocks have many openings?
5. Which rocks have layers?
6. Which rocks have a distinct odor?
7. Which rocks look like glass?
8. Which rocks are made of pebbles?
9. Which rocks make a mark on your hand or paper?
10. Which rocks may be used in arrowheads?
11. Which rocks can you use for writing?

Classify the rocks into igneous, metamorphic, and sedimentary groups. List each group and its members in your notebook. Compare your unmarked samples with the set of identified and labeled rocks. Examine your unmarked rocks and classify them into the three types. Put a small square of white, waterproof paint on your samples. Use India ink to number each rock to correspond with the number on the known sample. In your notebook, list the number and the name of each rock sample.

Table 7-1.   *Metamorphic Rock*

Texture		Name	Rank	Origin
Arrangement of Grains	Size of Grains			
FOLIATED Layers almost invisible	Microscopic	Slate	Lowest	Shale and siltstone
	Microscopic (except for mica flakes)	Phyllite	Low	Shale and siltstone
Layers visible to ½ in. apart	Recognizable	Schists	Intermediate to high	Extrusive igneous rock; shale, siltstone, impure sandstone, impure limestone
Layers ½ in. to several feet apart	Easily recognizable	Gneiss	Highest	Shale, siltstone, sandstone(impure), conglomerate, intrusive igneous rock
NONFOLIATED No layers	Calcite minerals easily recognizable	Marble	All ranks	Pure limestone
	Quartz minerals easily recognizable	Quartzite	All ranks	Pure sandstone
	Serpentine minerals easily recognizable; occasionally calcite is present	Serpentine	All ranks	Basalt, peridotite

Figure 7-11.   **Slate.**

University of Houston

Figure 7-12.   **Schist.**

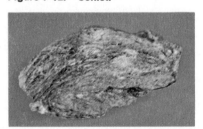

University of Houston

Figure 7-13.   **Gneiss.**

University of Houston

Figure 7-14.   **Marble (spinel-chrondrodite).**

Ward's Natural Science Establishment, Inc.

MAIN IDEAS

1. Metamorphic rocks are less abundant than either igneous or sedimentary rocks. They are formed at temperatures as high as 800°C and under great pressure while the rocks remain in a solid state.

2. The heat which causes metamorphism is produced by radioactive decay, friction during mountain building, pressure, or intrusions of magma.

3. Pressure is caused by a heavy burden of overlying rocks, crustal movement or uplift, or intruding magma.

4. Thermal metamorphism (metamorphism by heat) may cause rocks to recrystallize or to form new minerals by rearrangement of ions.

5. Igneous intrusions of liquid rock may cause the exchange of ions along points of contact with other rocks (metasomatism).

6. Dynamic metamorphism (metamorphism by pressure) plus heat causes foliation or rearrangement of minerals in layers.

7. Regional metamorphism, which may cover large areas, occurs where mountain building or crustal activity is taking place.

8. Contact metamorphism, the result of igneous intrusions, is of the highest rank.

9. The minerals in metamorphic rocks are the same ones found in igneous rocks with a few rare additions.

10. Metamorphic rocks showing various degrees of metamorphism and foliation are: *slates*, lowest degree of metamorphism and fine foliation; *phyllites*, much like slates only with visible mica flakes; *schists*, with both foliation and recrystallization, moderate metamorphism, often confused with gneisses; *gneiss*, some foliation, and complete recrystallization, high rank metamorphism.

11. Metamorphic rocks which do not show foliation are classified as recrystallized. Nonfoliated rocks include: marble, from limestone; quartzite, from sandstone; serpentine, possibly from basalt.

VOCABULARY

Write a sentence in which you use correctly each of the following words or terms.

contact metamorphism   radioactive elements

dynamic metamorphism   rank

foliation   recrystallization

gneiss   regional metamorphism

metasomatism   schists

migmatites   serpentine

phyllites   slates

quartzite   thermal metamorphism

STUDY QUESTIONS

A. True or False

Determine whether each of the following sentences is true or false. (Do not write in this book.)

1. The banding of metamorphic rocks is called foliation.

2. The hardest rocks may become pliable under pressure and high temperatures.

3. Metamorphic rocks closest to a mountain core are slate.

4. Slates are foliated metamorphic rocks.

5. During recrystallization, combinations of atoms adopt new geometric shapes that require less space than the former shape.

6. Gems, such as rubies, are produced during metasomatism.

7. Metamorphic changes are common at the surface of the earth.

8. Low rank metamorphism occurs at temperatures of approximately 800°C.

9. High rank metamorphism is due to pressure alone.

10. Metamorphism does not involve melting.

B. Multiple Choice

Choose the word or phrase which completes correctly each of the following sentences. (Do not write in this book.)

1. A metamorphic rock which closely resembles granite is (*slate, marble, gneiss*).

2. Metamorphism in which pressure is the dominant controlling factor is called (*dynamic, thermal, contact*) metamorphism.

3. The three most common minerals formed during recrystallization are (*mica, calcite, feldspar, amphibole, rubies, quartz, garnets*).

4. Slate is a metamorphic rock derived from (*basalt, sandstone, shale*).

5. The metamorphic rock that forms from limestone is (*gneiss, schist, marble*).

6. Metamorphic rock which contains alternating layers of metamorphic and igneous rock is called a (*geode, gneiss, migmatite*).

7. Phyllites can be differentiated from slates by the presence of (*mica flakes, quartz crystals, wide banding*).

8. Thermal metamorphism includes metamorphic changes due mainly to (*heat, pressure, ion exchange*).

9. A zone of contact metamorphism is associated with (*low rank metamorphism, dynamic metamorphism, metasomatism*).

10. The foliated rock which would be found closest to a mountain core is (*slate, gneiss, schist*).

C. Completion

Complete each of the following sentences with a word or phrase which will make the sentence correct. (Do not write in this book.)

1. The agents of metamorphism are __?__ and __?__.

2. Regional metamorphism often takes place during periods of __?__.

3. Two precious minerals associated with metamorphic rocks are __?__ and __?__.

4. Textures of metamorphic rocks are either __?__ or __?__.

5. Most minerals in metamorphic rocks are the same as the rock-forming minerals found in __?__ rocks.

6. The enlargement of old minerals and the forming of new ones during metamorphism is called __?__.

7. If new ions are added to the rock, or ions are removed from a rock during metamorphism, the process is called __?__.

8. Marble and quartzite are formed by ___?___.

9. Igneous intrusions may be associated with both pressure and high temperatures. In the vicinity of the intrusion, the effects of ___?___ are most evident.

10. The amount of metamorphism, or degree of change, is called ___?___.

D. How and Why

1. By what simple test can you distinguish between marble and quartzite? Can you use the same test to distinguish between marble and limestone?

2. Why should minerals in both metamorphic and igneous rocks be the same?

3. What is the most important source of heat for metamorphic processes? Is there any relationship between this heat source and pressure?

4. You have not yet studied mountain building, but you have been given some clues in this chapter to the relationship between mountain building and metamorphism. What information has been developed up to this point to indicate that sedimentary rocks may be buried and then uplifted?

5. Sometimes gneiss layering has several feet between bands. If you had a specimen taken from the section between bands, how would you classify the rock?

6. Schists have the greatest variety of minerals of any of the metamorphic rocks. Can you account for the variety? Contrast the origin of a schist with the origin of marble or quartzite.

INVESTIGATIONS

1. Draw a diagram illustrating the cycle of changes which rocks undergo to become sedimentary, metamorphic, and igneous rock. Remember that the cycle does not necessarily follow the same pattern every time .

2. Prepare a report on the quarrying of marble, limestone, slate, or granite.

3. Make a classification chart for metamorphic rocks on the order of those given for igneous and sedimentary rocks. Be sure to use "foliated" and "nonfoliated" as main divisions.

Indicate the parent rock for each metamorphic rock type and show what minerals are present. Use the igneous chart (Table 5–3) and the sedimentary chart (Table 6–1) to identify the minerals.

INTERESTING READING

Croneis, Carey, and Krumbein, William, *Down to Earth: An Introduction to Geology*. Chicago, University of Chicago Press, 1961.

English, George L., and Jensen, D. E., *Getting Acquainted with Minerals*, rev. ed. New York, McGraw-Hill Book Company, 1958.

Gamow, George, *A Planet Called Earth*. New York, Bantam Books, Inc., 1970.

Hyler, Nelson, *The How and Why Wonder Book of Rocks and Minerals*. Columbus, Ohio, Charles E. Merrill Publishing Co., 1960.

Parker, Bertha M., *Stories Read from the Rocks*. New York, Harper & Row, Publishers, 1958.

Pearl, Richard M., *How to Know the Minerals and Rocks*. New York, The New American Library, Inc., 1957.

8 Products of the Lithosphere

As man has learned to use minerals and rocks, civilization has become industrialized. Earth's matter is used for tools, machinery, chemicals, construction materials, and fertilizers. Some products always have been valued for their beauty alone.

During the Stone Age, weapons and tools were made of stone. Since then, innumerable tools and weapons have been designed. But, like the stone objects, all of them have come from minerals or rocks found in the earth's crust. Our world has changed greatly from the days of the Stone Age because man has learned to use a variety of ores. Chert, clay, copper, and iron are products from the earth's crust that have been used for thousands of years. Today these products are still among the most useful economic minerals. But in the thousands of years since the discovery of iron, many other minerals have become important. For example, until 1930 man used only about 17 elements from the crust. Today about 84 elements are being used. Sixteen of these elements have become important only in the last 10 years.

8:1 *Utilization*

During the Stone Age, weapons and tools were made of flint, chert, or any ordinary stone found on the earth's surface.

Early man did not attempt to classify the kind of rock he picked up. He was concerned only with its usefulness. By accident or by trial and error, man found that he could chip certain rocks. In this way he could make a sharp edge that was useful for cutting and scraping. *Chert*, also called *flint*, made the best edge. Thus, chert became the first eagerly sought industrial mineral. Many Indians traveled to Ohio or to Texas to find the right kind of chert for their arrowheads.

Later, man discovered that by rubbing flint against a fine-grained sandstone, he produced an even sharper edge. Thus, he discovered another industrial mineral, the grindstone. *Fine-grained sandstone* is still in demand as a grinding tool.

During the Stone Age, man discovered that he could store and preserve food in a container. He experimented with clay and learned to make pottery. Thus, he added *clay* to the economic products of the time.

The Bronze Age began when man discovered *copper* and *tin*. Bronze is a mixture of tin and copper which is harder than copper alone. However, in many areas that had copper, there was no tin. In these regions, copper was used alone for tools, weapons, and ornaments. Copper was hammered when cold to make it harder.

The Bronze Age began when man discovered how to make weapons and tools of copper or combinations of copper and tin.

Next, the use of iron was discovered. Probably primitive man first obtained metallic iron when he built great campfires against banks of rock containing hematite, an ore of iron. (Table 4–4.) Heat and gases from the fire could have released iron from its combination with oxygen. The carbon monoxide given off by the burning wood would unite with oxygen from the iron. This new gas would escape into the air and leave metallic iron behind in the ashes.

The Iron Age began when primitive man learned that iron could be shaped while it was white hot.

Iron is not naturally soft and malleable like copper. However, iron can be shaped if it is treated while white-hot. Repeated heating and pounding binds the particles of iron together into a hard, strong material. The Iron Age began when early man discovered the use of iron.

Modern civilization depends on a wide variety of metallic and nonmetallic minerals.

Figure 8-1. Rocks and minerals have both functional and aesthetic uses: a. carved bowls (top row, l to r) lapis, amazonite, agate (bottom row, l to r) rhodonite, malachite; b. hand ax of igneous rock.

Ward's Natural Science Establishment, Inc.

University of Houston

At first, iron was considered so precious that its use was limited to rings and ornaments. But minerals that contain iron are plentiful and widespread in occurrence. Soon many ways were found to use the new metal. For example, chariot wheels were made of iron. Iron was used in the construction of Solomon's temple. Today, steel is manufactured from iron. Steel is one of the most important materials in our industrial world. Cars, airplanes, machinery, buildings, and tools are among the many steel products.

During World War II, man first learned to use the metal uranium. Then uranium was used in bombs. Today uranium is used as a source of energy, mainly in the production of electricity. Probably the use of nuclear energy will expand rapidly to satisfy the great need for more electrical power. But important as uranium is, and although we often call the present time the Atomic Age, iron still is the major industrial and economic metal in the world.

8:2 Ores

Ores are metallic or nonmetallic minerals which can be mined at a profit.

Minerals or groups of minerals that can be mined at a profit are called **ores.** Originally the term ore was limited to minerals containing metals. Today, the term includes both metallic

The Anaconda Company

Figure 8-2.   Ores that occur near the surface are mined in open pits from which the overlying soil has been removed. Great quantities of rock are carried away as the mine is deepened.

and nonmetallic minerals that have economic use. However, only those minerals that contain a sufficiently large amount of the useful product are classed as ores. In general, mining and treating of ores yields a relatively small amount of the valuable product compared to the amount of valueless rock that must be handled. For example, one ton of ore may yield only four pounds of copper. Copper ores also may contain other metals, such as gold. The Utah Copper Mine at Bingham, Utah, recovers about 35 cents worth of gold from one ton of copper ore. If the rock contains less than 35 cents worth of gold per ton, it is too low grade to be mined. Low grade deposits become ores if the price of the valuable metal increases enough. More efficient mining and treating methods also may make it profitable to work low grade deposits.

Valuable ores almost always are mixed with lower grade mineral deposits and waste rock. During mining operations, these useless minerals and rock are brought to the surface along with the ore. The waste rock, or *gangue* (gang), is removed by crushing and treating. The concentrated ore then is smelted and refined. The smelting process consists mainly of chemical treatment to remove sulfur, oxygen, and other impurities from the wanted product.

Margaret S. Bishop

Figure 8-3. Butte, Montana, the "world's greatest mining town," had its beginning in 1874. Gold, silver, and copper have been mined from this area. The head frame of an underground mine marks the entrance to the "richest hill on earth."

Gangue is the low-grade mineral and waste rock removed with an ore during mining.

8:3　*Metals*

Metals are heavy elements that are *malleable* (mal'ee a bl) ; that is, they can be shaped by pounding without a loss in strength. Metals differ from one another in many of their properties, but all metals are malleable to some degree. Metals also are *conductors of electricity*, and some metals are especially useful because of this property.

Most metallic ores are found in regions where igneous rocks are exposed. Igneous rocks outcrop most often in the mountains or in regions where mountains once existed. Favorable regions for prospecting for ores include the Rocky Mountains, the Sierra Nevadas, and the Appalachian Mountains in the United States. The Canadian Shield is another good place to search for metallic ores. It previously was mountainous but now has been eroded to a low plane.

Metallic elements often are present in the gases and liquids that rise to the top of a magma. Magma in some respects resembles a thick pudding. Steam rises and bursts the surface in big bubbles as it escapes from a pudding. Like pudding steam,

Metallic ore bodies are most common in regions of igneous intrusions.

Figure 8-4. The low density rocks that occur with gold placers may be floated away, leaving the heavier gold on the bottom of the sluice box.

Figure 8-5. Gases and liquids from the magma follow cracks in the country rock where they are consolidated to form veins. Veins often are ore-bearing.

fluids from the magma rise to the top. These high temperature fluids then escape into surrounding rock openings. As the escaped fluids cool, minerals form and are deposited in rock openings next to the magma. *Veins* are filled former openings with minerals crystallized from the high temperature fluids. In contrast, dikes are cracks in which the magma itself hardens. Sometimes veins are so numerous and branching that they resemble blood veins of the human body. (Figure 8–5.) However, some ore veins are too narrow or too short to be worked at a profit. In some veins, metals occur in combination with other elements that cannot be removed profitably. All veins contain gangue. The most common gangue minerals are quartz and calcite.

Some metallic deposits remain unchanged after they are deposited. Other deposits are near enough to the surface to be affected by weathering. Copper ores often are concentrated by percolating waters. Copper sulfides are insoluble. However, they may be changed to copper sulfates in the zone of weathering. The copper sulfates are soluble and are carried downward in solution. At some depth they undergo other chemical reactions which change them into copper sulfides once more. The sulfides then precipitate from solution and are added to any copper sulfides which have not undergone weathering. In this way, the amount of copper in a vein is increased, and the deposit becomes more concentrated.

Like copper ores, the great iron deposits of North America have been concentrated by weathering. But unlike copper deposits, the unwanted substances were removed in solution. Iron was left behind. Iron ores were exposed at the surface of the earth for millions of years. Rocks containing the iron ores were weathered and clay and silica were carried away. The percentage of iron increased as the other material was removed.

Gold is another metal which is concentrated into profitable deposits by weathering and erosion. In 1848, sedimentary gold deposits, called *placers* (plas'erz), were discovered in California.

Placer deposits are found along stream beds where minerals of high density have been deposited with sand and gravel as the stream's velocity decreases.

The great western migration in the United States followed in 1849. Originally, gold occurred in veins high in the California mountains. Weathering caused the exposed rocks containing the gold veins to crumble. Streams flowing down the mountainsides carried gold grains and nuggets, along with rock fragments, to the foot of the mountains. When the streams reached the foot of the mountains, their velocity decreased. Gold was deposited along with sand and gravel in the stream beds. Miners came and panned the gravels to separate them from the gold. Many prospectors followed streams up to the mountaintops. Occasionally they found the original veins from which the gold had been weathered. The great Mother Lode vein in California was discovered in this way. Many veins, however, had been completely eroded away, and the gold had been carried down to the foot of the mountains.

Ward's Natural Science Establishment, Inc.

Figure 8-6. **Large gold nugget 1½ inches long.**

Tin, iron, platinum, and even diamonds have been found in riverbeds and along shores. But only metals that are heavy tend to be deposited as placers. The finer, less dense sediments are carried away by waves and currents or by rivers.

Lead, zinc, copper, and many other metallic ores do not occur as placer deposits because they decompose. These ores occur in veins, however, or as masses within country rock. They must be mined by means of shafts driven into the rock or from great open pits.

8:4 *Nonmetals*

Nonmetals are products of the lithosphere that do not contain metal. They include many products that have no common characteristics. Nonmetals, or industrial minerals, include a

Nonmetals are products of the lithosphere that do not contain metal. They include many products that have no common characteristics.

Figure 8-7.   Blasting in an Ohio limestone quarry.

Sulfur is a source for many products and an index to the industrial activity of a nation.

wide variety of products from the lithosphere. They include building stones, clay, limestone, fertilizers, and the source rock for many chemical products. Many industrial minerals are widely distributed and relatively abundant. Because so many of the nonmetals are used every day, they seldom are recognized as valuable economic products. They are very important, however, because they are used in such large quantities.

Sand is used in making glass and cement. Lime is used in cement, as fertilizer, and in hundreds of other common products. Gravel is used for roads. Sandstone, limestone, granite, marble, and serpentine are all useful as building materials. Table salt comes from halite. Graphite is a component of pencil lead. Potash, nitrates, and phosphates are used in commercial fertilizers. Sulfur is used to manufacture sulfuric acid. Fluorite yields fluorine. Sodium compounds play a part in the preparing, processing, or manufacturing of many of the things you eat, drink, or touch. The list of industrial products from the crust of the earth is almost endless.

Sulfur alone has thousands of uses, and the number constantly increases. Sulfur is used in dyes, fertilizers, pharmaceuticals, rubber, and in iron and steel. The amount of sulfur

Figure 8-8.   Salt is an industrial mineral which may be mined or dissolved and brought to the surface as a brine from which salt is then precipitated.

Caterpillar Tractor Co.

Figure 8-9. **Evenly bedded sandstone is an important building stone. The bedding planes make it possible to remove the stone in large blocks which are cut from the quarry face and lifted to the surface by cranes. The blocks are then shipped to the construction site.**

Figure 8-10. **Sulfur being loaded at Galveston, Texas docks.**

Figure 8-11. **Rough diamonds occur in nature in octahedral (8-sided) crystals. These diamonds are faceted and polished before being mounted in jewelry.**

used by a nation is said to indicate that nation's industrial activity. The United States leads all other nations in the consumption of sulfur.

Gems are products of the lithosphere that are used for decoration. Minerals must have beauty, durability, and rarity to be regarded as gems. Of the more than 2,000 known minerals, only about 80 have the attributes required of gems. From the beginning of recorded history, and probably even before, certain crystalline minerals have been highly prized. The most desirable gems are called *precious stones*. Gems that are less rare and less costly are called *semiprecious stones*. Only the hardest minerals and those resistant to chemical change are durable enough to be precious stones.

Precious stones in ancient Egypt, India, and China attracted trade from Europe. Probably the desire for gems, as well as spices, was responsible for the opening of early trade routes between China, India, and Europe. The Incas of the New World had stores of emeralds, diamonds, amethysts, and other precious and semiprecious stones in their temples. Gems never seem to lose their value and desirability. Men have fought and died trying to obtain them. Yet gems are valuable only because

Allan Roberts

Gems are valuable because of beauty, durability, and rarity.

of their appeal to a sense of beauty. Greatest values are attached to gems that are rare, free from defects, and perfectly cut. Diamonds, emeralds, rubies, and sapphires continue to be the most highly prized gems.

Semiprecious stones, although not as valuable as precious gems, are very popular. Many varieties of crystalline quartz— including citrine (yellow), amethyst (purple), rose quartz (pink), and colorless quartz—are cut, polished, and mounted to make jewelry. *Agate*, the banded quartz, and *chalcedony* (kal sed'en ee), the colored microcrystalline variety of quartz, are in great demand. The golden variety of *topaz*, a crystalline mineral, is highly prized. *Opals*, especially those known as fire opals, rank close to the precious gems. In the past, opals were believed to bring bad luck. This superstition has largely disappeared and opals are in great demand because of their beauty.

Figure 8-12. Cabochon of quartz with arborescent moss agate pattern.

Most gems are silicates. This group includes emerald, tourmaline, topaz, and quartz. Oxides, the next largest group of gems, include ruby and sapphire. Diamond is made of the element carbon.

Amorphous, or cryptocrystalline gem materials, are commonly cut and polished into a smooth, convex form called *cabochons* (kab'a shahns). First the gem is sawed into a small slab. Then it is ground into the desired shape, sanded, and finally polished. Gem materials of least value are often tumbled with a polishing material in a container. Irregular shapes, called *baroques* (ba rohks'), are formed by tumbling. Transparent, crystalline gems such as diamonds are usually *faceted* (fas'et ed), or cut into smooth, plane surfaces. Gems should have a hardness of 7 or above in order to be cut. Facet cutting is an art in which gems are cut into many small faces. Some gems have as many as 104 faces, cut and polished to reflect and refract light and thus give the crystal a brilliant appearance.

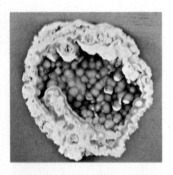

Figure 8-13.   Half of large geode of chalcedony.

8:5 *Mineral Fuels*

Metals and nonmetals may be found in any kind of rock. Mineral fuels almost always are found in sedimentary rock. They are products of organic decay in the absence of oxygen. The usual environment for the forming of fuels is quiet water, a swamp, or, a deep hole on the sea bottom, away from sunlight and scavengers. *Scavengers* (skav'in jers) are animals that live on dead matter and, thus, destroy it. Wave action also pre-

Ward's Natural Science Establishment, Inc.

Figure 8-14.   A 93 carat cut yellow sapphire gem.

vents the preservation of organic matter by breaking it up and allowing it to combine with oxygen. Organic matter contains the elements carbon, hydrogen, oxygen, and nitrogen. If decay occurs where oxygen is present, the organic matter is oxidized; that is, it combines with oxygen. If decay occurs where oxygen is absent, both nitrogen and oxygen are lost and only carbon and hydrogen remain. When used as fuel, carbon and hydrogen reunite with oxygen. During this process, called *burning*, light and heat are given off. Consequently, *hydrocarbons* (hie dra kahr′bons) are important sources of heat energy.

Examples of mineral fuels include coal, petroleum or oil, and natural gas. All these substances are hydrocarbons. *Coal* is a sedimentary rock made from the decayed remains of vegetation. Tree roots, twigs, leaves, and stems are subjected to pressure by overlying sediments when they are buried in a swamp environment. Water is squeezed out by the weight of sediments above the vegetation. *Peat* is the first form in coal formation. Twigs and leaves that can be seen in peat indicate that little change beyond compaction has occurred. *Lignite*, also called brown coal, is low grade coal which has lost most of its moisture. It is a compact mass in which only occasional pieces of vegetation can be seen. Lignite requires a longer time and deeper burial for its formation than peat. *Bituminous coal*, or soft coal, represents even longer burial and more pressure from overlying sediments. Bituminous coal has lost much of its original oxygen and nitrogen, as well as its original moisture. *Anthracite* is called hard coal. It occurs only in regions of mountain building or near igneous intrusions. Anthracite is a metamorphic rock rather than a sedimentary rock. Much greater heat and pressure are required for the transformation into anthracite than for the forming of bituminous coal.

Petroleum, or oil, is a liquid fuel. It comes from the decay of marine organisms, and perhaps from *diatoms* (die′a tahms), abundant one-celled organisms that float on the surface of the sea. Oil usually forms in muds, in parts of the sea where water circulation is limited and oxygen is absent. Oil also may form in lagoons cut off from strong wave action.

As muds are covered with younger sediments, organic matter and water are squeezed out and shales are formed. Shales are neither porous nor permeable. Their fluids are forced into adjacent beds of porous and permeable rock, such as sandstone or limestone. Oil collects between the grains of sandstone, or along the bedding planes of either sandstone or limestone.

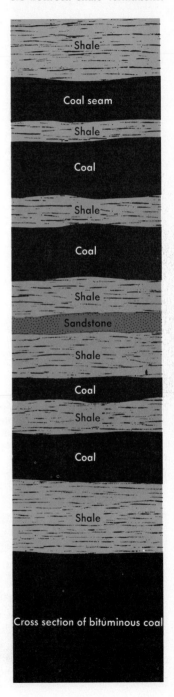

Figure 8-15. Swamp conditions alternating with marine conditions give rise to coal layers between shale formations.

Shale

Coal seam

Shale

Coal

Shale

Coal

Shale

Sandstone

Shale

Coal

Shale

Coal

Shale

Cross section of bituminous coal

Margaret S. Bishop

Figure 8-16. Modern derrick capable of drilling from 15,000 to 20,000 ft.

Oil is found in permeable rocks, usually at the highest position of such beds or where permeable rocks grade into impermeable materials.

Oil may be changed to gas by heat and pressure, or the change may occur over long periods of time.

When water moves through the rocks, it carries oil along with it. Because oil is less dense than water, it rises to the highest position in the permeable bed. Rock bodies in which oil collects are called *oil pools*. Although oil may be present in large quantities, it is distributed among the small openings between grains. Petroleum occurrence is limited because some change in rock position, or in rock permeability, is necessary for large quantities to accumulate. If the rocks are bent upward into a large arch, or *anticline*, oil tends to rise to the top of the arch and remain there. (Figure 8–17.) Where permeable rock grades into impermeable rock, the oil accumulates at the boundary between them. Oil often is trapped where sandstones grade into shales. (Figure 8–18.)

Natural gas, another form of hydrocarbon, is similar to oil. Some combinations of hydrogen and carbon tend to be gases instead of liquids. The gaseous hydrocarbons usually take longer to form than the liquid hydrocarbons. Great heat tends to turn the liquids into gases. Gas is less dense than oil. Where both oil and gas are present, the gas rises above the oil and accumulates at the top of the oil pool.

A few shales, known as *oil shales*, have retained organic matter. The organic matter can be extracted as oil, but at present the process is too expensive for general use. As oil resources diminish, oil shales may be utilized as a source of petroleum.

Figure 8-17. Gas, oil, and water are arranged in a reservoir rock according to their respective densities. In structural traps, the oil and gas occupy the highest position within the permeable rock.

Figure 8-18. In stratigraphic traps, oil and gas are held within lenses of permeable rock (thick in the middle and thin at the edges) surrounded by impermeable layers.

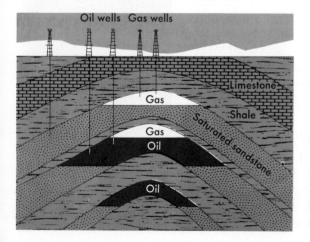

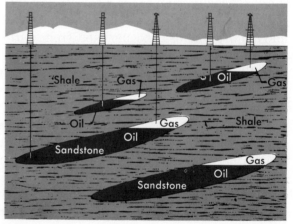

ACTIVITY. Prepare a report on material you have been collecting during the school term. The report may cover a variety of products of economic importance. You may approach the subject from the standpoint of its history, its mining and preparation for industrial use, or its geographic distribution. Samples of the products should be mounted for display. If you treat the topic from the standpoint of preparation, the sequence of mining and treatment makes an excellent display. If you treat the topic from the geographic standpoint, prepare a map of the area and its products.

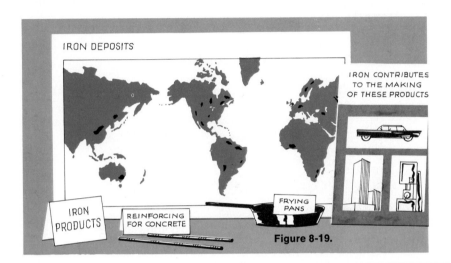

Figure 8-19.

MAIN IDEAS

1. Man's use of products of the lithosphere progressed from the Stone Age, through the Bronze Age, into the Iron Age and the present.
2. Valuable products of the lithosphere (ores) include metals and nonmetals.
3. Many metallic ores occur in veins associated with igneous intrusions.
4. Percolating water may concentrate some metallic ores in veins; streams may distribute ores in placer deposits in their beds, or expose them in place by wearing away the covering sediments.
5. Gems are the most precious of the nonmetallic ores.

6. Nonmetals include building materials, fertilizers, chemical source materials, and many other earth products.

7. Most mineral fuels are associated with sedimentary rock formations.

8. Most coal, formed of decayed plants, is found in sedimentary rock layers.

9. Anthracite coal is found where mountain building has metamorphosed the plant remains.

10. Petroleum and natural gas, formed from decayed marine animals and plants, are found in sandstone and/or limestone deposits.

VOCABULARY

Write a sentence in which you use correctly each of the following words or terms.

cabochons	nonmetals
diatoms	ores
gangue	peat
gems	petroleum
hydrocarbons	placers
industrial minerals	precious stones
lignite	scavengers
metals	semiprecious stones
native metals	veins

STUDY QUESTIONS

A. True or False

Determine whether each of the following sentences is true or false. (Do not write in this book.)

1. The Stone Age immediately preceded the Iron Age.

2. Stone Age men discovered the principle of the grindstone.

3. Bronze is a good substance for weapons because it is harder than iron.

4. Minerals containing iron are widely distributed.

5. Minerals containing metals can be mined at a profit.

6. Profitable construction materials come from sedimentary rocks.

7. Natural gas is found on top of petroleum in an oil field.

8. A large amount of ore yields a relatively small percentage of valuable metal.

9. Native metals occur as elements, not chemical compounds.

10. The most desirable gems are called semiprecious stones.

B. Multiple Choice

Choose the word or phrase which completes correctly each of the following sentences. (Do not write in this book.)

1. Stone Age weapons were made of (*calcite, chert, copper*).

2. Metals are closely associated with a(n) (*igneous, sedimentary, metamorphic*) rock origin.

3. Placer deposits may include (*gold, halite, sulfur*).

4. Nonmetallic ores that occur as evaporites include (*copper, rock salt, chert*).

5. Most of the mineral fuels are found associated with (*igneous, sedimentary, metamorphic*) rocks.

6. Precious gems are minerals which occur most often in (*sedimentary and igneous, sedimentary and metamorphic, metamorphic and igneous*) rocks.

7. Clay, chert, and fine-grained sandstones were the first industrial minerals which were discovered during the (*Bronze Age, Stone Age, Iron Age*).

8. The two most common gangue minerals are (*tin and copper, hematite and limonite, quartz and calcite*).

9. Petroleum forms during the decay of (*marine organisms, scavengers, swamp vegetation*).

10. (*Mineral fuels, Industrial minerals, Native metals*) may be classified as hydrocarbons.

C. Completion

Complete each of the following sentences with a word or phrase which will make the sentence correct. (Do not write in this book.)

1. Stone Age men used ___?___ to sharpen their tools and weapons.

2. Bronze is an alloy of ___?___ and ___?___.

3. The term ore includes both ___?___ and ___?___.

4. Waste minerals removed along with ore during mining are called __?__.

5. The nonmetallic source for bricks is __?__, for cement is __?__ and __?__, for glass is __?__, for salt is __?__, and for pencil lead is __?__.

6. Anthracite coal is a(n) __?__ rock.

7. A future source for oil may be found in __?__.

8. Metals are heavy elements that conduct electricity and are __?__.

9. Diamond is made of the element __?__.

10. The amount of __?__ used by a nation is said to indicate its industrial activity.

D. How and Why

1. Why was it natural for early men to choose flint for weapon making?

2. How do you suppose early men discovered that clay can be shaped into fairly permanent dishes and containers?

3. Why was copper in its native form a natural choice as the first metal used by primitive man?

4. Discuss the relative importance of metals and nonmetals in today's world.

5. Why are veins of copper, gold, and most other metals found near rock bodies of igneous origin?

6. How is copper concentrated by water?

7. Why is anthracite coal more valuable than lignite?

8. Why is oil shale not used extensively as fuel at present?

9. Discuss conditions under which a presently low-grade mineral deposit might become an ore.

10. Silver and gold are often recovered as by-products during the refining of lead or copper. What effect does the presence of silver and gold have on the grade of ore that can be profitably mined?

INVESTIGATIONS

1. Prepare a display of tools and weapons of the Stone Age. You might include pictures of modern weapons and some

modern tools for a distinct contrast to your Stone Age tools and weapons.

2. List at least 15 lithospheric materials which you have observed in use in your home or in a public building. Tell where you saw each material used.

3. Choose one of the following topics for an oral report. Use library references to research your topic.

   (a) Quarrying and using: marble, limestone, slate, granite, sandstone.

   (b) Source of supply, manufacturing, and using steel.

   (c) Mining or producing: iron, copper, gold, silver, diamonds, salt.

   (d) Locating and drilling oil wells.

   (e) Procuring and using commercially: flint chert, peat, coal, gypsum, anhydrite, coral, mica, kaolinite, oil shale.

   (f) Preparing and marketing any gem.

   (g) Producing, transporting (include information on modern pipe lines), marketing, and storing natural gas.

   (h) Using petroleum in manufacturing plastics or rubber.

INTERESTING READING

Ernst, W. G., *Earth Materials*. Englewood Cliffs, N. J., Prentice-Hall, Inc., 1969.

Heaps, Willard A., *Birthstones*. New York, Hawthorn Books, Inc., 1969.

*Huxley, Julian, ed., *Science Applied—Man and Science*. The Illustrated Libraries of Human Knowledge. Columbus, Ohio, Charles E. Merrill Publishing Co., 1968.

*Huxley, Julian, ed., *Technology—Creative Man*. The Illustrated Libraries of Human Knowledge. Columbus, Ohio, Charles E. Merrill Publishing Co., 1968.

Kunz, George F., *Gems & Precious Stones of North America*. New York, Dover Publications, Inc., 1968.

Shepherd, Walter, *Wealth From the Ground*. New York, John Day Co., 1962.

Skinner, Brian J., *Earth Resources*. Englewood Cliffs, N. J., Prentice-Hall, Inc., 1969.

* Well-illustrated material.

The Atmosphere
and the Hydrosphere

Seas roll to wraft me, suns to light me rise;
My footstool earth, my canopy the skies.

Alexander Pope (1688-1744)

The atmosphere and hydrosphere inspire many questions in those who study the earth. Where does the atmosphere end? What are clouds and why are there different types of clouds? How can the ocean floor be mapped? What causes tides, rain, winds, tornadoes . . . ?

Air and water are important agents in changing the appearance of the earth. Erosion reshapes the land. Air and water determine climates and weather. Planets without atmosphere are barren. Land without water is desert.

Man is probing the limits of the atmosphere and the bottoms of the oceans. He looks to the oceans for new sources of both food and minerals. He monitors the atmosphere from land, sky, and space to predict weather. Yet earnest investigation of many factors in the atmosphere and hydrosphere is just beginning.

The Atmosphere

Air is a mixture of gases. It contains oxygen which is used by plants and animals, carbon dioxide which is used by plants, and water vapor which is used by both animals and plants. Air also serves as a blanket that protects the earth from extreme heat and cold and from meteors that fall from outer space. Earth is not a barren planet because its air supports and protects life. Some elements necessary to life are supplied directly by the air. Other life-supporting elements are released during chemical reactions between air and rocks.

9:1 *Atmosphere of the Earth*

The **atmosphere** is an ocean of air surrounding the earth and extending into space for about 100,000 miles.

Earth is surrounded by a huge mass of gases called the *atmosphere* (at'mu sfir). No other planet is known to have a similar atmosphere, although many scientists believe that such planets may exist beyond our solar system. Earth's envelope of air is essential to life. Yet man is seldom aware of the importance of air until it is polluted with dust or smog.

The atmosphere extends outward for approximately 100,000 mi, and downward for hundreds of feet through rock openings that connect with the surface. Air is also dissolved in inland lakes and open oceans. Air and water cause chemical changes and physical changes in surface rocks where the lithosphere, atmosphere, and *hydrosphere* (hie'dru sfir) are in contact.

EXPERIMENT. *Fill five glasses with water. Set one glass in the sun and a second glass in the shade. Gently drop a small amount of soil into the third glass, a small piece of porous brick into the fourth glass, and a piece of granite into the fifth glass. What rises to the top of the glass when soil and brick are dropped into the water? What happens when the granite is added to the water? Explain your answer. Now look at the glass of water that was warmed by the sun. Explain what has happened. Examine the glass that was in the shade. Are any air bubbles present in that glass? Why?*

Granite

Brick

Earth

Figure 9-1.

9:2   *Air Pressure*

Earth's atmosphere consists of gases which cannot be seen. But the gases have volume and weight and, therefore, exert pressure on the lithosphere. At sea level, the weight of one cubic foot (1 ft³) of air is approximately one ounce (1 oz). At sea level, the gas molecules are packed closely together because the weight of the air above the molecules compresses the air at sea level. Air pressure decreases as altitude increases because molecules are freer to move and fewer molecules are present within a given volume of air.

Air pressure is measured by an instrument called a *barometer* (ba rahm′et er). The principle of an **aneroid** (an′e rawid) **barometer** is similar to that of a bathroom scale. When you step on a bathroom scale, your weight puts pressure on a spring. A needle attached to the spring moves across a scale of numbers and records the amount of pressure in terms of your weight. An aneroid barometer is a metal box from which air has been removed. The top of the box is a metal *diaphragm* (die′a fram), a thin metal disk. The diaphragm is supported by a spring. When air pressure increases, the diaphragm is bent inward, causing the spring to move. This movement is indicated by a needle which is attached to the spring. The needle moves across a scale which indicates the amount of pressure exerted by the air column.

Figure 9-2. This cutaway view of an aneroid barometer shows the needle that responds to compression of the diaphragm.

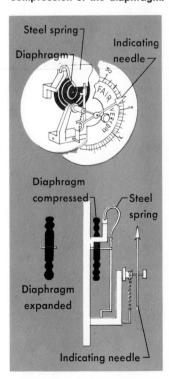

Steel spring

Diaphragm

Indicating needle

Diaphragm compressed

Steel spring

Diaphragm expanded

Indicating needle

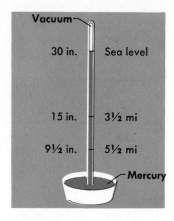

Vacuum

30 in.   Sea level

15 in.   3½ mi

9½ in.   5½ mi

Mercury

Figure 9-3. Increased air density is indicated by the increased height of the mercury column at sea level.

Units on a **mercury barometer** are based on the height in inches that a column of mercury rises in a closed tube. (Figure 9–3.) An open end of the tube is inserted in a dish of mercury. Mercury rises in the tube due to the air pressure exerted on the mercury that surrounds the tube. The space above the mercury in the tube is a vacuum. The tube is closed at the end exposed to the air. Thus, the mercury within the tube is protected from air pressure. The height of the mercury is read on a scale on the tube. This indicates the amount of pressure exerted by the column of air above the mercury in the dish. Normal readings on a mercury barometer are approximately 30 in. at sea level, 15 in. at an altitude of 3½ mi, and 9½ in. at 5½ mi (the elevation of Mt. Everest). Barometric readings vary from time to time for any given place because of temperature changes and wind movements. Pressure exerted by air at sea level is approximately 15 pounds for every square inch of surface (15 lb/in.²).

ACTIVITY. Hold an empty bottle upside down, and force its opening below the surface of water in a large pan. Try the same thing with an empty glass. Be sure to keep both the bottle and glass vertical. Does the water fill the glass or the bottle? What properties of air have you discovered in this activity?

EXPERIMENT. Attach a string to the center of a long, straight stick such as a yardstick. Be sure that the stick balances when you hold it up by the string. Inflate two balloons of the same size. Tie their openings with strings of the same length. Suspend a balloon from each end of the balanced stick. Keep the stick level and make certain that the balloons balance. Now touch a long, lighted match, preferably a fireplace match, to one balloon. What happens? Explain.

Figure 9-4.

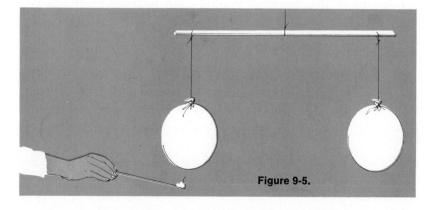

Figure 9-5.

ACTIVITY.   Place a container half full of water at a higher level than an empty container. Bend a flexible drinking straw or a small rubber tube into a U shape. Fill the tube with water from the faucet. Put a finger over each end of the tube and carefully insert one end in each of the containers. Remove your finger from the end, and let the tube hang on the side of the higher container. What happens to the water? Why? What are some practical applications of this siphoning (sief'uh ning) process?

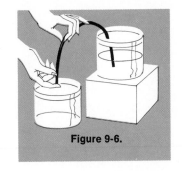

Figure 9-6.

9:3   *Composition of the Atmosphere*

USDA Photo

Air is a mixture of gases. *Nitrogen* (nie'tra jen), *oxygen, carbon dioxide,* and *argon* (ahr'gahn) are always present. Water vapor and traces of other gases are also present in small amounts. Dust particles are suspended in the spaces between molecules of gas.

Nitrogen makes up 78 percent of the atmosphere. Free nitrogen is not chemically active; that is, it seldom combines with other elements. Occasionally, lightning provides enough heat energy to cause free nitrogen of the air to unite with oxygen. But the major effect of the nitrogen in the air is to prevent the rapid uniting of oxygen with other substances in the process called burning. Nitrogen compounds enter the soil and nourish plant life. Soil algae and nitrogen-fixing bacteria live within the roots of plants called *legumes* (le'geums). These algae and bacteria produce nitrogen compounds in a form that can be used by plants. Animals eat the plants and return nitrogen compounds to the soil in their body wastes. Nitrogen compounds also are added to the soil during decay of plant and animal matter.

Figure 9-7.   The characteristic nodules on the roots of leguminous plants are caused by the nitrogen-fixing bacteria which live within them.

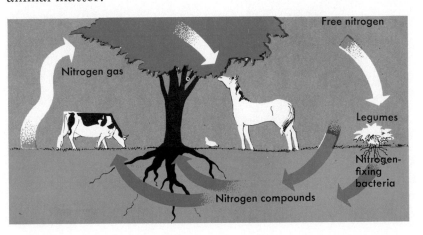

Figure 9-8.   Both plants and animals utilize the nitrogen compounds produced by the nitrogen-fixing algae and bacteria in the soil and return nitrogen to the soil or air after death.

Oxygen constitutes 21 percent of the air and is essential to various life processes. Land animals take oxygen directly from the air. Marine animals take dissolved oxygen from seawater. During burning, oxygen combines rapidly with other substances. During the decomposition of rocks, oxygen combines slowly to form new compounds. But the amount of oxygen in the air remains fairly constant because plants release oxygen during their life processes.

The small amount of argon in the air dilutes the oxygen and consequently slows decay.

Argon constitutes 0.93 percent, or almost one percent, of the air. Like nitrogen, argon is not chemically active; it does not combine readily with other substances. Argon in the atmosphere dilutes the amount of oxygen and, thereby, prevents rapid decay.

Although carbon dioxide is present in the air in small amounts, it is used by plants and insulates the earth against loss of heat.

Carbon dioxide composes 0.03 percent of the atmosphere. Plants convert carbon dioxide to organic matter and give off oxygen. Carbon dioxide helps to conserve the earth's heat. It prevents the escape of much of the heat that is radiated to earth from the sun.

Water vapor serves as insulation and furnishes needed humidity for plants and animals.

Water vapor is present in the atmosphere in small, variable amounts. About 0.04 percent of the air is water vapor. Thus, components of the air total 100 percent. Like carbon dioxide, water vapor prevents the loss of heat from the earth. Water vapor enters the air through *evaporation* from bodies of water. It also enters through *transpiration* (trans pa rae'shun), the emission of water from plant surfaces. Water returns to the surface of the earth as rain, snow, sleet, or hail, or it condenses on cool surfaces as dew or frost.

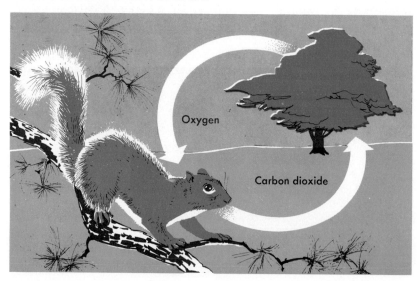

Figure 9-9. Plants and animals supply each other with substances necessary for their life processes.

Air that contains only nitrogen, oxygen, argon, carbon dioxide, and water vapor is "pure." Other gases such as carbon monoxide, sulfur dioxide, and nitrogen in various combinations with oxygen may enter the air. These gases, as well as dust and smoke, cause pollution. (Section 19:2.)

PROBLEM

1. Make a chart showing the comparative percentages of the components in the air. Does your total equal 100 percent? What components should you add to make 100 percent?

9:4 *Structure of the Atmosphere*

Five layers have been recognized in the atmosphere. Each layer has different characteristics. Closest to the earth is the *troposphere*, then the *stratosphere*, the *mesosphere*, the *ionosphere*, and finally the *exosphere*. These layers are of variable thickness and blend into one another. Much information has been gathered about the troposphere and the stratosphere because these layers have been investigated for many years. Recently, satellites and rockets have made it possible to reach the upper atmosphere and to obtain information about it. But much remains to be discovered.

The **troposphere** is the layer of air in which we live. It extends upward 7 mi above the earth and contains 75 percent of the atmospheric gases. Due to the weight of the air (Section 9:2), it is most dense at or below sea level. The troposphere contains almost all the water vapor of the atmosphere. Thus, clouds and storms are present in this zone, but not in the higher zones.

In the troposphere, air currents rise and fall because this is the zone where temperature differences are common. Warm air is less dense than cold air. Therefore, warm air rises. Then cold air moves in to take its place. (Section 10:1.) As air rises, it loses heat at about the rate of 2°C per 1000 ft. Thus, by the time air currents reach altitudes of around 35,000 ft, the temperature has dropped about 60°C or 70°C.

The boundary between the troposphere, the zone of turbulence, and the stratosphere, the zone of quiet, is called the *tropopause*. The elevation of the tropopause varies from equator to poles. In the zone of the equator, currents of air rise to about 55,000 ft. Over the poles, where air is descending, the

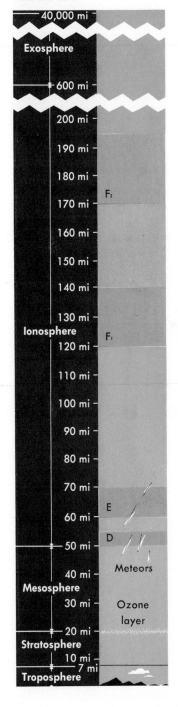

Figure 9-10. Earth's atmosphere decreases in density with distance from earth because particles are farther apart. In D, E, F₁, and F₂ Zones particles have been ionized by radiation from the sun.

tropopause is at about 20,000 ft. The average elevation of the tropopause between these two extremes is about 35,000 ft. Rising currents, together with the effect of centrifugal force, cause the higher elevation of the tropopause near the equator.

The tropopause shades into the **stratosphere** which extends from 7 mi to about 20 mi above the earth. Air in the stratosphere is dry, cold, and exceedingly thin. Temperatures are relatively constant at −54°C (−65°F). Temperatures vary so little in the stratosphere that there is almost no air movement. Because most water vapor is condensed within the troposphere, few clouds are present in the stratosphere.

The **mesosphere** extends from about 20 mi to about 50 mi above the earth. Its temperature of 77°C (170°F) makes the mesosphere a dangerous zone for spacemen. Space capsules must be protected from frictional heating by specially designed

The **mesosphere** is a 30 mile band, has extremely high temperatures, and protects the earth from ultraviolet rays and space debris called meteors.

Figure 9-11. A simulated heat shield glows in the high temperatures expected in the mesosphere.

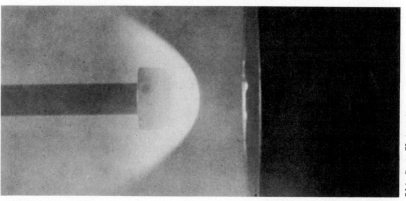

Ohio State University

heat shields for their reentry to earth's atmosphere. Several space explorers have described the fiery glow given off by the heat shield of a space capsule as it passes through the mesosphere.

In large amounts, *ultraviolet rays*, or rays of radiant energy from the sun, can cause death. However, they are beneficial in small doses. In the mesosphere, ultraviolet rays change free oxygen to *ozone* (O_3), a form of gas containing three atoms of oxygen in each molecule. Ordinary oxygen (O_2) in the troposphere contains only two atoms in each oxygen molecule. Ozone in the mesosphere absorbs ultraviolet rays and changes them so that they are harmless when they reach the earth. Thus, the mesosphere protects the earth from excessive ultraviolet radiation.

Heat in the mesosphere also protects the earth from large quantities of meteoric material. *Meteoroids* are the dust and rubble of outer space. They may be pieces of exploded stars or they may be original space matter that has never been a part of stars or planets. Most meteors are melted and burned in the layer of ozone in the mesosphere. *Shooting stars* are not stars at all but are meteors burning in the mesosphere. Occasionally, a meteor reaches the earth, but most meteors are burned up 40 mi or 50 mi above the earth. *Meteorites*, the name given to meteors that reach earth, travel with a velocity up to 40 mi/sec. Meteorites occasionally do great damage when they collide with earth. More often, they fall unnoticed because of their small size.

The **ionosphere** begins about 50 mi above the earth and extends outward for 500 mi to 600 mi. In the ionosphere, radiation from the sun changes the widely separated gas atoms into electrically charged particles called *ions*. (Section 3:3.) At this height, the air is so thin that objects passing through the ionosphere do not become heated.

Molecules in the ionosphere are too far apart to affect objects moving through the zone. But radio waves from the earth may come in contact with the rapidly moving ions. They are then bounced back to earth in much the same way that a ball is bounced back from a wall. Long radio waves have greater wavelength than short radio waves. But long waves do not travel as high in the air as short waves. Thus, short waves can reach a greater horizontal distance than long waves. (Figure 9–12.) Radio waves are reflected from the ionosphere at an angle and return to earth far from their point of origin. Radio reception

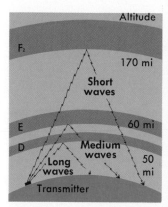

Figure 9-12.   Ionized layers of the ionosphere, known as the D, E, and F_2 zones, reflect radio waves toward the earth. Note that the long wavelengths have the least penetration of the ionosphere.

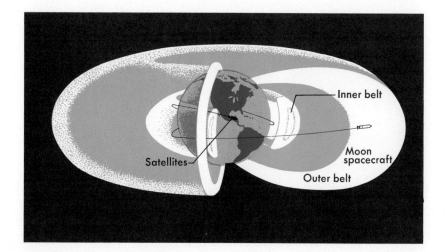

Figure 9-13.   Rockets that penetrate the exosphere and encounter bands of radioactive particles.

is disrupted temporarily from time to time as the position of the ionized layers shifts. Shifts of the ionized layers are due to changes in the sun's activity.

At the greatest distance from the earth is the layer called the **exosphere.** The exosphere begins about 500 mi to 600 mi above the earth with a band of helium gas approximately 900 mi thick. This helium-rich band is surrounded by a layer of hydrogen gas which extends outward for possibly another 40,000 mi. Little is known about the exosphere except that it contains radioactive particles which originated in the sun. In 1958, Dr. James Van Allen, an American physicist, identified bands of radiation in the exosphere. These bands now are known as the *Van Allen belts.* Radioactive particles in the exosphere would be as dangerous to life as radioactive fallout from a nuclear bomb. Manned space vehicles to the moon or planets must pass through these belts rapidly to be safe from radioactive particles. Satellites that are expected to stay up for many years are given orbits which do not pass through this zone.

Beyond the exosphere, gases may be somewhat more concentrated than they are in outer space. Scientists are studying the atmosphere above 40,000 mi, but the outer limits of the atmosphere may be as distant as 100,000 mi. Above 40,000 mi, molecules of gas are so widely separated that the exosphere often is considered the outermost layer of the atmosphere.

PROBLEMS

2. Make a scale diagram of the layers of the atmosphere surrounding the earth. If you find it impossible to represent

The **exosphere,** the most distant layer, is a band of helium 900 miles thick surrounded by hydrogen which may extend for another 40,000 miles.

Van Allen belts in the exosphere are bands of radiation which have been explored with rockets.

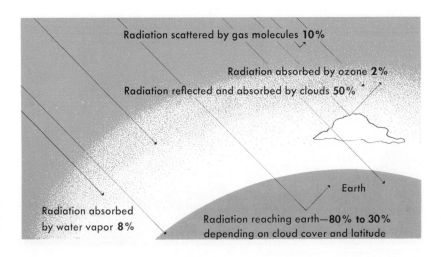

Figure 9-14. A varying percent of the sun's radiant energy reaches earth through the protective blanket of the earth's atmosphere.

the true relationship among the various zones, explain the reason for your difficulty.

3. Make a separate chart of the troposphere showing the relative densities of air at various altitudes.

9:5 *Heat*

Heat that strikes earth and atmosphere comes from the sun. It is thought that the sun emits a fairly constant amount of *radiant energy* in the form of waves. These waves may pass through the atmosphere and reach the earth in much the same way that light from a lamp travels across a room. However, the amount of radiant energy that reaches the earth is affected by several factors. Some radiant energy is reflected into space by gas molecules. Some is reflected by dust particles in the air. Some is reflected by clouds. Some is absorbed by ozone in the mesosphere. Radiant energy that is reflected into space is lost and never reaches the earth.

Radiant energy from the sun that is absorbed by the earth is transformed from light rays and infrared rays into heat.

Different areas of the earth receive different amounts of energy from the sun. Areas near the equator, where the sun's rays strike the earth at 90°, receive the most energy. Areas near the poles, where the sun's rays strike the earth at 0°, receive the least energy. Between these zones, the amount of energy received decreases as the angle of the sun's rays decreases. (Section 9:6.)

Radiant energy that reaches the earth is absorbed and changed into heat, or *infrared waves*. Different areas of the earth absorb different amounts of heat. At the poles, much of the radiant energy is reflected into the atmosphere by ice. Little of the sun's energy is changed, or converted, to heat in the polar regions. Oceans also reflect more of the sun's energy than is reflected by land. Dark areas of the earth absorb more heat energy than other areas. However, land areas tend to lose their heat to the atmosphere more readily than oceans do. Radiant energy that is absorbed by the earth and converted to heat becomes a source of heat for the atmosphere. Heat would be lost at night if it were not for the atmosphere. Like the moon, the earth would have extreme differences between day and night temperatures.

Differences in the surface of the earth cause differences in heat absorption.

Carbon dioxide and water vapor are important in keeping heat near the earth. They absorb heat and reradiate it toward the earth. Few infrared waves are reflected toward the earth if water vapor and carbon dioxide are absent from the atmosphere. Instead, heat is lost to outer space. Deserts and mountain regions, where water vapor is absent, lose more heat at night than is lost in humid regions. To some extent, gas molecules also help retain heat. On high mountains, where gas molecules are far apart, more heat is lost than in adjacent valleys.

Heat for the atmosphere comes indirectly from the sun, but directly from the earth. Processes of heating the atmosphere are similar to processes used in heating homes. Heat is transferred from one body to another by *radiation, conduction,* and *convection.*

Radiation is the process by which heat from a warm mass is transferred to a cold mass by heat waves. Heat flows in waves from the warm mass and causes the molecules of the cold mass to move more rapidly. The increased velocity of the molecules raises the temperature of the cold mass. Eventually both masses reach the same temperature. Radiation ceases when molecules of both masses are moving with the same velocity.

Fireplaces radiate heat. Although you do not touch the fire, your body is warmed on the side turned toward the fire because that side absorbs heat waves. However, this method of heating is not efficient because it does not distribute heat beyond the immediate area of the fire.

When the sun sets, a portion of the earth and its atmosphere no longer receives heat from the sun. The atmosphere begins to lose heat more rapidly than the earth. Thus, the earth remains warmer than the air. Earth then radiates heat into the atmosphere. As the earth cools, dew forms on the cold soil and plants. *Dew* is moisture from the air that condenses when it comes in contact with the colder earth. *Frost* forms if the temperature is below freezing. Frost occurs on cold, clear nights when heat is lost rapidly from the earth. If a cloud cover is present, heat radiated from the earth to the atmosphere is reradiated to the earth, and frost is less likely to form.

Figure 9-15. Waves of heat flow outward from a warm body toward a cold body.

Radiating heat waves

Heat waves

PROBLEMS

4. The *dew point* is the temperature at which dew forms on an object. What factors influence the dew point?
5. The *relative humidity* in Phoenix, Arizona, is normally 10%. Explain what this figure means.
6. The relative humidity in Houston, Texas, is often 70% to 80%. At which location, Phoenix or Houston, would a greater drop in temperature be required for dew to form?

7. Why does dew or frost form on clear, still nights rather than on windy nights, even though the temperature may be lower on windy nights?

EXPERIMENT. Fill an empty glass with ice cubes and water. Set it in a warm place and stir. Place another glass of water in the sun. What happens on the outside of each glass? From what you have observed, explain why dew forms on clear nights. Put the glass covered with moisture in front of an operating electric fan. What happens after several minutes?

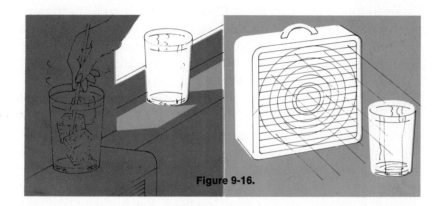

Figure 9-16.

Conduction (kan duk′shun) is the process by which heat from one mass is transferred to another mass through actual contact of molecules. Molecules of air in contact with the earth

Heat by conduction requires contact of molecules.

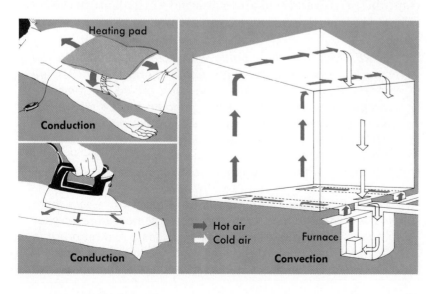

Figure 9-17. Heat may be transferred by direct contact or by circulating currents of warm air.

receive heat from the surface of the earth. Heat passes from molecule to molecule. Then molecules pass the heat to the cooler molecules above them, until all molecules reach the same temperature. Because both rocks and air are poor conductors of heat, this process is relatively unimportant in heating the atmosphere.

An example of heating by conduction is the transfer of heat to molecules of your skin when you touch a stove. Heating pads and hot water bottles warm a small area of your body by conduction, but the rest of your body is not affected.

Convection (kan vek′shun) is the transfer of heat energy by actual movement of heated matter. It is the most effective method of heating the atmosphere. Air near the surface of the earth is heated by radiation and conduction. As the air is warmed, its molecules tend to move farther and faster. Molecules are farther apart in warm air than in cold air and, therefore, warm air is less dense than cold air. Warm air rises and the heavier cold air flows in to replace it. *Convection currents* cause a constant exchange of air masses until heat is distributed equally over a wide area.

In convection heating, air is warmed, rises, is replaced by cool air, is cooled, and sinks again until heat is evenly distributed.

Most modern heating systems use the principle of convection to distribute heat. Air which has been heated by a furnace flows into a room, usually near the floor. Air in the path of the warm air is heated, and the warm air rises toward the ceiling, replacing cool air. Meanwhile, cold air moves downward toward the floor, where it too is heated. In efficient heating systems, cold air flows out of the room through cold air ducts. Warm air continues to rise and cold air to descend until all air in the room is heated to nearly the same temperature.

EXPERIMENT. *Fill a bottle with cold water. Record the temperature of the cold water with a thermometer. Set the bottle in direct sunlight. After one hour, record the temperature again. Is it the same? If not, account for the difference. Record the temperature in your notebook and indicate the method by which the water was heated.*

Heat a small pan of water over a Bunsen burner. Place a metal spoon in the pan and hold onto the handle. What happens? Why?

Place a thermometer on the floor. Allow it to remain there for a few minutes and then record the temperature in your notebook. Then take a reading at your desk, and record it in your notebook. Place the thermometer as close as possible to the ceiling. After a few minutes, read the temperature and record it. Is the temperature higher near the ceiling? Why? What is the temperature about halfway between the ceiling and the desk? Discuss the method by which the room is heated.

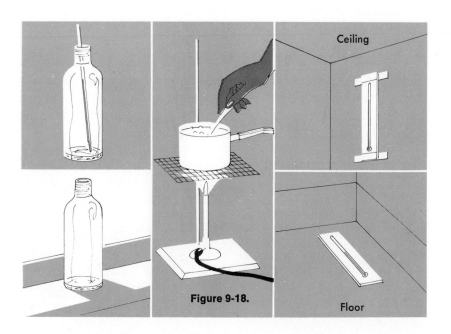

Figure 9-18.

9:6 *Seasons*

Giant convection currents in the atmosphere tend to distribute heat evenly around the earth. In spite of these convection currents, some regions of the earth are always hot, some regions are always cold, and other regions have alternate seasons of warm summers and cold winters. The amount of radiant energy given off by the sun is relatively constant. But the amount of heat received on earth varies with the length of daylight and the angle at which the sun's rays strike the earth.

Recall that the earth turns on its axis once in about 24 hours. The earth revolves around the sun once in approximately 365 days. Variations in the amount of daylight and the angle of the sun's rays are due to these motions of the earth. (Section 1:4.) There would be no seasons if it were not for the earth's motions and the tilt of the earth's axis away from a line vertical to its orbital plane.

As the earth rotates on its axis, the side facing the sun is in daylight; the side away from the sun is in darkness. If the earth's axis were vertical to its orbital plane, the number of

Heat distribution depends upon the length of time and the angle at which the sun's rays strike various areas.

Because of the tilt of the earth's axis and revolution and rotation, different areas receive varying amounts of exposure to the sun.

daylight hours always would be the same for any given latitude. Recall that the earth's axis is tilted 23½° from the vertical to its orbital plane. Thus the number of daylight hours varies throughout the year for any latitude. From March to September, the north pole is tilted toward the sun. From September to March, the south pole is tilted toward the sun. The seasons in the southern hemisphere are the opposite of those of the northern hemisphere. The northern hemisphere has summer, and the southern hemisphere has winter, when the north pole is tipped toward the sun. When the south pole is tipped toward the sun, the southern hemisphere has summer and the northern hemisphere has winter. (Figure 9–19.)

Figure 9-19. The amount of radiation received at different latitudes varies with the position of the earth in its orbit.

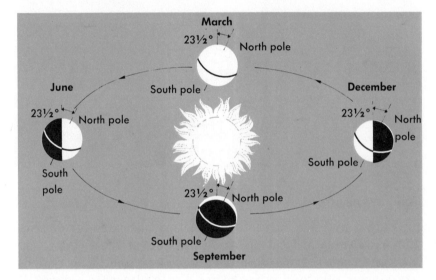

When a pole is tipped toward the sun, the polar region has 24 hours of daylight. When a pole is tipped away from the sun, the polar region has darkness for 24 hours. At the equator, day and night are always of equal length. Between the equator and the poles, the length of daylight or darkness ranges from a few seconds to 24 hours, depending on latitude and time of year.

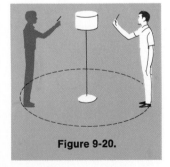

Figure 9-20.

EXPERIMENT. Hold a pencil 23½° from a vertical line to the floor. Keep the pencil at this angle and pointed toward the same place on the ceiling as you walk in a circle around a lamp. Compare the amount of light that falls on the eraser end of the pencil with the amount that falls on the pencil point. Are there any positions in which the amount of light received by both ends is approximately equal? Explain your answer.

Hours of sunshine only partly determine the amount of radiant energy received by the earth. Another important factor influences the amount of energy received by the earth. This factor is the angle at which the sun's rays strike the earth. The more atmosphere the radiant energy passes through, the more energy is lost before it reaches the earth. The more surface that a given amount of radiant energy strikes, the less heat per unit of area is transferred to the earth. Rays of the sun that strike the earth at 90° pass through the least amount of air. They bring the most radiant energy to the earth and cover the smallest surface area. Rays of the sun that strike the earth at angles of less than 90° pass through more atmosphere. They lose more energy and transfer less heat per unit area as the angles decrease.

If the earth did not tilt on its axis, the sun's rays would always strike the equator at 90°. They would strike the poles at 0°. Rays would strike other latitudes at angles ranging from 90° to 0°. Because the earth's axis is tilted from the vertical to the plane of orbit, the direct rays of the sun do not always strike the earth at the equator. As the earth moves around the sun between March and June, the direct rays shift gradually from the equator to 23½° north latitude. From June to September, the direct rays move back toward the equator. From September to December, the direct rays shift toward 23½° south latitude. From December to March, the direct rays move back toward the equator. (Figure 9–19.) Twice each year the direct rays of the sun are at the equator. At no time do the sun's rays strike the equator at less than 66½°.

EXPERIMENT. Find the center of an 8-in. square block of wood by drawing diagonals across one surface. From the center point, draw a straight line to the center of one edge of the wood block. Place the block in the sun where it will not be disturbed. Using a compass, locate north and arrange the block with the straight line pointing due north. Drive a nail into the center of the block so it casts a shadow on the block of wood. Check the time and mark the hours on the block as indicated by the shadow. Check the sundial the next day. Is it still telling the correct time? After a few weeks, does the sundial still indicate the correct time?

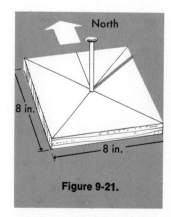

Figure 9-21.

The zone in which the sun's rays strike the earth most directly lies from 23½° south of the equator to 23½° north of the

The Tropics of Cancer and Capricorn at 23½° north and south of the equator are the boundaries of the area of the sun's direct rays.

equator. This zone is known as the *tropics*. The northern boundary of the tropics is the latitude called the Tropic of Cancer. The southern boundary is the latitude called the Tropic of Capricorn. *Temperate zones* lie between 23½° and 66½° latitude both north and south. *Frigid zones* lie from 66½° latitude to 90° at the poles. (Figure 9–22.)

Temperate zones lie between 23½° and 66½° latitude north and south. The polar zones lie north and south of the 66½° latitudes.

Polar regions have 24 hours of daylight part of the year, but they remain cold because the rays of the sun strike the region at such small angles. Furthermore, the ice cover tends to reflect much of the heat received during the summer season. Heat is lost continuously during the period of darkness.

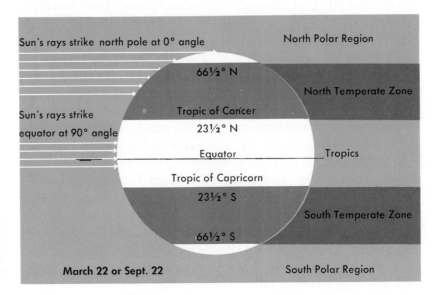

Figure 9-22. Rays from the sun are perpendicular to the equator and days and nights are of equal length throughout the earth at the spring and autumnal equinoxes.

PROBLEM

8. On a map that gives latitude and longitude, determine the zone in which you live.

9. Does any place in continental U. S. ever receive the rays of the sun at 90°? Why? What city comes closest to receiving the direct rays of the sun? What is the latitude of this city? Estimate the approximate angle at which the sun's rays strike this city on June 21.

10. What is the angle of the sun's rays that strike Rio de Janeiro, Brazil, on December 21?

Climates are classified according to presence of water vapor, temperature range, wind direction, and air pressure.

Climate is the term used to refer to weather conditions over long periods of time and in large areas. **Weather** refers to day-to-day changes in temperature, wind, and humidity. Weather is so variable and complex that it requires detailed discussion. (Chapter 10.) Weather records of ten or more years are averaged to determine the climate for a given area. Weather and climate are controlled by the amount of water vapor, range of temperature, kind and direction of wind movements, and variations in air pressure.

Climatic regions blend into one another, but geographers divide the earth into three general types, which agree with the three seasonal zones. North and south *polar climates* lie in the frigid zone. *Temperate climates* are characteristic of the temperate zone. *Tropical climates* are typical of the tropical zone. Within these three regions, local climatic conditions also occur. They include *marine climates* along shore zones, *continental climates* in the interior of the continents, and *mountain climates* and *desert climates* in limited regions of the continents. Climate for any region depends upon its location, the amount of radiant energy received from the sun, and the circulation pattern of the atmosphere.

MAIN IDEAS

1. Earth's atmosphere is a layer of air, perhaps 100,000 mi in extent, held in place by the earth's gravity.

2. The atmosphere, which is necessary to life, has weight and exerts pressure. Pressure and weight decrease as distance from the surface of the earth increases.

3. Air pressure is measured by a barometer and is 15 lb/in.^{2} at sea level.

4. Air is composed of the gases nitrogen, oxygen, carbon dioxide, argon, and water vapor plus suspended dust particles.

5. Nitrogen nourishes plants; oxygen sustains life; carbon dioxide is used by plants and conserves the heat of the earth; argon dilutes the oxygen; and water vapor insulates and provides humidity.

6. Scientists have concluded that the atmosphere is composed of five indistinctly separated layers.

7. The layer in which you live, the troposphere, extends outward for about 7 mi and contains almost three-fourths of the gases of the atmosphere.

8. The second layer, the stratosphere, extends from about 7 mi to about 20 mi above the earth. The air in this zone is quiet, cold, dry, and thin.

9. Beyond the stratosphere lies the mesosphere, a band of ozone about 30 mi thick, which protects the earth from ultraviolet rays and showers of meteoritic fragments.

10. In the ionosphere, extending from the mesosphere for about 500 mi to 600 mi, atoms are changed to ions by radiation. These electrically charged particles reflect radio waves back to earth at some distance from their point of origin.

11. Little is known about the exosphere, the most distant layer of the atmosphere, except that it contains the Van Allen belts, which consist of bands of dangerous radioactive particles.

12. The atmosphere and the earth are heated by radiant energy from the sun when infrared rays and light rays are absorbed by the earth. Absorption depends upon the water vapor and carbon dioxide present in the atmosphere and upon the surface conditions of the earth.

13. Heat is transferred to the atmosphere by radiation (waves of energy), conduction (contact of molecules), and convection (exchange of air currents).

14. Exposure to the sun's rays and the angle at which the rays strike different regions depends upon revolution and rotation of the earth and the tilt of the earth's axis.

15. Changing seasons and climatic zones are due to differences in the amount of sunshine received, and in the angle at which the sun's rays strike the earth.

VOCABULARY

Write a sentence in which you use correctly each of the following words or terms.

atmosphere	hydrosphere	stratosphere
barometer	ionosphere	temperate zones
climate	marine climate	transpiration
conduction	mesosphere	tropics
convection	nitrogen	troposphere

STUDY QUESTIONS

A. True or False

Determine whether each of the following sentences is true or false. (Do not write in this book.)

1. Air is a mixture of gases.
2. Air is dissolved in all the waters of the earth.
3. Air pressure increases with altitude.
4. The atmosphere contains several layers which are separated distinctly.
5. Radioactive particles and "shooting stars" are matter from space which could be dangerous to life on earth.
6. Carbon dioxide composes a very large and unimportant part of the atmosphere.
7. Summer in Argentina comes between December and February.
8. The equator has two periods of summer when the sun shines directly on it.
9. Temperate climates of the earth lie between $23\frac{1}{2}°$ and $66\frac{1}{2}°$ north and south latitudes.
10. Climates and weather depend upon the circulation of the atmosphere.

B. Multiple Choice

Choose the word or phrase which completes correctly each of the following sentences. (Do not write in this book.)

1. Much energy from the sun which becomes heat for the planet earth is first changed into (*ozone, ultraviolet rays, infrared rays*).
2. Plants help supply animals with (*carbon dioxide, oxygen, nitrogen*).
3. Animals add (*carbon dioxide, oxygen, nitrogen*) to the earth's atmosphere.
4. The atmosphere contains at least (*5, 7, 9*) layers.
5. The troposphere is the layer which contains ($\frac{1}{2}$, $\frac{2}{3}$, $\frac{3}{4}$) of the earth's atmosphere.
6. Molecules of oxygen in the mesosphere contain (*2, 3, 4*) atoms.

7. The most plentiful gas in the air is (*carbon dioxide, oxygen, nitrogen*).

8. The most important heating process for the atmosphere is (*radiation, conduction, convection*).

9. The axis of the earth is tilted from a perpendicular to its plane of orbit at an angle of (*23½°, 33⅓° 66⅔°*).

10. The longest period of daylight at the equator is (*8, 12, 16*) hours.

C. Completion

Complete each of the following sentences with a word or phrase which will make the sentence correct. (Do not write in this book.)

1. The pressure of the atmosphere at sea level is ___?___.

2. You live in the layer of air called the ___?___.

3. The layer of air called the ___?___ is important to radio reception.

4. The layer of air which protects you from harmful rays and fragments from outer space is the ___?___.

5. Jet planes ordinarily fly just below the ___?___.

6. The form of atmospheric gas which absorbs ultraviolet radiation is ___?___.

7. The earth's atmosphere is held in place near the earth by ___?___.

8. The thermal blanket which regulates the heat of the earth is mainly composed of ___?___ and ___?___.

9. The major climatic regions of the world are ___?___, ___?___, and ___?___.

10. The latitude which marks the southern limit of the sun's direct rays is called the ___?___.

D. How and Why

1. How much air is pressing on the cover of your closed book? (Use air pressure at sea level.)

2. Why is man's greatest interest concentrated on the layer of the atmosphere known as the troposphere?

3. Why is the zone beyond the mesosphere called the ionosphere?

4. Why do shifts in the ionosphere affect radio reception?

5. Why must space vehicles have protective heat shields?

6. Why are there few or no clouds in the stratosphere?

7. In what way do pressurized cabins and pressurized suits protect humans in the upper atmosphere?

8. The lower layer of the atmosphere plus that part of the crust to the depth of the oceans is often called the *biosphere*. Suggest some reasons for this term.

9. Why is nitrogen sometimes called the "element which doesn't do anything?" Is this idea a fact?

10. How is the process of heat radiation related to the formation of dew or frost?

INVESTIGATIONS

1. Refer to a magazine, such as *Holiday*, which gives average temperatures for cities in different parts of the world. Compare average temperatures for Honolulu, Buenos Aires, Athens, Mexico City, Toronto, Moscow, Juneau, and Phoenix. Indicate in which climatic region each city is located. From information in a geography book or an atlas, decide whether any other factors, such as marine, mountain, mid-continent, or desert location, or low altitude, have any influence on the temperatures. In what season is each city at the time you made the chart?

2. Refer to the daily paper and keep a daily weather chart on six cities for one week. Choose one city in a desert climate, one city in the extreme north, one city in a mountain region, one city on either the west coast or the east coast, and one city in the middle of the continent. This chart should include daily high temperature and low temperature. Compare temperatures for daily variance and day-to-night variance.

INTERESTING READING

Adler, Irving and Ruth, *Air*. New York, The John Day Company, Inc., 1962.

Loebsack, Theo, *Our Atmosphere*. New York, The New American Library, Inc., 1961.

Rosenfeld, Sam, *Science Experiments With Air*. Irvington-on-Hudson, N. Y., Harvey House, Inc., Publishers, 1969.

Wolfe, L., *Wonders of the Atmosphere*. New York, G. P. Putnam's Sons, 1962.

Winds and Weather

Air is constantly in motion. Horizontal movements of air are called winds; vertical movements are called currents. Winds and currents distribute the sun's radiant energy which has been transformed into heat by absorption at the earth's surface. They also determine the circulation pattern of the atmosphere. Winds and currents carry air from regions of high pressure and great density to regions of low pressure and less density. Air is relatively cold in areas of high pressure and relatively warm in areas of low pressure.

Water vapor weighs less than an equal volume of air. In moist air, molecules of oxygen, nitrogen, and other gases are displaced by water vapor. Consequently, dry air is more dense than moist air. Elevation also affects density. But, in general, temperature accounts for most differences in density.

10:1 *Air Circulation*

The equator is a zone of high temperature and low pressure.

Near the equator, between latitudes 23½° north and south, the earth receives more radiant energy than in any other re-

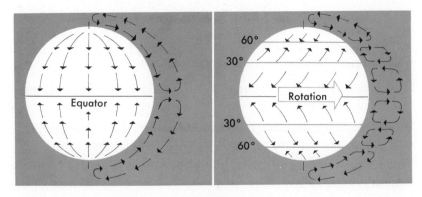

Figure 10-1. Major north-south convection currents in earth's atmosphere are broken into eddies by the earth's rotation, forming the wind pattern of the globe.

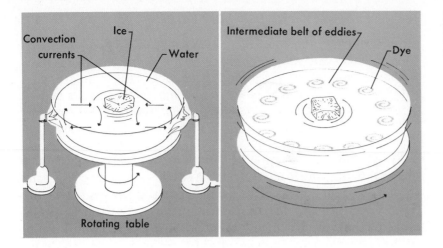

gion. Consequently, air at the equator is warmer and lighter than the air in adjacent latitudes. Motion of air in this region of low pressure is upward. Cold surface air flows toward the equator to replace the rising currents of warm air. Warm air rises and eventually flows poleward to take the place of the polar air that flows toward the equator. Circulation of the atmosphere spreads heat from the equatorial region to the rest of the earth. If the earth did not rotate on its axis, the atmosphere would be like a giant hot air heating system in which currents move north and south.

Because the earth rotates and because the earth has an unequal amount of land and water areas, circulation of air is extremely complicated. Victor P. Starr, an American meteorologist, developed a model of heat and cold exchange in an attempt to understand the major wind systems. Starr's model consisted of a shallow pan of water which contained ice at the center. By heating the outer rim of the pan, Starr set up a convection current. Warm water flowed across the surface toward the cold center. Cold water from the center flowed across the bottom and rose at the outer rim. After the simple convection pattern was established, Starr started the pan rotating. He discovered that the faster the pan rotated, the more the water broke up into eddies. He added dye to the water so he could trace movements of the currents. After the dye had circulated, the eddies looked like the lines on a weather map. Eddies moved toward a belt midway between the outer warm rim and the cold center. Starr's experiment suggests that the major wind patterns on earth are controlled by unequal heating of the earth and by the earth's rotation.

Winds move from high to low pressure areas. High pressure is associated with cold air, low pressure with warm air.

Warm air rises because it is less dense than cold air.

As applied to air masses, cold and warm are relative terms.

Eddies are circular currents.

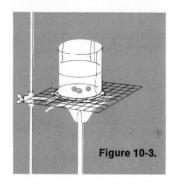

Figure 10-3.

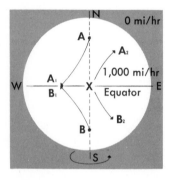

Figure 10-4. As an air particle travels from *A* toward *X*, *X* is carried eastward and the particle arrives at *A₁*. An air particle moving from *X* toward the north pole would arrive at *A₂*.

ACTIVITY. Put some cinnamon candy drops in the bottom of a beaker and fill the beaker half full with water. Heat the beaker over a Bunsen burner. What happens to the color from the candy as the water nears the boiling point? In your notebook, draw the circulation pattern of the water. Which kind of heating that also occurs in the air do you observe in the water?

The **Coriolis** (kohr ee oh'lis) **force** is the apparent force that causes moving bodies on or near the earth's surface to be turned from a straight course. The Coriolis force is caused by the differences in velocity of rotation at different latitudes. At the equator the velocity of rotation is at its maximum (1,000 mi/hr). At the poles the velocity of rotation is at its minimum (0 mi/hr). The velocity of rotation gradually decreases from the equator to the poles.

The original circulation of air caused by convection is in a north-south direction. But because the earth turns toward the east, all winds veer from this north-south direction. A particle of air that moves directly *south* in the northern hemisphere appears to be deflected toward the *west*. A particle of air that moves directly *north* in the southern hemisphere appears to be deflected toward the *west*. These apparent changes in direction are related to the motion of the earth below the particle.

Consider what happens to a particle of air moving on a north-south line from the north pole to the equator. The point on the equator moves eastward faster than the points lying farther north. Consequently, when the air particle reaches the equator, the point toward which it was moving has already moved some distance eastward. Although the air particle has actually been traveling directly southward, its apparent direction of travel appears to be from northeast to southwest.

ACTIVITY. On a classroom world globe, determine how a north-south line is affected by the turning of the earth beneath it. With a grease pencil, begin marking lightly on the globe at the north pole as another student turns the globe from left to right. Hold the grease pencil erect, maintain a steady pressure, and move the pencil directly toward the equator. Attempt to make a straight line from the north pole to the equator while the globe turns. What is the direction of the line? What determines the direction of the line? Repeat the experiment and move the grease pencil from the south pole toward the equator. Are the lines the same in both hemispheres? How do they differ? Which lines represent surface wind movements?

Figure 10-5.

10:2 *Major Wind Systems*

Rising currents of warm air produce a quiet, almost wind-less zone on the surface at the equator. This zone of quiet is known as the *doldrums* (dohl'drums). In the days of sailing ships, vessels often were stranded in the doldrums for many days. On either side of the doldrums, winds blow toward the equator. These winds bring cool air to replace the warm air that rises over the equator. (Figure 10–6.)

The **doldrums** is a windless zone at the equator where air seems to be motionless because it is rising.

Trade wind belts extend from the doldrums to about 30° latitude both north and south of the equator. In the northern hemisphere, the trade winds blow from northeast to southwest. In the southern hemisphere, trade winds blow from southeast to northwest. Trade winds also are known as the **easterlies.** Notice that winds are named for the direction *from* which they blow. In the zone of the easterlies, winds are deflected toward the west. Here the air flows from a zone in which the rotational velocity is less than it is at the equator.

Winds blowing toward the equator are deflected toward the west, and are called easterlies.

The zone of the **westerlies** lies between 30° and 60° latitude. Air currents descend to the earth's surface at 30° latitude. Part of the air turns southward as the trade winds; part of the

Winds blowing toward the poles are deflected toward the east, and are called westerlies.

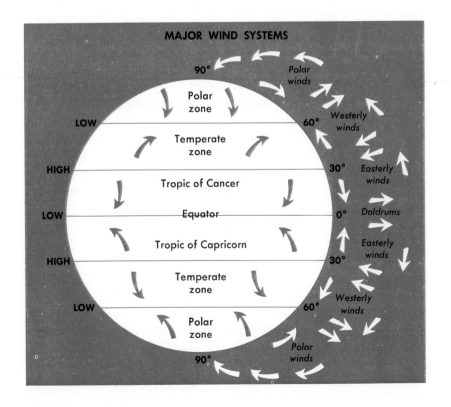

Figure 10-6. **Surface winds blow from regions of high-density descending currents toward regions of low-density ascending currents.**

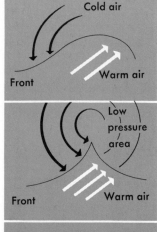

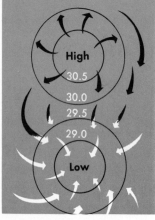

Figure 10-7. Cold air blows outward from the center of an anticyclone toward the low-pressure cyclone center, often causing warm air to rise above the cold air.

Weather in the zone of the westerlies depends on winds and air masses from both the tropics and the polar regions.

Clouds, rain, or snow may occur when highs and lows overtake one another.

air flows northward as the westerlies. Westerly winds blow from a zone in which the velocity of rotation is greater than the velocity of the zone toward which the air is flowing. Winds are deflected toward the east. In the northern hemisphere, westerly winds blow from southwest to northeast. In the southern hemisphere, westerly winds blow from northwest to southeast.

The zone of the westerly winds is noted for its changeable weather. Individual eddies, like those produced in Dr. Starr's experiment, form in the middle latitudes. Eddies are revolving masses of air called *cyclones* (sie'klohns) and *anticyclones*. Cyclones are local areas of low pressure and warm air. Anticyclones are local areas of high pressure and cold air. Cyclones and anticyclones tend to follow one another across the continents from west to east. They travel with the major wind system. Locally, winds blow from the high pressure center of an anticyclone toward the low pressure center of a cyclone. Cold and warm air are brought into contact by the winds of the cyclones and anticyclones. Day to day weather changes result from this mingling. The masses of cold air drift into the zone of the westerlies from the polar regions. Masses of warm air reach the westerly zone from the tropics. Storms and turbulence result from the mingling of air masses in the zone of the westerlies.

Polar wind zones lie between 60° latitude and the poles. Upper air currents flowing poleward from the equator are cooled during their journey. As the currents approach the poles, they are cold, dry, and dense. These air currents descend to the earth's surface in the neighborhood of the poles. From the poles, the air flows toward warmer latitudes. Polar winds are turned westward by the Coriolis force as they move into regions of increasing rotational velocity. Polar zones are relatively small compared to the area of the westerlies. But polar winds contribute large amounts of energy to the zone of the westerlies.

At about 60° latitude, the cold polar air at the surface displaces the warmer air of the westerly zone. This forces the warm air to rise. Eventually, this rising current of air joins the other poleward-moving currents from the equator. Radiant energy from the sun keeps the atmosphere in constant motion. Thus, daily changes in wind, moisture, and temperature ranges result.

Atmospheric turbulence is most noticeable in the troposphere, the layer of air closest to the earth. Air is constantly rising, descending, and moving horizontally. Wind velocities often are measured in several miles per hour at the earth's surface. However, both the easterlies and westerlies reach their maximum velocities at some distance above the earth. Easterlies have their greatest velocity at about 1 mi or 2 mi above the earth's surface. Westerlies have their maximum velocity at an altitude of about 7 mi.

Just above all this turbulence is a zone of relative quiet called the *tropopause* (troh'pa pawz). Jet planes often escape the clouds and winds of the troposphere by flying in the tropopause. However, near the upper boundary of the tropopause, where it merges with the stratosphere, air movement begins again. Here a stream of air, called the *jet stream*, flows from west to east at high velocities. In the jet stream, winds may reach a speed of 35 mi/hr in the summer and 90 mi/hr in winter. Occasionally, however, velocities of 200 mi/hr are reached. The jet stream may be 300 mi wide and 1 mi or 2 mi deep.

Polar winds that are deflected toward the west are called polar easterlies.

The **tropopause** is a zone of relative quiet between the troposphere and stratosphere.

Jet streams are strong winds blowing from west to east at the top of the tropopause.

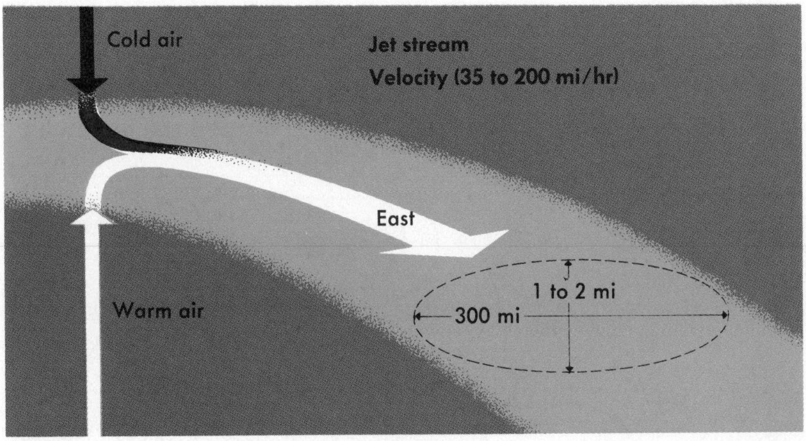

Figure 10-8. The jet stream forms when rising warm air currents meet descending cold air currents at the lower boundary of the stratosphere.

Cold air

Jet stream
Velocity (35 to 200 mi/hr)

East

Warm air

1 to 2 mi

300 mi

Jet pilots often use the jet stream to increase their speed when they are flying eastward. But they avoid the jet stream when flying westward. The jet stream is not in a fixed position; it may wander north or south, or upward and downward. The force of the jet stream decreases with time. Then winds wobble from side to side and up and down until their energy is spent. Eventually, the jet stream may settle downward into the path of the wind system of the troposphere. The jet stream sinks toward the earth if warm air slides over the stream. Unusually severe storms occur in the zone of the westerlies when the jet stream interferes with the surface wind system.

10:3 *Weather*

Weather refers to temperature, amount of moisture, air pressure, wind direction, and wind velocity.

Weather includes the day-to-day changes in wind, temperature, humidity, and pressure. Weather changes little from day to day or from winter to summer in the tropics. But in the zone of the westerlies, weather is indeed changeable.

Surface conditions determine the character of an air mass that remains stationary for several days above the area.

Masses of air that stay in place for some length of time take on characteristics of temperature and humidity from the surface of the earth over which the air stands. Masses of air that originate over the ocean tend to be moist. If the mass originates over the ocean in the tropics, the mass is both warm and moist. Large masses of cold, dry air originate in the temperate zone in winter and near the Arctic Circle at any time of year. Small masses of hot, dry air may form over deserts. Warm, moist air masses may develop over large inland lakes. Air masses are carried from regions of high pressure to regions of low pressure by major wind movements. The forward edge of a cold air mass is known as a *cold front*. The forward edge of a warm air mass is called a *warm front*. Weather forecasters predict local weather changes on the basis of the movement of cold fronts and warm fronts.

Forward edges of cold and warm masses are known as cold fronts and warm fronts, respectively.

In North America cold air masses tend to move toward the southeast. Warm air masses tend to move toward the northeast.

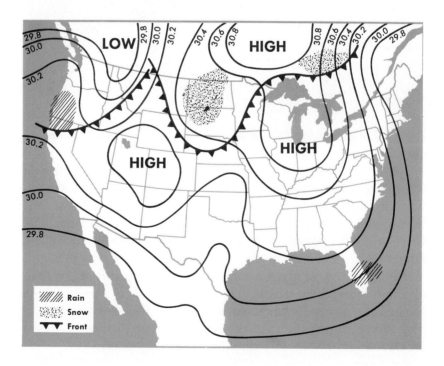

Figure 10-9. Local weather conditions are determined by the passage of high pressure and low pressure areas which follow each other in the zone of the westerlies.

When cold fronts collide with warm fronts, thunderstorms are common. Cold air pushes under the warm air and causes the warm air to rise rapidly. As the warm air rises, it cools, and its moisture condenses. If a warm front follows a cold front and overtakes it, rain occurs. In this case, however, rains are usually gentle and last for a longer time. (Figure 10–9.)

ACTIVITY. Make a weather vane. Cut a triangular piece of sheet aluminum for a pointer and a square piece of aluminum for a tail. Attach these pieces to the opposite ends of a piece of wood 1 in. wide and 1 in. thick. Drill a ¼ in. hole in the stick at its balance point. Oil the hole and with a long screw, mount the vane on a piece of wood 2 in. thick and 4 in. wide. You can improve the rotation of the vane by placing a well-oiled skate bearing or a washer between the wood surfaces. Set the vane in the wind and let it adjust to the wind direction. Use a compass to determine the direction of the wind. For one week, record the wind direction at the same hour. Check your readings with the local weather report. If the readings differ, does it mean your data are wrong?

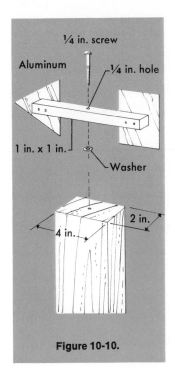

Figure 10-10.

Thunderstorms occur when warm (at least 0°C or 32°F) air masses or fronts are forced vertically upward. The most common type of thunderstorm occurs in temperate latitudes during the warm summer season. Convection currents cause most thunderstorms. Warm air rises when unequal heating of the earth's surface causes a local disturbance of the near-surface air. Upward momentum carries the rising air to higher and colder heights. Eventually, the current of air loses momentum, spills over, and starts to fall. Then cold temperatures may cause the water vapor to condense and fall as rain, hail, sleet, or snow.

In 1752, Benjamin Franklin proved by his famous kite experiment that a thundercloud generates electricity. The process by which the electricity is generated is not entirely understood, but it is known that positive and negative electrical charges are generated within the cloud. Negative charges usually collect on the lower surface of the cloud. Positive charges usually accumulate in the upper parts of the cloud. Electrical charges may build up in large quantities in clouds. Then the electricity may suddenly discharge by leaping from cloud to cloud, or from cloud to earth. Such sudden electrical discharges create bright flashes of light called *lightning*. Lightning strokes cause sudden heating of the air along their paths. Sudden heating expands the air so rapidly that abrupt pressure waves are formed.

If warm fronts overtake cold air masses, slow gentle rainfall results.

Lightning is an electrical discharge in the atmosphere.

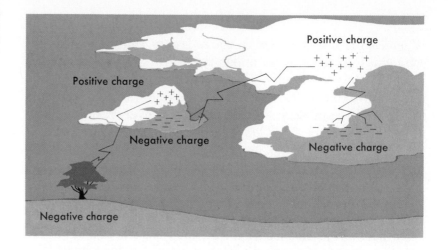

Figure 10-11. The presence of both positive and negative electrical charges within clouds may cause a sudden discharge of electricity, or lightning.

Explosions of any kind create similar waves, accompanied by loud noise. *Thunder* is the loud noise created by pressure waves formed by strokes of lightning. Thunder may be heard long after the flash of lightning has disappeared. The noise may continue because sound waves travel more slowly than light waves. Also multiple lightning strokes produce multiple pressure waves. Rumbling and various other sounds associated with thunder are partly the result of differences in the distances traveled by lightning strokes. The noise may be that reflected from both clouds and the earth.

Figure 10-12. When earth's negative electrical charges react with a cloud's positive charges, lightning may strike the earth.

Lightning strokes may carry large quantities of electric current which can be dangerous to life and property. Destructive forces due to lightning are of several different types. In addition to the heating effect, there are also explosive, crushing, and electrical effects. Magnetic and chemical effects are also associated with lightning.

Use of lightning rods to protect buildings from lightning damage was originated by Benjamin Franklin. Pointed metal rods are placed at intervals of 25 ft around the tops of buildings. The lightning rods attract the lightning stroke before it can reach the building. The electrical charge at the pointed ends of the rods is the same as that of the earth with which they are connected. Opposite charges between thunder clouds and the pointed rods attract each other. The electrical charge is carried from the rods by copper conductors to grounded metal plates in the earth. There it becomes harmless. In properly protected buildings, human life is in little danger from lightning.

ACTIVITY. Blow into a paper bag until it appears to be filled. Break the bag quickly. Explain what happens.

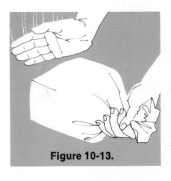

Figure 10-13.

Rainbows often are associated with rainfall. If the sun appears during the rainfall, an arc of color may spread across the sky. Water droplets suspended in the air act as prisms and separate the sunlight into all its colors. The colors, known as the **spectrum** (spek'trum), always occur in the same order: violet, indigo, blue, green, yellow, orange, and red. The center of a rainbow is always 180° from the sun. When the sun is setting, the rainbow is fairly high in the eastern sky. If the sun is high in the sky, the rainbow may not be visible above the horizon.

Rainbows occur when drops of water in the atmosphere separate the sunlight into its spectrum.

Tornadoes are violent, destructive storms. Tornadoes form when a mass of warm air becomes trapped between two layers of cold air. If an opening is present in the upper layer of cold air, the warm air rushes upward in a spiral pattern. The center of the spiral is an area of low pressure toward which the surrounding air rushes. Violent winds are associated with a tornado. They result from the vast difference between the pressure at the center of the tornado and the pressure in the surrounding air. When the air spirals upward suddenly, the pressure drops rapidly and causes the great difference in pressures. The center of the tornado is most dangerous. Pressures

Tornadoes are whirling storm centers of extremely low air pressure.

there are much lower than the pressures in closed buildings. Buildings located in the center of an updraft may burst outward. Opening windows and doors helps to equalize the pressure within and without. This lessens the effects of the tornado. The path of a tornado is usually only about ⅛ mi to ¼ mi wide.

Official U.S. Navy Photo

Figure 10-14. Here a tornado is forming as warm air spirals upward through a break in the upper cool layer. The greatest number of tornadoes occurs in the United States.

Hurricanes are large masses of low pressure with violent winds blowing toward the center, or **eye.**

Hurricanes are violent storms of lower wind velocity than tornadoes, but they affect a greater area. Low pressure areas form over water in the zone of the trade winds. These masses of warm moist air begin to move, carried forward by the major wind system. As the masses move, they rotate. Hurricane winds blow inward toward the low-pressure center, or the "eye." Velocities may be as high as 150 mi/hr. At the center of the hurricane, the eye is a zone of relative quiet because air currents are rising. The *squall line* is the area where cold and warm fronts meet. It may cover hundreds of miles and remain in place for several days. Hurricanes often bring violent weather to the Gulf of Mexico and the eastern half of the United States during the early fall.

Hurricanes originate over water in the trade wind belt during the fall season.

Much of the damage associated with hurricanes comes from the waters that pile up along the shore in front of the wind. As a hurricane moves landward, it blocks the return of water

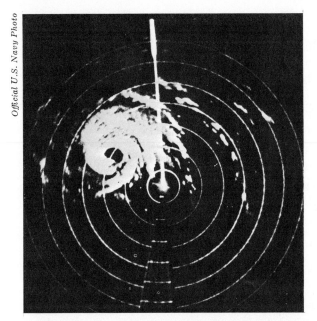
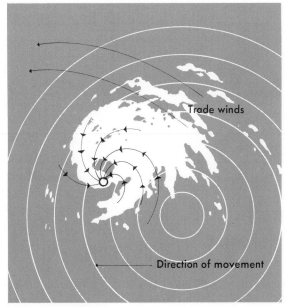

Trade winds

Direction of movement

Figure 10-15. Radar shows a spiral of warm air forming into a hurricane in the zone of the Trade Winds. Maintaining its unique spiral form, the hurricane is carried westward by the Trade Winds.

to the open ocean. Then water spills across the shore zone in great waves. Streams also are affected by the hurricane. Normally, their waters are emptied into the sea. But if the mouth is dammed by high water, a stream may back up, overflow its banks, and flood the surrounding land.

Convective storms are storms typical of the tropics. Air flows toward the equator from adjacent latitudes. This air is cooler than air at the equator, although the air is not cold. At the equator, the trade winds join the rising column of air. As the air rises, it is cooled, and eventually its moisture condenses and falls as rain. Rainfall is a daily occurrence in the equatorial zone wherever moisture is available. Trade winds that blow across the land are dry and have little water vapor. But winds that blow across the ocean supply abundant moisture for the tropical rain forests.

Convective storms occur in the doldrums as the rising air is cooled.

Monsoons (mahn soonz′) are seasonal winds. They are well known for their effect on the seasons in India. But monsoon winds occur in other places as well. Monsoons blow from land to sea when high pressure zones develop over the land. Monsoons blow from sea to land when high pressure zones develop over the sea. From June to September, the land area of India is warmer than the Indian Ocean, which lies south of the continent. The direct rays of the sun fall on India as the sun moves

Monsoons are seasonal winds blowing from land to sea during a part of the year and from sea to land during the rest of the year.

northward during the summer, and the land heats faster than the water. Then winds blow from the cool Indian Ocean toward the warm land. When the winds reach northern India, they rise to cross the mountains. Air cools as it rises, and its moisture condenses and falls on the lands south of the mountains. During the winter, the direct rays of the sun strike the Indian Ocean instead of the continent. The land mass of India becomes colder than the adjacent ocean, and winds then blow toward the sea. Winter winds are evaporating winds because they become warmer as they travel southward, and they are able to hold more and more moisture. Because of the monsoon winds, India has alternating wet and dry seasons.

Figure 10-16. As the summer sun heats the Asian continent, moist winds blow landward and cause rain. Dry winds blow seaward as the sun's direct rays move southward and heat the Indian Ocean.

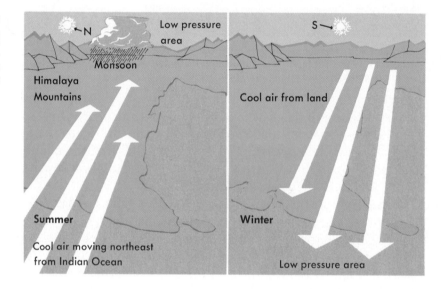

10:4   *Clouds*

Rain, hail, and snow occur if enough moisture condenses and droplets become large enough to overcome the buoyancy of air.

Clouds are condensed moisture suspended in the air. Moisture condenses around dust particles or salt crystals when the air is cooled below its dew point or saturation point. (Section 9:5.) The *dew point* is the temperature at which air is holding all the water vapor possible. At this point the air is 100 percent saturated with moisture. When clouds collect enough moisture, their droplets become large and heavy enough to overcome the buoyancy of air. Then the moisture falls as rain. Many clouds do not bring rain. Some clouds even disappear during the day as the temperature rises and the air is able to hold more moisture. Cooling of the atmosphere results from radiation of heat, from mixing of cold and warm fronts, and from rising air currents.

Cumulus (keu'mya lus) clouds are the white fluffy masses commonly formed on summer afternoons. Cumulus clouds seldom collect enough moisture to be rain clouds. *Cirrus* (sir'us) clouds are wispy, high, thin clouds formed in the upper part of the troposphere. Cirrus clouds consist of ice crystals, instead of water droplets. Their moisture condenses because temperatures are below freezing. *Stratus* (straet'us) clouds are low, widespread layers of condensation. Commonly, stratus clouds bring rain because cold and warm layers of air are being mixed. Slow, gentle, long-lasting rainfall often is associated with stratus clouds. *Cumulonimbus* (keu mya loh nim'bus) clouds are masses, often called thunderheads, that rise to great heights. They commonly bring thunderstorms with them. Cumulonimbus clouds begin as cumulus forms. As more and more moisture collects, their shape changes. Cumulonimbus clouds are black and large, and commonly cover much of the sky.

Figure 10-17. a. Cumulus clouds form as warm air rises, cools, and condenses; b. layers of dense stratus clouds often bring rain; c. high cirrus clouds contain ice crystals; d. cumulonimbus clouds often bring lightning and thunderstorms.

a.

b.

USDA Photo

Official U.S. Air Force Photo

c.

d.

Official U.S. Air Force Photo

Official U.S. Air Force Photo

American Airlines

Figure 10-18. Winds that reach deserts in the interiors of continents have lost most of their moisture. Winds also lose moisture as they rise to cross over mountains. Rain forests are present on the windward side, deserts on the leeward side of high mountain chains.

Local climates depend on the temperatures, rainfall, and wind directions averaged for at least a 10-year period.

Leeward sides are sides protected from the wind. **Windward** sides are sides which face the direction from which the wind blows.

The Gobi Desert and Sahara Desert occur where winds blow across land with no available moisture.

Clouds affect weather by screening the sun's rays. Daytime temperatures are usually lower when clouds cover the sky. On the other hand, a cloud cover prevents loss of heat during the night. Consequently, day and night temperatures tend to be less variable under cloudy skies than under clear skies.

Rain, hail, sleet, and snow are associated with storm clouds. *Snow* forms if moisture condenses in air in which the temperature is below freezing. Cirrus clouds are so high that they do not produce snow. Other types of clouds nearer the earth may bring snow during the winter. *Hail* forms if rain falls through a layer of cold air where the temperature is below freezing. Ice forms from the drops of water, and hail may occur even on warm summer days. *Sleet* is smaller particles of ice formed in much the same way as hail. However, sleet occurs only in winter because in summer the particles melt and form raindrops as they pass through warm air.

10:5   *Local Climates*

Within the major climatic regions of the earth, **local climates** are determined by local weather conditions. Temperature, rainfall, and wind conditions of at least a 10-year period are averaged to determine the classification. In general, weather of continental areas is controlled mostly by the wind belts in which they lie. However, certain types of local climates are influenced by particular conditions.

Deserts are regions in which annual rainfall is less than 10 in. Little water vapor is present to prevent loss of heat at night. No cloud cover screens the sun's rays during the day. Deserts heat quickly in the day and cool quickly at night. The temperature range between day and night may be as much as 40°F or 50°F (4.4°C to 10°C).

Deserts occur in almost all latitudes. They are found on the leeward sides of mountains that lie across wind directions. Deserts also occur in the interior of continents. Winds that travel long distances across dry land tend to lose their moisture early and have little opportunity to absorb more moisture. Consequently, continental interiors are often deserts. The Gobi (goh'bee) Desert of China is a good example of an interior continental desert. The Sahara Desert of Africa is another region where winds bring little moisture to the land. In fact, winds that blow across the Sahara Desert are evaporating winds. The 30° north latitude line lies about midway across the Sahara. The trade winds become warmer and warmer as they approach the equator. Thus, they are capable of absorbing more and more moisture as they blow southward. But because the winds travel across land areas, little moisture is available to them. Such winds are evaporating winds that take away moisture, rather than bring rain.

Mountains influence the amount of rainfall in their vicinity. They may cause desert conditions on their leeward slopes if the winds cross the mountains. Rain forests may occur on the windward slopes where winds lose moisture before they cross the mountains.

Rain forests may occur on windward slopes of the mountains that lie in the path of the major wind belts.

In California, the westerly winds rise to cross the Coast Ranges and the Sierra Nevada. As the air rises, it cools, and its moisture condenses. Moisture then falls as rain on the western slopes of the mountains. In northern California and Oregon, lush vegetation results from the abundant rainfall on the windward side of the mountains. On the leeward slopes of the mountains, winds are dry, and desert or semi-desert conditions are common.

Death Valley is a desert lying on the leeward side of the California mountains. Winds descend the mountain slopes into the valley. Gradually, the air becomes warmer and able to hold more and more moisture. However, little water is present, and desert conditions result. An evaporating wind that blows across the mountains in Wyoming is so dry that it often absorbs the spring snows without melting them. The wind is named the Chinook (shi nuhk') wind for the Indians of the area.

Death Valley lies on the leeward slope of the California mountains where winds are dry because they have lost their moisture in crossing the mountain slopes.

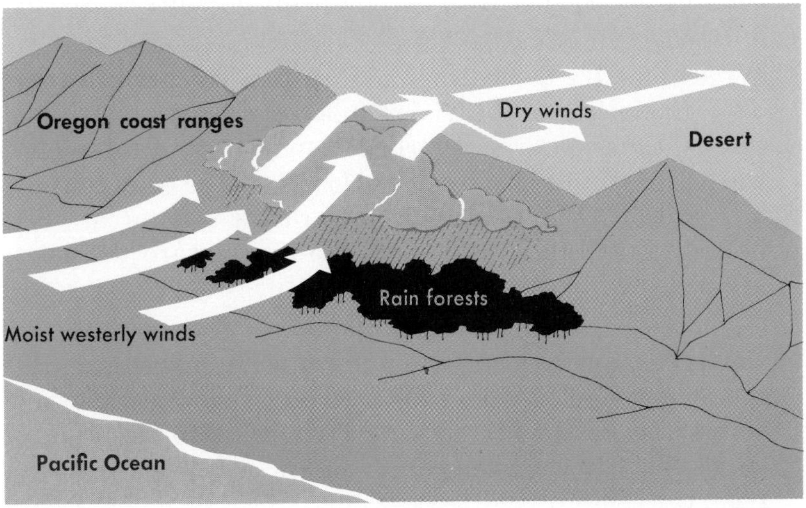

Figure 10-19. Winds lose their moisture as they rise to cross the mountains; they become evaporating winds as they descend into the desert.

Marine climates are typical of regions lying near the ocean. Moisture is abundant in the atmosphere, and rain is common. Temperature variations from night to day are commonly only 2°F or 3°F. This is a great contrast to the 40°F to 50°F variation of the desert regions.

Oceans tend to equalize the day and night temperature because they absorb and radiate heat less quickly than the land.

Bodies of water absorb and radiate heat more slowly than adjacent land areas. During the day, the land heats and the water remains cool. Winds, called *sea breezes*, then blow from the cool water to the warm land. During the night, heat from the land is radiated, and the land becomes colder than the body of water. A high pressure area develops on the land. Winds called *land breezes* blow toward the warm, low pressure zone over the water. Marine climates affect all shore zones near large bodies of water.

MAIN IDEAS

1. Radiant energy from the sun is transformed into heat by absorption at the earth's surface and the heat is then distributed by the atmosphere.

2. Rotation of the earth, distribution of land and water areas, and the exchange of heat between warm and cold areas causes the circulation patterns of the atmosphere.

3. The entire envelope of air surrounding the earth turns eastward as the earth rotates. However, segments of air within the troposphere move upward, downward, or horizontally in response to variations in air pressure caused by differences in temperature.

4. Wind belts are named for the direction *from* which they blow. Easterlies, or the trade winds, blow from 30° latitude toward the equator; westerlies blow from 30° latitude toward 60° latitude; polar winds blow from the poles toward 60° latitude. Winds blowing toward the equator are deflected toward the west; winds blowing toward the poles are deflected toward the east.

5. Cyclones and anticyclones, common in the zone of the westerlies, are local areas of low and high pressure, respectively. Cyclones and anticyclones follow each other across the continents, moving from west to east. Local winds blow toward the center of the cyclone and away from the center of the anticyclone.

6. The tropopause is a zone of quiet air at the upper level of the troposphere. The jet stream is a high velocity wind located at the boundary between the tropopause and the stratosphere.

7. The zone of the westerlies has changeable weather because warm air masses from the tropics and cold air masses from the polar regions come into contact.

8. Tornadoes are violent storms formed occasionally in the zone of the westerlies. Hurricanes are violent storms formed usually in the fall season in the zone of the trade winds. Both hurricanes and tornadoes result from the presence of low pressure zones toward which winds blow from adjacent high pressure zones. Great differences in pressure are responsible for the violence of the winds.

9. Rainforests occur where rainfall is especially abundant. They are found in the tropics, associated with daily rainfall, and on the windward slopes of mountain barriers, both in the tropics and the zone of the westerlies.

10. Rainfall in deserts is less than 10 in./yr. Deserts occur on the leeward side of mountain barriers and in the interior of continents where winds become warmer and are able to absorb more moisture.

11. Monsoons are seasonal winds in the trade wind belt. Monsoons bring rain when they blow from the ocean toward the land. They are drying winds when they blow from the land toward the ocean. Monsoons in India bring a wet season during the summer, a dry season during the winter.

12. Clouds are condensed moisture. They are less dense than the surrounding air. Many clouds do not produce rain, but eventually droplets in stratus and cumulonimbus clouds may become too large to be supported by the air. Then moisture falls as rain, snow, sleet, or hail.

13. Dew point is the temperature at which air is saturated; that is, it holds all the water vapor possible. Cooling below the dew point causes condensation of excess moisture.

14. Marine climates are relatively constant in temperature during both day and night. Changes from winter to summer temperatures are less than in the interior. Moisture in the atmosphere and slow absorption and radiation from the body of water tend to keep temperatures more even than on the continent.

VOCABULARY

Write a sentence in which you use correctly each of the following words or terms.

anticyclone	doldrums	saturate
Chinook wind	leeward	spectrum
Coriolis force	monsoon	tropopause
cyclone	prism	turbulence

STUDY QUESTIONS

A. True or False

Determine whether each of the following sentences is true or false. (Do not write in this book.)

1. Circulation of the air is affected by heat from the sun.

2. An upward current of air exists at the poles.

3. Cyclones and anticyclones are typical of the zone of the westerlies.

4. Winds blow toward the center of a high pressure area.

5. Both tornadoes and cyclones are high pressure areas.

6. Warm air masses tend to be less dense than cold air masses.

7. Hurricanes originate in huge low pressure areas of warm moist air.

8. Monsoon winds occur only in India.

9. There is a greater daily range of temperature in desert climates than in marine climates.

10. Thunderstorms frequently are associated with cumulonimbus clouds.

B. Multiple Choice

Choose the word or phrase which completes correctly each of the following sentences. (Do not write in this book.)

1. Rotation of the earth creates an apparent deflection of poleward moving winds from (*east to west, west to east, north to south*).

2. Heating of the atmosphere results in (*rising, stationary, descending*) currents.

3. The trade wind belt begins at (*the equator, 30° latitude, 60° latitude*).

4. Westerly winds are associated with the (*tropic, temperate, arctic*) zone.

5. Most warm air masses originate in the (*tropic, temperate, arctic*) zone.

6. The center of a(n) (*tornado, rainbow, anticyclone*) is an area of low pressure.

7. Hurricanes are most common in the zone of the (*westerly, trade, polar*) winds.

8. Convective storms are typical of the (*arctic, tropic, temperate*) zone.

9. India has droughts in (*winter, summer, spring*) due to the influence of the monsoon winds.

10. Along seacoasts, (*morning, afternoon, night*) winds tend to blow from the shore.

C.   Completion

Complete each of the following sentences with a word or phrase which will make the sentence correct. (Do not write in this book.)

1. The force that causes moving bodies to be deflected by the rotation of the earth is the ___?___ force.

2. The zone near the equator where air is relatively motionless is called the ___?___.

3. Winds are named for the direction ___?___ which they blow.

4. Westerly winds blow between latitudes of ___?___ and ___?___.

5. The jet stream of the tropopause blows from ___?___ to ___?___.

6. Tornadoes are most common in the ___?___ wind belt.

7. Dry winds that evaporate snow without melting are called ___?___ winds.

8. Mountains lying in the path of winds may cause heavy rainfall on the ___?___ side and arid conditions on the ___?___ side of the mountains.

9. Two deserts located in continental interiors are the ___?___ and the ___?___.

10. A rainbow is caused by the separation of light into a band of color by water droplets which act as a(n) ___?___.

D. How and Why

1. Why does the rotation of the earth deflect winds moving toward the equator? Would the deflection be apparent if you observed the wind movements from a stationary position in space?

2. Why is a cold air mass usually considered a high pressure area?

3. What is the difference between a hurricane and a tornado?

4. Why are weather patterns of the westerlies more complex than those in the trade wind zone?

5. Why are hurricanes accompanied by heavy rain and water damage?

6. Why do the snows of western Montana and Wyoming often disappear without causing runoff waters?

7. Why can tropical rainforests and desert conditions exist at the same latitude?

8. Why are you relatively safe in a steel frame building during a thunderstorm accompanied by lightning?

9. Why do day and night temperatures in a desert have such a wide range, whereas the temperatures along a coast have less change from day to night?

10. Why is the equator the location of warm air currents?

11. Discuss the reason why air moves from high pressure areas to low pressure areas.

12. Why did the Spanish explorers find it easier to get their sailing vessels to Central and South America than to North America?

INVESTIGATIONS

1. On an outline map of the world, draw and label the wind belts in each hemisphere. Explain why the easterlies are also called the trade winds.

2. Watch the weather report on television or get the information from the newspaper. On an outline map of the United States, point out the cold and warm fronts and the high and low pressure areas. If a storm is progressing across the United States, watch its development. Does it make a steady progress, or does it become stationary? If fog is common in your area, explain its formation.

3. Report on the tornado season in the United States. What part of the country is most affected and at what season of the year? Is anything being done to locate and chart tornadoes? Report on the hurricanes of North America. How are hurricanes studied? Is any effort being made to halt hurricanes or to divert them from populated areas?

4. Place a prism in the sunlight so that the sun's rays are diverted onto a sheet of white paper. Note the rainbow colors. Why is a rainbow arched while the colors lie in straight lines on the paper?

INTERESTING READING

Battan, Louis J., *Radar Observes the Weather*. Garden City, N. Y., Doubleday & Company, Inc., 1962.

Bonsall, George, *The How and Why Wonder Book of Weather*. Columbus, Ohio, Charles E. Merrill Publishing Co., 1960.

Holmes, David C., U.S.N., *Weather Made Clear*. New York, Sterling Publishing Co., Inc., 1965.

Irving, Robert, *Hurricanes and Twisters*. New York, Alfred A. Knopf, Inc., 1961.

Lehr, Paul E. R., Burnett, Will, and Zim, Herbert S., *Weather*. New York, Golden Press, 1957.

Longstreth, T. Morris, *Understanding the Weather*. New York, The Macmillan Company, 1962.

Ross, Frank Jr., *Weather: Science of Meterology from Ancient Times to the Space Age*. New York, Lothrop, Lee & Shepherd Co., 1964.

Sloane, Eric, *Folklore of American Weather*. Des Moines, Iowa, Meredith Corporation, 1963.

*Thompson, P. D., and O'Brien, R., *Weather*. Life Science Library. New York, Time Inc., 1965.

* Well-illustrated material.

The Hydrosphere

In addition to the lithosphere and atmosphere, the earth contains another sphere of matter called the hydrosphere. The hydrosphere includes all water standing in lakes and swamps, all water flowing on the surface in rivers, all water trapped within the rocks below the surface, and all water contained in the ocean basins. The ocean is a continuous body of salt water that covers two-thirds of the earth's surface. Bays, seas, gulfs, and oceans together constitute one vast expanse of water from which continents emerge like islands.

11:1 *The Hydrologic Cycle*

The **hydrologic** (hie dra lahj′ik) **cycle** is the cycle through which water passes from sea to land, and from land to sea. Water vapor enters the air through the evaporation of water. Water vapor in the air eventually condenses and falls as rain, snow, sleet, or hail. Water that falls on land collects in rivers which carry it back to the ocean. The return of water to the ocean may be slowed when water becomes trapped in lakes, swamps, or openings in the rocks. Eventually, however, most water returns to the ocean. Like the atmospheric circulation, the hydrologic cycle receives its energy from the sun. Evaporation could not occur without radiant energy from the sun.

> The **hydrologic cycle** is the continuous movement of moisture from ocean to land and land to ocean.

Destruction of the land through weathering and erosion accompanies the hydrologic cycle. Materials from land are carried to the ocean and deposited there. In the ocean, many of the materials are solidified into sedimentary rock. Other materials remain in solution in the ocean waters. Between land and sea, the hydrologic cycle produces a never-ending exchange of matter. Both destruction and construction of land forms accompany the hydrologic cycle.

> Water returning to the ocean carries material from the land to the sea and, thus, erodes the continents.

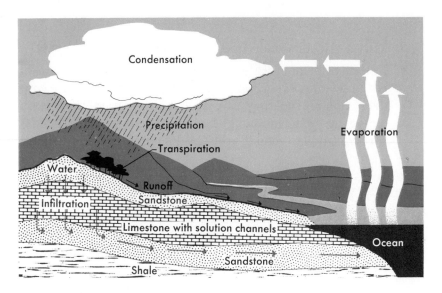

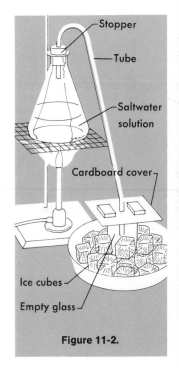

EXPERIMENT. *Dissolve 1 tablespoon of table salt in 1 cup of water and taste the solution. Pour this solution into a flask. Place the flask on a ring stand over a Bunsen burner, using wire gauze or screen to support the flask on the ring. Insert a flexible drinking straw or plastic or rubber tubing in the hole of a one-hole rubber stopper. Seal the hole with moist clay, if necessary, to insure a closed system. Close the flask with the stopper. Make sure that the straw or tubing is above the surface of the solution. Bend the straw or tubing, and insert the free end through a small hole in a piece of cardboard. Place the cardboard over a water tumbler. Add weight to the cardboard, if necessary, to keep it in place. Surround the tumbler with ice in a shallow pan. (Figure 11–2.)*

Bring the solution to a boil. What happens in the straw or tubing? What happens in the tumbler? Continue the boiling until the solution is almost, but not quite, boiled away. Then remove the burner. (Continued application of heat may break the flask.) When the tumbler and the water in it are cool, taste the water in the tumbler. Is it salty? What remains in the flask? Is the combined volume of water left in the tumbler and in the flask the same as the volume you placed in the flask at the beginning of the experiment? Explain your answer.

Figure 11-2.

PROBLEMS

1. Relate this experiment to the hydrologic cycle. What heat source near the equator is represented by the Bunsen burner in this experiment?

2. In one million years, will the ocean be slightly less salty or slightly more salty than it is now? Why?

3. Why are clouds sometimes seeded with dry ice?

4. You have demonstrated condensation or precipitation in the preceding experiment. You can also demonstrate condensation by holding a cold dish or pan in the steam emerging from the spout of a boiling teakettle. Will moisture continue to condense on the dish until there is no more water?

5. Which would be safer to drink, pond water or freshly collected rainwater? Why?

6. Seawater passing into the air as vapor and later condensing to fall as rain is an example of simple distillation. Distillation, an essential natural process, is also important in industry and is used in the chemical, oil refining, and drug industries as well as in many other applications. Can you name some products of distillation?

11:2 *Composition of the Ocean*

Water is derived from volcanic eruptions and from the consolidation of magma at depth below the surface.

Water for the ocean basins has been formed by consolidation of the earth's matter. When magma cools and solidifies to form igneous rocks, water vapor is given off. Some of this water vapor finds its way to the surface along cracks or bedding planes. Most of the water vapor is carried to the surface during volcanic eruptions. During the 4.5 billion years of the earth's existence, enough water has collected to more than fill the ocean basins. Water still is being added to the surface of the earth, but yearly additions are small.

Elements in solution in seawater are derived from weathering of rocks, volcanic eruptions, and the gases of the earth's atmosphere.

Water which is carried to the surface by volcanic eruptions has a number of elements in solution. These elements are present in ocean waters in relatively large quantities. Other elements are added to ocean waters by rivers that carry products of rock weathering in solution. Sodium chloride is the most abundant compound in solution in seawater. Sodium is a product of rock weathering. Chlorine is added to the ocean by volcanic eruptions. Ocean water is called *brine* because of the presence of sodium chloride and other salts. When sodium chloride is precipitated, it forms the mineral *halite*, or common salt.

Other substances in seawater are calcium chloride, magnesium chloride, sodium sulfate, and potassium chloride. Traces of silicon, bromine (broh'meen), and strontium (strahn'chee um) are present along with minute amounts of many other

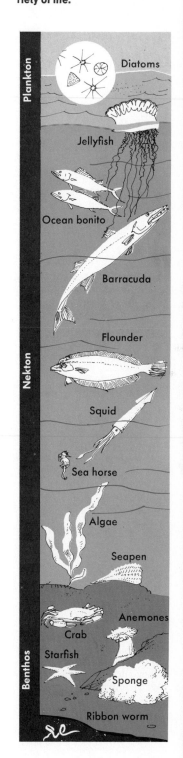

elements. Gases from the atmosphere, including oxygen, carbon dioxide, and nitrogen, are dissolved in seawater.

Most of the water in the ocean has traveled over the earth's surface as river water. However, river water and seawater differ in composition. One reason for the difference is that marine life removes some elements from ocean water. River water has a high content of silica (SiO_2) and calcium in solution. Ocean waters are low in silica and calcium because marine life uses these substances for shells, bones, and coverings. Most marine animals use calcium. Microscopic marine plants, called *diatoms* (die'a tahms), use silica in their coverings.

Rivers carry small amounts of salt compared to the volume of water. Nevertheless, enough salt is present in river water so that salt lakes may form by the concentration of salt through evaporation. Evaporation of ocean water has concentrated the amount of salt in solution until ocean water has become a brine. On a smaller scale, the Great Salt Lake of Utah is undergoing the same process of salt concentration and is now more concentrated than ocean brine.

A comparison between the composition of river water and ocean water is difficult. A river's dissolved materials are determined by the kind of rock and soil over which the river and its tributary streams flow. Each river tends to have a different concentration of soluble material. On the other hand, ocean waters undergo a thorough mixing. This distributes the soluble material almost uniformly. Thus, oceans contain similar substances, whether at the equator or at the poles.

11:3 *Life in the Ocean*

Living things abound in the oceans. They are classified according to their habits and to the part of the ocean they inhabit. *Nekton* (nek'tan) includes all the swimming forms, from tiny herring to huge whales. *Benthos* (ben'thahs) are creatures such as corals, snails, starfish, and clams that live on the sea floor. Forms of plant and animal life that float at or near the ocean surface are called *plankton* (plangk'tan).

Life activities are performed more easily in the ocean than on land. Oxygen for animals and carbon dioxide for plants are dissolved in seawater. Organisms can absorb what they require from the abundant and easily obtainable food supply. Many animals get their nourishment by circulating the food-bearing water through structures of their bodies which filter out the nutrients. Movement requires little energy because of the buoyancy of water. Daily surface temperature range of the ocean is small, between 1°F and 2°F. The annual range is about the same. Average temperatures range between 80°F at the equator and 30°F at the poles. Little protection against heat or cold is needed. But in spite of the advantages of the sea, few animals in the sea have a long life. Some other sea animal is always ready to use its unwary neighbor for food.

Plants are at the bottom of the food chain in the ocean, as they are on land. They are the food on which all animal life depends, either directly or indirectly. Plants convert sunlight, carbon dioxide, and water into proteins, carbohydrates, and starches by a process called *photosynthesis* (foht a sin'tha sis). This food energy is used directly by plant-eating animals

Figure 11-4. Animals derive most of their food energy from lower forms of life.

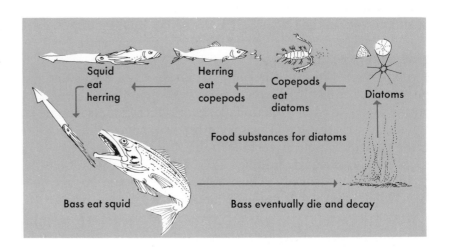

and indirectly by flesh-eating animals. Energy from the sun is necessary for the life processes of plants. Thus plant life is confined to the upper zone of ocean water that is penetrated by sunlight. Many plants belong to the plankton, but some seaweeds live attached to the bottom near the shore.

Plankton include several types of floating organisms, many of which are too small to be seen by the naked eye. Microscopic plants and animals, as well as tiny *larvae* (lahr'vee), or young forms of larger animals, belong to the plankton. Some plankton have characteristics of both plants and animals. Like plants, they can manufacture food from sunlight, carbon dioxide, and water. Like animals, they can capture food.

Microscopic organisms having some characteristics of both plants and animals are classified as **protists.**

Diatoms are small, one-celled plants that make up a large proportion of plankton. Diatoms are important sources of food for many sea animals, including some whales. During spring storms, ocean waters undergo a thorough mixing which brings nutrients and minerals to the surface in large quantities. This abundance of nutrients brings about a rapid growth of diatoms. In fact, diatoms multiply so rapidly that they may form a colored blanket on the ocean surface. This living blanket provides food for great numbers of marine animals. But the nutrients are soon used up, and within a few weeks the blanket of diatoms disappears.

Diatoms form important food supplies for all sea animals.

Benthos, or bottom dwellers, live in shallow water where sunlight penetrates to the bottom. Here food is abundant and little effort or movement is necessary to obtain it. Many animals attach themselves to the sea floor. Others crawl or swim slowly about in search of prey. Slow moving animals and those attached to the bottom usually have heavy *calcitic* (kal sit′ik) *shells* covering their soft bodies. Oysters, clams, snails, and several other shelled animals are familiar inhabitants of the shore zone. There food-getting is easy, but shells are needed for protection from their neighbors. A shell is little protection against the starfish. A starfish can open another animal's shell, insert a part of its digestive system, and consume the animal without breaking the shell.

American Museum of Natural History

Figure 11-5. The bottom-dwelling sea anemone is shown with its tentacles extended for food gathering (top and right) and withdrawn when disturbed (left).

Figure 11-6. The research vessel Trieste has made many journeys to the ocean bottom.

Nekton are swimmers and are not limited to a particular environment. Nekton move from one depth to another and from one place to another. Some prefer cold water, and others thrive in warm regions. Still others roam the entire ocean. Most flesh-eating nekton live just below the surface, where food is plentiful. Many plant-eating nekton come to the surface only at night to feed on plankton.

Diatoms are at the bottom of the food chain; nekton are at the top of the food chain.

Food becomes more and more scarce as water deepens, but probably no part of the ocean is without some organisms. Observers who descended to the bottom of the Mariana Trench in a *bathysphere* (bath'i sfir), a submarine observatory, were amazed to find life at a depth of nearly 36,000 ft. No light penetrates this great depth and water pressures are tremendous, yet organisms manage to exist.

11:4 *Topography of the Ocean Floor*

In the past, the ocean bottom was considered to be a smooth, plane surface where no erosion and little deposition occurred. Now oceanographers are beginning to realize how irregular the bottom of the ocean really is. (Figure 11–8.) The first scientific attempt to map the ocean bottom was undertaken by the Challenger expedition which set out from England in 1872. The Challenger collected a vast amount of data during its four years of travel. However, relatively few readings were made on ocean depths, considering the vast size of the ocean. Getting even one sample required many hours of difficult work. Reel

Challenger expedition was the first scientific exploration of the ocean bottom.

after reel of rope or wire had to be unwound and then rewound. Often, just the weight of the wire and the pressure of water broke the line. Then the procedure had to be repeated. Incomplete as it was, data from the Challenger expedition changed many old ideas about the ocean bottom. Unexpected irregularities were discovered and important oceanographic research had begun. Now many expeditions have crisscrossed the ocean and new instruments have been devised for mapping the relief of the ocean bottom.

Mapping the ocean floor requires methods different from those used on land. Land surveyors measure distance and elevation directly. Only indirect methods can be used in the ocean. Mapping is based on echo sounding, seismographic surveys, and sonar or radar methods. All of these methods depend on a similar principle. (Figure 11–7.) Sound, or any other kind of vibration, will pass from the surface to the ocean bottom at a given angle. Then it will be reflected to the surface at the same angle. In a given length of time, the vibration will be received by the surface receiver. The velocity of sound in water is approximately 5,000 ft/sec. Depth can be computed by the following formula:

$$D = \tfrac{1}{2}t \times V$$

Where D represents depth, t represents time elapsed between sending and receiving the vibrations, and V represents the velocity of the vibrations in water.

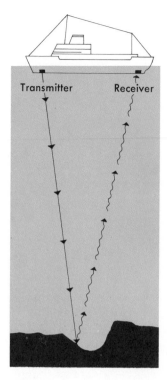

Figure 11-7. Sound waves sent out from the vessel are reflected surfaceward from the ocean bottom.

Figure 11-8. Mountains, plains, and deep trenches of the ocean floor.

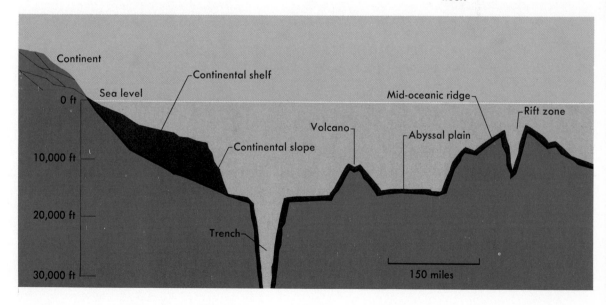

Problems

7. Through its sonar device, a ship determines that a submarine is nearby. How far from the ship is the submarine if the signal is received 4 sec after the initial sound impulse is sent?

8. A mapping ship sends a sound impulse and receives the reflection from the ocean floor 6 sec later. What is the depth of the ocean at this point?

Depth is measured from **sea level,** the zero elevation where land and sea meet. Sea level is the average height of the sea, measured over a long period of time, disregarding tides and waves. Land elevations are measured above sea level. Ocean depths are measured below sea level.

Echo sounding, sonar, radar, and seismograph surveys are useful in mapping the ocean.

Echo sounding is used to measure depth directly from sound waves. A bell or beeper is sounded at one end of the investigating vessel. The *echo,* or returning sound, is recorded at the other end of the ship. Sound strikes the ocean bottom at a given angle and is reflected or bounced back to the surface at the same angle. *Sonar* detection systems also use this principle. Submarines, for example, are equipped with control devices that pick up and record the return of sound.

Figure 11-9. The Atlantis Seamount rising 5,400 ft above the sea floor is recorded by this seismic profile.

Seismographic (siez'moh graf ik) *surveys* require two ships. One ship sets off a charge of dynamite. Another ship records the

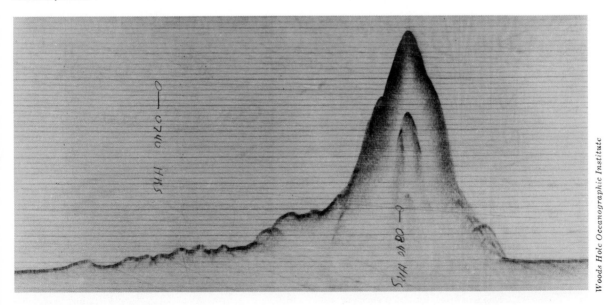

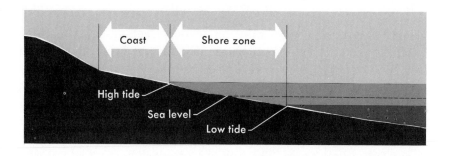

Figure 11-10. The shore zone is alternately covered and exposed as sea level changes with the tides.

time of arrival of seismic vibrations, which are similar to sound waves. Seismographic surveys provide more information than echo sounding or sonar. Seismic vibrations penetrate rock and have a different velocity in each different density of rock. Information about the kind of rock and the depths of different kinds of rock can be determined. From seismographic studies, oceanographers know that, above the mantle, continents are composed mostly of granitic-type rock. The crystalline rock layer above the mantle in the ocean basin is composed of basaltic-type rock.

Submarines, with their delicate sonar instruments, are used in mapping details of ocean topography. Submarines also have mapped the shape of overlying ice masses in polar regions. Through the use of echo sounding, sonar, and seismographic surveys, the ocean floor has been found to have as varied relief as the continents. Mountain ranges, deep canyons, volcanoes, and plains are found in the ocean depths.

The **shoreline** is the line where land and sea meet. Shorelines represent the average position of sea level, determined over long periods of time. During the geologic past, sea level has not been constant. Seawater moved over the continents and covered much of the land which is now exposed. Seas also have retreated to much lower levels than they now occupy. But during historical times, sea level is considered to have been a relatively constant surface. Thus, it remains the most useful plane of reference from which to measure elevations.

Shorelines always lie within shore zones. They represent a mid-position between maximum tide and minimum tide. The shore zone includes the region lying between high and low tide. This zone varies from day to day, or sometimes from hour to hour, depending on wave height as well as maximum tide. Within the shore zone, materials are in constant motion, moved back and forth by incoming and outgoing waters.

Extending inland from the shoreline to the first major change in the land surface lies a strip of land known as the

coast. A coastal region may be several feet or several miles wide. It actually belongs to the continent, but it is linked to the sea by contact with waves and currents.

The **continental shelf** is that part of the continent which is covered by seawater. (Figure 11–8.) The shelf extends from the exposed rocks of the continent to the edge of the true ocean basin. At the present time, water overflows onto the shelf from a too-full ocean basin. The amount of overflow depends on the amount of water in the ocean basin, as well as on the size of the basin. During past geologic time, the width of the submerged shelf has varied with changes in sea level. Changes in sea level occur during periods of glaciation when water in the form of ice is trapped on the land. Sea level also rises or falls if the ocean basin is filled or enlarged. During mountain uplift, sea level falls. After erosion of the continents, the sea rises.

The **continental slope** is an abruptly sloping surface that separates the continents from the ocean basin. On its landward side, the continental slope merges with the continental shelf. On its seaward side, the continental slope descends to the ocean basin, where it joins the abyssal plain.

The **abyss** (a bis′) is the deepest part of the ocean. Its average depth is approximately 15,000 ft. Features of the ocean floor include mountains, trenches, volcanoes, and plains. *Abyssal plains* are almost level areas in the deepest portion of the ocean basin. Great gashes, or *trenches*, cut into the abyssal plain. Trenches of the ocean basin resemble the Grand Canyon of the Colorado River, the most notable surface feature of North America. However, many oceanic canyons are longer and deeper. The Grand Canyon is 4,000 ft to 5,500 ft or about one mile deep. The *Mariana* (mar ee an′a) *Trench*, which lies just off the Mariana Islands in the western Pacific Ocean, is at least 36,000 ft or about 7 mi deep. The *Tonga* (tahng′a) *Trench*, in the South Pacific Ocean, is about 35,000 ft deep. Many other trenches are known to be almost as deep as these two. Most of the deep trenches lie close to the edge of the ocean basin. They often are associated with volcanic islands just off the mainland.

Numerous *volcanic peaks* rise from the abyssal plain. Peaks may occur alone or in chains, and some of them extend above sea level to form islands. Other volcanoes that once were islands have sunk below the surface of the sea. Former islands can be recognized by their flat tops, which were eroded by waves while the land was above sea level.

The **continental shelf** is that part of the continent submerged beneath ocean waters.

Figure 11-11. Since the great ice age, returning meltwater has raised sea level about 400 feet; melting of all polar ice would raise sea level another 150 to 200 feet. What U.S. cities would be inundated?

The *mid-oceanic ridge* is the most extensive and grandest feature that rises from the abyssal plain. This ridge ranges from 300 mi to 1,200 mi across and extends for 40,000 mi. Its course wanders, or meanders, from the Atlantic Ocean through the Pacific Ocean. Starting from Iceland in the North Atlantic, the mid-oceanic ridge extends southward through the Atlantic Ocean. Then it turns eastward around Africa, and northward into the Indian Ocean. From there, the ridge turns southward again and passes between Australia and Antarctica and out into the South Pacific Ocean. The ridge passes northward and eventually reaches the coast of Alaska. One branch extends northward to the coast of North America, where it ends. Some peaks of the ridge reach the surface and form islands. Others are covered by several thousand feet of water.

A *rift zone*, or central crack, marks the middle of the ridge throughout its length. Earthquakes and volcanic activity are common within the rift zone. The crack is 20 mi to 30 mi wide and is bordered by vertical walls that plunge downward for approximately one mile. Many other ridges are present on the floor of the Pacific Ocean, but the mid-oceanic ridge is the grandest mountain chain on the planet earth!

The Pacific Ocean floor is broken by four major cracks, or *faults*. They extend for thousands of miles, roughly parallel to

The mid-oceanic range is broken by a steep-walled crack along its axis.

Figure 11-12.   Great faults parallel to latitude break the floor of the Pacific Ocean into huge segments.

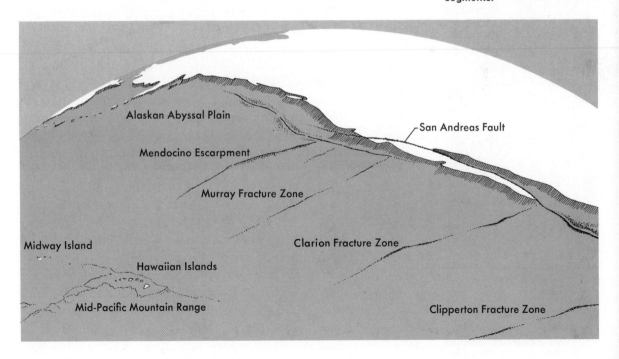

Alaskan Abyssal Plain

San Andreas Fault

Mendocino Escarpment

Murray Fracture Zone

Clarion Fracture Zone

Midway Island

Hawaiian Islands

Mid-Pacific Mountain Range

Clipperton Fracture Zone

lines of latitude. Many faults are bordered by steep cliffs that indicate vertical movement along the crack. The Hawaiian group of volcanic islands is associated with one of those great cracks. Along the fault, many earthquakes have been recorded just before volcanic eruptions. Such observations suggest that volcanic activity and earthquakes have related causes.

The ocean basin is not a quiet, uneventful environment. Instead, mountains rise from time to time, cracks form, and volcanic eruptions occur. Furthermore, the ocean basin receives sediments both from the land and from volcanic activity on the ocean floor.

11:5 *Deep-Sea Deposits*

Deposits in the ocean originate in the erosional debris of the continent, volcanic eruptions on the sea floor, falls of meteoric dust, and shells and coverings of marine organisms.

Sediments cover the ocean floor, except where the slopes of submarine mountains are too steep for the debris to withstand the pull of gravity. The average thickness of sediment is about 2,000 ft in the Atlantic Ocean and 1,000 ft in the Pacific Ocean. Many small submarine hills have been completely covered by sediments.

Approximately 3 billion tons of sediment are dumped into the oceans each year by the rivers of the world. Much of this material remains trapped on the continental shelf, but some is carried into the abyss. Deep-ocean sediment consists of meteoric dust, volcanic ash, some organic matter, and fine material carried seaward by winds.

Deposits on the abyssal plain are called **oozes** (ooz'es). At ocean depths of 2,000 ft to 13,000 ft oozes come primarily from plankton. At depths of 13,000 ft to 27,000 ft, these deposits contain mostly clay, with some quartz, mica, and iron stain. This material is so fine that individual grains can be identified only by use of X rays. Deep-ocean clay contains little organic matter, because calcitic shells are dissolved in deep waters. Carbon dioxide, which is in solution in relatively large amounts, plus the great pressure of the water help to dissolve calcite. Shark teeth and fish ear bones are two of the few recognizable animal remains.

Shells of calcite and coverings of silica overlay about half the ocean floor. This material is called **calcareous** (kal kar'ee us) **ooze** or **siliceous** (si lish'us) **ooze,** depending on which material is more abundant. Siliceous ooze, most of which comes from diatom coverings, is less abundant than calcareous ooze. However, some deposits of *diatomaceous* (die et a mae'shus) *earth* have been found on what is now land area. This proves that

Figure 11-13. Ball-shaped manganese nodules lie on the sea floor in the abyssal hills at a depth of 3,000 fathoms.

Bell Telephone Laboratories, Inc.

these deposits have been uplifted above sea level. Diatomaceous earth is a fine material which is used in filters and as an abrasive in toothpaste.

Meteoric dust, or "star dust," falls into the ocean and accumulates as part of ocean sediment. On land, such materials mingle with the soil and cannot be recognized. The meteoric origin of the dust in the ocean is quite apparent. Measuring this gives a clue to the total amount received by the earth. Other interesting materials found in the deep sea are manganese and iron **nodules** (nahj′ools), or lumps. Both manganese and iron are precipitated around cores of animal remains. Manganese is necessary to the manufacture of steel. Since little manganese is found on land, perhaps eventually the steel industry will turn to nodules from the sea floor for its manganese.

Coral reefs are deposits which usually occur in relatively shallow water and around mid-ocean volcanic islands in the Pacific. Reefs grow on solid rock in water below low tide level and no deeper than 150 ft. Coral is made from the skeletons and shells of tiny marine animals that live in colonies or apartment-like structures. Reefs occur only where water is salty, shallow, and clear. The water must be between 20°C and 26°C (68°F and 78°F) and be circulating freely to bring food to the stationary animals. Conditions favorable for reef growth occur in only a few parts of the ocean.

Reefs are begun when a coral attaches itself to a rock and then builds a shell around its body. This first shell serves as a base on which other marine animals can build. If the water is too deep, sunshine is not available. Then the organisms cannot live. If the water is too shallow, organisms may die because water circulation is insufficient to bring them their food. As corals multiply, many kinds of marine life are attracted to the reef. *Fringing reefs* grow on the borders of islands in mid-ocean or along the borders of continents where the continental shelf is especially narrow. *Barrier reefs* are built offshore at the edge of a wide continental shelf. They are separated from the mainland by a stretch of open, quiet water called a *lagoon*. An *atoll* (a′ tawl) is a ring of coral surrounding a lagoon. An atoll may be the last remnants of a fringing reef built around a sinking volcanic island. It also may be a new reef just beginning to be built around a rising island.

Geologists are especially interested in reefs because much of the world's oil has been found in ancient reefs. In many regions, these reefs have been buried beneath later sediments. Then

Figure 11-14. Coral reefs growing upward on the slopes of a subsiding volcanic island.

Fringing reef

Barrier reef

Atoll

wells must be drilled to depths of thousands of feet. Reefs record changes in sea level in their pattern of growth. In shallow water, reefs tend to grow outward toward the deeper ocean. In deepening water, reefs grow upward, sometimes for several thousand feet. If sea level rises, reefs may grow landward.

In spite of the vast size of the ocean and the great variety of its topography, ocean waters are surprisingly uniform in composition. Currents, tides, and waves are in constant motion, distributing heat and nutrients throughout the length and breadth of the ocean.

MAIN IDEAS

1. The hydrosphere includes water in the oceans, water vapor in the atmosphere, and all surface and near-surface water of the continents.

2. Sediments that accumulate on the continental shelves originate on the continents as a result of weathering and erosion of exposed rocks. These materials are carried to the ocean by wind and rivers and are deposited.

3. Most of the water of the hydrosphere probably was formed during volcanic eruptions and the cooling of the magma.

4. Ocean water contains elements derived from weathering of rocks, and from volcanic eruptions on the sea floor. Sodium chloride is the dominant compound in solution in seawater.

5. Marine life is classified by its habits and its environment. Plankton include floating protists, plants, and animals; nekton include swimming marine life; benthos include bottom dwellers.

6. Energy from the sun is made available to all marine life through photosynthesis, a life process of plants.

7. Shoreline is that line where land and sea meet along the average sea level.

8. The shore zone includes the region between high and low tide where sands are constantly moved about.

9. The continental slope is the steeply sloping boundary between continental shelf and ocean bottom.

10. The abyss is the deep part of the ocean, averaging about 12,000 ft to 15,000 ft deep, and marked by trenches 30,000 ft to over 36,000 ft deep. From the floor of the abyss rise

volcanic mountains and mountainous ridges which extend for thousands of miles. The major ridge is the mid-oceanic ridge that extends through both the Atlantic and Pacific oceans forming a continuous mountain range that is about 40,000 mi long.

11. Deep-ocean sediments include clay, calcareous and siliceous oozes, small amounts of organic matter, and nodules of iron and manganese.

12. Shallow water sediments include rock fragments, sand, and mud carried to the.sea by rivers, and limestone derived from shells and precipitates of marine organisms.

13. Marine organisms may build extensive reefs in warm, freely circulating, salt water which is no deeper than 150 ft. Ancient buried reefs often contain important petroleum deposits.

14. Although the ocean has many different characteristics, its composition remains fairly constant because of its continual circulation.

VOCABULARY

Write a sentence in which you use correctly each of the following words or terms.

abyss	lagoon	nutrient
atoll	larvae	ooze
benthos	mid-oceanic ridge	plankton
diatom	nekton	seismic
hydrologic cycle	nodule	shoreline

STUDY QUESTIONS

A. True or False

Determine whether each of the following sentences is true or false. (Do not write in this book.)

1. Water vapor in the atmosphere is a part of the hydrologic cycle.

2. Gases from the atmosphere are dissolved in ocean water.

3. Most river water contains only small amounts of salt in solution.

4. The Challenger survey proved that the ocean floor is not a smooth, plane surface.

5. Sea level never changes.

6. Volcanic activity and earthquakes are associated with the rift zone of the mid-oceanic ridge.

7. The amount of carbon dioxide in seawater increases as depth increases.

8. The Hawaiian Islands are true coral reefs.

9. Diatomaceous ooze is made of silica and clay.

10. No meteoric dust can be recognized in deep-sea sediments.

B. Multiple Choice

Choose the word or phrase which completes correctly each of the following sentences. (Do not write in this book.)

1. Whales are members of the (*plankton, benthos, nekton*).

2. Diatoms are classified as (*plankton, benthos, nekton*).

3. Oysters are classified as (*plankton, benthos, nekton*).

4. Water from the ocean basin overflows the continent on the (*continental shelf, continental slope, abyss*).

5. An island that lies on the mid-oceanic ridge is (*Greenland, Iceland, Newfoundland*).

6. Eventually the steel industry may use deep-sea deposits of (*manganese, calcium carbonate, magnesium*).

7. Rock density of the ocean floor is determined by means of (*seismic surveys, echo sounding, sonar devices*).

8. Ocean floor deposits at depths over 20,000 ft might contain (*shark teeth, oyster shells, whale skeletons*).

9. Most of the sediment from the land is deposited in the ocean on the (*continental shelf, continental slope, abyss*).

10. Reefs built around volcanic islands of the Pacific are called (*fringing reefs, barrier reefs, atolls*).

C. Completion

Complete each of the following sentences with a word or phrase which will make the sentence correct. (Do not write in this book.)

1. When sodium chloride crystallizes from a solution, it forms the mineral ___?___.

2. Fish use less energy for food-getting than land animals because of the ___?___ of the water.

3. The most abundant plankton are the ___?___.

4. Animals that attach themselves to the bottom of the ocean in the near-shore zone are called ___?___.

5. Echo sounding is a method of mapping the ocean bottom which uses ___?___.

6. Coverings of diatoms are made of ___?___.

7. Coral reefs are predominantly made of ___?___.

8. Fine-grained deposits on the ocean floor are called ___?___.

9. Velocity of sound in water is ___?___.

10. The average height of the sea or zero elevation where land and sea meet is called ___?___.

D. How and Why

1. Folklore tells about the mysterious appearance or disappearance of islands in the ocean. Is there any basis for such tales? Discuss possible reasons for occurrences of such islands.

2. If the hydrologic cycle continuously brings fresh water to the continents, why should desalting of ocean water be considered necessary for future water demands?

3. If you planned to take a core sample from the mantle of the earth, where would you drill in order to go through the least amount of crustal material?

4. Discuss some of the difficulties of underwater exploration.

5. Would you expect to find coral reefs growing around the volcanoes off the coast of Alaska? Explain your answer.

6. What information can be obtained from a seismographic survey that cannot be determined by echo sounding or sonar recording?

7. What is the origin of the sediments that accumulate in the shore zone? Discuss the changes that granite undergoes in order to furnish sediment to the continental shelf area.

8. What happens to the carbon dioxide in solution in seawater? Why is carbon dioxide less abundant in the near-surface waters?

9. Why can the percentage of meteoric dust in deep-sea ooze be determined although there is little evidence of meteoric dust on the continents?

10. Suggest reasons why Florida has its coral reefs growing around the area of the Keys, but the Louisiana and Texas coasts have no comparable coral development.

INVESTIGATIONS

1. Report on some inhabitant of the sea that you find especially interesting.

2. Read the authentic information about whales in the complete edition of *Moby Dick* by Herman Melville.

3. Arrange a display of various seashells or fossil shells and plant impressions from lake shores.

4. Prepare a report discussing either a potential food or a mineral resource which eventually may be derived from the ocean.

INTERESTING READING

Berrill, Norman J., *The Living Tide*. New York, Fawcett Publications, Inc., 1956.

Berganst, Erik, and Foss, William, *Oceanographers in Action*. New York, G. P. Putnam's Sons, 1968.

Blanchard, Duncan C., *From Raindrops to Volcanoes: Adventures With Sea Surface Meteorology*. Garden City, N. Y., Doubleday & Company, Inc., 1967.

Carson, Rachel, *The Sea Around Us*, rev. ed. New York, Oxford University Press, Inc., 1961.

Cromie, W. J., *Living World of the Sea*. Englewood Cliffs, N.J., Prentice-Hall, Inc., 1966.

Dubach, Harold W., and Taber, Robert W., *Questions About The Oceans*. U. S. Naval Oceanographic Office Publication G-13, 1968.

Guberlet, Muriel L., *Explorers of the Sea: Famous Oceanographic Expeditions*. New York, Ronald Press Company, 1964.

Idyll, C. P., *Abyss: The Deep Sea and the Creatures that Live in it*. New York, Thomas Y. Crowell Company, 1964.

Marx, Wesley, *The Frail Ocean*. New York, Coward-McCann, Inc., 1967.

Telfer, Dorothy, *Exploring the World of Oceanography*. Chicago, Children's Press, 1968.

Circulation of Ocean Water

12

Circulation of ocean water resembles the circulation pattern of the atmosphere. Water, heated at the equator, expands and spreads out on the surface. At the poles, cold, dense water sinks to the ocean floor and flows toward the less dense waters of the equator. But currents are not simple north-south movements. Like air, ocean waters are deflected by the rotation of the earth.

Circulation of ocean water influences the climate of the earth and warms the land adjacent to the sea. Currents distribute both heat and dissolved substances from place to place. Currents are responsible for distributing food to marine animals.

12:1 *Major Circulation Patterns*

Surface currents are set in motion in the tropics by the powerful trade winds and by differences between the density of tropical waters and polar waters. Cold water is more dense than warm water. Furthermore, sea level is slightly higher in the tropics than in polar latitudes and water tends to flow down this slight decline. Sea level is a few inches higher in the tropics because daily rainfall adds water to the surface of the sea faster than the water can spread out horizontally. Also, heat from the sun causes tropical waters to expand and to have a greater volume than polar waters.

Trade winds, the easterlies, blow steadily from northeast to southwest in the northern hemisphere. They blow from southeast to northwest in the southern hemisphere. Trade winds drive the ocean waters before them. But rotation of the earth deflects ocean currents even more than it does air currents.

In the tropics, currents flow westward until they meet the continents, then poleward, then eastward, and finally southward to the tropics.

Movement at the surface of the sea is almost due west in both hemispheres in the zone of the trade winds.

The westward moving currents meet the continents which form barriers. Water is turned toward the north and toward the south. Along the eastern coast of North America, the Gulf Stream, a warm, swift current, carries water northward. The Brazil Current moves water southward along the eastern coast of South America. Similar currents in the Pacific Ocean carry water along the eastern coast of Asia. (Figure 12–1.)

In both hemispheres, the surface currents move poleward until they reach the zone of the westerly winds. Then the currents are carried eastward in front of the westerlies until they meet another continent. When eastward moving currents come in contact with a continent, some water flows poleward. The rest flows toward the equator. In the zone of the trade winds, this water meets and joins the westward flowing currents. Major surface currents follow a circular path around a central,

Figure 12-1. The complicated patterns of ocean surface currents are determined by the force and direction of the winds and by land masses which act as barriers to the currents.

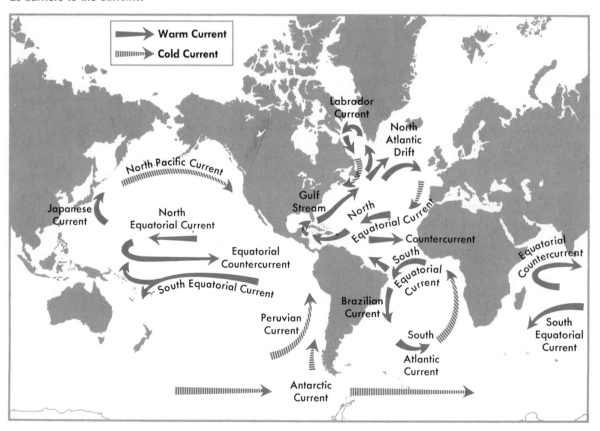

relatively quiet body of water in both the Atlantic and Pacific oceans. (Figure 12–1.) Within this quiet zone, circulation is too slow to supply food for marine organisms.

Deep ocean currents begin their movement in the polar regions. Cold, dense water slides toward the bottom of the sea and then flows slowly toward the equator. However, some water flows just beneath the surface currents but in a direction opposite to the surface currents. Movement of cold, dense water is always toward regions of lower density. As water moves at depth toward regions of lower density, some of the replaced water is forced toward the surface.

Upwellings or **rising currents** of cold water carry unused nutrients to the surface. There the nutrients are available to plankton. The Grand Banks of the North Atlantic have an abundant fish population due to such upwellings. Another famous upwelling occurs in the Pacific Ocean just off the coast of Peru. Here strong winds blow from the coast and send surface waters flowing oceanward. Water rises from great depths to replace the surface water which has moved away from the shore.

Upwellings of cold water bring a supply of food for plankton. Plankton, in turn, become food for fish. Because of the abundance of fish, hosts of birds nest along the nearby coast. Bird droppings are the basis for a large-scale fertilizer business. The abundance of fish makes fishing an important industry. Occasionally, the upwelling ceases. This causes a widespread depression in both the fertilizer and the fish industries throughout coastal areas of Peru and Chile.

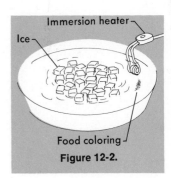

Figure 12-2.

ACTIVITY. Put several dozen ice cubes in the center of a large pan and fill it with water. Heat the water with an immersion heater placed just below the surface, or with a Bunsen burner placed at one side of the container. Add a cinnamon candy or food coloring to the water close to the heater. Draw a diagram to illustrate the movement of the color. What kind of currents are these? What causes the movement?

12:2 *Local Currents*

Both major surface currents and deep ocean currents are due to differences in density. But **density currents** occur whenever and wherever some ocean water becomes heavier than adjacent water. Many local density currents are present in the

Differences in density cause the major circulation pattern and many local currents in the ocean.

Seawater becomes less dense as it is heated, or diluted by fresh water from rivers or rain.

Seawater becomes more dense as it is cooled, as evaporation occurs, and as surface waters freeze and leave salt behind.

ocean. Some of these currents are complex and cannot be traced by present methods. Others have been recognized by navigators for many years.

Differences in density may have several causes. Surface waters become less dense than average seawater. For example, surface waters may be diluted by melting ice in polar regions. They also may be diluted by rivers that empty into the sea. Or excessive rainfall, such as occurs near the equator, may freshen the surface of the ocean.

On the other hand, density may be increased when salts are added to average seawater. When seawater freezes, its salts are left behind in the water just below the ice. Thus, this water becomes heavy and dense. Evaporation also causes concentration of brines. The dissolved salts are concentrated in a smaller volume of seawater.

A density current caused by evaporation is located in the Mediterranean Sea. A submerged ridge lies across the Straits of Gibraltar. This ridge makes the Mediterranean Sea an evaporite basin almost isolated from the Atlantic Ocean. Because few rivers flow into the Mediterranean Sea, little fresh water is added. Furthermore, the warm dry climate of the region causes evaporation of an enormous quantity of water. Without additions of fresh water, the Mediterranean brine becomes more and more dense. As the dense surface brine sinks to the bottom, it pushes the bottom layer of water across the ridge and out into the Atlantic Ocean. This deep current of heavy brine spreads westward as far as the Bahama Islands. At the surface, less dense water from the Atlantic flows across the ridge into the Mediterranean Sea. There it replaces water lost at depth.

Figure 12-3. In the Mediterranean Sea, currents flow toward the Atlantic at depth, and from the Atlantic at the surface due to difference in density.

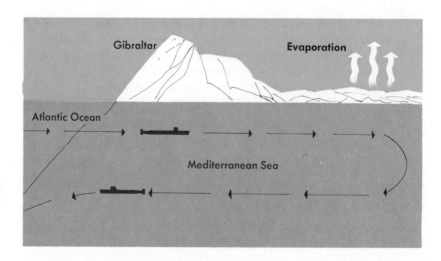

During World War II, many submerged German submarines escaped detection by turning off their engines and silently riding the currents into and out of the Mediterranean.

Turbidity (tur bid'it ee) **currents** are unique density currents. They are made dense by suspended mud and sand. Turbidity currents flow across and erode the ocean bottom. Turbidity currents have cut many gorges on the continental shelf, on the slopes of submerged volcanoes, and on the continental slope. These gorges resemble river valleys. Some of them appear to be extensions of channels of large rivers such as the Mississippi, the Congo, and the Ganges. During flooding, such rivers carry large quantities of sediment from the land to the sea. Flood waters then may be heavier than the ocean brine. They continue to flow across the shelf and slope as rivers of mud. Such rivers of mud are called turbidity currents. They scour out channels on the ocean bottom as they flow across it.

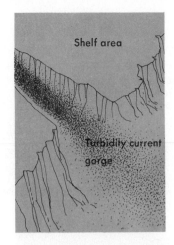

Figure 12-4. Turbidity currents erode channels along the continental slope.

Not all gorges or channels, however, are associated with rivers. Many channels begin rather abruptly at the edge of the continental slope. They may occur on submerged volcanoes in mid-ocean. The first clue to the origin of such channels was supplied in 1929 during an earthquake off the coast of Newfoundland. Immediately following the quake, telephone and telegraph cables on the ocean floor broke. Cables nearest the center of the earthquake snapped first. Others broke at successive intervals and distances. In regular succession, breaks occurred in cables lying farther and farther away from the center of the quake. Apparently the earthquake vibrations caused sediments lying on the steep continental slopes to slump downward. At the foot of the continental slope, a great bulge of debris was deposited. Deposits consisted of coarse sand, gravel, and shallow-water fossils. These coarse materials were out of place among the ooze and clay of the abyss. Undoubtedly, this debris had been carried to the ocean depths by turbidity currents. The velocity of the currents was reduced at the foot of the slope. There the materials were dropped in a fan-shaped bulge. Similarly shaped deposits may be found at the foot of steep mountain slopes on land.

Discovery of turbidity current deposits has helped geologists to interpret many deposits of rock now found exposed on continents. For example, similar rocks now exposed in the California mountains appear to be deposits made by turbidity currents. Apparently the rocks were uplifted during mountain building and later uncovered by weathering and erosion.

Some turbidity currents are associated with rivers from the continent; some result from landslide-type slumps.

Turbidity currents deposit fan-shaped bulges at the foot of the continental slope.

12:3　Ocean Waves

Oscillatory waves are deep water waves in which water particles orbit in a circle.

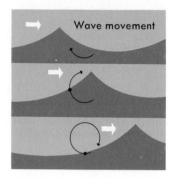

Figure 12-5. A water particle moves upward with the wave crest, then downward with the trough.

Ocean waves are *undulating* (un'ja laet ing), or alternately rising and falling, movements of seawater. Similar waves may be produced in any body of water. In the sea, waves may be initiated by winds, earthquakes, or tides.

Deep-water waves are called **oscillatory** (ah sil'a tohr ee) **waves** because the water fluctuates. It swings from a high to a low to a high point. In deep water, the wave itself moves forward, but the water particles remain in place. Water particles travel in circles and return to their starting points as the wave moves onward. The diameter of the orbit of the surface water particles is exactly equal to the height of the wave. Below the surface, water particles move in smaller and smaller circles. (Figure 12–6.) Motion is passed downward from one water particle to another. But eventually, motion ceases.

Waves are described by several features. The *crest* is the highest point of a wave. Its lowest point is the *trough*. *Wave height* is the vertical distance between crest and trough. *Wavelength* is the horizontal distance between successive crests, or successive troughs. *Wave period* is the length of time required for successive crests (or troughs) to travel past a given point. Therefore, wavelength and wave period are dependent upon one another. *Wave base* is the depth at which wave motion ceases. This is one-half the wavelength. (Figure 12–6.)

In mid-ocean depths, most water particles complete their orbits without contacting the ocean bottom. There most waves are deep-water waves. **Shallow-water waves** form where water depth is less than half the wavelength. Tides are shallow-water waves, even in mid-ocean. Their wave base is so deep that even

Figure 12-6. In deep water, a particle orbits in place, but the wave form moves onward.

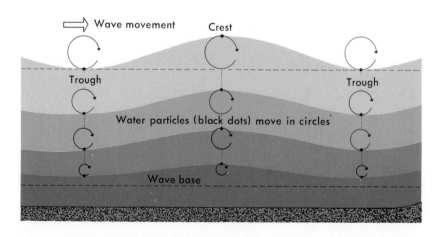

Wave movement　　Crest

Trough　　　　　　　　　　　　　　　　　Trough

Water particles (black dots) move in circles

Wave base

15,000 ft of water is less than half the wavelength. Unlike deep-water waves, shallow-water waves come in contact with the bottom. Thus, water particles cannot complete their circular orbits. Instead, the water particles are slowed down at the bottom of the orbit, which becomes an ellipse. The elliptical shape of the orbit increases the wave height. (Figure 12–7.)

Tides are shallow-water waves in mid-ocean, but wind-formed waves are oscillatory or deep-water waves. Wind-formed waves become shallow-water waves only when they reach the continental shelf. There water depths range from about 200 ft to zero feet at the shoreline. Waves strike bottom somewhere within these depth ranges.

The first line of waves to strike bottom is slowed down. But the velocity of the following waves is not changed, and the distance between waves is shortened. As wavelength decreases, wave height increases. The volume of water that originally was spread out over the longer wavelength is compressed into the shorter distance. Water can only rise and, as a result, water piles higher and higher until it is pulled down by gravity. As the crest falls, all the wave energy is directed toward the bottom. Each wave tumbles, strikes bottom, and stirs up loose debris. The zone in which waves first fall is known as the *breaker zone*. Between the first breaking wave and the shore is the *surf zone*. There waves form and re-form many times. Each new wave eventually arrives in water too shallow for its wavelength. It falls, re-forms, and falls again. Loose debris is tossed into the following wave and carried forward a short distance. Sand is always in motion in the water between the breaker zone and the shoreline.

Shallow-water waves come in contact with the ocean bottom and break, or topple over.

Energy of breaking waves is directed toward the bottom where loose material is eroded.

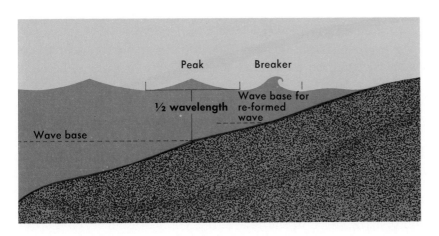

Figure 12-7. In shallow water, the wave base comes in contact with the bottom, causing waves to break.

Wind waves are caused by air that blows across bodies of standing water. Wind moves in a turbulent or tumbling fashion because of differences in temperature and pressure from place to place. Warm air rises, cold air descends, and air moves toward areas of least pressure. Many of these differences are local. Consequently, air is always in motion—upward, downward, and forward. Turbulent motion is passed on to the surface of the water as water particles are pushed downward and forward by the wind. Once waves are started, they increase in height as more and more surface comes in contact with the wind. Some time is required before waves develop a regular pattern. But once established, waves continue to move forward long after the wind ceases to blow. Energy is transferred from wind to water. Movement persists until all of the energy has dissipated by motion or by friction. The height of the waves depends on wind velocity, size of the water body, and length of time the wind blows.

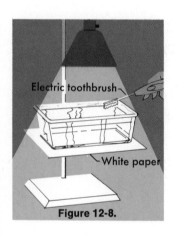

Figure 12-8.

ACTIVITY. Put a large piece of white paper on a ring stand. Set a Pyrex loaf cake pan filled with water on the paper. Turn on an overhead light source so that it shines directly on the pan without casting a shadow. Now start an electric toothbrush vibrating and immerse the brush just beneath the surface of the water. Observe the waves as they begin to move, and as they reach the edge of the pan. What happens to the waves as they reach the far end of the pan? What happens to the waves as they reach the sides of the pan? Observe the white paper beneath the pan. What pattern do the shadows of the waves make? Which waves are reflected? Does the speed of the waves increase or decrease with distance from the source of vibration?

A **tsunami** (seu nahm′ee) is a unique wave that is caused by a rapid shift of the ocean floor during an earthquake. Some tsunamis may be associated with volcanic eruptions, because volcanic activity often is preceded by a crack in the earth's crust. Vibrations set up by an earthquake cause water to move back and forth, or oscillate. Minor earthquakes initiate small waves, but major earthquakes produce waves that may travel halfway around the earth.

In mid-ocean, the tsunami is no higher than many wind waves. But the wavelength is great and the wave base is deep. Each wave includes tremendous amounts of water that crash against the shore in shallow water. On shore, no ocean distur-

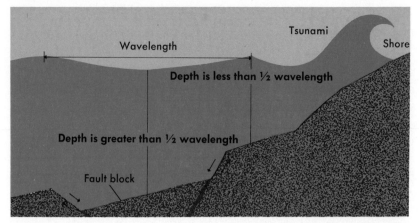

Figure 12-9. As the tsunami approaches shallow water, the wave crest heightens and a great wall of water washes over the shore.

bance is more destructive than a tsunami, or *seismic sea wave.* The first indication of the approach of a tsunami is withdrawal of water from the shore zone. Withdrawal accompanies the arrival of a low trough. Next a great crest arrives. This is often a towering wave capable of carrying ocean liners onto the shore and leaving them stranded. No protection is possible from such immense waves. Safety lies in leaving the area before the waves arrive.

Today when an earthquake occurs, it is recorded by seismographic stations. These stations cooperate throughout the world to warn coastal towns of the danger of an approaching tsunami. Notice of the earthquake is sent to all coastal stations that measure tides. Stations are requested to report unusual water levels which might indicate that a seismic sea wave is developing. If any unusual wave heights are reported, all coastal cities and towns are warned. Close cooperation between seismographic stations makes it possible to estimate the travel time of the wave. Thus, it is possible to predict when the tsunami will arrive at various cities in its path. During the Chilean earthquake of 1960, early warning of the approach of the tsunami saved many lives. Hilo, Hawaii, suffered extensive damage from 15-ft waves that swept away much of the city. However, the warning arrived in time, and there were few victims. When the same great wave reached Japan, either the warnings were not heard or they were ignored, and 180 people died.

Tsunami waves cause great destruction when they reach shore because their wave base is very deep, and the waves are very high.

12:4 *Tides*

Tides, like tsunamis, are waves that travel across the ocean. Unlike tsunamis, tides are a daily occurrence and not destructive. **Tides** are rhythmic movements of ocean water caused by the gravitational attraction between the earth, moon, and sun. Tides are waves with exceptionally long periods and great wavelengths. Crests reach shore approximately 12 hours apart, although this period varies somewhat from day to day. Tides affect the ocean from surface to bottom. Actually, tides are shallow-water waves, because their wave base comes in contact with the ocean floor. However, in mid-ocean the tide cannot be distinguished from a normal wind wave. Only when the tide approaches the shoreline, can the rise and fall of water be observed.

On low, gently sloping shores, tides move in and out with little effect. But on irregular coastlines, tides may be exceptionally high. For example, tides rise over 40 ft in the Bay of Fundy, Nova Scotia. Here the incoming water advances through a small opening into a funnel-shaped bay. Water cannot return readily to the ocean. It is confined by the land along

Tides are shallow-water waves because their wave bases reach bottom, even in mid-ocean.

Figure 12-10. Bay of Fundy tides are among the highest in the world: a. high tide, b. low tide.

NFB Photos by G. Blouin

the opening and blocked by the advancing tide. Eventually, the water returns to normal sea level, as the tide goes out. Along the nearby coast, where the shore is wide and smooth, the tide rises only one or two feet. Such irregular heights in the tides are due to the shape of the coast.

Tides are bulges of water which form on earth at all times. A large bulge forms on the side of the earth facing the moon. A smaller bulge forms on the side away from the moon. Water to fill the bulges is drawn from the area between them.

High tides occur on the side of the earth facing the moon.

Both the moon and the sun attract the earth and produce tides. However, the effect of the moon on the tides is much greater than the effect of the sun. This is because the moon is so much closer to the earth. The distance from earth to sun is approximately 93,000,000 mi. Compared to these millions of miles, the 8,000-mi diameter of the earth is extremely small. Consequently, the sun's gravitational attraction for the earth is distributed fairly evenly over the entire earth. By contrast, the moon is only about 238,800 mi from the earth. The moon has a strong attraction for the near side of the earth and a weaker attraction for the far side. Recall that the gravitational attraction between two bodies decreases in proportion to the square of the distance between them. (Section 1:3.)

Due to the moon's gravitational attraction, a bulge of ocean water always faces the moon. Water particles from adjacent areas add to the bulge as they flow toward this position of greatest attraction. All the earth's matter is attracted to the moon, but solid rock particles cannot flow readily. The portion of the earth's crust facing the moon rises only a few inches in response to the moon's attraction. On the other hand, water rises several feet. A major high tide represents the difference between the crust and ocean bulges.

On the side of the earth away from the moon, a second bulge of water occurs. This bulge results partly from centrifugal force developed during the earth's revolution around the sun. Recall that centrifugal force causes a revolving object to tend to fly away from the center around which the object revolves. (Section 2:1.) The earth itself has developed an equatorial bulge due to the centrifugal force developed by rotation on its axis. (Section 2:1.) The tidal bulge, however, results from the centrifugal force that tends to carry the earth away from its position in the solar system. At the same time, earth's position is fixed by the gravitational attraction between earth and its moon and between earth and the sun.

A lesser high tide occurs on the side of the earth away from the moon.

On the far side of the earth, centrifugal force overbalances, to some extent, the effect of gravity. A bulge of water occurs as water from adjacent areas moves toward this position of maximum centrifugal force. Some scientists believe that rock particles on the ocean floor are pulled toward the moon. This is because the ocean floor on the side away from the moon is closer to the moon than the ocean surface. (Figure 12–11.) Thus, a slight depression exists on the sea floor. Water rushes in and piles up to form the bulge. However, centrifugal force is probably the controlling or major influence in this tug-of-war between opposing forces.

Although the moon is the dominant force causing tides, the sun also has some effect on the tides. When earth, sun, and moon are in line with each other, the added gravitational attraction of the sun causes especially high tides. These tides are called **spring tides** but they are not related to the spring season. Instead spring tides occur twice each month, when the sun and moon are lined up on the same side or on opposite sides of the earth. When the sun and moon are at right angles to each other, their forces of gravity tend to counterbalance. Then bulges are less than normal and the tide is called a **neap tide.** Spring tides occur during the full moon and new moon positions. Neap tides are associated with first-quarter and third-quarter moon positions.

Figure 12-11. Maximum tides occur when sun and moon combine their gravitational pull; minimum tides occur when they pull at right angles.

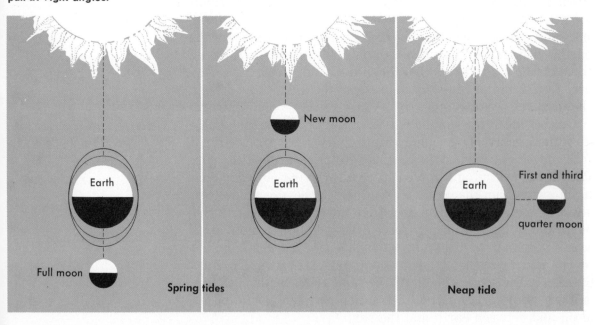

New moon

Earth

Earth

Earth

First and third

quarter moon

Full moon

Spring tides

Neap tide

Tidal bulges remain in approximately the same position relative to the earth, sun, and moon. But because the earth turns on its axis, different points on earth are affected by the high and low positions of the tides. As the earth turns on its axis, first it passes beneath the bulge facing the moon. Then it passes beneath a low tide. Continuing, it passes beneath a second high tide, a second low tide, and back to high tide again. This complete tidal cycle requires approximately 24½ hours. Recall that it requires about 29 days for the moon to orbit the earth. Consequently, during the 24 hours required for the rotation of the earth, the moon has changed its position slightly. It has moved in its orbit beyond the position from which rotation started.

Elapsed time between two successive maximum high tides is approximately 24½ hours.

ACTIVITY. Locate daily tide listings for a port city such as New York, Miami, Galveston, San Francisco, or Los Angeles. If such listings are not readily available, use the following data.

Low	High	Low	High
2:38 A.M.	8:56 A.M.	3:09 P.M.	10:32 P.M.
3:08 A.M.	9:30 A.M.	5:00 P.M.	11:34 P.M.
3:43 A.M.	10:11 A.M.	5:57 P.M.	12:56 A.M.
4:26 A.M.			

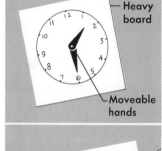

Make a large clock face on a piece of heavy cardboard. Show the time at which each tide occurs, indicating by H or L the kind of tide. If you live near a coast, record the tides for one month. Otherwise, determine from the listings given the number of days for which you have data. How much time elapses between high tides? Compare the time elapsed from high tide to high tide over a full day for each of the above cycles. Why do the tides require more than 24 hours in their cycle? How does the elapsed time between high tides compare to the elapsed time between low tides?

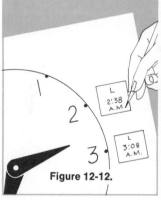

Figure 12-12.

12:5 *Shore Processes*

Tides, wind waves, and ocean currents cause ocean water to be continuously in motion. Waves carry water onto the shore, but water moved onto the shore returns to the sea. Along the shore, retreating water creates local currents unrelated to the major circulation pattern of the ocean.

Figure 12-13. At Cape Kiwanda, Oregon, Pacific Ocean waves have worn away rock shores to form these steep walls.

Waves erode by the force of water dashing against the coast and by abrasion.

Tidal scour deepens narrow channels.

Waves tend to wear away coastal materials. Boulders are broken off from rocky shores by the force of water dashed against the coast. During storms, waves pound the shore zone with tremendous force. Before flowing back to sea, water may enter cracks and crevices and enlarge the openings into caves. Waves also have *abrasive* (a brae'siv), or cutting, *action* as they roll rock fragments back and forth across the shore zone. Rock fragments are worn smaller and smaller in the shore zone. Eventually, the fragments may be carried away. Some solution also occurs, but abrasion causes most coastal destruction.

Flat, smooth *benches* are carved into rocky shores just below sea level. Above sea level, storm waves cut *notched cliffs* into the hard rock of some coasts. Occasionally, *stacks* are left as isolated, upstanding blocks of rock which remain after less resistant (ri zis'tent) rock has been worn away.

Tides scour deep *gouges* (gauhj'es) in narrow channels. The velocity of the water is increased when the tide is confined to small, narrow openings. Both incoming and outgoing tides tend to deepen such channels in a process called *tidal scour*. This process is effective even in hard rock if sediments are available for abrasive action. Tidal scour cuts many channels in soft rock and in reef materials.

When tides and storm waves move in the same direction, surges of water pile up on shore and do great damage. Especially during hurricanes the damage is great. Then water is

Figure 12-14. In this case, storm waves have undercut a rocky shore and produced a notched cliff above the bench carved beneath the waves. Offshore a stack has escaped the forces of erosion.

Stack forming

Bench (not observed at high tide—extends about to breaker line)

Notched cliff (reached only by storm wave)

Stack

a.

b.

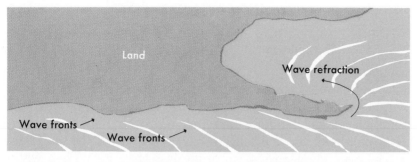

Figure 12-15. Waves approaching the shore at an angle are bent parallel to the coastline.

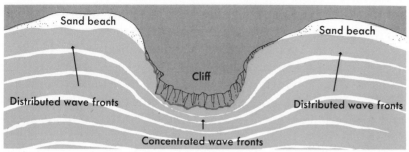

Figure 12-16. As headlands are eroded, they supply sediment for beaches in adjacent bays.

prevented from returning to the sea by the force of onshore winds. Eventually, water flows back to the ocean, carrying debris with it.

Along irregular coasts, wave energy is concentrated on headlands. *Headlands* are projections of land that extend into deep water. Waves wear headlands down faster than adjacent indentations or bays. Because waves tend to concentrate their energy on headlands, the energy of the waves is spent by the time they reach the bays. Some coasts have steep cliffs which are eroded slowly because waves strike the shore at an angle of 90°. If waves strike a steep cliff head-on, they are reflected toward the ocean and die out. Such waves cause little erosion along a shore. For this reason, vertical breakwaters are built along some shores. *Breakwaters*, like steep cliffs, reflect waves and protect the shore zone behind them. However, this type of protection is effective only if wind direction is relatively constant. If winds blow first from one direction, then from another, waves at some time strike breakwaters at an angle and erode them.

Waves are bent, or *refracted* (ri frakt'ed), as they swing around headlands. The velocity of the waves decreases when they collide with these projections of land. In adjacent bays, waves continue to move forward with their original speed. Wave fronts resemble marching groups that swing around pivot men to turn a corner. No matter what their original direction, when waves reach shore they tend to align nearly parallel

Headlands are eroded by waves that strike them at an angle.

Loose material eroded from headlands is deposited as beaches in adjacent bays.

Waves are refracted when a part of the wave reaches shallow water and is slowed down; the rest of the wave continues moving at its original velocity and catches up.

Waves may be reflected oceanward if they strike the shore at a 90° angle. Waves that strike the shore at an angle of less than 90° are deflected at an angle to the shore.

to it. However, even a small angle of reflection means that water returns to the sea some distance from where the wave carried it onshore.

Gravity pulls water back down the shore slope toward the sea. Movement of water as it returns to the sea forms local currents known as **longshore currents.** Waves that strike the shore at an angle of 90° are reflected directly toward the sea. Some waves meet the shore at an angle less than 90°. Then water returns to the sea some distance from the place where it strikes the shore. Incoming waves interfere with the return of water to the sea and turn the current aside. Reflection of the wave and interference by approaching waves causes longshore currents to flow downwind almost parallel to the shore. (Figure 12–17.) Longshore currents increase in strength as headlands and projections are worn away. Eventually, currents cease to follow the indentations of the shore. Instead, they flow down the beach in the direction in which they started. When the longshore current reaches deep water at the mouth of an indentation, its velocity decreases. Then debris carried by the current is dropped to the ocean floor.

Longshore currents transport sediment parallel to the shore in a downwind direction.

Because water is always pulled seaward by gravity, even longshore currents eventually move toward the open ocean. When the current finds a break in the wave front, it escapes seaward through the break and becomes a **rip current.** Rip currents are not a hazard on gently sloping shores. Rip currents are dangerous if wave action is strong or if the slope of the sea floor is steep, as it is along some parts of the California coast. These narrow currents flow perpendicular to the shoreline. If

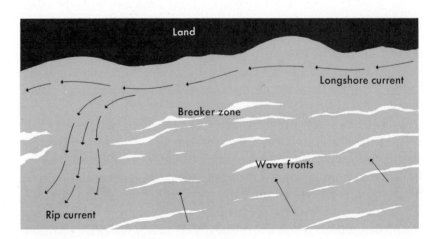

Figure 12-17. **Rip currents carry water seaward as they break through an opening in the approaching wave front.**

a person swims across the rip current, he soon should be able to reach less dangerous waters.

Not all water moves seaward as longshore currents or as rip currents. Some water moves seaward in a thin layer near the bottom. This movement is slow, but even a gentle **bottom current** moves sediment across the shelf toward the ocean basin. Dangerous surface currents are common around *jetties* (jet'ees) and breakwaters where these artificial projections interfere with normal wave motion.

Some water returns seaward along the ocean bottom.

12:6 *Shore Deposits*

Coasts consisting of hard rock usually have steep cliffs. Coasts consisting of sand usually have gentle slopes toward the sea.

Steep cliffs commonly occur where hard rock is exposed along the coast. Around the base of the cliff, boulders eroded from the cliffs often form ridges or beaches. Shores that consist of sand have relatively gentle slopes because sand cannot withstand wave action or support itself on steep slopes.

Loose material along the shore zone is brought to the shore by rivers. Other debris is eroded from the coast by wave action. Waves and currents sort these shore materials according to size. Fragments too large to be carried are left in place. Smaller fragments are carried along the shore, onto the continental shelf, or even to the continental slope. Some of the finest particles reach the abyss. Weak waves remove little debris. Strong waves and currents may remove and redeposit large quantities of sediment. Both the energy of the waves and currents and the amount of material in the shore zone determine what happens to the debris.

Beaches are deposits of loose material laid down parallel to the shore line. Beaches extend seaward to about 30 ft below mean tide level. They extend landward to the coastline. Much of the material in the upper part of the beach is kept in motion by waves.

Beach materials vary with the source rock.

Beach materials depend on the kind of rock which is exposed along the coast. If the rock is limestone, the beach will consist of lime fragments. Lime sand often is called "coral sand," although the material may not come from coral deposits. If basalt is exposed at the shore, beaches will consist of black sands or fragments of basalt. Some parts of the Oregon Coast and the Islands of Hawaii have black sand beaches. If waves erode granite or sandstone, the dominant beach material will be quartz grains, possibly with some feldspar. Most beaches in

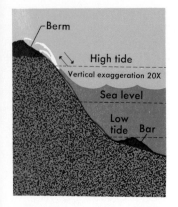

Figure 12-18. Storm waves leave a ridge of sand or gravel on the shore above the high tide level.

the United States are made of quartz sand grains. In the Bahama Islands, white beaches, often called "coral sand," are made of limestone.

Recently formed beaches are usually narrow and shallow. They form only a thin cover over the hard rocks below. Such beaches commonly consist of large boulders or gravel. New beaches often are swept away by winter storms, then built during the summer.

Beaches that have been exposed to the waves for a long time consist of fine sediments. In time, beaches become a permanent part of the shore, with a broad, deep berm. A **berm** is a ridge made of gravel or sand carried onto the shore during exceptional storms. It is the most familiar part of the beach, because the berm is above sea level. Berms are deposited above the shoreline by waves that splash over them continually. Waves keep the seaward slope of the berm gentle. However, the back slope is steep because materials are pushed over the high point of the ridge and then roll down the landward side. (Figure 12–18.)

Bars and spits are deposits of sand across a bay or indentation of the shore. *Spits* are deposits attached to the land at only one end. *Bars* are built completely across the mouth of a bay and are attached to the mainland at both ends. Bars and spits are composed of material that is eroded from the headlands and carried into the bays by the longshore current. Debris is deposited at the head of a bay where the current flows into quiet water.

Figure 12-19. Longshore currents lose velocity and drop their load of sediment in the deeper water of the bays and indentations.

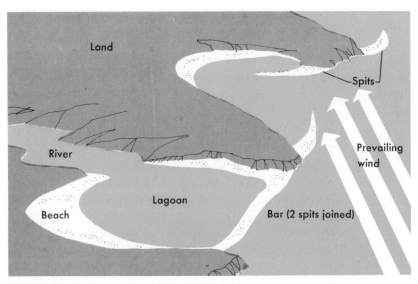

During the development of a shore, headlands are worn away and bays are cut off by bars and spits. In the early stages of development, headlands are prominent. Then the longshore current sweeps into the bay and deposits beaches adjacent to the headland. Later in the history of the shoreline, bars and spits are deposited across the mouth of the bay. Then the longshore current no longer enters the bay.

Bars and spits also may be built where rivers empty great quantities of sediment at the shore. This material is redistributed beyond the river mouth by the longshore current. Eventually, the river mouth may be completely blocked by a bar. Water trapped behind the bar forms a lagoon. The lagoon may become filled by river deposits or organic material, or by evaporites. If strong tidal currents are present, a connection with the sea may be maintained by the process of tidal scour.

Lagoons are bodies of water parallel to the shore and behind a bar or spit.

Barrier islands are offshore deposits of sand that parallel the shore. Barrier islands develop from sand ridges that are formed under water by breaking waves. Such ridges form at various depths, depending on where the waves tend to break. Underwater ridges near shore are only about one foot below mean water level. Occasionally, hurricanes dump great quantities of sand on these ridges and raise them above sea level. Once exposed, sand from the ridge may be blown into dunes. Then the ridge becomes a true *island* and presents a new shore zone to the sea. The new shore zone is widened by the growth of a berm, and the island is lengthened by the growth of spits.

Barrier islands are deposits of sand lying seaward from the mainland and separate from it.

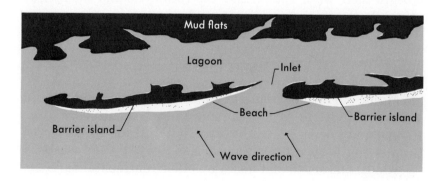

Figure 12-20. **The mainland will be extended outward to the barrier island as mud continues to fill the lagoon.**

Some underwater ridges become barrier islands through a lowering of sea level. Both the Atlantic Coast and the Gulf Coast of North America have many barrier islands. These islands extend for miles parallel to the shore but are separated

An **island** is a small tract of land surrounded by water.

from the mainland. These barrier islands probably formed during the changes of sea level associated with the advance and retreat of great ice sheets.

Both deposition and erosion may be observed along the seashore. The onrush of waves brings debris to the shore. The slowly returning water forms little *rills* that branch out like trees whose trunks point landward. *Ripple marks* are formed as waves push some sand toward the shore, and outgoing currents push the grains back toward the sea. Tiny ridges of sand are left behind as a result of the back and forth movement of the water. Some ripple marks are symmetrical (sa me'tri kal) with similar slopes on both sides of the ridge. Some ripple marks are asymmetrical; that is, one slope is much steeper than the other. Asymmetrical ripple marks are like miniature sand dunes. They may be formed by the wind or by currents that meet the shore at an angle.

Erosion and deposition constitute a never-ending cycle. Waves smooth the shore by eroding the headlands. Currents smooth the shore by depositing bars and spits across indentations. Eventually, erosion and deposition should fashion a balanced or static shore zone. Then all headlands would be worn away, all indentations cut off, and cliffs worn back so far inland that wave action would no longer be effective. This ideal state of balance or equilibrium never exists for long. Crustal movements raise or lower portions of the coast. Glaciers develop on land and sea level is lowered. When the ice melts, sea level rises. Any change in the position of sea level causes shore processes to begin their work again. Like the rock cycle and the hydrologic cycle, the *erosion cycle* has no end.

A **rill** is a minute stream of water, especially one that flows away from a beach as a wave subsides.

Erosion and deposition constantly change the shore zone.

MAIN IDEAS

1. Major surface currents begin in the tropics and flow in great circles in each ocean and in each hemisphere. Currents are deflected to the west by the trade winds, north and south by continental barriers, east by the westerly winds, and south and north by other continental barriers.

2. Surface currents distribute heat along shores and carry nutrients from place to place.

3. Deep ocean currents move toward the equator and beneath the surface. These currents are cold and dense compared to surface currents.

4. Tides on the side of the earth facing the moon are due to the moon's gravitational attraction. On the far side of the earth, the centrifugal force is probably the major cause of tides.

5. Spring tides occur when the moon, earth, and sun are in line with each other. Neap tides result when the sun and moon are at right angles to each other.

6. Waves are rhythmic movements of water caused by the gravitational attraction of the moon, submarine vibrations, or by wind.

7. Wave base of deep water waves is above the ocean bottom. Shallow water waves form in water that is less deep than half of the wavelength.

8. Water carried onto the shore by waves returns to the ocean basin due to the pull of gravity.

9. Waves and currents carve rocky shores into notched cliffs, cut benches, isolated stacks, and caves. Boulders carved from the shore are ground smaller and smaller by abrasion. Eventually the loose material may be transported to another location.

10. Shore deposits include beaches, berms, bars, spits, and barrier islands.

11. Destruction and construction by waves and currents are never-ending processes.

VOCABULARY

Write a sentence in which you use correctly each of the following words or terms.

abrasive	refract
berm	resistant
crest	rip current
density current	spring tide
jetty	stack
longshore current	tidal scour
neap tide	tsunami
notched cliff	turbidity current
oscillatory wave	upwellings

STUDY QUESTIONS

A. True or False

Determine whether each of the following sentences is true or false. (Do not write in this book.)

1. Rotation of the earth deflects ocean currents as well as air currents.

2. Channels formed by turbidity currents never are related to rivers from the continents.

3. Tides are shallow-water waves.

4. Spring tides take place in the spring, summer, fall, and winter.

5. Tsunami, sometimes called tidal waves, have no connection with tides.

6. Water particles are never carried forward onto the shore by oscillatory waves.

7. Beach sand always is composed of quartz grains.

8. Spits are deposited by a longshore current.

9. Motion of the waves is greatest at wave base.

10. Wave size depends on the depth of water alone.

B. Multiple Choice

Choose the word or phrase which completes correctly each of the following sentences. (Do not write in this book.)

1. Currents flowing toward the equator beneath the surface are (*turbidity, density, longshore*) currents.

2. Wavelength is measured horizontally from (*crest to crest, crest to trough, trough to wave base*).

3. Wave height is measured vertically from (*crest to trough, trough to wave base, crest to crest*).

4. Sand deposits built across the mouths of indentations along the shore are called (*bars, spits, berms*).

5. Currents that flow parallel to the shore are called (*rip currents, density currents, longshore currents*).

6. Turbidity currents are dense due to (*suspended sediments, evaporation, freezing of surface sea ice*).

7. Shore zone deposits include (*turbidity sediments, coral sands, ooze*).

8. The gravitational attraction of the moon causes (*tsunami, rip currents, neap tides*).

9. Barrier islands are due to (*erosion by waves, deposition across bays, ridges formed by breaking waves*).

10. Spring tides are caused by (*gravitational attraction of moon and sun working together, gravitational attraction of moon and sun working in opposite directions, excess rainfall during the spring*).

C. Completion

Complete each of the following sentences with a word or phrase which will make the sentence correct. (Do not write in this book.)

1. Two ocean currents in the Atlantic Ocean that follow the east coast of the American continents are the __?__ and the __?__.

2. Ocean tides are primarily the result of the gravitational attraction of the __?__.

3. New moon and full moon are associated with __?__ tides.

4. First-quarter and third-quarter moon positions are associated with __?__ tides.

5. Waves caused by submarine earthquakes are called __?__.

6. Shallow water waves occur in water that is half the __?__.

7. Ridges of sand that lie parallel to the shore but are separated from the mainland are called __?__.

8. Beaches in Hawaii and Oregon are black because they contain __?__ fragments.

9. Water pushed onto the shore by the waves becomes a __?__ current, flowing parallel to the shore before it returns to the deep ocean basin.

10. Currents flowing in and out of the Mediterranean Sea are __?__ currents.

D. How and Why

1. What conditions cause differences in the density of seawater? Suggest at least two reasons why water at the equator is less dense than water at other latitudes.

2. What conditions determine the size of wind waves? Suggest reasons why wind waves are never shallow-water waves in mid-ocean.

3. Explain why upwellings of cold water contain nutrients which may be lacking in warm surface water. What is the origin of upwellings and why do they sometimes fail to occur in the usual places?

4. Define abrasion and list several examples of abrasion. Discuss the process of abrasion along a shore. What is the source of the "tools" of abrasion in turbidity currents?

5. Why do shallow water waves erode the bottom of the ocean, but deep water waves do not?

6. During the 1964 Alaskan earthquake, Crescent City, California, was damaged by a huge wave. Was there any connection between these events? Explain your answer.

7. Why are tides higher in some places than in other places? For example, the Bay of Fundy has a 40 ft tide, whereas the Gulf of Mexico has a high tide about 2 ft above normal.

8. What two processes tend to smooth the shoreline?

9. Why do waves break only along the shore zone?

10. What evidence would indicate whether or not a shore zone had been uplifted?

11. What would happen to tides on the earth if there were no moon? What would happen to tides on the earth if the earth did not rotate? Explain your answers.

INVESTIGATIONS

1. On an outline map of the world, draw the major ocean currents. Compare them with the wind belts of the world. (Chapter 10.) Note any similarities or differences.

2. Discuss types of shorelines and ocean features using pictures or illustrations which you have drawn. Include wave action, notched cliffs, types of beaches, atolls and lagoons, barrier islands and reefs, stacks, benches, berms, spits, and bars.

3. On a map of the United States or of North America, locate barrier islands in the Atlantic Ocean and the Gulf of Mexico. Discuss why such islands are found in these localities but not on the west coast of the United States.

INTERESTING READING

Bascom, Willard, *Waves and Beaches: The Dynamics of the Ocean Surface*. Garden City, N.Y., Doubleday & Company, Inc., 1964.

Coker, R., *This Great and Wide Sea: An Introduction to Oceanography and Marine Biology*. New York, Harper & Row, Publishers, 1962.

Defant, Albert, *Ebb and Flow: The Tides of Earth, Air and Water*. Ann Arbor, Mich., The University of Michigan Press, 1958.

*Engel, Leonard, *The Sea*. Life Nature Library. New York, Time Inc., 1968.

Marx, Wesley, *The Frail Ocean*. New York, Ballentine Books, 1969.

Pell, Claiborne, *Challenge of the Seven Seas*. New York, William Morrow & Co., Inc., 1966.

Pincus, Howard, *Secrets of the Sea: Oceanography for the Young Scientist*. Columbus, American Education Publications, 1966.

Soule, Gardner, *Ocean Adventure: Science Explores the Depths of the Sea*. New York, Hawthorn Books, Inc., 1966.

Turekian, K. K., *Oceans*. Englewood Cliffs, N.J., Prentice-Hall, Inc., 1968.

* Well-illustrated material.

The Earth's Crust Redesigned

There is nothing constant in the Universe
All ebb and flow, and every shape that's born
Bears in its womb the seeds of change.

Ovid (43 B.C.-18 A.D.)

How are mountains formed? Why do rivers change their courses? Why are the remains of ancient sea creatures often found thousands of miles from present oceans? What causes an earthquake?

The earth is constantly changing. Sometimes it changes violently because of earthquakes or volcanic eruptions. More often, it changes gradually. Eons of weathering, erosion, mountain building, and subsidence have altered the earth's surface.

Through careful observation and experiments, man is constantly seeking insight into the processes which change the earth. Man has learned that he influences and to some degree can even predict and control change in the earth. He changes the course of rivers, the content of air, and even the quality of the oceans. Now to protect the quality of his environment he needs to know more about how the earth changes.

UNIT
Four

Mass Movements and Running Water

Processes of destruction and construction, so obvious along shore zones, are constantly changing the lithosphere. Water and air change materials of the crust and loosen and transport fragments. Finally, the fragments are consolidated into new forms. Although these processes are slow, they are constant. They would reduce the surface of the earth to sea level if neither crustal nor internal movements counterbalanced the removal of material. Look about you for signs of these processes at work.

13:1 *Erosion*

Weathered material is transported, deposited, and resolidified into new rock.

Recall that weathering is the change of rock material *in place.* (Section 6:2.) It is most effective on level ground in humid climates. Here vegetation holds the rock material until it has been disintegrated and decomposed by water and air.

Erosion is the process of wearing down the land surface. Rivers, wind, underground water, ocean waves and currents, and glaciers are agents of erosion.

Erosion (i roh'zhun) is the loosening and transporting of material by *moving* agents. It includes the work done by waves and currents as they tear down shorelines and transport debris to other locations. Percolating groundwater beneath the surface, slow-moving glaciers, and winds and currents of air also wear away the land. Most important is erosion done by running water in surface streams. Compared to streams and rivers, all other erosional agents are of minor importance.

Sometimes these forces work quietly and slowly for long periods. Often their work is dramatic and startling. Because sand dunes and glaciers inch along, their movement is almost unnoticed. Some rivers glide along their banks, but others rush in torrents which deepen their valleys rapidly and form deep canyons and *gorges* (gawrj'es). Groundwater works so silently that its action remains unnoticed until huge under-

Union Pacific Railroad Photo

Figure 13-1. A youthful stream plunging down a steep slope in Yellowstone Park forms one of the Park's famous waterfalls.

ground caverns are discovered. Sudden storms cause streams to carve channels in level land. Long periods of slow rainfall soak, or saturate, loose soil and cause hillsides to slump and move downward under the influence of gravity.

13:2 *Runoff*

Most of the water in the hydrologic cycle falls on the land surface as rain, snow, sleet, or hail. Some of this water evaporates into the air. Some is used by animals and plants. Some sinks into the ground, where it is held in the openings in rocks for a time. But nearly 40 percent of the water that falls on the land flows back to the sea by way of surface and underground streams. The water which flows on the surface in streams and rivers is called **runoff,** or running water.

Several factors affect runoff. The amount and type of rainfall and the slope, or *gradient* (graed'ee ent), of the area receiving the rainfall are important. In addition, the type of material over which the water flows and the amount and kind of vegetation present have an effect.

Runoff is also water flowing across the surface of the land.

Figure 13-2. Average annual rainfall in the United States ranges from 80 inches to less than 10 inches.

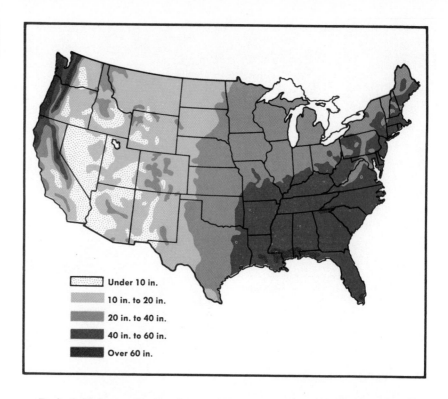

Under 10 in.
10 in. to 20 in.
20 in. to 40 in.
40 in. to 60 in.
Over 60 in.

Relief is the variation in the height of earth's surface.

Rainfall depends on the amount of moisture carried by the winds, and upon the relief of the land. The United States has five rainfall zones from east to west. (Figure 13–2.) The Atlantic Coast receives about 40 in. of rainfall per year. About 30 in. of rain falls in the Mississippi River drainage basin. The Western Plains receive about 20 in. Between the Rocky Mountains and the Sierra Nevada, the Great Basin has about 10 in. of rain. The Pacific Coast receives between 40 in. and 80 in. of rain per year. These figures represent an average amount of rainfall for a period of at least 10 years.

In addition to the amount of rainfall, runoff is affected by many other factors. The *rate of precipitation* and the *temperature* influence the amount of runoff. Snow and gentle showers promote evaporation and absorption of moisture rather than runoff. However, torrential (taw ren′chal), or violent, rains cause rapid runoff which results in severe erosion. Warm temperatures increase the rate of evaporation. Cold temperatures promote runoff. When temperatures are low enough for freezing, precipitation may become trapped as ice or snow. Then, when thawing occurs, runoff will be slow or rapid, depending upon the rate of melting.

Gradient is an important factor in determining the amount and rate of runoff. Steep slopes shed rain quickly before it can be absorbed by the ground. Gentle slopes and plains retain water temporarily, but eventually lose it to the underlying groundwater zone.

The *type of rock* on which the rain falls also influences the amount of runoff. Porous rocks allow water to sink into the ground. Loose material may become saturated with water. On hillsides, sheets of saturated soil often creep slowly toward the valley. Steep hillsides made of loose particles show the most destructive effect of runoff. Here raindrops form rills, rills become gullies (gul'ees), and gullies deepen rapidly into ravines. Coarse, rocky material has little effect on slowing the flow of water downslope.

Vegetation also determines whether runoff or absorption occurs. Ground that is covered by trees, grass, or shrubs has little runoff. Streams flowing through forest areas are usually clear because little soil is suspended in them and carried away. Such streams have a fairly constant rate of flow because movement of water into the streams is gradual.

Runoff is rapid on steep slopes and slow on plains.

Vegetation cover retards runoff.

Figure 13-3. Runoff can be especially destructive on a steep hillside.

Brown Brothers

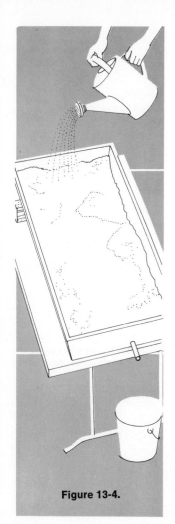

Figure 13-4.

ACTIVITY.   Prepare a stream table from a rubber or plastic tub, or from a wooden nursery flat about 3 ft × 2 ft × 4 in. Waterproof the wooden box with caulking compound. Make an opening at one end of the tub or box equal to the diameter of a piece of rubber tubing. Insert the tubing and seal the joint. Pack sand in the stream table to a depth of 2 in. If the sand contains clay, be sure to wash out the clay, or it will clog the outlet from the stream table. Create some surface features with the gravel and sand. With wooden blocks or books, raise the end of the stream table opposite the outlet. Put a container below the outlet to catch the runoff.

Fill a sprinkling can with water. Sprinkle the surface at the raised end of the stream table. Vary the rate of rainfall and observe the patterns that develop. Is the pattern dendritic (den-drit'ik), similar to the branches of a tree, or does the pattern have sharp bends? Is this the most common stream pattern? To answer this question, examine topographic maps of the United States.

In the stream table, how does the rate of rainfall affect the depth of the stream channel? How does the location of gravel affect the stream flow? What force causes the water to flow down the slope?

EXPERIMENT.   Using the same stream table, observe the effect of a change in slope on stream velocity. It is necessary to maintain a constant rate of flow so that the slope is the only variable. Arrange the stream table so that you can place a container of water at a higher elevation. (Figure 13–5.) Use a piece of tubing to siphon the water from the container to the river system in the stream table.

Now increase the height of the high end of the stream table. What changes in pattern and velocity occur? Raise the outlet end of the stream table. What is the effect of this change in slope? Note: Keep the stream table for future experiments.

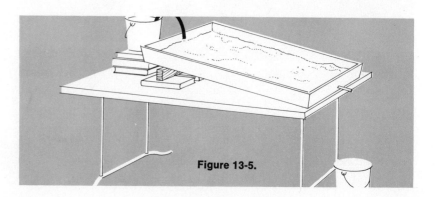

Figure 13-5.

Problems

1. If the stream table is 3 ft long and it is raised 6 in. above the table, what is its gradient? What is the gradient if one end of the stream table is 1 ft above the table?

2. What changes in stream pattern and velocity follow an increased gradient? What changes in stream pattern and velocity follow a decreased gradient?

3. What are two variables that influence the amount of erosion done by a stream?

4. Using only the materials required for the preceding experiments, discover another variable that determines how rapidly the stream can cut down its bed.

13:3 *Erosion in Arid and Humid Climates*

Comparison of the erosional effects of running water in arid (ar'id) and humid climates shows clearly the importance of factors which influence runoff. *Arid regions* usually have less than 10 in. of annual rainfall. This amount is insufficient to support much vegetation. In arid regions, evaporation exceeds rainfall. *Semiarid regions* have approximately 15 in. to 20 in. of rainfall per year. This supports only short grasses. In *humid regions*, rainfall ranges up to 80 in. per year. Here, rainfall exceeds both evaporation and transpiration.

In arid or semiarid regions, little vegetation is present. Although rainfall occurs only occasionally, it is usually violent. Under these conditions, runoff causes widespread erosion. The effects are especially striking in soft clay or sand. Ridges become more pronounced and gullies deepen with every rain. The Badlands of South Dakota is an excellent example of this type of landscape, or *topography* (ta pahg′ ra fee) .

In areas where both weak rock and resistant rock are present at the surface, soft or soluble rock may be carried away. Masses of resistant rock are left behind. Steep-sided, bare rocky remnants of various sizes often rise abruptly from desert plains. These remnants of erosion are called *inselbergs* (in′sel burgs) . (Figure 13–8.) On dry level land, erosion is less rapid than on steep slopes. Nevertheless, large masses of rock may be worn away, leaving high erosional remnants between the valleys. *Buttes* (beuts) may remain as streams cut deeper and deeper into a region. In the Southwest, masses capped by hard, resistant layers of lava, limestone, or sandstone form flat-topped

Figure 13-6. **Mud cracks in the channel of an intermittent stream during the dry season.**

Figure 13-7.   **In semiarid regions the fertile soil of farms and ranches can be washed away by rainstorms.**

William Huber

Figure 13-8. Steep-sided inselbergs rising from desert plains are remnants of long-term erosion.

Buttes and mesas have identical rock layers. Buttes are smaller with a narrower top than the broad-topped mesas.

table lands. These are called *mesas* (mae'sas), the Spanish word for tables. The resistant layer protects the soft layers beneath it from erosion. The height of a mesa is a measure of the thickness of material that has been removed by erosion.

In humid areas, erosion caused by runoff is less dramatic, but probably more effective, than in arid country. Rainfall is seldom violent, but it is frequent. Usually enough vegetation covers the surface to retard the flow of water and to allow time for the formation of a network of streams. Slopes, even if they are steep, are often wooded. Surface materials usually have had an opportunity to become weathered. Under these conditions, small rills tend to flow together to form creeks. Creeks become brooks, brooks join to form streams, and streams form a complex network called a **river system.**

Erosion is most complete in humid regions if river systems have had sufficient periods of time to develop.

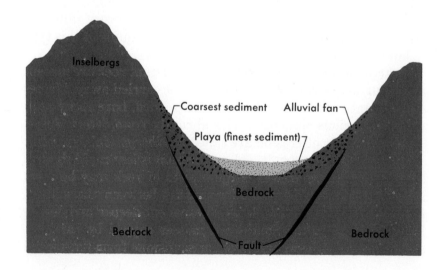

Figure 13-9. This cross section shows the development of alluvial fans along the mountain front. Only inselbergs extend above the sediments.

13:4 *Humid River Systems*

Development of a river system depends upon the force of gravity. In humid regions, gravity causes runoff to flow to lower and lower levels. Eventually, it reaches the sea. A typical river system begins in mountains and gathers speed as it reaches the lower hilly country. Finally, the river emerges on the plains. It flows steadily across the plains toward the ocean. From mountains to plains, gradient lessens but volume increases. Velocity is dependent upon both gradient and volume. Little mountain streams seem to bubble along at a rapid rate. But their velocity is actually less because they lack the volume of the mature stream. For a given volume of water, the steeper the slope over which water flows, the more rapid is its velocity. In the early stages of stream development, gradient is the important cause of rapid flow. Later, when the stream has a greater volume, it flows rapidly in spite of its reduced gradient. Streams have their greatest volume and swiftest velocity during spring floods.

Humid climate drainage systems often are described in terms of youth, maturity, and old age. However, the *age of a river* does not refer to its age in years. Age refers to the amount of work remaining to be accomplished in reducing the region to sea level. Billions of tons of debris must be removed from a mountainous region. Even an inland prairie that is thousands of feet above sea level must be eroded. On the other hand, rivers flowing through coastal plains have few youthful characteristics, because the land is already close to sea level. A stream flowing over resistant rock remains youthful much longer than one flowing through regions of soft, loose, easily moved material. Also, those parts of a drainage system that are closest to the sea are older than the parts higher up in the mountains.

Youth of a river begins when runoff is directed toward a definite channel after each rainfall. Water always flows toward any natural depression in the land surface. Here water may remain in a puddle, or even in a lake if the depression is large. However, when the depression is full, water overflows and moves downward to lower levels. Usually, water follows the shortest distance. But if resistant material is present, water follows the easiest path. The water flows around the obstruction and goes through soft material. Runoff continues to follow the same path after every rainfall. Eventually, the connections between depressions become channels, and a river is born.

Figure 13-10. River valleys widen as a stream approaches old age. However, the river channel occupies only a small portion of the river valley.

In youth, rivers flow rapidly through narrow, straight V-shaped valleys.

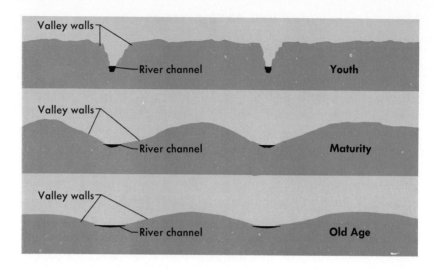

Figure 13-11. Drainage patterns become increasingly complex as a stream develops.

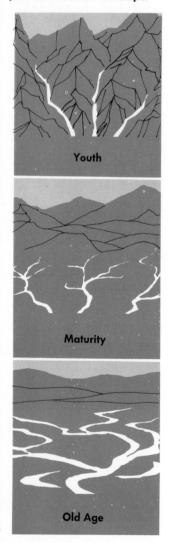

During the youthful stage, channels are short and relatively straight. Valleys are V-shaped and just wide enough to hold the available water. In early youth, a stream may flow swiftly, but it has little material in suspension with which to erode its channel. As the river flows onward, it picks up more and more fragments from the sides and bottom of the channel. Particles of silt and sand serve as tools with which the stream *abrades*, or grinds off, rocks from the stream channel. Fragments are carried upward and downward with the river currents. These particles strike the sides and bottom of the stream channel. They wear away the rock in the same way that wood is smoothed by rubbing it with sandpaper. At the same time, the particles themselves become rounded. By examining the shapes and sizes of the fragments, geologists often can judge the distance that the fragments have been carried.

Youthful streams erode their beds downward. Their tools are particles carried within the stream itself, as well as material that is rolled along the bottom of the channel. These particles make up what is called the *stream load*. The amount of material that a stream can carry depends upon its velocity. In youth, a stream usually can carry a larger load if the material is available. As a stream develops from late youth into early maturity, its load begins to equal its capacity to carry materials. Then, if its velocity is decreased, the stream deposits some of its suspended material.

Maturity of a river is reached when the river has reduced its slope until its velocity is just great enough to carry its load. By this time, the river channel is well established. Downward erosion is almost complete, and the stream is cutting sideward and widening its valley. The river gradient is slight. Any irregularities, such as resistant rocks, fallen trees, slumps of material from the valley walls, or depressions below the normal channel level, cause the water to swing from side to side in the channel. As the water travels sideward, it develops S-shaped curves called *meanders* (mee an'ders). A meandering stream (Figure 13–13) cuts on the outside of the curves where velocity is swift. It deposits on the inside of the curves, where velocity is reduced. The river channel gradually is moved back and forth over a wide area, called the *river valley*. By maturity, a river system has developed tributaries. *Tributaries* (trib'ye ter ees) are small streams which flow into larger streams. A mature river together with its tributaries forms a complicated network of streams. These streams drain a vast region called a *drainage basin*. As maturity approaches old age, the region between streams is worn down closer and closer to sea level.

Figure 13-12. A stream erodes sideward as it meanders.

Figure 13-13. This meandering stream has widened its valley through sideward erosion.

W. T. Lee, U.S. Geological Survey

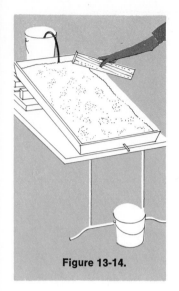

Figure 13-14.

Crustal movement may rejuvenate an old stream and renew its erosional ability.

EXPERIMENT. Use gravel or a piece of wood or plastic to build a dam across the stream in the stream table used in Section 13:2. Describe the stream both above and below the dam in terms of its velocity, its ability to transport materials, and its volume. Is the erosional ability of the stream changed?

Do dams increase or decrease the danger of floods? To answer this question, rapidly pour water into the stream table above the dam until water spills over the dam. Then, while still pouring the flood waters, make a diversion channel around the dam.

A river system reaches **old age** when its highlands are worn down nearly to sea level. Then the river flows within a channel that makes up only a small part of a wide valley. (Figure 13–10.) Resistant rocks, called *monadnocks* (ma nad'nahks), are the high land forms on a wide, eroded plain. *Oxbow lakes* are formed where the river cuts across its meanders and leaves arc-shaped bodies of water isolated from the main stream.

Rejuvenation (ri joova nae'shun) may occur when shifts in the elevation of the crust change the stream gradient. If an uplift of land occurs near the headwaters of a stream, the gradient is increased. Then the stream starts cutting downward again. Finally the stream develops a youthful V-shaped channel within its old meanders. Flood plains are left at an upper level in the form of *terraces* as the stream cuts downward. Such a stream is said to be rejuvenated, or made young again.

Figure 13-15. Uplift of the land has caused this stream to erode its channel downward, forming a steep V-shaped valley within its meanders.

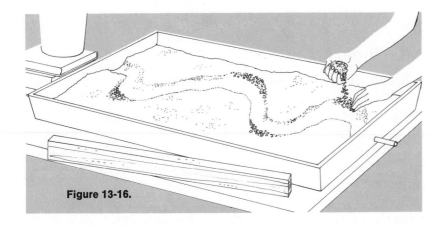

Figure 13-16.

ACTIVITY. *If the stream in the stream table has not developed some curves, fashion them in the sand and line a few of the banks with gravel. Adjust the gradient of the stream table or the velocity of the stream so that the water is moving just rapidly enough to move around the gravel. In which stage is this river system? Is it doing any erosional work?*

Union Pacific Railroad Photo

Figure 13-17. Streams flowing in old glaciated valleys often become overloaded and form a braided pattern as they drop sediment within their channels.

13:5 *River Deposits*

Recall that the stream load is determined by the stream's velocity. A decrease in velocity thus results in **deposition.** Few youthful streams are loaded to capacity. Consequently, youthful streams seldom deposit sediment except at the foot of an abrupt slope. Mature streams, however, transport sediment to the limit of their energy. Even slight reductions in velocity cause mature streams to deposit sediment.

Rivers remove approximately one foot of surface debris from the continents in 9,000 years. But only one-fourth of this sediment reaches the sea. The rest is redeposited locally within depressions of the drainage basins. Some material may be left within the stream channel itself. Some may be deposited along the sides, and some may be dropped at the mouth of the river.

Every time the velocity of a loaded stream is decreased, some material is dropped. The flood plains built by mature rivers adjacent to their channels are familiar examples of deposition. When excess water pours into the stream channel, some water spills over the sides. The velocity of the spilled water is reduced and deposition begins. The coarsest materials are dropped close to the river banks. These raised banks, or mounds, are called natural *levees* (lev'ees). Beyond the levees are *alluvial* (a loo' vee ul) *plains* made of fine mud which settles from the standing flood waters. These plains are swampy and covered with excel-

Much of the material eroded by rivers is redeposited before the river reaches the sea.

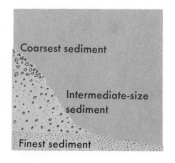

Figure 13-18. As a delta builds outward, coarse layers are laid down over fine sediments.

Coarsest sediment

Intermediate-size sediment

Finest sediment

Figure 13-19. The Missisquoi River is building a delta at its mouth where it flows into a quiet lake.

lent soil. In Egypt, most of the land available for cultivation comes from the yearly flood deposits of the Nile River. In the Mississippi River Valley, flooding adds a layer of fine rich soil to produce good farmland.

Another example of sediment deposition by rivers is the *delta* (del'ta). The shape of the Greek capital letter delta (Δ) gives rise to the term delta for the triangular deposits at the mouth of a river. When the stream enters a quiet body of water, its velocity is decreased. Sediment is dropped, and new land is formed. Coarse material is dropped first, fine silt is carried farther, and mud is spread out a greater distance into the quiet water. (Figure 13–19.)

In mountainous areas, streams form *alluvial cones*, or fan-shaped deposits, when they drop their loads quickly at the foot of a mountain slope. Abrupt changes in slope cause rapid decreases in velocity, and sorting is not as complete as it is in a delta. However, gravels are dropped nearest to the mountains, and fine silts and mud are deposited farthest away. Alluvial cones are common deposits along mountain fronts in arid regions. Often the cones spread out and join along the mountain front to form a continuous deposit called a *bajada* (bah hah' dah). (Figure 13–20.) Fine sediments are carried into the shallow, central basin between mountains. Since these desert basins, called *playas* (plie'as), are undrained, the water evaporates and deposits silt and sand in place. (Figure 13–9.)

Levees and alluvial plains are deposited by both mature and old rivers during flood periods.

Deltas are formed where rivers flow into quiet, standing water.

Alluvial cones or fans of unsorted material are deposited at the foot of steep slopes in arid or semiarid regions.

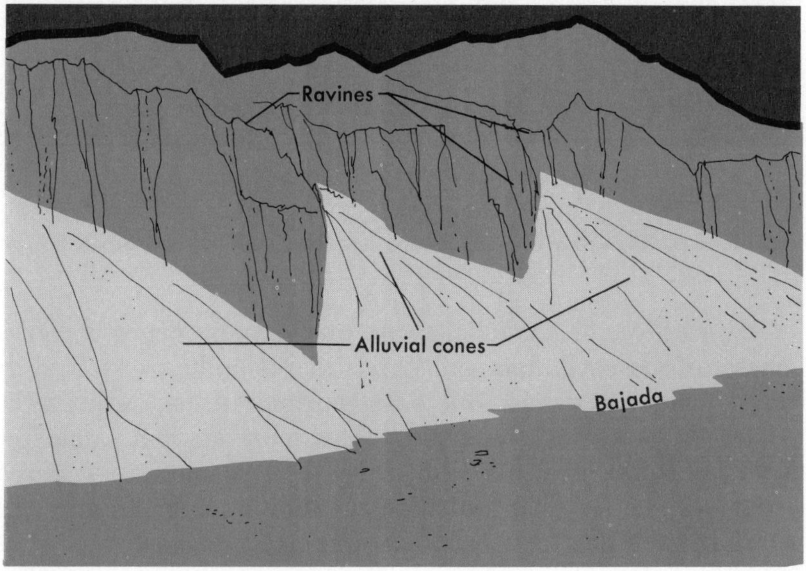

Figure 13-20. Loose material eroded from the mountain slopes forms alluvial cones at the mouths of the ravines through which the water flows.

13:6 *Mass Movements*

Masses of rock, ranging in size from particles which are barely visible to huge boulders, are loosened by weathering. When steep slopes become saturated with water, rock masses move down the slope in response to the force of gravity. The rock masses may slide as a thin sheet. This movement is called *creep*. Also, the rock masses may move as a rapid avalanche (av'a lanch), or landslide.

Creep occurs in humid climates where vegetation prevents rapid runoff and the soil becomes saturated. Apparently, clay swells with moisture. Then it becomes more subject to the pull of gravity. Fence posts, telephone poles, and trees that tip away from the vertical on hillsides are evidence that soil creep has taken place.

Figure 13-21. Spring rains helped to lubricate loose material on the steep slope causing a dangerous landslide on this mountain road.

National Park Service Photo by Jack E. Boucher

In humid areas, soil creep and landslides result when material on steep slopes becomes saturated with water.

Avalanches, or *landslides*, are rapid movements of large masses of loosened material. Landslides usually are started by earthquake vibrations. But on steep mountains, such as the Andes or the Alps, the spring thaw may start a landslide. Most landslides are small, but several large ones have caused great destruction. Much of the devastation accompanying the Alaskan earthquake of 1964 was due to landslides.

In arid regions, torrential rains bring down piles of weathered fragments that form heaps of debris at the foot of a slope. These *talus* (tae'lus) *slopes* consist of unsorted fragments and may contain huge boulders as well as small bits of rock.

Talus is the pile of loose rock that accumulates at the foot of a steep slope due to gravity.

In Arctic regions, freezing and thawing of surface rock creates a loose rock mantle of many different-sized fragments. The surface thaws in the spring. But the ground below the upper few feet remains frozen, and water cannot drain downward. Immediately after the spring thaw, a mass movement of rock debris starts downslope due to the pull of gravity. The mass moves slowly on the gentle slopes and swiftly on the steep slopes. Material may move as a single unit, or it may join other units in a jumbled massive flow.

Runoff and downslope movements are the major agents of land erosion. Together, these two agents cover more area and work longer than all other erosional agents combined.

Most erosion of the earth's surface is caused by runoff aided by downslope movements.

MAIN IDEAS

1. Weathering breaks down materials at the earth's surface. Erosion transports and redeposits weathered material by means of runoff, underground water, glaciers, and wind.

2. Erosion by runoff depends upon the amount and type of rainfall and the surface on which the rain falls.

3. In arid climates, runoff is usually rapid and destructive.

4. Inselbergs, buttes, and mesas are erosional remnants of resistant rock found in arid and semiarid climates.

5. In humid climates, erosion is most complete as river systems develop from maturity to old age.

6. Rivers are called young when much erosion remains to be done to reduce the land to sea level. During youth, rivers deepen their channels. During maturity and old age, rivers widen their valleys and reduce the area between streams to near sea level.

7. When streams have reduced most of the slopes of their drainage basin and are following a winding course, they are called mature.

8. In old age, rivers flow slowly through plains which are reduced nearly to sea level. Monadnocks, or remnants of a higher earlier surface, may rise about the plains.

9. Rivers in maturity or old age may be rejuvenated by an increase in gradient or an increase in volume. The streams begin to deepen their channels again.

10. Depositional features of rivers include alluvial plains, levees, deltas, and alluvial cones.

11. Soil creep, landslides, and accumulations of talus result from mass movements of rock and soil on steep slopes.

12. Runoff and downslope movements are the two most effective erosional agents.

VOCABULARY

Write a sentence in which you use correctly each of the following words or terms.

alluvial	dendritic	inselberg	rejuvenate
arid	erosion	levee	runoff
avalanche	gorge	meander	talus
butte	gradient	mesa	topography
delta	gully	monadnock	tributary

STUDY QUESTIONS

A. True or False

Determine whether each of the following sentences is true or false. (Do not write in this book.)

1. Erosion is a process which requires moving agents to accomplish its work.

2. Rainfall in the United States ranges from 10 in. to 80 in. per year.

3. Youthful streams are characteristic of mountains.

4. Clear streams are most likely to be found in level forest lands.

5. Rainfall accomplishes more erosion in arid regions than in humid regions.

6. The development of a river system is due to the pull of gravity.

7. Rejuvenation of a stream may cause a mature stream to regain certain characteristics of its youthful stage.

8. As a stream loses velocity, it deposits dissolved material.

9. Levees may be formed by rivers or built by man.

10. Deltas, alluvial fans, and talus slopes are deposits formed where a river flows into the ocean.

B. Multiple Choice

Choose the word or phrase which completes correctly each of the following sentences. (Do not write in this book.)

1. Erosion is most rapid on (*level plains, steep slopes, gentle slopes*).

2. The zone in the United States which receives the greatest amount of rainfall per area of land is the (*Mississippi River Valley, Atlantic Coast, Pacific Coast*).

3. Rejuvenation accompanies uplift of the headwaters of a stream because there is an increase in the stream's (*velocity, volume, suspended load*).

4. A V-shaped channel is typical of the (*mature, young, old*) stream.

5. High, flat-topped hills in arid country are called (*inselbergs, mesas, alluvial cones*).

6. Erosion is most effective if a stream carries (*no, suspended, dissolved*) material.

7. A drainage basin is established by a river in its (*youth, maturity, old age*).

8. Monadnocks and oxbow lakes are characteristics of (*youth, maturity, old age*).

9. The flood plain of a rejuvenated stream is (*above, at the same level as, below*) the stream channel.

10. Away from the river mouth, sediment in a delta is deposited in this order: (*silt, mud, sand; sand, silt, mud; mud, silt, sand*).

C. Completion

Complete each of the following sentences with a word or phrase which will make the sentence correct. (Do not write in this book.)

1. Gullies are features of the ___?___ stage of a river system.

2. Much of the rain which falls on gentle slopes and plains joins the ___?___ rather than the runoff.

3. Four agents of erosion are __?__, __?__, __?__, and __?__.

4. Factors which influence the effectiveness of erosion are __?__, __?__, __?__, and __?__.

5. Rainfall in arid and semiarid climates is likely to be __?__ and __?__.

6. Meanders are not likely to appear until a stream reaches the stage of __?__.

7. When meanders are cut off from the river, they form __?__.

8. A meandering stream cuts on the __?__ and deposits on the __?__ of the curves.

9. Features constructed by mature rivers include __?__, __?__, and __?__.

10. Downslope movements may be __?__ or __?__ depending on the speed of movement.

D. How and Why

1. In a humid climate, would surface materials of sand or clay favor runoff? Why? (Assume that the two materials have the same slope.)

2. Would you expect to find the least runoff in the uncultivated prairies of central Kansas, or in the desert of the Southwest, or in the heavily forested areas of the Pacific Coast? Why?

3. In what stage of development would a stream flow in a deep V-shaped, relatively straight channel?

4. Along the Mississippi River, where would you expect to find oxbow lakes?

5. Does construction counterbalance destruction in a drainage basin? Explain your answer.

6. Does flooding occur in desert regions, or only in humid climates?

7. Would flooding along the Rio Grande River of Texas enrich the soil as flooding along the Nile River and the Mississippi River does?

8. Stream gradients are usually steepest during early youth. Why are these streams less effective erosional agents than mature streams?

9. Why does the elevation of the playa region tend to rise in arid regions, but the elevation of the drainage basin in humid regions is continually lowered?

10. Discuss the permeability of granite compared to sandstone, conglomerate compared to shale, and coral sands compared to clay. (Refer to Chapter 5 and Chapter 6.) Which of these rocks would encourage runoff, and which would favor seepage into the ground?

INVESTIGATIONS

1. On an outline map of the United States, indicate the five rainfall zones.

2. On an outline map of the United States, show the Colorado River system. Indicate the humid and arid regions through which the river passes. Include all large dams and storage lakes and the Grand Canyon area. In what areas are new dams proposed or being built?

3. On an outline map of the United States, trace the entire Mississippi River system and the Missouri River system. Indicate areas of youth, maturity, and old age. Do you think a mistake was made in naming the system? Explain your answer.

4. Look for examples and pictures of soil creep as shown by tipping fence posts, telephone poles, trees, and houses. Discuss the causes and remedies.

INTERESTING READING

Bloom, A. L., *The Surface of the Earth*. Englewood Cliffs, N.J., Prentice-Hall, Inc., 1969.

Jauss, Anne Marie, *The River's Journey*. Philadelphia, J. B. Lippincott Co., 1957.

Kuenen, Philip H., *Realms of Water: Some Aspects of Its Cycle in Nature*. New York, John Wiley & Sons, Inc., 1955.

Leopold, L. B., and Langbein, W. B., *A Primer on Water*. Washington, D.C., U. S. Government Printing Office, 1960.

*Leopold, L. B., and Davis, K., *Water*. Life Science Library. New York, Time Inc., 1966.

Price, Willard, *Rivers I Have Known*. New York, The John Day Company, Inc., 1965.

* Well-illustrated material.

Underground Water

Rainfall which sinks into the ground is known as underground water. Erosional effects of underground water are not recognized as easily as the erosional effects of runoff. But underground water causes many important changes in the appearance of the landscape.

Some underground water is used by plants, some is evaporated, and some is stored in rocks. But most of the water that sinks underground returns eventually to the surface and joins the river systems.

14:1 *Zones*

Percolate means to pass or seep through permeable rocks.

Water percolates downward through underground cracks and through spaces between rock or mineral grains. Eventually, it reaches a layer of rock with no openings. At this depth, water begins to gather in the rock openings in the same way that water fills a glass.

Weathering occurs in the zone of aeration where air is present in rock openings.

The upper rock zone through which water can trickle easily is called the **zone of aeration** (aer ae′shun), or the *zone of oxidation*. In this zone, rock openings are filled with air, except immediately after a rain. Rainwater does not remain in the upper zone but continues downward. Then air returns to fill the openings. The presence of air gives the zone the name aeration. But the zone also is known as the zone of oxidation because oxygen and water react with elements in the rock to form new compounds. Most of the new compounds are combinations of oxygen and some other element. They also may be combinations of carbon dioxide—another constituent of air—and an element. Recall that similar processes of decomposition occur on the surface. (Section 6:4.)

At the bottom of the zone of aeration, some water is held in tiny tube-like openings in the rock by **capillary** (kap'e ler ee) **attraction.** A *capillary* is a fine, hair-like tube. This tube is capable of holding liquids because of the attraction between molecules of a liquid and a solid. Water is held in the small openings between rock grains in much the same way because of the attraction of the rock for the water.

Capillary attraction holds some underground water in the soil near the surface.

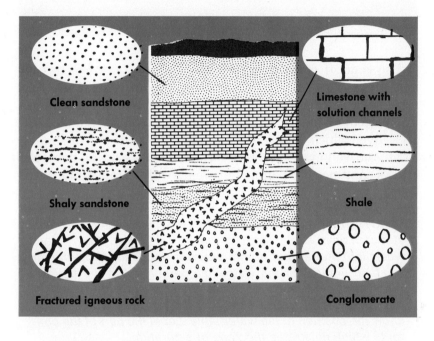

Clean sandstone

Limestone with solution channels

Shaly sandstone

Shale

Fractured igneous rock

Conglomerate

Figure 14-1. Permeability in rocks may originate during deposition as in sandstone, or after consolidation as in fractured rock or limestone solution channels.

ACTIVITY. Fill two open-ended glass tubes with dry sand. Use a clamp and stand to hold them upright in a shallow pan or plate. Carefully pour water into one tube until the sand is saturated and some water runs down onto the plate. What happens in the tube of dry sand when the water in the plate reaches it?

ACTIVITY. Place a stalk of celery or a white carnation in a glass jar. Partly fill the jar with water and add a few drops of red food coloring. Let this activity continue for several days. What happens to the celery or flower?

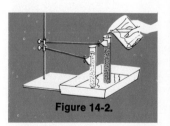

Figure 14-2.

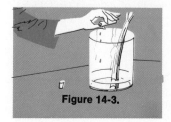

Figure 14-3.

PROBLEM

1. Some agricultural scientists doubt the benefits of plowing and hoeing during a dry summer. What is their reasoning?

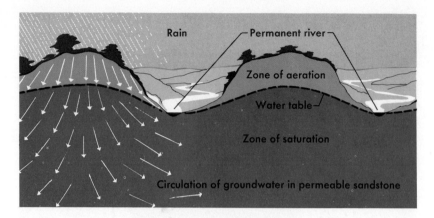

Rain — Permanent river
Zone of aeration
Water table
Zone of saturation
Circulation of groundwater in permeable sandstone

Water fills all spaces in the zone of saturation.

The **zone of saturation,** or the *groundwater zone,* lies immediately below the zone of aeration. The upper surface of the zone of saturation is known as the **water table.** (Figure 14–4.) The bottom of the zone of saturation is the upper surface of a rock layer which has no openings. At depths of approximately 12 mi, the weight of overlying rocks probably seals all pores and cracks. Absence of openings prevents water from sinking any deeper.

> *ACTIVITY. Fill a glass jar with a mixture of sand and small stones. Leave some room in the jar for water. Slowly pour water into the jar, but do not saturate the sand. Allow the jar to stand until all of the water has percolated to the bottom. When the upper sand becomes dry, measure the height of the damp sand. Draw a sketch of the jar and its contents to show the position of the water table. Label the part of the contents which illustrates the zone of saturation.*
>
> *Now add more water to the jar. What effect does it have on the water table? If, instead of a glass jar, you used a cardboard carton with a small hole in the bottom, what would happen to the water table? Why, in most places, does the water table fall during the summer?*

Figure 14-5.

Relief refers to the variation in height of different land forms.

The water table is approximately parallel to the ground surface although its relief is somewhat more gentle. On hilltops, the water table is farther below the surface of the ground than it is in adjacent valleys. Water wells drilled to the water table must penetrate more rock on the hilltop than in the valley.

The water table follows the surface relief at some depth below the surface.

Depth of the water table is not constant. It changes, or fluctuates, with the amount of rainfall. Each rainfall supplies water to the underground zone of saturation. The water table rises temporarily. Light showers seldom supply enough water to percolate downward beyond the zone of soil moisture, where it may be evaporated or used by plants. But during the spring in some areas, rainfall is at a maximum. Melting snow also adds to the amount of available water. In this period, the water table tends to be higher than during the rest of the year. During especially wet seasons, the water table may be close to, or even at, the surface of the ground. In periods of drought, the water table is far below the surface. Permanent rivers have water flowing through their channels throughout the year. These rivers, as well as lakes and swamps, are areas where the water table is above the surface of the ground.

14:2   *Movement of Groundwater*

Gravity causes groundwater to move from higher elevations to lower elevations, always following the path of least resistance. Groundwater flows in the same general direction as surface water, but much more slowly. Groundwater moves slowly because its speed is decreased by friction between the water and the rocks through which it flows. Eventually, water may emerge at the surface in springs, seeps, or man-made wells. (Figure 14–6.)

Water can flow through rock layers only if the rocks are *permeable* (pur'mee a bul). Permeable rocks have connected openings so that water can move through them. Rocks may be *porous*, with many openings, but unless the openings are connected, water cannot flow. Rocks which have no openings between grains are said to be *impermeable*. Movement of groundwater depends on several factors. These factors include the

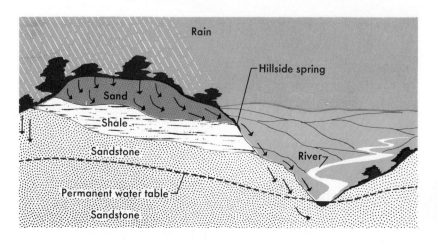

Figure 14-6. Because some rocks are impermeable, the circulation of underground water may be quite complex in regions of alternating permeable and impermeable rock.

slope of the rock layers, the supply of water, and the permeability of the rock layers. Rocks that have large pores which are connected so that water can flow freely are called *aquifers* (ak'wa fers). Most aquifers are made of sandstone, gravel, limestone, or sand. Wells must be sunk deep into an aquifer to insure a dependable supply of water. This type of aquifer yields water only when pumped.

Artesian (ahr tee'zhan) **water** is a natural upwelling of water under hydrostatic pressure. Sometimes a layer of permeable rock lies between dense, impermeable rock layers. Then water moves through the permeable rock in the same way that water moves through a pipe. If the upper part of the aquifer is exposed at the surface, its water supply is continually renewed. Then water will rise toward the surface by any available opening. Some openings are cracks or fractures in the rock layers. Other openings are man-made wells. In either case, water escapes upward under pressure. The pressure is due to the weight of the column of water in the aquifer. Water does not rise quite as high in these openings as the elevation at which it entered the permeable layer. Water loses some energy due to friction as it flows through the aquifer. (Figure 14–7.)

Springs occur where water reaches the surface under pressure and flows through a natural rock opening. **Seeps** are places where water oozes out only enough to moisten the ground,

Aquifers are rocks which store water in connected pores.

Artesian water, held under pressure between layers of impermeable rock, may be forced upward through any openings to the surface.

Hydrostatic pressure is pressure exerted by water.

Seeps and springs are present where the water table meets the surface.

Figure 14-7. Water under pressure rises through either natural or man-made openings to form artesian springs or wells. Artesian wells were first discovered in Artois province in France about 1100.

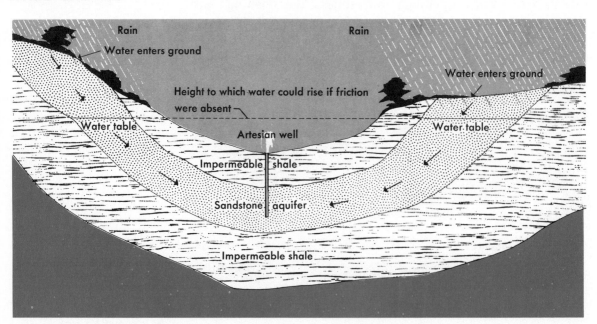

but there is no distinct water flow. Both springs and seeps are points at which the water table meets the surface of the ground.

> *EXPERIMENT. Use three 8-oz paper cups or three ½-pt milk containers with their tops cut off. Fill one container half full of sand, another half full of a mixture of sand, clay, and gravel, and the third container half full of clay. Punch a few holes in the bottom of each container and a few on the sides above the bottom. Be sure that the holes are all the same diameter and in the same places in each container. Stand the three containers on stilts made from swab sticks or on supports made of small blocks. Place all of the containers over a pan or in the sink. Pour about ¾ cup of water in each container. Does any water run out of the containers? If so, describe the appearance of the water (clear, cloudy, and so on).*
>
> *Allow the containers to stand for at least one hour. Examine them again. Are any of them still dripping? Is water standing on the top of any of the sediments? Has all of the water drained from any of the containers? Is the water that passed through the clay clear? What do you conclude about the relative permeability of the sand, the clay, and the sand-clay-gravel mixture?*

Figure 14-8.

14:3 *Composition of Groundwater*

Rainwater is a weak acid which contains carbon dioxide in solution. Limestone rocks, which consist of calcium carbonate, go into solution as long as rainwater flows over them and carries away the dissolved substance. Groundwater that contains more than 8 grains of mineral matter per gallon is called **"hard water."** **"Soft water"** contains little mineral matter in solution. The dissolved substances in soft water tend to remain in solution. Rainwater is "soft" when it falls on the land. But if it flows through a limestone region, it soon becomes "hard." Water is called "hard" if it contains calcium sulfate and calcium, magnesium, and iron carbonates in solution. Of these minerals, calcium carbonate is the most abundant in hard water.

Deposits on the inside of water heaters and teakettles are composed of calcium carbonate which precipitates from solution when hard water is heated. A disadvantage of hard water is that it makes soap ineffective as a cleaning agent. Calcium tends to precipitate from the soap solution, leaving a scum of dirt and oil along with it.

Rainwater is a weak acid which may dissolve calcium carbonate and calcium sulfate and carry these compounds away in solution.

Grain is a unit of weight equal to 0.0648 g.

Rainwater is a weak acid and may dissolve calcium carbonate, sodium carbonate, or salt and carry these compounds away in solution.

In the semiarid southwestern United States, evaporating water often leaves crusts of calcium carbonate on or near the surface of the ground. Such deposits are known as *caliche* (ka lee'chee). Sodium carbonate is another common component of the soil in arid regions. Calcium carbonate and sodium carbonate are usually absent in the soils of humid regions. These substances are dissolved and carried away in the runoff. Sodium carbonate gives the waters of arid regions a bitter taste. After a rain, or even after irrigation, thin white layers of sodium carbonate cover the surface where water remained for a while before it evaporated. Sodium chloride, or common salt, is another substance often found on the surface of the ground in arid regions. Salt that is dissolved in groundwater may come from layers of salt which were deposited in evaporite basins such as the Salton Sea of California. Other possible sources are saltwater trapped in sediments during their formation on the sea floor, or saltwater that infiltrated areas near the sea.

Because they are porous and permeable, volcanic rocks are often the sites of mineral springs and geysers (gie'zers). Many

Figure 14-9. When water turns to steam, pressure lifts the whole column and forces it out at the surface opening to form a geyser.

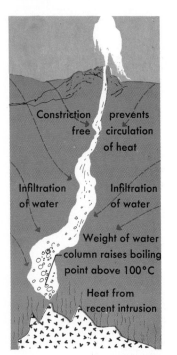

Constriction prevents
free circulation
of heat

Infiltration
of water

Infiltration
of water

Weight of water
column raises boiling
point above 100°C

Heat from
recent intrusion

Figure 14-10. Eruption of White Dome Geyser has built up a cone of siliceous sinter around the surface opening.

National Park Service

of the springs in volcanic formations are heated by contact with hot magma far below the surface. Because of their high temperatures, these waters are able to dissolve large amounts of matter. Hot springs which contain calcium carbonate, calcium sulfate, or sulfur often have a conspicuous color, taste, or odor and are called *mineral springs.* *Geysers* are named for the hot gushing springs of Iceland. These hot springs erupt through small openings at intervals. As water accumulates in the tube or underground chamber of the geyser, it is heated. Eventually the water turns to steam at the bottom of the chamber. When the steam pressure reaches a certain value, the water in the upper end of the tube flows out onto the surface. This lowers the pressure on the column of water. As the pressure on the water in the geyser tube is released, all water in the chamber begins to boil. Finally, a jet of steam is thrown into the air, sometimes as high as 200 ft. The geyser continues to spew forth steam until its pressure is reduced. This process is repeated at intervals as steam pressure rebuilds and escapes.

Geysers are hot springs in which water is forced upward by steam pressure. Narrow openings at the surface cause water and steam to erupt at given intervals.

14:4 *Underground Water Deposits*

Hot springs, including geysers, contain large quantities of dissolved minerals. These minerals may be precipitated as the water cools. Precipitates around hot springs commonly contain abundant calcium carbonate. These sediments are called *travertine* (trav′er teen), if compact; *tufa* (teu′fa), if porous. They are called *onyx* (ahn′iks) if composed of translucent or semi-transparent layers. Sometimes the spring water has traveled through igneous rock. Then deposits may consist of a milky colored silicate called *siliceous* (sa lish′as) *sinter.*

Groundwater transports, deposits, and concentrates valuable minerals such as copper, lead, zinc, silver, and gold. Such concentrations occur along rock fractures and faults, or between rock layers. Groundwater also helps to consolidate sediments into hard rock layers. Sediments may be cemented by the precipitation of minerals between grains of sand, gravel, or lime. Some of these sedimentary rocks become valuable building stone.

Groundwater may help to concentrate certain ores and some minerals.

Replacement is another process by which groundwater changes rocks and minerals. Some elements of the rock go into solution and are replaced by elements from the groundwater. *Petrified wood* results from the replacement of wood fibers by

Meston's Travels

Figure 14-12. This petrified wood is a silica replacement of the wood cells of a tree that probably was covered by flood waters. Burial on a river flood plain allowed time for the replacement to occur.

Wood cells replaced by silica become petrified wood.

National Park Service

Figure 14-13.

silica (SiO_2). As the wood fibers decay, silica takes the place of the original woody materials. Gradual replacement preserves the exact shape of the bark, tree rings, and cellular structure. Complete petrification usually requires many years. Under favorable circumstances, it may occur within a few months or even weeks. Petrified wood of gem hardness is found in flood plain sediments once submerged beneath waters that carried large amounts of volcanic ash.

> *EXPERIMENT. Pour ¼ cup of salt into a clear glass or plastic container, ¼ cup of clay into a second container, and ¼ cup of sand into a third container. Add water to each container and stir well. What happens in each container?*
>
> *From your observations, explain the distribution of sandy materials and clay in the soil. What happens to the salt, clay, and sand that is carried away by streams? If water does not run off the surface, but trickles through the soil to some depth, what happens to the clay and to the sand?*

PROBLEM

2. Recall the principles you learned about the solution of sedimentary rocks in Chapter 6. Which sedimentary rocks might go into solution? (To answer this question, you may wish to repeat the experiment in Section 6:8 using dilute hydrochloric acid on several sedimentary rocks.)

14:5 *Topography of Limestone Areas*

Limestone regions offer the best evidence of the chemical action of groundwater. Limestone consists mainly of calcium carbonate, which is soluble in a weak acid such as rainwater. Much of the soluble limestone may be carried away by groundwater, leaving features known as sink holes, caves, caverns, solution valleys, and natural bridges. The resulting landscape is called *karst topography*, after the honeycombed limestone Karst area on the eastern side of the Adriatic Sea.

Sink holes may appear in a level, dry landscape where water descends from the surface along joints, cracks, and other openings in the rock. *Sink holes* are depressions shaped like large funnels with their outlets downward. Surface waters drain into these sinks. Then if mud collects and blocks the outlet, deep lakes are formed. The Bottomless Lakes in New Mexico are actually water-filled sink holes.

Sink holes are circular, funnel-shaped depressions formed in rock joints where water has descended to join the underground water.

Water may seep downward slowly, dissolving soluble materials and forming *caves* and *caverns* in rock which is particularly soluble. Caverns, such as those at Carlsbad, New Mexico, consist of a number of caves. These caves are joined by narrow passageways. Often the true extent of such a system of caves is unknown. Once a cavern system has developed, a stream of water often flows through the large tunnel-like opening. Eventually, the water emerges at the surface to join the runoff. Mammoth Cave, Kentucky, has such a stream flowing through it. Florida's springs are also outflowing underground streams. Most underground water moves slowly between layers of rock or through rock pores, instead of flowing swiftly like a river. However, it still is an effective erosional agent.

Caves and caverns are common underground features in limestone areas.

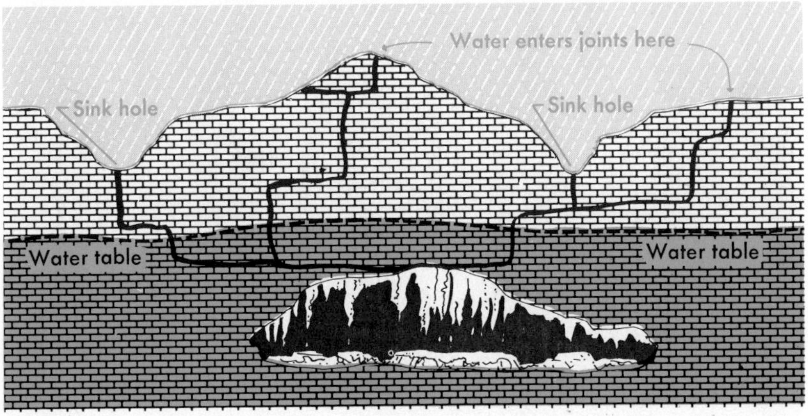

Figure 14-14. **Limestone that goes into solution along joints and bedding planes above the water table is often precipitated in caves in the zone of saturation.**

William Huber

Figure 14-15. Weathering and erosion have left the more resistant rock suspended above a deep gorge worn in the weaker rock below.

Solution valleys and natural bridges are formed when the roofs of caves and caverns collapse. A *natural bridge* is the section which remains when adjoining roof sections have collapsed. If an underground stream flowed through the cavern, it now becomes a river flowing in a *solution valley*. The river eventually removes the collapsed-roof material of its former tunnel.

Stalactites and stalagmites are deposits of calcite formed by water dripping slowly from the ceiling of caves.

Deposits suspended from the ceilings of caves are called *stalactites* (sta lak'tiets). Deposits built up from the floor are called *stalagmites* (sta lag'miets). These formations result from slow precipitation of the mineral calcite ($CaCO_3$). As water loaded with calcite drips from the roof of a cave, some

Figure 14-16. As water containing dissolved calcium carbonate drips from a cave's roof, calcite is deposited in the form of stalactites and stalagmites.

Allan Roberts

of it evaporates and leaves the hanging stalactite. As the stalactite continues to drip like a melting icicle, a stalagmite is built up from the floor below it. When the two forms meet, they become a pillar or column. Carlsbad Caverns, New Mexico, contain beautiful examples of these formations.

14:6 *Importance of Groundwater*

Transportation, deposition, and concentration of minerals are important functions of groundwater. Many industries utilize these deposits of silver, copper, lead, zinc, and other ores. However, the most vital use of groundwater is to add to supplement surface water for human consumption.

At present, rainfall is the major source of water available for use by man. A large portion of rainfall is lost to the atmosphere by evaporation and transpiration of plants. The remainder becomes either runoff or groundwater. Runoff supplies water to surface bodies such as rivers, lakes, and man-made reservoirs (rez'urv wahrs). Groundwater is stored in the zone of saturation. But recall that both runoff water and groundwater return to the oceans during the hydrologic cycle.

More than half the runoff and groundwater of the world is outside man's living area. It returns to the ocean unused by man. The remainder of earth's water supply is used in industry, in agriculture, and for domestic purposes before it is returned to the sea. When surface water supplies are inadequate or polluted, groundwater must be tapped. One of today's challenges is finding enough pure water for the needs of our growing population and industry. Surface water not only is being used at an increasing rate, but also is being heavily polluted by industrial, agricultural, and urban wastes. Polluted water cannot be used until it is purified. Because groundwater accumulates slowly, pumping water from the zone of saturation lowers the water table at an alarming rate in many regions.

Several possible solutions to our water problems are under study. Attempts are being made to remove salt from ocean water at reasonable costs. Studies have been undertaken of methods for purifying surface water and returning some processed water to ground storage. Scientists are trying to find more efficient ways to use irrigation water in arid regions and to prevent evaporation and seepage of water from reservoirs. One of the more promising solutions is the diversion to cities of the presently unused rainfall which flows back to the ocean.

Figure 14-17.   Carlsbad Caverns in New Mexico.

The water table is being lowered by the excessive use of water.

The supply of pure water must be increased and must be used more efficiently.

MAIN IDEAS

1. Water which sinks into the ground is part of the hydrologic cycle.

2. Some underground water is held near the surface by capillary attraction; some underground water percolates through the zone of aeration and collects as groundwater in the zone of saturation.

3. The water table is the upper surface of the zone of saturation, and lies almost parallel to the surface relief.

4. Groundwater joins surface water through springs, seeps, and wells. Seeps and springs appear where the water table intersects the surface of the ground. Artesian water, confined between layers of impermeable rock, is under great pressure. Artesian flow occurs when a well, or some other opening, extends from the surface to the aquifer in which the water is confined.

5. Aquifers are rocks with connected pore spaces in which water can be stored effectively.

6. Because rainwater is a weak acid, it will dissolve calcium carbonate, sodium carbonate, salt, and certain other minerals. These substances may be redeposited in a different environment due to evaporation or a chemical reaction of the water in which they are contained.

7. Hot springs often contain calcium carbonate, calcium sulfate, sulfur, and silica in solution. Water of these springs may be heated by contact with hot magma in regions of volcanic activity.

8. Geysers are hot springs which erupt at intervals. Because openings to the surface are narrow, water cannot flow continuously as it does in other hot springs. Eruptions occur when steam pressure builds up sufficiently to force the water through the narrow opening.

9. Topographic features in limestone areas include sink holes, natural bridges, underground river tunnels, solution valleys, and caves. These features are formed during solution of limestone by groundwater.

10. Stored groundwater should be conserved and used more efficiently because it is of vital importance to life on earth. Studies are being made of new and better ways to control water for future use.

VOCABULARY

Write a sentence in which you use correctly each of the following words or terms.

aeration	capillary	saturation
aquifer	geyser	stalactite
artesian	permeable	stalagmite

STUDY QUESTIONS

A. True or False

Determine whether each of the following sentences is true or false. (Do not write in this book.)

1. Groundwater is one part of the hydrologic cycle.

2. Air is present in the zone of oxidation.

3. Water table is the upper surface of the zone of aeration.

4. The water table is almost parallel to the surface relief.

5. Artesian water is stored in an impermeable rock layer.

6. Most groundwater moves toward sea level.

7. Gravity is the force which causes groundwater to flow.

8. Sediments are cemented by substances precipitated from groundwater.

9. Sand commonly is carried downward farther than clay by percolating groundwater.

10. Most of the rain and snow which fall on land become groundwater.

B. Multiple Choice

Choose the word or phrase which completes correctly each of the following sentences. (Do not write in this book.)

1. A small hair-like tube is called a(n) (*aquifer, reservoir, capillary*).

2. Groundwater is stored in the zone of (*oxidation, saturation, aeration*).

3. Rock which has connected openings through which water can percolate is (*impermeable, permeable, impervious*).

4. In a (*seep, geyser, stalactite*), water is forced to the surface by steam pressure.

5. The water table is closest to the surface of the ground (*on a hilltop, on a hillside, in a valley*).

6. The most impermeable type of rock is (*shale, sandstone, limestone*).

7. Hot springs are commonly associated with regions of (*volcanic rock, shore deposits, karst topography*).

8. Two of the following which are most likely to be concentrated by groundwater action are (*coal, copper, lead, diamonds, emeralds*).

9. In arid regions, a hard crust of calcium carbonate is often left on the ground when groundwater is evaporated. This substance is called (*travertine, onyx, caliche*).

10. Karst topography is in areas of (*limestone, granite, lava*).

C. Completion

Complete each of the following sentences with a word or phrase which will make the sentence correct. (Do not write in this book.)

1. Water which collects below the water table is called ___?___.

2. Rock capable of storing water is called a(n) ___?___.

3. Some underground water is held near the surface by ___?___ attraction.

4. A lake made by man for water storage is called a(n) ___?___.

5. Hot springs that erupt at intervals are called ___?___.

6. Many hot springs contain ___?___, ___?___, and ___?___.

7. Calcium carbonate deposits found near hot springs include ___?___, ___?___, and ___?___.

8. Petrified wood is formed when wood fibers are replaced by ___?___.

9. Three features commonly found in karst topography are ___?___, ___?___, and ___?___.

10. As groundwater that contains calcite drips from the roofs of caves and caverns it forms ___?___ and ___?___.

D. How and Why

1. Why does water erupt from a geyser? Use a diagram to illustrate your answer.

2. Why do some citrus growers in semiarid climates plow between trees, or plant grass cover?

3. Why is the zone of aeration called the zone of oxidation?

4. Why do authorities in some arid and semiarid localities prohibit the sinking of wells on private property?

5. Why should sand overlie clay layers in a flower bed?

6. Why are layers of caliche and salt found on the surface in arid and semiarid climates but not in humid climates?

7. Why do wells along the seashore sometimes become salty?

8. What kind of rock underlies the Florida Peninsula? (Clues to the kind of rock are found in the presence of disappearing rivers, springs, and funnel-shaped lake beds.)

9. What conditions along the Florida seacoast indicate the possible presence of great thicknesses of limestone? Explain your answer.

10. What is hard water, and where is it found?

INVESTIGATIONS

1. Investigate the depth of the water table in your locality. Contact your local water department or your state department of natural resources for maps and data. Discuss the problems of supplying pure water for your community. In addition to human consumption, how is water used in your community?

2. Report on water witching or dowsing. Is it based on scientific facts or is it superstition?

3. What is spelunking? Is it of any scientific value? What are some of the dangers and how should they be avoided? Report on the work of some discoverers of famous caves.

4. If you have seen the springs and geysers of Yellowstone Park or some other place, report on your observations.

INTERESTING READING

Folsom, Franklin, *Exploring American Caves*. New York, P. F. Collier, Inc., 1962.

King, Thompson, *Water: Miracle of Nature*. New York, The Macmillan Company, 1961.

Longsworth, Polly, *Exploring Caves*. New York, Thomas Y. Crowell Company, 1959.

Stone, A. Harris, and Igmanson, Dale, *Drop by Drop*. Englewood Cliffs, N. J., Prentice-Hall, Inc., 1969.

Glaciers

Like surface water and underground water, masses of ice move under the influence of gravity. Although the ice masses move more slowly than water, they are more abrasive because of their great weight and stiffness, or rigidity.

Rivers are far more important than glaciers in erosional work. But in some regions glaciers have played a significant part in changing the surface of the earth. In fact, much of northern North America has been shaped by glaciers.

15:1 *Glacier Origin*

Glaciers are masses of ice in motion. They are formed by collection or accumulation of snow and ice. On the surface of a glacier, snow remains in flakes, just as it fell. Below the soft, new snow, some melting occurs. Here, the flakes combine to form rounded *granules* (gran'euls), or grains. Below this zone, pressure from the overlying layer compacts the granules into a permeable mass. This permeable mass is called *firn*, or névé (nae vae'). If snow accumulates for several seasons and reaches a depth of 100 ft to 200 ft, the buried snow layer becomes an impermeable block of interlocking ice crystals. This is *glacier ice*. The process which changes snow to firn ice resembles the compaction of sediments to form sedimentary rock. Recrystallization of firn ice under pressure resembles the recrystallization of sedimentary rock to form metamorphic rock under pressure.

In a *snowfield*, snow remains on the ground from year to year. Snowfields extend down mountain slopes to an altitude where melting offsets additions of new snow. This altitude is called the *snow line*. Below the snow line, melting prevents accumulation of snow. Above the snow line, snow is always pres-

Glaciers are composed of four layers: new snow, ice granules, firn, and interlocking crystals of ice.

A **snowfield** is an area of permanent snow. A **snow line** is the lower boundary of a snowfield.

Figure 15-1. When a sufficient thickness of ice accumulates, valley glaciers move downslope usually following a previous river channel.

ent. The extent of a snowfield depends upon topography, temperature, and the amount of precipitation. Steep slopes are made bare by snowslides, wind scour, and exposure to the sun. Hollows that shade the snow prevent melting and promote glacier formation. In humid regions, where temperatures are below freezing, snowfields may be large and extend to low altitudes. In warmer or drier regions, snowfields are found only at high altitudes.

Figure 15-2. High mountains often have snow all year because temperatures are too low for melting to occur.

As snow accumulates on the surface of a snowfield, pressure from the overlying layer changes buried snow into ice. Bottom ice becomes plastic or pliable and begins to flow. Surface ice remains brittle because it is not under such a heavy load. As the glacier moves downward, friction with the rock wall slows movement at the sides of the glacier. Thus the center portion of the glacier moves more rapidly than the sides. This creates tension in the surface ice. Also as the bottom plastic ice of the glacier glides over irregularities, tension develops in the upper zone. These tensional stresses cause the brittle surface ice to crack. The cracks, or *crevasses* (kri vas′ses), which form may be 100 ft to 200 ft deep. Meltwater drips into these cracks and forms rivers within and beneath the ice. *Eskers* are deposits of sand and gravel formed by such rivers. When a glacier melts,

287

Edward J. Webster

Figure 15-3. Below the snow-line, glacial meltwaters carry away great quantities of debris.

eskers are left as mounds on the rock surface beneath the ice. Such mounds tell the position of former rivers in the glacier.

Some surface snow is lost by evaporation. At its lowest limit, a glacier loses some ice by melting. If the ice melts faster than snow accumulates, the glacier recedes. If melting is balanced by the forward movement of ice, the glacier front remains stationary. If snowfall in the snowfield exceeds the rate of melting throughout the glacier, the glacier increases in size. Then it spreads to lower elevations or lower latitudes.

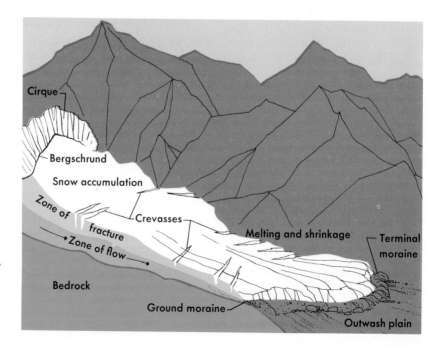

Cirque

Bergschrund

Snow accumulation

Zone of fracture

Zone of flow

Crevasses

Melting and shrinkage

Terminal moraine

Bedrock

Ground moraine

Outwash plain

Figure 15-4. As a glacier moves downslope over an uneven channel, the surface ice is broken into deep crevasses; the bottom ice flows over the irregularities.

EXPERIMENT. Place two large ice cubes in a shallow pan. Put a large piece of iron or a brick on one of them. Which cube melts faster?

Put two more ice cubes in the pan. Cover one ice cube with a square of heavy white paper. Cover the other ice cube with a square of heavy black paper. Which cube melts faster?

Now place two large ice cubes in a shallow pan. Place a key or heavy nail on one ice cube and put the pan in the freezing compartment of a refrigerator. Leave the pan in the refrigerator for several hours or overnight. Examine the ice cubes. Where is the key or nail? Explain what has happened. If you live in a region where freezing occurs, list some examples which illustrate this principle.

Summarize your conclusions regarding the influence of heat absorption and pressure on melting.

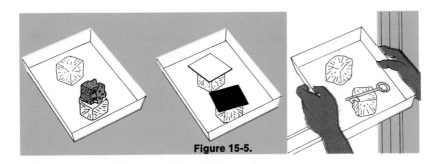

Figure 15-5.

15:2 *Location*

Glaciers form in high latitudes or at high altitudes. These are places where heavy snowfall collects and remains throughout the year. Glaciers that originate on mountains are called *mountain*, or alpine, *glaciers*. Mountain glaciers become *valley glaciers* when they move down major mountain valleys. This movement is in response to the pull of gravity. Mountain glaciers are more extensive in high latitudes than in low latitudes. In Alaska, valley glaciers extend downward to the base, or foot, of the mountains. There they join to form a continuous mass of ice. These glaciers, known as *piedmont* (peed' mahnt) *glaciers*, form a plain of ice at the foot of the mountains.

Continental glaciers form in high latitudes where snowfall is heavy and little melting occurs. Today continental glaciers exist only in Antarctica and Greenland. Because these glaciers are small compared to the continental glaciers of the past, they usually are called *ice caps*. Antarctica and Greenland, however,

Figure 15-6. Wilson Piedmont glacier, marked by numerous meltwater gullies, ends abruptly at the mountain foot where melting counterbalances ice movement.

Ward's Natural Science Establishment, Inc.

are covered continuously with ice that moves out in all directions due to its weight. Both of these areas have true continental glaciers.

Continental glaciers cover valleys, plains, and even mountains with ice that is thousands of feet thick. Greenland's ice cap now is only a small remnant of an enormous ice blanket. The ice blanket once covered northern Europe, northern Asia, and North America as far south as the Ohio River Valley. During the advance of this great continental glacier, snow probably accumulated near the present Hudson Bay. Ice formed thousands of feet thick and its weight caused the bottom ice to move outward in all directions. Movement was most rapid around the outside edge. There the ice was thinnest. As this great mass of ice moved across the rock beneath it, it removed all loose fragments. The glacier also scoured basins in soft rock. Resistant rock was polished and sometimes scratched by debris carried in the bottom of the ice. Because mountain glaciers occupy channels and move downward, they could not have eroded the New England mountaintops. But the tops of New England's hills were planed, gouged, and polished by ice action.

Evidence from both erosion and deposition indicates the former presence of a continental glacier over much of Canada and northern United States.

Figure 15-7. Angel Glacier, in the Canadian Rocky Mountains just north of Banff, is only a small remnant of the glacier which once occupied the large cirque from which Angel Glacier spills.

William Huber

Edward J. Webster

The height of these hills is a good measure of the thickness of North America's continental glaciers. Continental glaciers 8,000 ft to 10,000 ft thick must have been present to cover these hilltops with enough weight to cause erosion on the hilltops.

15:3 *Glacial Erosion*

Running water has affected large areas since the earth was first formed. Therefore, it has been more effective than glaciers in reducing continents to sea level. But glaciers erode more deeply than rivers, because glaciers carry a much more massive load of boulders, gravel, and sand.

Continental glaciers acquire their load of sediments at the bottom of the ice. Valley glaciers gather their loads from above and from the bottom and sides as well. Sediments are frozen into the ice of valley glaciers and carried forward as the ice moves downslope. In continental glaciers, the sediments are carried beneath the ice and outward from the center.

The erosive power of a glacier depends on its thickness. Ice that is thousands of feet thick can transport boulders tens of feet in diameter. Many of these boulders are plucked from the bedrock and carried along by the ice as it moves forward. Meltwater from the surface or from within the ice mass flows downward until it penetrates joints in the rock over which the ice is moving. When the meltwater freezes, it becomes a part of the moving glacier. So does the rock which meltwater has penetrated. This process is called *plucking*. Glaciers accumulate massive loads of boulders, gravel, and sand. White, gleaming ice soon changes into a dark, muddy, flowing mass. These rock materials act as abrasives.

A valley glacier scrapes the sides and bottom of its channel as a giant sharp file might gouge a hollow in a log. Because continental glaciers are not confined to channels, they scrape rock surfaces beneath the ice over a wide area.

In mountains, snow collects in *cirques* (surks). These are bowl-shaped hollows which are shielded from winds and shaded from the sun. Meltwater trickles down the opening between the snow and the rock wall of the mountain. In these cracks, meltwater freezes and expands with force. Its wedging action breaks the mountain face into rock fragments, which are added to the ice. Between the ice and the rock wall a crack, called the *bergschrund* (burg′ schrund), is repeatedly filled with new

Figure 15-8. Glacial lakes formed in depressions left by the retreating glacier.

Figure 15-9. This cirque, a natural amphitheater, was formed by alternate thawing and freezing of ice during Pleistocene glaciation.

Phyllis G. Lewis

Figure 15-10. Features formed above and beneath the ice remain as clues to glacial erosion long after the ice disappears.

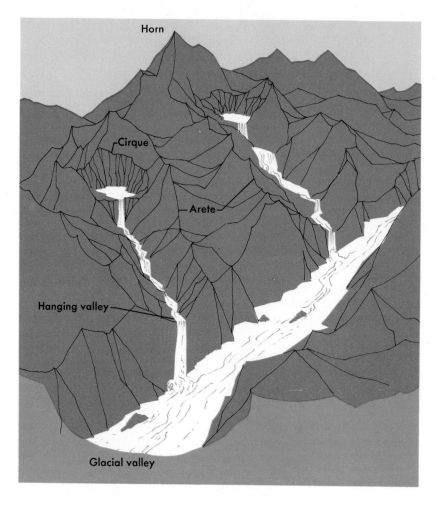

Figure 15-11. The Matterhorn is a typical remnant of erosion extending above the highest cirques.

Glacial valleys are U-shaped.

snow. As ice wedging recurs, the original cirque becomes larger. Thus, the rock wall of the mountain is eroded.

Many mountain summits have rock remnants with steep-sided, three-cornered peaks above the highest cirques. Such rock remnants are called *horns*. The Matterhorn in the Alps is a familiar example. Thin rock walls with upward pointing jagged edges separate one glacier from another. These *aretes* (a raets') add debris to the valley glacier surface.

Glaciers that begin on mountain summits occupy channels that originally were mountain stream beds. As the glacier moves downslope, the V-shaped stream channels are abraded into steep-sided U-shaped valleys. Tributary channels from side ravines join the main glacier. Because the main glacier is much thicker than its tributaries, the main channel is eroded more deeply. Thus, tributaries may join the main glacier at much higher elevations than the main channel. Small glaciers

Ohio Division of Geological Survey

from side valleys enter at right angles, because ice cannot turn corners easily. Special features of valley glaciers are not apparent until the ice melts. Then the channels of side glaciers are left as *hanging valleys* above the main channel. Yosemite (yoh sem' it ee) Park, California, is famous for its hanging valleys and beautiful waterfalls.

Because ice is rigid, it acts much like a bulldozer. The glacier gouges out soft areas and leaves step-like irregularities of resistant rock in its bed. High areas are planed, smoothed, and polished. Rock surfaces, and even individual boulders carried by the ice, are marked by grooves and *striations* (strie'ae shuns), or scratches, showing that the ice contained debris with sharp edges.

Figure 15-12.   Grooves and striations on rocks help to indicate the directions of past glacial movements.

United Air Lines, Inc.

Figure 15-13.   Yosemite National Park is famous for its hanging valleys, its waterfalls, and its ice-carved U-shaped valleys.

Canada's Shield area consists of polished and striated bed-rock which has been uncovered by continental glaciation.

The Canadian Shield area, which was covered by the continental glacier in Canada, exhibits many evidences of glacial erosion. The continental glacier scraped loose debris from the hard rock floor. It carried the debris southward to the northern United States. Rocks of the Canadian Shield are polished, grooved, and striated. Many small depressions were gouged from soft materials. These basins now are filled with water. Because ice covered this region until about 11,000 years ago, weathering and erosion have not had time to destroy the marks of the glacier.

EXPERIMENT. Arrange a board at an angle that will support a flat, heavy rock and not let it roll down the slope. Different angles and different sizes of rock should be used in the experiment and results compared. Form a thick slab of "silly putty" and place it at the top of the sloping board, a short distance above the position of the rock. After 24 hours, observe what has happened to the putty. What has happened to the rock? After several days, observe what has happened to the putty and to the rock. Remove the rock from the board and place some pieces of gravel or broken shell in the path of the putty. If flat, angular pieces are used, they will tend to remain on the board without rolling. After 24 hours, observe what has happened to the gravel or shells.

Why is putty instead of ice used in this experiment? What force moves the putty down the slope? Will the same force move ice?

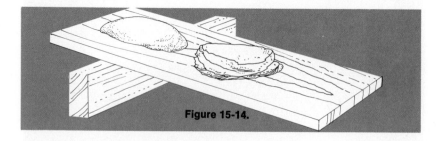

Figure 15-14.

15:4 *Glacial Deposits*

At some time in the life of a glacier, melting occurs. Then the ice can no longer retain its debris. If its valleys empty into the sea, fronts, or *snouts*, of the glacier break off and float away as *icebergs*. Snouts of other valley glaciers melt as they reach lower altitudes and warmer temperatures. The outermost edges

Ewing Galloway

Figure 15-15. Portage Glacier, Alaska, where the snouts or lower extremity of the glacier extends into open water, breaks off, then floats away.

Edward J. Webster

Figure 15-16. This Greenland valley is filled with rock fragments left behind by the melting glacier.

Figure 15-17. The pile of debris on which people are walking represents an end moraine of the Athabaska Glacier in the Columbia Ice Fields of Alberta, Canada. The dark ridge to the right of the glacier is a lateral moraine. Beneath this pile of rock and mud, ice still is present.

of ice sheets recede as climates become warmer. Eventually the entire glacier shrinks.

As ice at the front of a glacier becomes water, the glacier drops much of its sediment load directly. This unsorted material, called *drift* or *till*, forms a ridge known as a *terminal moraine* (term'nal · ma raen'). A terminal moraine within a valley dams its channel and creates a lake. Terminal moraines also are formed by continental glaciers. Such moraines indicate the farthest advance of the glacial ice.

Moraines are built higher and higher as long as the forward movement of the ice equals its rate of melting. But if melting exceeds forward movement, the ice front recedes. Then debris is scattered over a wide area in a *ground moraine*. Ground moraines have relatively smooth plane surfaces. The deposits are a mixture of boulders, gravel, sand, and clay. Beneath the ground moraine, old river valleys have been filled and hills have been planed. Occasionally, small clusters of hills, called *drumlins* (drum' lins), dot the ground moraine. Drumlins are fine glacial clay hills of drift shaped like cigars. The highest elevations associated with glacial deposits usually are terminal moraines. Sometimes the ice front halted and retreated repeatedly. Then other high ridges, called *recessional moraines*, parallel the terminal moraine.

Meltwater flows off the ice front as a sheet. It drops sand and gravel in wide gently sloping deposits which fan outward from

William Huber

Figure 15-18. The topography of a glaciated region is fashioned by deposits beneath and in front of the ice.

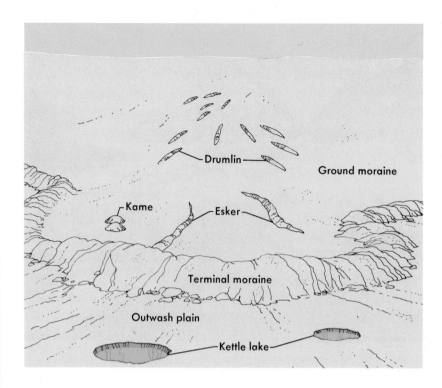

Figure 15-19. An outwash plain, consisting of sand and gravel which was deposited by water flowing off the front of a retreating glacier, is located downslope from the moraine.

Figure 15-20. Kames like this one sometimes are formed near a terminal moraine.

the terminal moraine. These deposits, called the *outwash plain*, merge with terminal moraines or with recessional moraines. Occasionally, rounded gravel hills, called *kames*, are built near the terminal moraine. Kames are formed by swirling water that pours off the ice front. Like eskers (Section 15:1), kames are composed of sand and gravel. But eskers are long ridges which are formed beneath or within the ice. They lie perpendicular to the terminal moraine and settle onto the ground moraine when the ice melts.

Sometimes blocks of ice become detached from a glacier and are buried by drift. As the ice block melts, material from above sags into the depression left after melting. *Kettle lakes*, which pit the surface of both outwash plains and ground moraines, are formed in such depressions.

Moraines are associated with both continental and valley glaciers. When formed by continental glaciers, moraines extend for hundreds of miles. They seldom are more than 100 ft high. Moraines formed in valleys are small features which do not usually remain long after the valley glacier melts. However, moraines may dam water that flows through former glacial valleys. Then such valleys become long, narrow lakes. The Finger Lakes of New York State occupy former tributaries which spread out like fingers.

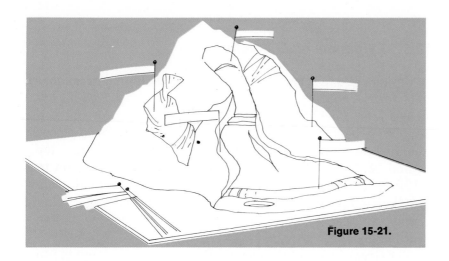

Figure 15-21.

ACTIVITY.   Make a model of a valley glacier, using several colors of modeling clay. Use a square of heavy cardboard as a permanent mounting. Form the mountain of the darkest clay and fashion hollows and valleys in which to show the presence of the glacier. Indicate the various features of the glacier, as well as deposits in front of the ice. Label each feature with a paper pennant. Be sure to include a cirque, crevasses, a terminal moraine, and a lateral moraine. Slice through the model in a vertical direction to show various features and layers.

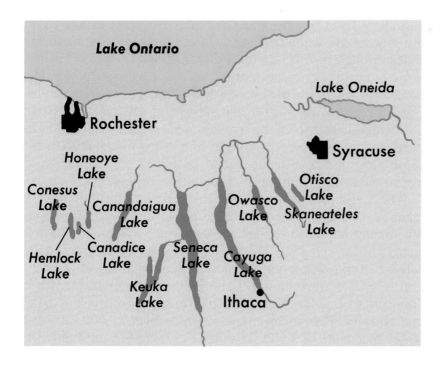

Figure 15-22. The Finger Lakes of New York State occupy old river valleys dammed up by glacial debris.

297

15:5   *Evidence of Glaciation*

Canada and northern United States show abundant evidence of a former continental glacier. The glacier removed all loose debris from the Canadian Shield and polished and striated the solid rock beneath. It planed New England's hills to smooth, rounded surfaces. In addition, the glacier moved large, individual boulders from their source area and striated and polished them. Some of these boulders are 6 ft to 10 ft in diameter. Further evidence of glaciation is found in drumlins, eskers, kames, and kettle lakes that dot the ground moraine and outwash plains.

Ancient river beds were enlarged into the Great Lakes during the last continental glacier.

The Great Lakes of the central Canadian border region illustrate how glacial erosion and deposition may change old river drainage patterns. Apparently, the present Great Lakes were former river valleys. These valleys were deepened and widened as the ice pushed southward. When melting occurred, the depressions filled with water and became great inland bodies of fresh water. At one time, the Great Lakes were much larger than at present. Beaches and other shore features were deposited in Michigan, Indiana, Illinois, and Wisconsin. These features are on land that is now far above lake level. Early drainage from the lakes flowed through the Chicago River to the Mississippi River drainage basin. Melting gradually removed ice from the Canadian region. Then the Chicago River drainage route was abandoned. Finally, the present drainage route through the St. Lawrence River was developed. This new route is at a lower level than that of the Chicago River route. Some changes in the drainage of the Great Lakes occurred because the crust rose after the retreat of the ice. The great downward pressure of the ice due to its weight depressed the northern area. When the weight of the ice was removed, the crust returned to its pre-glacial position. This elevation is higher than the elevation of the earlier drainage pattern.

The world had a pluvial climate during the melting of the continental glaciers.

World climates were affected by melting of the ice. Even climates in regions not involved directly in glaciation became much more humid than they are now. Such a humid climate is called *pluvial* (ploo' vee al), a term which means rainy. During retreat of the ice, even the now semiarid areas of western United States were humid. Lake Bonneville spread westward from the foot of the Wasatch Mountains across much of Utah and Nevada. This former lake covered about 20,000 mi^2 with water to a depth of 1,000. The lake has dwindled until only the

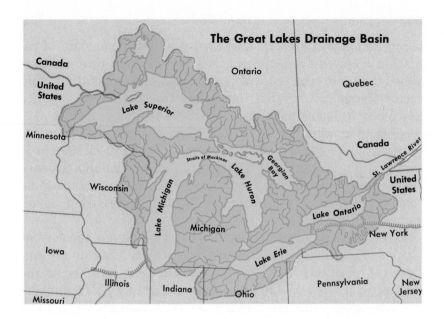

The Great Lakes Drainage Basin

Canada
United States
Minnesota
Lake Superior
Ontario
Quebec
Canada
St. Lawrence River
United States
Straits of Mackinac
Georgian Bay
Lake Huron
Wisconsin
Lake Michigan
Michigan
Lake Ontario
New York
Iowa
Lake Erie
Illinois
Indiana
Ohio
Pennsylvania
New Jersey
Missouri

Figure 15-23. As the Pleistocene glacier advanced southward, it followed a former drainage system and deepened and widened old river channels in which lakes now stand.

Great Salt Lake of Utah remains. The former size of Lake Bonneville is revealed by shore features now stranded high above the Great Salt Lake. Because weathering and erosion are exceptionally slow in a desert climate, the old lake features have been preserved.

15:6 *Theories of Glacial Origin*

At least three times during the earth's history, continental glaciers have appeared, made their mark, and then departed. The earliest glacier appeared over 600,000,000 years ago. The next period of glaciation occurred about 200,000,000 years ago. However, this glaciation did not affect the northern hemisphere. Only Africa, South America, India, and Australia were glaciated. The most recent glaciation began less than 1,000,000 years ago. The ice retreated from North America about 11,000 years ago. Ice caps at the poles are remnants of this most recent glacial event.

At least three ice ages have occurred during the geologic past.

Many theories have been suggested to explain why glaciers have occurred at such widely separated times, and in such widely separated places. One suggestion is that the earth's poles have not always been in the same position with respect to the continents. If continents have moved (Section 17:3), then it may be that at some time in the past the oceans were over the poles. Ice could not accumulate in the water, and no glaciers could form. But when land was over the poles, or very near the poles, then snowfall could remain, and eventually

Ice ages may be related to a shift in position of the earth's poles.

Decreased radiation may have caused lower temperatures and growth of ice fields.

Increased radiation received by earth may have resulted in increased evaporation and more snowfall at the poles.

become a glacier. Another idea suggests that the amount of radiation received from the sun has varied from time to time. When the earth received less heat than normal, glaciation could occur. Temperatures fell, more snow accumulated, and ice advanced to lower and lower latitudes before it melted. According to another theory, glaciers formed during an increase in radiation from the sun. The increased heat caused increased evaporation, and increased precipitation. Eventually, a dense cloud cover shut out heat from the sun. Then the earth became colder. Increased precipitation resulted in increased snow accumulation at the poles.

Like the theories of the earth's origin, present theories of glacier origin are not completely acceptable. They do not answer all questions about glaciation. However, studies of the Antarctic, as well as other research concerning polar wandering, may eventually provide the answers. Certainly much has been learned about glaciation since the middle of the last century. Louis Agassiz (ag'a see), a Swiss-American naturalist of the nineteenth century, first recognized that continental glaciation had occurred. Agassiz had studied the behavior of glaciers in his native Switzerland. He learned to identify both erosional and depositional features of valley glaciers. When Agassiz visited the United States, he traveled across the northern states. There he recognized many features similar to those of his home area. He found widespread ground moraines, eskers, terminal moraines, and polished and striated bedrock in a region where no mountains were present. Following the theory of uniformitarianism (Section 6:1), Agassiz suggested that a massive ice sheet must have covered the northern United

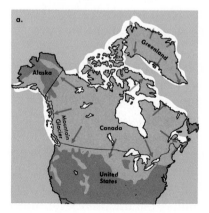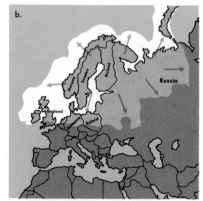

Figure 15-24. Only 11,000 years ago, millions of square miles of North America (a.) and Europe (b.) were covered by ice.

States. Many scientists have studied this region and have come to the same conclusion. The behavior and features of existing glaciers help scientists to recognize the presence of glaciation in the past.

MAIN IDEAS

1. Snow becomes granular, firn, and finally true glacier ice if the thickness of ice is great enough, and if it remains in place for several seasons.

2. Snow collects in a snowfield and extends to the snow line where melting counterbalances deposits of new snow.

3. Glaciers form in high latitudes and/or high altitudes if precipitation is available and temperatures are below freezing.

4. Bottom ice of a glacier becomes plastic under pressure. Surface ice remains brittle and cracks when bottom ice begins to flow.

5. High altitude glaciers are called valley glaciers. High latitude glaciers that cover vast areas are called continental glaciers.

6. Glaciers erode by abrading with debris plucked from beneath them and frozen into the bottom ice.

7. Erosional features of valley glaciers include cirques, horns, aretes, U-shaped channels, and hanging valleys.

8. The Canadian Shield was covered by a continental glacier from about 1 million to 11,000 years ago.

9. Depositional features of glaciers include terminal moraine, ground moraine, drumlins, outwash plains, eskers, kames, kettle lakes, and finger lakes.

10. A continental glacier which covered part of North America apparently gouged out river valleys to form the present Great Lakes.

11. Ancient Lake Bonneville was present in Utah during the retreat of the continental glacier. Changes in climate caused this great lake to dwindle until all that remains is the Great Salt Lake.

12. Ice ages may result from a shift in the position of the earth's poles with respect to the continents, from changes in the atmosphere due to volcanic activity, or from changes in the amount of sun's radiation received on earth. More heat may have led to greater evaporation, more precipitation, and a filtering of the sun's radiation. Less heat may have led to an increase in the accumulation of ice.

VOCABULARY

Write a sentence in which you use correctly each of the following words or terms.

cirque	meltwater	recede
crevasse	moraine	shield
firn	piedmont	striated
granule	pluvial	terminal

STUDY QUESTIONS

A. True or False

Determine whether each of the following sentences is true or false. (Do not write in this book.)

1. Erosion by glaciers covers more area than erosion by any other agent.
2. The snow line is the line where melting counterbalances addition of snow.
3. Glaciers form in mountains if snow reaches a depth of 100 ft to 200 ft and stays in place for several seasons.
4. Temperature and precipitation determine the formation of glaciers.
5. An ice field is not a glacier until the ice begins to move.
6. Movement in a valley glacier is most rapid at its center.
7. Some material in a ground moraine may have been deposited by meltwater.
8. The outwash plain is formed by meltwater alone.
9. The Finger Lakes of New York State were formed by moraines left in their valleys by former glaciers.
10. The Great Salt Lake is a remnant of Lake Bonneville.

B. Multiple Choice

Choose the word or phrase which completes correctly each of the following sentences. (Do not write in this book.)

1. Formation of true glacier ice resembles the formation of (*igneous, sedimentary, metamorphic*) rock.

2. An ice cap covers much of (*Canada, Greenland, Ireland*).

3. The hollow in which a mountain glacier starts is called a(n) (*cirque, bergschrund, arete*).

4. Openings or cracks between rock walls and glaciers on mountain summits are called (*bergschrunds, aretes, horns*).

5. Unsorted material, dropped directly by melting ice, is called (*loess, till, outwash*).

6. When melting exceeds forward movement, the glacier deposits a (*lateral, terminal, ground*) moraine.

7. Small hills composed of drift and left on the ground moraine are called (*kettle lakes, drumlins, cirques*).

8. Before the last continental glacier melted, the Great Lakes drained into the (*Hudson Bay, St. Lawrence River, Mississippi River*).

9. At one time, the Great Lakes covered much more of the area of (*New Jersey, Pennsylvania, Michigan*) than they do today.

10. The last ice age began about (*6, 2, 1*) million years ago.

C. Completion

Complete each of the following sentences with a word or phrase which will make the sentence correct. (Do not write in this book.)

1. Rounded granules of ice become compacted by pressure into __?__ or __?__.

2. Valley glaciers are also called __?__ or __?__.

3. A glacier at the foot of a mountain is called a(n) __?__ glacier.

4. Erosion of the tops of hills indicates that the area was once covered by a(n) __?__ glacier.

5. Tributary glaciers leave __?__ above the main glacier channel.

6. The farthest advance of a glacier is marked by a(n) __?__ .

7. Melting of buried blocks of ice leaves __?__ lakes in a glaciated area.

8. Ground moraine may contain small serpentine hills of sorted material called __?__ or rounded gravel hills called __?__ .

9. The glaciated area of Canada is known as the __?__ .

10. __?__ is the term that describes a rainy climate.

D. How and Why

1. What determines the erosive capability of a valley glacier? How does this differ from the erosive capability of a river?

2. Why might exceedingly low temperatures make the formation of a glacier impossible?

3. Why is the snow line at a higher altitude in the Rocky Mountains of Montana than in the Cascades of Washington even though these mountains are located in almost the same latitude?

4. Would you expect a greater snowfield on Mt. McKinley (elevation 20,320 ft) in Alaska, or on Mt. Chimborazo (elevation 20,551 ft) in Ecuador? Why?

5. Why does a continental glacier move in areas of little or no gradient?

6. How might the melting of ice caps affect sea level and the seacoasts?

7. How might melting of ice caps affect the circulation of seawater and climates of seacoasts?

8. How might melting of the ice caps change the altitude of continents?

9. Why was the drainage pattern of the Great Lakes changed after the last continental glacier melted?

10. How are the salt water bays (fiords) of Norway related to glaciers?

INVESTIGATIONS

1. (a) On an outline map of the world, indicate the present position of ice caps and glaciers.

(b) On a map of the United States, indicate the present drainage pattern of the Great Lakes. Using a different colored pencil, show them before the glacier melted and the present drainage pattern developed.

(c) On a map of North America, show the area covered by the last glacier (Pleistocene).

2. Examine the ice in the freezing compartment of a refrigerator. What kinds of ice do you find there? How are they formed?

3. (a) Report on any military bases which are located on an ice cap. Discuss the problems of living under glacial conditions.

(b) Report on any story (fact or fiction) which tells of an animal or person being frozen in a glacier or ice cap.

(c) Report on the life of Louis Agassiz and his study of glaciers.

INTERESTING READING

Agassiz, Louis, *Studies on Glaciers*, Albert Carozzi, ed. Darien, Conn., Hafner Publishing Co., 1967.

"Antarctica: The World's Most Fascinating Icebox," *Reader's Digest* (September, 1965), pp. 119–23.

Baum, Allyn, *Antarctica: The Worst Place in the World*. New York, The Macmillan Company, 1967.

Davis, K. S., and Day, J. A., *Water: The Mirror of Science*. Garden City, N.Y., Doubleday & Co., Inc., 1961.

Eklund, Carl D., and Beckman, Joan, *Antarctica*. New York, Holt, Rinehart & Winston, Inc., 1963.

Fenton, Carroll L. and Mildred A., *Giants of Geology*. Garden City, N.Y., Doubleday & Company, Inc., 1952.

*Ley, Willy, *The Poles*. Life Nature Library. New York, Time Inc., 1962.

Schultz, Gwen, *Glaciers and the Ice Age*. New York, Holt, Rinehart & Winston, Inc., 1963.

Sharp, Robert P., *Glaciers*. Eugene, Ore., University of Oregon Press, 1960.

---

* Well-illustrated material.

16 Wind

Wind erosion is neither as widespread as water erosion nor as deeply abrasive as glacial erosion. However, wind is an important erosional agent in climates and areas where water and ice are not abundant.

Unlike the flow of water and of valley glaciers, wind is not confined to channels. Instead, wind blows freely over the landscape in all directions and at varying speeds. But little erosion occurs unless the wind has materials which act as tools to abrade and undercut the obstacles in its path.

16:1 *Wind-Borne Material*

Wind carries in suspension or sweeps along before it materials which cause wind erosion. Recall that large-scale air movements and currents are caused by temperature differences between the equator and the poles of the earth. The direction of the air movements is affected by the earth's rotation as well as by temperatures. These movements constitute the major wind systems of the earth. (Section 10:2.) Wind moves forward constantly. But it also moves in a turbulent fashion, with updrafts, downdrafts, and local eddies.

Wind includes large wind systems and local turbulent air movements.

Wind-borne material is called **eolian** (ee oh' lee an) **material.** It is composed of sand, silt, and dust particles. These particles are picked up from the surface over which the wind blows. Plowed fields, river flood plains, volcanoes, and glaciated areas furnish rock debris, or *detritus* (di triet' us), to the wind. Deserts and shore zones are the most common sources of wind-blown particles. There loose material is available and water action is intermittent, or periodic. By contrast, moist areas and lands covered by vegetation contribute little material to the wind.

Winds transport any available detritus, particularly from desert and shore zones.

Most sand grains carried by the wind are quartz. But some grains are gypsum such as the White Sands of New Mexico. Other grains, such as the "coral sands" of Bermuda, are calcite. Volcanic ash or glass, finer than either quartz or gypsum grains, also is carried by the wind. *Loess* (les) is the fine material carried by the wind. It consists of silt-size particles and dust gathered from deserts, alluvial plains, or glaciated areas, especially from old, dry glacial lake beds.

Loess is composed of silt and dust-size particles.

Turbulent action carries the sediments at varying heights and in many directions. If the wind is gentle, heavy grains bump along the ground and bounce other grains out of place. Dislodged grains then can be moved easily by the wind. These grains are carried forward until the pull of gravity or a downdraft overcomes their forward movement. At times, blowing sand appears to form a moving blanket near the ground. Sometimes ground currents form miniature whirlwinds, called "dust devils."

Distance and height to which material is carried depend upon several factors. These factors include the size of the grains, the velocity of the wind, and the length of time the wind blows. The upper range of wind action is limited by the height to which the wind can carry the grains. Because it is heavier than dust, sand stays close to the ground and falls quickly. Updrafts carry fine silt and dust into the upper air currents. There strong winds can transport these fine particles far from their place of origin. Study of eolian deposits may furnish clues to ancient climates and geologic formation.

Wind action depends on size of grains, speed of wind, and period of time it blows.

Wind constantly redistributes loose sediments. In the process, the wind etches (ech'es) and cuts surface rocks and, thus, makes more fragments available as tools of erosion.

Phyllis G. Lewis

Figure 16-1. White dunes in the background are deposits of gypsum at White Sands, New Mexico.

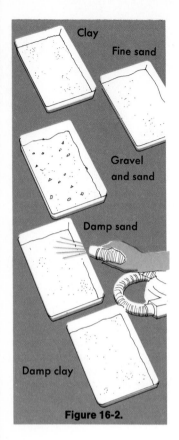

Clay

Fine sand

Gravel and sand

Damp sand

Damp clay

Figure 16-2.

EXPERIMENT. Obtain various types of detrital material, including clay, fine sand, and a mixture of gravel and sand. Arrange each type of material in a separate flat pan. Fill a fourth pan with damp sand and a fifth pan with damp clay. Direct a stream of air from an electric fan, a hair dryer, or a vacuum cleaner blower onto each of the pans. Be sure that the distance between the blower and the pan is the same for each test. Note what happens to each type of material. Now vary the distance to the blower. Then change the angle at which the air strikes the materials in the pans. Put obstacles (a few twigs, some gravel, a pencil, etc.) in the pans and observe the effect on the material. Sift some sand in front of the blower. What happens? If you use a hair dryer, what effect does time have on the behavior of the damp sand and damp clay? Why?

Record your observations in your notebook. What type of material is picked up most easily by the wind? What is the effect of moisture on the ability of the wind to pick up materials? How does an obstacle affect the action of the wind? What effect does the gravel have on the wind erosion of the sand-gravel mixture? What shape of dune did you form? What effect would vegetation have had on the experiment? In which pan(s) were dunes formed? If dunes were not formed in all pans, explain why.

16:2 *Erosion*

Wind erosion removes loose topsoil in semihumid and semi-arid lands.

Removal of material by wind is called **deflation.** It is an important process in wind erosion. In semiarid and semihumid lands, wind removes tremendous amounts of topsoil in periods of drought. During the 1930's, parts of the bared land in the drought-stricken Middle West became known as the "dust bowl." Enormous quantities of wind-blown sediments were removed. Cultivated land, no longer held in place by vegetation, lost more than three feet of topsoil. Some fine silt was carried as far east as the Atlantic Coast. Larger grains often came to rest in the source area. Trees, houses, fences, and barns were buried under worthless sand. Eventually, all of this wind-blown material came to rest. But the land laid bare by erosion was of little value for many years.

Wind erosion in deserts may leave bare desert pavements or oases at water table level.

Loose material may be removed so completely in desert areas that bedrock or a "desert pavement" of flat pebbles is exposed. Occasionally, the wind erodes material down to the water table. When water is available near the surface, trees, shrubs, and

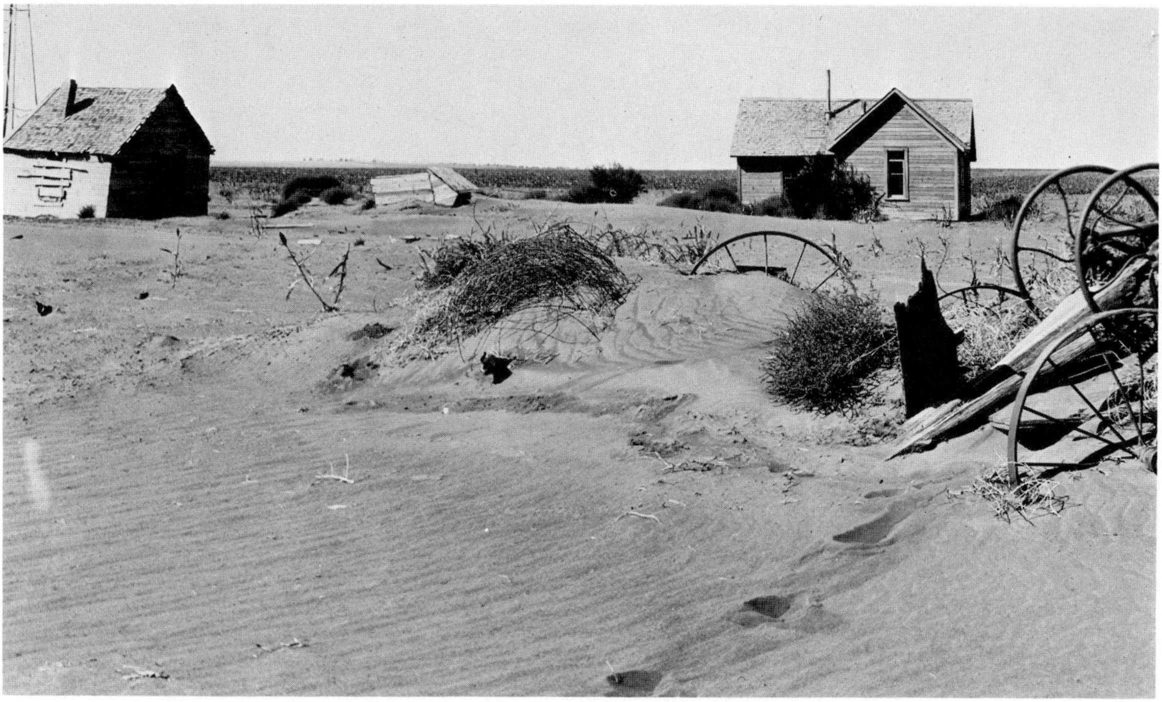

Figure 16-3. A typical dust bowl scene in which wind has piled sand and silt around all obstructions.

Figure 16-4. Ventifacts are shaped by the abrasive action of wind-blown sand.

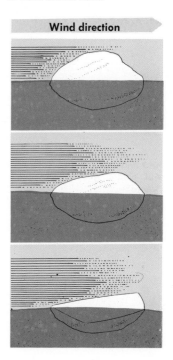

Wind direction

grasses take root and form an *oasis* (oh ae'sis), or fertile green spot within the desert waste. The trees act as a barrier against further erosion or additions of materials to the oasis. But occasionally, during especially severe storms, sand dunes may overtake an oasis and bury it. Oases prove that deserts can be very fertile where water is available.

Abrasion by wind polishes resistant rock and carves out soft layers. Wind caves, natural arches, rock windows, and bridges result from the sandblasting type of wind action. Even rock faces are etched into lace-like surfaces. Boulders left in the path of the wind are polished and etched. Desert boulders and pebbles too large to be carried by the wind have flat sides which meet at a sharp angle. These rocks are quite unlike the rounded shapes of water-worn pebbles. Each side of the rock facing the wind becomes flat. Then as the rock turns, another side is worn down. Such rocks are called *ventifacts* (vent' a fakts).

Sand-size particles carried by the wind develop spherical, pitted surfaces. Water-borne sand is angular because each grain is protected by a thin film of water. In contrast, eolian

Figure 16-5.   Weathering and erosional processes have combined to form these unique rock shapes in the Arizona desert.

grains collide with each other so often that all angles disappear and the surface of each grain has a frosted, or pitted appearance. Geologists can distinguish between eolian fragments and fluvial fragments by their shapes and surface appearance.

16:3   *Wind Deposits*

Wind-blown material comes to rest when winds die down. Sand bumps and bounces along the ground. Eventually it comes to rest near the place where it was picked up by the wind. Silt includes the largest particles which wind can carry in suspension for any distance. Silt is moved farther than sand and deposited separately. Fine dust particles may be carried great distances and for long periods of time. They are deposited only during rain or snow storms.

Loess may be gathered from alluvial plains, glacial deposits, or deserts.

Loess, unlike most wind-blown grains, consists of particles so fine that they have retained their angular shape. Loess particles tend to lock together to form densely packed soil. This is fertile soil because it retains minerals that would be dissolved and removed if carried by water. In North America, loess deposits are found on hilltops and valleys near the Mississippi River. These deposits probably originated in glacial lake clays, or perhaps on the outwash plains of the last Ice Age. Fine material was carried down into the Mississippi Valley by strong winds blowing across the remains of the ice sheet. Winds resorted the material and left silt near the Mississippi River.

Meston's Travels

Figure 16-6. Small plants catch and hold blowing sand. Thus, they often start the formation of a dune or prevent a dune from moving leeward.

Fine clay particles were carried beyond the Mississippi Valley. Loess deposits of China consist of wind-borne material from the Gobi (goh'bee) Desert and the Ordos (orh'dohs) Desert. These deposits are much thicker than those of the Mississippi Valley.

Sand dunes are the most common wind deposits. Dunes form in semiarid and desert regions and on shores where sand is plentiful and dry. Coarse sand is piled relatively close to its place of origin. Fine silt may be blown some distance. Any obstacle in the wind's path slows its velocity and causes it to deposit its load. Since obstacles need not be large to produce this effect, small plants often start the growth of dunes. (Figure 16–6.)

Along shores or in semiarid regions, plants may take root in the piled sand. Then the loose sand, which once threatened to bury everything in its path, becomes a fixed dune. Grass- and tree-covered ridges, once migrating dunes, have formed parallel to the shores of some of the Great Lakes. Unanchored dunes continue to migrate inland along neighboring shores.

If the wind's path is not obstructed, dunes move in the direction toward which the wind is blowing. Bare, hard surfaces are swept clean and every available particle of sand is added to the growing dune. Each wind scours sand from the windward side of the dune. The sand is carried across the crest to the leeward side. The leeward slope is called the *slipface*. The loose sand slips and slides down its steep face, but eventually the sand is piled too high. Then sand slides downward as a thin sheet until the slope is gentle enough to withstand the pull of gravity. Dunes have a gentle slope on the windward side and a steep slope on the leeward side. Dune shapes may be changed from time to time as the direction of the wind changes. Rounded, symmetrical dunes may form, but they tend to shift from place to place. Such dunes do not reach the height of dunes in a prevailing wind belt. (Figure 16–8.)

Ward's Natural Science Est.

Figure 16-7. Dead trees show the destructive effect of the advance of a sand dune into the forest area.

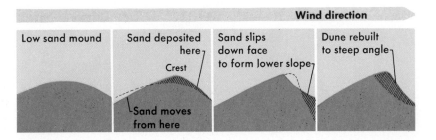

Wind direction

| Low sand mound | Sand deposited here | Sand slips down face to form lower slope | Dune rebuilt to steep angle |

Crest

Sand moves from here

Figure 16-8. Dunes advance leeward as sand is blown from the windward slope over the crest to the slipface.

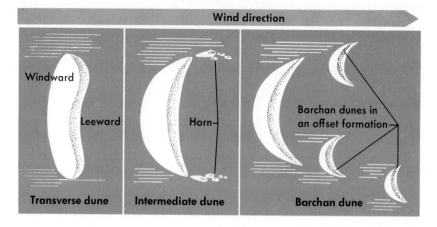

Wind direction

Windward

Leeward

Transverse dune

Horn

Intermediate dune

Barchan dunes in an offset formation →

Barchan dune

Free moving dunes form barchan dunes with a convex side toward the wind.

Transverse dunes form on a hard, dry surface where wind direction is constant. Commonly, transverse dunes become crescent (kres'ent) shaped and are called *barchan* (bahr'kahn) *dunes.* As winds continue to blow, sand from the ends of the growing dune is carried forward into horn-like projections. The convex side of the dune is toward the wind. Because the inside curve is protected on all sides but one, the slipface is steep. Over long periods of time, migrating sand is carried from the ends. Then new barchans appear near the projections in an offset pattern. (Figure 16–9.)

Anchored dunes form parabolic dunes with a concave side toward the wind.

Another type of crescent-shaped dune is the *parabolic* (par a bahl'ik) *dune.* It is formed in a prevailing wind belt if vegetation holds down the end of a transverse dune. Winds move the central part of the dune forward into a concave curve. If the wind continues to blow steadily, the center of the dune may be carried away and later re-formed as a new dune.

Figure 16-10. Ripple marks on these dunes at White Sands, New Mexico indicate the prevailing wind direction.

Meston's Travels

16:4   *Evidence of Eolian Erosion*

Etched rock faces, polished boulders, wind caves and windows are evidence of wind erosion. Rounded grains and excellent sorting by size distinguish wind-borne debris from debris carried by water or glaciers. Migrating dunes or fixed dunes are composed of unconsolidated sand grains. They are ample proof of the continuing work of the wind.

Evidence of past wind erosion and deposition is found in consolidated sand dunes. Dunes which formed millions of years ago were covered and cemented into hard sandstone layers. Such dunes are recognizable by their cross bedding. The layers lie at steep angles to each other, unlike the horizontal stratified layers of most sedimentary rock formations. Eolian deposits are laid down with a gentle slope on the windward side and a steep slope on the leeward side. Although successive layers are composed of rounded grains of uniform size, shifts in wind direction are registered by layers laid down at different angles. Road cuts and renewed erosion have exposed ancient dunes in many parts of the arid and semiarid West.

Eolian erosion is recognized by characteristic rock formations, etched boulders, and rounded rock fragments.

Petrified sand dunes are wind deposits of ancient geologic periods.

Ward's Natural Science Establishment, Inc.

Figure 16-11. This cross section shows how a dune is built up layer upon layer.

MAIN IDEAS

1. Wind is movement of air in large systems, in local turbulence, in any direction, and at any velocity.

2. Wind erosion is particularly common in arid, semiarid, or shore areas where detritus is available. Plants help to keep materials from being carried away by the wind.

3. Wind-borne materials are quartz, gypsum, volcanic or calcite sand, dust, and silt.

4. Size of grains, velocity of wind, and length of time wind blows determine how high and how far detritus can be carried.

5. Wind removes topsoil in semihumid and semiarid lands and may sweep desert surfaces down to hard rock layers or to water tables. Oases form where the water table is exposed.

6. Wind abrasion removes soft rock to form windows, leaves resistant rock in arches and bridges, etches boulders, and smooths and sorts sand grains.

7. Deposits of silt and fine clay derived from glacial lake beds, alluvial plains, or deserts form compact soil called loess.

8. Sand dunes form transverse to the wind with a gentle slope facing the wind and a steep slope away from the wind.

9. All dunes migrate unless tied down by vegetation. Barchans have the convex side toward the wind. Parabolic dunes have the concave side facing the wind because the ends are anchored by vegetation.

10. Eolian erosion creates abraded rock, spherical sand grains, and petrified sand dunes.

VOCABULARY

Write a sentence in which you use correctly each of the following words or terms.

barchan	eolian	oasis
concave	fluvial	parabolic dune
convex	loess	slipface
detritus	migrating dunes	transverse dune

STUDY QUESTIONS

A. True or False

Determine whether each of the following sentences is true or false. (Do not write in this book.)

1. Wind erosion is not as widespread as water erosion.
2. Winds blow in the direction of the large wind systems.
3. Winds commonly blow in a turbulent fashion.
4. Sand grains are seldom lifted aloft except by strong winds.
5. "Dust devils" are miniature whirlwinds.
6. Dust storms of the 1930's originated in the fertile farms of the Mississippi Valley.
7. Eolian sand grains are angular and of many different sizes.
8. A crescent dune concave to the wind results if vegetation grows on the dune ends.
9. Shore dunes develop parallel to the waterline.
10. The slipface of a dune faces the windward direction.

B. Multiple Choice

Choose the word or phrase which completes correctly each of the following sentences. (Do not write in this book.)

1. Wind-borne material is called (*fluvial, pluvial, eolian*).
2. Sediments deposited by water are (*fluvial, pluvial, eolian*) sediments.
3. Most common sand grains are (*gypsum, quartz, calcite*).
4. Bermuda's white beaches are grains of (*gypsum, quartz, calcite*).
5. China's large deposits of loess came from (*glacial deposits, deserts, alluvial plains*).
6. A crescent dune convex to the wind is a (*barchan, parabolic, transverse*) dune.
7. Migrating dunes commonly begin as (*barchan, parabolic, transverse*) dunes.
8. The dune which usually has the steepest slipface is the (*barchan, parabolic, transverse*) dune.

9. The gentle slope of a dune is on the (*windward side, leeward side, slipface*).

10. Loess deposits in the Mississippi Valley are mainly from (*glacial lake deposits, desert dust, fluvial deposits*).

C. Completion

Complete each of the following sentences with a word or phrase which will make the sentence correct. (Do not write in this book.)

1. A general term for rock debris from weathering and erosion is ___?___.

2. Wind deposits of dust and silt are called ___?___.

3. During droughts, cultivated lands may lose ___?___ which is no longer held in place by vegetation.

4. The wind cuts and ___?___ rock surfaces.

5. A small grove of trees and shrubs in a desert is called a(n) ___?___.

6. The steep slope of a sand dune is called the ___?___.

7. Crescent dunes convex to the wind are called ___?___.

8. The White Sands of New Mexico are deposits of ___?___.

9. Fine silt and dust are removed from deserts by the process of ___?___.

10. Irregular ___?___ in certain sandstone layers may indicate that the layers belong to ancient hardened sand dunes.

D. How and Why

1. Do all ocean shore zones have sand dunes parallel to the coast? Why?

2. Why can the wind sort material so completely that sand and silt are seldom found together?

3. Why do particles of loess retain their angles, but sand grains become rounded?

4. Why are sand dunes along the eastern shore of Lake Michigan larger and more prevalent than sand dunes on the western shore of Lake Michigan? Why do the Michigan and Indiana dunes migrate inland?

5. Why are "dust devils" more common in southwestern deserts than in northern, sandy areas?

6. In what type of rock are wind caves and windows formed? Why?

7. How could you recognize a hardened sand dune?

8. Why do Great Sand Dunes of Colorado and White Sands of New Mexico remain localized instead of migrating?

9. Dust from the eruption in 1883 of the volcano Krakatoa in Indonesia is said to have been carried around the entire world. How would this have been possible?

10. Would quartz, gypsum, or calcite particles be most effective for wind scour and abrasion? (Refer to Table 4–2.)

11. Explain why telephone poles, light poles, etc., in desert regions are protected by piles of boulders around their bases, but this protection does not extend upward beyond one to two feet.

INVESTIGATIONS

1. Report on wind blown volcanic ash from the volcano Irazu in Costa Rica (1963-64) or Mt. Katmai in Alaska (1912).

2. Report on the effect of the "dust bowl" of the 1930's. Discuss the conditions that existed, reasons for the conditions, and possible safeguards against their repetition.

3. Report on the effect of wind on Cape Cod, Cape Hatteras, and Padre Island on the Gulf Coast.

4. On a world map, indicate all desert regions and all known loess deposits. Relate the deserts to major wind systems and land features.

5. Report on the sand dunes of the Great Lakes, Southern California, and Colorado. What are the problems created by these dunes? How can they be controlled?

INTERESTING READING

Bendick, Jeanne, *The Wind*. Chicago, Rand McNally & Co., n.d.

Bloom, A. L., *The Surface of the Earth*. Englewood Cliffs, N.J., Prentice-Hall, Inc., 1969.

*Leopold, A. Starker, *The Desert*. Life Nature Library. New York, Time Inc., 1967.

*Shimer, John, *This Sculptured Earth, The Landscape of America*. New York, Columbia University Press, 1959.

* Well-illustrated material.

Crustal Movements

Winds, rivers, glaciers, and ocean waves have eroded the surface of the earth since its formation. Yet mountains still reach toward the sky, and continents remain above the sea. What forces maintain mountains and continents? What forces offset the effects of weathering and erosion?

Ancient Greeks and Romans believed that mountains were formed by giants who were trying to reach the heavens. According to one myth, the giants piled one peak on top of another to form a stairway to the sky. Zeus, the king of the gods, struck down the peaks with his thunderbolts and scattered the remains into rugged, mountain chains. Zeus then imprisoned the giants beneath the mountains. During their struggle to escape, the giants broke the earth's crust and hurled liquid rock against their enemy, Zeus.

17:1 *Diastrophism*

These Greek and Roman myths are not acceptable scientific explanations. They do not account for upheavals of the earth's crust or for eruptions of volcanoes. But the myths show that ancient peoples recognized some relationship between volcanoes and earthquakes and the earth's interior. Today, many scientists believe that most crustal movements are caused by the release of heat energy. The heat results from decay of radioactive elements within the earth. (Appendix E, p. 533.)

Mountains display rocks of every kind in every possible position. Rock formations may be horizontal, twisted, torn, tilted, or folded. Geologists go to mountains to study the relationships among different rock layers. From such studies, they hope to understand the processes by which rocks are moved from one position to another.

Diastrophism (die as'tra fiz em) includes all processes by which rocks are moved from one place to another or from one position to another. The term diastrophism comes from a Greek word which means "to deform or twist." The effects of diastrophism are most evident in sedimentary rocks. Sedimentary rocks are laid down in layers in nearly a horizontal position. Furthermore, most sedimentary rocks were deposited in the sea. Therefore, sedimentary rocks that are found in mountains or plateaus thousands of feet above the sea are evidence that uplift has occurred. Sedimentary rocks that lie in a horizontal position at high levels show that movement must have been vertically upward. Rocks that are folded, twisted, or broken reveal that direction of crustal movements may be upward, downward, or horizontal.

Horizontal movement may be recognized if rock layers end abruptly, then reappear some distance away. Sometimes houses, fences, and other man-made installations attached to solid rock are broken and the parts are separated. The rocks also must have shifted.

Diastrophism includes all processes by which rocks are broken, folded, uplifted, or depressed.

Deformation can be recognized in sedimentary rocks that were laid down in horizontal layers at sea level.

Figure 17-1. Majestic peaks of the Grand Teton Mountains, Wyoming, represent a series of fault blocks tilted downward toward the right.

Ned Schreiner

Uplift and subsidence often can be recognized where shore features are above or below present sea level.

Even slight crustal movements may be observed along shore zones. Beaches and undercut cliffs now high above the present water level suggest an upward movement of the land or a lowering of sea level. Flooded river mouths, known as *estuaries* (es'cha wer eez), suggest either a downward movement of land or a rise of sea level. Sometimes it is impossible to determine whether land has risen or sea level has lowered. Movement measured as the difference between the old and new positions of certain features is known as *relative movement.*

Evidence of alternating uplift and *subsidence* (sub sied' ens), or sinking, of a shore zone is found in a temple near Naples, Italy. The temple was built on land above sea level. Eventually, the land sank, and underwater clams bored holes in the marble columns of the temple. Today the temple is again above sea level, and the clam borings can be seen halfway up the temple columns. The old temple has a record of the subsidence and uplift of the Mediterranean shore bored into its marble columns.

Figure 17-2. In the Panorama Hills, northeast of Maricopa, California, drainage is offset to the right where streams cross the San Andreas fault. Movement along the fault is toward the northwest on the southwestern side of the fault. This horizontal movement is an example of a strike-slip fault.

Few records of crustal movement can be recognized as easily as the one in the temple at Naples. But examples of displacement are found in many areas. The *San Andreas* (san · ahn drae'ahs) *fault* is a line of weakness along the Pacific Coast. Many earthquakes have occurred along this zone. During the San Francisco earthquake in 1906, horizontal movement along

U.S. Forest Service

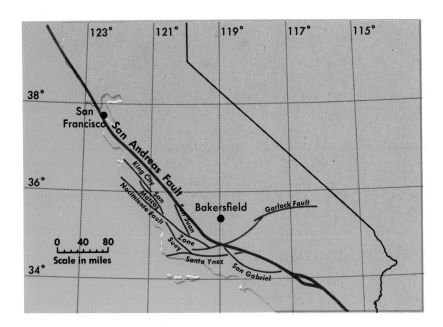

Figure 17-3. The San Andreas strike-slip fault accounts for many earthquakes as the oceanward block moves northward from time to time.

the San Andreas fault measured between 16 ft and 21 ft. Along the Baltic Sea, measurements of movement have been recorded for many years. These measurements show that the coast is rising at the rate of about 1 in./yr.

Movement still occurs along the San Andreas Fault in California.

Sometimes displacements occur rapidly. They may require only a few seconds for several feet of movement. Other movements occur slowly and require thousands of years for a few inches of change. Regardless of the direction or rate of crustal movements, any change in rock position is outward evidence of the work of internal forces.

17:2   *Internal Forces*

Materials within the earth are like other solids. They hold together, or cohere (koh hir′), because of the mutual attraction between molecules. This resistance to change in shape or volume is called **cohesive force**. External force must be exerted against a solid body to cause a change in shape or volume. *Elastic bodies* recover their original shape and volume when the external force is removed. But every body has a limit of resistance to force. If this limit is exceeded, the body changes shape or volume, or both. Then the body does not return to its original shape or volume. A force may change the shape or volume of a given body permanently. In this case, the force exceeds the *elastic limit* of that body. Such forces include tension, compression, shearing, and buoyancy. (Figure 17–4.)

Tension is a stretching force which may pull rocks apart.

Tension (ten'chun) is a pulling force. A body under tension is stretched, or pulled in opposite directions. Tension is illustrated by the stretching of a rubber band. When tension is removed, the rubber band returns to its original shape and size because it is elastic. But the elasticity of even a rubber band is limited. A rubber band breaks if it is stretched beyond its limit of elasticity. Rocks also are elastic. But if the tension is greater than their elasticity, rocks will pull apart. In general, rocks tend to have great strength. Their elastic limit is exceeded only by tremendous forces.

Compression is a squeezing force that may cause bending or breaking.

In contrast to tension, **compression** is a system of forces pushing against a body from directly opposite sides. For example, a soft rubber ball may be compressed or squeezed until it changes from a sphere to an elongated shape. The rubber ball tends to return to its original shape when the compressional forces are removed. Rocks also change shape when squeezed or compressed. However, rocks are less elastic than rubber. They tend to retain their changed shape or volume. Rocks may even break if they are compressed beyond a given point. Compression tends to squeeze rocks into accordion-like forms. These forms occupy less space than the original shapes.

Shearing forces are directed against a body from two directions. But the opposing forces are not directly opposite the same point of the body. Shearing causes bodies to become twisted or torn. During shearing, parts of the body slide past one another. Many rocks of the earth are sheared during crustal movements.

Buoyancy is an upward force exerted by a liquid on a floating or submerged body. The force is always equal to the weight

Figure 17-4. Stresses within the earth cause movement of the crust and often rupture rocks along lines of weakness.

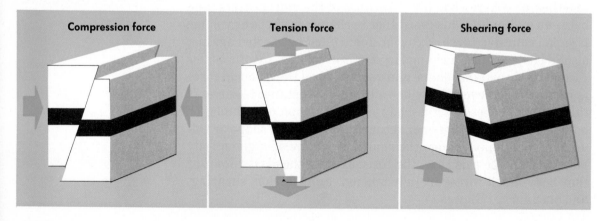

of the displaced liquid. A body that is less dense than a liquid will float in that liquid. Some vertical movements of the earth's crust are due to buoyancy. Great crustal blocks float on the plastic, pliable mantle (density 3.3 g/cm³) as blocks of wood float on water. Blocks composed of sedimentary rock have a density of about 2.5 g/cm³. Sedimentary rocks would float higher than blocks composed of granite which has a density of 2.7 g/cm³. Either sedimentary or granite would float higher than blocks composed of basalt which has a density of about 3.0 g/cm³. Actually, blocks of the crust may contain more than one kind of rock. But continental rocks are mostly granite with some sedimentary rock. Oceanic blocks are mostly basalt. During erosion, material is removed from the elevated blocks of the continent. This sediment is deposited in great deltas along the seacoast. As the continental blocks are reduced in weight, they tend to float higher on the mantle. But beneath the delta, the added weight causes the crust to sink, or subside. This state of *equilibrium* (ee kwa lib'ree um), or balance, among blocks of the earth's crust is called **isostasy** (ie sahs'ta see).

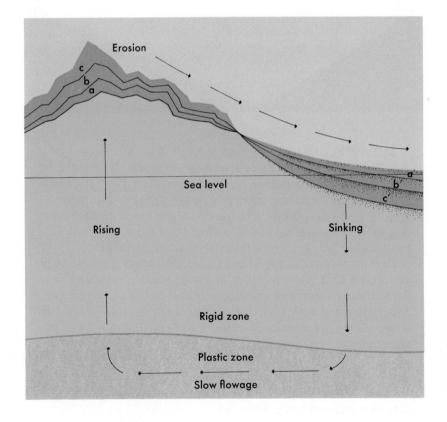

Figure 17-5.   As layers c, b, and a are removed by erosion, they are redeposited to form layers c', b', and a'. Due to isostasy, the mountain rises after erosion and the sea floor sinks after deposition.

Figure 17-6.

ACTIVITY. Fill a durable plastic bag with water and tie it tightly. Press on the bag. What happens to its shape? How does this illustrate isostasy? What happens when you release the pressure?

EXPERIMENT. Float two blocks of wood in a pan of water. With a grease pencil or crayon, mark the water line on the sides of the pan and on each block. Add some sawdust, pencil shavings, or other small items on top of one of the floating blocks. Is there any change in the water level? With another color, mark the new water line on the pan and on the block. What do the blocks of wood represent? What does the water represent? How does this experiment illustrate isostasy?

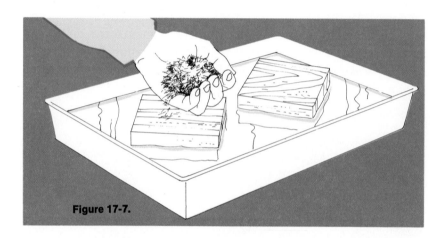

Figure 17-7.

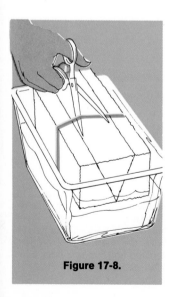

Figure 17-8.

ACTIVITY. Cut an inverted triangle from the center of a 9-in. × 5-in. × 3-in. block of styrofoam. (Figure 17–8.) Hold the parts of the block together with a rubber band. Float the block in a plastic or Pyrex loaf-cake pan no larger than 10 in. × 6 in. × 5 in. (If you use a larger pan, use a larger block so that there is only 1 in. clearance on each side.) Cut the rubber band on the floating block. Carefully observe what happens.

Determine the density of the styrofoam. Measure a block of styrofoam and determine its volume. Float it in water and measure the volume of styrofoam that is below the water line. The block will sink until it just displaces its own weight in water. Since the density of water is 1 g/cm^3, the density of the styrofoam will be the weight of the block divided by the volume of the block. To determine the specific gravity of the styrofoam, its density must be divided by 1 g/cm^3, the density of water. Suggest another way in which the volume of the displaced water can be determined.

Internal forces cause many surface effects on the earth. Scientists have offered a number of hypotheses to account for these effects.

The **shrinking earth theory** is one of the older ideas. According to this theory, the earth originally was much hotter than it is now. Cooling began in the crust, and now extends to about 500 mi below the surface. Within the zone of cooling in the upper mantle, contraction causes tensional forces to develop. The crust adjusts to the shrinking upper mantle by buckling and wrinkling like the skin of a drying apple.

The **expanding earth theory** proposes that heat from the decay of radioactive elements is accumulating within the earth. As the heat increases beneath the crust, the earth expands. Expansion causes cracks in earth's outer layer. The great rift zone (Section 11:4) in the ocean basin is used as evidence for the expanding earth theory.

Another explanation is called the **convection theory.** According to this idea, radioactive elements are distributed unequally within the mantle. An excess of heat develops where radioactive elements are most abundant. Rocks in this region soften, expand, and flow upward. Recall that convection currents are present in the atmosphere (Section 10:1) and in the ocean (Section 12:1) due to excessive heating at the equator. The atmosphere and ocean receive their heat from the sun. But convection currents within mantle materials receive their heat from radioactive decay. Currents rise, cool, move horizontally and then downward, like those of the air and the ocean. In the mantle, horizontal convection currents may oppose one another and cause compression. As they move upward or downward, they may cause tension or shearing in the crust. Theoretically,

Earth's internal forces result from its unequal heating and cooling.

Figure 17-9. Mountain building is attributed to stresses that originate beneath the crust. Various theories have been developed to account for these stresses.

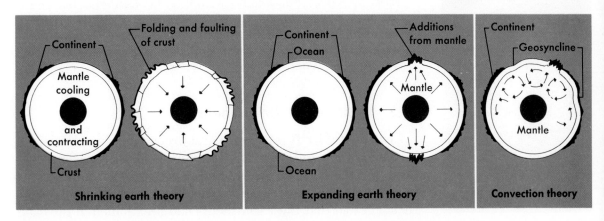

Shrinking earth theory — Continent, Folding and faulting of crust, Mantle cooling and contracting, Crust

Expanding earth theory — Continent, Ocean, Additions from mantle, Mantle, Ocean

Convection theory — Continent, Geosyncline, Mantle

ascending and descending currents oppose the cohesive forces in the solid crust and cause crustal movement.

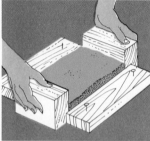

EXPERIMENT. Arrange a slab of "silly putty" and one of plasticine or modeling clay between two blocks of wood so the slabs cannot spread sideways. With two other blocks of wood, push against the slabs until they buckle. Is there any difference in the way the silly putty and the plasticine clay react to pressure?

Mix clay and water into a thick, rather dry mass, and mold it into a brick. Allow the brick to dry. Then put it between two blocks of wood so it cannot spread sideways. Push against the brick with the other two blocks of wood. What happens?

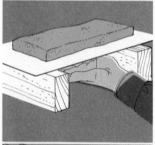

Now put a piece of heavy cardboard on two blocks of wood with a space between them. Moisten some clay and fashion it into a brick. Place it on the cardboard above the space between the blocks. Now push vertically upward on the cardboard until it bends. What happens to the brick? Repeat with modeling clay on the cardboard. Is there any difference in the way modeling clay and the clay brick react to pressure? What is the effect of moisture on clay?

Put a piece of hardened road tar in a pan in an oven (250°F) for a few minutes. Remove the tar and describe any changes that occurred. Strike the tar a sharp blow with a hammer. Does it break? Now put the same piece of tar in the refrigerator freezing compartment for several hours. Remove the tar and strike it with a hammer. What happens? What conclusions can you draw about the effect of heat and the effect of pressure on the state of matter?

Place a square of modeling clay on a table. Put a heavy weight on the clay for one or two hours. The surface of the weight should have nearly the same dimensions as the clay. What happens? Put a heavy weight on the hardened tar. The surfaces should be nearly equal. Leave the weight on the tar in the refrigerator overnight. What happens? Leave the weight on the tar in a warm room overnight or in the sun for a few hours. What happens?

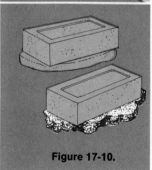

Figure 17-10.

17:3 *Continental Drift Theory*

Continental Drift is a theory first proposed in 1911 by Alfred Wegener (Vay'guh ner), a German geologist. Wegener noticed that the coasts of Africa and South America can be made to fit together like pieces of a jigsaw puzzle. (Figure 17–11.) He suggested that these continents had been joined in the past.

Then they split apart and moved away from each other. Recently this idea has received much support. Today the theory is widely accepted by many scientists.

Recent studies of the ocean bottom have lent support to the idea that at one time all the continents were joined together. This single continent is called *Pangaea*. Pangaea was located nearer to the south pole than any of the continents except Antarctica. That is, Africa, South America, Australia, India, North America, and Eurasia are presumed to have drifted both northward and sideward. The American continents were carried westward. Europe, Asia, and Australia may have been carried eastward. There is no way to tell exactly where Pangaea was located along longitude, so these movements and directions are relative.

Studies of the ocean bottom show that heat is escaping along the mid-oceanic ridge. New crust is being introduced along the rift that separates the ridge. (Figure 11–12.) Rising convection currents carry mantle material upward and add it

Figure 17-11. The good fit between the coastlines of South America and Africa suggests that these continents were once part of the same land mass.

Figure 17-12. Convection currents rising from within the mantle may have carried the continents away from their former positions.

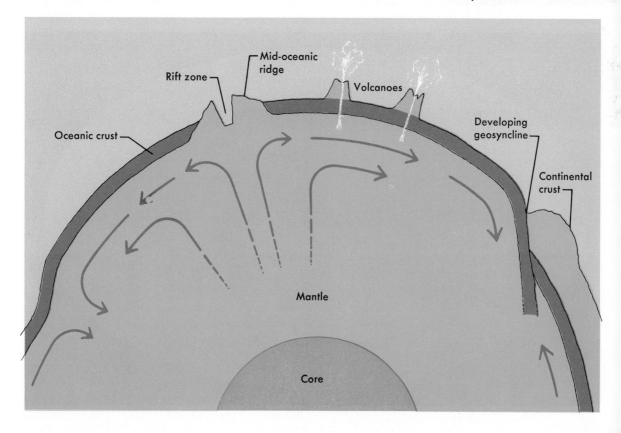

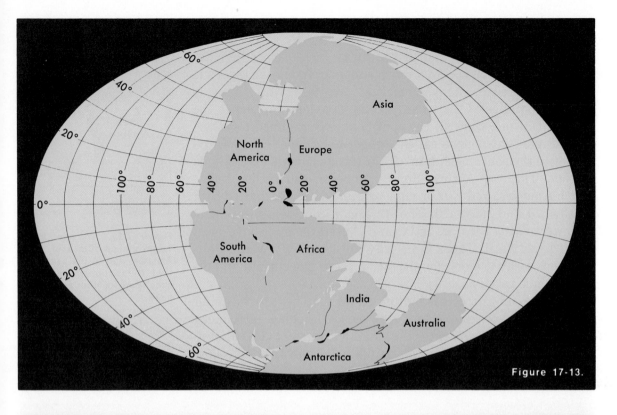

Figure 17-13.

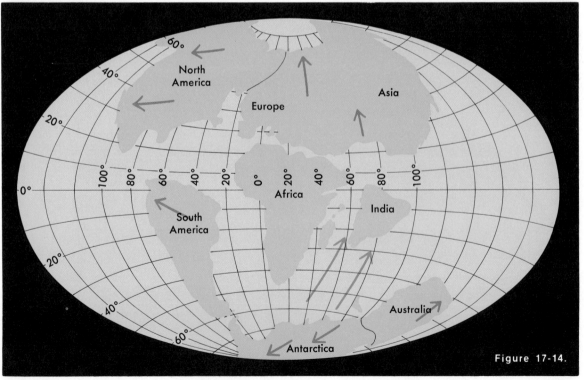

Figure 17-14.

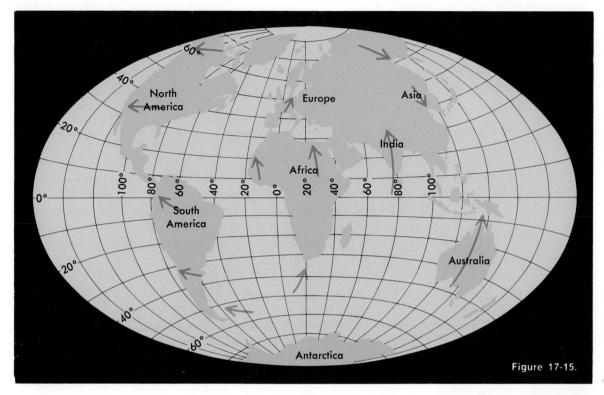

Figure 17-15.

Figure 17-13. 200 million years ago, all continents of the earth may have been joined in one large landmass called Pangaea.

Figure 17-14. As the continents drifted apart, some of them rotated slightly. About 65 million years ago, the earth may have looked like this.

Figure 17-15. If the theory of continental drift is correct, the continents have reached their present positions through millions of years of drifting.

ACTIVITY. Determine the amount and direction of movement for the following areas. The present latitude and longitude readings are given for reference.

	Latitude	Longitude
North America	70°N to 10°N	165°W to 60°W
South America	10°N to 55°S	75°W to 35°W
Eurasia	70°N to 10°N	0° to 180°E
Australia	10°S to 35°S	125°E to 150°E
Africa and Arabia	35°N to 35°S	15°W to 60°E
India	30°N to 10°N	70°E to 90°E

Use Figure 17–13 for latitude and longitude of the areas while part of Pangaea.

to the crust, thus widening the ocean floor. Continents that once were close together are separated farther and farther with each new addition of mantle material. Dating of the oceanic crust shows the youngest material to be in the rift zone. On each side of the ridge, age increases with distance. This process by which the Atlantic Ocean has been widened is known as *sea floor spreading*. The Pacific Ocean is presumed to have been in existence from the earliest accumulation of water.

One variation of the sea floor spreading idea is the suggestion that the ocean floor is broken into blocks similar to ice floes. These blocks move about with little change in the layers of sediment. When two blocks move apart, mantle material moves upward between them to form a ridge. If two blocks approach each other, one block may slip beneath the other. Or, moving toward one another, the blocks may push up a mountain belt. Overriding of one block by another appears to be happening on the west coast of North America. An example both of overriding and mountain building is found in the Himalayas.

ACTIVITY. Gently heat a pan of water over a candle or Bunsen burner. Place the heat source beneath the center of the pan. Add a few drops of food coloring or a cinnamon candy to the water just above the heat source. When the color shows that convection currents are established, place two small blocks of balsa wood side by side over the rising current. Observe movement of the blocks. Relate your observations to the problem of continental drift. Now take several small balsa blocks. Again place them in the water directly over the heat source. Arrange the blocks as close together as possible in the water. Using an immersion heater (Figure 12–2) add a second heat source at one side of the pan. What effect does the second heat source have on the movement of the blocks? Try this activity with several different sizes of pans. Compare the effect on the movements among the blocks.

Belief in the drift of continents is supported by several kinds of evidence. Magnetism of older rocks suggests that the position of the magnetic pole was different from what it is today. The alignment of magnetic particles in the old rocks still points in the direction of the original pole even though the continents have moved. Data from the rocks suggests that poles have wandered or that the crust has moved. Most scientists believe that it is the crust that has moved although they talk about *polar wandering*. (Section 15:6.)

During Permian glaciation 250 million years ago, only the southern hemisphere was affected. (Chapter 21.) Glaciation was limited to a region which now lies close to the equator. This suggests a northward drift of Africa and South America. Furthermore, great salt beds were deposited in West Texas and Germany during the time glaciers occupied Africa and South America. The position of these evaporite regions would have been in the tropics if the continents were positioned farther south. Today evaporites are forming only in tropical regions.

Figure 17-16. Millions of years ago, Africa and Antarctica may have been connected. Their climates may then have been similar. Today, after drifting apart for millions of years, the climates of these two continents are very different.

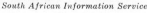
South African Information Service

Wide World Photos

Fossil remains of land animals that lived before the Cenozoic Era show many similarities. This is true whether the fossils are found in Europe, Asia, Africa, or North and South America. The remains of Lystrosaurus (Figure 17–17) have been discovered in Antarctica, Africa, South America, India, China, and Russia. This animal was about 2 to 4 feet long and fed on aquatic vegetation. It lived around rivers and lakes more than 200 million years ago. Lystrosaurus is considered the best biological evidence of the theory of continental drift yet discovered. Obviously this small hippopotamus-like reptile could not have swum the Atlantic Ocean. Apparently, prior to the separation of the continents, animals could roam freely from one area to another. Today, on the separated continents, animals have developed many differences.

Figure 17-17. The remains of lystrosaurus, a reptile that lived about 200 million years ago, have been found in Antarctica, South America, Asia, and Africa. The distribution of these remains supports the continental drift theory.

Structures and glacial striations in South America appear to be broken off at the edge of the continent. These features seem to match structural and glacial features in Africa.

These lines of evidence are used by scientists who believe that the continents have moved away from one another. These scientists suggest convection currents in mid-ocean as the cause of movement. Upward rise is followed by horizontal movement away from mid-ocean ridge. The crust is broken and then carried along by the mantle convection currents. Downward moving currents are presumed to be present at the continental edge. Many of the arguments for continental drift are complicated. They require understanding of engineering and geophysics. But evidence in favor of continental drift seems to be increasing as more is learned about the ocean basins.

Figure 17-18. New ocean crust appears to be added to the lithosphere from time to time. Mantle material reaches the ocean floor along the mid-ocean ridge which surrounds the earth.

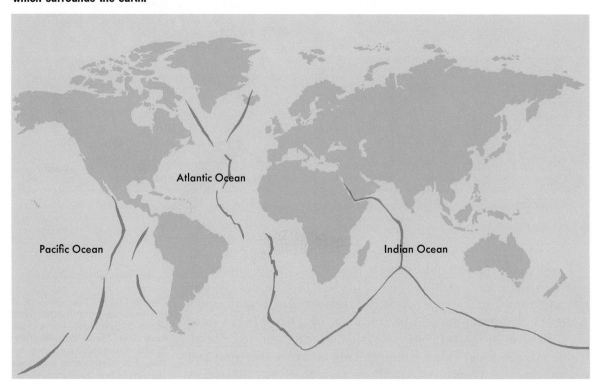

None of the proposed hypotheses is entirely satisfactory. More knowledge about the mantle is needed before internal forces can be understood fully. The effect of various forces on the position of rock layers is evident, however, even though the origin of the forces is not known.

17:4 *Rock Structures*

Structure refers to the position of rock layers. Tensional, compressional, and shearing forces cause changes in the position or structure of rocks. Most sedimentary rocks originally were deposited in a horizontal position at or near sea level. But, like a layer cake, sedimentary rocks consist of different layers which may be recognized by differences in color, grain size, or kind of sediment. The upper or lower surface of each layer is known as a **bedding plane.** Bedding planes provide reference planes by which movement can be recognized. Bedding planes originally are horizontal. If they are broken or bent, it is apparent that movement occurred after deposition.

A variety of structures occurs. The kind of structure depends on the amount of force applied, the rate at which the force is applied, and the kind of rock that is subjected to the force. Many rocks yield to compressional or shearing forces by folding. If enough force is applied, eventually the rocks may yield by breaking. Compressional or shearing forces, if applied slowly, tend to bend rocks. But the same amount of force applied in rapid blows tends to break rocks. Certain kinds of rock break more readily than other kinds. For example, limestone breaks more readily than shale. On the other hand, rock salt always flows when subjected to even a slight compressional or shearing force. At depth, rocks are covered by a great load of overlying material. There compressional and shearing forces cause bending rather than breaking. Near the surface, the same forces usually cause rocks to break.

Different kinds and amounts of force are applied against different kinds of rock. Thus, a great variety of structures occurs. Rocks may be broken into blocks. The blocks may remain stationary, or they may move up, down, or horizontally. Rocks sometimes are bent into gentle wavelike forms. Under other conditions they are folded until formerly horizontal bedding planes become vertical or overturned.

Fractures in rocks are simple breaks in which no movement is involved. Most uplifted rocks are fractured. Fractures may occur in rectangular patterns, known as *joint systems.* (Figure 17–19.) Basaltic flows, however, commonly exhibit hexagonal fracture patterns called *columnar joints.* Hexagonal fractures form during cooling and contraction.

Faults are breaks accompanied by movement. Some faults can be recognized at the surface because rocks on one side of a

Structure refers to the position of rock layers.

Rocks may bend, break, or move in any direction under sufficient pressure.

Figure 17-19.   Pattern of joints in limestone.

J. C. Russell, U.S. Geological Survey

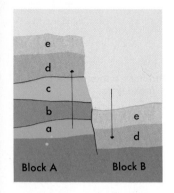

Figure 17-20.   Block B has moved downward along a vertical fault relative to Block A.

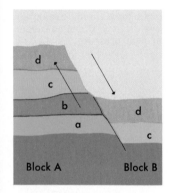

Figure 17-21.   Block B has moved downward along a normal fault plane.

Figure 17-22.   Block A has moved upward relative to Block B, and erosion has removed Bed e.

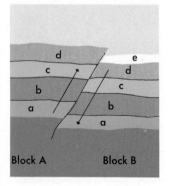

break have been pushed upward to form sheer cliffs. Other faults occur deep within the crust and cannot be seen.

Many faults have been discovered during the drilling of wells. Some faults on the ocean floor have been found by sounding devices. (Section 11:4.)

Movement along faults may result in complex patterns of rock distribution. Layers sometimes stop abruptly at the fault plane. The same layers then continue at some distance away. They may be above, below, or horizontally removed from the position in which the layers normally would occur. Movement along the fault plane may be in any direction. Movement also may be in a combination of directions. Commonly, one side of a fault plane moves upward and the other moves downward. But some movement may be horizontal as well. *Fault blocks* are blocks of rock bounded on at least two sides by faults. Such blocks may be a few feet or several miles wide. (Figure 6–2.)

Fault planes may be at any angle from vertical to nearly horizontal. Fault angles are measured between an imaginary horizontal plane and the plane along which movement occurs. Broken layers of rock may lie in a horizontal position, or may be tilted or folded.

Figure 17-23.   A normal fault in the Wasatch sandstone with downward movement on the left.

D. E. Winchester, U.S. Geological Survey

Folds are bends in rock layers. Most folding probably occurs below the surface of the earth. At depth, heat causes rocks to become pliable or plastic. When pliable rock is subjected to compression, it is bent into a new, shorter shape. Folds may require thousands of years to form. Gradually, rock layers change from horizontal positions to a series of alternating arches and troughs. (Figure 17–24.) Similar structures may be formed on an accordion by squeezing it. Arches are called *anticlines* (an'ti kliens). Troughs are called *synclines* (sin' kliens). Folds may be a few feet or several miles wide. Folds may be squeezed together until the bedding planes are nearly vertical. Sometimes a fold is pushed over until it lies on its side. Complex folds may be broken by both fractures and faults. Tensional, compressional, and shearing forces combine to form the complex structures associated with areas of mountain building.

Figure 17-25. **From the cross-sectional sketch (a.) it is evident that the sedimentary beds have been tilted to an almost vertical position during mountain building (b.).**

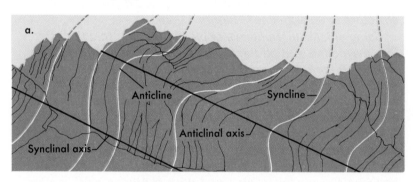

U.S. Forest Service

Figure 17-24. Undisturbed layers of sedimentary rock are normally horizontal. When subjected to stress, they may be folded into a variety of shapes.

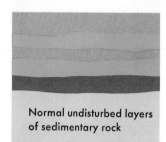

Normal undisturbed layers of sedimentary rock

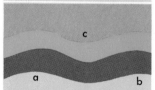

Gently folded sedimentary rock a and b—symmetrical anticlines c—syncline

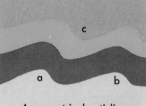

Asymmetrical anticlines and syncline

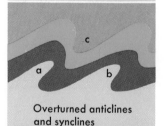

Overturned anticlines and synclines

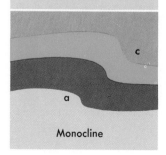

Monocline

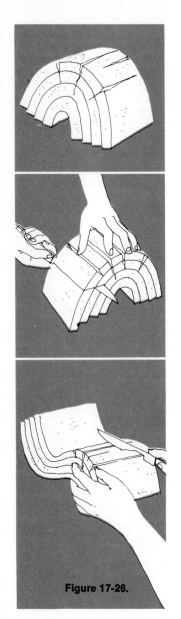

Figure 17-26.

ACTIVITY. In paper cups, make four different mixtures resembling shale, sandstone, conglomerate, and limestone. Use mud, sand, bits of rock or small pebbles, patching plaster, and water. Color three of the mixtures with cake coloring so they can be easily identified. Arrange the "sedimentary rocks" in layers on a cardboard base. Allow the rocks to dry, then push or pull them until you have illustrated folds, faults, and fractures. Cut through the folds and faults with a sharp knife so you can see them in cross section. Label the layers to indicate which is shale, sandstone, conglomerate, and limestone. Now bend a piece of plasticine clay into folds. Is the clay more resistant to bending than the sedimentary rocks?

Use several colors of plasticine clay to resemble different sedimentary layers. Fold the sequence into an anticline. If small cracks appear in the clay, do not be concerned; they are common in nature. When you have a fold, cut off its tip so that you can view several layers of your model. Now, on a sheet of paper, draw the layers as they appear from above. Add a legend to your map to indicate the order in which the beds were deposited. For example, blue—oldest layer; green —next older layer; red—youngest layer. From the distribution of beds as indicated on your map, how could you tell that the structure is an anticline? (Figure 17–26.)

Using at least three colors of plasticine clay, fold the layers into a syncline. Cut off the top so you can see all three layers when you look down on the model. Summarize your findings so that, with the aid of a geological map, you could recognize a syncline from the distribution of beds. What must you know about the beds to use this method?

With a sharp knife, cut vertically through the anticline and the syncline deep enough to show how the beds would look if a river cut across their surfaces. What are some differences between the modeling clay and your synthetic sedimentary rocks? Based on your answer, why do rocks fold instead of break? Why do some folds end in faults near the surface?

17:5 Structural Mountains

Mountain chains contain complex folds, fractures, and faults.

Any part of the earth's surface that rises above the surrounding area is called either a mountain or a hill, regardless of its origin. *Mountains* rise 2,000 ft or higher above the adjacent area. *Hills* have elevations of less than 2,000 ft. The major classes of mountains include structural mountains, volcanic cones, and dissected mountains. Structural mountains are produced by uplift. Volcanoes result from igneous activity. Dissected mountains are produced by erosion.

Figure 17-27. Absoraka Range, overlooking Yellowstone Valley near Livingston, Montana, is only a small part of the vast Rocky Mountain system.

Mountain systems are great masses of nearly parallel rock ridges. The ridges rise sharply above the surrounding plains. Mountain systems include every kind of mountain. The system as a whole results primarily from uplift.

The great mountain systems of the world are roughly parallel to the continental coastlines. The width of a mountain system is measured in hundreds of miles. Its length is measured in thousands of miles. Mountain systems exhibit every kind of disastrophism, every type of structural feature, and all stages of erosion. Rocks in mountainous regions include igneous, metamorphic, and sedimentary materials. Sedimentary rocks contain evidence of shallow water deposition. The evidence includes fossils, ripple marks, and mud cracks. Most metamorphic rocks retain features that suggest a sedimentary origin. Igneous bodies include lava flows, and often dikes, sills, and laccoliths of granites, diorite, or gabbro. Because they are difficult to cross, mountain systems have influenced the history of mankind. For example, in North America the Appalachian Mountains lie parallel to the Atlantic Coast. Because of these mountains, early settlement was limited to the coastal region. The Rocky Mountains and Coast Ranges, which lie parallel to the Pacific Coast, are part of a mountain system that extends from Alaska through Mexico and southward into the southern tip of South America. Early settlers of California came by sea, rather than by the difficult land route.

Today mountains rise above the plains. But at one time a trough existed on the sea floor where mountains now exist. These sinking troughs that eventually develop into mountains are called **geosynclines** (jee oh sin′kliens). Most geosynclines probably form close to shore at the foot of the continental slope. Often the position of the geosyncline marks the position of a major fault which extends downward into the mantle. The troughs parallel the shore for hundreds, or even thousands of

Thousands of feet of sediment from the continent and offshore volcanoes accumulate in a geosyncline prior to uplift.

miles. Their width ranges from 300 to 500 miles. Geosynclines persist as sinking troughs for thousands or even millions of years before being uplifted into mountains.

Sediments are carried into a developing geosyncline from the continent on one side and from volcanic islands on the oceanward side. Eventually thousands of feet of sediment and volcanic debris accumulate in the sinking trough.

At depth, heat is produced by radioactive decay of certain elements. The heat cannot escape through the great blanket of overlying sediments. Instead, the heat energy is used up in metamorphism of the buried sediments. Or, if the temperature rises sufficiently, the sediments may melt.

Igneous intrusions move upward from the mantle and from the melted zone within the crust. When the magma eventually cools, it forms great batholiths. During this period of intrusion,

Magma may form at the bottom of a geosyncline if temperatures exceed the melting point of rock under pressure.

Intrusions of magma accompany the uplift of mountains from a geosyncline.

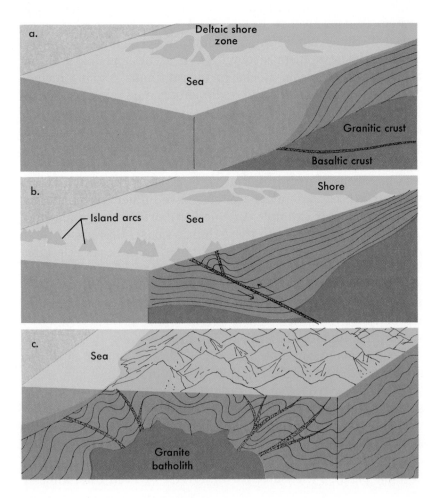

Figure 17-28. Great mountain chains eventually rise from geosynclines along the edges of continents. (a.) sediments accumulate, (b.) faulting and volcanic eruptions, (c.) uplift.

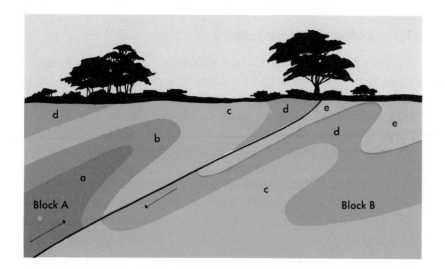

materials within the geosyncline are uplifted, folded, and faulted. Tensional, compressional, and shearing forces cause complex patterns to develop. The complicated folded and faulted forms resulting from activity within a geosyncline are **structural mountains.**

Mountain cores are areas of great uplift. Here the batholith is surrounded by high rank metamorphic rocks. Folding is complex and *thrust faults* are common. Along thrust faults, older rock has been pushed upward and over younger rocks. Folding becomes less and less complex as distance from the mountain core increases. Eventually folds disappear. Near the mountain region lies the *plateau area.* Here rocks are elevated but still horizontal. A steep cliff commonly forms the border of the plateau. Here rocks have been torn apart by tension during uplift. The uplift of mountains affects a continent far beyond the area of the mountain system itself. A plateau is one of the more visible effects of uplift. The Colorado Plateau of Arizona, New Mexico, Colorado, and Utah is associated with the Rocky Mountains. The Allegheny and Cumberland Plateaus of Pennsylvania, Kentucky, and Tennessee are plateau areas associated with the Appalachian Mountains.

Block fault mountains are other structural features associated with regions of mountain building. As igneous rocks cool, they contract. Contraction causes tension, and tension causes steep fractures to form. When movement occurs along these fractures, great crustal blocks may be raised or lowered. Mountains throughout Nevada, Utah, and parts of California are block fault mountains. Movement still continues along many of these crustal blocks.

Volcanic activity, igneous intrusions, and metamorphism are characteristic of the mountain core.

Plateaus are uplifted regions in which sedimentary layers remain approximately horizontal.

17:6 *Volcanic Mountains*

Volcanic mountains are formed by surface eruptions of lava. Batholiths are formed by intrusions of magma that do not reach the surface.

Volcanic eruptions and lava flows are common in areas of mountain building. But volcanoes are found on plateaus as well. Volcanic eruptions tend to be explosive if lava contains large quantities of gas. Lava is blown out of the *vent*, or opening, at the summit of the volcano. It cools quickly and forms cinders. Cinders pile up in steep *cinder cones* at the foot of the opening. If lava does not flow readily, it forms dome-like volcanoes. **Dome volcanoes** usually are composed of rhyolite. Volcanic eruptions in which lava flows out quietly form **strato-volcanoes.** Strato-volcanoes usually are made of andesite, and are layered flows with gentle slopes. **Shield volcanoes,** like strato-volcanoes, are built up layer upon layer. However, shield volcanoes have a much wider base than strato-volcanoes. Shield volcanoes are formed of basalt, which flows readily and spreads over a wide area before it hardens.

Figure 17-30.   A cinder cone rises in the background. In the foreground small spatter cones have been formed along cracks leading away from the larger vent. The spatter cones are made from the same type of material as the cinder cone, but they lacked sufficient gas for explosive action.

William Huber

Paricutin is an explosive volcano built of cinders.

In 1943, a new volcano resulted from an explosive eruption in a field in Michoacan (mee cha wah kahn'), Mexico. This volcano, named Paricutin (pa ree ke teen'), erupted about one billion tons of ash, cinders, and bombs, or large fragments, during its first year. Bombs were thrown about 4,000 ft into the air. Today, Paricutin is a cinder cone volcano which rises 9,000 ft above sea level. Many years ago, a similar eruption formed Sunset Crater, a volcano near Flagstaff, Arizona.

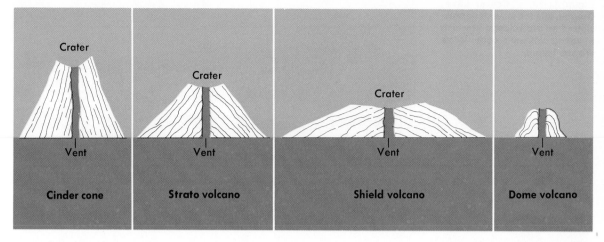

| Cinder cone | Strato volcano | Shield volcano | Dome volcano |

Mount Shasta, a strato-volcano in northern California, may have been active only a few thousand years ago. Its flows of andesite have accumulated to a height of 14,162 ft. In this volcano, lava welled up from a central vent and oozed out quietly, layer upon layer. Mount Shasta is associated with the mountain building of the West Coast.

The Hawaiian Islands are the peaks of a submerged major mountain chain rising from the ocean floor. These volcanic islands erupted from five vents along a major fault line in the Pacific Ocean floor. Because basalt flows readily and spreads out, the Hawaiian Islands have the wide base common to shield volcanoes.

Most volcanic mountains have depressions at their summits. Some depressions may be formed by collapse of volcanic debris

Figure 17-31. The composition of a volcano determines its shape. Free-flowing basalt forms a low volcano with a wide base; viscous lavas form high volcanoes on a relatively narrow base.

Hawaiian Islands are shield volcanoes built of layers of basalt.

Figure 17-32. Basalt cools in many weird shapes as it pours down a steep slope.

W. C. Mendenhall, U.S. Geological Survey

Figure 17-33. Crater Lake, Oregon, fills the summit depression of an old volcano in which a young volcanic cone forms Wizard Island.

into the vent during a period of quiet. Other depressions may result from violent explosion. Crater Lake, Oregon, for example, has a depression resulting from an explosion that literally blew off the top of the volcano. Sometimes erosion also causes some subsidence of the vent area. Depressions are particularly characteristic of periods of quiet. When the volcano is not erupting the lava hardens and contracts. The consolidated lava occupies less volume than the molten lava.

EXPERIMENT. Set a metal funnel upside down in a deep container that is one-quarter full of water. (A coffee percolator pipe also may be used.) Build a slope of modeling clay around the funnel, to the edge of the pan, but just below the rim, to allow space for water. Set the pan on a ring stand and heat it with a Bunsen burner. What happens? How is this model like a volcano or a geyser? What happens at great depths below the earth's surface where no openings are present? What are the possible effects of heating rock, or the fluids within the rock, so that melting occurs or steam forms? (Figure 17–34.)

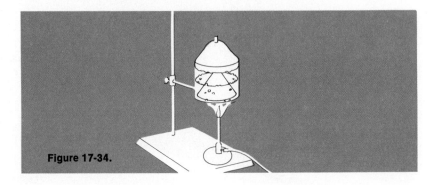

Figure 17-34.

17:7 *Dissected Mountains*

Volcanoes, block fault mountains, and mountains due to folding and faulting produce a variety of landscapes. But landscapes also may have a variety of hills, valleys, and even mountains that result from erosion instead of mountain building processes. Because they are high above sea level, plateaus are especially subject to erosion.

Many mountains and hills have been formed during the development of a drainage system. Rivers flow down slopes, cut channels, and remove material to form valleys. As the valleys widen, the region between them becomes a series of mountains or hills. These mountains or hills are now higher than the surrounding area only because erosion has cut valleys below the original height of the area. Mountain summits represent the original elevation above sea level.

Mountains and hills, known as **dissected mountains,** have been dissected, or cut, from the original landscape. (Figure 17–35.) As drainage systems are enlarged, they erode even the summits of the mountains. Then mountains become hills, and, eventually, hills become plains.

Plateaus eroded to form hills and mountains are known as **dissected mountains.**

Plateaus become noticeably dissected, but structural mountains also are subject to erosion. Anticlines often are stretched and broken at their crests. Valleys commonly form in the weakened crest of an anticline. When the anticline is eroded, the adjacent syncline becomes a mountain. Many such synclinal ridges remain in the Appalachian Mountains. The adjacent anticlines, however, are worn away.

Valleys are eroded from soft, unresistant layers. Hard, resistant layers form ridges which extend high above the valleys. The ridges are called **cuestas** (kwes′tas) if the resistant layers slope gently. If the resistant layers slope steeply, the ridges are called **hogbacks.** Some dissected mountains are remnants of resistant igneous rock. These rocks were intruded into less resistant sedimentary layers. Then the sedimentary rock was removed by erosion. Resistant laccoliths and volcanic necks often form isolated hills which rise above the surrounding plains.

Resistant rock layers may form cuestas and hogback ridges after nonresistant rock layers have been eroded.

In summary, some mountains are rock that has escaped erosion. Other mountains have been pushed above their surroundings. Still other mountains consist of piles of debris poured, or blown, out of vents to form volcanoes. Each mountain or system of mountains was formed by one or more of

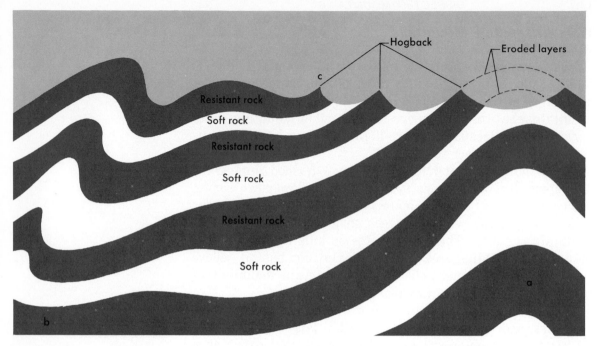

Hogback

Eroded layers

c

Resistant rock

Soft rock

Resistant rock

Soft rock

Resistant rock

Soft rock

b

a

Figure 17-35. Erosion has removed a number of layers to form a valley at the crest of anticline *a*, but anticline *b* is still protected by the resistant layer that forms a hogback at *c*.

these processes of diastrophism, igneous activity, or erosion. The kinds of rock, the amount of tilting, and the degree of erosion determine the history of mountains.

Figure 17-36.

ACTIVITY.   Mold each of four colors of modeling clay into four slabs exactly 1 in. thick. Cut one slab into a circle that will just fit into the cake pan used in an experiment in Section 17:2. Cut the other slabs into circles with decreasing diameters. Pile them in the pan with the largest at the bottom and the smallest at the top, to represent a hill. Add water to the pan until the lower slab is covered. To make a map of the hill, look down on the cake pan. The first contour line is the line of contact between the water and the hill. To draw the line accurately, make an outline on paper that is the same size as the upper rim of the pan. A clear plastic pan cover aids in plotting contour intervals. Measure out from each corner of the pan to find the horizontal position of the point of contact between hill and water. Plot this position as a dot on your map. Take several readings from different points along the edge of the pan to the hill, and then join the dots to form a line. This line is a contour line. (See Figure 17–38.) It represents the line of intersection between a horizontal plane (the water) and the surface of the hill. If 1 in. of clay represents 100 ft, and if the bottom of the pan represents sea level, what is the elevation of this contour line? To determine the second contour line, add water until the second slab of clay is covered. Repeat the mapping procedure until you have completed the contour map of the hill. How many contour lines are there on your map? What would be the shape of the contour lines if you were drawing a depression instead of a hill? Assuming that each color of clay represents 100 ft, number the contours on your map. Why is there no 400-ft contour?

Now turn the hill over and set it in the pan. This time start with sea level; that is, the contact between the upper surface of the inverted model and water added to this level in the pan. Repeat the activity by removing water to the contact with the next lower slab. Remove the slab and draw contours at each of these depths. Using a scale of 100 ft, what are the numbers on these contours? Why are they negative numbers?

Assume that each color of clay represents a different layer of sedimentary rock. How would you describe the position of the layers in the original hill? Were they flat, horizontal, tilted, or sloping? Which of the layers was the oldest? Which layer was the youngest?

When you understand the principle of contouring, use the hill model to demonstrate the outcrop pattern of sedimentary layers that are more complex than those of the original model.

ACTIVITY. Use the hill and the pan from the preceding activity. Separate the layers of the hill, but do not change the outline. Carefully shave off part of the surface of the bottom layer so that the thickness is ¼ in. on one side, but 1 in. on the other side. Do the same with the second layer, and put them together with the thin part of the second layer above the thick part of the first layer. Do not change the third layer. On the fourth layer, make channels similar to erosion channels. These channels should extend down the entire hill, as a river channel or a gulley would. Now repeat the procedure outlined in the preceding activity. But this time, mark the cake pan in inches and add water first to the 1-in. line, 2-in. line, and so on. Draw the contours as directed before.

Refer to your map and to the hill in the cake pan and answer the following questions. Does the presence of the channels affect your contour lines? If not, why not? Do the channels affect the pattern of the water? In the preceding activity, the height of the water indicated not only the contact between different colors of clay, but also the position of the surface of the hill. Is this true in this activity? Do the surface contours or the topographic contours show the positions of the rock layers? Could you draw contours to show the positions of the rock layers?

Figure 17-37.

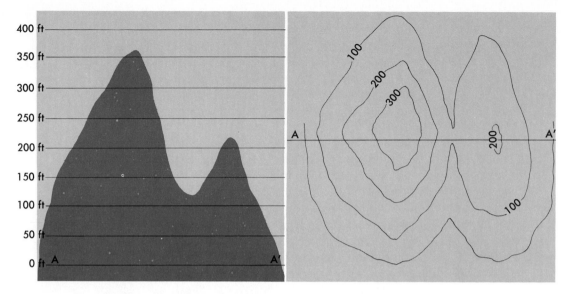

Figure 17-38. On the right, contour lines show the elevation of the hills shown in profile on the left.

Figure 17-39.   Hingham Bay, Hull, Mass.
Scale 1:31680   Contour Interval 10 ft

Figure 17-40.   Oceanside, Calif.
Scale 1:62500   Contour Interval 25 ft

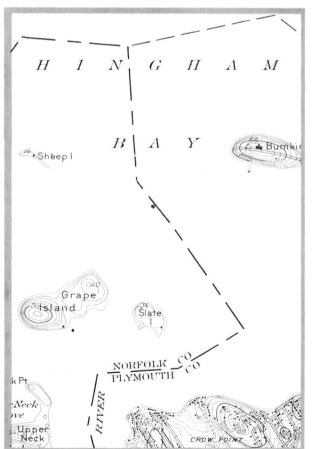

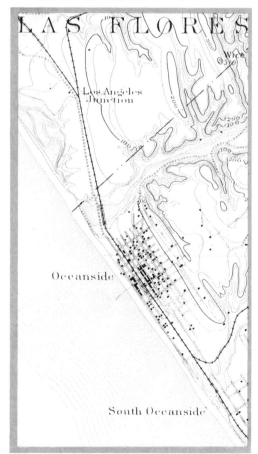

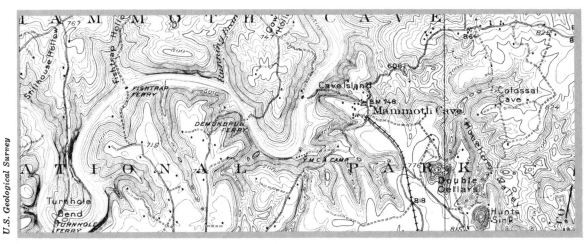

Figure 17-41.   Mammoth Cave, Kentucky   Scale 1:62500   Contour Interval 25 ft

Figure 17-42.   Loveland, Colorado   Scale 1:62500   Contour Interval 20 ft

Figure 17-43.   Kaatersill, New York   Scale 1:62500   Contour Interval 20 ft

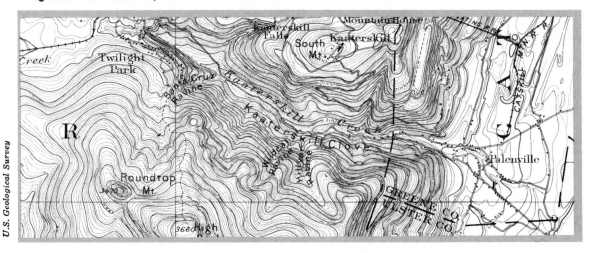

MAIN IDEAS

1. Many geologists believe that decay of radioactive elements in the earth's interior is the major cause of diastrophism.

2. Sedimentary rocks, which were laid down in horizontal layers, exhibit diastrophism in twisted, broken, and uplifted layers. Shore zones serve as a reference point for relative movements.

3. Vertical movements of the earth's crust due to buoyancy maintain a state of isostasy.

4. Internal heating or cooling causes tension to pull, compression to push, and shearing to twist rocks and distort their positions.

5. Some scientists believe diastrophism is caused by cooling and shrinking in the outer layers of the earth. Others believe that crustal movements are caused by heating and expanding. Still other scientists theorize that heating causes convection currents in the mantle to displace rocks of the crust.

6. The theory of continental drift suggests that all the continents were joined at one time. Convection currents caused breaks in the earth's crust which allowed continents to drift apart.

7. Structural changes in rock layers depend upon the amount of pressure, how long or how suddenly the pressure is applied, and the kind of rock involved.

8. Rock fractures become faults if movement occurs along the fractures.

9. Mountain chains contain every type of rock and structure. Mountains develop from geosynclines which lie adjacent to and parallel to coastlines of continents. The greatest diastrophism occurs on the oceanward side of the geosyncline. The least diastrophism occurs on the continental side of the geosyncline.

10. Volcanic mountains include cinder cone, strato-volcano, dome, and shield types. Paracutin is a cinder cone, Mt. Shasta is a strato-volcano, and the Hawaiian Islands are shield volcanoes.

11. Plateaus of the earth are regions that are raised vertically but which escape intense folding and faulting during mountain building. Plateaus are on the continental side of a mountain chain.

12. In time, erosion dissects plateaus into hills and mountains. Mountains and hills eventually are eroded into plains.

VOCABULARY

Write a sentence in which you use correctly each of the following words or terms.

anticline	fault	joint
buoyancy	folds	plateau
compression	fracture	shearing
cuesta	geosyncline	subsidence
diastrophism	hogback	syncline
dissected mountains	isostasy	tension

STUDY QUESTIONS

A. True or False

Determine whether each of the following sentences is true or false. (Do not write in this book.)

1. Diastrophism is believed to be caused by decay of radioactive elements in the earth's matter.
2. Movement along the San Andreas fault illustrates block faulting.
3. Shearing of rocks causes tremendous twisting.
4. Melting of glaciers causes uplift.
5. Expansion of the earth's crust accompanies cooling in the mantle.
6. Structures are influenced by the kind of rock involved.
7. Brittle rocks tend to fold rather than break.
8. Deeply buried rock layers tend to break rather than fold.
9. Mountain ranges commonly appear near to and parallel to the continental coastline.
10. The Hawaiian Islands are examples of shield volcanoes.

B. Multiple Choice

Choose the word or phrase which completes correctly each of the following sentences. (Do not write in this book.)

1. Crustal movements are most easily recognized in (*igneous, sedimentary, metamorphic*) rock.

2. Rocks which are bent into troughs are called (*anticlines, synclines, block faults*).

3. According to the theory of (*isostasy, diastrophism, convection*), buoyancy of crustal blocks may result in uplift.

4. According to the (*shrinking earth, convection, expanding earth*) theory, decay of radioactive elements causes rising and descending currents in the mantle of the earth.

5. A joint system occurs in rock layers which have simple (*folds, faults, fractures*).

6. A break in a rock combined with either upward or downward movement is called a (*fault, fold, fracture*).

7. A huge, sinking trough developed off a coastline and parallel to it is a (*syncline, anticline, geosyncline*).

8. Slow-moving, widespread layers of lava form a volcano known as a (*cinder cone, strato-volcano, shield volcano*).

9. Dissected mountains result from (*erosion, folding, faulting*).

10. Hogbacks are resistant rock layers which are (*steeply dipping, horizontal, gently dipping*).

C. Completion

Complete each of the following sentences with a word or phrase which will make the sentence correct. (Do not write in this book.)

1. Twisted, folded, faulted, and tilted rocks show the effects of __?__.

2. Differences between the old and new position of shore features is called __?__ movement.

3. Force that pulls rocks apart is called __?__.

4. Force that twists rocks is called __?__.

5. The dominant force associated with a shrinking earth would be __?__.

6. The position of rock layers is called __?__.

7. An upward arch in a series of rock layers is a(n) __?__.

8. The volcanic form which results from an explosive eruption is a(n) __?__.

9. Crater Lake, Oregon, is a body of water that collected in the ____?____ of an extinct volcano.

10. Eroded plateaus become ____?____ mountains.

D. How and Why

1. If you were to find beaches and benches along the California coast 20 ft to 30 ft above sea level, what could you conclude about the former position of the Coast?

2. Why do sedimentary rocks provide the most information about diastrophism?

3. Why are sedimentary layers occasionally found below igneous and metamorphic rocks in parts of mountain chains?

4. If rocks that formerly were deeply buried in a geosyncline are brought to the surface, would you expect them to be folded and faulted, or just faulted? Explain your answer.

5. What forces are dominant in block faulting?

6. Why is volcanic activity often associated with mountain building?

7. Why do volcanoes adopt different shapes at the surface?

8. How might the theory of a heating and expanding earth lead to the idea that continents once were connected and then split apart into their present shapes?

9. What are the major events in the life of a geosyncline?

10. What is the reason that some hills are formed from synclines, and some valleys are called anticlines?

INVESTIGATIONS

1. Recount a Greek myth or a Japanese tale used to explain earth movements. Report on the rising of a volcano such as Krakatoa, Pelee, Mauna Loa, Kilauea, Vesuvius, or Etna.

2. Observe road cuts, river banks, or mountain areas in your region and photograph or draw a picture of an anticline, a syncline, or a fault. Make a sketch map of its location.

3. Send to the U. S. Geological Survey (Washington, D. C. 20242 or Denver, Colorado 80225) for topographic maps of mountain and plateau areas. Locate faulting, folding, volcanic peaks, plateaus, and dissected mountains on the maps.

4. On a world map, indicate major mountain ranges and volcanic areas. Save for a comparison with a map of earthquake areas. (Chapter 18.)

INTERESTING READING

America's Wonderlands, The National Parks, rev. ed. Washington, D.C., National Geographic Society, 1966.

Bloch, M. H., *Mountains on the Move*. New York, Coward-McCann, Inc., 1960.

Bullard, Fred M., *Volcanoes*. Austin, Tex., University of Texas Press, 1962.

Clark, S. P., *Structures of the Earth*. Englewood Cliffs, N. J., Prentice-Hall, Inc., 1969.

Drury, G. H., *The Face of the Earth*. Baltimore, Penguin Books, Inc., 1959.

Macklin, J. G., and Cary, A. S., *Origin of Cascade Landscapes*. Information Circular 41. Olympia, Wash., Washington Division of Mines and Geology, 1965.

Marsh, Susan, *All About Maps and Mapmaking*. Westminster, Md., Random House, Inc., 1963.

Matthews, William H., *The Story of Volcanoes and Earthquakes*. Irvington-on-Hudson, N. Y., Harvey House, Inc., Publishers, 1969.

*Milne, Lorus J. and Margery, *The Mountains*. Life Nature Library. New York, Time Inc., 1962.

Pearl, R. M., *Seven Keys to the Rocky Mountains*. Colorado Springs, Colo., Maxwell Publishing Co., 1968.

Upton, W. B., Jr., *Land Forms and Topographic Maps*. New York, John Wiley & Sons, Inc., 1970.

Volcanoes. U. S. Department of the Interior, Geological Survey, 1964.

Volcanoes of the United States. U. S. Department of the Interior, Geological Survey, 1965.

Wyckoff, Jerome, *The Adirondack Landscape, Its Geology and Landforms*. Gabriels, N. Y., Adirondack Mountain Club, 1967.

---

* Well-illustrated material.

Earthquakes

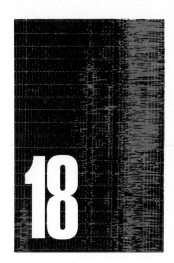

18

Tremblings of the earth's surface are obvious evidence of diastrophism. Widespread devastation often accompanies the violent shakings of the so-called solid earth. Earthquakes along the Pacific Coast, along the Mediterranean Sea, and in the West Indies are especially frequent and have been noted for centuries. Early Mediterranean civilizations recorded tremblings of the earth, as well as the cracking and buckling that accompanied the quakes. These are minor changes in the earth's surface compared to changes caused by rivers, glaciers, and wind. But, because they are often disastrous, earthquakes are an important area of study.

18:1 *Origin*

Earthquakes are tremblings or shaking of the ground. They are caused by a sudden break in rocks below the earth's surface or slippage along an old fracture. When rocks are pulled apart by tension, or broken by compression, tremors or vibrations spread out in ever-widening patterns. Grasp the ends of a stick in your hands. Now break the stick. Did you feel the vibrations of the breaking process? Drop a pebble in still water. Did you observe an ever-widening circle of waves? Both actions represent, on a small scale, what happens when rocks within the earth are broken.

When rocks break because of tension or compression, vibrations start.

Within the earth, rock particles immediately next to a break are set in motion. The motion is passed on to adjacent particles. These particles in turn pass the motion on to the next particles. Eventually, the vibration reaches the surface. If the rock break occurs in the upper mantle or deep within the crust, vibrations that reach the surface usually are too weak to cause much damage. But even weak vibrations are recorded. If the

Vibrations pass from rock particles to rock particles.

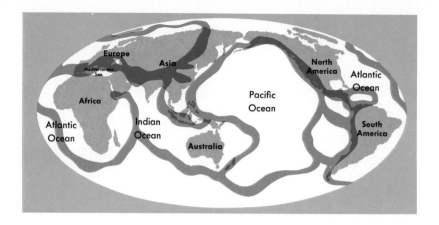

rock break is near the earth's surface, rocks are set in motion. Surface rocks move up and down somewhat like waves in a body of water. Unlike water, most rocks are brittle and cannot change shape easily to form waves. Instead, rocks buckle, bend, or break when the motion is strong and vibrations are great.

ACTIVITY. Measure the length of a thick rubber band without stretching it. Now stretch it until the band breaks and measure its length. Does the stretching and breaking of the rubber band change its length? What force breaks the band?

Stand a yardstick on edge and brace it so it cannot move. Try to bend the stick in an arc. What kind of force are you applying to the yardstick? Now grasp one end of a yardstick in each hand and break it. Describe the sensation in your hands.

Place two large wooden blocks on a table so they are touching one another. Push one block in one direction and the other block in the opposite direction, so that they slide past one another. This movement in a horizontal direction is like the movement along a strike fault, *such as the San Andreas fault in California. What kind of force are you applying to the blocks? What is the relationship between the rubber band and faulting?*

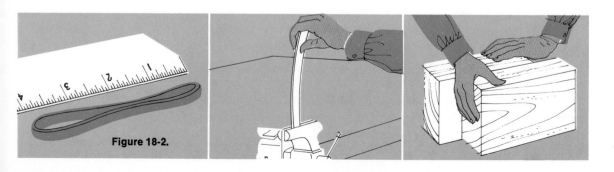

Figure 18-2.

Surface damage following earthquakes occurs in linear patterns, or along generally straight lines. This linear or straight pattern suggests that vibrations come from the breaking and movement of rocks along faults. (Section 17:4.)

Earthquakes sometimes are caused by volcanic action or by the collapse of caverns and mine tunnels. Such quakes, however, affect only local areas. These shocks are minor compared to the violent vibrations caused by movement along faults. For example, horizontal movement occurred during the San Francisco earthquake in 1906. The coastal side of the San Andreas fault moved northward in relation to the landward side. On opposite sides of the fault, movement ranged from 16 ft to 21 ft. Movement extended along the break for about 270 mi.

Studies of the San Francisco earthquake suggest that internal forces tend to drag the coastal side of the land northward along the fault zone. When these forces overcome the strength of the rocks, the rocks break. Prior to the break, internal forces store elastic energy within the rocks, as energy is stored in a tightly coiled spring. Sudden movement releases the stored energy in the form of earthquake waves. Heat also is released. The heat is caused by friction between masses of rock sliding along the fault. The forces and energy involved in seismic activity are enormous. Compare the energy required to tear down a large building with the destruction that accompanies an earthquake. This will give you an idea of the energy released by an earthquake.

Movement of rocks occurs along faults.

Internal forces cause elastic energy to be stored in rocks.

Figure 18-3. Movement of one rock mass against another causes vibrations known as earthquakes.

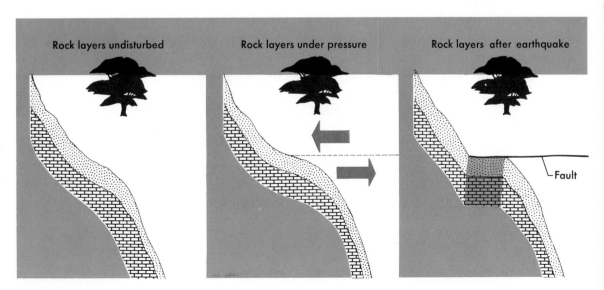

Rock layers undisturbed

Rock layers under pressure

Rock layers after earthquake

Fault

The San Francisco earthquake occurred when stored elastic energy overcame the strength of the rocks. The result was like pulling the trigger of a giant gun. But what is the source of the energy that pulls the trigger? Heat is the most probable energy source. Several theories that may account for crustal movements were described in Section 17:2. Heat is involved in all of these explanations. It, therefore, is considered the most probable source of earthquake energy.

Heat is probable source for energy resulting in earthquakes.

18:2 *Seismographs*

Earthquakes that originate at great depth may not affect the surface visibly. Earthquakes that reach the surface in uninhabited regions also may escape notice. But a seismograph (seiz′ma graf) records even the faintest earth tremors.

Modern **seismographs** are instruments that record, measure, and analyze vibrations in the earth's crust. Operation of a seismograph requires that some point or line within it shall remain steady or at rest. These steady points usually are some form of pendulum. A heavy mass is suspended on a wire or rod from a fixed frame or support. The supporting frames are fastened to the earth. They move with the earth vibrations. During earthquakes the pendulum tends to remain at rest because of its inertia. (Section 1:3.) Thus, the pendulum acts as the fixed reference point.

Earthquake vibrations are recorded by seismographs.

A simple seismograph consists of a mass suspended at the end of a vertical wire. A small sharp point, or *stylus* (stie′lus), projects from the bottom of the mass. The stylus barely touches a smoke-coated paper tape which is pulled forward or rotated on a large drum. (Figure 18–4.) Such a device will detect an earthquake and record the relative movement of the ground. The motion of the ground is transmitted to the supporting frame. But due to its inertia, the suspended mass tends to remain motionless. This type of seismograph is affected most by horizontal ground motion. It is classed as a *horizontal seismograph*.

Seismograph consists of fixed frame and suspended pendulum which hangs at rest because of inertia.

A *vertical seismograph* uses a different type of suspension. A simple vertical seismograph consists of a heavy mass suspended from an elongated coiled spring. A pencil or stylus projects from the side of the mass. The pencil just barely touches the surface of a smoked paper tape. The paper tape is pulled along a vertical plane or rotated on a large drum. (Figure 18–4.)

Modern instruments at a seismic observatory are more elaborate and refined than the simple devices described. But the principles of operation are the same. Commonly, three seismographs are used together. One records vertical movements, a second records north-south horizontal movements, and a third records east-west horizontal movements.

Sensitive seismographs commonly record *background noise*, or unwanted vibrations. Sources of such noise are ocean waves, surf, trains, and heavy trucks. Unwanted vibrations are reduced by careful selection of observatory sites and careful construction of observatory piers. Concrete piers support the instruments, but they have no mechanical contact with the observatory buildings. This isolation protects the instruments from unwanted building vibrations.

Seismograms are lines recorded by a seismograph. These lines indicate earthquake intensity by their wave-like patterns. Wave height, or *amplitude* (am'pli teud), is measured on the Richter scale which is used by all seismic observatories. The magnitude of an earthquake is indicated by the amount of amplitude. When stations within 60 mi of the center of the earthquake record 7 to 8 units on this scale, a major earthquake is in progress.

Seismic observatories are equipped to record two types of vibrations. These vibrations travel outward through the earth from the site of the earthquake. Horizontal waves are called *P waves*, or *primary waves*. *P* waves also are known as longitudinal or compressional waves. In *P* waves particles vibrate back and forth lengthwise, or in the direction of wave travel. Movement passes from rock particle to rock particle. Regions of

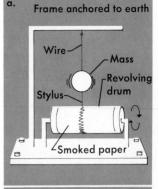

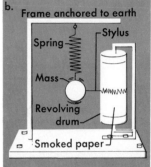

Figure 18-4.   (a.) Horizontal movement of the earth causes the mass to move from side to side as the drum revolves. (b.) Vertical movement of the earth causes the mass to move up and down as the drum revolves.

Figure 18-5.   During the 1964 Alaskan earthquake, this seismogram recorded vibrations.

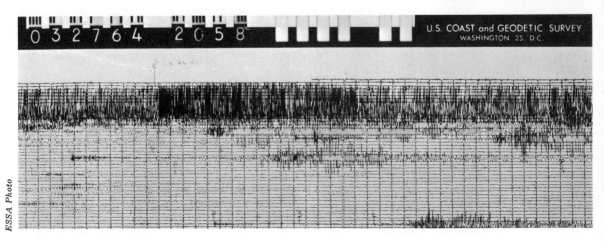

compressed rock particles alternate with regions of separated rock particles. A "slinky" toy that is held at one end, then given a slight jerk, illustrates the movement of the *P* wave.

Vertical waves are called *S waves*, or *secondary waves*. *S* waves also are known as transverse or oscillatory waves. Vibrating particles move up and down. Movement is at right angles, or transverse to the direction of vibration of the *P* wave. By moving the free end of a rope up and down rapidly, *S* waves can be produced in a rope which is fixed at one end. *P* waves and *S* waves travel within the earth, but never along the surface.

EXPERIMENT.   Place eight glasses in a row. Strike each of them gently with a pencil. Arrange them so their sounds reproduce a musical scale. If the glasses do not produce all the notes of the scale, add water to each glass until you duplicate the sounds of the scale. Why does water change the sound? What is the relationship between earthquakes and sound waves? Why do we not hear earthquake vibrations?

Have two students hold a "slinky" toy stretched loosely between them. To send vibrations along the toy, pluck the spring near one end. What happens? Compare this movement with earthquake vibrations. How do builders muffle sounds in large rooms? How do different materials in the interior of the earth affect the vibrations of an earthquake?

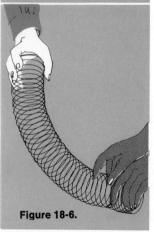

Figure 18-6.

The *focus* of an earthquake is the actual location of the rock break or fault within the earth. The focus may be as deep as 400 mi to 500 mi below the earth's surface. The *epicenter* (ep i sent'er) is a point on the earth's surface directly above the focus. The location of an earthquake's epicenter can be interpreted from the *P* and *S* wave arrival times. *P* waves travel almost twice as fast as *S* waves. Therefore, the *P* waves always arrive at the seismograph station before the *S* waves.

A seismologist can determine from time-distance tables or curves how far from his station the earthquake originated. The time-distance tables are calculated from data recorded and plotted from numerous earthquakes. These tables show the miles from epicenter to observatory for any time interval between the *P* and *S* waves. A seismologist reads the time of arrival for both the *P* wave and the *S* wave from the seismogram. He then determines the difference between the two arrival times. Using this difference, he can read the distance from observatory to epicenter from the tables. The calculated location is really an estimate because an epicenter is assumed to be a point. Actually epicenters may involve large areas. For example, recall that the San Francisco earthquake was caused by a fault 270 mi in length.

If observatories have two horizontal seismographs, one can record waves from the north-south direction. The other can record waves from the east-west direction. Comparison of the two seismograms is an aid in determining the direction of the epicenter from the observatory.

When three or more observatories exchange records of the same earthquake, the location of the epicenter can be determined with greater accuracy. On a world map, each recording observatory is plotted as a center point. A circular arc is drawn from each of these points. The radius of each arc is the distance from observatory to epicenter as determined from time-distance tables. The point of intersection of three or more arcs is the location of the epicenter. (Figure 18–7.)

P and *S* waves travel away from fault zones and spread out in circles in every direction. These waves do not take the shortest path between fault and seismograph station. Instead, they follow the shortest *time-path*. The shortest time-path depends on the changes in wave velocities within the earth. If wave velocity were uniform throughout the earth, the shortest time-path would be a straight line between fault and seismograph.

Distance between observatory and epicenter is calculated on basis of time elapsed between arrival of P waves and S waves.

Intersection of arcs based on distance from three observatories, when inscribed on a world map, indicates epicenter of an earthquake.

Shortest time-path of P and S waves depends upon wave velocities of material within the earth.

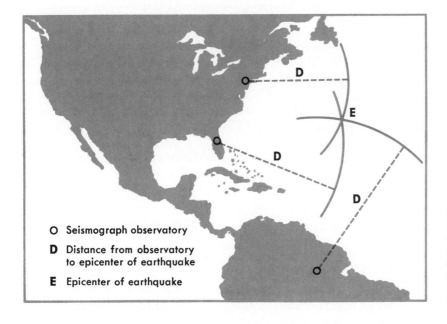

O   Seismograph observatory

D   Distance from observatory to epicenter of earthquake

E   Epicenter of earthquake

Figure 18-7. Three seismic observatories locate the epicenter of an earthquake by drawing circles, using the observatories as centers and a radius equal to the computed distance from earthquake to observatory.

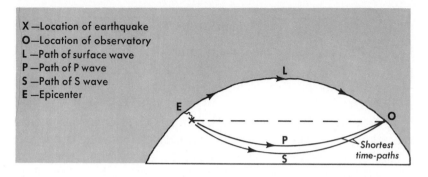

Figure 18-8. Earthquake waves are separated into the L, S, and P waves which travel at different speeds through the earth.

X —Location of earthquake
O —Location of observatory
L —Path of surface wave
P —Path of P wave
S —Path of S wave
E —Epicenter

But velocity is not uniformly distributed; it actually increases with depth. P and S waves follow somewhat similar, but not identical, paths. Recall that the P wave travels almost twice as fast as the S wave.

A third type of vibration is the *surface wave* or *L wave*. This wave moves directly upward from focus to surface. Then it follows along the surface or perimeter of the earth. The L waves often are destructive. The earth surface sways as the wave passes along, much as a boat rises and falls with the waves in a lake. But buildings generally are not built to withstand much vibration. They may be shaken and sometimes destroyed. Arrival time and amplitude of P, S, and L waves of an imaginary earthquake are shown in Figure 18–9. Notice that maximum amplitude, indicated by the letter M, occurs during passage of the L wave. Amplitude gradually decreases after passage of the maximum until earth movements finally cease.

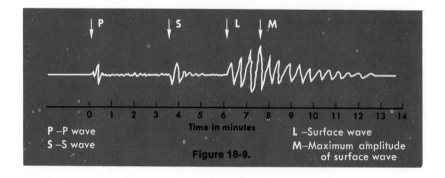

P —P wave
S —S wave

Time in minutes

L —Surface wave
M —Maximum amplitude of surface wave

Figure 18-9.

PROBLEMS

Refer to Figure 18–9 to answer these questions.

1. Estimate the elapsed time between the arrival of the P wave and the S wave.

2. Estimate the elapsed time between the arrival of the P wave and the time of the greatest surface damage.

3. Assume that P waves travel twice as fast as S waves. What is the total travel time required for the S wave to travel from the earthquake focus to the seismograph?

4. Assume that S waves travel 2 mi/sec. How far from the seismograph is the earthquake focus? What is the distance from seismograph to earthquake focus in kilometers?

5. Assume that P waves travel twice as fast as S waves. What is the total travel time required for the P wave to travel from the earthquake focus to the seismograph?

6. Assume that the P wave travels 4 mi/sec. How far from the seismograph is the earthquake focus?

7. A velocity of 2 mi/sec is equivalent to how many kilometers per second?

8. Is the velocity of the L waves faster or slower than the velocity of the P waves and the S waves?

9. Estimate the elapsed time between the arrival of the P wave and the L wave.

10. You calculated the travel time of the P wave from focus to seismograph in Problem 5. Use this time and the elapsed time as determined in Problem 9, to estimate the total travel time required by the L wave to travel from focus to seismograph.

11. On a separate sheet of paper, draw a time scale with minute intervals every ½ in. Draw a vertical arrow above zero and label with an X. Zero time (X) indicates the time the earthquake occurred. Recall from Problem 5 the total travel time required for the P wave to travel from earthquake focus to seismograph. Draw a vertical arrow at the correct point on the time scale. Label it P to indicate the correct arrival time of the P wave at the seismograph as compared with the time of the earthquake. Draw and label similar vertical arrows indicating the correct arrival time of S, L, and M. Assume that the earthquake occurred at 3:09 P.M. From the new time scale, prepare a table listing the time of the earthquake occurrence and the arrival time of P, S, L, and M.

12. Assume that the earthquake focus was close to the earth's surface. Also assume that the distance to the epicenter was 840 mi. What is the velocity of the L wave in miles per second? What is the velocity of the L wave in kilometers per second?

18:3 *Effects of Earthquakes*

Earthquake vibrations cause much indirect damage.

Earthquake vibrations may affect large areas and cause tremendous damage to large cities. Indirect damage resulting from a quake often causes almost as much loss as the earthquake itself. Damage to railroads, highways, and utilities may cause interruptions of public services, such as transportation, electricity, communications, water, and sewers. Fires resulting from broken gas mains may rage out of control because broken water mains cannot supply water for fire fighting. Lack of water and shattered sewer systems interfere with sanitation and create health hazards. Food delivery may be interrupted or prevented; food losses may be high due to breaks in power lines which supply electricity to refrigeration systems.

Figure 18-10. Earthquake damage at Anchorage, Alaska, caused by surface waves.

U.S. Dept. of the Interior

During an earthquake, buildings may vibrate and sway so violently that they crumble and collapse. Buildings of stone or brick are especially subject to collapse.

Flexible buildings permit swaying without breaking or separating. They are best suited for construction in earthquake areas such as Japan and the Pacific Coast. Reinforced concrete and steel framing in large buildings and wood in small structures withstand most earthquake shocks. But these materials have flexibility within a limited range and damage may be expected during severe earthquakes. In 1971, the Los Angeles area earthquake damaged some buildings constructed to withstand these shocks.

Buildings in areas subject to earthquakes should be of flexible materials.

Coastal cities are subject to severe damage by sea waves called *tsunamis*. (Section 12:3.) Tsunamis are caused by earthquakes under the ocean or under the land area near the coast. Submarine landslides triggered by shaking of the sea floor also may cause tsunamis.

Tsunamis may be only a few feet high near their origin. However, a large volume of water is set in motion. Wave fronts may be 100 mi wide and wave heights about 5 ft. Waves 5 ft high are not unusual at sea, and may pass a ship unnoticed. But this huge wave of water moves at a high speed, often 400 mi/hr to 500 mi/hr. When the waves reach shallow water along the coast, the water suddenly piles up. In V-shaped bays, a sudden increase in wave height to 100 ft is likely to occur. Such a wall of water moving at high speed is so destructive that few man-made shore structures can withstand its force.

Earthquakes commonly are regarded as disastrous events. They may cause enormous loss of life and property destruction. But, during all of geologic time, earthquakes have not changed the earth's surface greatly. Some earthquakes have formed cliffs. Some have altered drainage systems. Some have caused landslides which dammed lakes. But, compared with the work of rivers and glaciers, earthquakes are relatively ineffective. Why then are geologists so interested in earthquakes?

U.S. Forest Service

If scientists could predict where and when earthquakes will occur, they could help prevent disaster. They know some areas where rocks are under stress and subject to earthquakes. But at present it is impossible to predict when the rocks will break and cause damaging vibrations. Based on present recordings of earthquakes, about one major earthquake occurs about every four years, on the average. From one to ten million earthquakes occur every year. This figure includes all magnitudes and depths of focus. Today's predictions are too generalized and widespread to be of much immediate help. About 80 percent of all earthquakes occur in the vast region of the Pacific Ocean. California, Alaska, Chile, Japan, and mid-ocean areas have experienced earthquakes. But there is no way to know which area will have the next earthquake.

Figure 18-11. A new lake is formed in Montana by a landslide that dammed up the outlet of Madison River during an earthquake.

18:4　*Interior of the Earth*

A study of earthquakes makes it possible to predict and warn of approaching tsunamis. Such a study also helps to locate the earthquake epicenter. These are important practical results. A more theoretical result of earthquake study is the understanding it provides of the character of the earth's interior.

Conditions in the earth's interior cannot be reconstructed in the laboratory. But velocity measurements on rocks can be made. These measurements are made under different conditions of temperature and pressure. Then an attempt is made to find conditions that produce the velocities observed during earthquakes.

Velocity of sound waves varies with rock density and elasticity. Elasticity is the more important of the two factors. Tables are available which list velocities of *P* and *S* waves in most types of rocks.

The values are computed for rock velocities under a variety of conditions. These conditions include: rocks at various depths, rocks of differing densities, and rocks of different ages. Seismograph stations are distributed throughout the world. Data from these stations are used to interpret the density of the earth.

Seismograms that show variations in velocity contain useful clues to rock characteristics. For example, seismic waves travel faster through igneous rocks than they do through sedimentary rocks.

Several types of rock are encountered by seismic waves that pass between an earthquake focus and a given seismograph

Rock density and elasticity determine velocity of seismic waves.

Variations in seismic velocities indicate variations in type of rock traversed between focus and station.

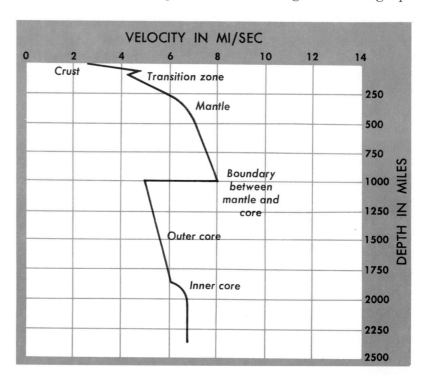

Figure 18-12.   Velocity of the P seismic wave varies with depth, indicating changes in both density and the state of matter.

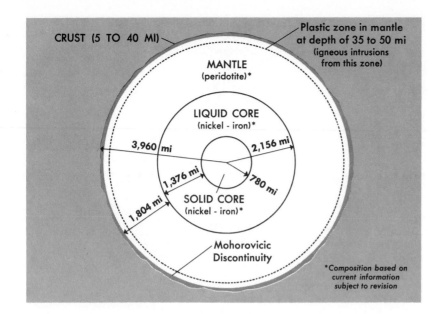

CRUST (5 TO 40 MI)

Plastic zone in mantle
at depth of 35 to 50 mi
(igneous intrusions
from this zone)

MANTLE
(peridotite)*

LIQUID CORE
(nickel - iron)*

3,960 mi   2,156 mi

1,376 mi   780 mi

1,804 mi

SOLID CORE
(nickel - iron)*

Mohorovicic
Discontinuity

*Composition based on
current information
subject to revision

Figure 18-13. The structure and composition of the earth's interior are suggested by earthquake vibrations received at many widely distributed seismograph stations.

station. Usually the velocity of the *P* wave gradually increases with depth. For example, velocities increase from about 3¾ mi/sec (normal for granite) to 4 mi/sec (normal for basalt) to a depth of about 25 mi. At this depth a sudden increase in *P* wave velocity occurs. This increase was first recognized by Andrija Mohorovicic, a Yugoslavian seismologist. The abrupt velocity increase from 4 mi/sec to 5 mi/sec observed by Mohorovicic indicated a sudden change in the density of material at this depth. The boundary where this change takes place is called *Mohorovicic* (moh ha roh'va chich) *discontinuity* (dis kahnt en eu'at ee), or simply *Moho*.

Sudden increase in seismic velocity 25 mi below the surface, recognized by Mohorovicic, indicates a change, or discontinuity, in rock character.

The velocity change at the Moho indicates that basalt is replaced by a more dense rock material. Scientists do not agree on the composition of rock at this depth. In fact, several rocks have velocities that fit the observed value. Some scientists have proposed drilling a deep hole to find out what kind of rock lies below the discontinuity. But such a hole would be extremely costly if it could be drilled successfully.

Seismology indicates that earth is composed of different materials in crust, mantle, and core.

The Mohorovicic discontinuity separates the outer layer, or *crust*, from a lower layer, the *mantle*. (Section 2:5.) The outer and inner *cores* are recognized below the mantle. Only through the interpretation of seismic data can we learn about the characteristics of the cores.

An earthquake would send both *P* and *S* waves directly through the earth's center *if the material were all solid*. Both waves would be recorded by seismographs located on the side

Figure 18-14. Earthquake waves encounter different materials and different conditions that affect their velocity. S waves will not pass through the liquid core; P waves indicate a solid inner core.

Figure 18-15. (a.) That temperature rises with depth is demonstrated by measurements in wells drilled for oil. (b.) Estimates for temperatures of the mantle and core are based on the known temperature increase and rock melting points.

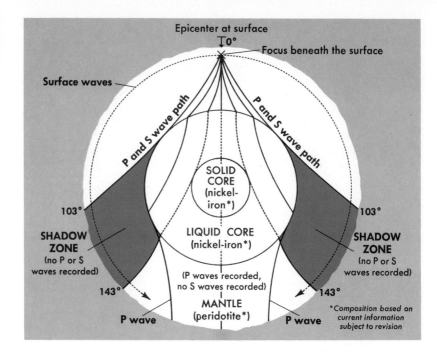

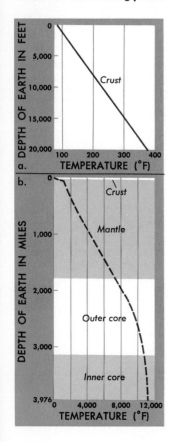

of the earth opposite the earthquake focus. Furthermore, the travel time of a seismic wave through the earth could be judged in advance. To make such a prediction, the *location* of the epicenter, the *time* at which the quake occurred, and the *velocity* of the seismic waves must be known.

But when seismic waves pass through the center of the earth, their travel time is too long for the expected travel time through a solid. This time lag suggests a velocity change and the presence of different materials below the mantle. (Figure 18–13.)

Seismographs located on either side of the earthquake focus at an angular distance of 103° to 143° do not receive either *P* or *S* waves. These are *shadow zones.* (Figure 18–14.) But seismographs located beyond 143° in either direction from the focus receive *P* waves but no *S* waves. This is a puzzling situation!

Drawing on their understanding of vibrations, scientists have concluded that the outer core must be a liquid. From laboratory experiments we know that *S* waves cannot pass through a liquid. A liquid core would account for the loss of the *S* waves. The radius of this liquid core is calculated to be 2156 mi. This calculation is based on the position of the shadow zone.

But *P* waves *do* pass through a liquid. Why are they absent from the shadow zone? Although *P* waves pass through a liquid, they move more slowly than they do through a solid. These waves then, appear to be bent as they pass through the outer core. The bending is sufficient to direct the *P* waves beyond the shadow zone. These *P* waves will be received by stations beyond 143°. (Figure 18–14.) Directly opposite the focus, stations pick up *P* waves that pass through the inner core. Their velocity is increased over the velocity of waves that pass only through the outer core. These data suggest that the inner core is solid with a radius of 780 mi.

In summary, seismic evidence suggests that the earth's crust ranges in thickness from 5 mi to 40 mi. (Section 2:5.) Compared to the rest of the earth, this outer layer is extremely thin. Below the crust is the mantle. It is separated from the crust by the Mohorovicic discontinuity. The mantle extends to a depth of about 1800 mi. At this depth the outer core's boundary is marked by a sharp decrease in velocity of seismic waves. *P* waves slow to about one-half the speed with which they travel through the mantle. *S* waves disappear. This outer part of the core is presumed to be a liquid. A solid inner core with a radius of 780 mi is present within the liquid core.

Seismic evidence indicates that earth consists of a solid outer crust, the mantle starting with Moho, a liquid outer core, and a solid inner core.

18:5   *Composition of Earth's Layers*

Seismology is useful in providing clues to the character of the earth's layers and in identifying their materials. But identification is not always positive. Many rock materials have similar values for velocity, rigidity, and density. Enormous pressures and high temperatures exist within the earth. These temperatures and pressures may change the physical properties of the earth's materials in ways not understood.

Problem

13. Examine the seismograph in Figure 18–16. Where do the vibrations of an earthquake cause movement? Which part remains steady during earthquake vibrations? If an earthquake occurred on the side of the earth opposite this seismograph, through what layers of the earth would the vibrations pass? How would the seismogram recorded by this seismograph differ from the seismogram at a station within 100 mi of the epicenter of the quake?

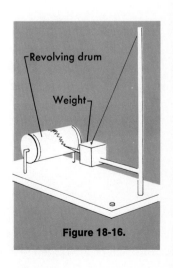

Figure 18-16.

Seismologists assume that the earth's composition changes with depth. This assumption is based on seismic data, on what is known about crustal materials, and on the composition of

Seismic information suggests an inner core of solid iron or nickel-iron and an outer core of liquid nickel-iron.

meteorites. Many scientists agree that the inner solid core probably is composed of iron or a nickel-iron alloy. The outer core also is thought to consist of iron or nickel-iron. But matter in the outer core is in the liquid state. This composition is similar to some meteorite material. In addition, seismic velocities for iron-nickel combinations agree with observed velocities in the core.

High-velocity earthquake waves are characteristic of the mantle. Similar velocities are associated with rocks of high density and rigidity. Peridotite, a magnesium-iron silicate, fits the high velocity requirements. But other rocks have similar properties. Positive identification of mantle material cannot be made at present, but peridotite seems the most likely material.

Recall that the outermost layer of the earth ranges in thickness from 5 mi to 40 mi and has an average thickness of 20 mi. *P* waves travel in this layer at the rate of 3¾ mi/sec, the normal velocity in granite. Velocities increase with depth to a speed of about 4 mi/sec which is normal in basalt. These values for velocity in granite and basalt are close to the observed *P*-wave velocity in the upper 20 mi of the earth. Therefore, granite appears to overlie basalt in the continental crust. But granite is absent in ocean basins where the crust is only 3 mi to 5 mi thick. Only velocities characteristic of basalt are present in the crustal layer of the ocean.

Seismic velocities indicate crustal material of granite overlying basalt on the continents and basalt alone beneath oceans.

PROBLEMS

14. Refer to Figure 18–13 and convert all of the dimensions for the layers of the earth from miles to kilometers.

15. Draw a cross section of the earth similar to Figure 18–13, but change the scale to 1 in. = 3,187.8 km. Use the conversions from Problem 14 and indicate all of the dimensions in kilometers. If your measuring device is not divided into ¹⁄₁₀-in. segments, convert the fractions ⅛ through ⅞ to decimals. Then estimate the radius measurements. You may wish to use a slide rule. Radius of earth in inches on the cross section may be found by simple proportion.

MAIN IDEAS

1. Internal forces of tension or compression cause rocks to break along fault lines and start vibrations which pass from rock particle to rock particle.

2. Elastic energy, probably produced by heat, is stored until rocks reach their limit of strength. Earthquakes release stored elastic energy.

3. Both horizontal and vertical seismographs consist of a fixed frame and a suspended pendulum which remains at rest because of inertia. The frame supports a tape on which vibrations are recorded by a stylus which is attached to the pendulum.

4. *P* or primary waves vibrate in the direction of wave movement. *S* or secondary waves vibrate at right angles to the direction of *P* waves. *P* and *S* waves spread out from the focus of the rock break. The epicenter is directly above the focus of the rock break.

5. Distance from seismic observatory to earthquake is determined by measuring the time elapsed between arrival of *P* waves and *S* waves. *P* waves travel almost twice as fast as *S* waves. Intersection of three circular arcs drawn on a world map locates the epicenter. The radius of each arc represents epicentral distance from an observatory.

6. *P* and *S* waves reach observatory by shortest time-path governed by material through which they pass. *L* waves travel through surface material and cause maximum amplitude of seismogram.

7. Earthquakes and tsunami from undersea disturbances are less effective in changing earth's surface than either rivers or glaciers.

8. Scientists study seismograms to detect variations in rock material. These variations are indicated by different seismic velocities.

9. Studies of seismic velocities indicate that a sudden change, called Mohorovicic discontinuity (Moho), occurs in earth's matter 25 mi below the surface. The Moho marks the boundary between basalt of the crust and an undetermined material of the mantle.

10. Seismic waves are screened out by shadow zones between 103° and 143° angular distance from an earthquake focus. *P* waves penetrate to the far side of earth.

11. Seismologists conclude from studies of seismic velocities that the earth is composed of four layers. They picture an outer solid crust about 20 mi thick, a plastic mantle about

1,800 mi thick, a liquid outer core 1,376 mi thick, and a solid inner core with a radius of about 780 mi.

12. Earth may consist of an inner core (iron or nickel-iron), a liquid outer core (nickel-iron), a plastic mantle (peridotite), and a solid crust (basalt under the sea with granite above basalt on the continents).

VOCABULARY

Write a sentence in which you use correctly each of the following words or terms.

amplitude	horizontal	seismic
background noise	seismograph	shadow zone
	Moho	time-path
discontinuity	opaque	vertical
epicenter	primary waves	seismograph
focus	secondary waves	vibration

STUDY QUESTIONS

A. True or False

Determine whether each of the following sentences is true or false. (Do not write in this book.)

1. Earthquakes are more common in some parts of the earth than in others.

2. Seismographs at one location permit accurate determination of the epicenter of an earthquake.

3. *P* waves travel faster than *S* waves.

4. Moho is a city that has experienced frequent, severe earthquake damage.

5. A suspended mass that tends to remain at rest during an earthquake is an essential part of a seismograph.

6. *P* waves and *S* waves are not recorded by seismographs located in shadow zones.

7. Average thickness of earth's crust is about 1,800 mi.

8. Sudden velocity changes of earthquake waves are evidence of a change in earth composition.

9. Large buildings with steel frames are usually more resistant to earthquake damage than buildings of similar size composed of brick or stone.

10. Earthquakes are evidence of diastrophism.

B. Multiple Choice

Choose the word or phrase which completes correctly each of the following sentences. (Do not write in this book.)

1. The seismic wave with greatest velocity is the (*P, S, L*) wave.

2. Earth's mantle is thought to be composed of (*granite, peridotite, basalt*).

3. Earth's core is composed of (*silicates, iron-nickel, iron-lead*).

4. Average horizontal movement along the San Andreas fault during the San Francisco earthquake was approximately (*18, 78, 108*) ft.

5. Focus is the location of a(n) (*rock-break, observatory, shadow zone*).

6. The *L* wave travels through material in the earth's (*core, surface, mantle*).

7. Maximum damage to cities comes from the (*P, S, L*) wave.

8. Greatest change in the earth's surface is caused by (*earthquakes, rivers, wind*).

9. The Mohorovicic discontinuity separates the crust from the (*solid core, liquid core, mantle*).

10. As depth increases, seismic wave velocity (*increases, remains the same, decreases*).

C. Completion

Complete each of the following sentences with a word or phrase which will make the sentence correct. (Do not write in this book.)

1. Most probable energy source for crustal movements or earthquakes is __?__.

2. The compressibility, rigidity, and density determine seismic wave __?__.

3. Earthquakes occur when stored __?__ energy exceeds the strength of rocks.

4. The larger the __?__ on a seismogram, the greater is the energy.

5. Epicenters are located directly above the __?__.

6. Earthquakes under the ocean or near the coast and submarine landslides may be the cause of seismic sea waves called __?__.

7. The boundary between the crust and mantle is called the ___?___.

8. Knowledge of the structure and composition of the earth's interior has been gained from ___?___.

9. *S* waves never travel along the earth's ___?___.

10. Earth's composition is assumed to change with ___?___.

D. How and Why

1. Why is epicentral distance, determined from time-distance tables from a single seismogram, only an approximation?

2. Explain why *P* waves and *S* waves do not follow the shortest path from earthquake focus to seismograph station.

3. Although 80 percent of all the earthquake energy is released in or along the Pacific Ocean, why is it difficult to predict the time and the location of the next earthquake?

4. If changes of seismic velocity can indicate changes in the type of rock in the crust as compared to the mantle, why is there interest in drilling into the mantle and sampling its rock?

5. Why may the arrival of the *P* wave on a seismogram be more positively identified than the arrival of the *S* wave or *L* wave?

6. If seismic sea waves, or tsunamis, can reach heights of 50 ft to 100 ft in bays and harbors, how can they pass ships at sea without being observed and reported?

7. Why are two horizontal seismographs usually installed in a well-equipped seismic observatory?

8. What is the nature of the stored energy in rocks that causes them to break?

9. How is diastrophism related to earthquakes?

10. What is the probable source of the stored elastic energy that causes quakes? How is the energy transferred and stored in the rocks?

INVESTIGATIONS

1. From library research, report on one of the following earthquakes: Lisbon, Portugal, 1755; San Francisco, 1906; Tokyo, 1923; Yellowstone Park, 1959; Alaska, 1964.

2. On a world map, show the areas of major earthquake activity. Compare this with your map of volcanic activity. (Chapter 17.)

3. List some recommendations for building specifications in areas subject to earthquakes. Investigate requirements in California compared to building requirements of neighboring states. Research the earthquake-proof hotel designed by Frank Lloyd Wright after Japan's 1923 earthquake. Did it withstand later earthquakes?

4. Locate a seismograph station and request some recordings to discuss with the class. Your local weather bureau might direct you to the nearest station.

INTERESTING READING

Earthquake Information Bulletin. National Earthquake Information Center, U. S. Coast and Geodetic Survey, (Sept./Oct., 1970.)

Eiby, George A., *About Earthquakes*. New York, Harper & Row, Publishers, 1957.

Ericksen, G. P., and Concha, J. F., *Peru Earthquake*. Circular 639. U. S. Geological Survey, 1970.

Hodgson, J. H., *Earthquakes and Earth Structure*. Englewood Cliffs, N. J., Prentice-Hall, Inc., 1964.

Leet, L. Don and Florence, *Earthquake: Discoveries in Seismology*. New York, Dell Publishing Co., Inc., 1964.

Macelwane, James Bernard, *When the Earth Quakes*. New York, The Bruce Publishing Company, 1947.

Pough, Frederick, *All About Volcanoes and Earthquakes*. Westminster, Md., Random House, Inc., 1953.

The San Andreas Fault. U. S. Department of the Interior, Geological Survey, 1965.

*Sunset Staff and Iacopi, Robert, eds., *Earthquake Country*. Menlo Park, Calif., Lane Magazine & Book Co., 1969.

Tazieff, Haroun, *When the Earth Trembles*. New York, Harcourt Brace Jovanovich, Inc., 1964.

Tsunami, the Story of the Seismic Seawave Warning System. U. S. Coast and Geodetic Survey, 1965.

"When the Earth Rang Like a Bell," *Reader's Digest* (August, 1965), pp. 179–84.

* Well-illustrated material.

Chapter 19 The Environment

Man has changed the atmosphere, rivers, lakes, oceans, and the local distribution of rocks and soil. Many living forms are destroyed because they cannot adapt quickly enough to new conditions. Changes in the atmosphere and hydrosphere are particularly important because their effect is worldwide. Man has made major changes in the earth's environment since the industrial revolution of the eighteenth century. But the increased rate of change has become alarming in the past fifteen to twenty years.

Man is increasingly important as a geologic agent.

19:1 *Man and the Environment*

Environment includes the conditions of climate, vegetation, animals, rivers, lakes, oceans, land forms, and soil of any given area. These conditions interact with one another to form the **biosphere** (bie′a sfir). The biosphere includes those places of the earth in which life can exist. Climate is reflected in the kind of soil. The kind of soil is reflected in the type of vegetation. Animals reflect the abundance of food and water. Every part of the environment affects every other part. Change in one condition is reflected by changes in other conditions.

As long as man lives on the earth, he must use its materials.

Man depends upon the soil for food. He depends upon lakes, rivers, and the sea for both food and water. He depends upon the atmosphere for oxygen. But man's use of minerals has taken him far beyond these simple uses of the earth. Since the early days of the industrial age, man has removed large quantities of minerals from the earth's crust. Millions, or even billions, of years are needed for concentrations of minerals to form. Once these ore concentrations are exhausted, they cannot re-form quickly enough to be of use to man. Furthermore, as man uses minerals from the earth, he creates vast quantities of waste rock and chemicals. Gases formed by the burning of fuels enter the atmosphere. Waste rock, chemicals, and gases pollute the environment and endanger life.

19:2 *Man and the Atmosphere*

Gases of the atmosphere are necessary to life. They also influence the amount of radiant energy that reaches the earth from the sun. In man's effort to control climate, he has used wood, coal, oil, and gas to produce heat energy. These fossil fuels, called *hydrocarbons* (Section 8:5), are being used up at

Figure 19-1. Gases emitted in the smoke from an industrial plant remain in the surrounding area until dispersed by the wind or washed to earth by rain.

Figure 19-2. Burning coal is still a major method used to produce electricity.

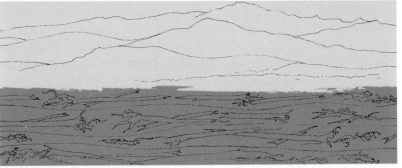

Figure 19-3. (a.) Today's coal began forming in swampy forests millions of years ago (b.) Eventually the plants died, fell into the swamp and began to decay (c.) As layer upon layer was buried, moisture, oxygen, and other gases were lost. Finally, only the form of hydrocarbon known as coal remained.

a rapid rate. Over a period of generations, wood may be replaced. But fuels that come from the burial and decay of organic matter require millions of years to form. While buried, these hydrocarbons store large quantities of hydrogen and carbon, and small amounts of sulfur and nitrogen. These elements return to the air when the fuels are burned.

Fossil fuels return a number of gases to the atmosphere when they are burned.

Carbon dioxide is used by plants. Thus, an increase in the amount of carbon dioxide in the atmosphere encourages an expansion of plant life. Carbon dioxide also dissolves in ocean and lake waters. There it is used by plankton. (Section 11:3.) But neither of these uses of carbon dioxide has increased fast enough to take care of the amount of carbon dioxide produced by the burning of fossil fuels. As the amount of carbon dioxide

Figure 19-4. If the percentage of carbon dioxide in the atmosphere should continue to increase, eventually the earth's temperature may rise enough to melt the polar ice caps.

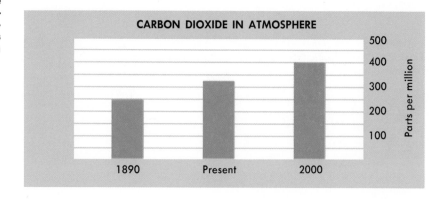

in the atmosphere increases, more heat is held near the earth. If worldwide temperatures continue to rise, many changes will occur on earth. Glaciers will melt and sea level will rise about 200 ft.

If glaciers melt, coastal cities will be drowned, land areas will be reduced, and ocean areas will be increased.

Sulfur is another element that enters the air from burning fuel. It reaches the air as sulfur dioxide, which damages paint, rubber, nylon, and our lungs. Governments now regulate the amount of sulfur that industry may release into the air. Sulfur (Section 8:4) is an important industrial product. Many industries emit sulfur as a waste product. But these industries recover as much sulfur as possible from their smokestacks. Companies are encouraged to build high stacks to put the unrecoverable sulfur into the upper atmosphere.

Figure 19-5. Dirt particles and smog combine to coat buildings with an oily layer that is difficult to remove. Acids that form in the atmosphere accelerate the weathering of stone buildings.

When sulfur dioxide remains in the air for a short time, it combines with water vapor to form sulfuric acid. This acid falls with rain. If concentrations of sulfur reach small lakes, fish cannot live in the lakes. But some sulfur is necessary for

Vincent McGuire

proteins to form. Nature maintains the proper circulation of sulfur. But man has not yet learned to regulate the amount of sulfur proper to maintain life.

Nitrogen is another gas which is abundant in the atmosphere. It is necessary to life, but only certain organisms can make nitrogen available for plants. (Section 9:3.) This process of *nitrogen fixation* by organisms is slow. It cannot supply enough nitrogen for man's farming needs. Therefore, man takes nitrogen from the atmosphere and treats it to make it into fertilizers for plants. Large quantities of nitrogen fertilizers then are carried from fields to rivers and lakes by runoff. Some of these nitrogen compounds return to the air along with water vapor.

The sun's radiant energy changes these nitrogen compounds, sulfur compounds, and hydrocarbons to **smog.** Elimination of smog has become one of our most pressing problems, especially in cities. Smog is harmful to life when poisonous gases such as nitrogen and sulfur compounds reach a high concentration. Four thousand people are reported to have died from smog in 1952 in London, England. Respiratory diseases and eye troubles often are caused by smog. Smog also tends to screen out the sun's radiant energy, causing cooler climates.

Dust is another material that helps to create smog. In some areas poor farming methods loosen soil. The soil then is carried away by winds. (Section 16:2.) Particles of dust also are released during burning. Large quantities of dust tend to screen out the sun's radiant energy and may change the climate.

Figure 19-6. Smog over Washington, D.C.

Courtesy of National Air Pollution Control

Figure 19-7. Smog over Denver, Colorado.

Courtesy of National Air Pollution Control

19:3 *Man and the Hydrosphere*

Rivers have been used by man throughout history. River mouths make good harbors, but sediments deposited by rivers tend to destroy the harbor. The Roman city of Ostia was an important port in the last century B.C. It is now 1.5 mi from the sea. An abandoned port city of about the same period in ancient Greece is now 15 mi inland. Huge amounts of money are spent maintaining harbors. But eventually most harbors are abandoned because the cost of keeping them open is too great.

Many rivers are straightened for flood control. But if meanders are cut off, a river travels a shorter path to the sea. As the distance a stream travels is decreased, the velocity increases.

Figure 19-8. Many harbors such as this one in Nice, France would eventually fill without constant maintenance.

Meston's Travels

As the velocity increases, the stream can carry more sediment and the river bottom is eroded more deeply.

Dams are built to help control floods. But dams change the normal river pattern. Upstream, velocity is decreased by the obstruction of the dam. Then silt is deposited. Below the dam, the river picks up a new load of sediment and again erodes its channel. If the deposit above the dam is large, however, the river may not carry much sediment to its mouth. Normally rivers supply sediment to the ocean's longshore current. (Section 12:5.) But if rivers do not supply sediment, the longshore current takes sediment from the shore and erodes the beaches.

Damming rivers upstream has an indirect effect on beaches.

Figure 19-9. Dams constructed on rivers can lead to a buildup of silt on one side of the dam and greater erosion of the riverbed on the other.

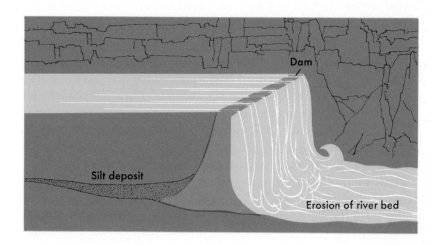

Dam

Silt deposit

Erosion of river bed

Dams also are constructed for storage of water to be used for irrigation. Irrigation water spreads over the land and sinks into the ground. Then the water table rises. Plant roots may become waterlogged and crops may be ruined. Also, as the water stands, it evaporates and leaves salts behind in the soil. But plants cannot tolerate salty soil. In some areas this problem has been solved by drilling wells. Instead of standing on the surface and evaporating, excess water drains off through wells. Water carries salts downward to deeper levels.

Stream water is also used for industrial cooling. Many manufacturing processes require high temperatures. Water from rivers is piped to the industry and made to flow across various pipes. The river water absorbs heat from the pipes then returns to the stream. *Thermal pollution* results from the higher temperature of the returned water. The heated water loses some of its dissolved oxygen. Lack of oxygen prevents de-

Figure 19-10. Improper irrigation practices can ruin both crops and soil.

Will Sheppard

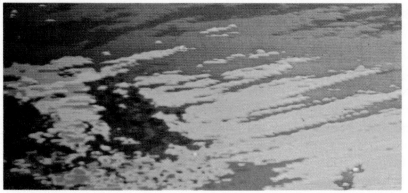

Barnes Engineering

Figure 19-11. This thermo-gram (made with a type of heat sensitive photography) shows thermal pollution in the Connecticut River. The red area shows hot water entering the river from an industrial plant. Where it mixes with cool water (black or dark green), the water temperature rises (yellow and light green).

composition of organic waste and increases bacterial action. Many fish cannot survive the high temperatures and lack of oxygen in our rivers.

Thermal pollution may affect all life in a stream.

Another more serious problem is the use of rivers for the disposal of sewage and industrial waste. Even rivers in rural areas are polluted by runoff containing fertilizers and pesticides. Streams that carry sewage, industrial waste, pesticides, and fertilizers may be dangerous to all life.

Vincent McGuire

Figure 19-12. In many lakes, rivers, and streams, fish can no longer survive the high temperature, lack of oxygen, and generally polluted conditions.

Figure 19-13. Sandstone can filter out bacteria and particles carried in groundwater, but limestone may have large openings which allow polluted groundwater to pass through too rapidly for purification.

Groundwater (Chapter 14), like surface streams, may become polluted by waste. Water that filters through sand or sandstone tends to become purified. But water that moves rapidly through large openings does not have time to lose its load of wastes. Fractures and bedding planes allow rapid movement of water. Limestone areas in particular are likely to have openings through which polluted water may be moving. In some areas, the water table is too close to the surface for filtering to occur. Groundwater around swamps and coastal regions requires special precautions before being used.

Figure 19-14. Eutrophication in a lake becomes apparent if the lake begins to fill with vegetation.

Polluted water cannot be used for domestic purposes nor for recreation.

La Berea Tar Pit in California is an example of a natural seep.

Figure 19-15. An oil globule leaving a natural oil seep.

Lakes, even more than streams and groundwater, have become polluted. Streams carry their burden of pollutants into lakes. There the waste collects. One of the pollutants of lakes is an oversupply of nitrogen. This excess nitrogen is used by algae. Various forms of life use the algae as food. As biologic activity increases, all available oxygen is used up. Then nothing can live but the algae. This sequence of events is known as **eutrophication** (eu trahf i kae' shun). Eutrophication means enrichment. But this kind of enrichment is bad for plants, animals, and man.

Phosphorus is another element which is overabundant in polluted lakes. It enters streams and lakes in large amounts from fertilizers, sewage, and detergents. Then pond weeds and floating organisms multiply rapidly. As they multiply, they use up both nitrogen and oxygen. Eventually, only algae can survive in the lake.

Because *oceans* are so vast, men have thought that their waters could tolerate waste without becoming polluted. But now some marine life cycles are being affected by the substances carried to the sea. Even oceans need time to redistribute solids and gases brought in by rivers. Waste products tend to remain near river mouths, in the shore zone, and on the surface for long periods of time. Thus bays and lagoons are affected most because circulation is slower there than in the open ocean.

A pollutant that has become increasingly significant is the *oil spill*. In addition to the oil spills from offshore drilling, much oil reaches the ocean from other sources. Ships pour waste oil into the sea. Discarded oil from cars and industry often is dumped into rivers and carried to the ocean. And natural oil seeps are present on land and on the ocean floor.

Natural seeps have contributed oil to the ocean for millions of years. This oil has not accumulated because some bacteria use oil in their life processes. But oil-consuming bacteria are not normally present in large enough numbers to use the millions of barrels of oil from spills. Scientists now are breeding oil-eating bacteria. They freeze them and hope to have quantities ready for the next spill. After disposing of the oil, the bacteria will die as they will have no food source.

Radioactive wastes and chemicals also may pollute the oceans. These waste materials are sealed in containers and dropped into the sea. Recently, governments have begun to require that such wastes be dropped into the abyss. In deep waters leakage probably would be diluted before it reached shore.

But scientists are working on ways to change harmful waste into harmless or even useful forms.

Not all oceanic problems are related to waste. Engineering projects along shorelines cause many changes in the marine environment. *Groins* are narrow piers which are built perpendicular to the shore. Their purpose is to protect a harbor or beach. As waves are turned seaward by a groin, their sediment is dropped. Normally longshore currents are supplied with materials carried shoreward by the waves. But lacking this sediment, the longshore current erodes the beaches.

Whenever currents are slowed down by construction, deposition occurs. Seawalls are built to protect cities from storms. But they often interfere with wave action. Bridges and fishing piers also change the wave and current movement. Changes in the shape of the shore reflect the influence of shore construction.

19:4　*Man and the Lithosphere*

In ancient times when men gathered food from fields and forests, the earth was supporting about 10 million people. Now the earth has about 3½ billion human beings. Modern agriculture probably could support about 10 billion people. But if the earth is to support this many, its soil and nutrients must be preserved. Proper plowing and crop rotation must be practiced to prevent runoff. Fertilizers must be recycled, not wasted, and not allowed to destroy lakes and streams. Particularly phosphorus must be conserved. When it is carried to the sea, phosphorus (unlike oxygen, carbon, sulfur, and nitrogen) does not return to the land. Other elements return to the air in water vapor. Then they return to the land with rainwater. But phosphorus stays dissolved in the sea. Or it becomes a part of marine organisms and eventually is deposited on the sea floor.

The growth of the cities is changing the land. Cities are expanded to house a growing population. Sources of industrial material often are buried beneath new buildings. Farmland is removed from cultivation. Parking lots, buildings, and paved highways prevent infiltration of rainwater. Then runoff is increased and flooding often becomes a problem. Cities also withdraw large amounts of groundwater for domestic purposes and for industry. In some areas the removal of groundwater has lowered the water table and even affected the earth's surface. Water in rock pores helps to support overlying material. When the water is removed, rock grains settle into the space once

Oceans, like the rest of the hydrosphere, are being polluted.

GAF Corporation

Figure 19-16.　The construction of bridges changes currents and shorelines.

Figure 19-17. In urban areas where a large portion of the land is paved, runoff can lead to mud slides.

Figure 19-18. Where land is not reclaimed, abandoned strip mines are barren because too little soil is left for vegetation to grow.

In mountainous regions, slopes must be protected against the downward movement of rocks and debris.

occupied by water. This settling causes cracks in the surface soil, in buildings resting on the soil, and in underground pipes.

In the Gulf Coast area, sediments are not yet consolidated. There removal of groundwater causes surface cracks in the soil and in buildings as the sediments become compacted. Limestone areas also are likely to weaken as groundwater is removed. Groundwater may dissolve out limestone beneath the surface. (Section 14:5.) Then if buildings are constructed on the overlying rock, the rock may collapse and carry the buildings downward.

Archaeologists (ahr kee ahl′ a jists) are men who study ancient buried cities. They report that primitive man built up the crust with waste much as we do today. In London, one foot of debris has been added to the city every century. The rate today is about the same as for ancient cities. Building of homes, offices, and industries brings about the redistribution of sand, clay, gravel, limestone, and other products. As the number of people increases, the demand for material also increases.

Much of the material needed by cities and commerce comes from mines. To obtain the material, millions of tons of rock must be moved. Many metallic ores, as well as sand, gravel, clay, and coal are dug from open pits. Limestone, marble, and granite are quarried or removed as large solid blocks from the earth.

Ores also are obtained from tunnel-like openings beneath the surface. While mining is going on, tunnels are braced. When mines are abandoned, however, they often are neglected. Then overlying rocks may collapse. Scranton, Pennsylvania, for example, lies above a coal mine. To save part of the city from sinking, the mine now must be filled at the cost of millions of dollars. Cleveland, Ohio, overlies a salt mine. Support of the roof rocks must be carefully maintained to avoid collapse.

In addition to rocks moved during mining, great quantities of soil and rock are moved when roads are built. Road building tends to steepen slopes and to upset their equilibrium. Then soil creep occurs in response to the pull of gravity. Another effect of road building is in the chemistry of the nearby area. A lead halo from traffic exhaust extends about two miles on either side of a major highway. Lead poisons the vegetation and the animals that forage along the road.

In addition to road building, slopes may be changed by residential developments. Then landslides are common. California has experienced many of these slides after major rainfall or slight earth tremors. Fill dirt and debris from excavations overload the slope. Water from cesspools, lawns, and gardens adds to the instability of the soil. Builders can learn to recognize old landslide areas and areas of faulting. Then they can avoid slopes which are apt to be unstable.

19:5   *Man and Energy*

Much of the energy which powers an industrial economy comes from electricity. But fuel is needed to generate this electricity. Generally, coal, oil, and gas are used in the production of electricity. Today nuclear energy also is being used. Supplies of coal probably will last for centuries. But supplies of gas and oil are limited. Present estimates of oil and gas supplies indicate they will last only about 75 years. Although processes that form coal, oil, and gas are still active, man is using earth's supplies of fossil fuels far faster than nature can replace them. In the 1800's, the world used about 250 million tons of coal per year. Now it uses 2.8 billion tons per year. Before 1890, use of oil was hardly measurable. Today man uses 12 billion barrels per year. About 25 years ago, most fuel gas was manufactured from coal. Now natural gas, the gas formed in nature, is an important fuel. Man can return to making gas from coal, but coal creates a serious pollution problem. The next major source of energy appears to be nuclear power. One gram of uranium 235 produces as much energy as 14 barrels of oil or 3 tons of coal. The supply of uranium 235, however, is expected to last only to the year 2000.

At present, nuclear energy is obtained from splitting uranium 235 atoms. This process is called **fission**. But if scientists can develop a method of **fusion,** or joining atoms, the supply of fuel will be almost unlimited. Seawater has innumerable atoms of *deuterium* (deu tir′ ee em), an isotope of hydrogen. Deuterium atoms can be joined much as hydrogen is changed to helium in the sun. (Section 22:4.) At present this method is too expensive, and it has not yet been done on a large scale. The waste from the fission process is stored underground as a liquid. Danger of leakage is always a possibility. Fusion waste is a solid that can be buried safely. Thus, adequate energy and an easier disposal method make it important to develop the fusion process as an energy source.

Although eventually nuclear energy may supply man's energy requirements, other sources are being studied. For example, the sun releases great quantities of radiant energy. This energy powers all of nature's surface processes on the

Figure 19-19.   **Coal and slate that lie just beneath the topsoil are being removed in this active strip mine.**

An industrial economy uses energy for transportation, manufacturing, heating, and cooling.

If nuclear fusion can be used as a source of energy, man will have an adequate supply of fuel for years and years.

Figure 19-20.   **Deuterium is an isotope of hydrogen which has a neutron in its nucleus. The more common hydrogen isotope has no neutrons.**

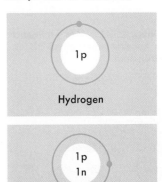

1p

Hydrogen

1p
1n

Deuterium
(heavy hydrogen)

William Huber

Figure 19-21. Waterfalls can be used to generate electricity; however, many are too remote for this purpose.

Ward's Natural Science Est.

Figure 19-22. Thermal springs provide energy in some regions.

Waterfalls, such as Niagara Falls, release large amounts of energy.

Figure 19-23. Man's influence is apparent throughout his environment.

Vincent McGuire

earth. But man has not made much direct use of this energy. In some areas energy from the sun is used to heat water or to evaporate water for cooling. The sun's energy also is used to heat some homes. But the sun does not always shine when heat is needed most, and so other methods of heating have proved more useful. Probably more of the sun's heat will be harnessed eventually.

Water is another possible source of energy. The farther water falls, the more energy it releases. Energy from large waterfalls such as Niagara Falls is used to generate electricity. Dams also may provide energy. Norris Dam in Tennessee and Hoover Dam in Nevada are examples of large dams built to furnish electricity. Other dams have been proposed. But conservationists, who, to preserve rivers and wilderness as they now are, often object to dams. Waters ponded by dams often cover farmland, deposits of industrial material, and places of beauty. Also, the weight of the water stored by dams may place too much stress on subsurface strata and cause movement of the rocks.

Other local sources of energy are thermal, or hot, springs. These springs are present in some areas of recent igneous activity. For example, California, Iceland, New Zealand, and Italy have thermal springs which are used to operate certain industries.

19:6 *Restoration of the Environment*

Modern civilization has done much to change the environment. Crustal materials cannot be renewed in less than millions of years. It is important to find ways to reuse old cars, refrigerators, tires, bottles, and other materials now collecting as waste. Long ago, when thousands, instead of billions, of people lived on earth, waste was not much of a problem. A crowded location could be abandoned. The air was still clean; water was still pure. Unused soil was still fertile. The surface of the land was the product of natural processes. Now man has become the most significant erosional agent of all time. He changes drainage systems and shorelines. He creates some lakes and destroys others. He even changes the composition of the atmosphere and of seawater. Man is changing the environment too rapidly for new life forms to replace life that cannot adapt to the changed environment.

Saving the environment does not mean that man must give up his modern technology. But man must learn to live within nature's cycles. Governments are beginning to take measures to clean the air and water. Costly changes are being made in the use of the earth in an attempt to preserve the natural environment. But we cannot leave all the solutions to the scientists. Every individual can help to prevent waste and litter. A serious effort can save the earth for use by all life that exists today.

MAIN IDEAS

1. Man is an agent of change for the atmosphere, hydrosphere, and lithosphere. The rate of change has increased drastically since the industrial revolution.

2. The environment includes all conditions of climate, life, runoff, lakes, topography, and soil for any given area.

3. Carbon dioxide has been added to the atmosphere by the burning of hydrocarbons. The additions of carbon dioxide have been absorbed only partly by solution in the oceans, lakes, and rivers and by the increase in vegetation. If the increase in amounts of carbon dioxide in the atmosphere continues, it may lead to general warming of the climate and eventually to melting of glaciers.

4. Acted upon by sunlight, sulfur dioxide, nitrogen compounds, and hydrocarbon compounds in the atmosphere produce smog, a condition dangerous to all forms of life.

5. Dust in the atmosphere has increased as a result of man's activities. Dust tends to screen out the sun's rays, causing the climate to cool.

6. Dams tend to have several effects on rivers and beaches. They bring about deposition of sediment on the upstream side of the dam, and erosion in the downstream channel and at the river mouth in the beach area.

7. Man's burning of fossil fuels has upset the natural cycling of elements needed by plants. An overabundance of nitrogen and phosphorus has been particularly disastrous for lakes and their various forms of life.

8. Oceans now are being polluted by radioactive wastes, by organic wastes carried in by rivers, and by oil spills. Changes in the production of nuclear power from the fission of uranium atoms to the fusion of deuterium atoms may solve man's energy needs and make radioactive waste less difficult to dispose of.

9. Mining for materials needed in industry and for the building of cities leads to redistribution of millions of tons of rock material. Collapse of the earth's surface may occur where underground mines are not properly filled or braced. Collapse also is a problem where cities are built above cavernous limestone or in areas where groundwater is being removed faster than it can be replenished.

VOCABULARY

Write a sentence in which you use correctly each of the following words or terms.

archaeologist	eutrophication	hydrocarbon
biosphere	fission	phosphorus
deuterium	fusion	smog
environment	groin	thermal pollution

STUDY QUESTIONS

A. True or False

Determine whether each of the following sentences is true or false. (Do not write in this book.)

1. The biosphere includes those places of the earth in which life can exist.
2. Thermal pollution means the addition of heat to a river.
3. Photosynthesis adds carbon dioxide to the atmosphere.
4. Sunlight causes smog to form from hydrocarbons and nitrogen compounds in the air.
5. Dams sometimes cause rivers to erode part of their channels more deeply.
6. The earth's unused coal supply is larger than the unused oil supply.
7. Water may be purified if it filters through sandstone.
8. Rivers tend to deepen the harbors at their mouths.
9. Nuclear waste from the fusion of atoms is a solid waste.
10. Hillsides always are the safest places for residences in periods of heavy rainfall.

B. Multiple Choice

Choose the word or phrase which completes correctly each of the following sentences. (Do not write in this book.)

1. Animals and plants on the earth live in the (*stratosphere, biosphere, ionosphere*).

2. Harbors often are protected by the construction of (*dams, bridges, groins*).

3. The important life-supporting element which is lost when washed into the sea is (*oxygen, nitrogen, phosphorus*).

4. The burning of fossil fuels releases large amounts of (*phosphorus and nitrogen, carbon and oxygen, nitrogen and oxygen*).

5. Roads tend to change hillsides by (*flattening the slope, steepening the slope, adding fill dirt*).

6. Heat is held near the earth by large concentrations of (*carbon dioxide, nitrogen, oxygen*) in the atmosphere.

7. An overabundance of nitrogen in lakes creates (*thermal pollution, photosynthesis, eutrophication*).

8. Scientists who study ancient civilizations are (*mineralogists, archaeologists, geologists*).

9. Cities deposit waste and trash at the rate of about (*1 foot, 5 feet, 10 feet*) per century.

10. Collapse of overlying rocks in limestone areas often results from (*underground water dissolving rock, removal of coal, compaction of the rock*).

C. Completion

Complete each of the following sentences with a word or phrase which will make the sentence correct. (Do not write in this book.)

1. Coal, oil, and natural gas are all __?__ fuels.

2. An increase in carbon dioxide in the atmosphere leads to an increase in __?__ life.

3. Additions of carbon dioxide to the atmosphere result from the burning of __?__.

4. Sulfur dioxide in the air combines with water vapor to form __?__.

5. Water which is returned to a river after cooling industrial pipes causes ___?___ pollution.

6. Oil has been added to the ocean for millions of years from ___?___.

7. Organisms take nitrogen from the soil in a process called ___?___.

8. The sun's radiant energy changes nitrogen oxides and hydrocarbons in the atmosphere to ___?___.

9. An isotope of hydrogen found in seawater is called ___?___.

10. Iceland and New Zealand make use of the natural energy of ___?___.

D. How and Why

1. Why are trees and meadows important in creating a healthy environment?

2. Along a lake shore, why should a water well be drilled between the lake and the septic tank?

3. Why do road construction crews cover the sides of steep cuts with burlap or tree branches?

4. Why should cities encourage bicycle riding to replace driving cars?

5. Why are paper containers better than plastic containers in relation to the environment?

6. How does irrigation sometimes kill crops and make land unusable?

7. Would irrigation be better for land and crops at the headwaters of a river or at the mouth of the river? Why?

8. Why are flood control dams sometimes harmful to a beach?

9. How are scientists trying to control oil spills?

10. Why is solar, or sun, heating impractical?

INVESTIGATIONS

1. Make a list of the ways your class can help to improve your local environment.

2. If gullies are present on public property near you, see if you can get permission to fill the gullies with trees and branches. Discarded Christmas trees make good material for this project. After a heavy rain, check to see how effective the cover is.

3. Make a list of mineral products that are accumulating in junkyards in your city. Try to discover ways this matter could be reused.

4. Contact authorities to find out the source of your water supply. Find out how and how often the purity of the water is checked. Discuss ways you can help to keep the water supply clean.

5. Find out who makes the rules that govern the treatment of sewage and industrial waste. If your water comes from shallow wells, find out what precautions are taken to locate uncontaminated water.

6. Find out what your local government is doing about air pollution.

INTERESTING READING

The Biosphere. A Scientific American Book. San Francisco, Calif., W. H. Freeman & Co., 1970.

Carlisle, N. Y., *Riches of the Sea: The Science of Oceanology.* New York, Sterling Publishing Co., Inc., 1967.

Cousteau, Jacques–Yves, *The Living Sea.* New York, Pocket Books, Inc., 1964.

Dubos, Rene, et. al., *Fitness of Man's Environment.* Smithsonian Institute Annual Symposium. New York, Harper & Row Publishers, Inc., 1970.

Fisher, James, et. al., *Wildlife in Danger.* New York, Viking Press, Inc., 1969.

Flawn, Peter, *Environmental Geology: Conservation, Land-Use Planning, and Resource Management.* New York, Harper & Row Publishers, Inc., 1970.

Marine Fouling and Its Prevention. Woods Hole Oceanographic Institution, 1952.

1970 National EQ Index. Educational Servicing, National Wildlife Federation, 1970.

Saline Water Conservation Report for 1965. U. S. Department of the Interior, Office of Saline Water, 1965.

Science and the Sea. U. S. Naval Oceanographic Office, 1967.

Scientific American. Vol. 233, No. 3 (September, 1970).

Earth History

The interest in a science such as geology must consist in the ability of making dead deposits represent living scenes.

Hugh Miller (1802-1856)

Many of the most difficult questions to answer about the earth concern its history. How old is the earth? What changes have produced the planet man now inhabits? What did the earth look like to prehistoric man or to dinosaurs?

Cave drawings offer clues about the world of prehistoric man but tell us nothing about the earth before man. With no written records of earth's early history, ancient scholars could merely speculate about the origins and development of the earth. Now questions about the earth's development often are answered through the study of rocks and the fossils they contain. Using information from rock layers, scientists can trace the earth's development and reconstruct events that happened before man existed.

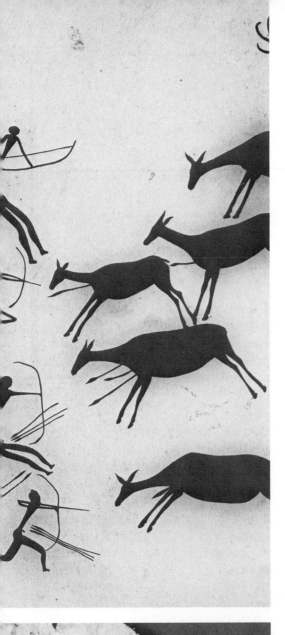

UNIT
Five

20

Dating Geologic Time

Knowledge of things and their properties, which Severinus advised his students to gain, depends on knowing their history. Two important questions about the history of the earth are: "How old is the earth?" and "How can you tell how old it is?"

20:1 *Units of Time*

Earth's age is determined by studying changes in rocks and former living organisms.

The age of the earth has been estimated from rates of change in earth materials. Some changes in earth materials require millions, or even billions, of years. Accurate methods for determining age based on such long-term processes are difficult to develop. Two branches of geology, **stratigraphy** (stra tig'ra fee) and **paleontology** (pae lee ahn tahl'a jee), work together to pry secrets of age from rocks of the earth's crust. *Stratigraphers* (stra tig'ra fers) study the composition and arrangement of layered, or stratified, rocks. *Paleontologists* (pae lee ahn tahl'a jists) study the remains of plants and animals which have been preserved in the earth's crust by natural processes. Remains of past life, called *fossils*, are found commonly in sedimentary rocks.

Scales for measuring age depend upon a regularly repeated action.

All measurements require an accurate scale. Common units of time meausrement are based on an action which is repeated at equal intervals. Earth's time units are based on the regularly repeated motions of rotations and revolution. (Section 1:4.) Earth's rotation on its axis gives rise to the unit called one *day. Months* are units related to the moon's revolution around earth. *Years* are units based on earth's revolution around the sun. Geologists cannot always determine the age of various earth periods in terms of years. Many divisions of geologic time are based on estimates and relationships among events.

Measured in earth years, the planet earth has had a long life. Scientists estimate that the earth is approximately 4.5 billion years old. Man's history on earth spans, at the most, less than one million years. Compared with some members of the universe outside our solar system, the earth may be extremely young. But compared with man's recorded history, 4.5 billion years is a long time.

The earth is approximately 4.5 billion years old.

20:2   *Estimates of Earth's Age*

One of the first attempts to measure the age of the earth was based on the **molten earth theory.** According to this theory, the earth was molten when it was first formed. The earth since has been cooling at a measurable rate. The yearly rate of heat loss at the surface then should be a measure of the age of the planet. Based on this theory, the earth has been estimated to be about *20 million years old.* But there is some evidence that the earth never was molten. Heat has been added to the earth by the decay of radioactive elements in the interior. The amounts of heat which have been added are unknown. Furthermore, the earth may have had a cold beginning. Thus, the molten earth theory cannot be accepted as an accurate estimate of the earth's age.

Heat loss from the crust is an unsatisfactory measure of earth's age because undetermined amounts of heat are being added constantly.

Another suggested method for establishing the earth's age is the **salt method.** This measurement is based on the amount of salt (NaCl) in seawater. Each year salt is carried to the ocean by rivers. Salt has accumulated in the ocean as a result of the evaporation of seawater. The amount of salt in ocean water can be divided by the amount of salt the rivers add to the ocean each year. Then, this should show how many years the ocean has been receiving salt and should show the age of the ocean. However, this method has many weaknesses. If the estimated age is to be correct, it must be assumed that the oceans originally contained only fresh water. Furthermore, thousands of cubic feet of salt now are buried on land where the seas once covered the continents. Scientists cannot be sure that all such land deposits have been discovered. Thus, the accuracy of such calculations is uncertain. Another problem is the fact that rivers are eroding the continents faster today than they did during much of past geologic time. Salt probably is being added to the oceans more rapidly now than in the past.

Weaknesses in the salt method include possible variation in the erosion rate, impossibility of measuring all salt deposits trapped on land, and the possibility that oceans and earth may not be the same age.

The **sedimentation method** is another means used to measure the earth's age. The sedimentation method uses the total thickness of all known rock layers as a measure of age. The amounts of sand, silt, and mud carried to the sea are measured yearly. From these measurements, the time required for the deposition of one foot of sediment can be computed. The rate at which limestone is deposited in reefs and along shores also is determined. The amounts of evaporites formed in evaporite basins are measured. By comparing the rates of deposition with the thickness of sedimentary rock layers, scientists can estimate the time required for such accumulations. But, like the salt method, the sedimentation method is inaccurate. Rivers now carry sediments to the sea at a more rapid rate than in the past. Differences in climate, topography, and sea level influence the rate of sedimentation. Therefore, an accurate estimate of geologic time cannot be made unless all geologic history is known. Erosion is the greatest obstacle to a correct estimate of the earth's age by the sedimentation method. Many layers of rock are removed by erosion. Remaining strata do not indicate how long deposition has continued nor how rapidly sediments were accumulated.

Errors in sedimentation method arise because rate of river erosion is not constant, layers of sedimentary rock may be missing, and rate of accumulation is not known.

20:3 *Radioactive Clocks*

The most accurate method for estimating the earth's age has been provided through the study of *radioactivity*. In 1896, Henri Becquerel, a French scientist, discovered the radioactive properties of the element uranium. In 1903, he shared the Nobel prize with the French chemists Pierre and Marie Curie for their work on radioactive elements. The Curies had discovered that certain elements undergo radioactive decay and form other elements, called *daughter products*. The decay is spontaneous (spahn tae'nee us), occurring without the application of heat or pressure, and it is not part of a chemical reaction. However, like a chemical reaction, radioactive decay either produces or absorbs energy.

Radioactive elements change into other elements by giving off streams of *alpha particles* or *beta particles*, and by *electron capture*. The changes affect the nucleus of an atom. (Section 3:2.) A loss of an alpha particle means that two protons and two neutrons are thrown out of the nucleus. Thus, the atomic number of the atom is reduced by 2; the mass number is reduced by 4. This decay of the nucleus is accompanied by a loss

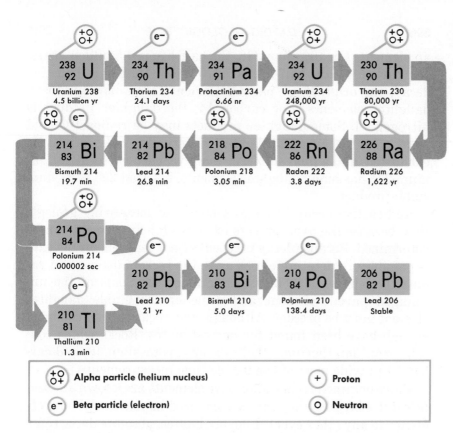

Figure 20-1. Through a series of steps, uranium 238 decays to its stable daughter product, lead 206.

of mass which is given off as a *gamma ray*. The mass is converted into energy in this process. When decay occurs through loss of a beta particle, an electron is lost from a neutron. The neutron changes into a proton, and the atomic number is increased by 1. The mass number remains unchanged. During electron capture an electron from the innermost electron shell joins a proton in the nucleus. The proton is changed into a neutron. The atomic number is reduced by 1, but the mass number remains the same. (Appendix E, p. 533.)

Only a few elements are radioactive. But if radioactive elements and their daughter products are found in measurable amounts in crustal rocks, they can be used to measure the age of rocks.

After the discovery of radioactivity, the rate of decay was determined for each radioactive element. Not all atoms of an element decay at the same time. But the same number of atoms decay within a given period of time. Thus, an average rate of decay can be determined. The time period in which one-half of the original number of atoms decays is called the **half-life** of an element. For uranium 238, the half-life is 4.5 billion years. For carbon 14, the half-life is 5,770 years. During radioactive decay, the original, or parent, element forms new products, daughter elements. For carbon 14, the daughter product is nitrogen 14. Some daughter products may be radioactive and form other decay products. But eventually, radioactivity is exhausted, and a final *stable*, or inactive, *element* results. Uranium 238 has many daughter elements, but lead 206 is its final stable product.

Radioactive elements decay at a measurable rate (half-life) to form daughter elements.

Radioactive decay provides a means of measuring geologic time because the average rate of decay for an element can be determined. Because decay is repeated, a measurement in years is possible. To determine rock ages, the rocks must contain radioactive elements in measurable amounts. Some of the unchanged parent element and some of the stable daughter element must be present. Although such rocks are not common, enough have been found for age estimates. Rocks which contain uranium, thorium (thohr'ee um), potassium 40, and carbon 14 provide most of the usable time measurements.

Half-life of uranium, thorium, potassium 40, and carbon 14 provide absolute dates.

Dates obtained from radioactive elements are known as *absolute dates* because they can be measured in years, without reference to any other event. Like birthdates, absolute dates refer to numbers of years before the present. But not all geologic time can be measured in years. Many events can be determined only with reference to other events. For example, you may know that a friend has an older brother and a younger sister. Even though you do not know any of their birthdates, you know the relative ages of your friend and his brother and sister. Many geologic events are expressed in *relative ages* rather than as absolute dates.

Relative dates indicate the order in which events happened.

20:4 *Dates from Rocks*

Compared with the vast length of geologic time, absolute dates have been established for relatively few rocks. But more dates are being determined. Eventually geologists will have a much more exact calendar of events.

Measurable amounts of uranium, thorium, or potassium 40 in a mineral may be used to date that mineral. Radioactive dates indicate the time when the mineral crystallized from a magma or precipitated from a solution. Rock ages are interpreted from the age of the minerals contained in the rock. Igneous rocks are most likely to contain uranium and thorium, and the most precise uranium dates come from granites. Potassium 40 occurs in all classes of rocks, and it is providing an increasing number of absolute dates.

The oldest known absolute dates belong to rocks found in Africa. Based on uranium dating, these rocks have been determined to be over 3 billion years old. In North America, the oldest rocks are found in the Canadian Shield (Section 15:3), where dates of 2.7 billion years have been determined. The date of 4.5 billion years for the planet earth has come from analysis of meteorites, not from crustal rocks. Meteorites are matter from space which falls to the earth's surface. The sun and its planets are thought to have formed at the same time. Thus the age of meteorites may indicate the age of the earth.

Carbon 14 is a radioactive element which is present in extremely small amounts in all living matter. Carbon 14 is formed by cosmic rays which stream from the sun. When these rays produce neutrons, the neutrons in turn knock a proton from the nitrogen 14 nucleus. When nitrogen 14 loses a proton from its nucleus, it becomes the element carbon 14. In turn,

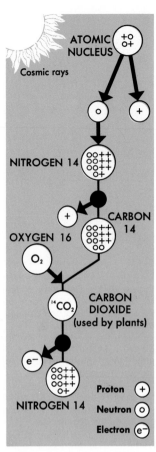

Figure 20-2. Nitrogen 14 is converted to radioactive carbon 14 by neutron bombardment; carbon 14 reverts to nitrogen 14 through loss of beta rays.

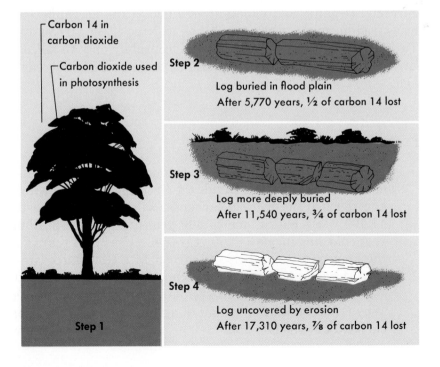

Carbon 14 in carbon dioxide

Carbon dioxide used in photosynthesis

Step 1

Step 2
Log buried in flood plain
After 5,770 years, ½ of carbon 14 lost

Step 3
Log more deeply buried
After 11,540 years, ¾ of carbon 14 lost

Step 4
Log uncovered by erosion
After 17,310 years, ⅞ of carbon 14 lost

Figure 20-3. Carbon 14 enters plants through photosynthesis; animals eat plants and distribute carbon 14 to the animal kingdom. After death, carbon 14 reverts to nitrogen 14 and is not renewed.

National Park Service

Figure 20-4. Recovery of fossil bones from solid rock involves the tedious and delicate process of chipping.

Carbon 14 indicates age of once-living matter. Half-life of carbon 14 is 5,770 years.

Nitrogen 14 becomes carbon 14 when bombarded by neutrons produced by cosmic rays.

Carbon 14 is produced in the upper atmosphere at a constant rate and enters all living matter as a result of plant activity. Carbon 14 decays to nitrogen 14, but the amount of carbon 14 is constantly renewed until an organism dies.

carbon 14 loses a beta particle from its nucleus and reverts to nitrogen 14. This process is continuous. Even though carbon 14 decays to nitrogen 14, the amount of carbon 14 in the atmosphere remains constant because it is always being renewed.

Most of the carbon in the air is present as carbon dioxide (CO_2). Carbon 12 makes up the largest proportion of the carbon (one carbon 14 atom is present for about 1 trillion carbon 12 atoms). Nevertheless, carbon 14 is distributed in approximately equal amounts everywhere on earth. Plants use carbon dioxide in their life processes, and the plants in turn are eaten by animals. Thus, carbon 14 is in all living organisms, and the amount remains approximately constant during their life. After death, carbon 14 is no longer renewed. The amount of carbon 14 remaining in a fossil can be compared with the amount present in living things. Then the date of the fossilized organism's death can be determined.

Carbon 14 has a half-life of 5,770 years. This means that in 5,770 years, half of the original amount of carbon 14 will have decayed to nitrogen 14. In another 5,770 years, half of the remaining carbon 14 atoms will have decayed to nitrogen 14. Only one-fourth of the original amount of carbon 14 will remain. In this way, organic matter such as charcoal, bones, and wood can be dated. However, organic matter that is older than 50,000 years contains too little carbon 14 to be measured accurately. Organic matter less than 1,000 years old cannot be measured accurately because it has lost too little carbon 14. Thus, carbon 14 can be used to date accurately only fossilized living things that died between 1,000 years and 50,000 years ago.

PROBLEM

1. Draw a circle to represent the amount of carbon 14 present in all living things. Divide the circle into units showing how much of the original carbon 14 will remain in a fossil 11,400 years old, in one 17,100 years old, in one 22,800 years old, and in one 34,200 years old. (Use 5,700 years as the approximate half-life of carbon 14.) How much carbon 14 would be left in approximately 50,000 years? If $\frac{1}{16}$ of the original carbon 14 remains, how old is the fossil? Why is 50,000 years the limit of age determination by the carbon 14 method?

Rocks containing organic matter often can be interpreted as being of the same age as the organic matter they contain. However, fossils of animals that died in caves or fell into ravines must be younger than the rock in which they are found. Such fossils provide relative dates rather than absolute dates for the enclosing rock. Under other circumstances, bones may provide absolute dates for enclosing rocks. For example, if an animal dies and is carried downstream and deposited on a flood plain or delta, its bones and the enclosing rock will be the same age.

Organisms dated by carbon 14 commonly indicate relative dates for enclosing rocks.

Absolute dating is a complicated process. It may be years before correct dates are established for all units of geologic time. Most geologic dates still are relative, rather than absolute. Recall that dates are called relative if the order of events can be determined, but not the length of time involved. **Relative dates** refer to the relationship between time of deposition and certain events in the geologic sequence.

Mountain building events are useful in determining divisions of geologic time.

Geologic events that are most easily recognized include faulting, folding, intrusions, and volcanic eruptions. Recall that changes in rock position can be recognized because sedimentary rocks are deposited in a horizontal position near sea level. Furthermore, sedimentary rocks are deposited in succession. The oldest layer is at the bottom of the series and the youngest on the top. Age determination by position of the rock layers in a vertical sequence is called the **law of superposition.** Ages of associated igneous rocks are determined by the **law of cross-cutting relationships.** For example, if a dike cuts across sedimentary beds, the sedimentary rock layers must have been

The **principle of superposition** states that the youngest rock layers are deposited above older rock layers.

Figure 20-5. In Stage 1, sediments were deposited on the continental shelf, buried, and intruded by magma. In Stage 2, erosion has removed the upper layers, and a new series of beds has been deposited following a second transgression of the sea.

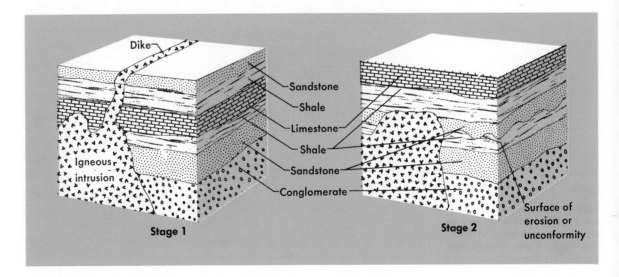

Dike — Sandstone — Shale — Limestone — Shale — Sandstone — Conglomerate — Igneous intrusion — Stage 1 — Stage 2 — Surface of erosion or unconformity

there when the dike was formed. If sedimentary layers are pushed up by laccoliths or sills, then the igneous rocks are younger than the sedimentary beds. If sedimentary beds are deposited above igneous rocks, the igneous rock must be older. Often a sedimentary bed overlying an igneous mass contains gravel, or even boulders, of the eroded igneous rock. Such sedimentary gravels indicate their source is the older igneous rock. Volcanic ash and lava flows are especially useful for establishing a time sequence. The ash or the lava may contain radioactive elements which furnish absolute dates. Then relative dates can be established for the layers above and below the volcanic material.

Both the law of superposition and the law of crosscutting relationships help to establish relative dates for certain rock layers. Other useful evidence in relative dating includes the presence of folding and faulting. Metamorphism indicates uplift from geosynclinal regions. The uplift of mountains provides a break in the continuity of rock layers. This break is useful for dating geologic events. The change from folded, metamorphosed rocks to overlying, horizontal sedimentary beds can be readily recognized. Often such major changes in the rock record are used to separate the geologic time scale into units.

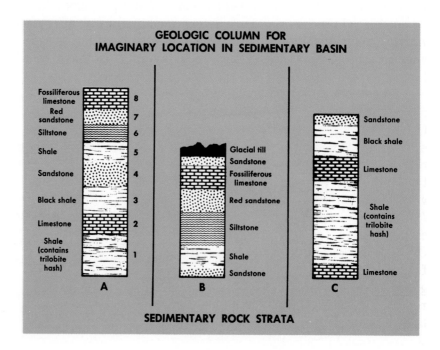

Figure 20-6. Columns A, B, and C indicate the thickness and kinds of rock found at three different locations in the same sedimentary basin.

PROBLEM

2. Use Figure 20–6 to correlate the rock layers in *B* and *C* with the layers in *A*. Which column represents the youngest rock formations? Is *C* an older or younger sequence than *A*? What layers are missing from *B* and *C* that are present in *A*? After you have studied Section 20:6, explain how the geologic column of the world has been assembled. Base your reasoning on the correlation of *A*, *B*, and *C*.

20:5   *Dates from Fossils*

Paleontologists study a variety of remains of past life. Occasionally, *entire animals* are preserved. For example, woolly mammoths have been buried and frozen into the ice sheet that has covered Siberia for thousands of years. Leaves or soft-bodied animals may leave imprints if they are buried quickly beneath soft mud. As the plant or animal matter decays, everything disappears except the element carbon. A *carbon impression* reproduces all the fine lines of the leaf or the animal. In fact, in some carbon imprints of worms even their fine whiskers can be recognized. Another type of fossil record is the *footprint*, the track left in soft mud. An animal track is like the footprint which you might leave in snow or wet cement. Snow tracks disappear during melting. But tracks in cement, like tracks in soft mud, are preserved when the material solidifies.

American Museum of Natural History

Figure 20-7.   Some fossils have been preserved by minerals deposited into their pore spaces; others press a record of their shapes into soft rock before they are dissolved.

Teeth, bones, and *shells* of animals may be preserved by prompt burial in materials which moisture cannot penetrate. Organic matter decays if it is not buried quickly. Decay is especially rapid in warm, humid climates. Sometimes mineral matter seeps into openings in bones or shells and replaces the original material. For example, petrified wood is formed when tree cellulose is replaced by silica. (Section 14:4.) *Permineralization* is the process in which the original shell or bone has its pore spaces filled with other mineral matter. Other fossil records are the mold and cast. A *mold* is a cavity formerly occupied by an organism. Molds are formed where groundwater dissolves an object. The surrounding material retains an impression of the object. Sometimes the mold is later filled with mud. The mud filling retains the imprint of the original object. The filling is known as a *cast*.

Figure 20-8.   An imprint of a fossil fern.

Norfolk & Western Railway

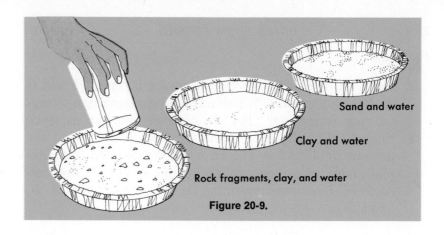

Sand and water

Clay and water

Rock fragments, clay, and water

Figure 20-9.

EXPERIMENT. In three small aluminum pie pans, make three very firm mixtures of sand and water, clay and water, and rock fragments mixed with clay and water. Allow the mixtures to stand for a few minutes. Then press a hard object such as a small block of wood or a glass into the mixtures with enough force to make an impression. Remove the object and compare the impressions made in the mud, in the sand, and in the gravel. In what kind of rock would you expect to find the best fossil impressions?

ACTIVITY. Shape a firm brick from a mixture of clay and a small amount of water, or from plasticine clay. Press a piece of bone or a shell firmly into the brick until most of the object is surrounded. Carefully remove the object so that you have a sharp impression in the brick. What is this hollow that shows the design of the fossil? Now mix patching plaster with water to a thick consistency and use this mixture to fill the impression in the brick. Allow the plaster to dry, and then break away the clay brick. What is the plaster object that duplicates the original bone or shell? Many similar casts are found in nature when limestone fills the hollows left by fossil shells. How could you distinguish between a cast and a true fossil shell?

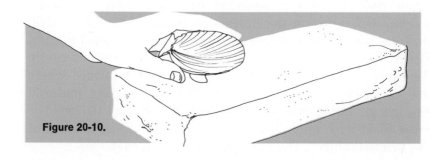

Figure 20-10.

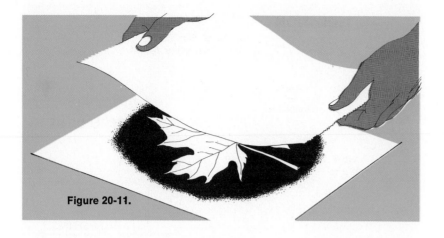

Figure 20-11.

ACTIVITY. Thoroughly coat a sheet of typing paper with white Vaseline or cooking oil. Remove any excess oil from the paper. Light a candle and hold it below the paper so that the carbon from the flame coats the paper. Be careful not to burn the paper. Place a perfect leaf from a tree or bush on the carbon-coated side of the paper. Cover the leaf with a paper towel and press gently. Lift the towel carefully and then remove the leaf with tweezers. Place the leaf, carbon-coated side down, on another sheet of typing paper. Press with a clean paper towel. Carefully remove the leaf. You should have a perfect carbon impression of the leaf. Cover the impression with a sheet of thin plastic (sandwich wrap) and save for experiments in Section 21:6. Do you have a true fossil?

Rock layers that contain fossils are called *fossiliferous* (fahs i lif'e ras). Fossiliferous limestone is fairly common. Reef environments are especially favorable for the preservation of numerous kinds of marine organisms. Plants and soft-bodied animals may be preserved in soft muds or in layers of volcanic ash. But most preservation of organic material occurs in marine sediments, flood plains, or lake beds. Prompt burial is most likely in such environments. Furthermore, oxygen is less abundant in the deeper parts of lakes or seas, and decay is less rapid than on land.

Some fossils represent organisms that lived in a limited environment. Such fossils are known as **facies** (fae'shee eez) **fossils.** For example, certain life forms live in shallow water, but not in deep water. Other organisms live in fresh water but not in seawater. Facies fossils are useful in understanding the conditions of deposition, as well as the sequence of events. For example, dinosaur bones indicate a land environment; bones of swimming reptiles indicate a marine environment.

Fossiliferous rocks contain remains of ancient life.

Figure 20-12. Species may develop through isolation, interbreeding of subspecies, or mutations.

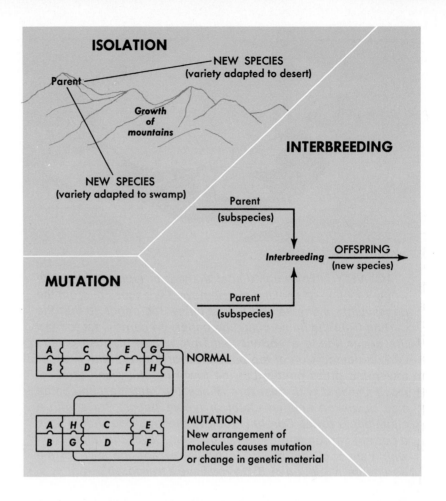

Figure 20-12. Species may develop through isolation, interbreeding of subspecies, or mutations.

To use fossil dating efficiently, paleontologists first separate fossils into groups. Grouping is based on similarities or differences among the fossils. The group most useful to paleontologists is called a species (spee'sheez). A **species** is a population of individuals that have similar characteristics, such as bone structure or surface markings. Although the individual members of a species are not identical, the living members can interbreed. They produce offspring that have the same general characteristics as the parents. Even small differences among individuals may result in the development of new species by a series of gradual changes. One such change is an increase in size. Other changes may involve bone structure, eye position, or ear structure. Some changes have involved body covering. The changes that may occur are almost numberless. But most changes occur gradually. If the fossil record is good, the changes can be traced from one geologic time division to another.

Reasons for change are not always the same. Sometimes a species is so isolated that its members can interbreed with only a limited number of individuals. Then any differences tend to become emphasized. Sometimes subspecies interbreed and they produce new varieties. Subspecies are difficult to define. In general, individuals that belong to a **subspecies** are slightly different from members of another subspecies. However, all members of both subspecies can interbreed. When subspecies interbreed, slight differences give rise to new forms. **Mutations** (meu tae′ shuns) are changes that occur suddenly in certain offspring of a species. These changes cannot be predicted, but sometimes they are passed on to succeeding generations. Thus, isolation, interbreeding of subspecies, and mutations bring about changes in a species. Changes in both plant and animal forms have occurred throughout geologic time. Fossil records suggest that most changes are in the direction of an increasing number of kinds of animals and plants. Changes also have brought about an increase in the complexity of the more recent forms. For example, trees are much more complex than algae (al′jee) which are among the earliest known plant-like organisms. Backboned animals are much more complex than the jellyfish-like forms, or the trilobites that are among the earliest known many-celled animal forms.

Both physical changes and biological features in rocks are used to separate the long history of the earth into time units. The fossil record contains many examples of the extinction of certain species and the rise, or emergence, of new species. Boundaries between time units are based on the life span of certain life forms. Such units contain varying numbers of years. They cannot be compared to the more common units of time such as hours, days, months, or years. Indeed, the life span of some species has covered only a few thousand years. Other species have lived for millions of years. But changes in life forms and patterns are useful for relative dating of geologic time.

Great changes in life patterns often accompany major changes in the physical character of the earth's surface. Boundaries of eras are related to the uplift of mountain systems. These boundaries are also dividing lines between the extinction of major groups of animals and the appearance of new groups. (Table 21–1.) In general, boundaries between eras mark times when continents were high above sea level. Oceans were mostly withdrawn from the land masses and

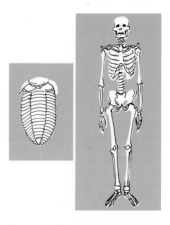

Figure 20-13. Throughout geologic time, life has become more complex and diversified. Note the complexity of the human skeleton as compared to the trilobite.

Most fossil forms have developed from simple to complex forms.

Field Museum of Nat'l History, Chicago
Artist, Charles R. Knight

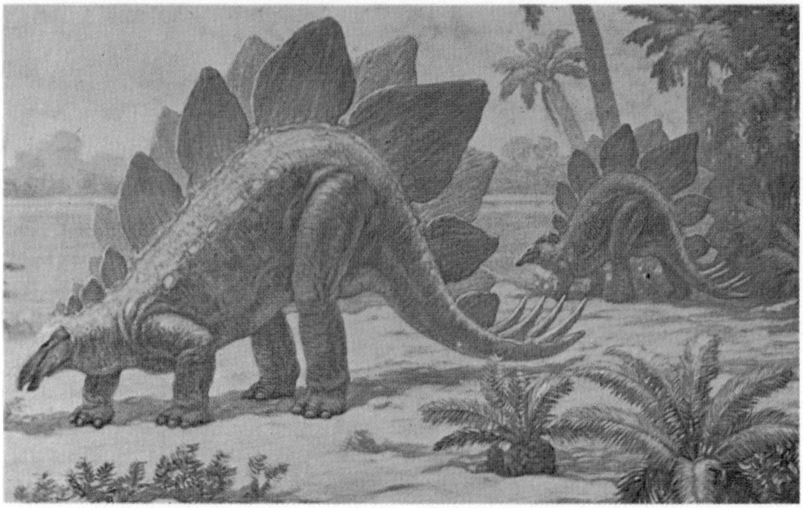

Figure 20-14. Stegasaurus was a unique dinosaur having plates on its back. It was only one among several kinds of dinosaurs of Jurassic age that were buried in the area now known as the Dinosaur National Monument. Probably most of these animals floated downstream after death and became lodged in the sandbar of an ancient river.

erosion was rapid. Folded metamorphic and igneous rocks were worn down and reduced to sea level. Seas gradually flooded the continents. Younger layers of sediments were deposited above the eroded surfaces of the continents. Such breaks in the rock record are called **unconformities.** They are evidence of physical changes in the earth's surface. Above such breaks, rocks contain fossils quite different from those contained in older rocks.

Index or guide fossils must be abundant, widespread, and limited in time span.

Besides being used to date rocks, fossils also provide information about the history of life on earth. Fossils that can be used to divide geologic time into small units are called **index fossils,** or **guide fossils.** Index fossils are remains of organisms that lived only a short time. They are found widely distributed in many different regions of the earth. In a sequence of rocks, the older layers contain forms of life that are simple compared with the increasingly complex forms of the younger layers. The relative ages of layers are determined by the law of super-

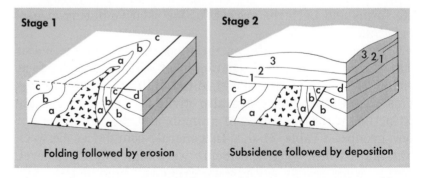

Figure 20-15. In Stage 1, rocks have been folded, uplifted, and eroded. In Stage 2, the folded beds of Stage 1 have been submerged and covered by younger sediments to form an angular unconformity.

position. Then the ages of fossils are determined from the position of the fossil beds within the sequence of rock layers. In regions where rock layers are folded or faulted, fossils themselves may be used to determine the relative ages of disturbed rock layers. Fossils found in the folded or faulted layers are compared with fossils found in horizontal beds. Thus, complex rock structures often can be *correlated*, or matched, with simple layers. Then their position within a sequence of beds can be determined.

20:6　*Geologic Column*

Stratigraphers and paleontologists have combined their efforts to determine the order in which sediments were deposited. Correlation of rock layers from place to place is based on the law of superposition and on the type of fossils contained in the rock layers. In the latter part of the eighteenth century, William Smith, an English engineer, traveled through England and Wales. Smith found that he could recognize rock layers from one place to another, based on the fossils in the rocks. Smith mapped the locations of these fossils. Later he matched the fossils of England with those of certain rock layers in France. Eventually, the English rocks were correlated with rocks in Holland, Belgium, and other regions, as a result of comparison of similar fossils.

By worldwide correlation of fossils and rock layers, geologists have attempted to reconstruct a complete record of deposition from the beginning of time. This model of all deposition is known as the **geologic column.** A geologic column is only an estimate of the thickness of deposits, because erosion has removed much of the record. Geologists can only guess at how much of the total rock record has been lost. However, erosion has not removed rocks from all regions at the same time. While one region was undergoing erosion, another region was receiving deposition. Like solving a giant jigsaw puzzle, the geologist attempts to match rock layers in one region with rock layers in another region. He fits deposits from one layer into missing layers in some other place. Eventually, he assembles a sequence of rocks into a column that represents all the known records of deposition.

Most of the dating of rocks is based on their relative position in the geologic column. But some absolute dates have been supplied by radioactive dating. Divisions of geologic time are known as the *geologic time scale.*

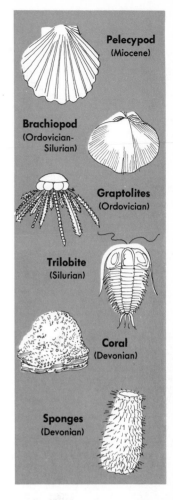

Figure 20-16. **Each unit of geologic time has unique life forms, called index fossils, by which the age of the rock can be recognized.**

Absolute dates may be determined for rocks that contain a radioactive element and its daughter products in measurable amounts.

MAIN IDEAS

1. An age of approximately 4.5 billion years has been estimated for the planet earth based on radioactive dating of meteorites. Fossils and rock layers are used in determining relative dates, and in determining position of rocks in the geologic column.

2. Suggested methods for determining earth's age include the rate of heat loss from molten rock, the rate of accumulations of salt in the ocean, and the rate of accumulation of sediments. None of these methods is accurate because they are all based on factors that cannot be measured precisely.

3. Decay of radioactive elements provides a satisfactory scale for determining the ages of some rocks.

4. Radioactive elements include uranium, thorium, potassium 40, and carbon 14 which decay spontaneously at a measurable rate (half-life) and produce daughter elements until a stable element is formed.

5. Radioactive dating requires that both the parent radioactive element and the stable daughter product be present in measurable amounts. A radioactive date indicates when minerals containing the radioactive element crystallized from a magma, or precipitated from a solution, or when an organism died. Oldest absolute dated rocks are in Africa; next oldest are in Canada.

6. Carbon 14 is used to date organic remains. Carbon 14 is maintained at a constant level in all living matter because it is renewed constantly until the organism dies. After death, decay of radioactive carbon occurs at a regular rate. Its half-life is 5,770 years.

7. Arrangement, or superposition, of rock strata indicates relative age of layered rocks.

8. Fossil records, tracks, impressions, molds, replacements, and preserved hard parts of plants and animals indicate that most species developed from simple to complex forms during geologic time.

9. Index or guide fossils are fossils that have a limited time span and widespread distribution. They are useful in correlation, and also in separating the geologic column into time units.

10. Mountain building helps divide geologic time into units. Such revolutions may have changed the environment to such an extent that many organisms could not survive, and new life forms developed.

VOCABULARY

Write a sentence in which you use correctly each of the following words or terms.

absolute date	index fossil
carbon 14	mutations
correlation	paleontology
crosscutting relationships	permineralize
daughter element	radioactive decay
facies fossils	relative ages
fossils	species
fossiliferous	stratigraphy
half-life	superposition

STUDY QUESTIONS

A. True or False

Determine whether each of the following sentences is true or false. (Do not write in this book.)

1. The salt method of age determination is used to determine relative dates.

2. Radioactive elements change into different elements in time.

3. Absolute dates are determined by fossil forms.

4. Daughter elements must be present to date minerals.

5. Some carbon 14 is present in all living organisms.

6. The age of the earth is judged to be approximately the same as some meteorites.

7. Man has existed on the earth for about 1 billion years.

8. Stable elements have lost their radioactivity.

9. Carbon 14 changes to nitrogen as it decays.

10. The earth is older than any member of the universe outside the solar system.

B. Multiple Choice

Choose the word or phrase which completes correctly each of the following sentences. (Do not write in this book.)

1. Scientists who specialize in age determination by study of rock layers are called (*paleontologists, stratigraphers, physicists*).

2. The age of the earth is calculated to be (*2.7, 3, 4.5*) billion years.

3. The method which seeks to determine earth's age by measuring thickness of deposits of silt, sand, and gravel is called the (*sedimentation, salt, heat loss*) method.

4. Uranium commonly is found in (*sedimentary, metamorphic, igneous*) rocks.

5. The oldest known rocks are found in (*Canada, Africa, Europe*).

6. Potassium 40 is found in (*sedimentary rocks only; metamorphic rocks only; metamorphic, igneous, and sedimentary rocks*).

7. Relative dates for igneous dikes may be determined by the law of (*uniformitarianism, superposition, crosscutting relationships*).

8. Age determination by carbon 14 is not reliable beyond (*5,770, 50,000, 1,000,000*) years before the present.

9. Geologists who specialize in the study of fossils are called (*paleontologists, stratigraphers, physicists*).

10. A radioactive element most useful in age determination of bones or wood is (*uranium 238, potassium 40, carbon 14*).

C. Completion

Complete each of the following sentences with a word or phrase which will make the sentence correct. (Do not write in this book.)

1. The most accurate method of age determination is through the study of ___?___ elements.

2. Rays given off during decay of the nuclei of atoms are ___?___, ___?___, and ___?___ rays.

3. Dates which serve as a record of only a sequence of events are ___?___ dates.

4. The rate at which radioactive elements decay spontaneously and become daughter elements is called their __?__.

5. A radioactive element which originates in the upper atmosphere is __?__.

6. The principle used to determine relative ages of layers in a series of undisturbed rocks is known as the law of __?__.

7. Rocks which contain many remains of past life are called __?__ rocks.

8. New elements which form during decay of radioactive elements are called __?__ elements.

9. Fossils which are preserved by permineralization or petrification are __?__ of one material by another.

10. If a fossil has a short time span, but is widespread, it makes a good __?__ fossil.

D. How and Why

1. What is the difference between relative and absolute dates of geologic age?

2. Would a fossil species which was abundant over a period of 400 million years be a useful index fossil? Explain your answer.

3. Why do only a few organisms become fossils after death?

4. Is petrified wood a fossil?

5. The last ice age began about 1 million years ago and retreated from North America 11,000 years ago. Could any of this time be dated by carbon 14?

6. Why are marine animals rather than land animals more likely to be preserved as fossils?

7. Tree trunks and leaves are often found in coal. What kind of environment has made their preservation possible?

8. Why are limestones rather than sandstones more likely to contain fossils?

9. Why are layers of volcanic ash unusually good indicators of time, as well as useful for relative dating of beds beneath them and above them?

10. How could you obtain dates for a sedimentary series of rocks cut by an igneous dike composed of granite? What kind of dates would you have for each rock?

INVESTIGATIONS

1. Report on the use of wood from campfires to determine some dates of rocks in the United States.

2. Report on the use of carbon 14 to date remains found in recent excavations in Mexico.

3. Make a list of animals of North America which should make good facies fossils.

INTERESTING READING

Beerbower, James R., *Search for the Past: An Introduction to Paleontology*, 2nd ed. Englewood Cliffs, N. J., Prentice-Hall, Inc., 1968.

Carrington, Richard A., *A Guide to Earth History*. New York, Mentor Press, 1961.

Eicher, D. L., *Geologic Time*. Englewood Cliffs, N. J., Prentice-Hall, Inc., 1968.

Farb, Peter, *The Story of Life*. Irvington-on-Hudson, N. Y., Harvey House, Inc., Publishers, 1962.

Fenton, Carroll L. and Mildred A., *In Prehistoric Seas*. Garden City, N. Y., Doubleday & Company, Inc., 1963.

*Fenton, Carroll L., *Tales Told by Fossils*. Garden City, N. Y., Doubleday & Company, Inc., 1966.

Folsom, Franklin, *Science and the Secret of Man's Past*. Irvington-on-Hudson, N. Y., Harvey House, Inc., Publishers, 1966.

Harland, W. B., *The Earth: Rocks, Minerals, and Fossils*. New York, Franklin Watts, Inc., 1960.

Laporte, Leo F., *Ancient Environments*. Englewood Cliffs, N. J., Prentice-Hall, Inc., 1968.

McAlester, Arcie L., *The History of Life*. Englewood Cliffs, N. J., Prentice-Hall, Inc., 1969.

Macgowan, Kenneth, and Hester, Joseph A., Jr., *Early Man in the New World*, rev. ed. Garden City, N. Y., Natural History Press, 1962.

Swinton, William E., *The Dinosaurs*. New York, John Wiley & Sons, Inc., 1970.

* Well-illustrated material.

The Geologic Time Scale

Using a combination of absolute dates and relative dates, geologists have constructed the geologic time scale. (Table 21–1.) The units of this scale are based on systematic correlation of sedimentary layers. Time is divided into units by the presence or absence of certain fossil forms, as well as by absolute dates. Geologic dating is not exact, because the time involved is so vast. Also, some rock formations may have been removed.

21:1 *Geologic Time Units*

Geologic time, from its beginning to the present, is divided into two major units called *eons* (ee'ans). The oldest, called the **Cryptozoic** (krip ta zoh'ik) **eon,** includes all of the time from the formation of the planet earth to 600 million years before the present (B.P.). The second eon, called the **Phanerozoic** (fan e ra zoh'ik) **eon,** includes all of the time from 600 million years B.P. to the present.

The term Cryptozoic comes from two Greek words: *cryptos* (krip' tohs), which means hidden or secret, and *zoion* (zoh'i on), which means animal. The name indicates that any life which may be present in Cryptozoic rocks is hidden. The second, or Phanerozoic, eon contains abundant evidence of past life. The term Phanerozoic comes from the Greek word *phaneros* (fan' er ohs), which means visible. Thus, time is divided into two eons: in one, evidence of life is lacking; in the other, an abundant record of life is present.

The Cryptozoic eon cannot be subdivided into smaller units that can be correlated from one place to another. The Phanerozoic eon, based on the abundant fossil content, is subdivided

Geologic time is divided into two eons, the Cryptozoic and the Phanerozoic.

Cryptozoic rocks contain few fossil forms.

Rocks of Phanerozoic eon contain much visible evidence of past life.

Table 21-1. *Geologic Time Scale*

Eon	Era	Period	Epoch	Life
PHANEROZOIC	Cenozoic	Quaternary	Recent Pleistocene	
		Tertiary	Pliocene Miocene Oligocene Eocene Paleocene	Angiosperms dominant Mammals dominant Birds
	Mesozoic	Cretaceous		Massive extinction of reptiles
		Jurassic		First angiosperms Reptiles dominant Conifers and cycads
		Triassic		First mammals
	Paleozoic	Permian		Great extinction of marine invertebrates
		Pennsylvanian		First reptiles Lycopod trees
		Mississippian		Amphibians dominant
		Devonian		First amphibians Age of fish
		Silurian		First land plants Age of corals
		Ordovician		
		Cambrian		Invertebrates dominant (trilobites and brachiopods)
CRYPTOZOIC		*Precambrian Time* (Not divisible into eras or periods)		Primitive plants Sponge spicules Primitive animals (similar to jellyfish)

Age Estimate (Absolute)

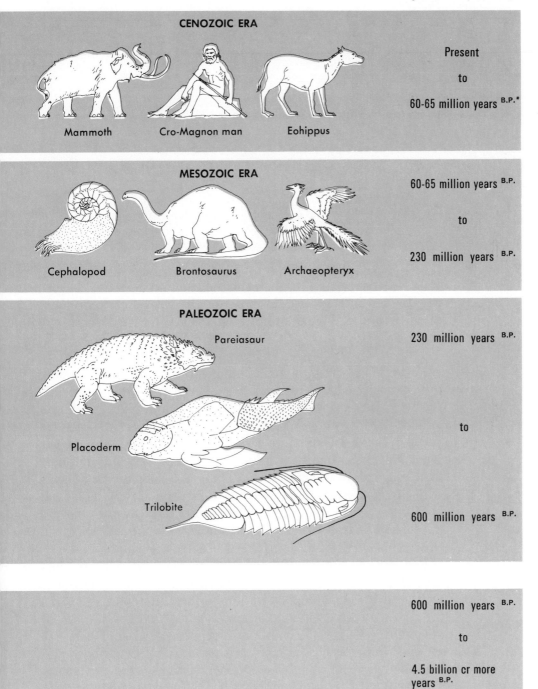

CENOZOIC ERA

Mammoth   Cro-Magnon man   Eohippus

Present

to

60-65 million years B.P.*

MESOZOIC ERA

Cephalopod   Brontosaurus   Archaeopteryx

60-65 million years B.P.

to

230 million years B.P.

PALEOZOIC ERA

Pareiasaur

Placoderm

Trilobite

230 million years B.P.

to

600 million years B.P.

600 million years B.P.

to

4.5 billion or more years B.P.

*Before Present

Figure 21-1.   Before life appeared on earth, the land was a barren waste.

into *eras*. Eras are further subdivided into *periods*. Periods are divided into *epochs*. All units of the Phanerozoic are subdivided into still smaller units on the basis of characteristic fossils.

Extinction of old life forms and emergence of new ones are recorded in the rock layers. Changes in life forms commonly are associated with changes in the elevation of continents. Such changes are reflected in the sedimentary deposits, as well as in the life forms. When worldwide mountain systems are formed, changes in climate occur. The sea withdraws from the land. Marine animals have less living area, but land animals have more room for expansion. These are some of the reasons why changes in the fossil record are associated with mountain building events. Major mountain building, however, covers millions of years. Although it affects many areas of the world, these areas are not all uplifted at exactly the same time.

Periods usually are the smallest divisions of geologic time that can be correlated on a worldwide basis. But paleontologists find it convenient to divide periods into epochs. Epochs are divided into even smaller units called *zones*, as an aid to assembling the geologic column for a local area. Zones are grouped into epochs, epochs are grouped into periods, and periods are grouped into eras. Each time division includes a group of animals and plants that are characteristic of that particular time. Such groups of life are known as **fossil as-**

semblages. The larger the number of fossils in an assemblage, the better is the chance that some of them will be found in another region. If the same fossils are found in more than one region, the areas can be correlated. Recall that facies fossils differ from place to place because they live only in a special kind of environment. But sometimes even facies fossils are transported to a location where they are mixed with another fossil assemblage. For example, during a storm, deepwater fossils may be carried to shore. If strong winds blow offshore, shallow water forms may move into deep water. Thus, organisms that ordinarily do not live in the same environment may be found together in the same fossil record.

21:2   *Cryptozoic Eon*

Rocks belonging to the Cryptozoic eon are present on every continent. The region in which such rocks are exposed at the surface is called the **continental nucleus.** But much of the Cryptozoic rock record is buried beneath younger rocks, or has been eroded away. Cryptozoic history is difficult to interpret from the rocks, because most of the rocks have been changed by extreme metamorphism. Again and again in this eon, mountains were uplifted. Then most of the younger rocks were eroded, leaving only the metamorphosed mountain roots. Even if fossils had been present in the rocks, in most regions it would be impossible to recognize them now.

Subdivision of the Cryptozoic eon on the basis of fossils is impossible. Thus, the first 4 billion years of earth history cannot be separated into meaningful units of time. Preservation of organic matter has occurred only during the last 600 million years of earth history. In the preceding 4 billion years, only a few microscopic plant fossils, such as algae, were preserved. Consequently, little is known about life in the Cryptozoic eon. In fact, paleontologists have hesitated to state that any life except the most primitive protists existed before the Phanerozoic eon. But in 1947, some impressions of soft-bodied organisms were discovered in Cryptozoic rocks of Australia. In many respects, these impressions appear to be ancient forms similar to modern jellyfish. A few stem-like prints suggest that algae was present in the Cryptozoic. Although some plants and animals may have lived during the Cryptozoic eon, fossils are rare. Cryptozoic life apparently lacked hard parts that could be preserved. Furthermore, metamorphism, to

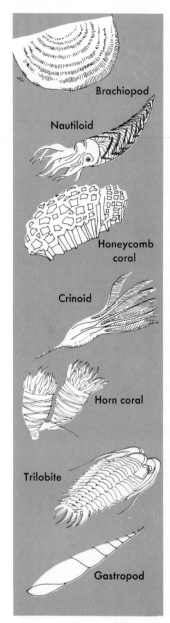

Figure 21-2. Typical fossil assemblage of the Silurian sea bottom.

Cryptozoic organisms may have had no hard parts that could be preserved.

which much of the rock was subjected, destroys evidence of fossils.

Rocks of the Canadian Shield area belong to the Cryptozoic eon. So do the rocks at the bottom of the Grand Canyon. But without fossils, it is impossible to correlate the rocks from these two regions. Nor can they be correlated with rocks of Australia or any other continent. All of these rocks are placed in the Cryptozoic eon because all of them lack fossils. When absolute dates are available for more of the Cryptozoic rocks, stratigraphers may be able to subdivide this long unit into smaller units of geologic time. Rocks of the Cryptozoic often are referred to as *Precambrian*. Most Early Precambrian rocks are metamorphic rocks intruded by great masses of igneous rock. In the Late Precambrian, igneous rocks and metamorphics are still common in some areas. In other regions, however, sedimentary rocks dominate. Then the contact between Precambrian and Cambrian may be difficult to recognize on the basis of rock type. But from the beginning of Cambrian time, fossils are present in the sedimentary rocks. The appearance of numerous fossils is an important time marker. These earliest forms of life mark the beginning of the Phanerozoic Eon and the Paleozoic Era.

Rocks of early Precambrian time are mostly metamorphic.

Figure 21-3. Seas have advanced, withdrawn, and advanced repeatedly throughout geologic time, leaving a complex record in their deposits.

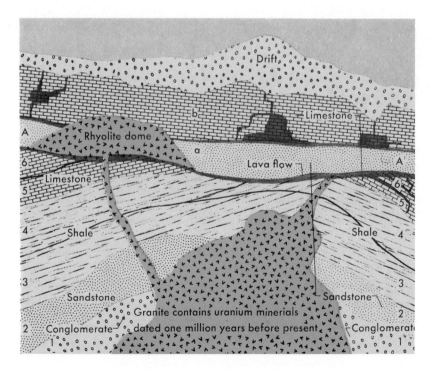

PROBLEM

1. Write the geologic history of the region illustrated in Figure 21–3. Indicate which beds are marine, which are continental, and which are igneous. Also indicate which dates are absolute and which are relative.

21:3   *Phanerozoic Eon*

The Phanerozoic eon began about 600 million years ago and continues today. Phanerozoic time is divided into three eras: **Paleozoic** (pae lee a zoh'ik), which means ancient life; **Mesozoic** (mes a zoh'ik), which means middle life; and **Cenozoic** (see na zoh'ik), which means recent life. Boundaries of eras are associated with geologic revolutions, or mountain building events. But the division into eras is based on the extinction of certain life forms. Volcanic activity and climatic or environmental changes commonly accompany mountain building. Such changes may have influenced the disappearance of certain life forms. Also, it is possible that the disappearance of animals and plants typical of a geological era was caused by events that paleontologists cannot interpret today.

Phanerozoic eon covering 600 million years is divided into Paleozoic, Mesozoic, and Cenozoic eras, on the basis of the contained fossils.

Geologic revolutions, or mountain building, commonly mark transitions from one era to the next.

Like the era, smaller divisions of geologic time also are based on the extinction of certain life forms and the appearance of new forms. The record of all animals and plants that lived and died during the 600 million years of the Phanerozoic era is incomplete. Enough evidence is available, however, to subdivide the eon into smaller units.

Eras are divided into periods based on changes in life forms.

PROBLEMS

Refer to Table 21–1 to answer these questions.

2. If the time covered by the Cenozoic era is accepted as 65 million years, approximately how many million years does the Paleozoic era represent? How many million years does the Mesozoic era represent?
3. Using the estimated age of the earth, approximately how many years does the Cryptozoic eon represent?
4. If you use the scale of 1 in. to represent the time covered by the Cenozoic era, approximately how many inches would represent each of the following: Mesozoic era, Paleozoic era, Phanerozoic eon, and Cryptozoic eon?

21:4   *Paleozoic Era*

With the beginning of the Paleozoic era, earth history becomes somewhat easier to interpret. The era is divided into seven periods. Each period is named for the geographic location in which it was first described. Because the earliest field studies were conducted in Wales and England, the oldest periods have British names. Adam Sedgwick, an English geologist, and Sir Roger Murchison, another English scientist, first described the lower Paleozoic sections. They named the Cambrian and Silurian periods. The Ordovician was named by Charles Lapworth.

Paleozoic era is divided into seven periods named for the regions where their rocks were described first.

The **Cambrian,** oldest of the periods, is given the old Roman name for Wales. **Ordovician** (awrd a vish'an), the next oldest, and **Silurian** (sie luhr'ee an), the third oldest, are named for ancient tribes of Wales. **Devonian** (di voh'nee an) is named for Devonshire, England. The next two period names come from locations in the United States. **Mississippian** is named for exposures along the Mississippi River, and **Pennsylvanian** is named for exposures in the mountains of Pennsylvania. **Permian** (pur'mee an) is named for a province in Russia where these rocks are exposed.

Earliest known records of animal life are marine **invertebrates** (in vert'e brats), or animals without backbones. Invertebrates probably lived in shallow water, near the shore. These ancient forms were soft-bodied, but had a covering of *phosphatic* (fahs fat'ik) material similar to your fingernails. Modern shrimp and soft-shelled crabs have similar coverings. Two important representatives of the ancient invertebrates were trilobites (trie'la biets) and brachiopods (brak'ee a pahds). *Trilobites* are distantly related to crabs and lobsters. *Brachiopods* resemble clams, but belong to a different subdivision of animal life.

Fossils are well preserved in Cambrian rocks of North America where deposition was undisturbed.

During the early Paleozoic era, shallow seas invaded the continents. Then abundant marine life existed over thousands of square miles. In many regions, the Cambrian period was one of quiet deposition. Animals lived, died, and were buried in the rocks. Sometimes whole bodies were kept intact. But because trilobites were jointed animals, their heads often became separated from their bodies after death. Rocks that contain numerous trilobite bodies and heads jumbled together are called *trilobite hash*. Most of the Cambrian fossils consist of trilobite and brachiopod coverings. But in one locality in British Colum-

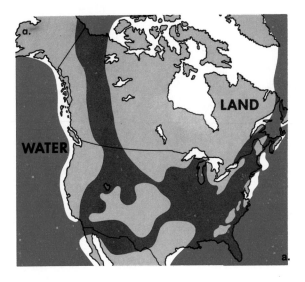
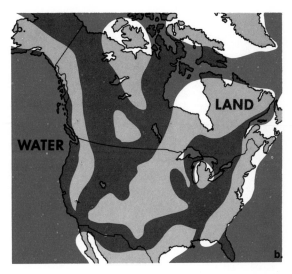

bia, *Burgess shale* preserved not only the coverings of animals but also carbon imprints of soft bodies. A great variety of life from the Cambrian period is preserved in this shale. Muds which formed the Burgess shale must have been deposited in a deep basin where there was little circulation. Thus, nothing disturbed the organisms that had accumulated. During the Ordovician period, calcitic shells replaced phosphatic coverings in most of the brachiopods. Calcitic shells were preserved in greater numbers than the earlier softer coverings. As the number and varieties of animals increased, limestones, consisting almost entirely of preserved shells, were deposited. During the

Figure 21-4. Seas advanced over the interior during Cambrian (a.) and Ordovician (b.) but retreated during the Taconic Mountain uplift at the end of the Ordovician.

Figure 21-5. During the Ordovician period, trilobites, straight and coiled shelled cephalopods, and various snails and corals were common.

Field Museum of Natural History
Artist, Charles R. Knight

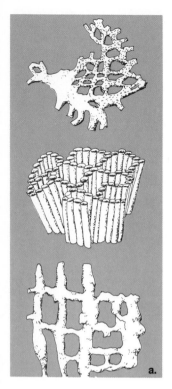

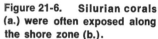

Figure 21-6. Silurian corals (a.) were often exposed along the shore zone (b.).

Figure 21-7. (a.) All of North America, except the evaporate basin of Michigan and New York, emerged from the sea by the end of the Silurian period. (b.) At the close of the Permian period, the continent, except for the Texas evaporite basin and the Pacific geosyncline, emerged again.

Silurian period, great limestone reefs were built by corals and other animals that found the reef a favorable environment for food and protection.

Changes in climate and environment and major changes in both the plant and the animal kingdoms occurred during the Devonian period. Mountain building caused seas to retreat from the land and to disappear from many regions. During this

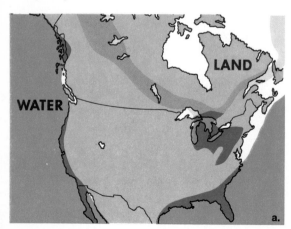

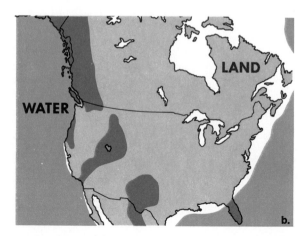

Figure 21-8. Vegetation characteristic of the Devonian forests of western New York including horsetail rushes, tree ferns, and early leafless plants.

time, land plants, which had appeared during the Silurian period, developed into large forms. The earliest trees are found in rocks of the Devonian period. Eventually, new varieties of vegetation covered the exposed, uplifted land areas. These new land plants, which resembled giant ferns and marsh plants, were forerunners of today's vegetation. When plants appeared on land, animals found a new environment. Until land plants were available for food, animals either did not venture upon the land, or if they did, they died from starvation.

During the Silurian period, the transition from marine animals to land animals occurred. Fish were the first backboned animals. They appeared at least as early as the Ordovician period. But they became the dominant occupants of the sea during the Devonian period. One kind of fish developed a lung that allowed it to survive out of water. In addition, some of these fish had fins that would support their weight. Fish that could obtain oxygen and food and move about on land were probably ancestors of amphibians (am fib′ee ans).

Amphibians cannot live far from water, because their eggs must be laid in water. Even adult amphibians must spend part of their time in water or lose their body fluids. Modern varieties of amphibians include frogs and toads. Amphibians have not been the dominant life form since the end of the Paleozoic era.

During the late Paleozoic era, one variety of amphibian may have developed the ability to survive without returning to the water. The first clue to the development of this new variety of animal was the discovery of an amniotic (am nee aht′ik) egg

Figure 21-9. Bones in the fish's lobe fin appear to be forerunners of the amphibian's limb bones.

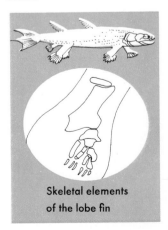

Skeletal elements
of the lobe fin

Figure 21-10. Fin-backed and other reptiles of the Permian period were mostly awkward, slow-moving animals.

along with amphibian-like bones. An *amniotic egg* has a hard, protective outer covering. This covering surrounds a watery material which nourishes the *embryo* (em'bree oh), or baby. This new development in reproduction meant that the adult no longer had to return to water to produce its young. Amphibians may have given rise to *reptiles*, the name given the new variety of animals that produced the amniotic egg. Along with this change in reproduction, reptiles developed hard scales that prevented the evaporation of their body fluids. These two changes allowed reptiles to roam the land except in frigid zones. Like fish and amphibians, reptiles are cold-blooded and must live in warm climates to maintain their body temperature.

During late Paleozoic time, fish dominated the seas, and amphibians or reptiles dominated the land. Many varieties of invertebrates were present, as they are today. But invertebrates were no longer the dominant life forms. All trilobites and nearly all amphibians became extinct at the end of the Paleozoic era. Numerous changes in the invertebrate groups also occurred. For these reasons, the Permian period is sometimes referred to as the *period of the great extinction*.

In addition to changes in life forms, physical changes in the earth also occurred toward the end of the Paleozoic era. Vast swamps, much like the Everglades of Florida, covered the interior of continents during the Pennsylvanian period. After burial, vegetation of these swamps became the great coal fields of the world. Mountains rose higher and higher around the edges of continents and prevented moisture-laden winds from reaching the interior. During the Permian period, desert conditions accompanied uplifting of mountains. Land vertebrates and land plants that survived were those that adapted to the new environment. As their living area increased, land animals increased in numbers and variety. But marine animals were crowded into smaller and smaller areas and many forms became extinct.

By the end of Paleozoic time, continental land masses were no longer submerged. Along the eastern coast of North America, high mountains, now known as the Appalachians, had arisen. Extensions of these mountains stretched as far south and west as the area which is now Texas. Mountain chains probably were also present along the west coast of North America. Mountain ranges joined Europe and Asia into one vast land mass. A large part of South America emerged from the sea, as did the continent of Australia. Great changes marked the end of the 370 million years of the Paleozoic era.

Continents were raised and mountain chains were formed as Paleozoic era ended and Mesozoic era began.

21:5 *Mesozoic Era*

The middle era of earth history covers less than half as much time as the Paleozoic era. The Mesozoic era is divided into three periods: Triassic (trie as'ik), Jurassic (juh ras'ik), and Cretaceous (kri tae'shus). The **Triassic period** is named for exposures in Germany. **Jurassic** is named for the range of Jura Mountains which borders France. **Cretaceous** is named for the great exposures of chalk formed during this time. Possibly the most famous of the Cretaceous chalk beds are the chalk cliffs of Dover, England.

Mesozoic era is divided into Triassic, Jurassic, and Cretaceous periods.

Figure 21-11. During the Triassic period (a.), the emergence begun in Permian time continued. Seas returned to the interior during the Cretaceous period (b.) for the last great submergence.

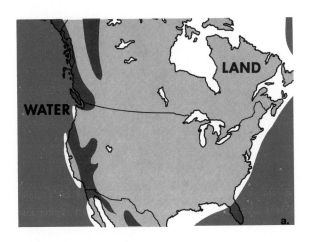
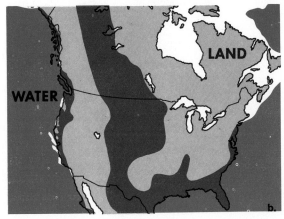

During the Mesozoic era, climatic changes occurred as mountains were worn down and the land was once more reduced to near sea level. Over much of the earth, an arid climate existed during Triassic time. Gradually, conditions changed, and by the Cretaceous period, a humid climate had returned. Seas reinvaded many land areas during Cretaceous time. East of the Mississippi River, the land remained above water except for a narrow border along the Atlantic Coast and the Gulf Coast. The western region was flooded from near the present location of the Mississippi River almost to the Pacific Ocean.

Great changes in animal and plant life accompanied changes in the Mesozoic environment. Plants of the Paleozoic era were adapted to a humid climate. New plant groups that developed during the Mesozoic era were adapted to a more varied environment. The first **angiosperms** (an'jee a spurms), or flowering plants, had developed by Cretaceous time and had become the dominant type of vegetation. Angiosperm seeds have a protective covering and they can survive hot, cold, wet, or dry seasons. The seeds could survive for long periods of time. Eventually they could take root and continue the life of the group, even though the parent plants died. These improvements in survival of offspring caused a rapid spread of angiosperms into all regions.

Many invertebrates also developed new forms and greater variety. One of these groups, the **ammonites** (am'a niets), is abundant in rocks which were deposited during the Mesozoic era. Ammonites could float on the sea, and thus were distributed over wide areas. Because their shell markings are distinctive, ammonites can be matched from Europe to Mexico to the United States. Paleontologists are able to divide the Mesozoic era into many zones based on ammonite index fossils.

Reptiles were the most characteristic and interesting of the Mesozoic animals. The dominant group of reptiles has been named **dinosaur** (die'na sawr), which means terrible lizard. Some varieties of dinosaurs were extremely large and became masters of the animal world. Some dinosaurs were *carnivorous* (kahr niv' a rus), or flesh-eaters. Others were *herbivorous* (er biv' a rus), or plant-eaters. Paleontologists have reconstructed the skeletons of many dinosaurs. From the structure of the jaws and teeth, scientists have determined the nature of the dinosaurs' diets.

Brontosaurus (brahnt a sawr'us) was 60 ft to 70 ft from nose to tail and weighed about 30 tons. Brontosaurus lived in

Erosion lowered land and allowed seas to cover large areas during the late Cretaceous.

Reptiles may be ancestors of both mammals and birds.

Brontosaurus was a vegetarian dinosaur; tyrannosaurus was a carnivorous dinosaur.

marsy lands and was herbivorous. It is difficult to imagine how these animals found enough plants for their enormous needs. *Tyrannosaurus* (ta ran a sawr'us) was the largest carnivorous land animal of all time. Tyrannosaurus was about 20 ft tall and 50 ft long and weighed about 10 tons. Brontosaurus could obtain food in the swamps and thereby conserve energy,

Field Museum of Natural History
Artist, Charles R. Knight

Figure 21-12. Brontosaurs, plant-eating dinosaurs of the Jurassic, probably spent much time in water in order to support their enormous weight of 30 to 40 tons.

Figure 21-13. Tyrannosaurus, the greatest of the Cretaceous carniverous dinosaurs, challenges Triceratops, the horned dinosaur.

Field Museum of Natural History
Artist, Charles R. Knight

but tyrannosaurus had to hunt food. Many small dinosaurs must have been required to satisfy tyrannosaurus' hunger.

Dinosaurs are not the only reptiles for which the Mesozoic era is famous. *Birds* and *mammals* may have developed from reptiles during the Mesozoic era. Reptiles became so numerous and so varied that they inhabited all environments. Some of them became flying reptiles. Others entered the sea and developed paddle-like feet or fins. Like the modern whale, which is a mammal, most reptiles of the sea looked more like fish than like reptiles. However, characteristics of their teeth and skeletons indicate that they were indeed reptiles and not fish.

One of the most interesting finds ever made by fossil hunters was the discovery of a probable link between reptiles and birds. The skeleton of this fossil looked like that of a flying reptile. But some perfectly preserved specimens had left imprints of feathers in the enclosing rock. Feathers had replaced scales on this variety of animal. Thus, it was akin to both reptiles and birds.

Another interesting change in Mesozoic life occurred in a group of reptiles. Formerly, reptiles had teeth in the shape of an overturned cone. But the new group of animals had some teeth that resembled modern molars. Some looked like canine teeth. Others were like the incisors of today's mammals. Another distinctive characteristic of this new reptile group was the position of their limbs. The legs of early reptiles extended from their sides, as do the legs of crocodiles. But the legs of this new group were attached under their bodies like the legs of mammals today. These probable ancestors of modern mammals were very unimportant in the Mesozoic, but they survived. Because of their mouse-like size, tyrannosaurus probably overlooked them in his search for food.

Like the Paleozoic era, the Mesozoic era ended with the extinction of many groups of animals. Dinosaurs disappeared, as did the flying reptiles and the marine reptiles. The surviving varieties of reptiles include turtles, snakes, lizards, and crocodiles. Modern reptiles, compared with the Mesozoic dinosaurs, seem insignificant in today's animal populations.

At the end of the Mesozoic era, the continents emerged once more and the seas withdrew from much of the submerged land. Mountain chains were uplifted along the borders of the Pacific Ocean in both North America and South America. Mountain ranges rose in other continents during this time. Many new life forms appeared and replaced extinct forms of Mesozoic life.

Reptiles may be ancestors of both mammals and birds.

Figure 21-14. Both shape and number of teeth differentiate the mammalian jaw from the reptilian jaw.

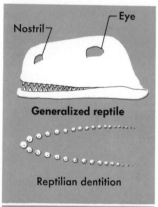

Generalized reptile

Reptilian dentition

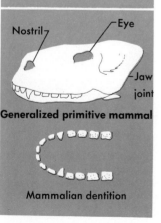

Generalized primitive mammal

Mammalian dentition

Figure 21-15.   Flying reptiles among the Cycad trees illustrate two life forms of the Jurassic period.

Figure 21-16.   Marine reptiles of the Mesozoic included the long-necked plesiosaurs and the finned ichthyosaurs.

21:6 *Cenozoic Era*

Cenozoic is divided into two periods, Tertiary and Quaternary.

The Cenozoic era is divided into only two periods, the **Tertiary** (tur'shee er ee) and the **Quaternary** (kwaht'er ner ee). These names have no particular meaning in the modern geologic time scale. The Cenozoic era began when ammonites and dinosaurs had disappeared. Rapid changes in the life of the Cenozoic followed and many new varieties appeared. Continents were enlarged and uplifted, bringing about the present distribution of land and sea, mountains and plains. The greatest changes during the Cenozoic occurred along the borders of the Pacific Ocean and at the present sites of the Alps and Himalaya.

Mammals have dominated the earth since the beginning of the Cenozoic era.

New life forms became prominent as the environment changed. The dominant marine invertebrates were members of the snail, starfish, and clam groups. Birds dominated the air; mammals dominated the land; fish still dominated the sea. Like the reptiles of the Mesozoic, the mammals adapted to all en-

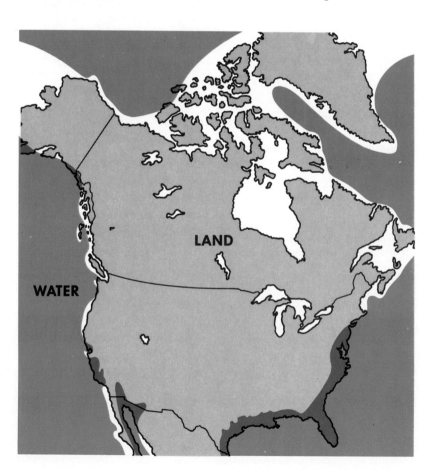

Figure 21-17. **By Miocene time, the continent of North America had emerged almost as it is today.**

Figure 21-18. The Australian kangaroos of the Quaternary period were giants compared to their modern descendants. Quaternary wombats were the size of the modern rhinocerous. Both kangaroo and wombat are marsupials unique to Australia.

vironments. Some mammals returned to the sea; others learned to fly. Whales and porpoises are mammals of the sea; bats are mammals of the air.

Because birds and mammals are warm-blooded animals, they could invade land environments which the reptiles could not tolerate. Mammals are the only vertebrates which bear their young alive and suckle their young. Thus, the mammal was better able to survive.

During Cenozoic time, many land areas became isolated. Australia and South America were separated from other land masses and were cut off from the general trends of mammal development. Several unusual **marsupials** (mahr seu′pee als) still exist in Australia. Female marsupials have a pouch in which they carry their young. South America also had a unique population of marsupials. In the late Cenozoic era, the Isthmus

Animals from North America migrated to South America when a land bridge was formed. Southern forms were eliminated as a result.

of Panama emerged from the sea. Then animals from North America moved south across this strip of land and entered South America. As North American animals occupied the South American continent, the unique groups originally living in South America disappeared.

It is difficult to determine why the invading animals from North America were more successful at survival in South America than the native animals. Perhaps animals migrating from their northern homelands already had adapted to new climates and new kinds of food. Or perhaps weaker groups had not survived the migration. Whatever the reason, the animals from the north dominated South America and most of the South American animals became extinct. Only a few, such as the armadillo (ahr ma dil'oh), moved northward and found a new place to live. Armadillos now inhabit much of Southwestern United States.

PROBLEM

5. Make a chart similar to Table 21–1, but allow more space for each geologic time division. Indicate where each of the fossils in Figure 21–19 belongs. If possible, place each fossil in the correct period as well as in the correct era or eon.

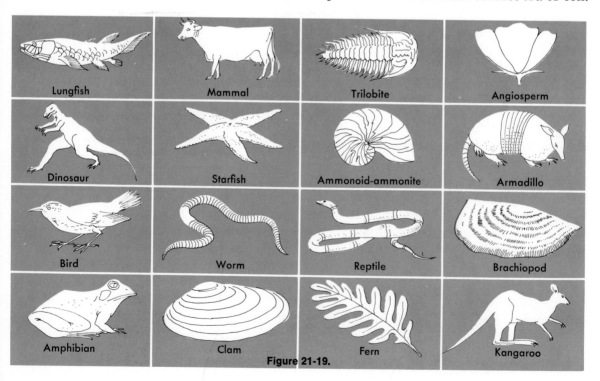

Figure 21-19.

A major event of the Cenozoic era was the invasion of a continental glacier. It spread from the region of Hudson Bay in North America south to the present location of the Ohio River. In Europe, ice covered much of what is now Scandinavia, Scotland, Germany, and Russia. This great ice age was present during the late Quaternary. Morainal hills mark the southern boundary where ice once stood. Just north of the moraines are deposits of widespread till. This material was dropped by the melting ice. The till was picked up by the ice when most of Canada was scoured and scraped by glaciation.

Figure 21-20.   Flesh-eating birds, as well as mammals, were trapped in the La Brea tar pool near Los Angeles, California, during the Pleistocene epoch.

Figure 21-21.   Remains of mammoths have been found from Siberia across North America. About 12 feet high, with long curved tusks and a woolly coat, the mammoth was characteristic of the Ice Age.

First indications of man's presence on the earth appear during the ice age in the late Quaternary period.

During the ice age, man left his first marks upon the land. His stone implements are clues to man's presence at a time for which there is no other record. The history of early man has been reconstructed from an extremely small amount of evidence. Occasionally, nearly complete skeletons have been found. But more often, only a few skulls or thigh bones were preserved. Most of our understanding of early man's appearance is based upon skull and thigh bones. Position of eye sockets in the skull suggest that man's eyes were adjusted to seeing three dimensions. This gave him an advantage over many other animals. Length and shape of thigh bones show that early man walked erect.

Fossil remains indicate that early man's diet was varied, that he could see in three dimensions, and that he walked erect.

Because teeth material resists decay better than bones, much of the information about early man is based on fossil teeth. From these fossils it is evident that early man could eat either flesh or grains as he does today. Short canine teeth indicate that man did not tear his food as some flesh-eaters do. Grinding molars indicate his ability to chew grains and other relatively hard materials.

Many scientists are searching for more remains of early man. The British anthropologist, Dr. Louis S. B. Leakey, has made many interesting discoveries in Olduvai Gorge in present Tanzania. Dr. Raymond Dart and Dr. Robert Broom also have found fossils of man's ancestors in limestone quarries of South Africa. But the most complete record of early man's life is in the caves of France. About 40,000 years ago, Cro-Magnon (kroh · mag′nan) people lived in this area. They left paintings of bulls, horses, antelope, and reindeer on the walls of the cave homes. These pictures tell much about Cro-Magnon man's way of life. Awls, needles, knives, and other tools found in the caves show that these early ancestors had reached a high level of development. Fortunately, they lived in caves that remained dry. Therefore, records of their culture have been preserved.

Rock layers contain records of past events and former inhabitants of the earth. Uplift, erosion, and deposition leave their marks. Volcanic activity, intrusions, and mountain building events are recorded. Sediments preserve the history of advances and withdrawals of the sea from the continent. Fossils in caves and on flood plains may indicate the presence of land animals. But many questions about earth history remain unanswered. Although each generation adds new understanding, much remains to be discovered.

Earthquakes on the western coast of North and South America indicate that we still live in a period of mountain building.

Thickness of sediments in the Gulf Coast region suggests the presence of a geosyncline. Some future day, these geosynclinal deposits may be uplifted into a young mountain chain. Many scientists believe that glaciers will advance once more across the land. Just when such events will occur cannot be predicted. But we know that eventually mountains will be worn down, seas will invade the land, and new mountains will be uplifted.

Severinus advised his students to "search the valleys, the deserts, the shores of the seas, and the deepest recesses of the world." He was suggesting the methods by which scientists attempt to unravel the puzzle of the history of the earth. Thousands of students have followed Severinus' advice since he first told his students to observe their world.

Tourisme—Courbeix   Courtesy France Actuelle

Figure 21-22. Early man left a record of his environment and artistic ability in some of the caves where he sought shelter. This Paleolithic painting is in the Lascaux Cave.

Figure 21-23.

Figure 21-24.

Figure 21-25.

ACTIVITY. *Examine a collection of fossiliferous rocks of various sizes and kinds. Look for fossil clues such as footprints, carbon imprints, casts, molds, or replacements. Some true preservations also may be present.*

Are the shells complete or broken? What do complete shells indicate? What do broken shells indicate? Are the shells in fine sediment or coarse sediment? If there are any casts, of what material are they formed? Compare the hardness of the shells to the hardness of the casts. How can you distinguish casts from preserved shells? How do the fossil imprints differ from the carbon imprint you made in Section 20:5?

Examine petrified wood samples. Are there any fossils? Compare the petrified wood to a block of natural wood. How do they differ?

EXPERIMENT. *Obtain several specimens of fresh leaves and flowers. Sprinkle borax or baking soda on a pad of paper towels. Arrange the specimens so that all of the surfaces touch the borax or soda. Cover the leaves and flowers with a thin layer of borax or soda, and place two or three paper towels over the specimens. Pile several heavy books on the covering towel and leave them in place until the specimens are completely dry. Describe their color and appearance.*

What is the purpose of the borax or soda? What type of fossil do the pressed leaves and flowers represent? Compare these fossils with the carbon imprint you made in Section 20:5. Would the specimens be the same if they had been buried in mud or silt?

ACTIVITY. *Collect leaves from as many different environments as possible. In most regions, it should be possible for you to obtain a variety of leaves from places such as swamps, gardens, and vacant lots. The leaves should include a flat-veined leaf, such as maple, oak, or elm; an African violet leaf (thick and moist); a fern leaf; pine needles; heads of grasses such as rye grass or wheat; a geranium leaf; and a hollow stalk, such as reed, bullrush, or miniature bamboo.*

Mount the leaves on bristol board for display, or press them and store them in containers, such as plastic boxes. Identify each leaf and include its environment on the label. Are the collections of your classmates similar to yours? If you were to correlate the leaves to determine whether they represented the same geologic unit of time, what problem would you have? Is any overlap of vegetation apparent in leaves from the different local environments? From a literature search, can you locate the ancestors of your modern plants?

MAIN IDEAS

1. Geologic time from earth's beginning is divided into two eons, the Cryptozoic and the Phanerozoic. Cryptozoic rocks contain little evidence of life, hence the name. Rocks of Phanerozoic time contain an increasing number of fossils.

2. Rocks of Australia contain some evidence of soft-bodied organisms that lived during Cryptozoic time. Absence of fossils does not mean a total absence of life. Instead it means that preservation was not possible under the conditions that existed.

3. The Phanerozoic eon lasted from 600 million years before the present to now. Phanerozoic eon is divided into three eras: Paleozoic, Mesozoic, and Cenozoic. Disappearance of old and appearance of new plant and animal groups is the basis for the division of the Phanerozoic eon into eras. Changes in fossil forms also are used to subdivide eras into periods. Changes from one era to another usually are associated with major mountain building events.

4. Fossils in Cambrian rocks include trilobites and brachiopods with phosphatic coverings.

5. Early Paleozoic fossils indicate that plants adapted to the land environment when the seas withdrew. Fish then developed a simple lung and may have evolved into amphibians that occupied a watery environment on the continent.

6. Amphibian development into reptiles may have accompanied the development of an amniotic egg. Reptiles have been found in late Paleozoic rocks.

7. Great mountain building occurred throughout the world at the end of the Paleozoic era. The Paleozoic era ended with the disappearance of the trilobites and the extinction of many other invertebrates.

8. During the Mesozoic era, dinosaurs emerged as dominant animals. Flying reptiles and the first mammals and birds appeared. Angiosperms became the dominant plants and ammonites were numerous.

9. Crustal changes which occurred during the Cenozoic era isolated Australia and South America and prevented migration of animals from one continent to another. Appearance of a land bridge between North and South America allowed northern forms to invade South America. Many South American groups disappeared.

10. Evidence of early man appears during the Late Quaternary. Cro-Magnon man left excellent records of his way of life in the dry caves of France. Cro-Magnon people lived about 40,000 years ago.

VOCABULARY

Write a sentence in which you use correctly each of the following words or terms.

algae	fossil assemblage
ammonite	geologic revolution
amniotic egg	herbivorous
amphibian	invertebrate
angiosperm	mammal
brachiopod	marsupial
carnivorous	reptile
continental nucleus	trilobite
epoch	zone

STUDY QUESTIONS

A. True or False

Determine whether each of the following sentences is true or false. (Do not write in this book.)

1. Apparently the first living animals were invertebrates.
2. Cryptozoic means hidden life.
3. Reptiles were the dominant life forms during the Cryptozoic eon.
4. Amphibians must spend part of their time in water.
5. Great crustal uplifts commonly are associated with the end of each era.
6. Uplift of high coastal mountains results in arid conditions in the interior of continents.
7. Cretaceous means a period of chalky limestone deposition.
8. Fish were the first animals to develop lungs.
9. Fossils of early man are numerous, complete, and widespread.
10. The Paleozoic is the longest unit of geologic time.

B. Multiple Choice

Choose the word or phrase which completes correctly each of the following sentences. (Do not write in this book.)

1. The oldest rocks that contain fossils in abundance belong to the (*Cambrian, Devonian, Permian*) period.

2. Earliest life forms are (*algae, angiosperms, invertebrates*).

3. The earliest work on the history of rocks was done by (*Adam Sedgwick, Pierre Curie, Dr. Louis Leakey*).

4. First flowering plants belong to the (*ammonites, algae, angiosperms*).

5. Female (*armadillos, marsupials, dinosaurs*) carry their young in a pouch.

6. The most useful marine index fossils of the Mesozoic era are (*ammonites, angiosperms, brachiopods*).

7. A dinosaur which fed on plants was (*tyrannosaurus, brontosaurus, armadillo*).

8. The first animal forms to develop teeth similar to those of modern mammals were members of the (*invertebrates, amphibians, reptiles*).

9. Rocks of the Early Precambrian are (*igneous and sedimentary, metamorphic and sedimentary, igneous and metamorphic*).

10. Whales are (*invertebrates, amphibians, mammals*).

C. Completion

Complete each of the following sentences with a word or phrase which will make the sentence correct. (Do not write in this book.)

1. The eon about which least is known is the ___?___ eon.

2. The era which includes the present is the ___?___ era.

3. Animals without backbones are called ___?___.

4. Tyrannosaurus was the largest ___?___ animal of all time.

5. Two fossil invertebrates found in Cambrian rocks are ___?___ and ___?___.

6. Recent discoveries in Australia of impressions of jellyfish-like forms suggest that life began in the ___?___ eon.

7. Dominant animal group of Cenozoic era is the ___?___.

8. The earliest indication of the development of reptiles came with the discovery of a(n) __?__ egg.

9. An animal which migrated north from South America is the __?__.

10. Evidence of man first appears in the __?__ era.

D. How and Why

1. Why did the development of land animals come after the development of land plants? Was it by chance, or was there some reason for this sequence?

2. Why do ammonites make excellent index fossils?

3. Could dinosaurs be used as index fossils? Could they be used as facies fossils? Explain your answers.

4. Rats are among the earliest known mammals. Would they be good index fossils? Would they be good facies fossils?

5. A great reef has been discovered during drilling in west Texas. Thousands of feet of reef have been drilled through. Compare this reef with the Great Barrier Reef of Australia and indicate what the conditions in Texas must have been when the reef was forming during Permian time.

6. How could you diagram the sequence of development in the vertebrates? Remember that although one group may be the ancestor to a new group, the original group may continue to exist.

7. In Texas, bones of mammoths, elephants, and other animals have been found among pieces of charcoal that have been dated at approximately 29,000 years B.P. Along with the charcoal that is dated, pieces of crude flint shaped like arrowheads have been found. How do you interpret this find, and how was the date determined?

8. Bones of a mammoth were discovered along a river bank in which the evidence suggested that the rocks were about 35,000 years old. However, the bones were dated at 17,000 years. How do you account for the difference between the dating of the bones and the enclosing rocks?

9. In what way would the uplift of mountains tend to affect the climate, if uplift occurred on the west coast in the path of the westerly winds?

10. In the Pacific Ocean, the isolated Galapagos Island has developed unique types of life. How can a paleontologist use

this observed phenomenon to explain the kind of life present in South America before the land bridge developed?

11. Indians and Eskimos have many similar characteristics and a resemblance to the Mongolian race of Asia. How have these similarities led to the belief that man migrated to North America from Asia?

INVESTIGATIONS

1. Report on the Cro-Magnon caves of France and caves containing traces of man in Africa. Discuss dates involved and fossils found.

2. Report on the latest findings concerning man's early history which suggest that Africa was his place of origin.

3. Discuss the authenticity of relics such as those of the Piltdown man.

INTERESTING READING

Adler, Irving, *How Life Began*. New York, The John Day Company, Inc., 1957.

Colbert, E. H., *Dinosaurs*. New York, E. P. Dutton & Co., Inc., 1961.

*Farb, Peter, *The Forest*. Life Nature Library. New York, Time Inc., 1961.

*Fenton, Carroll L. and Mildred A., *The Fossil Book: A Record of Prehistoric Life*. Garden City, N. Y., Doubleday & Company, Inc., 1959.

Geis, Darlene, *The How and Why Wonder Book of Dinosaurs*. Columbus, Ohio, Charles E. Merrill Publishing Co., 1960.

Kurten, Bjorn, *The Age of the Dinosaurs*. New York, McGraw-Hill Book Company, 1968.

Matthews, William H., *Wonders of the Dinosaur World*. New York, Dodd, Mead & Co., 1968.

Pringle, Laurence, *Dinosaurs and Their World*. New York, Harcourt Brace Jovanovich, Inc., 1964.

*Rhodes, Frank H., et. al., *Fossils*. New York, Golden Press, 1962.

---

* Well-illustrated material.

The Universe

Astronomy compels the soul to look upwards and leads us from this world to another.

Plato (428/427-348/347 B.C.)

Today man wonders, as he did in ancient times, about the nature of the universe. Where did the moon come from? What is a star? Does life exist on other planets?

Many ancient questions about the moon, the solar system, and the stars remain unanswered, but our present knowledge of the universe is greater than Plato's. Scientists today have large optical and radio telescopes to search the sky. Powerful listening devices collect radio waves from distant points in space. Unmanned and manned vehicles venture farther and farther into space searching for information about the universe.

With modern techniques, scientists are learning more and more about stars, planets, comets, and galaxies. Although man has answered some ancient questions, he has found many new problems to solve as he continues to study the universe.

UNIT
Six

22 The Solar System

Long before the present Space Age, men watched and wondered about the sun by day and the stars by night. Early sky watchers named and mapped the celestial bodies they could see with the unaided eye. The pinpoints of light which seemed to be fixed in the heavens they called stars. Other bodies which seemed to wander were called planets. Mapping of the heavens was based on the belief that the earth was the center around which the planets, stars, sun, and moon revolved.

22:1 *Sky Mapping*

After the invention of the telescope, man concluded from his observations that the sun, not the earth, is the center of the nearby celestial bodies. The earth is just one of a group of planets which revolve around the sun. The **solar system** includes the sun, the planets, their satellites, planetoids, comets, meteoroids, asteroids, and interplanetary cosmic dust and gas. Modern telescopes and methods of study have shown that our solar system is only a part, and not the center, of a vast multitude of stars. These stars form a group called a *galaxy* (gal'ak see). Beyond the galaxy to which our solar system belongs, other galaxies extend into space to form the **universe.** All celestial bodies are moving, but disances to stars are so great that they seem to be standing still. No wonder the word *astronomical* (as tra nahm'i kal) has come to mean numbers or distance beyond man's power to grasp or ability to calculate.

In the second century A.D., Ptolemy (tahl'a mee), a scientist in the city of Alexandria, Egypt, decided to plot or map the movement of heavenly bodies. He was particularly interested in observing the planets because they are closer to the earth than the stars. Also, the planets seemed to be moving, but the

Official U.S. Naval Observatory Photograph

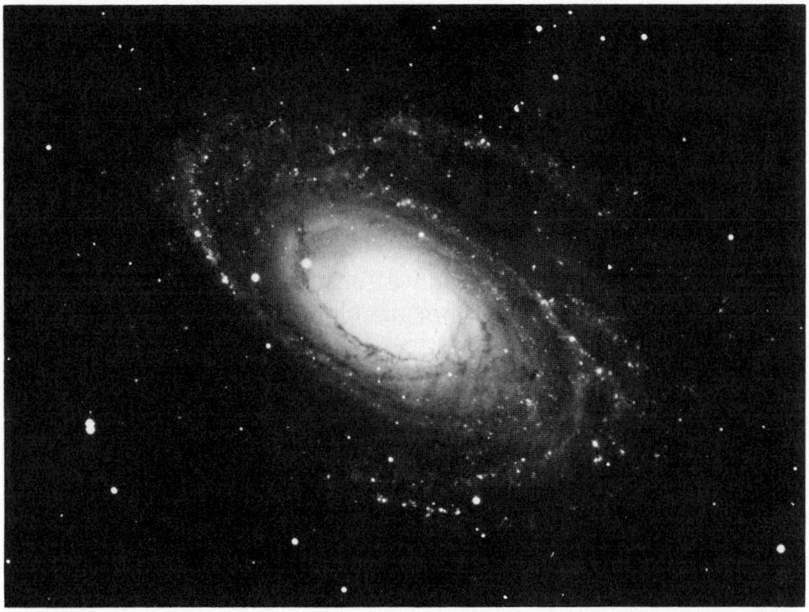

Figure 22-1. The spiral galaxy Messier 81, a vast multitude of stars, has great arms surrounding the central stellar nucleus.

stars appeared to stand still. To explain the movements of planets, Ptolemy worked out a mathematical model. The model placed the earth at the center of all movement. Ptolemy found that the planets appeared to move around the earth in a complex fashion. At times, some planets appeared to be moving forward. At other times, some planets seemed to move backward in the sky. In order to explain these apparent movements, Ptolemy decided that each planet revolved around a point. He reasoned that as it revolved, each planet made a series of small circles in its major orbit around the earth.

Ptolemy's idea of the universe used the earth as the center of all celestial bodies with planets revolving in small circles as they moved in their orbits around the earth.

ACTIVITY. Roll a small wheel or ride a bicycle in a circular path. Note that the wheel makes the orbit suggested by Ptolemy. The rim of the wheel or the tire of the bicycle makes small circles as it moves in the large circle.

Figure 22-2.

Ptolemy used 40 circles to explain the movements that he observed. As more astronomers observed the planets and gathered more accurate data, even more circles were required. Astronomers suggested circles within circles until the system became extremely complicated.

In 1530, Copernicus (koh per′ ni kas), the Polish founder of modern astronomy, suggested a simpler system than the Ptolemaic circles. Copernicus correctly assumed that the planets of the solar system revolved around the sun. However, he still thought that the planets moved in circles. Their true orbits

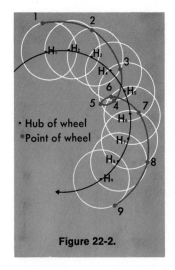

were not understood until the seventeenth century. Then Johannes Kepler, a German astronomer, plotted their elliptical paths.

Galileo (gal a lee' oh) was an Italian scientist who lived from 1564 to 1642. He is most famous for his contributions to the fields of mathematics and physics. But also he is remembered for his insistence on experimentation to prove an idea. In 1609, Galileo heard about a telescope developed by Hans Lippershey, a Dutch spectacle maker. Galileo perfected his own telescope with which he studied the stars. He concluded that planets moved around the sun rather than around the earth. Galileo published his findings to confirm what Copernicus already had suggested. Scholars of the day were not ready to accept Galileo's interpretation and his publications were suppressed. The Ptolemaic system remained the accepted explanation of the universe until the seventeenth century.

Fortunately, Galileo's manuscript was not lost. His and Copernicus' theories were read and considered by seventeenth century scientists who were willing to accept new ideas. Within the last 300 years, astronomers finally have accepted the idea that the earth is only a small member of a vast universe. The universe is composed of almost numberless stars, some of which may have their own planets.

> Galileo observed the skies through the earliest telescope, and found Copernicus' idea to be correct. Galileo's manuscript, which showed the sun to be the center of the solar system, was suppressed until the 17th century.

22:2 Motions in the Universe

The movement of heavenly bodies is difficult to understand because everything is in motion. Nothing stands still to form a point of reference. If you have been in a car or bus that is standing still, you may have had the sensation of movement as a neighboring car starts to move. If both cars are moving, your judgment of relationships becomes even more difficult. To you, the earth seems to be standing still. All other objects in space seem to be in motion. Actually, this planet is whirling through space at a great rate of speed. The illusion of being stationary makes the plotting of motions of other celestial bodies difficult.

> Movement of heavenly bodies is difficult to understand because all heavenly bodies are in motion and no fixed reference point is possible.

When viewed from earth, stars seem to be fixed in their positions. But stars move slowly compared to their distance from earth. Thus, measurement of their movement requires many years. Movement of planets, which are much closer to earth, can be recognized from one month to the next. Movement of moons around their planets can be traced in a matter of days.

> Stars appear to be stationary because of their great distance from the earth.

Astronomers know that day-to-day observations may lead to false conclusions. But data gathered over centuries provides a basis for an accurate interpretation of the motions of celestial bodies.

22:3 *The Celestial Sphere*

In order to plot movements of celestial bodies, astronomers have devised a **celestial sphere** which resembles a world globe. (Figure 22-3.) The movements of stars and planets as seen from earth are plotted on the sphere. Astronomers use the earth as the center of the sphere. The sky is divided into units similar to latitude and longitude on the world globe.

Poles of the earth are extended outward to where they intersect the celestial sphere. These positions are known as the **celestial poles.** All midpoints between the two poles lie on the plane of the **celestial equator.** Degrees north and south of the celestial equator are determined by planes. The planes pass through the celestial sphere parallel to its equator. These planes are similar to latitude planes on earth. Celestial circles corresponding to latitude lines on earth are called *declination* (dek le nae′ shun). Positions north of the celestial equator are known as *plus declination*. Positions south of the celestial equator are known as *minus declination* on the celestial sphere.

Stars and planets are plotted on the celestial sphere (an imaginary sphere using the earth as the center) in order to locate them in the sky.

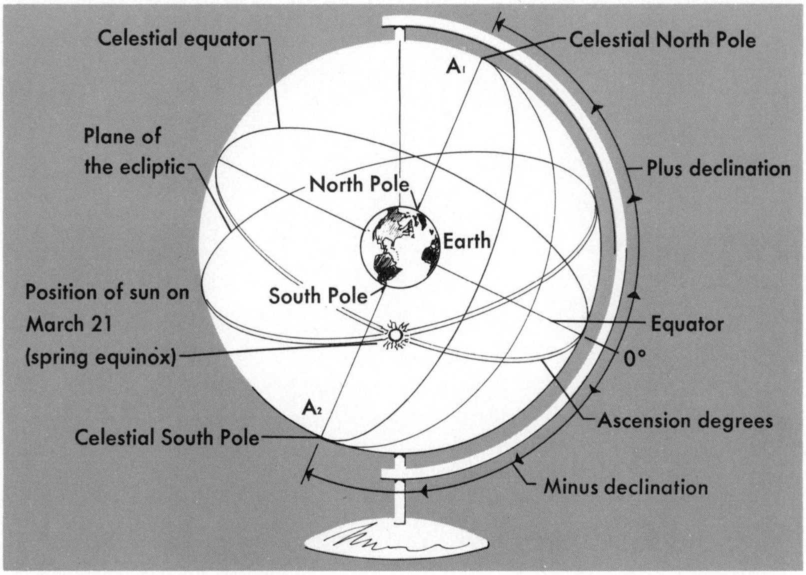

Figure 22-3. On a clear plastic sphere, stars and planetary orbits may be plotted to show the sky as it appears from earth, which is located at the center of the sphere.

Figure 22-4. The constellation Scorpius.

Day and night are of equal length at equinox.

On an earth globe, longitude is measured from a plane that passes through both poles and Greenwich, England. Distances are given in degrees both east and west of the longitude (0°) which passes through Greenwich. The celestial circle which corresponds to longitude on earth is called *right ascension*. Right ascension is measured on the celestial equator from the *vernal equinox* (ee′ kwa nahks). This is the point where the sun crosses the celestial equator going from south to north about March 21. Drawings of the celestial sphere show a great circle, called the **ecliptic** (i klip′ tik). The ecliptic is the plane of the earth's orbit extended to meet the celestial sphere. Because the earth is used for the center of the celestial sphere, the sun *appears* to be moving around the earth on the path of the ecliptic. The ecliptic and the celestial equator intersect at two points. One of the points is the autumnal equinox. The other point is the vernal equinox. Right ascension is measured continuously in an easterly direction from the vernal equinox or zero point. This measurement is divided into 24 large units, each representing one hour.

Maps of the heavens illustrate star positions so that any given star may be located at any time of the year. Charts have

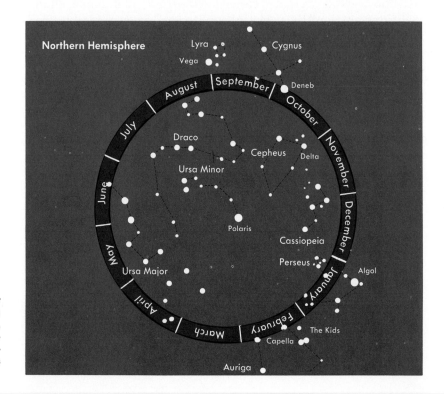

Figure 22-5. With the proper month at the bottom and with the top turned toward the north, the position of the stars overhead in the northern hemisphere will be the same as those of the chart.

Yerkes Observatory

the months indicated around the perimeter. If the chart is held in the proper position for the current month, stars may be located quickly and identified.

Some stars appear to be close together as viewed from earth. These stars have been grouped into **constellations** (kahn sta lae' shuns). Constellations, to imaginative early observers, seemed to resemble familiar objects. The Big Dipper and the Little Dipper are parts of constellations called Ursa Major and Ursa Minor (Great Bear and Little Bear). It is easier to recognize and learn the names of groups or constellations than single stars.

Planets are not shown on star charts because they change position in relation to the stars. The **zodiac** (zohd' ee ak) is an imaginary belt about 18° wide with the ecliptic in its center. The zodiac contains the apparent path of the principal planets except Pluto.

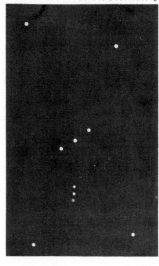

Figure 22-6. The constellation Orion.

Figure 22-7. A belt called the zodiac includes the apparent paths of all planets, except Pluto.

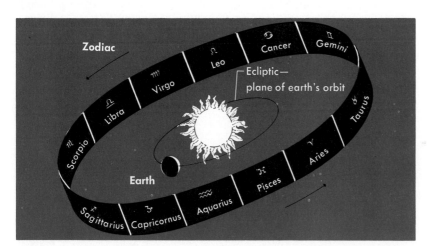

Constellations are groups of stars named for objects familiar to early Greek and Roman sky watchers.

22:4 *The Sun*

The solar system is known to consist of nine planets, their satellites (sat' el iets), asteroids (as'te rawids), meteoroids (meet'ee a rawids), and comets. All these bodies revolve around the sun. The sun's mass is 2×10^{33} grams. The sun holds members of the solar system in orbit by its gravitational attraction. Although the sun is composed mainly of hydrogen and helium, the two lightest elements, it accounts for 99.86 percent of the solar system's mass.

Planets of the solar system rotate on their axes and revolve around the sun at various rates.

Traces of most elements found on earth are also present in the sun. The average density of the sun is only 1.41 g/cm³ compared to 5.5 g/cm³ for the earth. The diameter of the sun is approximately 864,600 mi. The sun has a rotation rate of 25 days at its equator, 34 to 35 days near its poles. Gases at the sun's equator move more rapidly than gases at its poles. Consequently, rotation rate is not the same for both positions.

Transmutation (trans meu tae'shun) is the changing of hydrogen gas into helium gas. This process is the source of the sun's energy. These nuclear changes are similar to processes that cause the explosion of a hydrogen bomb. The process of transmutation is called hydrogen "burning" and the product helium is known as "ash." Temperatures are approximately 15,000,000°C in the sun's interior. At these temperatures, particles move at tremendous speeds. Protons which normally would repel one another are forced to combine. The resulting combinations usually are unstable. But the combined protons may be joined by other particles. Then a stable helium nucleus of 2 protons and 2 neutrons may be formed. Mass is converted to energy during transmutation. This energy is the source of the sun's heat and light. The process of transmutation in the sun will continue until most of the sun's hydrogen has been changed to helium.

Average rotation period for the sun is 27 days.

Radiant energy originates in the sun.

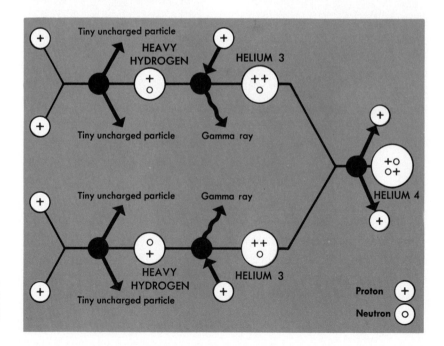

Figure 22-8.   High temperatures in the sun cause protons to unite with such velocity that they combine in a sequence of reactions to form helium.

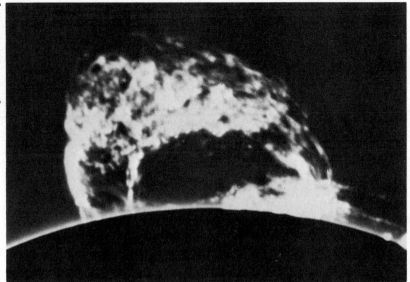

High Altitude Observatory

Figure 22-9. Activity of solar flares, protons and electrons streaming outward from the sun, affect radio reception on earth.

Within the sun's interior, great pressures exist. They result from the transmutation of hydrogen and the high temperature of the sun's gases. These internal pressures are counterbalanced by the weight of overlying gases. But radiation passes outward from the sun's interior to the surface. There it escapes into space. In this way, equilibrium is maintained.

The **photosphere** (foht'a sfir) is the surface of the sun which we see. This layer gives off visible radiation. Lying outside the photosphere is the **chromosphere** (kroh'ma sfir). The chromosphere is a layer of hot gas which can be seen only during an eclipse or with a telescopic device which blots out the photosphere. Seen through a telescope the chromosphere is a brilliant red halo extending about 6,000 mi beyond the photosphere. From the chromosphere, *prominences* of gas shoot outward sometimes for millions of miles. Some of them fall back toward the sun; some may be propelled outward into space.

Beyond the chromosphere is a still thinner and more transparent zone, called the **corona** (ka roh'na). This filmy envelope is highly ionized gas. It can be observed only during a total eclipse of the sun.

Sunspots are dark areas on the sun's surface. The spots consist of gases which are cooler than the surrounding gas. They first appear on the photosphere as small areas. They are less brilliant than the photosphere, although their diameters may be over 1,000 mi. Temperatures are about 4,000°C (7,200°F) in sunspots. This compares to 5,480°C (9,900°F) for the surrounding materials. Within a few days, sunspots may expand

The sun's surface contains the visible photosphere, a transparent layer of gas called the chromosphere, and the corona, an outer layer of widely separated protons and electrons.

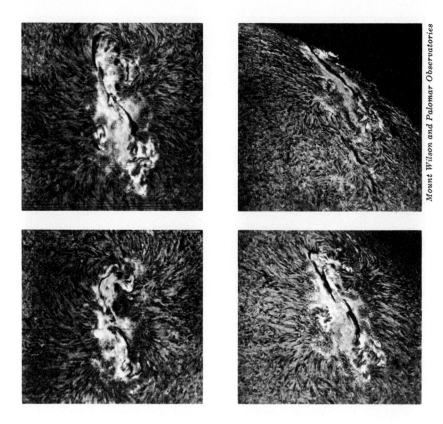

Figure 22-11. Sunspots, the
dark areas of the photosphere
where temperatures are lower
than the surrounding gases, expand as they move across the
sun.

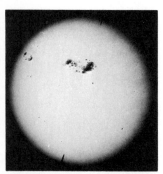

to several thousand mi in diameter. One of the largest sunspot
areas ever observed appeared from February 5 to May 11,
1947. It covered approximately 7 billion square miles of the
photosphere. Sunspots may last a day or as long as several
months. Sunspot activity seems to occur in cycles of about 11
years. The longest observed period was 17 years. The shortest
was a little over 7 years.

Solar flares are sudden increases in brightness of areas near
sunspot groups. From these flares, protons and electrons stream
outward. Their velocity ranges from 200 mi/sec to 500 mi/sec.
Many of the protons and electrons reach the earth. Some of
them may travel to the limits of the solar system. While flares
are active, they cause disturbances in radio reception and affect
the earth's magnetic field. The *solar wind* consists of charged
atomic particles (ions) that constantly escape from the sun.
But the most intense rain of these particles on earth follows the
activity of solar flares. The rain of particles excites gases in
earth's upper atmosphere. As the gases are excited, they give
off light. These colored streamers of light are known as the
aurora, or northern lights. These lights are 50 mi to 100 mi
above the earth and most brilliant in the arctic regions.

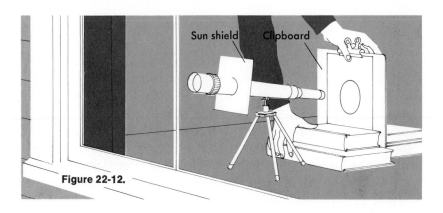

Figure 22-12.

Sun shield   Clipboard

EXPERIMENT. Caution: Never look directly at the sun with unprotected eyes or through telescopes or binoculars unless they have special lenses. Ordinary sunglasses or photographic negatives are not sufficient protection against the sun's rays. The best way to examine the sun is by looking at its image on a sheet of white paper. Make your observations at sunrise or sunset when the earth's atmosphere filters some of the dangerous rays. Never look at the morning sun after it changes from red to orange, or at the evening sun before it changes to red.

Put a telescope on a tripod or stand it in a window facing the sun. Prop a clipboard holding a sheet of white drawing paper opposite the eyepiece of the telescope. Arrange a sun shield (a square of heavy cardboard) on the telescope as illustrated in Figure 22–12. Move the clipboard back and forth until the largest possible image of the sun appears on the board. Focus the lens so that the image is distinct. Trace the outline of the sun's image and include any sunspots. Sometimes there are no sunspots, but usually several are present and they can be observed as they move across the sun.

Keep the telescope in position so you can make observations on succeeding days. Repeat the examination of the sun's image each day and draw the image and any sunspots on a new piece of paper each day. Compare the location of the spots from day to day for at least one week. Do the sunspots have the same shape each day?

Planets, their moons, meteoroids, comets, and a belt of asteroids move around the sun. (Figure 1–8.) All are members of the solar system. Their motions are determined by their position relative to the sun. (Table 22–1.) Planets rotate on their axes as they move around the sun. All their axes appear to be tilted at some angle to the sun's equator. As the planets revolve around the sun, most of them orbit in nearly the same plane as the earth.

22:5   *Mercury*

Mercury, the smallest planet of the solar system, is closest to the sun. Its day is equal to 58.6 earth days, but its year is only 88 days long.

Mercury is the smallest planet of the solar system. It orbits closest to the sun at an average distance of 36,000,000 mi. Because of Mercury's small size, dark appearance, and nearness to the sun, telescopic observation and photography are quite difficult. Astronomers thought that Mercury had a rate of rotation equal to its year of 88 earth days. They also believed that one side always faced the sun. But radar measurements in 1965 proved that Mercury rotates once during ⅔ of the time required for its revolution around the sun. Therefore, Mercury's period of rotation is equal to 58.65 earth days. Thus one side of Mercury faces the sun every second revolution at perihelion, the orbital position nearest the sun. (Section 1:4.) The opposite side of the planet faces the sun at perihelion every other revolution.

The side of Mercury turned away from the sun is cold. The sunny side is hot. Because there is little or no atmosphere, the solar heat is not distributed by convection as it is on earth. When Mercury is at its mean distance from the sun, its temperature is about 340°C (650°F). Mercury is so small that its surface gravity is only ⅜ that of the planet earth.

22:6   *Venus*

Venus is the second planet outward from the sun. It is at a mean distance of 67,200,000 mi from the sun. Venus is earth's nearest planetary neighbor and approaches the earth within 26,000,000 mi.

Earth and Venus often are called twin planets because of their similar characteristics. Both Venus and earth have an atmosphere. Many attempts have been made to determine the composition and temperature of Venus' atmosphere and the character of its surface. But Venus' atmosphere is so dense and cloudy that telescopic observation of its surface is impossible. Every known observational method of investigation has been used, but many questions concerning Venus' atmosphere and surface remain unanswered.

Surface temperatures on Venus have been difficult to determine because of the cloud cover. A Russian probe, however, reported temperatures ranging from approximately 45°C (114°F) to 280°C (536°F). The higher temperature prob-

Figure 22-13.   **Venus, earth's twin planet, as seen through the telescope at Mount Wilson.**

Mount Wilson and Palomar Observatories

ably represents the surface of Venus. The lower temperature readings probably are from the atmosphere above Venus.

Venus rotates clockwise, or *retrograde*, compared to the other planets. Radar echoes from a reflecting "feature" on the surface of Venus were tracked from day to day. Thus, it was possible to determine the period of rotation. This period is approximately 243 days. Measurements are repeated every 19 months when Venus passes between the earth and the sun. Then all three bodies are in alignment.

Although Venus and earth are similar in many respects, there are some important differences. Russian probes report that no magnetic field or radiation belt is present. American flybys suggest an extremely weak magnetic field.

Present evidence indicates that Venus' atmosphere is mostly carbon dioxide. Estimates range from 72 percent to 98 percent carbon dioxide. Water vapor, oxygen, and carbon monoxide have been identified tentatively. But there is no general agreement on these minor constituents. The presumed high temperatures on Venus and the absence of oxygen make earth-like life an impossibility for earth's twin planet. Estimates of atmospheric pressure range from 7 to 15 times earth's pressure. Venus' atmosphere is so dense that light from the sun probably is refracted away from its surface.

Venus' day is equal to 243 earth days. Its year is equal to 224 earth days.

22:7 *Earth*

Earth is the third planet outward from the sun. It is at a mean distance of 93,000,000 mi from the sun. Earth differs from other members of the solar system. Its atmosphere contains oxygen, and its temperature range of about 85°C (185°F) allows water to exist as a gas, liquid, or solid. Stars in other galaxies may have planets with conditions similar to conditions on earth. But within our solar system, earth may be the only planet where life exists.

Earth rotates on its axis once in approximately 24 hours. It revolves around the sun once in approximately 365 days. These repeated motions are the basis for our measurement of time. Earth's one natural satellite, or moon, revolves around the earth in 27⅓ days. (Section 1:4.) Density of the earth is 5.5 g/cm³. Possibly earth's original gases have been lost. But other gases have formed during the solidification of igneous rock. Most of these gases have been retained to form earth's unique atmosphere.

Figure 22-14. This view of the earth from 98,000 miles in space shows parts of Africa, Asia, and Europe.

NASA

Figure 22-15. Mars photographed by Mariner 7 at a distance of more than 1 million miles.

22:8 *Mars*

Mars' color, brightness, and nearness to earth have attracted the attention of astronomers for many centuries. The orange to reddish color of Mars is easily recognizable with the unaided eye. As early as 1610, Galileo observed Mars through the first astronomical telescope.

Mars orbits the sun at an average distance of 142,000,000 mi. Its orbit departs from a true circle more than any other planet except Mercury and Pluto. In 1666, the Italian astronomer Cassini determined the rotational period of Mars with less than a 3 minute error. Today, the accepted rotational period for Mars is 24 hours, 37 minutes, and 22.6 seconds. Mars revolves around the sun in approximately 687 earth days.

White patches are present near Mars' poles of rotation. They are known as polar caps because of their apparent similarity to earth's polar ice caps. Ice, snow, frost, or frozen carbon dioxide have been suggested as the polar cap material. The white patches expand at one pole and shrink at the other pole at the same time. This suggests a relationship to changing seasons.

In 1877, the Italian astronomer Schiaparelli (skahp a rel′ ee) interpreted large light and dark areas as land and sea, respectively. He also named many straight line markings *canali* which means channels. Others translated this word as canals. Based on the supposed presence of canals, many people came to believe that Mars supported intelligent life. Recent photos of Mars' surface have supplied no evidence of a true canal system.

Schiaparelli's idea of Martian canals influenced Percival Lowell of Boston, Massachusetts. In 1894, Lowell founded the Lowell Observatory at Flagstaff, Arizona. For many years, Lowell studied there and mapped Mars. He believed that meltwater from the polar caps was distributed through a vast irrigation system. He thought the system was built by intelligent life to support vegetation. Lowell's theories concerning Mars were not well accepted. But he is noted for predicting the existence of a ninth planet. Such a planet, called Pluto, was discovered in 1930, 14 years after Lowell's death.

In spite of all the attention given to Mars, the question of the presence of life persists. Biologists and chemists have found no positive evidence that Mars cannot support life which is chemically similar to life on earth. But if life is present on Mars, it need not resemble life on earth. Martian life forms might consist of microorganisms, microbes, or even molds or mosses. Or life might be completely different from life on earth. Experiments have been made with earth soil organisms under artificial weather conditions similar to those of Mars. Those experiments have proved that microorganisms would be more likely to survive than larger organisms. Microorganisms are more resistant to freezing and thawing than large organisms. Because of the low temperatures on Mars, ice crystals would tend to form in the cells of large organisms.

Measured surface temperatures of Mars have a wide range. At the south polar cap, temperatures go down to about $-100°C$ ($-150°F$) during the winter. The average temperature range from $-70°$ to $+31°C$ ($-100°F$ to $+80°F$) is comparable to ranges of temperature on earth. However, the daily temperature range on Mars may reach $80°C$ ($180°F$) in some areas. On earth the maximum daily range is approximately $10°C$ ($50°F$). But some areas of Mars might be located favorably with respect to climate. Thus, the presence of life cannot be ruled out on the basis of temperature.

Because of the masking effect of earth's atmosphere, various analyses of Mars' atmosphere have given conflicting results. Measurements from a high-altitude, unmanned balloon suggest the presence of water vapor and carbon dioxide in Mars' atmosphere. Evidence from an unmanned spacecraft flyby also indicated that Mars' atmosphere is mostly carbon dioxide. Atmospheric temperature was found to be about $-90°C$ ($-130°F$). Surface atmospheric pressure was measured as less than 0.75 percent of the pressure at the earth's surface.

Data indicate that Mars has neither a magnetic field nor radiation belts of any significance. If a magnetic field is absent, charged particles are not trapped outside the planet. Thus, the planet is exposed to cosmic rays and to the solar wind. Ultraviolet radiation from the sun is not absorbed or filtered by the thin Martian atmosphere. The presence of harmful cosmic and solar radiation reduces the chance for the survival of even simple organisms, such as bacteria, spores, or fungi.

More than 70 craters have been discovered within less than one percent of Mars' photographed surface. Martian craters resemble craters on earth's moon. The presence of craters supports the theory that the Martian surface has been struck by meteorites. The surface has melted, cooled, and cracked along lines that join the impact craters. Several astronomers believe the so-called canals are these crustal faults.

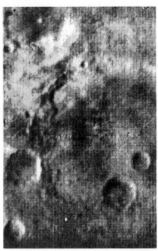

NASA

Figure 22-16. The surface of Mars between Mare Sirenum and Mars Cimmerium, showing Atlantis.

Mars' surface contains many impact craters and straight line markings which may be faults.

Phobos and Deimos are satellites of Mars which were predicted by Jonathan Swift but not discovered until 150 years later.

Mars' two moons were discovered in 1877 by Hall, an American astronomer. He named the Martian moons Phobos (foh'bohs), meaning fear, and Deimos (dee'mohs), meaning panic. The moons were named after the horses that pulled the chariot of Mars, the mythical Roman god of war. Phobos, the larger moon, is unique among the satellites of the solar system. It is the only satellite that revolves around its primary (Mars) in less time than the rotation period of its primary.

Hall did not discover the Martian satellites until 1877. But Jonathan Swift mentioned such satellites 151 years earlier in his book called *Travels into Several Remote Nations of the World by Captain Lemuel Gulliver*, commonly known as *Gulliver's Travels*.

"They [the astronomers of Laputa] have likewise discovered two lesser stars, or satellites, which revolve about Mars, whereof the innermost is distant from the center of the primary planet exactly three of the diameters, and the outermost five; the former revolves in the space of ten hours, and the latter in twenty-one and an half; so that the squares of their periodical times are very near to the same proportion with the cubes of their distance from the center of Mars, which evidently shows them to be governed by the same law of gravitation, that influences the other heavenly bodies."*

Swift's nearly accurate statement in 1726 of the periods of revolution for Phobos and Deimos is startling! Had Swift used ancient writings now lost that contained an advanced knowledge of astronomy? The source of his knowledge of the moons remains one of the major mysteries of science and literature.

22:9 *Asteroids*

Asteroids are fragments of cosmic matter which orbit the sun between Mars and Jupiter.

Beyond the planet Mars, moves a belt of asteroids. **Asteroids** are fragments that orbit the sun. They are in a position generally between Mars and Jupiter. Material in the asteroid belt is similar to matter in other planets. In this region fragments apparently did not unite. Probably no one fragment or mass was large enough to dominate the belt and collect other fragments. Or possibly the fragments are the remains of a planet that broke apart millions of years ago.

---

* Jonathan Swift, *Gulliver's Travels* (New York, The Modern Library, 1931), p. 193.

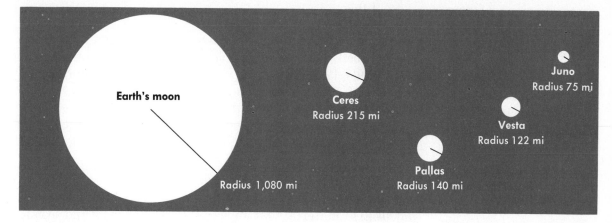

Earth's moon

Radius 1,080 mi

Ceres
Radius 215 mi

Pallas
Radius 140 mi

Vesta
Radius 122 mi

Juno
Radius 75 mi

Thousands of asteroids are present in the asteroid belt. Their size ranges from particles of dust to fragments 430 mi in diameter. The largest asteroid is named Ceres. Most asteroids are too small to be observed through a telescope, but they appear in photographic series in which movement can be detected. Some asteroids have been pulled into the gravitational field of the planet Jupiter, which lies beyond them in the solar system. These asteroids are known as the Trojan asteroids. They either follow or precede Jupiter in its orbit around the sun. From time to time, Jupiter may cause other asteroids to change their orbital paths. Then some fragments are sent flying toward the sun. Others are forced outward toward more distant planets. A few asteroids follow eccentric paths that bring them close to earth. Icarus passed within 4,000,000 mi of earth in 1968. Geographos passed within 6,000,000 mi of earth in 1969.

Figure 22-17. Four of the largest asteroids are drawn to the same scale as a portion of the moon's surface.

Most asteroids cannot be observed in a telescope but can be photographed.

22:10 *The Distant Planets*

Jupiter orbits at a mean distance of 484,000,000 mi from the sun. It is a massive planet with a volume 1,300 times that of the earth. Its density is only one-fourth that of earth. Jupiter has an atmosphere hundreds of miles deep. This atmosphere consists of hydrogen, ammonia (NH_3), and methane (CH_4) gases. Jupiter's surface gravity is about 2.5 times as strong as that of earth because of Jupiter's tremendous mass. Jupiter consists largely of gas. But it may have portions that are liquid or even solid because of the tremendous pressures which are present. A unique feature of Jupiter's surface is its Great Red Spot. This area is 30,000 mi across, but it changes size and shape as well as color. Its origin is unknown. Jupiter rotates on its axis once every 9 hr 50 min and orbits the sun once in 11.9

Figure 22-18. Massive Jupiter has an atmosphere hundreds of miles deep.

Mount Wilson and Palomar Observatories

Figure 22-19.   Saturn's unique rings can be seen clearly through the telescope.

years. Like earth, Jupiter is surrounded by radiation belts. Jupiter's belts emit powerful radio waves that reach the earth. Jupiter has 12 known moons. This is the largest number of natural satellites of any planet. Four of Jupiter's satellites were discovered by Galileo in 1610.

Saturn moves beyond Jupiter at a mean distance of 889 million mi from the sun. Saturn is 95 times as massive as the earth. Its density is only 0.127 that of earth. Saturn requires about 29½ earth years for its orbit around the sun. Rotation on its axis requires 10 hours and 14 minutes. Saturn is surrounded by 3 rings of material that appear to consist of snow and cosmic grit. The diameter of the ring system is 171,000 mi. But the rings are only 10 mi to 20 mi thick. Some scientists believe that the *cosmic grit* is material which was left behind by Saturn during formation of the planet. Or the grit may be the remains of moons torn apart by Saturn's tidal action. Saturn's surface is obscured by clouds. It has 10 moons. Its largest satellite is called Titan. Titan is as big as Mercury and has an atmosphere of methane gas. This is the only moon known to have its own atmosphere.

Uranus is another massive gaseous planet. It consists principally of hydrogen, methane, and ammonia gases. Its mass is 14½ times that of earth, and its diameter is nearly 4 times greater. Uranus moves beyond Saturn at a mean distance of 1,784,000,000 mi from the sun. It has 5 natural satellites. Uranus is barely visible to the unaided eye. It first was observed with the aid of a telescope in 1781. Uranus revolves around the sun once every 84 earth years. It rotates on its axis once every 10 hours and 49 minutes. Its axis of rotation lies

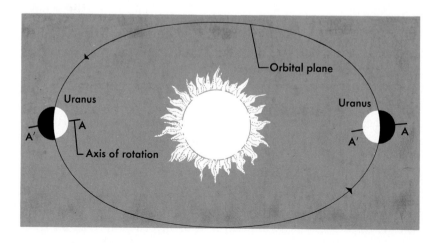

Figure 22-20.   Uranus' axis of rotation is almost parallel to its orbital plane, causing alternate poles (A, A′) to point toward the sun every half revolution.

in its orbital plane which is unique among the planets. With the completion of a half-revolution, alternate poles of Uranus point toward the sun.

Astronomers observed that Uranus' orbit has certain irregularities that suggested the gravitational attraction of another body. The resulting search for another planet beyond Uranus led to the discovery of Neptune.

Neptune is at a mean distance of 2,800,000,000 mi from the sun. Its orbit of the sun requires 165 years. Neptune is not visible to the unaided eye. Seen through a telescope, it appears to have a pale green color. Its atmosphere probably is similar to that of Uranus. Like Saturn and Uranus, Neptune is a gaseous planet. Its diameter is 28,000 mi, but its density is only 0.4 times that of the earth. Neptune has 2 natural satellites.

Pluto was discovered in 1930. It appears to be the most distant planet in our solar system. Because Pluto is so far away, it reflects less light than planets closer to the sun. Although its measurements are uncertain, its diameter has been estimated to be approximately 3,600 mi. Pluto's orbit is the most eccentric of all the planets. It ranges from 2,700,000,000 mi at perihelion to 4,600,000,000 mi at aphelion. During its 248-year orbit around the sun, Pluto passes within Neptune's plane of orbit. In spite of intensive study of the sky beyond Pluto, no other planets have been discovered.

22:11 *Comets, Meteoroids, Meteors, and Meteorites*

In addition to the planets and their satellites, the solar system includes comets and meteoroids. Comets are not satellites

Mount Wilson and Palomar Observatories

Figure 22-21.   Pluto, is difficult to see even with the most powerful telescopes.

Pluto is a small planet whose orbit may represent the outer limit of the sun's gravitational field.

Figure 22-22.   Halley's comet, observed since 240 B.C., last appeared in 1910. On April 26 (a.) the comet was barely visible; on May 8 (b.) its approach to the sun was accompanied by vaporization of its head and the formation of a tail millions of miles long. As the comet moved away from the sun by May 28 (c.), the tail began to dissipate; on June 11 (d.) the comet was barely visible.

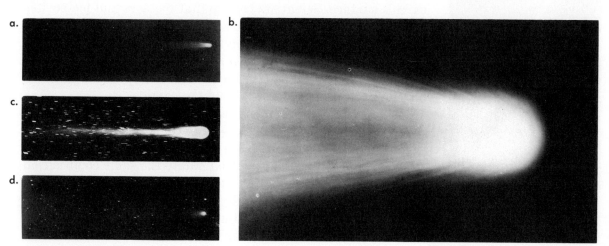

Mount Wilson and Palomar Observatories

Comets orbit within the solar system, but they are independent of the planets and have various orbital paths.

of any planet. Instead, **comets** are independent accumulations of cosmic grit and ice. They may or may not orbit in the same plane as the planets. Comets follow elliptical orbits which possibly may range 10 trillion miles (1.5 light-years) from the sun. Some comets follow paths that bring them close to the sun. There they may be broken into small pieces. Comets are most spectacular as they approach the sun. The comet's mass is in the nucleus. The nucleus consists of masses of frozen methane, ammonia, and water as well as meteoritic particles. As a comet approaches the sun, sometimes solid portions of the nucleus are vaporized. The resulting gases are given off explosively and trail behind the head for millions of miles. This trail always points away from the sun. The head of the comet includes both the nucleus and the coma, a foggy envelope surrounding the nucleus.

Meteoroids consist of fragments formed during the disintegration of either comets or asteroids. Some meteoroids remain in space. Others rain down on the sun and planets. Approximately 2 million tons of "star dust" are added to the earth every year. (Section 11:5.) This amount of cosmic dust would form a layer 10 ft deep if it had been distributed evenly during the 4.5 billion years of earth's existence. Compared to the 6.6 trillion ton mass of the earth, the amount of meteoritic material is insignificant. But as a clue to matter in space, "star dust" is indeed significant.

Meteoroids are too small to be observed in space, but they may be photographed. They also may be detected by radar as they approach earth's atmosphere. **Meteors** are meteoroids that reach our atmosphere; **meteorites** are meteors that reach the earth's surface. Scientists believe that meteors and meteorites are similar to the cosmic materials from which the planets were formed. Most meteors burn up as they pass through the atmosphere and do not reach the earth's surface. Some meteorites, however, reach the earth. These are valuable sources of information about the universe beyond the earth.

Meteorites are classified according to their composition. **Siderites** (sid' a riets) are meteorites composed of iron, or iron and nickel combinations. These are the largest known meteorites. They may represent approximately the same composition as the earth's core. **Aerolites** (ar' a liets), or stony meteorites, are smaller and more difficult to identify than the siderites. These stony meteorites are similar to materials found on the earth's surface. Probably many more fall to earth than are

Figure 22-23.   In September, 1966, this giant meteor streaked across the sky in the eastern half of the nation and trailed flames described as a combination of red, orange, green, and blue.

Photo by James C. Fish

recognized as coming from space. Stony meteorites usually contain some iron particles and consist mostly of iron-magnesium silicates. They appear to be somewhat like basaltic volcanic rocks. **Siderolites** (sid' e ra liets) are the rarest meteorites. They resemble a sponge made of iron. Between the iron particles, spaces are filled with minerals similar to the stony meteorites. Siderolites are intermediate in composition between stony and iron meteorites. They contain both iron-nickel and iron-magnesium silicates.

Meteorites are rarely found—only 1,500 have been recovered. Undoubtedly, many more have fallen. But only experts can recognize stony meteorites after they have begun to weather. The type of iron, however, is a clue. Meteorites contain iron and nickel alloys. Iron formed on earth occurs in combination with oxygen. But unusual looking rocks that *appear to have been melted* on the surface may be worth investigating. This is especially true if the rock has a cone shape. Most meteorites are found only after a "fireball" has been observed in the sky. Observed falls account for most of the discoveries of meteorites. A search of the area where the meteorite seems to burn out often leads to finding remnants of the fireball. Because of heating as they pass through earth's atmosphere, meteorites are black when they reach the earth's surface. But weathering of the iron changes them to rusty brown. Surface crusts on stony meteorites resemble space capsules that have been burned or fused as they returned to earth. Meteorites may plunge through earth's atmosphere with velocities as high as 45 mi/sec. The impact velocity with which a meteorite strikes depends on the speed and direction of the meteorite relative to the earth's motion. Great craters in the earth's surface have been formed by the impact of meteorites. In 1908, an impact in Siberia created such an explosive force that a forest was flattened. Damage extended over a radius of 100 mi. Meteor Crater, Arizona, is another great depression in the earth caused by the impact of a meteorite. Probably many such craters have been formed during the earth's existence.

The surface of Mars and of the moon suggest how earth's surface may have appeared before water vapor was present in the earth's atmosphere. Weathering and erosion have erased the marks of many impacts. Some craters formed early in the history of the earth may have been covered by later deposits. On the surface of Mars and the moon, however, weathering and erosion have not erased these meteorite marks.

Exceptionally large meteorites may form craters like those on Mars and the moon.

Figure 22-24. Meteor Crater at Winslow, Arizona, is estimated to have been formed 20,000 to 75,000 years ago. Millions of tons of pulverized sandstone as well as 15 to 20 tons of meteoritic iron-nickel fragments represent the impact effects of a large mass meeting the earth at meteoritic velocities.

Official U.S. Air Force Photo

Problem

1. Diagrams of the distance relationships between members of the solar system cannot be drawn to scale because of the great distances involved. However, a diagram can give you an idea of their respective positions. Using the scale ⅛ in = 2,000 mi, calculate the size of the paper needed to draw a scale diagram of the sun, the earth, and the moon. Round off the figures to the nearest whole number. Use the following approximations for the computations.

Earth's diameter	8,000 mi
Sun's diameter	865,000 mi
Moon's diameter	2,000 mi
Distance from earth to sun	93,000,000 mi
Distance from earth to moon	240,000 mi

Using the same scale and Table 22–1, calculate the length of the paper needed to diagram the approximate distances to the other planets.

Table 22-1. The Planets

PLANET	Satellites	Mean Distance from Sun	Length of Year	Sidereal Rotation	Diameter at Equator	Relative Volume (earth = 1)	Relative Mass (earth = 1)	Mean Density (water = 1)
MERCURY	0	35,983,000 mi	87.969^d*	58^d 39^m	3,100 mi	0.06	0.0543	5.2
VENUS	0	67,235,000 mi	224.70^d	243^d 9^m 36^s	7,550 mi	0.86	0.81485	5.1
EARTH	1	92,956,000 mi	365.24^d	23^h 56^m 4.1^s	7,927 mi	1.00	1.00	5.52
MARS	2	141,637,000 mi	686.98^d	23^h 37^m 22.67^s	4,220 mi	0.15	0.1069	4.0
ASTEROIDS**								
JUPITER	12	484,000,000 mi	11.86^y	9^h 50^m 30^s	88,700 mi	1,317.00	317.8	1.34
SATURN	10 and 3 rings	887,100,000 mi	29.46^y	10^h 14^m	75,000 mi 171,000 mi***	762.00	95.22	0.68
URANUS	5	1,784,000,000 mi	84.02^y	10^h 49^m	29,000 mi	50.00	14.54	1.6
NEPTUNE	2	2,797,000,000 mi	164.8^y	15^h 48^m	28,000 mi	42.00	17.23	2.2
PLUTO	0	3,675,000,000 mi	248.31^y	6.4^d	3,600 mi?	0.09?	0.8?	?

*y=year, d=day, h=hour, m=minute, s=second (in earth time units)

**Asteroids have orbits that vary and, therefore, their mean distances from the sun are only approximate. Almost all asteroids are found between 142,000,000 mi and 484,000,000 mi from the sun; that is, they lie between Mars and Jupiter. Because of the number and variety of asteroids, their measurements have been omitted.

***Diameter of ring system.

MAIN IDEAS

1. Ptolemy was an early astronomer who believed that the earth was the center of the universe around which the sun, planets, and stars revolved.

2. Galileo was the first scientist to use the telescope for observation of the moon and planets. He believed that the sun was the center of the solar system and supported the idea first expressed by Copernicus, that the earth was but one of the planets controlled by the sun. By the 17th century, scientists generally accepted Galileo's theory of the solar system.

3. The celestial sphere is used for charting star positions. Declination indicates distances north and south of the celestial equator. Plus declination readings are north, minus declination readings are south of the celestial equator. Right ascension measures positions eastward from the point where the celestial equator and the ecliptic (sun's apparent path) intersect on the spring equinox.

4. Constellations are groups of stars named by Greek and Roman astronomers for objects familiar to them.

5. The gravitational attraction of the sun holds the planets in their orbits.

6. Radiant energy is emitted by the sun during the transmutation of hydrogen into helium gas.

7. The sun consists of the interior, where transmutation of hydrogen occurs; the photosphere, which is the luminous surface we see; the chromosphere, a zone of hot gas surrounding the photosphere, and the corona, a zone of thin gas in which protons and electrons are widely dispersed.

8. Sunspots are areas on the sun's surface in which temperatures are lower than surrounding gases. Sunspots have cyclic periods of activity which affect earth's magnetic field.

9. Planets of the solar system include Mercury, Venus, Earth, Mars, Jupiter, Saturn, Uranus, Neptune, and Pluto in this order outward from the sun.

10. Asteroids are fragments of cosmic matter which orbit in a position between Jupiter and Mars.

11. Mars does not appear to have a magnetic field or radiation belts similar to those of earth.

12. Venus' surface is obscured by dense clouds.

13. Photographs of a portion of the Martian surface show many craters similar to those of the moon. Mars atmosphere, which is exceedingly thin, appears to consist principally of carbon dioxide.

14. Jupiter, Uranus, Neptune, and Saturn are known as gas giants because of their great size and low density.

15. Comets follow orbits which are independent of other members of the solar system. If comets collide with other celestial bodies, they may disintegrate into small fragments called meteoroids.

16. Meteoroids are called meteors if they enter the earth's atmosphere. Meteoroids are called meteorites if they reach the earth's surface.

17. Meteorites furnish clues to the kind of material from which the planets were formed. The earth's core is thought to be similar to iron meteorites. The earth's mantle may be similar to the stony meteorites.

VOCABULARY

Write a sentence in which you use correctly each of the following words or terms.

ascension	corona	photosphere
asteroid	declination	satellite
celestial sphere	ecliptic	siderites
chromosphere	equinox	transmutation
constellation	meteoroid	zodiac

STUDY QUESTIONS

A. True or False

Determine whether each of the following sentences is true or false. (Do not write in this book.)

1. Ptolemy and Galileo agreed that the earth is the center of the universe.

2. The sun is the star which supplies radiant energy to the solar system.

3. Other planets orbit the sun in nearly the same plane as the planet earth.

4. Stars appear to be stationary because they are very distant.

5. A constellation is composed of several planets.

6. The solar system contains the sun and seven planets.

7. The celestial sphere has the earth at its center.

8. The surface of Venus is obscured by clouds.

9. Planets may be located easily on a star chart.

10. Planets appear to move more rapidly than stars.

B. Multiple Choice

Choose the word or phrase which completes correctly each of the following sentences. (Do not write in this book.)

1. The first astronomer to use the telescope in his study of the stars was (*Ptolemy, Galileo, Kepler*).

2. The idea that the sun is the center of the solar system was first suggested by (*Copernicus, Galileo, Lowell*).

3. The sun's apparent path in the sky is called the (*celestial equator, zodiac, ecliptic*).

4. Planets orbit the sun within an area called the (*celestial equator, zodiac, ecliptic*).

5. Density of the sun is (*greater than, less than, the same as*) the density of the earth.

6. Transmutation takes place in the sun's (*interior, chromosphere, corona*).

7. Of all the planets in the solar system, (*Saturn, Uranus, Earth*) has conditions that are necessary to supporting complex forms of life.

8. The largest planet in the solar system is (*Jupiter, Saturn, Uranus*).

9. Cosmic materials which are burned as they pass through earth's atmosphere are called (*asteroids, meteoroids, meteors*).

10. Siderites, aerolites, and siderolites are types of (*meteorites, meteoroids, meteors*).

C. Completion

Complete each of the following sentences with a word or phrase which will make the sentence correct. (Do not write in this book.)

1. Measurements in angular degrees north and south of the equator of the celestial sphere are called ___?___.

2. The scientist known as the founder of modern astronomy was __?__.

3. Measurements eastward from the position of the intersection of the ecliptic and celestial equator are called __?__.

4. The Big Dipper and Little Dipper are found in constellations known as __?__ and __?__.

5. The sun contains __?__ per cent of the mass of the solar system.

6. Transmutation is a process by which __?__ is changed to __?__ gas.

7. __?__ is the planet which is closest to the sun.

8. A belt containing many __?__ lies between Jupiter and Mars.

9. Three planets which are not visible without a telescope are __?__, __?__ and __?__.

10. __?__ are celestial bodies of cosmic grit and ice which may orbit far into outer space.

D. How and Why

1. How may an observer distinguish a star from a planet?

2. Why was it difficult for people to accept Copernicus' idea that the earth and planets revolve around the sun?

3. Although astronomers know that earth is not the center of the universe, why do they continue to use earth as the center of the celestial sphere?

4. Why is the ecliptic called the "apparent path of the sun"?

5. Why is intersection of the ecliptic and celestial equator used as the starting point for measuring right ascension?

6. What conditions on the surface of Venus make the existence of earth-like life impossible?

7. What conditions on Mars make it seem improbable that animal life as we know it could exist?

8. What kinds of information may be obtained from a study of meteorites?

9. Why does the tail of a comet trail away from the sun?

10. Suggest two reasons why Mercury has not retained a detectable atmosphere although both Venus and Earth have retained their atmospheres.

INVESTIGATIONS

1. Find information on the latest comet and report to the class.
2. Report on Meteor Crater, Arizona. Is the crater correctly named? Do scientists agree on the cause of the crater?
3. Select one of the planets and report on the latest information available.
4. Discuss the work of Clyde Tombaugh, Percival Lowell, or another astronomer.

INTERESTING READING

Adler, Irving, *The Sun and Its Family*, rev. ed. New York, John Day Co., 1969.

Asimov, Isaac, *Environments Out There*. New York, Abelard-Schuman, Ltd., 1968.

*Bergamini, David, *The Universe*. Life Nature Library. New York, Time Inc., 1968.

Branley, Franklyn M., *A Book of Venus for You*. New York, Thomas Y. Crowell Co., 1969.

Edgar, Robert A., *Have You Seen a Meteorite?* Tempe, Ariz., Arizona State University Press, 1966.

Highland, Harold J., *The How and Why Wonder Book of Planets and Interplanetary Travel*. Columbus, Ohio, Charles E. Merrill Publishing Co., 1962.

Knight, David C., *The First Book of Mars*. New York, Franklin Watts, Inc., 1966.

*Leonard, Jonathan, and Sagan, Carl, *Planets*. Life Science Library. New York, Time Inc., 1966.

Ley, Willy, *Inside the Orbit of the Earth*. New York, McGraw-Hill Book Co., 1968.

Moffat, Samuel, Schneour, Elie A., and Lederberg, Joshua, *Life Beyond the Earth*. New York, Four Winds Press, 1966.

Page, Thornton and Lou W., *Wanderers in the Sky*. New York, The Macmillan Company, 1964.

*Wilson, Mitchell, *Energy*. Life Science Library. New York, Time Inc., 1967.

Wyler, Rose, and Ames, Gerald, *The New Golden Book of Astronomy*. New York, Golden Press, 1965.

---

* Well-illustrated material.

23 The Moon

Earth's natural satellite and nearest celestial neighbor is the moon. Compared to the planets and stars, the moon can be observed quite easily with the unaided eye. The moon has aroused man's curiosity from the beginning of time. Now that men with scientific instruments have made landings on the moon, eventually we may learn to understand our satellite's history and origin.

23:1 *Properties*

In 1610, Galileo trained a telescope on the moon. For the first time, man saw details of the moon's rugged surface. Galileo named the low, dark, flat areas *maria* (mae′ ree a), the Latin word for seas. Each "sea" or *mare* (mae′ ree) that has been observed has been given a special name, such as *Mare Nubium* (Sea of Clouds) and *Mare Tranquillitatis* (Sea of Tranquility). Although scientists now realize that no water is present in the maria, the original term still is used. Bright areas of the moon are highlands.

On July 20, 1969 Neil Armstrong and Edwin Aldrin walked on the moon. Their partner, Michael Collins, orbited above them in a mothership. For two hours, Armstrong and Aldrin walked about and gathered rocks and dust in *Mare Tranquillitatis*. The forty pounds of moon rock they brought back, plus rocks gathered by later landings, will be studied by earth scientists for many years.

Some of the rocks are quite similar to earth's marine basalts. Moon rocks are most like basalts associated with the mid-ocean ridges and the Hawaiian lavas. These rocks have been dated as about 3.7 billion years old. Moon dust has been dated at about

4.6 billion years. Moon dust is so fine it can be studied best by X-ray and electron microscopes or various other instruments. The dust contains numerous glass spheres. These glass spheres are presumed to form when a meteorite hits the moon. The contact melts some of the material and splashes this melted material up from the surface. The glass spheres themselves are covered with tiny high-velocity impact craters which are visible under the microscope. The dust includes meteoritic material as well as moon material which has been pulverized by the impact of meteorites.

The moon's diameter of 2,160 mi is small compared to most members of the solar system. Nevertheless, in proportion to the size of the earth, the moon is extremely large for a satellite. Jupiter, Neptune, and Saturn have moons that are larger than earth's moon, but these satellites are extremely small compared to the size of their respective planets.

The moon's mass is 7.35×10^{22} kg; its density is 3.3 g/cm³. Because the moon does not have enough gravitational attraction to hold an atmosphere, few earth-like weathering processes occur. Little or no air and moisture are present on the moon. Consequently, the moon's surface features have remained nearly unchanged, in contrast to the earth's surface where little remains exactly the same from one day to the next. Temperature on the moon varies greatly. Parts of the moon in shadow may have temperatures as low as $-173°C$ ($-280°F$).

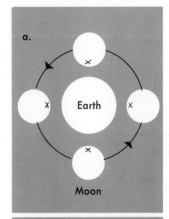

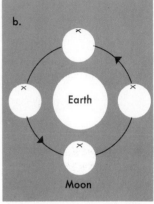

Figure 23-1. **(a.) Revolution and rotation periods of the moon are the same. Therefore, the same side always faces the earth. (b.) If revolution interval were the same but the moon did not rotate, both sides would be visible from earth.**

Earth's moon is exceptionally large compared to its planet.

Surface features of the moon have changed little because erosion and weathering are not effective. Temperature range on the moon is greater than on earth due to the lack of a lunar atmosphere.

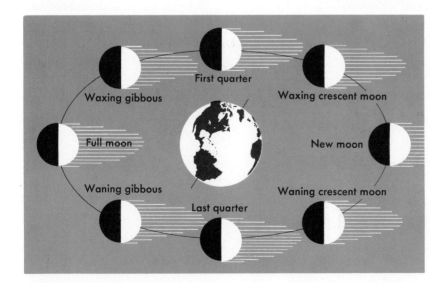

Figure 23-2. **Relative position of earth and moon with respect to the sun determines the moon's phase. A complete cycle from new moon to new moon is 29½ days.**

In direct sunlight, moon temperatures may range from 110°C to 130°C (230°F to 266°F).

23:2 *Motions*

The moon completes one revolution of the earth in 27.3 days, measured in relation to a sighting on a star. At the same time, earth moves forward in its orbit around the sun. Thus, 29½ days pass before the moon arrives opposite the same position of earth from which it started.

During the moon's 27.3-day revolution around the earth, it makes one complete rotation on its axis. (Figure 23–1.) Consequently, the same side of the moon always faces the earth.

Figure 23-3.   The sun's corona seen during an eclipse.

Ewing Galloway

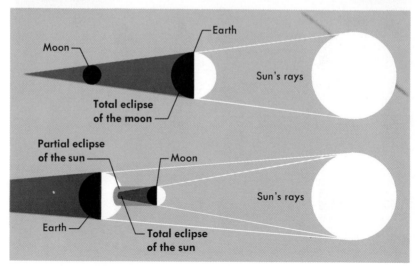

Figure 23-4.   An eclipse of the sun occurs when the moon is between the earth and the sun. An eclipse of the moon occurs when the earth is between the moon and the sun.

When that side of the moon is illuminated by sunlight, it reflects some light to the earth as moonlight. A *full moon* occurs when the earth is between the sun and moon. When the moon is between the earth and sun, the *new moon* or the dark period of the moon occurs. *First quarter* and *last quarter* moon occur halfway between the full and dark positions. Less than a quarter is a *crescent moon;* more than a quarter is a *gibbous* (gib′ us) *moon*. (Figure 23–2.) These particular appearances in the cycle of changes are known as the *phases* of the moon.

Its size and elliptical orbit make earth's moon unique among the satellites of the solar system. Satellites of other planets have nearly circular orbits. The moon's orbit, an ellipse, carries it 253,000 mi from the earth at apogee (ap′a jee) and 221,000 mi at perigee (per′a jee). The angle between the moon's orbital plane and the celestial equator varies from $18\frac{1}{2}°$ to $28\frac{1}{2}°$ in a period of 18.6 years. Satellites of other planets orbit in the plane of the equator of their respective planets. Some scientists regard the earth and moon as twin planets because the moon is so different from other moons in the solar system.

An interesting phenomenon related to our moon is the shadow which it casts on earth. At times the earth also casts a shadow on the moon. Such shadows are called eclipses.

An eclipse of the moon is called a *lunar eclipse*. It occurs when sun, earth, and moon are lined up so that the moon lies in earth's shadow. (Figure 23–4.) A lunar eclipse would occur with every revolution of the moon if the moon's orbit were around earth's equator and if the moon's axis were not tilted. Three or fewer lunar eclipses occur per year. However, many people have seen them because a lunar eclipse may be viewed from about half of the earth. The earth's orbit and the moon's orbit are known precisely. Thus, their positions for casting shadows on one another can be calculated and the eclipse can be predicted.

When the moon lies directly between earth and sun, an eclipse of the sun, or *solar eclipse*, occurs. Then the moon shuts out the sun's rays over some portion of the earth. Because the moon is smaller than the earth, only a small segment of earth lies in the path of a total solar eclipse. A larger area has a partial eclipse. Some parts of the earth have no eclipse. During a total solar eclipse, the sun's corona can be studied. Then the brilliant photosphere is blacked out and only the corona is visible. (Figure 23–3.) Total solar eclipses are relatively rare. One occurred on March 7, 1970. The next eclipse will be in 1979.

Because of its size the sun is never in total eclipse over the whole earth.

Figure 23-5.

ACTIVITY. Place a large ball in the middle of a desk or table. Be sure that there is enough room for you to walk around the table. Through the middle of a smaller ball, push a spindle or long nail as an axis. Hold the smaller ball with its axis perpendicular to the table, and mark the side facing the larger ball. Carry the smaller ball around the table and turn it slowly on its axis so that it rotates once during your orbit around the larger ball. Observe the marked side as you turn the smaller ball on its axis. During the orbit, is the mark always in the same position with respect to the larger ball? Discuss why only one side of the moon is visible from earth. How would the view of the moon from earth differ if the moon did not rotate? How would it differ if the moon rotated more rapidly?

Darken the room and again orbit the smaller ball around the larger one. Have another student direct a flashlight beam toward the larger ball on the table. His position should allow you to move the smaller ball between the light and the larger ball. Hold the smaller ball so your body does not shade it from the flashlight beam.

Draw diagrams to show the amount of light reflected from the smaller ball, as seen from the position of the larger ball. What is the position of the smaller ball with respect to the flashlight beam during the phases? On your diagrams, label the various phases of the moon as full moon, crescent moon, quarter moon, gibbous moon, and new moon.

23:3 Earth-Moon System

Center of gravity for the earth-moon system lies 3,000 mi from the earth's center, on the side facing the moon.

Planet earth and its moon revolve around the sun somewhat like a single body. The earth-moon system has a common center of gravity, called the *barycenter*. The barycenter is located on the side of earth facing the moon. (Section 1:4.) The moon orbits the earth due to the gravitational attraction between earth and moon. Without gravity, the moon's inertia would cause the moon to continue moving forward in a straight line. But the gravitational attraction of the earth pulls the moon inward and keeps it moving in an elliptical path around the earth.

The gravitational attraction of the moon for the earth causes tides to rise and fall within and on the earth. Tides are most apparent in ocean waters. (Section 12:4.) But tidal energy, estimated at about two billion horsepower, is lost to the earth. Some energy loss is caused by friction between adjacent water particles. Other energy is lost by friction between water particles and ocean bottom, and between water particles and the shore. This loss of energy causes earth's rate of rotation to decrease slightly. Recall that the length of day depends on the time required for one complete rotation of the earth. Thus, any decrease in the rate of rotation results in a longer day.

Energy loss due to tidal friction causes the earth to rotate more slowly with age.

Our day is estimated to be growing at the rate of about 0.0016 sec per century. The loss of even this small amount means that the position of bodies in the solar system calculated a century ago are now slightly in error. Future positions of planets still may be calculated accurately if corrections that take tidal friction into account are made.

George Darwin, a British astronomer and son of Charles Darwin, was an authority on tidal energy. He demonstrated that the slowing of the earth's rotation has an important, long-term effect on the angular momentum of the earth-moon system. **Angular momentum** is equal to the mass of the body times the velocity times the distance of the body from its axis of rotation. It may be written mathematically as follows:

Angular momentum of a rotating body is not lost but may be redistributed.

$$A_m = M \, V \, R$$

In this equation, A_m represents angular momentum, M represents mass, V represents angular velocity, and R represents the distance of the body from the axis of rotation.

Conservation of angular momentum applies to the solar system and to the earth-moon system. It applies to any bodies that rotate on their axes and revolve around each other. The total angular momentum of the system must always remain constant. Ice skaters, ballet dancers, and acrobats use this law while spinning on skates, on their toes, or when suspended from a rope. These performers spin at a low rate of speed with arms extended sideways. If they bring their arms to their sides quickly, they spin at a much higher rate. Entertainers present a spectacular appearance when they go into a fast spin.

Mass of the earth-moon system remains constant, as does its angular momentum.

EXPERIMENT. Use a turntable capable of supporting your weight. The platform should be less than 1 ft above the floor. Oil all bearings to reduce friction; the platform should spin freely with minimum effort. Hold weights of about 5 lb in each hand. Stand in the center of the platform and have another student gently and slowly start the platform rotating.

While rotating, extend your arms and the weights about half-way to your shoulders, making a 45° angle with the floor. What happens? Raise your arms and the weights to shoulder height, parallel to the floor. What happens? Continue to rotate and return your arms and the weights to your sides. What happens to the rate of rotation?

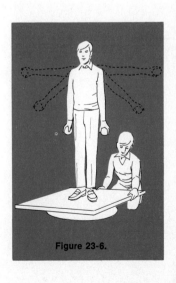

Figure 23-6.

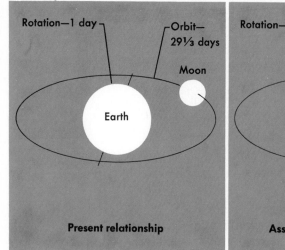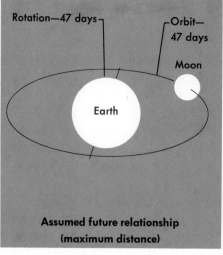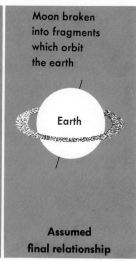

| Rotation—1 day | Orbit—29⅓ days | Rotation—47 days | Orbit—47 days | Moon broken into fragments which orbit the earth |

Present relationship

Assumed future relationship
(maximum distance)

Assumed
final relationship

Figure 23-7. The earth-moon system would readjust to a change in angular momentum.

Changes in rotational velocity of the earth result in changes of the radius between earth and moon.

The earth-moon system is controlled by the law of conservation of angular momentum. Recall from the experiment in Section 1:4 that the velocity of the washer decreases as the length of the string increases. In the earth-moon system, the distance automatically adjusts to any changes in velocity. The radius between earth and moon increases as the earth loses rotational velocity.

The rotational slowing of the earth has been determined from the position of the planets. The planets now arrive at calculated positions ahead of schedule. Calculations show the moon to be moving away from earth at the rate of about ½ in/yr. Even these small changes have become significant during earth's approximately 4.5 billion-year life. Probably the life of the earth-moon system has been about the same as earth's life.

Eventually earth's period of rotation may equal moon's period of orbit.

Because the moon is moving away from earth, the month as well as the day is lengthening. Many astronomers believe that earth's period of rotation will equal the orbital period of the moon in the distant future. They estimate that eventually the month will equal 47 of our present days. At that time, one earth day would equal 1128 hours.

$$\left(\frac{47\ \text{days}}{}\ \Big|\ \frac{24\ \text{hr}}{\text{day}} = 1128\ \text{hr}\right)$$

PROBLEMS

Recall the law of conservation of angular momentum and the formula for angular momentum: $A_m = M\,V\,R$

1. If the distance R is doubled and there is no change in mass M, what happens to the velocity V? Why? Prove that your answer is correct by replacing M, V, and R with numbers.
2. If the distance R is halved and there is no change in mass M, what happens to the velocity V? Why? Prove that your answer is correct by replacing M, V, and R with numbers.

If earth's rotation period ever equals the moon's revolution period, there will be fixed tides on both moon and earth. Then there will be no tidal friction. But from what is known today, the earth-moon system would not then be stable because of the effect of the sun's gravitation. The sun's gravitation would become the dominant tidal influence. Tidal friction would cause the earth's rotational period to become longer than the moon's period of revolution. Then the system would readjust to the change in angular momentum and the moon would move back toward earth. If the moon approached within a few thousand miles of the earth, the earth's gravitational field would develop strong tidal forces in the moon. Such stresses would cause the moon to break up into small particles. These particles could orbit the earth as a ringcloud. Astronomers predict that disruption of the moon would occur when the moon was still about 10,000 mi from earth.

Tidal friction caused by the sun's gravitational attraction would reverse the outward movement of the moon.

Destruction of the moon might be expected as it approached within 10,000 mi of the earth.

Although the earth's gravitational attraction would hold the earth together, tides of tremendous size would change the shape of earth's surface. Mathematically, the disruption of the moon can be predicted. But the time involved is many billions of years. The sun may have burned itself out before these changes in the earth-moon system could occur.

Some original energy already has been lost from the earth-moon system. The lengthening rotational period of the earth has caused the moon to recede and our day to grow longer. Paleontologists have found evidence of the previously shorter day in fossil shells millions of years old. Yearly growth rings on ancient shells indicate that formerly an earth day was shorter than it is at present.

23:4 *Origin*

As a result of his studies of tidal friction, George Darwin suggested a theory for the origin of the moon. His theory was accepted by astronomers of his day. Today it is regarded as improbable. Darwin believed that tidal calculations could be projected backward in time to an unknown date when earth and moon formed a pear shaped liquid mass. This mass then separated. At that time, day and month were equal, and both were about 3 hours to 5 hours long. Because day and month were the same, the only tidal friction was due to the sun's gravitational attraction. Eventually, the solar tides upset the earth-moon equilibrium and tidal friction carried the moon away from the earth and has continued to do so.

Kuiper (Section 1:2) suggested that planets originated in a great mass of rotating gas and dust. Eddies or centers of condensation, called *protoplanets*, developed within the major dust cloud. Eventually the eddies became planets. The eddy which became earth may have had two centers of condensation. The larger center condensed to form earth. The smaller center became the moon. Kuiper's theory accounts for a satellite of large size which does not necessarily orbit the nearby planet's equator. But only a rigid material could have retained its nearly

Kuiper's theory of moon origin suggests that the eddy containing earth's protoplanet developed a second eddy which became the moon.

Figure 23-8.   The crater Copernicus from a distance of 28.4 miles. The distance from the horizon to the base of the photograph is about 150 miles.

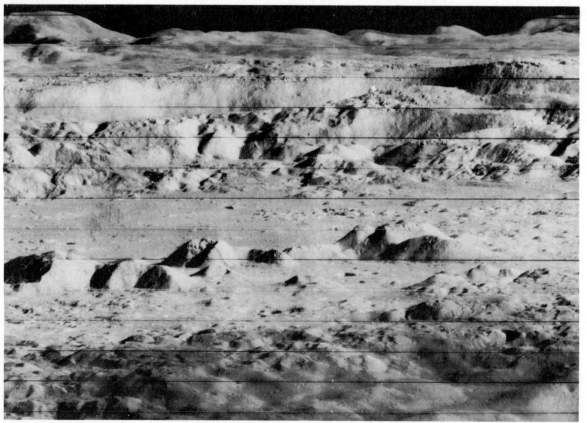

spherical shape in spite of tides caused by the nearby planet. Thus, according to Kuiper's theory the moon was rigid when it joined the earth in the earth-moon system.

Harold Clayton Urey, an American chemist and astronomer, has suggested that at one time the moon was an independent small planet. This rigid planet orbited close enough to earth to be captured by earth's gravitation. Urey believes that recent evidence from moon samples supports his idea.

23:5 *Surface Features*

Although questions concerning moon material remain, great progress has been made in the study of the moon's surface through the use of both manned and unmanned spacecraft. Features of the visible side of the moon have been assembled on a lunar reference mosaic or lunar map prepared by the U.S. Air Force.

Because the moon has an elliptical orbit and rotates at a constant speed, only 59 percent of the moon's surface is visible from the earth. But in October, 1959, the Russian Lunik III orbiting spacecraft supplied the first, indistinct pictures of the back of the moon. More recently, spacecraft from the U.S. have taken pictures of both the front and back of the moon. These pictures are used to map the lunar surface.

Mountains, plains, and craters mark the moon's surface. Some craters are so small they cannot be seen from earth even with the best telescopes. These small craters have been photographed by U. S. spacecraft of the Ranger, Surveyor, Lunar Orbiter series, and crews of the Apollo flights. Some craters are extremely large, and some have craters within craters. The southern portion of the moon's visible side is especially rugged. The back side of the moon has fewer craters than the side facing earth. Craters, mountains, and steep cliffs cover hundreds of square miles. Some mountains are estimated to rise 30,000 ft above the moon's surface, higher than any mountains on earth. Straight cliffs appear to be great fault lines, perhaps similar to the San Andreas fault line of California. (Section 18:1.) One cliff, the Straight Wall located in Mare Nubium, is about 60 mi long and 1,200 ft high. Photographs returned by Lunar Orbiter 4 revealed a trough about 200 mi long and 10 mi wide. This trough is on the back side of the moon near the limb, or outer edge.

Only 59% of the moon's surface can be seen from earth, but over 75% of the back side and 99% of the front side have been photographed. Maria make up about one-third of the moon's surface.

Figure 23-9. Astronaut footprint in lunar soil.

NASA

Maria are the most prominent moon features. These depressions make up about one half of the visible surface of the moon. Maria often are nearly 2 mi below the brighter, light-colored highlands. The dark central region of the maria may represent subsidence of a central volcanic vent. But some scientists suggest that the subsidence might be due to the impact of large meteorites or even asteroids.

Mare Imbrium is one of fourteen principal seas. According to R. B. Baldwin, an American scientist, Mare Imbrium (diameter 700 mi) probably was caused by the impact of a small, low-velocity asteroid. The diameter of the asteroid is estimated to have been approximately 100 mi and its velocity 2 mi/sec. A smaller asteroid moving at a higher velocity is another possible cause of the depresion.

Mare Serenitatis, Mare Humorum, Mare Nectaris, and Mare Crisium are other circular maria. **Circular Maria** are surrounded by rims or ring anticlines beyond which lie the plains. Their craters are filled with dark gray material which is presumed to be lava like that of Mare Tranquillitatis. The age of the lava flow in Mare Tranquillitatis is about 3.6 billion years. This may be much less than the age of the craters.

Rills are markings on the moon's surface which have steep sides, flat bottoms, and varying widths. Some rills extend for hundreds of miles and cut across mountains, maria, and other moon landscape features. Because rills often outline the maria, the rills may be associated with lava flows. Some astronomers believe the rills are cracks produced by faulting when the moon material was in the cooling stage.

In contrast to the rills, **wrinkle ridges** rise above the surface of the moon. Wrinkle ridges have irregular, complex shapes and rather uniform widths. They average less than 1,000 ft in height and perhaps 10 mi to 20 mi in width. They may extend for great distances. Wrinkle ridges may be caused by compression, in contrast to rills which probably are due to tension. Compressional ridges, or wrinkle ridges, may have formed in the central part of the maria during movement of moon's surface.

Rays constitute one of the most distinctive features of the moon. Rays are the bright streaks that radiate from craters like the spokes of a wheel from the hub. These rays may extend up to 2,000 mi. Ranger spacecraft photographs show small craters located on some rays. A generally accepted theory suggests that rays consist of pulverized rock. This *rock flour* was

---

Maria are depressions that may represent subsidence resulting from the internal character of the moon, or possibly due to impact of large meteorites or asteroids.

Maria are thought to be filled by lava from beneath the moon's surface.

Trenches in the moon's surface which extend across other moon features sometimes for hundreds of miles are called **rills.**

Wrinkle ridges are complex forms 10 to 20 mi wide that extend for great distances.

Rays are bright areas on the moon's surface radiating outward from a center like the spokes of a wheel.

NASA

Figure 23-10. Around Crater Tycho, the prominent ray system is brightened during the full moon.

blasted from the moon's surface material during the formation of a crater. Light-colored rays may darken with age or during bombardment by cosmic material. Not all craters appear to have rays. It may be that a darkening process makes old rays impossible to recognize. Rays may be a clue to the relative ages of ray craters as compared to rayless craters. Crater Tycho, which has a spectacular ray system, is considered one of the youngest of the craters.

Walled plains are among the most conspicuous craters. They are from 40 mi to 150 mi in diameter. Within a walled plain, the terrain is almost level except for an occasional crater or mound. They resemble volcanic craters formed by collapse along fault lines. They may have been broken down by gradual erosion due to temperature changes, cosmic rays, or meteoritic bombardment. Some walled plains appear to be the oldest observable features on the moon, but like other moon features, their origin is unknown.

Walled plains on the moon are craters that appear to be due to internal activity.

Figure 23-11. Astronaut setting up experiments on the surface of the moon.

NASA

Moon features may be due to both volcanic activity and meteoritic impact.

Explosion craters are numerous and found in all kinds of moon terrain. Their walls are definite, and small craters, called *craterlets*, are common around their rims. Most explosion craters tend to be circular. In contrast, walled plains tend to be polygonal. Ray systems are characteristic of explosion craters. The outer edge or limb of the moon that leads, as the satellite moves in its orbit, contains a concentration of explosion craters. This concentration suggests that the moon meets many meteoroids head-on.

From a study of moon rocks, it appears that both volcanic activity and meteoritic impact account for the moon's features. Some scientists believe that all of the depressions are due to impact. Others believe that all depressions are due to volcanic activity. But a careful evaluation of all features seems to require different interpretations for different kinds of depressions.

Evidence for the meteoritic origin of many lunar craters has been gathered during studies of meteorite craters found on earth. Craters formed by chemical and nuclear explosions have received much attention in recent years. The ratio of depth to diameter characteristic of meteorite craters on earth

Figure 23-12. A 50-mile diameter crater on the far side of the moon.

seems to apply to many lunar craters as well. Sizes of craters involved in this study range from 26 ft to about 20 mi. Shapes and relative dimensions of moon craters have been photographed by several spacecrafts and by ground-based telescopes. These dimensions agree with dimensions of meteorite craters on earth. Dimensions of volcanic craters on earth do

Figure 23-13. Domes on the moon similar to the volcanic domes of Northern California rise 1,000 to 1,500 ft above the surface; diameters are 2 to 10 miles.

not appear to duplicate normal lunar craters. Based on this reasoning, the moon's explosion craters appear to be the result of meteoritic impact.

Chain craters do not seem to have a meteoritic impact origin. These small pits in the moon's surface are less than 3 ft in diameter. They are aligned in chains extending more than 100 mi. Chain craters are found within the maria. A few extend into the higher, light-colored surrounding area. Chain craters have low rims and probably resulted from violent eruptions of gas which threw out dust and fragments of surface material.

Some observers of the moon have noted that a mist or fog occasionally appears over local areas. Surface details are not visible during periods of fog. Because surface water is not present on the moon, the fog has been attributed to the presence of gas clouds. In 1958, N. A. Kozyrev, a Russian astronomer, obtained spectrograms that indicated weak emissions of gas containing carbon. The gas seemed to come from the central peak of the crater Alphonsus. Kozyrev interpreted the gas as due to volcanic activity. More recent observations by astronomers at New Mexico's Corral Observatory have found ultraviolet radiation coming from Crater Aristarchus. Seismic evidence seems to support the idea that volcanic activity may occur on the moon.

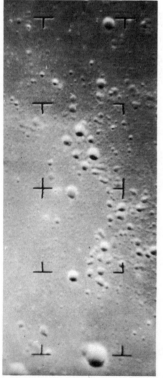

Figure 23-14. Crater Copernicus contains numerous secondary craters and this outlying ray.

NASA

Seismometers left behind on the moon by astronauts have recorded moonquakes every 28.4 days. These quakes occur when earth and moon are closest, or at perigee. The quakes appear to be centered in Fra Mauro, a highland crater first explored during the Apollo 14 mission.

The moonquakes suggest that faulting occurs on the moon as it does on earth. Apparently, the faulting on the moon is related to tides caused by the gravitational attraction of the earth. The escaping of gas in certain areas of the moon suggests that some internal heat is present. Thus, the moon may not be quite the cold, lifeless body that it has seemed.

Magnetic effects have been recorded by a magnetometer stationed on the moon. Readings from the Explorer 35 satellite were higher than expected. Although the magnetism of the moon is extremely low compared to earth, the moon may have a small magnetic field. It is also possible that magnetic rocks, such as great masses of iron, may be concentrated in the area near the magnetometer.

One of the more important results of the moon study has been the application of geology to a mapping project by the

Astrogeology Branch of the United States Geological Survey. At first their work was limited to telescope measurements and photographs. But the high quality photographs from spacecraft of the Ranger, Surveyor, and Lunar Orbiter series have aided this project. E. M. Shoemaker, an American astronomer, heads a group which has devised a time scale for major events on the moon. Using the law of superposition (Page 399), the group has determined the ages of various moon features.

The geologic time scale of the moon has been worked out by using the law of superposition.

Large craters, called **primary craters,** are surrounded by a pattern of small craters known as **secondary craters.** Secondary craters appear on top of some surface features and disappear beneath others. If secondary craters are above, they are younger than the features. If secondary craters are below, they are older than the other features. Based on this kind of information, the Geological Survey has named the lunar periods. The oldest period is called *Pre-Imbrian.* Next oldest is known as *Imbrian. Eratosthenian period* and *Copernican period* follow in that order. This sequence of events was developed for the region of the Mare Imbrium. Shoemaker believes that in time, lunar events can be related to events on earth.

Figure 23-15. The Apollo 12 Lunar Module as it heads toward its landing site in the Sea of Storms.

NASA

Figure 23-16. The earth viewed from the surface of the moon.

Figure 23-17. Simplified diagram of the internal combustion system of a rocket.

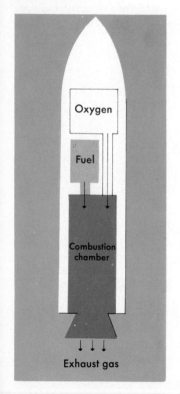

Oxygen

Fuel

Combustion chamber

Exhaust gas

23:6 Travel to the Moon

Astronomers hope that travel to the moon will answer questions about the universe as well as about the moon. If telescopes can be landed on the moon, scientists can have an unobstructed view of the universe. Earth's atmosphere interferes with telescopic viewing. Dust and water vapor make it difficult to see the sky. Air also tends to be in motion much of the time, and motion distorts the view of the heavens from the earth.

Scientists, engineers, and technologists have cooperated in building spaceships that can make a safe round trip to the moon. A spaceship leaving the earth must attain a speed of about 25,000 mi/hr to escape the earth's gravitational pull. However, if the spacecraft left the earth at this velocity, it would bypass the moon and go into orbit around the sun. To hit its target, a spaceship begins its journey to the moon at a slower speed. A number of rockets then are used to control the speed of the spacecraft and to provide thrust at the proper moment.

The principle of rocketry depends on Newton's law of physics. This law states that for every action there is an equal and opposite reaction. The recoil of a gun illustrates this principle. When an explosion sends a bullet forward, the gun recoils or moves backward. The recoil has the same amount of energy as the forward moving bullet. Burning and expelling of gas causes a rocket to move forward with an amount of energy equal to that given off by the gas.

Figure 23-18. Photographs of the moon: (a.) from earth through a 36-in. refracting telescope, (b.) the crater Kepler from Apollo 12 in lunar orbit, (c.) terrain near the Apollo 11 lunar module as it stands on the surface of the moon, (d.) microscopic view of lunar soil.

Travel to the moon was first accomplished on July 20, 1969. The spacecraft had three sections. One section held rockets and fuel used in maneuvering the spacecraft into lunar orbit. Another section, the moonship, carried two astronauts to the moon and back to rejoin a third astronaut in the mothership. Only the mothership returned to earth. The moonship remained in orbit around the moon. The rocket fuel section was abandoned just before reentry to the earth's atmosphere.

EXPERIMENT.   On a piece of drawing paper, draw a large semi-circle. Divide the arc into fourteen even divisions. Indicate east at the left and west at the right of the arc. (These are not the usual positions for these directions, but because you will face south during your observations, east will be to your left.) Mark the top of the arc as zenith. *Draw a silhouette of the buildings or landscape features visible when you face south. Include the tallest tree or building as a marker.*

Refer to the daily paper, an almanac, or calendar for the date of the next new moon. Begin your moon watch about two days after new moon. Make your observations at exactly the same time each evening (6:30 is recommended). When the first sliver of the crescent moon appears, add it to your diagram exactly as it appears in the sky. Be sure the points are in the correct position. Locate the moon every night at the same time for at least two weeks. After each sighting, sketch the moon on your diagram. Date each sketch. If clouds obstruct your view, leave a dated space in your diagram. In what

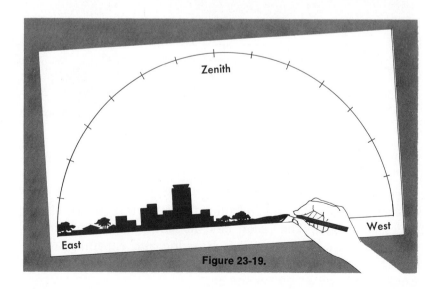

Figure 23-19.

direction do the sketches progress? At the end of two weeks, what is the position of the moon in the diagram? What is its shape? Continue to watch the evening sky at the same time. What do you observe about the moon?

EXPERIMENT.　Draw a chart similar to Figure 23–20. Locate the date of full moon and the time at which the moon will rise on that date. Begin your observations on the day when the moonrise is at sunset. On your chart, record the date and the exact minute at which you see the moon rise. Does your data agree with the official time for moonrise? For one week, record the date, the time of moonrise, and the shape of the moon on your chart. Use information from a newspaper to complete the moonset column. How much later is moonrise each night? If the moon rose at 6:00 PM on Monday, what time would it rise on the following Sunday? Did you observe the moonset at any time during the week?

Use binoculars or a telescope to observe the full moon and its surface features. What features account for the moon's "face"? Why does the moon's face seem to turn from side to side on succeeding nights?

MOON CHART			
Date	Moon rise	Moon set	Moon shape
10/5/68	6:32 P.M.	7:10 A.M.	Full moon

Figure 23-20.

Table 23–1.　*The Moon*

Mean distance from earth	238,857 mi
Mean diameter	2,160 mi
Volume	53×10^8 mi³
Mass	7.35×10^{22} kilograms
Density	3.3 g/cm³
Temperature　　　Noon	110°C to 130°C (230°F to 266°F)
Midnight	−173°C (−280°F)
Synodic month (from new moon to new moon)	$29^d\ 12^h\ 44^m\ 2.8^{s}$*
Sidereal month (measured from star position)	$27^d\ 7^h\ 43^m\ 11.5^s$
Axial rotation	$27^d\ 7^h\ 43^m\ 11.5^s$
Mean orbital velocity	2,287 mi/hr
Inclination of equator to orbital plane	6° 41′
Inclination of orbital plane to ecliptic	5° 08′ 43″
Nutation	18.6 y
Surface　　{ Observable	59%
Always visible	41%
Never visible	41%
Alternately visible	18%

*y=year, d=day, h=hour, s=second (in earth time units)

MAIN IDEAS

1. The moon is a celestial body which orbits the earth in an elliptical path. The moon's orbital plane intersects the celestial equator at an angle varying from 18½° to 28½° within an 18.6 year cycle.

2. Because of its large size compared to earth and the oddities of its orbit, astronomers suggest that earth and moon may at one time have been separate planets. Possibly they may have originated in separated eddies or within a larger eddy during formation of the solar system.

3. Center of gravity for the earth-moon system lies on the side of the earth facing the moon. The system has a constant angular velocity. Changes in the rate of rotation of earth have caused the distance between earth and moon to increase.

4. An increase in the length of day on earth has resulted from tidal friction. Astronomers have predicted that, in billions of years, day and month will be approximately the same length and tides due to the moon will be fixed. Tides caused by the sun then will be a dominant influence and will upset the equilibrium of the earth-moon system. An earth day then will be shorter than a month. The moon will approach the earth to within 10,000 mi and break up into small pieces which will continue to orbit the earth.

5. Darwin believed that at one time earth and moon were part of a large liquid mass which separated, and the moon moved away from earth to its present position.

6. Only 59 percent of the moon's surface is visible from earth. Orbiting spacecraft have photographed the back and the front of the moon.

7. The surface of the moon is marked by mountains and various sized depressions. Maria are the largest depressions. Walled plains are next largest and probably the oldest features of the moon.

8. Surface materials of the moon include basaltic type lava, gravel, and meteoritic particles.

9. A geologic time scale for the moon has been worked out by using the law of superposition.

10. The spaceships which carry men to the moon contain three sections. The mothership makes the round trip but does not

land on the moon. A section carrying rockets is abandoned upon reentry into the earth's atmosphere. The moonship which carries astronauts to the moon and back to the mothership also is abandoned.

11. Escape velocity of 25,000 mi/hr is required to leave the earth's gravitational field. This velocity is attained in space after the initial thrust has sent the spaceship into orbit. Rockets operate on the Newtonian principle that for every action there is an equal and opposite reaction. Expulsion of gas from the rear of the ship causes forward thrust.

VOCABULARY

Write a sentence in which you use correctly each of the following words or terms.

angular momentum	eclipse	rays
chain craters	gibbous moon	rills
cohesive	maria	walled plains
crescent moon	protoplanet	wrinkle ridges

STUDY QUESTIONS

A. True or False

Determine whether each of the following sentences is true or false. (Do not write in this book.)

1. Dark areas on the moon which sometimes look like seas are really depressions.

2. Earth's calendar month is longer than the time required for moon's orbit around the earth.

3. The moon is the smallest planet in the solar system.

4. Moon's atmosphere is humid.

5. Earth is the only planet which has a moon.

6. Some scientists believe that the moon was once an independent planet.

7. The same side of the moon always faces the earth because the moon does not rotate.

8. An eclipse of the moon occurs when the moon is in the earth's shadow.

9. Ocean tides on earth are caused mainly by the moon's attraction for the earth.

10. Earth's rotation rate is being slowed because of tides.

B. Multiple Choice

Choose the word or phrase which completes correctly each of the following sentences. (Do not write in this book.)

1. The moon's density is (*less than, the same as, greater than*) the density of the earth.

2. The moon's surface is weathered (*more than, about the same as, less than*) the earth's surface.

3. Moon's rotational period is (*24 hours, 708 hours, 27.3 days*).

4. A total solar eclipse may be observed occasionally (*over all, in a small part, in no part*) of the earth.

5. Moon's diameter is approximately (*1,560, 2,160, 25,600*) miles.

6. When half of the moon is seen from earth, it is the (*crescent, gibbous, full*) moon.

7. Travel to the moon requires the use of the principle of (*superposition, rocketry, dominance*).

8. Astronomers will be able to study the universe better from the moon because (*planets and stars will be closer, the moon has little or no atmosphere, the moon does not rotate*).

9. At the present time, (*the moon is moving away from the earth, the moon is approaching the earth, the earth is increasing its velocity of rotation*).

10. Moon surface features which resemble spokes of a wheel are called (*rills, wrinkle ridges, rays*).

C. Completion

Complete each of the following sentences with a word or phrase which will make the sentence correct. (Do not write in this book.)

1. Because of earth's gravitational attraction and the moon's inertia, moon's orbit is ___?___.

2. A solar eclipse aids the study of the sun's ___?___.

3. The center of gravity of the earth-moon system is called the ___?___.

4. The moon returns to the same place in its orbit of the earth in __?__ days.

5. When the lighted portion of the moon appears to be convex, but not quite round, it is called a __?__ moon.

6. Mass of a body times velocity times distance of the body from the axis of rotation give the __?__.

7. The most prominent and first observed features of the moon's surface are the __?__.

8. Explosion craters on the moon appear to have been caused by __?__.

9. Astrogeologic study has determined the age of moon features by using the law of __?__.

10. The principle of physics which says that for every action there is an equal reaction, first stated by __?__, is used in the study of __?__.

D. How and Why

1. Why is the moon's surface more ancient than the present surface of the earth, if both earth and moon were formed at the same time?

2. Compare the age of the moon's surface with the age of Mars' surface.

3. What forces are acting on the moon's orbit that cause it to be an ellipse?

4. How does a study of earth's meteorite craters help interpret the craters of the moon?

5. What is the significance of the alignment of chain craters? Why are these craters not generally thought to be of meteoritic origin?

6. Why is the fog noted occasionally in some areas of the moon interpreted as a gas other than water vapor?

7. If the velocity of earth's rotation were to increase, what effect would it have on the moon's distance from earth? What theory of moon origin is based on a backward in time projection of this relationship?

8. How can the Astrogeology Branch of the U. S. Geological Survey set up a geologic time scale for the moon events?

9. Before Surveyor landings on the moon, some astronomers expected the surface to be covered with a layer of dust, per-

haps a hundred or more feet deep. What evidence has changed their minds?

10. Why did Galileo call the large depressions on the moon maria?

11. Why must the moon spaceship carry rockets?

INVESTIGATIONS

1. Report on the latest solar eclipse. Discuss the dangers in observing the sun during an eclipse. What advice could you give to an observer?

2. Through library reading, investigate myths about the moon. Find an Indian myth as well as the more common Greek and Roman myths.

3. Report on recent hard and soft landings on the moon. Discuss Russia's explorations as well as those of the United States.

INTERESTING READING

Asimov, Isaac, *The Double Planet,* rev. ed. New York, Abelard-Schuman, Ltd., 1966.

Branley, Franklyn M., *Experiments in the Principles of Space Travel.* New York, Thomas Y. Crowell Co., 1955.

Cooper, Henry S., Jr., *Moon Rocks.* New York, Dial Press, Inc., 1970.

Kosofsky, L. J., and Farouk, El-Baz, *The Moon as Viewed by Lunar Orbiter SP-200.* Washington, D. C., U. S. Government Printing Office, 1970.

*Ley, Willy, *The Conquest of Space.* New York, The Viking Press, 1949.

Page, Thornton and Lou W., *Neighbors of the Earth.* New York, The Macmillan Company, 1965.

Sutton, Felix, *The How and Why Wonder Book of the Moon.* Columbus, Ohio, Charles E. Merrill Publishing Co., 1963.

Warshofsky, Fred, *Target Moon.* New York, Four Winds Press, 1966.

---

* Well-illustrated material.

Stars and Galaxies

Beyond the solar system are countless stars. Some stars are visible to the unaided eye. Some can be seen only with the aid of a telescope. Still others can be located only through instruments such as radio telescopes. Man has devised a number of instruments with which to investigate the universe. Astronomical distance remains a barrier to travel to the stars.

24:1 *Radiant Energy*

Our knowledge of the universe depends on observing, recording, or measuring some kind of radiant energy. Light, heat, and radio waves are familiar forms of this energy. But radiant energy also includes television waves, infrared radiation, ultra-violet rays, X rays, and gamma rays. The **electromagnetic spectrum** includes all radiant energy forms arranged in the order of their wavelengths. These wavelengths range from trillionths of a millimeter to thousands of kilometers. For convenience, the spectrum has been divided into regions of different wavelengths. (Table 24-1.) Note that only part of the electromagnetic spectrum is visible.

All known forms of radiant energy travel with a velocity of approximately 186,000 mi/sec. Each form of radiant energy can be distinguished by its wavelength or frequency. **Wavelength** is the distance between successive wave crests. **Frequency** is the number of radiated waves per second.

With the aid of powerful telescopes, astronomers can see distant stars and recognize differences in their size, color, and brightness. With other instruments, astronomers also have identified elements within the stars and have discovered the process by which stars radiate energy. Each element in a star radiates energy with its own wavelength or frequency. There-

Most present knowledge about the universe is based on observations and measurements of radiant energy.

Forms of radiant energy are distinguished by wavelength or frequency.

Elements may be identified in a star's spectrum by wavelength or frequency.

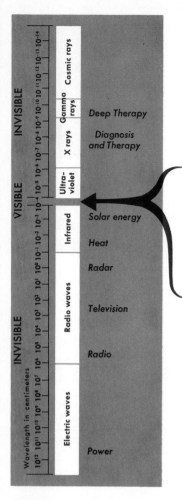

Figure 24-1. Electromagnetic spectrum.

Table 24–1. The Electromagnetic Spectrum

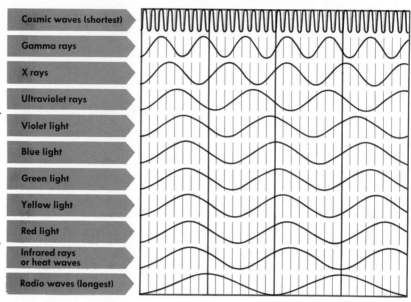

Figure 24-2.

fore, elements can be recognized in the star's spectrum by their characteristic wavelengths.

By means of an instrument called the **spectroscope** (spek′ tra skohp), visible light may be separated into a pattern called the *visible spectrum*. A similar separation of sunlight occurs after a rainstorm. Raindrops disperse light into many colors to form a rainbow. Each color of the visible spectrum has a distinct wavelength or frequency. Colors always appear in the same order—violet, indigo, blue, green, yellow, orange, and red. Violet light is at one end of the spectrum with the shortest wavelength or the highest frequency. Red light, at the other end of the visible spectrum, has the longest wavelength or the lowest frequency.

ACTIVITY. Cut a narrow slit in a square of cardboard so a thin beam of light shines through. Place a prism and the cardboard in the sun so a beam of light strikes the prism. Attach a piece of drawing paper to a clipboard and place it perpendicular to the beam of light so light will be dispersed on the paper. Indicate the bands of color on the paper. (Figure 24–2.) Do colors blend into each other or do they have distinct divisions? Use matching colors of chalk to color the bands of light as they appear in the spectrum. Which color is refracted, or bent, the most? Which color is refracted least? Which color has the longest wavelength? Which color has the shortest wavelength? Why does the sun appear to be red dur-

ing sunset and sunrise? Why does the sky often appear to be blue during the day? Which colors in a rainbow are most distinct and persist longest in the sky?

One **light-year** is the distance that light travels during one year. Light travels at approximately 186,000 mi/sec. Thus, a light-year is equal to 5,865,696,000,000 mi/yr or nearly six trillion mi/yr (6×10^{12} mi/yr). Light from even the closest stars requires several years to reach earth. You see stars and galaxies in the heavens as they were years ago, not as they exist today! Astronomers use light-years in measuring astronomical distances beyond the solar system.

One light-year equals six trillion mi/yr.

Light from the stars is studied by means of the spectroscope. This instrument separates light into its various wavelengths and frequencies. Each star gives off a *continuous spectrum*. This spectrum includes most light wavelengths or frequencies. But radiant energy from a star's interior passes outward through the star's cool surface gases. There certain wavelengths or frequencies are absorbed by the surface gases of the same wavelengths. Dark lines called *absorption lines* occur in the star's continuous spectrum where certain wavelengths of light are absorbed. These absorption lines represent the presence of a given wavelength in the surface gases. If these wavelengths match the known wavelength or frequency of a certain element, that element is known to be present in the star. Thus, astronomers can use the star's spectrum to determine its chemical composition. They also use the spectrum to determine the star's speed and direction of movement.

Stars emit light wavelengths or frequencies in a continuous spectrum crossed by dark lines.

Elements whose wavelengths or frequencies match a star's spectrum are present in the star.

Spectral lines shift toward the violet end of the spectrum if a star is approaching earth. They shift toward the red end of the spectrum if movement is away from earth. These shifts are

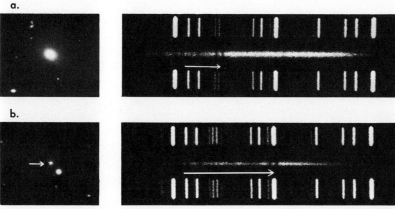

Mount Wilson and Palomar Observatories

Figure 24-3.   (a.) The red shift for Ursa Major is 9,300 miles per second. Its distance from earth is estimated to be 560 million light-years. (b.) Bootes' red shift is 24,400 miles per second. Its distance from earth is estimated to be 1,290 million light-years. Note the spreading of the spectral lines.

called the **Doppler** (dahp′ ler) **effect** for a well-known Austrian physicist. They have been observed for thousands of stars over a period of many years.

When the wave source is approaching the observer, waves are crowded together. Then the wavelength is shortened. When the wave source is receding, waves are spread apart. Then the wavelength is increased. (Figure 24–3.) The Doppler effect may be compared to the characteristics of approaching and receding sound waves. As you wait for a train to approach, the frequency of the sound waves increases. Then the pitch becomes higher and higher. As the train passes and moves farther away, the frequency of the waves decreases and the pitch becomes lower and lower.

Violet light has high frequencies or short wavelengths. Red light has low frequencies or long wavelengths. Approaching stars produce lines shifted toward the violet end of the spectrum. Stars receding from earth produce lines shifted toward the red end of the spectrum. Galaxies show only a red shift, according to present observations. Thus, they seem to be moving away from earth.

24:2   *Stars*

Figure 24-4. Surfaces A, B, C, and D illustrate that the amount of light reaching an object varies inversely as the square of the distance (*d*) from the light source (I_s). The brightness (*I*) at any distance from the source may be written mathematically as $I = \dfrac{I_s}{d^2}$.

Stars are self-luminous spheres of gas. Some stars appear bright because they are relatively near the earth. Others appear bright because they are massive and give off more radiant energy. Stars are classified according to their brightness or *magnitude* (mag′ na teud). In order to compare the brightness among stars, astronomers need a common standard. For this standard, astronomers calculate the brightness of a star at

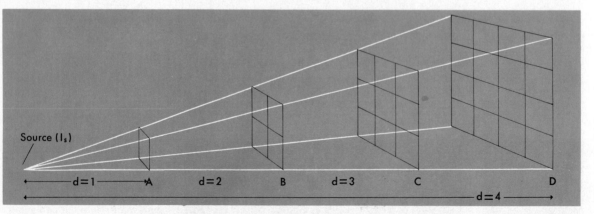

Source (I_s)

d=1   A   d=2   B   d=3   C   D

d=4

Figure 24-5. The great cluster of Hercules, at least 100 light-years across, contains more than 50,000 stars bright enough for observation and probably many dwarf stars too small to be recognized at a distance of 35,000 light-years from earth.

a distance of 32.6 light-years (10 parsecs). This brightness is called **absolute magnitude. Apparent magnitude** is the brightness of a star observed at its actual distance from earth. The apparent brightness of a light source decreases with the square of the distance from the observer. Thus, absolute magnitude can be computed from the apparent magnitude if the distance to a star is known. (Figure 24–4.)

According to present theory, stars are formed from nebulae, or concentrations of interstellar matter. Dense clouds of dust and gas as small as one light-year in diameter condense to form some stars. But masses of interstellar material equal to about 1,000 suns also form stars. During condensation, a nebula this large may break up into many parts. The parts then condense into clusters of stars instead of into a single star.

As condensation takes place within a nebula, temperatures rise higher and higher. Eventually the temperature is high enough for transmutation of hydrogen to helium to occur. Then the mass begins to give off radiant energy, and a star is born. The radiant energy is formed in the star's interior and released at the star's surface at the same rate at which it forms. Thus, a star maintains a relatively constant size, shape, and brightness during most of its life. But when most of the hydrogen in the star's interior has been changed to helium, the core collapses. During collapse, the temperature rises. Then transmutation of hydrogen begins in the star's outer gases. These gases expand during transmutation, and the star brightens.

Parsec is a unit of measure for interstellar space, equal to 3.26 light-years.

Stars form when concentrations of interstellar matter condense and become self-luminous.

Stars become luminous when transmutation of hydrogen to helium begins.

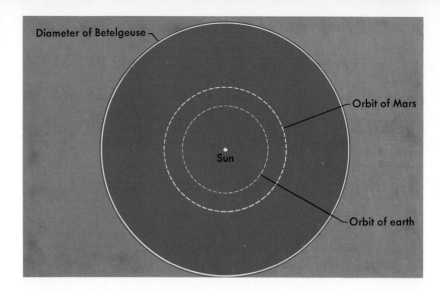

Diameter of Betelgeuse

Orbit of Mars

Sun

Orbit of earth

Figure 24-7. A star's position in this Hertzsprung-Russell diagram is determined by plotting its absolute magnitude and its temperature.

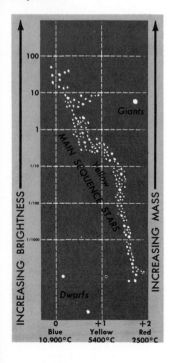

In the final stages of a star's life history, all fuel for nuclear reactions has been consumed. Then the star collapses into an extremely dense sphere. This sphere continues to shine until its internal heat is lost to space. When all its heat is lost, the star becomes dark. This entire process may take over 10 billion years.

Astronomers recognize several different kinds of stars. One way of classifying stars is to plot them on a diagram according to absolute magnitude and temperature. (Figure 24–7.) A narrow band of points runs from the upper left corner to the lower right corner of the diagram. Stars that fall within this band are called **main sequence stars.** Main sequence stars are in a state of equilibrium or balance. Hot, bright stars are in the upper left. Cool, less bright stars are in the lower right. Color varies with temperature. Blue stars have surface temperatures of 20,000°C (36,000°F). Blue stars are the most massive and have the highest temperatures. White stars have surface temperatures of about 9,000°C (17,000°F). Yellow star temperatures are about 6,000°C (10,000°F). Red stars range from 2,200°C to 3,700°C (7,000°F). Red stars are the smallest and coolest of the main sequence stars.

Giants and **supergiants** fall outside the main sequence. They are abnormally large, massive, bright stars. Supergiants are brighter and more massive than giants. They also are more rare, but otherwise the stars are the same. Giants and supergiants are in an advanced stage of evolution. Hydrogen in the core of such stars already has been consumed. Nuclear reactions now are in progress in the outer gases. Giants may be either red or yellow. Supergiants may be white, blue, yellow, or red.

White dwarfs also fall outside the main sequence. They are faint stars in the last stage of stellar evolution. In white dwarfs all particles of matter are tightly packed. One cubic inch of their material would weigh about one ton. Too little space is avaliable for electrons and protons to form normal atoms. Probably all matter in the white dwarfs is in the form of tightly packed neutrons.

Variable stars are stars that vary in brightness. The variations may be due to some characteristics within the star, or the variation may result from conditions outside the star. Variable stars include novae, supernovae, Cepheids, and eclipsing stars.

Novae (noh' vee) and **supernovae** brighten rapidly, then gradually dim. In some stars the magnitude increases only once. In other stars recurring bursts of brightness take place. Supernovae are more massive than novae, but otherwise the two are similar. Supernovae lose mass and some may disappear after a period of exceptional brightness. Supernovae explode only once in a lifetime, during which they add tremendous amounts of gaseous material to space. Novae appear to be stars in the process of collapsing to become white dwarfs.

Novae and supernovae differ in mass, but otherwise are similar.

Supernovae lose mass and some disappear after a period of exceptional brightness.

Mount Wilson and Palomar Observatories

Figure 24-8. Crab Nebula in Taurus, a remnant of a supernova, consists of rapidly moving electrons at the center surrounded by outward expanding gases.

The Crab Nebula is a remnant of a supernova observed by Chinese astronomers in 1054 A.D. The Chinese observed this exceptionally bright star over a period of two years. Then the star disappeared from view. Now the Crab Nebula is recognized as a source of radio noise, X rays, and visible light. The Crab Nebula is now only a mass of expanding gases. A similar brilliant star was observed in 1572 by Tycho Brahe, a Danish astronomer. Six or seven such supernovae have been reported during the past 2,000 years. Although such stars may become invisible, their radio waves and X rays persist. Eventually they may become white dwarfs.

Cepheids (see' fee ids) belong to the class of variable stars that have periodic pulsation. These stars are not in equilibrium. The star's outer layers alternately expand and contract. During expansion, surface temperatures decrease. During contraction, surface temperatures increase. Differences between the maximum and minimum temperatures may be about 700°C to 1,200°C (1,300°F to 2,200°F). When the star is hottest, it is yellow. As it cools, it becomes orange.

Cepheids are variable stars that have regular pulsations.

Cepheids pulsate with almost perfect regularity. Harlow Shapley of the Mount Wilson Observatory discovered that bright, massive Cepheids have longer cycles than small, dim Cepheids. Astronomers assume that Cepheids in distant galaxies have the same relationship between brightness and length of cycle that is shown by nearby Cepheids. Therefore,

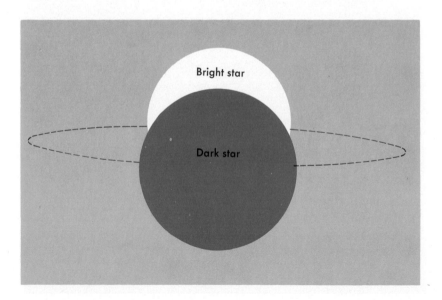

Figure 24-9. Eclipsing variables change magnitude as the brighter star of a pair passes behind the darker star.

the length of its cycle is a clue to the true brightness of a Cepheid and to its distance from earth.

An astronomer finds the apparent magnitude of a Cepheid by observation. He then determines absolute magnitude from the length of its cycle. Brightness decreases with the square of the distance from the source of light. (Figure 24–4.) Thus, the following formula can be used to calculate distance to a star, if its apparent magnitude and true magnitude are known.

$$I = \frac{I_0}{d^2}$$

Where I_0 represents brightness at a distance of 32.6 light-years; I represents brightness at a distance d from observer.

Eclipsing variables are stars that appear to change magnitude because they have partners that are dim. The two stars orbit around a common point. Therefore, an observer alternately sees a bright light followed by a dim light. Both lights appear to come from the same point in the sky.

Cycle of a Cepheid is used to calculate a star's distance from earth.

Eclipsing variables are two stars of different brightness that orbit a common point.

EXPERIMENT. Study a star chart until you can locate at least four major constellations in the northern sky. These northern constellations seem to circle the North Star, Polaris *(pa lar'us). Polaris is the apparent extension of the North Pole into the celestial sphere.*

Make the following observations of the sky with the help of one or two companions. On a clear, moonless night at 8:00, stand outside where you have an unobstructed view to the north. Use a compass to find true north. Starting at the horizon, look gradually toward the zenith until you locate Polaris, the bright star exactly north of your position. Two patterns of stars will guide you. Polaris is the last bright star in the handle of the constellation called the Little Dipper. *The two bright stars that make up the bowl of the* Big Dipper *are called the* Pointers *because they are always in a straight line with Polaris.*

Use a string with a weight on one end and a pencil on the other. Point the pencil at Polaris and let the string hang free for a guideline to the position of the stars. Plot these positions on a sheet of drawing paper and mark each star with X_1. You should have plotted the stars of both the Little Dipper and the Big Dipper. Repeat this procedure again at 9:00. This time mark each star position with X_2. Do the X_1 stars and the X_2 stars form the same pattern? If there is any change, what is it? Does this prove that the stars are moving?

Yerkes Observatory Photograph

Figure 24-11. Compare these star trails with yours.

ACTIVITY. Use a camera which has a time exposure control and which can be braced, and the most sensitive film available. Go outside just after dark on a clear, moonless night. Locate Polaris and arrange the camera so that Polaris is in the center of the lens. Brace the camera in this position and set the focus on infinity. (Figure 24–12.) Open shutter for a time exposure. Leave the camera set up for two hours and then close the shutter.

Note: Explain the nature of the film to your dealer and request that the film be developed with great care. What does the print show? What are the lines in the picture and why do they curve? What is the most central point of light?

EXPERIMENT. On a piece of drawing paper 10 inches square, draw a circle with a diameter of 8 in. Put an X in the center of the circle to indicate the North Star, Polaris. Divide the circumference of the circle into twelve equal sections and label the sections for the months of the year in sequence. Put thirty dots along each arc to represent the days of the month.

Go outside just after dark on a clear, moonless night. Be sure to make your observations at the same time every night. Face north and hold the diagram up with the dot which represents the date of your observation at the top of the chart. Note the positions of Ursa Major and Ursa Minor and put them on the diagram. Be sure to locate them in relation to Polaris. Add Cassiopeia (kas ee a pee'a), Cepheus (see'feus), and Draco (drae'koh). In two weeks, compare your calendar and the star positions to see if the constellations are correct for that date. Remember, the correct date is always at the top of the chart as you face north. If you did not know today's date, how could you use a star calendar to determine the approximate date? Could you use this star chart in the Southern Hemisphere? Explain your answer.

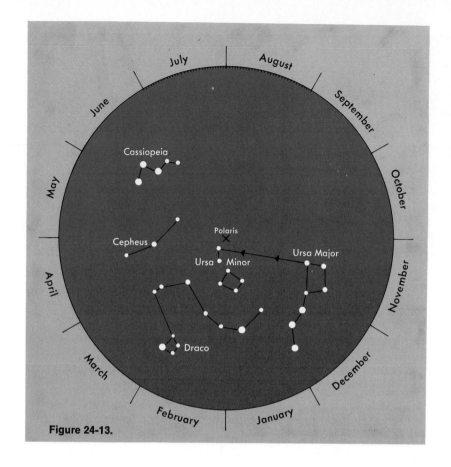

Figure 24-13.

24:3 *Galaxies*

Galaxies are very large groups of stars. They contain billions of stars. Galaxies are observed outward in space in all directions as far as man can see with modern telescopes. They have not always been recognized as groups of stars because they are so far away. A 100-inch telescope was installed in 1920 at Mount Wilson, California. Then for the first time, stars could be seen in regions of the sky that formerly had appeared as faintly glowing spots call *nebulae.* In 1924 Edwin Hubble, a California astronomer, examined certain gaseous nebulae which were thought to be within our Galaxy. He was able to see stars in many of these areas. By noting the presence of Cepheids, Hubble was able to show that the nebulae were outside our Galaxy. He believed the nebulae were star systems similar to our Galaxy. He concluded that such galaxies continued to the visible limits of the universe. Hubble estimated the universe to extend outward approximately one billion light-years.

Mount Wilson and Palomar Observatories

Figure 24-14. Spiral galaxy in Virgo as seen on edge.

Today, most astronomers estimate the visible limits of the universe to be more than ten billion light-years away.

PROBLEM

1. Our nearest star, other than the sun, is 4.3 light-years away from earth. Calculate this distance in miles.

Galaxies have been classified according to their appearance. **Irregular galaxies,** as their name implies, have irregular boundaries. They contain an abundance of gas and dust and some of them appear to be developing spiral arms. Gases are somewhat more concentrated in these developing arms which seem to be rotating around a center. Most stars in irregular galaxies appear to be large. They probably are in an early

Figure 24-15. Mosaic of the Milky Way from Sagittarius to Cassiopeia.

Mount Wilson and Palomar Observatories

stage of stellar evolution. **Spiral galaxies** consist of one or more spiral arms that rotate around a distinct, relatively dense nucleus. Stars in the central hub are probably older than stars in the spiral arms. The spiral arms contain great quantities of cosmic dust and gas. Possibly these concentrations of cosmic matter have not yet been formed into true stars. **Elliptical galaxies** are symmetrical. They range from spheres to flattened ellipsoids or disks. Such galaxies contain little dust and gas. These cosmic materials may already have been formed into stars.

The **Milky Way,** which appears in the sky as a band of indistinct light, is the galaxy to which our solar system belongs. The Milky Way is a spiral galaxy, with a diameter of about 80,000 light-years. It contains approximately 100 billion to 200 billion stars. Almost all of them are at least 100 light-years distant from earth. Light which today reaches earth from the star *Alpha Centauri* (al'fa · sen tawr'ee) left there 4.3 years ago. Yet Alpha Centauri is the nearest star to our solar system! Our sun is about ⅔ of the way between the center and outer edge of our Galaxy. The sun travels at a rate of approximately 500,000 mi/hr and carries the rest of the solar system along with it. About 250 million years are required for the sun and its planets to complete a revolution of our Galaxy.

Two nearby galaxies are known as the *Magellanic* (maj e lan'ik) *Clouds.* The Large Magellanic Cloud, the exterior galaxy closest to us, is 160,000 light-years from earth. The Small Magellanic Cloud is at a distance of 180,000 light-years. *Andromeda* (an drahm'ed a) *Galaxy*, about 2,200,000 light-years away, is the most distant galaxy visible to the unaided eye. It is a spiral galaxy similar to our Galaxy in size and shape.

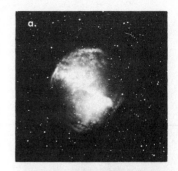

Mount Wilson and Palomar Observatories

Figure 24-16. **(a.) Dumbell Nebula in Vulpecula ejects gases at a relatively low velocity. (b.) Horsehead Nebula in Orion is a large mass of interstellar gas and dust that obscures the stars behind it.**

Revolution of the Milky Way by the sun requires 250 million years.

Figure 24-17. **Normal spiral galaxies representing evolutionary stages from the young tightly wound type (a.) through the more loosely wound older types (b.), (c.), and (d.).**

24:4 Radio Sources

Mount Wilson and Palomar Observatories

Figure 24-18. In 1961, Allan R. Sandage discovered 3 C 48, the first star-like object found at the location of a strong well-known radio source.

Apparent red shift of quasars suggests that they are the most distant celestial objects, according to some astronomers.

Quasars are small compared to galaxies but produce vast amounts of energy.

Astronomers have been familiar with stars for centuries and with the concept of galaxies for almost 50 years. But recently, another type of celestial body has been observed. These newly recognized bodies are called **quasars** (kwae′sars). This name was coined by Dr. H. Y. Chiu of Goddard Institute for Space Studies. The name is a substitute for the term **"quasi stellar radio sources."** Quasars are powerful sources of radio energy. They have been called "quasi stellar" because they seem to be starlike objects but actually do not appear to be stars. Quasars are celestial objects different from anything known previously.

Quasars were discovered in March, 1963. Radio astronomers in Australia and California pinpointed the location of five sources of radio noise in space. These five locations then were photographed from the Mount Wilson and Palomar Observatories. Faint, starlike objects appeared on the photographic plates at the locations of the radio noise. Except for the sun, these were the first so-called "radio stars" to be photographed and identified as local radio sources.

Astronomers at Mount Wilson and Palomar Observatories recorded the light spectrum from two of the quasars. Wavelengths of light emitted by hydrogen were recognized. However, they were at longer wavelengths than similar lines emitted in earth laboratories. The increase in wavelength toward the red part of the light spectrum is known as the **red shift.** Astronomers showed that as the distance to a galaxy increased, the shift toward the red end of the spectrum became faster. Thus, apparently the faster a galaxy appears to move away from earth, from the solar system, or from our Galaxy, the more distant the galaxy is.

Astronomers have found the red shifts of quasars to be greater than the shift for visible galaxies. Their shifts suggest that quasars may be the most distant and brightest objects in the universe. But quasars are only three light-years or less in diameter. Diameters of typical galaxies measure in tens of thousands of light-years. Typical galaxies contain 100 billion stars or more. Quasar light may appear faint on photographic plates because quasars are so distant. But if quasars are as distant as they seem, they must give off many times more light than the brightest galaxies. It is difficult to understand how any object can outshine 100 billion stars.

Some astronomers believe that quasars are not as distant as their red shifts suggest. They think that quasars possess enormous speed but are less than 100 million light-years from earth. If quasars are this close, then normal processes within stars may account for their release of energy. But no one has accounted for the high rate of speed suggested. The problem of the red shift is still unsolved.

Pulsars are other newly discovered radio sources. They are neutron stars which are extremely dense. Probably pulsars are residues of exploded stars or supernova. They pulse at an extremely uniform rate from 0.25 sec to 1.96 sec. These rates are so constant that they are expected not to vary even one sec in 30 billion years.

Pulsars have been discovered in the Crab Nebula by several astronomers. John Coche, Michael Disney, and Donald Taylor from Arizona searched Crab Nebula because it is a well-known source of radio waves. But these radio waves were not known to be connected with a starlike body. The Arizona astronomers trained their telescope on a small pinpoint of light in Crab Nebula. They found that the light flashed 30 times per second. These flashes agreed with radio pulses previously recorded. Now several astronomers from other observatories have confirmed the presence of pulsars in Crab Nebula.

> Some astronomers believe quasars are within one hundred million light years of earth but moving away at enormous speed.

24:5 *Optical Telescopes*

Modern astronomers have learned much about the chemical composition and physical state of celestial bodies. They also have been able to draw conclusions about the motions of stars, galaxies, and quasars. This new understanding was made possible by the development of astronomical tools.

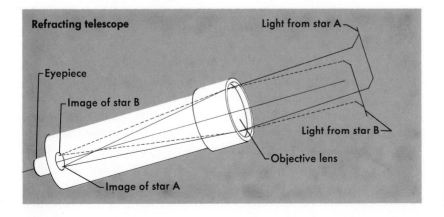

Refracting telescope

Light from star A

Eyepiece

Image of star B

Light from star B

Objective lens

Image of star A

Figure 24-19. Starlight that enters the objective lens of a refracting telescope is observed through the eyepiece.

Figure 24-20.   By sighting through the eyepiece of this astronomical quadrant, a star's altitude could be determined.

Problems associated with producing flawless glass of large area limits the size of refracting telescope lenses.

The earliest astronomical tool was the **quadrant** (kwahd′rant), or quarter circle. It was used to measure the altitude of stars. A quadrant consists of an arc divided into 90°. A simple sighting index is used to measure the position of a celestial body above the horizon.

Then Galileo developed an "optik tube," a type of telescope called a **refractor** or **refracting telescope.** It has a large front lens, or *objective*. A second lens, called the *ocular*, forms the eyepiece at the opposite end of the tube. The objective lens collects light and bends or refracts light rays toward a focal point. A *focal point* is the position where a small image of an object is formed. *Focal length* is the distance between the focal point and the lens. Ocular lenses magnify an image formed by the objective. Image size is proportional to the focal length of the objective and the ocular lens.

Refracting telescopes are usually long and rather unwieldy. Astronomical refracting telescopes are similar to spyglasses. However, in a spyglass both the objective and ocular lenses are mounted in sliding metal tubes. Sliding tubes make it possible to adjust the position of an image to the focal length of each lens. Also, spyglasses usually are fitted with an additional lens to turn the image right side up for the viewer. In astronomical telescopes, the additional lens is omitted and the star's image is inverted. Stars appear much the same whether or not they are upside down. The extra lens would reduce the efficiency of the telescope by causing a loss of light.

Refracting telescopes used by amateur astronomers are limited in size. Usually the diameter of the objective lens is 3 in. or less. The tube length is about 5 ft. Galileo's telescope had a paper tube 4 ft long. Its objective was 2 in. in diameter. Magnification with Galileo's telescope was 32 times, but its field of view was small. Yerkes Observatory in Wisconsin has the largest refractor telescope. Its focal length is 60 ft and its objective has a 40 in. diameter.

The size of the objective of a refracting telescope is limited because preparing bubble-free optical glass of large area is so difficult. Costs rise rapidly as lens size increases. Grinding and polishing a large lens is difficult and expensive, and there is a practical limit to the diameter of a lens. But large diameter lenses are desirable because they collect more light than small lenses. Collection of light is the basic function of the telescope. The amount of light collected depends on the area of the objective. As the amount of collected light increases, stars that are too faint or too distant to be seen with smaller telescopes can be observed and photographed.

To overcome the size limitation of an objective lens, *concave mirrors* are used. Mirrors are easier and cheaper to produce than lenses because mirrors do not require bubble-free glass. An aluminum reflective coating on the front surface of a mirror prevents light from passing through the glass. Bubbles and flaws within the glass are relatively unimportant if the light does not pass through it. Telescopes that use concave mirrors instead of lenses are called **reflector telescopes.** Sir Isaac Newton invented the reflector telescope in 1668.

Mirrors do not require flawless glass, and may be larger than lenses.

In a reflector telescope, a concave mirror collects light from a star and produces a small image at the focal point of the mirror. Most reflectors have a mirror, tilted at a 45° angle to the axis of the concave mirror. The mirror reflects the image to the eyepiece. The eyepiece is mounted on the side of the tube housing the concave mirror. The eyepiece magnifies the star's image.

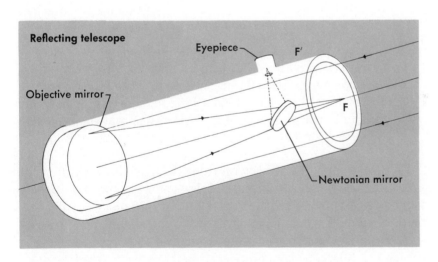

Figure 24-21. In the reflecting telescope, light is reflected from objective to eyepiece.

A reflector mirror is cheaper and easier to build than a lens of equal diameter. Large mirrors are ground from optical glass which has been cast in a mold. Cooling is carefully controlled at a slow rate to avoid internal strain. Palomar Mountain Observatory has the world's largest optical telescope. Its mirror has a diameter of 200 in. Cooling of the cast mirror blank continued for almost one and a half years after the molten glass was poured into the mold.

Figure 24-22. Dome of the 200-inch Hale telescope, largest in the world, at Mount Wilson and Palomar Observatories.

Mount Wilson and Palomar Observatories

Figure 24-23. The equatorial mounting permits the telescope to point to any spot in the sky and to compensate for rotation of the earth.

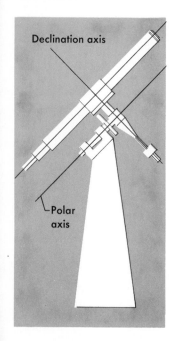

Declination axis

Polar axis

PROBLEM

2. Yerkes Observatory has the world's largest refracting telescope with a lens diameter of 40 in. Palomar Mountain Observatory has the world's largest reflecting telescope with a mirror diameter of 200 in. Which telescope collects the most light? How much more light is collected?

Telescopes must be readily movable in order to view different areas of the sky. In a stationary telescope a star would appear to move westward. Eventually, the star would move beyond the field of view. This apparent westward movement of stars results from the earth's rotation. To cancel the effect of earth's rotation, a telescope is mounted so that it runs on an axis called the *polar axis*. The polar axis of a telescope is parallel to the earth's axis. The ends of the axis point toward the celestial poles. (Section 22:3.) Usually a clock or motor drive turns the telescope on its polar axis. It moves at the same rate of speed as the rotation of the earth but in the opposite direction. A telescope is mounted at an angle with a horizontal plane equal to the latitude of the observatory.

The second axis of the telescope is called the *declination axis*. This axis is perpendicular to the polar axis. As a telescope turns on the declination axis, it moves northward or southward. The polar axis and declination axis make it possible to aim a telescope at any point in the sky. This type of telescopic mounting is known as an *equatorial mounting*.

Astronomers use telescopes to study celestial objects through both visual observation and photography. Photography of the night sky has become increasingly common since 1850. Reflector telescopes are adapted to camera work better than refractor telescopes. Refractor lenses cannot transmit ultraviolet radiation. But ultraviolet radiation is important in astronomical photography. Reflective coatings of mirrors have been improved to the point where photography of the whole ultraviolet range of the light spectrum is possible. Photographic plates are especially sensitive to this part of the spectrum. All major observatories now have cameras or plateholders attached to their telescopes.

Cameras have many advantages over direct observation. Pictures may record light which the eye cannot see. Long time exposures allow the effect of faint light rays to accumulate

Movement of a telescope on the polar axis compensates for earth's rotation.

Yerkes Observatory Photograph

Figure 24-24. Yerkes Observatory, Wisconsin, has a 40-inch refracting telescope, the largest refracting telescope in the world.

until light becomes visible on a developed photographic plate. Plates also provide permanent records. From plates, measurements of stars may be determined and rechecked at a later date. With the help of a microscope, distance between stars can be measured accurately and their positions determined on a photographic plate. Measurements of similar accuracy would be almost impossible with direct viewing alone. Furthermore, special processes permit computation of a star's distance from earth. Combined camera and telescopic observations have produced a great expansion in astronomical knowledge.

New methods and types of cameras continue to be adapted to telescopic work. For example, **television cameras** may be attached to the eyepiece of a telescope. The star's image is brightened and improved on a television screen. Pictures can be made from this bright image. Still another improvement in photographic equipment is the **Schmidt camera.** This camera has been useful in discovering many new stars. Before 1930, it was impossible to photograph large areas of the sky successfully. Blurred images always appeared at the edge of the field of view. In 1930, Bernhard Schmidt, a German astronomer, devised a specially shaped glass plate which he placed in front of the reflector mirror. This type of plate prevents a blurred image. Palomar Mountain Observatory now uses a 48-in. Schmidt camera.

Schmidt's camera improved the quality of wide-area photographs.

Another useful device is the **photometer** (foh tahm′e ter). Photometers measure the intensity of light received from celestial objects. In 1725, the brightness of sun and moon was compared to candlelight. But after 1830, several devices for measuring light intensity became available. One early photometer used an electric light bulb to create a starlike image. Brightness of this image could be adjusted to match the brightness of stars or planets under observation. This early instrument depended upon visual comparison. Today, highly accurate photometers are used. They depend on photoelectric methods of measurement.

Actual photographs of celestial bodies are of great interest to astronomers. But from a scientific viewpoint, perhaps even more information is obtained from photographs of the spectra of stars.

Spectroscopes are instruments that separate visible light into various wavelengths or frequencies. Separation is done by means of either glass prisms or ruled gratings. Ruled gratings are pieces of glass or highly polished metal on which a large

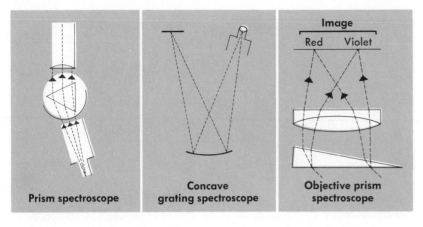

Image

Red   Violet

Prism spectroscope

Concave grating spectroscope

Objective prism spectroscope

number of closely spaced, fine parallel lines have been drawn. Small spectroscopes may have glass prisms, glass gratings, or aluminum-coated glass. Large spectroscopes usually have metal gratings. Standard grating spacing varies from 5,000 to 30,000 lines/in.

A *slit* admits light to the spectroscope. Usually the width of the slit can be adjusted to between 1.0 mm and 0.005 mm. Each line in the spectrum is a single color image of the slit. Although slits are used with most spectroscopes, slitless spectroscopes have been developed for special kinds of work with stars.

Spectroscopes in which cameras or plate holders replace the eyepiece are called **spectrographs.** Spectrographs are used to photograph the spectra of stars. These photographs are known as **spectrograms.**

Spectrograms of stars are interpreted by comparing them with the spectrum of iron. The iron spectrum is used for comparison because iron produces spectral lines through the entire visible light range. This comparison aids astronomers in recognizing the presence of the red shift for stars or galaxies. Usually iron's spectrum is photographed first and placed at the top of the photograph. Next the star's spectrum is photographed and placed in the middle. Then another photograph of iron's spectrum is placed at the bottom. Before and after pictures show any changes in temperature or air movements. Such changes distort the star's spectrum during photographing. Comparison of the star's spectrum with the iron spectrum shows if corrections are necessary for changed conditions. Spectrum lines of a star are identified by measuring wavelengths. Astronomers use either specially designed measuring instruments or microscopes.

Heat sensitive spectrographs have been designed to measure the infrared spectrum. Infrared has a longer wavelength than

Spectrographs are spectroscopes which use cameras in place of eyepieces.

A star's spectrum is compared to the spectrum of iron as a standard.

Figure 24-26. Most of the large solar telescope at Kitt Peak, Arizona, is beneath the surface of the earth.

Figure 24-27. The length of the solar telescope at Kitt Peak is 500 feet. This great length reduces the intensity of sunlight so it can be studied.

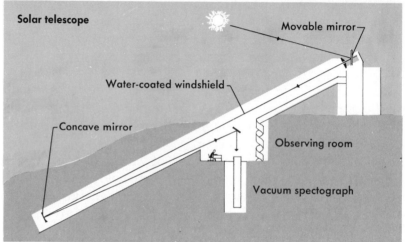

Solar telescope

Movable mirror

Water-coated windshield

Concave mirror

Observing room

Vacuum spectograph

Figure 24-28. The interior of a large reflecting telescope at Kitt Peak National Observatory.

Radiometers are used with reflector telescopes to study the infrared portion of a star's spectrum.

the red end of the visible spectrum. A sensitive heat detector called a **radiometer** is placed at the focal point of a reflector telescope. Radiometers measure the amount of heat produced by the incoming radiant energy from a celestial object. Various types of radiometers include *bolometers, vacuum thermocouples,* or *thermopiles.* These devices convert radiant energy to electrical output. Output is amplified and automatically recorded. At the same time, the celestial body is being scanned by the telescope. Infrared spectrograms have been used to identify gases in planetary atmospheres and to measure the temperature of planets and stars.

Infrared spectrograms are used in identification of planetary atmospheric gases and to measure temperatures of planets and stars.

Some astronomical devices have been designed especially for studying the sun. The sun's spectrum has been compared with the standard laboratory spectra of known elements and 67 elements have been identified.

At Mount Wilson Observatory, a specially designed 150-ft tower has been constructed for the study of the sun. A mirror is placed at the top of the tower in order to avoid air movements caused by the sun's heating of the ground surface. Precautions are taken to avoid the effect of air currents because they might distort the sun's spectrum. The laboratory is located below ground level. There a uniform temperature is maintained. A mirror system transmits a beam of parallel sunlight through an insulated tube from the top of the tower to the laboratory.

An instrument called the **spectroheliograph** makes it possible to photograph the sun in the light of a single wavelength. Spectroheliographs are similar to spectrographs except that the spectroheliograph has two slits instead of one. The second slit is located in front of the photographic plate. It allows light from only one element to strike the photographic plate. Thus, the sun can be photographed with the light of elements such as calcium, potassium, or hydrogen in the sun's surface. Distribution and movement of these elements in the sun can be recorded and studied.

Spectroheliographs make it possible to photograph the sun in the light of a single element.

Coronographs are instruments which are used in photographing the sun's corona, solar prominences, and chromosphere. Coronographs eliminate light from the photosphere in photographs. By creating an artificial eclipse of the photosphere, the coronograph makes it possible to take spectacular motion pictures, particularly of the prominences.

Coronographs act as artificial eclipses to eliminate light from the photosphere in photographs of the sun.

24:6   *Radio Astronomy*

Radio astronomy is a study of radio waves that originate from celestial bodies. Radio astronomy began in 1932. Then Karl Jensky of Bell Telephone Laboratories discovered radio

Radio astronomy is a study of radio waves originating from celestial bodies.

Figure 24-29. This radio telescope at Goldstone, California, a part of the Deep Space Network, is engaged in collecting radio signals from outer space.

Unlike visible waves, many radio waves are not blocked out by cosmic dust and gas.

wavelengths coming from the Milky Way. In 1939, Grote Reber, an amateur radio operator at Wheaton, Illinois, built the first radio telescope.

The importance of radio astronomy is great. Unlike visible waves, few radio waves are blocked out by cosmic dust and gas. Radio waves also move through clouds and turbulent air. Dust in outer space hides much of the universe from view. In the earth's atmosphere, clouds and turbulent air movements disturb visual observations and photography of the sky. But radio observations can be carried out night and day without interference.

Radio astronomy is also important in exploring the universe beyond the reaches of optical telescopes. Indeed, radio astronomy is the only way in which the invisible, most distant parts of our universe can be studied. Two types of radio waves reach earth from space. These are thermal waves and non-thermal waves. Like light, thermal radiation is generated by hot particles or objects. Non-thermal radio waves probably occur when high speed electrons react with a magnetic field.

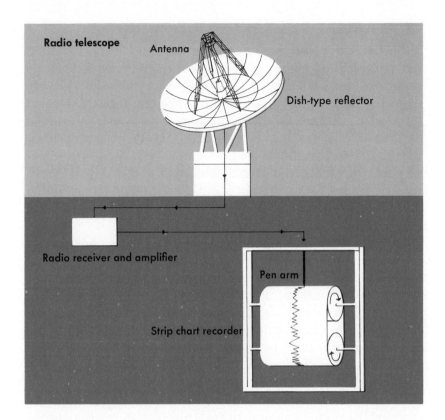

Figure 24-30. The radio telescope consists of a dish for concentrating radio waves on the antenna, an amplifier, and a recorder which transcribes the signals.

A radio telescope consists of a *reflector*, or *dish*, a *directional antenna*, and a highly sensitive *radio receiver*. Receivers are used to detect and amplify radio waves. They also select wavelengths within narrow limits or bands. Receivers are connected to a recording meter. The meter charts the power of incoming radio waves. The efficiency of the receiver depends on the power of incoming radio waves compared to the noise created within the receiver.

Antennas of radio telescopes collect radio waves in the way that optical telescopes collect light waves. Radio waves are collected from a desired direction and focused for the receiver. Each antenna has a *dipole* which consists of two insulated metal rods or wires placed in line. Dipoles receive best those wavelengths that come from a direction perpendicular to the rods or wires.

The radio telescope reflector, often called a *dish*, is concave. Its function is similar to that of the reflector of an optical telescope. In order to collect radio waves of many wavelengths, reflectors must have a large diameter. Solid metal reflectors are costly and difficult to build, but reflectors need not be of solid

Radio telescopes have directional antennas which collect radio waves.

Dipoles consist of two insulated metal rods placed at the focal point of a reflector mirror.

metal. Instead, metal mesh or screen wire may be used. Use of wire reduces the weight and the area of the reflector exposed to wind pressure. Like optical telescopes, radio telescopes need to be built so they can be aimed toward different areas of the sky. But as size is increased, it becomes more and more difficult to construct a reflector that is steerable. The Jodrell Bank, England, radio telescope has a steerable dish with a 250-ft diameter. Other large, steerable radio telescopes in the United States have diameters ranging from about 20 ft to more than 200 ft. The 1,000-ft diameter dish of the telescope at Arecibo, Puerto Rico, however, is not steerable.

The only drawback of radio telescopes is that they do not distinguish between energy sources as efficiently as optical telescopes. Radio telescopes can separate sources of power that are degrees, or perhaps minutes, apart. But Palomar's 200-in. reflector telescope can identify sources of light that are only a few hundredths of a second apart. The larger the dish of a radio telescope, the greater its ability to distinguish between separate sources of radiation. But unlimited increase in dish size is impractical.

A radio **interferometer** is a device used to improve the efficiency of the radio telescope. In fact, quasars were located first through the interferometer. When separate dishes are attached to the same receiver, they have the effect of a single dish of huge proportions. The *resolving power*, or ability to distinguish between sources of radiation, is improved. An interferometer may have two or more antennas separated by several thousand feet. All antennas are connected to the same radio receiver. Astronomers at the University of Manchester, Australia, use antennas that are separated by about 75 mi.

Radio spectroscopy is a tool which astronomers have used since 1951. Through the use of the Doppler shift of hydrogen lines, the velocity of radio sources can be measured. In this way the velocity of quasars and radio galaxies has been determined. The spiral arms of the Milky Way Galaxy were traced through radio spectroscopy.

Radar is a method of finding objects through the use of radio waves. Originally radar was known as *r*adio *d*etecting *a*nd *r*anging. Radar waves are pulses sent out from a transmitter and reflected to a receiver placed near the transmitter. An object beyond the range of sight can be found, and its distance determined by radar.

Radar measures the travel time of wavelengths from 0.1 cm up to 10 meters. Pulses are sent out in search of a given object.

When the object is located, pulses are reflected to the receiver. Travel time of the pulse from transmitter to receiver can be measured to about one millionth of a second. One half the travel time is a measure of the distance between transmitter and object. Like the sound of an echo, only a small fraction of energy returns to the receiver. (Section 11:4.)

Radar originally was designed to detect objects on or near earth. But astronomers now make use of radar waves for finding celestial objects. Microwaves are particularly useful in studying the planets. (Section 22:5.) Radar is being used to determine distances to planets. The rate and direction of rotation and the characteristics of planetary surfaces also can be determined by radar.

Galileo with his telescope made observations that opened an era of research and scientific understanding. Many scientists have followed in his footsteps or found new paths to travel in attempting to solve problems concerning the universe. Each new instrument and each new measurement opens further possibilities of knowledge. But every discovery brings new questions. Pursuit of scientific knowledge and understanding remains a never-ending quest.

Radar waves are pulses sent out from a transmitter and reflected to a receiver placed near the transmitter.

Radar waves are used to measure distances, rotation, and surface characteristics of the planets.

Arecibo Observatory, Puerto Rico

Figure 24-31. Beginning with visual observation of his environment, man has progressed to the instruments of radio astronomy like this one at Arecibo, Puerto Rico, by which he probes the invisible and most distant parts of his universe.

MAIN IDEAS

1. Different forms of radiant energy may be recognized by their wavelengths or frequencies. An electromagnetic spectrum includes all radiant energy forms and is arranged according to wavelengths or frequencies. Visible light makes up a small portion of the electromagnetic spectrum. Other forms of radiant energy include cosmic waves, gamma rays, X rays, ultraviolet rays, infrared rays, and radio waves. Knowledge about space depends upon a study of radiant energy.

2. Stars emit continuous spectra crossed by dark absorption lines. From the spectra, astronomers determine which elements are present in a star and which wavelengths or frequencies have been absorbed by the outer gases of the star. Shifting of spectral lines indicates whether stars are approaching the earth (shift to the violet end of the spectrum) or receding from earth (shift toward the red end of the spectrum).

3. Stars are formed from interstellar matter which condenses and eventually reaches temperatures at which transmutation of hydrogen to helium occurs. Stars probably evolve from condensing masses of cosmic material, which achieve equilibrium when radiant energy is released at the surface at the same rate it is produced within the star's interior. Stars in equilibrium are known as main sequence stars. When hydrogen of the core is consumed, the core collapses and transmutation of hydrogen occurs in the outer envelope. At this stage, stars may become novae or supernovae. Last stage in stellar evolution is the white dwarf, a star in which almost all transmutation of hydrogen to helium has been completed.

4. Cepheids are stars that have periodically increasing brightness followed by decreasing brightness. The period of a Cepheid is related to its absolute magnitude and can be used to calculate a star's distance from earth.

5. Galaxies contain billions of stars. Galaxies in early, middle, and late stages of stellar evolution are called irregular, spiral, and elliptical, respectively. Irregular galaxies have abundant cosmic dust and gas; elliptical galaxies have very little cosmic dust and gas.

6. Our Galaxy is the Milky Way, a spiral galaxy containing over 100 billion stars and revolving around a central mass of stars. This revolution takes our sun about 250 million years to complete.

7. Quasars are starlike objects that emit radio energy and which appear to be moving away from the earth at an exceptionally rapid rate. Astronomers do not agree on their interpretation of why quasars have such small volumes. About 200 quasars have been located and half of them have been interpreted as showing a red shift indicative of recession from earth, solar system, and galaxy.

8. Optical telescopes may be refractor or reflector types. Refractors use lenses; reflectors use mirrors.

9. Spectroscopes and spectrographs are used in study of the visible and near visible spectrum. With radiometers, the infrared portion of the spectrum can be studied.

10. Radio waves originating in cosmic bodies have been studied by means of radio telescopes. This type of telescope uses a concave metal-mesh dish or a broad flat antenna to collect radio waves.

11. Radar waves, as used in astronomy, are pulses sent into space to probe celestial bodies, which reflect the waves to receivers placed near the transmitter. Radar has been useful in studies of the moon and planets.

12. Today's scientists seek new knowledge as did Galileo and Severinus. Each new instrument and each new measurement furthers the never-ending pursuit of scientific knowledge.

VOCABULARY

Write a sentence in which you use correctly each of the following words or terms.

absorption lines	light-year	radar
Cepheids	magnitude	red shift
coronograph	objective	slit
dipoles	ocular	spectrum
frequency	photometer	supernovae
galaxies	quasars	wavelength

STUDY QUESTIONS

A.   True or False

Determine whether each of the following sentences is true or false. (Do not write in this book.)

1. Galaxies were first recognized as extremely large groups of stars by Hubble.
2. Galaxies extend less than two billion miles into space.
3. Earth is part of an elliptical galaxy.
4. Earth's nearest star, other than the sun, is 4.3 light years away.
5. In main sequence stars, contraction and expansion produce supernovae.
6. Small red dwarfs and red giants are cooler than the sun.
7. Exceptionally bright stars that disappear from view after a period of brightness are called novae or supernovae.
8. White dwarfs are extremely dense.
9. In the electromagnetic spectrum, radiant energy forms are arranged in the order of their wavelengths or frequencies.
10. Stars are formed from clouds of expanding cosmic gas.

B.   Multiple Choice

Choose the word or phrase which completes correctly each of the following sentences. (Do not write in this book.)

1. Light travels at the rate of approximately 186,000 (*feet, yards, miles*) per second.
2. The sun is a (*blue, yellow, red*) main sequence star.
3. Stars in which brightness varies in a predictable cycle are (*Cepheids, quasars, supernovae*).
4. Visible forms of radiant energy are (*television waves, X rays, light waves*).
5. The color with the longest wavelength or lowest frequency is (*violet, blue, red*).
6. A star's spectrum is known as a (*separate, color, continuous*) spectrum.
7. Absolute magnitude refers to the brightness of a star (*as seen from earth, at the star's actual distance from earth, at 32.6 light years from earth*).

8. Stars in the last stage of stellar evolution in the main sequence are called (*white dwarfs, red dwarfs, supergiants*).

9. Variable stars include (*Cepheids, main sequence stars, white dwarfs*).

10. Color of a star is determined by a star's (*density, temperature, mass*).

C. Completion

Complete each of the following sentences with a word or phrase which will make the sentence correct. (Do not write in this book.)

1. The earth belongs to the ___?___ Galaxy.

2. Galaxies are classified according to their stage of stellar evolution as ___?___, ___?___, or ___?___.

3. The most distant galaxy which is visible to the unaided eye is ___?___.

4. Most massive stars with the highest temperatures are of ___?___ color.

5. Quasars appear to be ___?___ earth, according to most astronomers' interpretation of the red shift data.

6. Crab Nebula is a cloud of expanding gas which is presumed to represent the remains of a ___?___.

7. Quasars were located by means of the ___?___.

8. A mirror is used in a reflecting telescope instead of a(n) ___?___, as is used in a refracting telescope.

9. Pairs of stars of differing brightness which orbit around a common point and block out the light of each other at times are called ___?___.

10. Visible light is separated into colors in the following order, from shortest to longest wavelength: ___?___, ___?___, ___?___, ___?___, ___?___, ___?___, ___?___.

D. How and Why

1. Why are boundaries of an irregular galaxy so indefinite?

2. Why does the contraction of a nebula cause a rise in temperature?

3. By observing a star, astronomers can estimate its relative temperature. On what basis can they make such estimates?

4. Distinguish between true and apparent brightness.

5. Explain how astronomers have determined that the sun has 67 elements present in its matter.

6. What methods or instruments do astronomers use to study celestial objects that are beyond the range of visibility?

7. What are the advantages of using wire mesh instead of solid metal reflectors on radio telescopes?

8. Suggest methods and instruments that could be used in a study of Venus' atmosphere and to obtain temperatures of Venus' clouds and surface.

9. How do astronomers determine whether a star is approaching, or receding from, the earth?

10. Travel time of a radar pulse sent on a certain date from Chicago to Venus and back to Chicago is 28.67383 min. How far was Venus from Chicago?

INVESTIGATIONS

1. From library research, report on a myth concerning the formation of a constellation. Discuss the naming of constellations. Have the outlines of the constellations changed since their imaginative naming? Explain your answer.

2. What is the difference between astronomy and astrology? Is either a true science? Locate the astrology chart in the daily paper and discuss its contents.

INTERESTING READING

Alter, Dinsmore, et. al., *Pictorial Astronomy*, 3rd ed. New York, Thomas Y. Crowell Co., 1969.

*Clarke, Arthur Charles, *Man and Space*. Life Science Library. New York, Time Inc., 1968.

Hoss, Norman, *The How and Why Wonder Book of Stars*. Columbus, Ohio, Charles E. Merrill Publishing Co., 1960.

*Huxley, Julian, ed., *Space—Man in His World*. The Illustrated Libraries of Human Knowledge. Columbus, Ohio, Charles E. Merrill Publishing Co., 1968.

Inglis, Stuart J., *Planets, Stars, and Galaxies*, 2nd ed. New York, John Wiley & Sons, Inc., 1967.

Page, Thornton and Lou W., *Telescopes: How to Make Them and Use Them*. New York, Macmillan Co., 1966.

* Well-illustrated material.

APPENDICES
GLOSSARY
and
INDEX

APPENDIX A
Metric System

The metric system is a convenient, widely-used system of measurement which has the advantage of units based on ten and multiples of ten. It was developed by using the mass of pure water in the shape of a cube. The "cube of water" was a cubic centimeter—a cube one centimeter long on each edge. The mass of the cubic centimeter of water was measured at an exact temperature of 3.98°C and was called one gram (g). Because ten grams is very small, the kilogram (kg) is sometimes used as the standard of mass in the metric system. A kilogram is equal to 1,000 grams.

The unit of length in the metric system is the meter (m). It is equal to 39.37 inches (in.). The unit of volume in the metric system is the liter (l). A liter is the volume of a kilogram (1,000 g) of pure water measured at an exact temperature of 3.98°C. A liter is equal to 1.06 quarts.

TABLE A–1. Frequently Used Metric Units

LENGTH

1 centimeter (cm)	=	10 millimeters (mm)
1 meter (m)	=	100 centimeters (cm)
1 kilometer (km)	=	1000 meters (m)

VOLUME

1 liter (l)	=	1000 milliliters (ml)

MASS

1 gram (g)	=	1000 milligrams (mg)
1 kilogram (kg)	=	1000 grams (g)

TABLE A–2. Metric Unit Prefixes and Their Definitions

kilo—	1,000	$= 10^3$
hecto—	100	$= 10^2$
deka—	10	$= 10$
deci—	0.1	$= 10^{-1}$
centi—	0.01	$= 10^{-2}$
milli—	0.001	$= 10^{-3}$
micro—	0.000001	$= 10^{-6}$

The metric system has been legal in the United States since 1866. Because both metric units and English units are used, it is helpful to know how to convert from one system to the other. The relationships of some metric units and English units are given in Table A–3.

TABLE A–3. **Metric-English Equivalents**

LENGTH

1 in. = 2.54 cm	1 cm = 0.3937 in.
1 ft = 0.3048 m	1 m = 39.37 in. = 3.2808 ft
1 mi = 1.609 km	1 km = 39,370 in. = 3,280 ft
	= 0.62137 mi

1 in.^{2} = 6.452 cm^2	1 cm^2 = 0.1550 in.^{2}
1 ft^2 = 0.09290 m^2	1 m^2 = 10.764 ft^2
1 mi^2 = 2.59 km^2	1 km^2 = 0.3861 mi^2

VOLUME

1 in.^{3} = 16.387 cm^3	1 cm^3 = 0.0610 in.^{3}
1 ft^3 = 0.02832 m^3	1 m^3 = 35.315 ft^3
1 mi^3 = 4.1681 km^3	1 km^3 = 0.2399 mi^3
1 qt = 0.946 l	1 l = 1.06 qt

MASS

1 slug* = 1.46 × 10^4 g	1 g = 6.9 × 10^{-5} slugs
	1 cm^3 of water = 1 g

---

* The *slug* is the unit of mass in the English system. The *pound* is an English unit used for expressing a force such as the pull of gravity (weight). At sea level, a mass of 1 slug has a weight of 32.170 pounds.

APPENDIX B
Temperature Scales

The scale of degrees devised by G. D. Fahrenheit is the one used on thermometers for homes. It is called the *Fahrenheit temperature scale*. It is abbreviated as F. The freezing point of pure water at one atmosphere of pressure is assigned a value of thirty-two degrees (32°). The boiling point of pure water at one atmosphere of pressure is assigned a value of two hundred and twelve degrees (212°).

The *centigrade or Celsius scale*, devised by the Swedish astronomer Celsius, is used by scientists throughout the world. It is abbreviated as C. The value of zero degrees (0°) is assigned to the freezing point of pure water at one atmosphere of pressure. The boiling point of pure water at one atmosphere of pressure is assigned the value of one hundred degrees (100°) on the centigrade scale. Centigrade means 100 degrees.

The Fahrenheit scale has exactly 180 equal divisions or degrees between the freezing point and boiling point of pure water at one atmosphere of pressure. The centigrade scale has exactly 100 equal divisions or degrees between the freezing point and boiling point of pure water at one atmosphere of pressure. Thus, a Fahrenheit degree is 5/9 of a centigrade degree ($\frac{100}{180} = 5/9$). A centigrade degree is 9/5 of a Fahrenheit degree ($\frac{180}{100} = 9/5$).

To change temperatures from one scale to another, these formulas can be used:

$$°F = (9/5 \times °C) + 32 \qquad °C = (°F - 32°) \times 5/9$$

Temperatures of interest to astronomers range from about —270°C to 50,000,000°C. Negative numbers, or temperatures expressed in degrees below zero, can be avoided by using the *Kelvin temperature scale*. This is one of many reasons that astronomical publications commonly refer to temperatures in °K. The symbol K is a tribute to Lord Kelvin, an English physicist who made many contributions to the theory and meaning of absolute zero. The Kelvin, or absolute, temperature scale is a Celsius or centigrade scale with zero equal to —273°C. Changing scales from Celsius to Kelvin is a matter of simple addition, as °K = °C + 273°.

TABLE B–1. Comparison of Temperature Scales

At one atmosphere of pressure	F	C	K
Freezing point of pure water	32°	0°	273°
Common point	− 40°	− 40°	233°
Boiling point of pure water	212°	100°	373°

Element	Symbol	Atomic number	Atomic weight	Element	Symbol	Atomic number	Atomic weight
Actinium	Ac	89	227*	Mercury	Hg	80	200.59
Aluminum	Al	13	26.9815	Molybdenum	Mo	42	95.94
Americium	Am	95	243*	Neodymium	Nd	60	144.24
Antimony	Sb	51	121.75	Neon	Ne	10	20.183
Argon	Ar	18	39.948	Neptunium	Np	93	237*
Arsenic	As	33	74.9216	Nickel	Ni	28	58.71
Astatine	At	85	210*	Niobium	Nb	41	92.906
Barium	Ba	56	137.34	Nitrogen	N	7	14.0067
Berkelium	Bk	97	247*	Nobelium	No	102	253*
Beryllium	Be	4	9.0122	Osmium	Os	76	190.2
Bismuth	Bi	83	208.980	Oxygen	O	8	15.9994[a]
Boron	B	5	10.811	Palladium	Pd	46	106.4
Bromine	Br	35	79.904	Phosphorus	P	15	30.9738
Cadmium	Cd	48	112.40	Platinum	Pt	78	195.09
Calcium	Ca	20	40.08	Plutonium	Pu	94	244*
Californium	Cf	98	251*	Polonium	Po	84	209*
Carbon	C	6	12.01115	Potassium	K	19	39.102
Cerium	Ce	58	140.12	Praseodymium	Pr	59	140.907
Cesium	Cs	55	132.905	Promethium	Pm	61	145*
Chlorine	Cl	17	35.453	Protactinium	Pa	91	231*
Chromium	Cr	24	51.996	Radium	Ra	88	226.05
Cobalt	Co	27	58.9332	Radon	Rn	86	222*
Copper	Cu	29	63.546	Rhenium	Re	75	186.2
Curium	Cm	96	247*	Rhodium	Rh	45	102.905
Dysprosium	Dy	66	162.50	Rubidium	Rb	37	85.47
Einsteinium	Es	99	254*	Ruthenium	Ru	44	101.07
Erbium	Er	68	167.26	Samarium	Sm	62	150.35
Europium	Eu	63	151.96	Scandium	Sc	21	44.956
Fermium	Fm	100	253*	Selenium	Se	34	78.96
Fluorine	F	9	18.9984	Silicon	Si	14	28.086
Francium	Fr	87	223*	Silver	Ag	47	107.868
Gadolinium	Gd	64	157.25	Sodium	Na	11	22.9898
Gallium	Ga	31	69.72	Strontium	Sr	38	87.62
Germanium	Ge	32	72.59	Sulfur	S	16	32.064
Gold	Au	79	196.967	Tantalum	Ta	73	180.948
Hafnium	Hf	72	178.49	Technetium	Tc	43	97*
Helium	He	2	4.0026	Tellurium	Te	52	127.60
Holmium	Ho	67	164.930	Terbium	Tb	65	158.924
Hydrogen	H	1	1.00797	Thallium	Tl	81	204.37
Indium	In	49	114.82	Thorium	Th	90	232.038
Iodine	I	53	126.9044	Thulium	Tm	69	168.934
Iridium	Ir	77	192.2	Tin	Sn	50	118.69
Iron	Fe	26	55.847	Titanium	Ti	22	47.90
Krypton	Kr	36	83.80	Tungsten	W	74	183.85
Lanthanum	La	57	138.91	Uranium	U	92	238.03
Lead	Pb	82	207.19	Vanadium	V	23	50.942
Lawrencium	Lr	103	257*	Xenon	Xe	54	131.30
Lithium	Li	3	6.939	Ytterbium	Yb	70	173.04
Lutetium	Lu	71	174.97	Yttrium	Y	39	88.905
Magnesium	Mg	12	24.312	Zinc	Zn	30	65.37
Manganese	Mn	25	54.9380	Zirconium	Zr	40	91.22
Mendelevium	Md	101	256*				

APPENDIX C
International
Atomic Weights

*The mass number of the isotope with the longest known half-life.

APPENDIX D
The Periodic Table

(BASED ON ^{12}C = 12.0000)

Light Metals

Heavy Metals

Metalloids and Nonmetals

I A	II A	III B	IV B	V B	VI B	VII B		VIII B		I B	II B	III A	IV A	V A	VI A	VII A	VIII A
1 H 1.00797																	2 He 4.0026
3 Li 6.939	4 Be 9.0122											5 B 10.811	6 C 12.01115	7 N 14.0067	8 O 15.9994	9 F 18.9984	10 Ne 20.183
11 Na 22.9898	12 Mg 24.312											13 Al 26.9815	14 Si 28.086	15 P 30.9738	16 S 32.064	17 Cl 35.453	18 Ar 39.948
19 K 39.102	20 Ca 40.08	21 Sc 44.956	22 Ti 47.90	23 V 50.942	24 Cr 51.996	25 Mn 54.9380	26 Fe 55.847	27 Co 58.9332	28 Ni 58.71	29 Cu 63.546	30 Zn 65.37	31 Ga 69.72	32 Ge 72.59	33 As 74.9216	34 Se 78.96	35 Br 79.904	36 Kr 83.80
37 Rb 85.47	38 Sr 87.62	39 Y 88.905	40 Zr 91.22	41 Nb 92.906	42 Mo 95.94	43 Tc 97	44 Ru 101.07	45 Rh 102.905	46 Pd 106.4	47 Ag 107.868	48 Cd 112.40	49 In 114.82	50 Sn 118.69	51 Sb 121.75	52 Te 127.60	53 I 126.9044	54 Xe 131.30
55 Cs 132.905	56 Ba 137.34	57 TO 71	72 Hf 178.49	73 Ta 180.948	74 W 183.85	75 Re 186.2	76 Os 190.2	77 Ir 192.2	78 Pt 195.09	79 Au 196.967	80 Hg 200.59	81 Tl 204.37	82 Pb 207.19	83 Bi 208.980	84 Po 209	85 At 210	86 Rn 222
87 Fr 223	88 Ra 226.05	89 TO 103	104 257														

Lanthanide series (Rare earth metals)

57 La 138.91	58 Ce 140.12	59 Pr 140.907	60 Nd 144.24	61 Pm 145	62 Sm 150.35	63 Eu 151.96	64 Gd 157.25	65 Tb 158.924	66 Dy 162.50	67 Ho 164.930	68 Er 167.26	69 Tm 168.934	70 Yb 173.04	71 Lu 174.97

Actinide series

89 Ac 227	90 Th 232.038	91 Pa 231	92 U 238.03	93 Np 237	94 Pu 244	95 Am 243	96 Cm 247	97 Bk 247	98 Cf 251	99 Es 254	100 Fm 253	101 Md 256	102 No 253	103 Lr 257

The following radioactive elements are mentioned in the text as being important in determining the absolute ages of various rocks in which the elements are found. A number of other elements are radioactive also, but the elements listed here are the ones most useful in geologic dating.

APPENDIX E
Radioactive
Elements

	Parent Element	Daughter Element(s)	Type of decay
Single step decay	Potassium 40	Argon 40	electron capture
		Calcium 40	beta
	Rubidium 87	Strontium 87	beta
Series decay	Thorium 232	Lead 208	6 alpha + 4 beta
	Uranium 235	Lead 207	7 alpha + 4 beta
	Uranium 238	Lead 206	8 alpha + 6 beta
Neutron induced decay	Carbon 14	Nitrogen 14	beta

During decay, excess energy is given off as *gamma rays* or *X rays. Gamma rays are formed in the nucleus. X rays are formed in electron cloud.*

Other single-step-decay radioactive elements include Vanadium 50; Indium 115; Tellurium 123; Lanthanum 138; Cerium 142; Neodymium 144; Samarium 147, 148, and 149; Gadolinium 152; Dysprosium 156; Hafnium 174; Lutetium 176; Rhenium 187; Platinum 190 and Lead 204.

A radioactive nucleus that decays by giving off an *alpha particle* loses two protons and two neutrons. The atomic number is reduced by *2*. The mass number is reduced by *4*.

A radioactive nucleus that decays by giving off a *beta particle* loses an electron from the decay of a neutron into a proton. The atomic number is increased by *1*. The mass number remains the same.

Electron capture changes the nucleus by adding an electron from the innermost electron shell. This electron from the electron cloud combines with a proton to form a neutron. The atomic number is reduced by *1*. The mass number remains the same.

APPENDIX F
Topographic Maps

Topographic maps are small scale representations of land-scape and cultural features. Landscape features include such things as streams, lakes, oceans, mountains, and plains. Cultural features include houses, roads, railroads, and other man-made objects. Some topographic maps even show vegetation.

This appendix contains maps of three different types of landscape. As you look at these maps, notice how the various features of each type of landscape are illustrated. Note how topographic maps can be used to describe gorges, mountains, plains, deserts, swamps, lakes, and other land features.

Grand Canyon, Arizona

The Grand Canyon of the Colorado River is perhaps the best known example of a youthful river valley in North America. Mexico has similar great canyons, but they are not as well documented and described. The Grand Canyon country illustrates important characteristics of erosion. The Colorado River is in a youthful V-shaped valley. The Granite Gorge portion of the valley is shown on this map. Notice how the steep walls of the valley are shown by the close spacing of contours on both sides of the valley.

Some horizontal layers have steeper valley walls than other layers. The valley slopes differ because some rock layers resist weathering better than others. All of the beds exposed along the river are approximately horizontal. Resistant beds do not weather readily so the contours are closely spaced along a steep cliff. Other layers weather easily. These tend to slump, or sheet flooding washes away the fragments of rock as they form. Contours on such beds are more widely spaced because the valley slope is gentle.

Along the line AA', compare the spacing between the contours for elevations of 7200 and 6800 feet with the spacing between 6800 and 6400 feet. Note the especially gentle slope between the 4400 ft contour and the 4000 ft contour. Between the 3600 ft contour and the 2800 ft contour near the bottom of the gorge, the valley slope is especially steep.

From the high point of Brahma Temple (near A'), the elevation of the region descends to approximately 2500 ft in Granite Gorge. The elevation then ascends from the valley to the bench mark point (BM) of 7129 near the southern third of the map on AA. From this BM, the surface slopes gently toward the southwest. The gentle slope is the plateau surface.

The steep slopes of the rest of the map represent a dissected surface where the Colorado River and its tributaries have cut into the plateau. The drainage pattern is dendritic. Valleys are V-shaped in cross section. They also have a V pattern in the map with the V pointing upstream. Generally, buttes (see Newton Butte) are triangular in shape because erosion (Chapter 13) has cut into them from three directions.

Antelope Peak, Arizona

This map shows the topography of the Sonoran Desert in Arizona. In addition to the contour lines, mountain areas have been shaded so the map looks more like a photograph.

In the southeast corner of the map are two small cinder cones on the Papago Indian Reservation. In the southcentral region, the Table Top Mountains are resistant erosional remnants. Mountains in sections 25 and 36 (T. 6 S., R. 2 E.) below Mesquite Road are typical examples of inselbergs (Figure 13–8). Surrounding these mountains are alluvial deposits which merge into the bajada of the northeast portion of the map.

Just north of Indian Butte (sections 17 and 18 of T. 7 S., R. 3 E.) an alluvial fan is present (Figure 13–20). Streams of the region are intermittent. However, they have dissected the mountains and deposited over a thousand feet of sediments on the mountain flanks.

A box canyon extends from near the N in the word MOUNTAIN, in the southcentral portion of the map, to section 10 of T. 7 S., R. 3 E. The sides of this canyon are over 100 feet high in many places. Streams end in the deposits of the alluvial fans. There water sinks into the ground or is evaporated. This map is one of the best in the United States for a view of alluvial plains, inselbergs, and other desert features described in Chapter 16.

Kettle Moraine Region in Wisconsin

This map shows an area in which topography is controlled by a receding continental glacier. The low hills in the middle portion of the map represent a terminal moraine. The 900 ft contour roughly outlines this moraine. Toward the southeast, Honey Creek drains the gently sloping outwash plain that fronts the moraine. Notice the number of kettle lakes bordering the moraine. Characteristic of the morainal type of deposits is the swampy area surrounding the line of lakes from Middle Lake on the southwest to Peters Lake in the east central portion of the map. Within the moraine itself are many circular hills. (Refer to Chapter 15, especially 15:4.)

GRAND CANYON, ARIZONA

Scale 1:62500
Contour Interval 80 ft

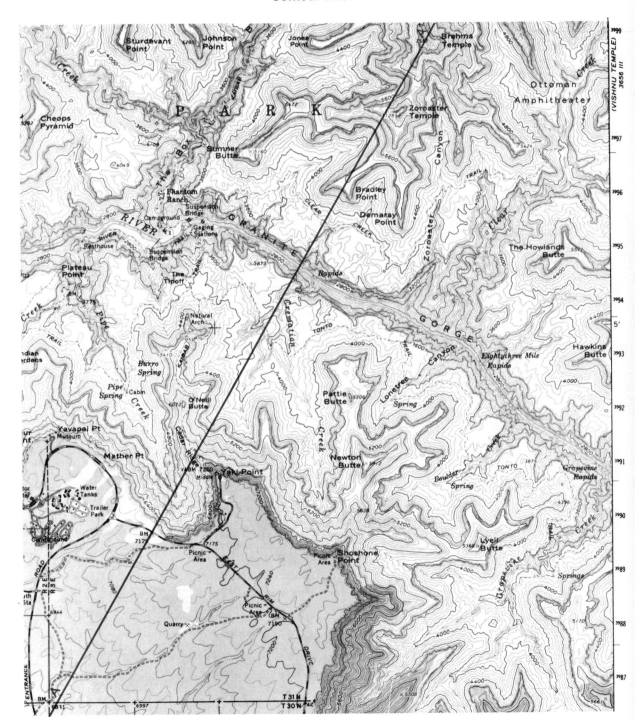

ANTELOPE PEAK, ARIZONA

Scale 1:62500
Contour Interval 25 ft

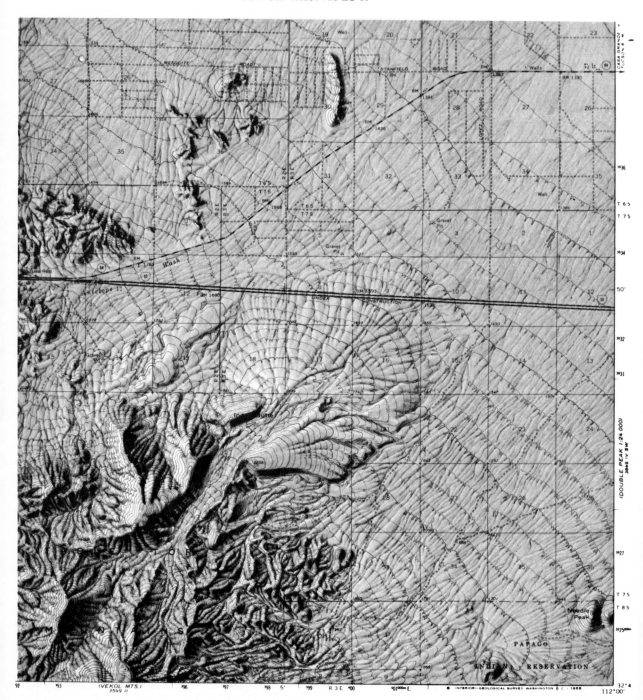

KETTLE MORAINE REGION IN WISCONSIN

Scale 1:62500
Contour Interval 20 ft

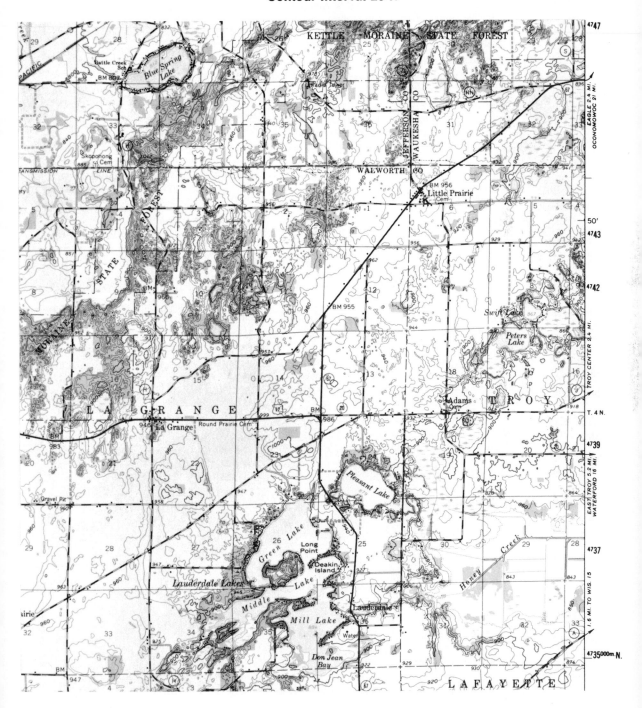

GLOSSARY

Pronunciation
Key

ae ... bake

ah ... father

a ... back

ee ... easy

e ... less

eu ... few

ie ... life

i ... trip

oh ... flow

aw ... soft

ah ... odd

oo ... food

uh ... foot

eu ... cube

u ... up

y ... yet

j ... judge

k ... cake

s ... sew

th ... thin

abrade (a braed'): to rub or to wear away by friction

abrasive (a brae' siv): tending to wear away by friction

absolute dates: dates in earth's history arrived at by dating radioactive rocks and measured without reference to any other event

absolute magnitude (mag' na teud): brightness a star would have at a distance of 32.6 light-years

absorption lines: dark lines crossing the continuous spectrum of stars showing where frequencies have been absorbed by surface gases

abyss (a bis'): deep part of the ocean floor

acceleration (ik sel a rae' shun): time rate of change of velocity

accessory (ik ses' e ree) **mineral:** mineral present in a minor amount and not necessary to the classification of a rock

aeration (aer ae' shun): exposing to the free action of air; treating of a substance with air

algae (al' jee): plants, such as seaweeds, which grow in water and possess chlorophyll often masked by red or brown pigment

alluvial (a loo' vee ul): deposits of sand, mud, and other materials transported by flowing water

Alpha Centauri (sen tawr' ee): star, other than the sun, nearest to earth

alpha (al' fa) **ray:** stream of positively-charged particles moving at high speed emitted from an atomic nucleus

ammonite (am' a niet): flat, spiral fossil shell of a group of invertebrates abundant in the Mesozoic era

amniotic (am nee aht' ik): having a membrane containing fluid in which the embryo is immersed

amorphous (a mawr' fus): shapeless; having no definite crystal structure

amphibian (am fib' ee an): cold-blooded vertebrate intermediate between fishes and reptiles

amphibole (am' fi bohl): one of the rock-forming mineral groups containing iron, magnesium, calcium, and aluminum silicates in which the silicate tetrahedra are arranged in double chains

amplitude (am' pli teud): vibratory movement of a pendulum as measured from the mean position to the extent of its arc

angiosperm (an' jee a spurm): flowering plant having seeds in a protective covering which enables them to survive and reproduce

angular momentum: momentum of a rotating body as it turns on its axis, governed by mass times velocity times the distance from axis of rotation

anticline (ant' i klien): upward fold or bend of rock strata

anticyclone (ant i sie' klohn): system of wind rotating about a center of high atmospheric pressure, turning clockwise in the northern hemisphere and counterclockwise in the southern hemisphere

aphelion (a feel' yan): point in a planet's orbit farthest from the sun

apogee (ap' a jee): point in the orbit of a satellite of the earth at the greatest distance from the center of the earth

apparent magnitude: brightness of a star observed at its actual distance from earth

aquifer (ak' wa fer): water-bearing rock

archeologist (ahr kee ahl' a jist): scientist who studies remains of past human life and activities

arete (a raet'): sharp ridge separating two glaciated valleys

argon (ar' gahn): colorless, odorless, inert gaseous element that composes 0.93 percent (by volume) of the earth's atmosphere

arid (ar' id) **climate:** climate having insufficient rainfall for vegetation

artesian (ahr tee' zhan) **water:** groundwater under enough pressure to rise above the aquifer containing it

asteroid (as' te rawid): fragment of material similar to planetary matter which orbits the sun between Mars and Jupiter

astronomical (as tra nahm' i kal) **unit:** mean distance between the earth and the sun, equal to 93,000,000 mi

atmosphere (at' mu sfir): gaseous mass surrounding the earth or other celestial body

atoll (a' tawl): ring-shaped coral reef often surrounding a body of water

atom (at' em): smallest particle of an element that enters into a chemical reaction

atomic number: total number of protons present in nucleus of atom of a given element

avalanche (av' a lanch): large mass of snow, rock, or other material in swift motion down a mountain slope

axis (ak' sis): imaginary straight line about which a rotating body turns

background noise: unwanted vibrations recorded by a seismograph

bajada (bah hah' dah): series of alluvial fans which are joined at the foot of a mountain range

barchan (bahr' kahn): dune with crescent shape when observed from above, having the convex side facing the wind

barometer (ba rahm' et er): instrument for determining pressure of the atmosphere

baroques (ba rohks'): irregular-shaped polished gems or semiprecious stones

batholith (bath' a lith): large shield-shaped mass of intrusive igneous rock extending to unknown depths

benthos (ben' thahs): organisms that live on the bottom of the ocean

bergschrund (burg' schrund): crevasse at the head of a mountain glacier which separates moving snow and ice from that which clings to the rock face

berm: narrow horizontal portion of a beach built of material deposited by wave action

beta (baet' a) **ray**: stream of electrons emitted from an atomic nucleus

binary (bie' na ree) **star**: system of two stars that revolve around each other under their mutual gravitation

biosphere (bie' a sfir): the part of the world in which life can exist

boiling point: temperature at which a liquid changes to a gas

brachiopod (brak' ee a pahd): phylum of marine invertebrates having two unequal shells or valves

buoyancy (bawi' an see): resultant of upward forces exerted by a fluid on a submerged or floating body, equal to the weight of the fluid displaced by the body

butte (beut): turret-like hills or ridges which rise abruptly from and stand above the surrounding plain

cabochon (kab' a shahn): gem or bead cut in convex form

caldera (kal der' a): large basin-shaped depression at the summit of a volcano

caliche (ka lee' chee): crust of calcium carbonate formed on soil in arid region by evaporation of moisture

Cambrian (kam' bree an): earliest geologic period of the Paleozoic era; rocks containing fossils of every animal type

canine (kae' nien): conical pointed tooth suited to tearing flesh

capillary (kap' e ler ee)**attraction**: rising of liquid in hair-like openings in a solid due to attraction between unlike molecules

carbonate (kahr' ba naet): compound containing the radical CO_3

carbon dioxide: heavy, colorless gas that composes 0.03 percent (by volume) of the earth's atmosphere

carnivorous (kahr niv' a rus): flesh-eating

celestial (se les' chal): pertaining to the sky or visible heavens

celestial sphere: globe with the earth as center on which movements of stars and planets are plotted or mapped

centrifugal (sen trif' ye gal) **force**: force which tends to impel an object outward from the center of rotation

Cepheid (see' fee id): pulsating star with regular light variations

chain craters: small pits on the moon's surface aligned in chains

chalcedony (kal sed' en ee): microscopic fibrous quartz or agate

Chinook (shi nuhk'): evaporating wind that blows downward on the eastern slopes of the Rocky mountains

chromosphere (kroh' ma sfir): layer of hot gas surrounding the photosphere of the sun

Pronunciation Key

ae . . . bake

ah . . . father

a . . . back

ee . . . easy

e . . . less

eu . . . few

ie . . . life

i . . . trip

oh . . . flow

aw . . . soft

ah . . . odd

oo . . . food

uh . . . foot

eu . . . cube

u . . . up

y . . . yet

j . . . judge

k . . . cake

s . . . sew

th . . . thin

cirque (surk): deep, steep-sided recess or hollow in a mountain caused by glacial erosion

clastic (klas' tik): rock composed of fragments derived from a pre-existing rock

cleavage (klee' vij): tendency to split along planes determined by the crystal structure of a mineral

climate (klie' met): average of local temperature, precipitation, and wind conditions over a period of years

cohesive (koh hee' siv): tendency of particles of a substance to be bound together as a unit

compaction (kam pak' shun): decrease in volume of sediments due to pressure of overlying material or drying

compound: two or more elements chemically joined

compression (kam presh' un): force or stress that tends to decrease the volume of a substance

concave (kahn' kaev): hollowed or rounded inward like the inside of a bowl

conchoidal (kahn kawid' l): curved like the inside of a shell

condense (kan dens'): make more dense or compact; to compress the volume of a substance; to change from gas to liquid or solid

conduction (kan duk' shun): movement of heat, light, electricity, or sound by contact among particles

conglomerate (kan glahm' e rit): rock consisting of rounded and water-worn pebble-sized fragments cemented by another mineral

consolidate (kan sahl' i daet): make solid or firm; to unite

constellation (kahn sta lae' shun): pattern produced by an arrangement of stars and named for some earth object

contact metamorphism: change in rock resulting from contact with hot magma or igneous rock

continental nucleus: region where rocks of the Cryptozoic eon are exposed at the surface

convection (kan vek' shun): movement of heat and matter (plastic, liquid, or gas) because of differences in density usually resulting from differences in temperature

Pronunciation Key

ae ... bake

ah ... father

a ... back

ee ... easy

e ... less

eu ... few

ie ... life

i ... trip

oh ... flow

aw ... soft

ah ... odd

oo ... food

uh ... foot

eu ... cube

u ... up

y ... yet

j ... judge

k ... cake

s ... sew

th ... thin

convex (kan veks'): curved or rounded outward like the outside of a bowl

Coriolis (kohr ee oh' lis) force: apparent force due to the earth's rotation that causes a body in motion to be deflected from its initial path

corona (ka roh' na): filmy envelope of highly ionized gas beyond the sun's chromosphere

correlate (kawr' e laet): to match the geologic age or stratigraphic position of one rock body with another

cosmic (kahz' mik): pertaining to that part of the universe beyond earth's atmosphere

crater (kraet' er): steep-walled depression at the summit of a volcanic vent

crescent (kres' ent): figure resembling a bow ending in points; the moon in its first or last quarter when both edges are nearly parallel

crest: highest natural point of a hill, mountain, anticline, or wave

crevasse (kri vas'): fissure or cleft in the ice of a glacier

crosscutting relationships: age relationships of rocks which cut across rocks already in place

crust: crystalline outer layer of the earth

crystal: solid body bounded by plane surfaces showing a regularly repeated arrangement of atoms

crystal faces: flat surfaces of a crystal which join at well-defined angles

cuesta (kwes' ta): hill or ridge with a steep face on one side and a gentle slope on the other

cyclone (sie' klohn): system of wind rotating about a center of low atmospheric pressure, turning clockwise in the southern hemisphere and counterclockwise in the northern hemisphere

daughter element: element formed from another by radioactive decay

debris (da bree'): loose material resulting from decay and disintegration

declination (dek le nae' shun): distance north or south from the celestial equator, measured along a great circle passing through the celestial poles; celestial coordinates corresponding to latitude on earth

decomposition (dee kahm pa zish' un): chemical separation of minerals and rocks into elements or simpler compounds

deflation (di flae' shun): removal by wind of loose material from the land surface

deflection (di flek' shun): act of bending or turning aside

delta: triangular-shaped alluvial deposit at the mouth of a river

dendritic (den drit' ik): branching figure resembling a tree

density (den' sit ee): mass per unit volume

density current: ocean current caused by differences in density due to unequal amounts of suspended or dissolved substances in water or due to differences in temperatures

deposition (dep u zish' un): laying down of possible rock-forming sediments; precipitation of dissolved substances

detritus (di triet' us): loose material resulting from rock disintegration

deuterium (deu tir' ee em): an isotope of hydrogen which is twice the mass of ordinary hydrogen and which occurs in water

diastrophism (die as' tra fiz em): process by which the crust of the earth is deformed causing continents, ocean basins, plateaus, mountains, folds, and faults

diatoms (die' a tahm): small one-celled algae which secrete siliceous material

dike: tabular body of igneous rock that cuts across another rock body

dinosaur (die' na sawr): group of large extinct reptiles

dipole (die' pohl): directional antenna for collecting radio waves

disintegration (dis int e grae' shun): mechanical breaking of material into small particles during weathering

displacement: relative movement of two sides of a fault measured in any specified direction

dissect (dis ekt'): to cut into hills and valleys during erosion of a plateau or uplifted peneplain

doldrums (dohl' drumz): calm, windless area near the equator

dominant (dahm' a nant): controlling or most influential

Doppler (dahp' ler) **effect**: change in the frequency with which waves from a given source reach the observer when the source and the observer are in rapid motion with respect to one another

drumlin: long, narrow, smoothly rounded hill of unstratified glacial drift

dynamic (die nam' ik) **metamorphism**: metamorphism resulting from rock folding or faulting

eccentric (ik sen' trik): not following a circular path; deviating from an established pattern

eclipse (i klips'): passing of a luminous body into the shadow of another body

eclipsing variables: two stars that orbit around a common point and appear to change magnitude because one of them is dimmer

ecliptic (i klip' tik): great circle inclined to the celestial equator at an angle of 23° 27' formed by the intersection of the plane of the earth's orbit with the celestial sphere

eddy: current of water, air, or gas running contrary to the main current

electron (i lek' trahn): nearly weightless subatomic particle with a negative electrical charge

electron cloud: portion of an atom consisting of negative electricity surrounding the nucleus

element: any substance which, in its pure form, cannot be separated into simpler substances

ellipse (i lips'): curved plane surface generated by a point that moves so the sum of its distance from two fixed points is constant

embryo (em' bree oh): organism in the early stages of development

energy level: one of a series of levels in which electrons vibrate around the nucleus of an atom

entrench: to erode downward so as to form a trench beneath the general surface of the adjacent upland

Pronunciation Key

ae . . . bake

ah . . . father

a . . . back

ee . . . easy

e . . . less

eu . . . few

ie . . . life

i . . . trip

oh . . . flow

aw . . . soft

ah . . . odd

oo . . . food

uh . . . foot

eu . . . cube

u . . . up

y . . . yet

j . . . judge

k . . . cake

s . . . sew

th . . . thin

Pronunciation
Key

ae . . . bake

ah . . . father

a . . . back

ee . . . easy

e . . . less

eu . . . few

ie . . . life

i . . . trip

oh . . . flow

aw . . . soft

ah . . . odd

oo . . . food

uh . . . foot

eu . . . cube

u . . . up

y . . . yet

j . . . judge

k . . . cake

s . . . sew

th . . . thin

environment (in vie'ran ment): sum total of all conditions surrounding an organism or community

eolian (ee oh' lee an): borne, deposited, or eroded by wind

eon (ee' an): one of the two largest divisions of geologic time

epicenter (ep' i sent er): point on the earth's surface directly above the focus of an earthquake

epoch: subdivision of a period in geologic time

equilibrium (ee kwa lib' ree um): state of balance between opposing forces

equinox (ee' kwa nahks): position where the center of the sun crosses the plane of the earth's equator making day and night of equal length

era (ir' a): large division of geologic time containing more than one period

erosion (i roh' shun): process by which materials of the earth's surface are loosened or dissolved and removed

erupt (i rupt'): to burst forth, as the violent outpouring of lava from a volcano

escarpment (is kahrp' ment): a steep slope separating two gently sloping surfaces

esker: a serpentine ridge or hill of sand or gravel deposited within stream channels in a decaying glacier ice sheet

essential mineral: mineral necessary to the classification of a rock

estuary (es' cha wer ee): bay at the lower end of a river where the river current meets the tide

etch: to pit or corrode a mineral or rock surface so as to produce a pattern of pits or lines

eutrophication (eu trahf i kae' shun): the process of becoming rich in dissolved nutrients but deficient in oxygen

evaporation (i vap e rae' shun): physical change from liquid to gas; process by which water becomes a vapor at a temperature below the boiling point

evaporite (i vap' e riet): product of evaporation; sediment left after evaporation of a solvent

exfoliation (eks foh lee ae' shun): the peeling off of thin, concentric layers from a bare rock surface

exosphere: outer layer of earth's atmosphere which contains helium, hydrogen, radioactive particles, and bands of radiation

extinct (ik stingkt'): no longer existing

extrusive (ik stroo' siv): igneous rocks which have been consolidated at or near the earth's surface

faceted (fas' et ed): polished with small, plane surfaces meeting at sharp angles

facies (fae' shee eez): areally differing characteristics (composition, fossil content, or texture) of a geologic unit of deposition

fault: fracture of the earth's crust along which displacement of one side of the fracture with respect to the other has occurred

firn: compact, permeable mass of granular snow which has remained for more than one season and forms the upper surface of the accumulation area of a glacier

fission (fish'en): a splitting or breaking up into parts, particularly the splitting of an atomic nucleus resulting in the release of large amounts of energy

fluvial (fleu' vee al): produced by stream action

focal length: distance between the focal point and the lens

focal point: point at which light rays converge to form a small image on a lens

focus: true center of an earthquake

fold: bend in rock strata

foliation (foh lee ae' shun): structure in certain metamorphic rocks resulting from segregation of different minerals into parallel layers

fossil (fahs' il): record of past life, such as a shell, bone, or impression, preserved in the earth's crust

fossil assemblage: fossils naturally associated in a stratum and possibly derived from more than one fossil community

fossiliferous (fahs i lif' e ras): containing organic remains

fracture (frak' chur): distinctive manner of breaking in a mineral other than along a plane surface; breaks in rocks due to intense folding and faulting

freezing point: temperature at which a liquid becomes a solid

frequency (free' kwan see): number of repetitions of a periodic wave per unit of time

fretwork: pattern of dark and light; a design worked by perforations

fuse: to combine or blend by melting together

fusion (fyeu'zhen): union by melting, particularly union of atomic nuclei to form heavier nuclei resulting in the release of enormous quantities of energy when certain light elements unite

galaxy (gal' ak see): system or community of stars

gamma ray: most penetrating and destructive atomic ray emitted by radioactive substances

gangue (gang): worthless rock surrounding valuable minerals

gas: form of matter without definite shape or volume

gem: precious or semiprecious stone which may be polished for ornament

geode (jee' ohd): hollow, globular body of rock often lined with inward growing mineral crystals

geodesists (jee ahd' e sists): scientists who measure earth's shape, size, gravity, and magnetism

geodetic (jee a det' ik) **surveys:** mathematical measurements of earth's dimensions

geologic revolution: time of major crustal deformations

geosyncline (jee oh sin' klien): great regional, subsiding, downward warp of the earth's crust in which thousands of feet of sediment and volcanic rock accumulate

geyser (gie' zer): spring that irregularly throws forth jets of hot water and steam

gibbous (gib' us): moon when more than half but not all its disc is illuminated

globule (glahb' eul): small, spherical body

gorge (gawrj): narrow, deep passage between rocky sides

gradient (graed' ee ent): slope, particularly of a stream or land surface

granule (gran' eul): rounded rock fragment larger than sand grains but smaller than pebbles

gravitation (grav i tae' shun): mutual attraction between all matter

gravity (grav' it ee): gravitational attraction of the earth for objects near its surface

groin (grawin): a projecting curved line along which two intersecting arches meet, particularly designed to protect a shore

gully (gul' ee): trench worn by running water

half-life: time in which half the initial number of atoms of a radioactive element disintegrate into atoms of a daughter element

hardness: resistance to scratching or abrasion

helium (hee' lee um): light, colorless gaseous element usually containing 2 protons, 2 neutrons, and 2 electrons

herbivorous (er biv' a rus): plant-eating

hexagonal (hek sag' an l): crystal system having three equal lateral axes intersecting at angles of 60° in one plane and a fourth unequal axis perpendicular to the others

hogback: ridge produced by sharply tilted resistant strata left exposed as adjacent weaker strata are eroded into deep ravines

horizontal seismograph: instrument used to record horizontal vibrations of earth

humic (heu' mik) **acid:** product of decomposition of plant or animal matter

hydraulic (hie draw' lik): operated or moved by means of water in motion

hydrocarbon (hie dra kahr' bon): organic compound of carbon and hydrogen

hydrogen (hie' dra jen): light, colorless gaseous element usually containing 1 proton, 1 electron, and no neutrons

hydrologic (hie dra lahj' ik) **cycle:** cycle of water circulation from sea to atmosphere, to land, to sea again

Pronunciation Key

ae . . . bake

ah . . . father

a . . . back

ee . . . easy

e . . . less

eu . . . few

ie . . . life

i . . . trip

oh . . . flow

aw . . . soft

ah . . . odd

oo . . . food

uh . . . foot

eu . . . cube

u . . . up

y . . . yet

j . . . judge

k . . . cake

s . . . sew

th . . . thin

hydrosphere (hie′ dru sfir): water portion of the earth including water vapor in air, seas, rivers, and groundwater

hypothesis (hie pahth′ e sis): proposition or an assumption based on available information offered as an explanation for a problem

igneous (ig′ nee us): rock formed by solidification of molten material produced under conditions of intense heat

impression: form or shape left on a soft surface by material which has come in contact with it; preserved form of a fossil

incisor (in sie′ zer): tooth adapted for cutting

index fossil: fossil with a narrow time range and wide distribution used to identify and date the rock layer in which it occurs

industrial mineral: nonmetallic mineral important in industry

inertia (in er′ shuh): resistance to motion or to change of direction

inorganic: not having the characteristics of living things; not capable of self-duplication or producing offspring

inselberg (in′ sel burg): bare, rocky, steep-sided residual hills rising from eroded plains

intact: unaltered, sound, or whole

interferometer (int er fa rahm′ et er): multiple-element antenna feeding a single receiver to aid in distinguishing between sources of radiation

intermittent (int er mit′ ent): alternately ceasing and beginning again

international date line: imaginary line at approximately the 180° meridian at which the date is adjusted, being one day later west of the line than east of it

intersect (int er sekt′): to pierce or divide by passing through or across

intrusive (in troo′ siv): rock which, while fluid, has penetrated into or between other rocks, but has solidified before reaching the surface of the earth

invertebrate (in vert′ e brat): animal lacking a spinal column

ion (ie′ an): electrically charged atom

ionosphere (ie ahn′ a sfir): layer of the earth's atmosphere about 50 mi to 600 mi above earth's surface containing free electrically charged particles by means of which radio waves are transmitted to distant areas

isostasy (ie sahs′ ta see): condition of equilibrium in the earth's crust in which masses of greatest density are lower than those of lesser density

isotopes (ie′ sa tohps): atoms of the same element having different mass because of differences in the number of neutrons

jetty (jet′ ee): projection built into a body of water to influence current or tide

kame: conical, irregular hill of sand or gravel deposited at the edge of a glacier ice sheet

laccolith (lack′ a lith): mushroom-shaped body of intrusive igneous rock which has domed up the overlying rock and has a floor that is usually horizontal in contrast to the larger batholith

lagoon (la goon′): area of shallow salt water possessing a restricted connection with the sea

larvae (lahr′ vee): early forms of any animal which is unlike its parents and must change before adulthood

lateral (lat′ e ral) **moraine**: body of unstratified drift or till lying on the surface near and parallel to the sides of a valley glacier

latitude (lat′ i teud): distance north or south of the earth's equator measured in degrees

lava (lahv′ a): fluid rock issuing from a volcano or fissure, or same material cooled and solidified

leeward: direction toward which the wind is blowing

legumes (le′ geums): plants whose nitrogen-fixing bacteria form usable nitrogen compounds

levee (lev′ ee): man-made or natural bank confining a stream channel

Pronunciation Key

ae . . . bake

ah . . . father

a . . . back

ee . . . easy

e . . . less

eu . . . few

ie . . . life

i . . . trip

oh . . . flow

aw . . . soft

ah . . . odd

oo . . . food

uh . . . foot

eu . . . cube

u . . . up

y . . . yet

j . . . judge

k . . . cake

s . . . sew

th . . . thin

light-year: distance that light travels in one year, equal to 6 x 10^{12} mi/yr

linear (lin′ ee ar): involving a single dimension; straight

liquid: form of matter without definite shape but having definite volume

lithium (lith′ ee em): soft, silver-white element; lightest known metal

lithology (lith ahl′ a jee): study of rocks

lithosphere (lith′ a sfir): solid outermost part of the earth; the earth's crust

loess (les): nonstratified silt and clay deposited by wind

longitude (lahn′ ji teud): distance east or west of the prime meridian at Greenwich, England, measured in degrees

longitudinal (lahn ji teud′ nal): of or relating to lengthwise dimension

longshore current: local current flowing parallel to the shore caused by waves breaking at an angle to the shore

luminosity (loo ma nahs′ at ee): quality of giving off light

luminous (loo′ ma nus): emitting light

luster: character of light reflected by a mineral

Magellanic (maj e lan′ ik) **Clouds:** two galaxies nearest the Milky Way and appearing as conspicuous patches of light

magma (mag′ ma): molten rock material which is formed beneath the earth's crust and from which igneous rocks are solidified

main sequence stars: normal stars or stars in equilibrium

malleable (mal′ ee a bul): capable of being shaped by pounding

mammal (mam′ el): any of a class of higher vertebrates that nourish their young with milk secreted from glands

mantle (mant′ ul): layer of the earth between the crust and the core

maria (mae′ ree a): depressions on the moon's surface once believed to be seas

marsupial (mahr seu′ pee al): lower mammal groups that have a pouch on the female in which the young are carried

mass: measure of the quantity of matter in a body

mass number: total number of protons and neutrons present in the nucleus of each atom of a given element

matter: anything that has mass and occupies space

meander (mee an′ der): turn or loop-like bend in a stream channel

melting point: temperature at which a solid becomes a liquid

meltwater: water from the melting of ice or snow

meridian (ma rid′ ee an): great circle on the surface of the earth passing through the poles and crossing the equator at a right angle

mesa (mae′ sa): isolated hill having steeply sloping sides and a level top protected by a resistant layer of rock

mesosphere (mez′ a sfir): layer of earth's atmosphere about 20 mi to about 50 mi above earth's surface containing ozone which absorbs ultraviolet rays

metal: opaque, fusible, ductile, lustrous element

metamorphic (met e mawr′ fik): rock changed in composition or texture after consolidation as a result of deformation and/or increased temperature

metasomatism (met a soh′ ma tiz um): metamorphic changes in chemical composition and texture by introduction of new material into a mineral or group of minerals

meteoroid (meet′ ee a rawid): fragment of cosmic material too small to be observed from earth

meteorology (meet ee a rahl′ a jee): science dealing with the atmosphere and its phenomena, particularly relating to weather

mid-oceanic ridge: mountain ridge in mid-ocean which extends for about 40,000 mi roughly parallel to continental margins

migmatites (mig′ ma tiets): rocks containing alternate layers of igneous and metamorphic rocks

migrating dune: dune which moves more or less as a unit because of wind action

mineral: inorganic substance which occurs in nature, in the solid state, with a definite chemical composition and characteristic internal atomic pattern

Pronunciation Key

ae . . . bake

ah . . . father

a . . . back

ee . . . easy

e . . . less

eu . . . few

ie . . . life

i . . . trip

oh . . . flow

aw . . . soft

ah . . . odd

oo . . . food

uh . . . foot

eu . . . cube

u . . . up

y . . . yet

j . . . judge

k . . . cake

s . . . sew

th . . . thin

mineraloid (min′ ra lawid): similar to a mineral except that it has no characteristic internal pattern

mixture: two or more substances combined in any proportion which, unlike a chemical compound, retain their identity and can be separated by mechanical means

Mohorovicic discontinuity (moh ha roh′ va chich · dis kahnt en eu′ et ee): position within the earth at which seismograph study indicates an abrupt change in density; boundary between the solid crust and the plastic mantle; often referred to as Moho

molar (moh′ lar): tooth with a flat surface suited to grinding

molecule (mahl′ i keul): smallest particle of a substance that can exist separately and retain its distinct characteristics

mollusk (mahl′ usk): phylum of invertebrate animals enclosed in a symmetrical calcareous shell

molten (mohlt′ en): liquified by heat

monadnock (ma nad′ nahk): residual rock, hill, or mountain standing on an eroded plain

monocline (mahn′ a klien): change in dip from horizontal strata downward and back to horizontal

monsoon (mahn soon′): wind which reverses with the seasons; wind established between water and adjoining land

moon phase: apparent change in the shape of the moon's disc because of the moon's revolution around the earth and change in its reflected light from the sun

moraine (ma raen′): deposit of unstratified gravel, sand, clay, and boulders left by direct melting of a glacier

mutation (meu tae′ shun): sudden fundamental change in heredity producing new individuals unlike the parents

myth: imaginative story used to explain a natural phenomenon

native metal: metal found in an uncombined state in nature

neap tide: tide of minimum range occurring at the first and third quarters of the moon

nebula (neb′ ye la): immense body of highly rarefied gas and dust in interstellar space

nebular (neb′ ye ler) **hypothesis:** proposition which states that the solar system evolved from hot gaseous nebulae

nekton (nek′ tan): free-swimming marine organisms

neutron (neu′ trahn): particle in the nucleus of an atom that has no electrical charge

neve (nae vae′): permeable mass of snow granules forming the upper surface of the accumulation area of a glacier

nitrogen (nie′ tra jen): colorless, tasteless, gaseous element constituting 78 percent (by volume) of the earth's atmosphere

nitrogen fixation: the assimilation of atmospheric nitrogen by soil microorganisms and its release for plant use by nitrification in the soil after the death of the microorganism; the industrial conversion of free nitrogen into combined forms as starting material for fertilizers or explosives

nodule (nahj′ ool): rounded body of irregular shape formed within certain sedimentary layers of rock

nonmetal: element that lacks metallic properties

notched cliff: cliff with indentation cut by wave action

nova (noh′ va): star that irregularly, yet suddenly, increases its light output tremendously and then fades to its former obscurity as it loses mass

nucleus (neu′ klee us): central point or portion of an atom around which electrons are gathered; central portion of a galaxy

nutation (neu tae′ shun): periodic oscillation or nodding of the earth's axis

nutrient (neu′ tree ent): substance that promotes growth

oasis (oh ae′ sis): fertile green spot in a waste or desert

objective lens: lens of a telescope which is exposed to the object under observation and which produces an image of the object for viewing with the eyepiece

Pronunciation
Key

ae . . . bake

ah . . . father

a . . . back

ee . . . easy

e . . . less

eu . . . few

ie . . . life

i . . . trip

oh . . . flow

aw . . . soft

ah . . . odd

oo . . . food

uh . . . foot

eu . . . cube

u . . . up

y . . . yet

j . . . judge

k . . . cake

s . . . sew

th . . . thin

oblate spheroid (ahb′ laet · sfir′ awid): spherical body that bulges at its equator and is flattened at its poles

octahedron (ahk ta hee′ dron) : solid bounded by eight plane faces

ocular (ahk′ ye lar) **lens:** lens of a telescope which is the eyepiece for magnifying

ooze: fine-grained mud of more than 30 percent organic origin which covers parts of the ocean floor

opaque (oh paek′): not capable of transmitting light or radiant energy

orbit (awr′ bit): path of a body in its revolution around another body

ore: mineral or groups of minerals which can be mined at a profit

orthoclase (awr′ tha klaes): potassium—containing mineral member of the feldspar family; most abundant mineral in granites

orthorhombic (awr tha rahm′ bik): crystal system having three unequal axes intersecting at right angles

oscillatory (ah sil′ a tohr ee) **wave:** wave in which particles move about a point with little permanent change in position; a deep water wave

oxide: chemical compound containing oxygen combined with a positive ion or ions

oxygen: colorless, tasteless, odorless gaseous element constituting 21 percent (by volume) of the earth's atmosphere

ozone (oh′ zohn): form of oxygen having three atoms to the molecule

paleontologist (pae lee ahn tahl′ a jist): scientist who studies the life of past geologic ages through fossils

parabolic (par a bahl′ ik) **dune:** curved dune with the concave side toward the wind

parsec: unit of measure for interstellar space, equal to 3.26 light-years

peat: partially carbonized vegetable tissue

pendant (pen′ dant): small solutional remnant projecting from the ceiling

pendulum (pen′ je lum): body suspended from a fixed point so as to swing back and forth in response to the action of gravity and momentum

perceptible (per sep′ ta bal): capable of being recognized or seen

percolating (per′ ka laet ing): oozing or trickling through fine openings in a permeable substance

peridotite (pa rid′ a tiet): igneous rocks composed of olivine and another ferromagnesian mineral, usually a pyroxene

perigee (per′ a jee): point in the orbit of a satellite of the earth at the least distance from the center of the earth

perihelion (per i heel′ yan): point in a planet's orbit nearest the sun

perimeter (pa rim′ et er): outer boundary of a two-dimensional figure; the circumference

period: fundamental unit of the geologic time scale; time required for a complete swing of a pendulum from maximum position to minimum position

periphery (pa rif′ a ree): external surface or boundary of an area

permeable (pur′ mee a bul): having a texture that permits liquid to move through the pores

permineralize: fossilization whereby original hard parts of an organism have additional mineral material deposited in their pores

petrify (pe′ tra fie): to change into stone or a stony substance

petroleum (pe troh′ lee am): liquid, flammable hydrocarbon

phenomenon (fi nahm′ e nahn): fact, occurrence, or circumstance observed

philosophy (fi lahs′ a fee): study or science of the principles of a particular branch of knowledge

phosphorus (fahs′ fares): a nonmetallic element of the nitrogen family that occurs widely, especially as phosphates

photometer (foh tahm′ et er): instrument for measuring intensity of light energy

photosphere (foht′ a sfir): luminous, visible part of the sun

photosynthesis (foht a sin′ tha sis): formation of carbohydrates from carbon dioxide in the tissues of plants exposed to sunlight

phylum (fie′ lem): primary division of a kingdom

physics (fiz′ iks): science dealing with natural laws and physical changes of matter

Pronunciation Key

ae . . . bake

ah . . . father

a . . . back

ee . . . easy

e . . . less

eu . . . few

ie . . . life

i . . . trip

oh . . . flow

aw . . . soft

ah . . . odd

oo . . . food

uh . . . foot

eu . . . cube

u . . . up

y . . . yet

j . . . judge

k . . . cake

s . . . sew

th . . . thin

piedmont (peed' mahnt): area lying along or near the foot of a mountain range

placer (plas' er): alluvial deposit, as of sand or gravel, containing gold or other valuable minerals

plagioclase (plae' jee a klaes): mineral group belonging to the feldspar family containing sodium silicate and/or calcium silicate

plane: flat or level surface

planetesimal (plan e tes' i mal): small, solid body in space revolving around a larger body

plankton (plangk' tan): marine organisms that float at or near the ocean surface

plateau (pla toh'): level land area rising above adjacent land

playa (plie' a): desert basin without drainage where water collects and evaporates

pluvial (ploo' vee al): characterized by abundant rain

porous: having openings which may or may not be connected

porphyry (pawr' fa ree): rock with distinct crystals in a fine-grained ground mass

precession (pree sesh' un): cone-shaped motion traced by the axis of a rotating body acted on by an outside force that tilts the axis away from the perpendicular to the plane of its orbit

precious stone: gem of great commercial value because of its rarity, beauty, and durability

precipitation (pri sip i tae' shan): discharge of water in liquid or solid state from the atmosphere; process of separating minerals from a solution or melt by chemical reaction or evaporation

prevailing (pri vael' ing): having superior power or influence

primary wave: earthquake wave which vibrates back and forth in direction of wave travel

prime meridian: meridian which passes through Greenwich, England, and from which distances east and west on the earth's surface are measured

prism (priz' em): transparent body having three or more similar plane faces which are parallel to a common axis and used to disperse a beam of light

protista: group of one-celled microscopic organisms having characteristics of either plants or animals

proton (proh' tahn): particle in the nucleus of an atom having a positive electrical charge; a unit of positive electricity

protoplanet: first form of a planet

pyroxene (pie rahk' seen): one of the rock-forming mineral groups containing iron, magnesium, calcium, sodium, and aluminum silicates in which the silicate tetrahedra are arranged in a single chain

quadrant (kwahd' rant): instrument for measuring altitudes consisting of a graduated arc of 90° with a plumb line for fixing the vertical direction

quasar (kwae' zar): from *quasi* stell*ar*; source of radio energy from outer space, not stars; celestial objects possessing certain attributes of stars, but which are not stars

radar (rae' dahr): from *r*adio *d*etecting *an*d *r*anging; instrument for detecting a target and measuring the travel time of a radio pulse sent out from a transmitter and reflected by the target in order to determine the distance and direction of the target

radiation (raed ee ae' shun): process of emitting radiant energy in the form of waves or particles

radioactive decay: changing one element into another element through loss of charged particles from the atomic nucleus without the influence of heat, pressure, or chemical reaction

radioactive element: element capable of changing spontaneously into another element by emission of charged particles from the nucleus of its atoms

radiometer (raed ee ahm' et er): instrument for measuring the intensity of radiant energy

rank: measure of intensity of metamorphism

Pronunciation Key

ae . . . bake

ah . . . father

a . . . back

ee . . . easy

e . . . less

eu . . . few

ie . . . life

i . . . trip

oh . . . flow

aw . . . soft

ah . . . odd

oo . . . food

uh . . . foot

eu . . . cube

u . . . up

y . . . yet

j . . . judge

k . . . cake

s . . . sew

th . . . thin

rays: bright streaks radiating from some moon craters

recede (ri seed'): withdraw or move back

recrystallization: formation of new mineral grains or enlargement of pre-existing mineral grains caused by thermal metamorphism

red shift: shift of all spectral lines in light from receding distant galaxies toward longer wavelengths or the red end of spectrum characteristic of all galaxies

reflecting telescope: telescope in which incoming light is converged into an image by a concave mirror rather than a lens

refract (ri frakt'): to bend or deflect from a straight line

refracting telescope: telescope using an objective lens to produce an image of the object under observation and an ocular lens through which the observer views the image

regional metamorphism: large scale metamorphism that affects an entire region, but need not be related to known igneous intrusions

rejuvenation (ri joo va nae' shun): to restore to a youthful state

relative dates: dates in earth's history determined with reference to other events

relief (ri leef'): difference between high and low elevations of a land surface

reptile (rep'tel): cold-blooded vertebrate that moves on its underside or on short legs

reservoir (rez' urv wahr): artificial lake where water is stored for use; a natural underground container of oil, water, or gas

residual (ri zidj' wal): that which remains in the place it was formed

resistant (ri zis' tent): that which withstands or opposes force

retrograde: having direction contrary to general direction of similar bodies

revolution (rev a loo' shun): moving of a body in a circular course about a central point; a time of major crustal deformations

rhombohedron (rahm boh hee' dron): solid with faces that are parallelograms with oblique angles

right ascension (a sen' chun): distance eastward from the point where the celestial equator and the ecliptic intersect on the spring equinox; celestial coordinate which corresponds to longitude on earth

rills: long, narrow markings on the moon's surface having steep sides, flat bottoms, and varying widths; minute stream channels on earth

rip current: seaward-moving current that returns water from the shore to greater depths

rotation (roh tae' shun): turning motion of a body on its axis

satellite (sat' el iet): body revolving about a larger body

saturate (sach' u raet): to soak thoroughly so that all openings are filled with fluid

saturation (sach u rae'shun): degree to which rock openings are filled with fluid or to which a solution contains all the dissolved material possible at a given temperature

scavenger (skav' en jer): organism that feeds on refuse or decaying flesh

scientific theory: general principle offered to explain observed facts and events

secondary crater: small crater near large crater on the moon's surface

secondary wave: earthquake wave which moves up and down perpendicular to direction of wave travel

sedimentary (sed a ment' a ree): rock formed of sediments—either fragments of other rock deposited by wind or water or material precipitated from solutions

seismic (sies' mik): characteristic of or produced by earth vibrations

seismograph (siez' ma graf): instrument to record vibrations of the earth

semiprecious stone: gem of less commercial value than a precious stone

shadow zone: area between 103° and 143° on either side of earthquake focus where no *P* or *S* waves are recorded

shearing: stress resulting from applied forces that cause two adjacent parts of a solid to slide past one another parallel to the plane of contact

Pronunciation Key

ae ... bake

ah ... father

a ... back

ee ... easy

e ... less

eu ... few

ie ... life

i ... trip

oh ... flow

aw ... soft

ah ... odd

oo ... food

uh ... foot

eu ... cube

u ... up

y ... yet

j ... judge

k ... cake

s ... sew

th ... thin

shield: continental block of the earth's crust that has been relatively stable since Precambrian time; a disc-shaped volcano

shoreline: average position of line where land and sea meet

sidereal (sie dir' ee al): pertaining to measurements determined by positions of stars

siderite (sid' a riet): meteorite of iron or iron and nickel

siderolite (sid' e ra liet): sponge-like iron meteorite with stony material in its pores

silicate (sil' i kaet): chemical compound which is a combination of silicon, oxygen, and some other element or elements

sill: tabular igneous rock body intruded between and also parallel to older rock layers

slip face: leeward slope of sand dune down which sand slides because of gravity

slit: narrow opening designed to let a minimum beam of light reach the spectroscope

smog (smahg): a fog made heavier and darker by smoke and chemical fumes

solid: state of matter which has a definite shape and volume because molecules cannot move freely from place to place

solstice (sahl' stis): point in the ecliptic at which the sun is farthest either north or south from the equator

solution (sa loo' shun): condition in which particles of a solid are dissolved in a liquid and cannot be separated by filtration

species (spee' sheez): class of individuals having common characteristics and capable of interbreeding

specific (spi sif' ik) **gravity:** ratio of the mass of a body to the mass of an equal volume of water

spectrogram (spek' tra gram): photograph of a spectrum

spectrograph (spek' tra graf): apparatus for dispersing radiation into a spectrum and photographing the spectrum

spectroheliograph (spek troh hee' lee a graf): apparatus for photographing the sun in the light of a single wavelength

spectroscope (spek' tra skohp): instrument for examining the visible spectrum

spectrum: band of visible colors formed when a beam of radiant energy is dispersed and its rays are arranged in the order of their wavelength or frequency

spheroidal (sfir awid' al): having a shape resembling a sphere

spiral: winding around a center and gradually receding from it

spontaneous (spahn tae' nee us): produced by natural causes

spring tide: high tide caused by position of sun, earth, and moon in a straight line

stable (stae' bel): able to continue or last; not changeable

stack: vertical block of resistant rock cut off from the mainland by wave action

stadium (staed' ee um): ancient measure of distance

stalactite (sta lak' tiet): deposit of calcium carbonate hanging from the roof or sides of a cavern

stalagmite (sta lag' miet): deposit of calcium carbonate built up from the floor of a cavern by the drip of water from above

stoping (stohp' ing): process in which magma engulfs blocks of overlying country rock and assimilates them

strata (strae' ta): layers of the same kind of rock material, usually applied to sedimentary rock layers

stratigraphy (stra tig' ra fee): science that deals with origin, composition, distribution, and succession of rock strata

stratosphere (strat' a sfir.): layer of earth's atmosphere from about 7 mi to about 20 mi above earth's surface having relatively constant temperature and little water content

streak: color of the fine powder of a mineral obtained by scratching it against a hard white surface

stress: amount of physical pressure, pull, or other force exerted per unit of area

striated (strie' aet ed): marked with usually parallel grooves or channels

striation (strie' ae shun): one of a group of parallel grooves caused by abrasion by ice or rock

Pronunciation
Key

ae ... bake

ah ... father

a ... back

ee ... easy

e ... less

eu ... few

ie ... life

i ... trip

oh ... flow

aw ... soft

ah ... odd

oo ... food

uh ... foot

eu ... cube

u ... up

y ... yet

j ... judge

k ... cake

s ... sew

th ... thin

stylus (stie' lus): hard-pointed, pen-shaped instrument for marking

subatomic particle: component of an atom too small to be seen with any instrument

subsidence (sub sied' ens): act of sinking or settling

substance: matter including both elements and compounds

summit: highest point or part of a hill or mountain

superficial (seu per fish' al): of or relating to or affecting only the surface

superposition: order in which rocks are deposited one above the other

suspension: state in which particles of a solid are mixed with a fluid but are undissolved

symmetrical (sa me' tri kal): having parts that correspond in size, shape, and relative position on opposite sides of a dividing line or axis

syncline (sin' klien): fold in rock in which strata dip inward from both sides

synodic (sa nahd' ik): interval of time required for a celestial body to complete one revolution as seen from the earth

talus (tae' lus): heap of rock debris at the base of a cliff

tangent (tan' jent): touching

tension (ten' chun): system of forces tending to pull a body apart; the stress resulting from such forces

terminal (term' nal) **moraine:** moraine situated at or forming the end of a glacier

terrace (ter' as): level surface bounded by a steep ascending slope on one side and a steep descending slope on the other

terrestrial (te res' tree al): consisting of or representing the earth

tetragonal (te trag' an l): crystal system having three axes at right angles to one another, two being of equal length and one longer or shorter

tetrahedron (te tra hee' dron): a solid bounded by four plane faces

texture (teks' cher): characteristics of rock particles including size, shape, and arrangement of the particles

thermal (ther' mal): of or pertaining to heat

thermal pollution: pollution caused when water from a stream is diverted for industrial cooling and then returned to the stream; as the temperature of the water rises, it loses oxygen in the process and bacterial growth is increased

tidal: of or pertaining to the periodic rise and fall of waters of the ocean

tidal scour: channels eroded by movement of tidal waters

time-path: shortest time from instant earthquake wave is initiated until it is received by a seismograph, governed by different wave velocities of earth material, but not always the shortest distance

topography (ta pahg' ra fee): surface features of an area

torrential (taw ren' chal): violent, having the nature of a torrent

transmutation (trans meu tae' shan): transformation of one element into another through nuclear reactions

transpiration (trans pa rae' shun): process by which water vapor escapes from a living plant into the atmosphere

transverse (trans vers') **dune:** dune lying across or at right angles to the wind

travertine (trav' er teen): mineral composed of calcium carbonate deposited by a hot spring

tremor (trem' er): vibratory movement; a quivering or trembling

tributary (trib' ye ter ee): stream contributing water to another larger stream

trilobite (trie' la biet) **hash:** undistinguishable mixture of broken segments of fossil trilobites

tropics: zone of the earth's surface extending $23\frac{1}{2}°$ north and $23\frac{1}{2}°$ south on either side of the equator

troposphere (troh' pa sfir): layer of the earth's atmosphere from the surface to about 7 mi above the earth containing about 75 percent of the gases of the atmosphere

tsunami (seu nahm' ee): great sea wave produced by a submarine earthquake

turbidity (tur bid' it ee) **current:** ocean current caused by density of water containing sediment in suspension

Pronunciation Key

ae ... bake

ah ... father

a ... back

ee ... easy

e ... less

eu ... few

ie ... life

i ... trip

oh ... flow

aw ... soft

ah ... odd

oo ... food

uh ... foot

eu ... cube

u ... up

y ... yet

j ... judge

k ... cake

s ... sew

th ... thin

turbulence (tur′ beu lans): haphazard, secondary motion caused by eddies in a moving fluid or air current

unconformity: break in the rock record

undulate (un′ ja laet): to move in rising and falling flowing waves

uniformitarianism (eu ni fawr mi ter′ ee a niz em): geological principle that states that processes of the present are similar to processes of the past

uranium (eu rae′ nee am): heavy, radioactive, metallic element found in pitchblende existing naturally as a mixture of three isotopes

variance (ver′ ee ans): disagreement between two parts

vein: narrow, well-defined zone containing mineral-bearing rock in place

velocity (ve lahs′ et ee): time rate of linear motion in a given direction

veneer (va nir′): overlay of thin sheets of some material

vertical seismograph: instrument used to record vibrations at right angles or up and down during an earthquake

vesicular (va sik′ ya ler): containing many small cavities due to the escape of gas or vapor

vibration: quiver or tremor; an oscillation

viscous (vis′ kus): pertaining to a fluid which resists flowing because of the cohesion of its molecules

wavelength: horizontal distance between similar points on two successive waves measured perpendicularly to the crest

weather: day-to-day changes in wind, temperature, humidity, and pressure

weathering: physical disintegration and chemical decomposition of earth material at or near the surface

weight: measure of gravitational pull of the earth on bodies near the surface of the earth

windward: direction from which the wind is blowing

wrinkle ridges: raised ridges on the surface of the moon probably caused by compression

zenith (zee′ neth): point on the celestial sphere directly above the observer; highest point reached in the heavens by a celestial body

zodiac: imaginary belt about 18° wide with the ecliptic in the center and containing the apparent path of the principal planets except Pluto

INDEX